ISSUES IN URBAN ECONOMICS

ISSUES
IN
URBAN
ECONOMICS

Based on Papers Presented at a Conference
Sponsored by the Committee on Urban Economics
of Resources for the Future, Inc.

Edited by Harvey S. Perloff and Lowdon Wingo, Jr.

*Published for Resources for the Future, Inc.
by The Johns Hopkins Press*

This book is based on papers prepared for presentation at a conference
sponsored by the Committee on Urban Economics of Resources for the Future,
Inc., Washington, D.C., January 1967. At the time of original publication
Harvey S. Perloff was director of RFF's regional and urban studies, and chairman
of CUE; Lowdon Wingo, Jr. was an RFF research associate. Mr. Perloff is now
dean of the School of Architecture and Urban Planning at the University of
California, Los Angeles, and a consultant to RFF. Mr. Wingo is director of RFF
regional and urban studies. Susan R. Zuckerman assisted in editing the manuscript.
Charts were drawn by Clare and Frank Ford. The index was prepared by
Adele Garrett.

RFF staff editors, Henry Jarrett, Vera W. Dodds, Nora E. Roots,
Sheila M. Ekers.

PREFACE

An infant among the traditional interests of economists, urban economics has a special need to identify what is germane to its special involvement with the city. Thus, the mission of this volume is to establish benchmarks at the outer limits of what is known in the hope that scholars will be stimulated to venture beyond them.

The book climaxes eight years of effort by the Committee on Urban Economics of Resources for the Future, Inc., to advance the field of urban economics. The Committee consists of university scholars and researchers in economics and the other social sciences who have been concerned with urban problems for many years. On one level it has sought to provide intellectual leadership for the more rapid development of the field; on another it has channeled funds for fellowships, research, conferences, and various overhead activities to build up the necessary "infrastructure." Moved by a sense of timeliness, the Committee has endeavored in this volume to capture the state of urban economics as it existed in 1967, but even more, to propagate the excitement of what is to be discovered in the coming years that can change the nature of cities. And for the great majority of us the city is the primal environmental fact of our lives.

Members of the Committee, joined by other interested scholars, prepared the papers in this volume. They were first presented at a conference held in Washington, D.C., in January 1967, to elicit critical review of the authors' appraisals of their sectors of the field and to introduce the viewpoints of other scholars. In our estimation, the papers, along with the viewpoints of their discussants, have provided an uncommonly clear view of this field and, more importantly, of its scholarly potential.

This book should be of particular interest not only to undergraduate and graduate students of economics, but also to those in other social sciences who are exploring for the first time the economic dimensions of urban growth and change. With this in mind, the volume is designed to provide (1) a broad overview of the state of the arts, in its introduction; (2) a more intensive description of the key areas of urban economics, in the papers and comments; and (3) clear paths into the literature that has accumulated in the areas, in the form of selected readings appended to each paper.

HARVEY S. PERLOFF and LOWDON WINGO, JR.

vii

CONTENTS

CONTENTS

ISSUES IN URBAN ECONOMICS

*Harvey S. Perloff and Lowdon Wingo, Jr.**

INTRODUCTION

As was probably the case with other special fields in economics, urban economics became a focus of interest among economists as a result of rising policy issues that were not only of great practical significance but were intellectually intriguing. Important among them have been the following problem areas:

a) *The economic growth and stagnation of cities.* After World War II the lagging growth and severe unemployment that afflicted a number of major urban centers as well as many smaller cities within depressed regions brought the problems of urban economic growth to the attention of the whole nation. General economic studies of such major cities as New York, St. Louis, Pittsburgh, and Boston were sponsored, and economists were brought in to tackle the analyses. Simultaneously, many of the 14,000 "area development" agencies identified by the Committee for Economic Development in the late fifties began to undertake more limited studies of area problems. Thus, by the early sixties there was vigorous activity among economists interested in the subnational economy, and this was given a further spur by such federal agencies as the Area Redevelopment Administration and the Housing and Home Finance Agency in sponsoring local economic studies as a pre-condition for federal aid.

b) *Local impact of national policies and expenditures.* Several federal government agencies, as well as individual researchers, became disturbed over possible distortions in the subnational economy that could be created inadvertently in carrying out massive federal programs. Clearly such programs had the capability of radically changing growth trends and the welfare dimensions of local areas. The Department of Defense in its procurement plans found it necessary to calculate the impacts of its vast expenditures on regions and local communities. In parallel fashion, the National Aeronautics and Space Administration combined with its responsibilities for outer space a concern for the consequences of its policies on "inner space," which it expressed in a significant program of research grants to universities across the nation to study the regional impacts of the space program.

c) *Transportation.* The exodus to the suburbs and the mounting congestion of the inner city generated pressures to build giant transpor-

* Director of Regional and Urban Studies, and Research Associate, Resources for the Future, Inc.

1

tation networks in and around the major metropolitan regions. The Bureau of Public Roads joined with state and local agencies to carry out costly general transportation studies in a number of large cities, including New York, Philadelphia, Chicago, Detroit, Pittsburgh, and San Francisco. The many factors and interrelationships involved—social, economic, technical—focused interest on large-scale mathematical models for "conditional" prediction and for "experiments on paper" with whole transportation systems. The special skills of the economist in such matters were indispensable. Their contributions to such efforts as the RAND Transportation Study and the Penn-Jersey and Chicago Area Transportation studies made the mathematical model a significant planning and policy tool.

d) *Public services and urban development policy.* A number of problems formerly treated in a functional context alone became grist for the economic analysis of urban issues. Programs to rehabilitate urban physical capital focused interest on the land, housing, and general real estate markets conceived in a metropolitan framework. Problems of educational equality generated new attention and interest in urban investment in human beings. Urban poverty issues brought about a restatement of conventional thought about urban income distribution and the labor market. The problems of public investment decisions generated new interest in the applicability of planning-programming-budgeting systems (PPBS) to rationalize policy-making and financial behavior of local governments. The pressure of rising demands for urban public services against the rigid financial systems of state and local governments revived interest in state and local finance. The Advisory Commission on Intergovernmental Relations has taken leadership in reexamining the needs and problems posed by the inherited system of financial relations among governmental units. In the academic world, The Brookings Institution, seizing the opportunity provided by a large-size project on public finance, has in several recent works advanced the knowledge and level of analysis of the local public economy.

e) These policy interests have received valuable support from recent work on *data problems and methodology.* Regional accounts, information systems, and data banks have been put forward as means to improve the data base for the analysis of policy issues. In 1959 Resources for the Future launched its program to promote the development of regional accounts. Guided by a committee under the leadership of Werner Hirsch, its purpose was to provide a sounder base of information for urban decision-making. Work on input-output analysis in its application to subnational economies has been pushed by Leontief and others as a related information system. Data banks to exploit computer technology have been developed with the aid of federal support and have sparked the interest of urban planners and administrators. Economists have been stimulated to work on substantively oriented information systems as a reaction to the indiscriminate storage of information sometimes characterized as GIGO—"garbage in, garbage out." At the federal level, a key regional analysis unit set up in the Department of Commerce is but one of several federal information efforts now in operation. Finally, important methodological advances in regional analysis have been produced by the regional science program directed by Walter Isard.

A Note on the Parochial Nature of this Volume

The contributions in this volume come out of the American urban experience. The parameters they incorporate stem from our market institutions and political processes. The empirical analyses are fed by the uniquely rich data sources of our public and private agencies. The fact is that most of what we do know about the economies of cities has proceeded from the study of the cities of the United States, and it has been a general principle of this volume to focus on what we know best.

This caution is not to be interpreted as reflecting a purely parochial interest. While the inputs to the papers flowed from this country's particular experience, knowledge about cities in other parts of the world and in other stages of development has been indirectly advanced. For example, suggestions for methodological procedure abound, and many of the conclusions reached offer good working hypotheses for the study of cities in other societies. Elements of theory emerge, the generality of which far transcends our national case. Scholars and researchers concerned with urban development in the less advanced as well as in the modern industrial nations should be able to profit from our state of the arts in urban economics, at least to the extent that they will be able to shortcut the tortuous path we have carved out to get just this far. Furthermore, it should be recorded here that numerous studies are now underway dealing with the economies of cities in other societies. It is likely that the rapidly expanding interest and the growth of knowledge on the American scene will stimulate and inform parallel developments elsewhere.

Classic Economic Questions

As economists began to focus attention on the city, it became evident that the classic problems of economics were at the core of the crucial urban problems, even though the city gave the analytical issues as well as the policy issues a somewhat unique character. Behind the question

3

of how a particular city might overcome a lag in economic growth and whether it should provide subsidies to attract industries, or how to build a metropolitan-wide transportation network, or whether to spend billions of public dollars to rebuild the central business district, is the basic question of *economic efficiency.* The city has become the production "shell" within which output efficiency is or is not to be achieved; the cost record of a highly efficient plant can be undone by a clogging of the movement of inputs and outputs and, say, inadequate water for cooling purposes. Consideration of *equity* or *distributive justice* are at the heart of the great issues of racial discrimination in jobs and housing markets. In the struggle for equity, modern urbanization has opened up new battlefronts; the relatively simple issues of tax categories and tax rates have given way to the far more complex problems of relative service burdens and tax jurisdictions in our segregated metropolitan regions. Issues of *welfare and quality of life,* which have begun to loom large in economics in recent years, are particularly dominant and particularly tough on the urban scene. Poverty in the city seems to be rigidly institutionalized. The divergence between private costs and benefits on one side, and social costs and benefits on the other, take recognizable forms in the polluted atmosphere and water of the city and in the housing market of the slum.

Thus, it has become evident that the mainstream of economic thought could be advantageously applied to the problems of the urban community and, in turn, that urban economics could contribute to the content and tools of the economic discipline.

Three Major Categories

The analytical aspects of those current urban policy issues which involve considerations of efficiency, equity, or welfare cluster more or less naturally into three large interrelated categories:

1. *The external relations of the urban community;* including the relation of the city to the nation as a whole of which the city is, after all, a subsystem; to companion urban units in the highly articulated "system of cities"; and to its hinterland, for which it serves nodal functions.

2. *The internal relations among its parts, or the intrametropolitan dimension.* The metropolitan area basically encompasses a labor market and a dense, interrelated communications system. As long as the production, consumption, and family-living functions have to take place in space, the handling of the friction of space and the operation of land, plant, and housing markets will continue to be significant subjects, not only for public policy but for study—for some, the heart of urban economics.

3. *The public economy of the urban community* and its intergovernmental dimensions. The demands for public services and activities have increased greatly as industries and people have clustered together, so that the efficiency, adequacy, and equity with which such services are provided have an ever increasing impact on the lives of the people, while simultaneously the lack of coincidence between the local governmental jurisdictions and the economic region and the plethora of local units which govern the metropolis vastly complicate matters and raise many difficult issues.

I. THE URBAN COMMUNITY WITHIN THE NATIONAL ECONOMY

Every significant feature of national socioeconomic change is reflected in urban change, but differentially as among the various communities. The size, functions, and specializations, and the city's linkages with its hinterland and with other cities would seem to have an influence on its development and on the jobs and income it provides for its residents. But what is the nature of this influence, and what determines the special character of any city's growth or of the growth of all the cities taken together?

Economists struggling with these questions can reach back into an extensive literature. One line of development can be traced back through the intellectual lineage of the German economic geographers. Johann Heinrich von Thünen's early nineteenth century analysis of the economic organization of the city's agricultural hinterland related access (or transportation costs) to rents, and rent to factor proportions in production, and so paved the way to an understanding of how the market structures the city. From the Thünen analysis stemmed two other branches—location and central-place theory. The partial equilibrium theory of industrial plant location was given its significant early formulation in the work of Alfred Weber (1909)—later elaborated into a more general theory of the shaping of the space economy by Walter Isard, who synthesized location theory and international trade theory. Central-place theory was first formulated in a meaningful way by Walter Christaller (1933) and greatly broadened and elaborated by August Lösch (1940–44). In recent years, central-place theory has been extended and applied by Brian Berry and others to a host of questions concerned with the spatial distribution of economic activities.

Another line of development evolved from the concept of the economic base with its implicit multiplier concept. Homer Hoyt pioneered the use of this concept as early as 1937. While the economic base theory has been the target of extensive criticism, it has retained a re-

5

markable durability and in one version or another is central to most urban growth projections. The debate centering on economic base theory has been a rich source of conceptualization about the nature of the relation of urban communities to the national economy or to the rest of the world.

Another line of work has sought to clarify the patterns of urban change within an integrated national economy by examining and explaining the patterns of regional deviations from the national average in rates of economic growth and in level, distribution, and stability of income. These studies, as John Meyer has traced through in his survey of regional economics,[1] have applied to the urban-regional field the well-established tradition of combining historical and economic explanations and reformulating tentative hypotheses as experience and data accumulate. Such an approach has characterized some of the major economic studies of recent decades, including the New York, Pittsburgh, and Upper Midwest economic studies, as well as the studies of Hanna, Borts, Fuchs, Dunn, and Sonenblum. In a similar tradition of hypothesis-testing have been the studies of the Duncans, Sjaastad, Lowry, Kusnets, Thomas, and Lee, which are concerned with human ecology and migration within the context of urban structure and national-urban change. Among other consequences, these studies have brought human resources into the urban economics picture in a significant manner and opened the way to a fruitful new line of research.

The Performance of Local Economies in a National Setting

In his recent path-breaking book,[2] Wilbur Thompson brought these various strands together and, in turn, linked them with the mainstream economic issues of income, employment, and growth. In his contribution to the present volume, Thompson takes up where his *Preface* left off, contending that the issues of national-to-urban change are indeed central to the field of urban economics. "Our charge in urban-regional economics," he suggests, "is to determine why some urban areas are richer or more egalitarian or more unstable—or all three (as in the case of Flint, Michigan). Urban-regional economics, freed in the beginning from explaining the general state of the national economy, becomes the study of variations within the system of cities. Product and income may be measured at the national level, but it is produced

[1] John R. Meyer, "Regional Economics: A Survey," *American Economic Review*, Vol. 53 (March 1963).
[2] *A Preface to Urban Economics* (The Johns Hopkins Press, for Resources for the Future, 1965).

at the local level more or less efficiently, depending on the form and functioning of our cities."

While many factors influence the performance of a local economy, the industrial structure dominates the rest. As Thompson puts it, "Tell me your industries and I will tell your (immediate) fortune." "How could a highly specialized economy," he asks, "fail to reflect in its level, distribution, and stability of income and growth rates its distinctive industry mix?" Thompson presents a graphic model which describes how these welfare characteristics emerge from the industrial structure of an urban community. Here the concept of industrial structure goes beyond a mere collection of industry categories to include even more basic characteristics: whether the local plants are old or modern, whether they produce products that are income elastic or not, whether they exert oligopolistic controls, whether they require a broad or narrow range of worker skills.

Local industrial characteristics, Thompson argues, shape the local income pattern not only directly, but also indirectly by influencing the rate of growth of the local economy. If a greater-than-average increase in the demand for local labor raises wages and provides opportunities for overtime earnings and part-time jobs, it will also attract workers from outside. Classical economic theory would predict an increase in the supply of labor in response to the attraction of the prosperous growing community. The seeming paradox of poverty amidst plenty in the booming locality, says Thompson, is quite in conformance with classical theory. Poor people are drawn to rich communities. Thus, measuring over-all averages, growth does not necessarily make a locality richer, only bigger. But this formulation, one should note, may well hide some significant facts. The status of the new migrants is more important than the averages. Even if their income is sufficiently below the income of the older residents to reduce the average family income below the pre-migration levels in a given locality, still each of the family units will often tend to be better off than before, without reducing the incomes of the older residents. Also, the large size that results from the growth of cities that are attracting migrants tends to reduce the incidence of poverty, as Ornati points out in another paper in this volume. The really nasty poverty is in the smaller, non-growing places.

Whatever its impact on *average* incomes, urban growth—that is, growth in population numbers and volume of activities—is itself an attraction for many. As a matter of fact, the beginnings of modern urban economics can be traced back to the concern with the base of

7

economic growth of New York in Haig and McCrea's classic study of the New York region.[3] What is behind the relative growth of the different urban communities? Once again, industrial structure is the key consideration. In the earlier formulations, which followed upon the development of the export base theory, the emphasis was on the urban area as a wide-open economy heavily dependent on external trade, not unlike the small industrially advanced country in the world market; and therefore growth was directly associated with the ability of a given urban community to attract "export" industries. The volume and rate of growth would be directly related to the projected export sector. But, as Thompson points out, analysts soon identified shortcomings in this formulation, some even arguing that the local services, not the export sector, provide the regenerative powers and growth possibilities for an established community.

More significant was the recognition that what made sense in the relatively short run did not hold for the longer run. Where the export and local service components of industrial structure are largely fixed, the primacy of the demand for export products in effecting change seems incontestable, but over time the export and service components come to resemble a chicken-and-egg condition; it is the totality of the supply factors in the given situation, the relative "cumulative advantage" of the area, that becomes critical for growth.

But when we get to the supply factors, many economists act as if they feel naked away from their short-term equilibrium tools and concepts, and hurry for cover. Still, some are willing to conjecture. Thompson wants to bring the argument away from industrial sectors to other fundamental considerations—population size, for instance. The size that a city has already achieved may well be the critical factor in the rate and character of future growth: for example, large size may virtually insure further growth at a near-average rate: "growth stability." A large sample of exports typical of a big city is likely to include the products of some new, fast-growing industries, some middle-aged slow-growing ones, and some old, declining ones. Accordingly, we would expect, says Thompson, to find the large diversified export sector generating neither unusually rapid growth nor very slow growth, but a good, steady type of growth.

Actually, the large metropolitan area is more distinguished by its depth than its breadth. The social overhead that has been amassed,

[3] Robert M. Haig and R. C. McCrea, *Major Economic Factors in Metropolitan Growth and Arrangement: A Study of Trends and Tendencies in the Economic Activities within the Region of New York and Its Environs* (*Regional Survey of New York and Its Environs*, Vol. I, 1927).

more than export diversification, provides the source of its vitality and endurance. The long-run viability of any area "must rest ultimately on its capacity to invent and innovate or otherwise acquire new export bases." Thompson concludes: "The economic base of the larger metropolis is, then, the creativity of its universities and research parks, the sophistication of its engineering firms and financial institutions, the persuasiveness of its public relations and advertising agencies, the flexibility of its transportation networks and utility systems, and all the other dimensions of 'infrastructure' that facilitate the quick and orderly transfer from old dying bases to new growing ones."

To explain some of the problems of the smaller communities, Thompson suggests "a filtering-down theory of industry location." Moving on beyond the Perloff-Dunn-Lampard-Muth industrial-mix-and-share concept that the growth of an area can stem from either a favorable *mix* of fast-growing industries or the acquisition of a larger *share* of the different industries (including the older slower-growing ones), he offers the hypothesis that the larger urban areas combine a favorable industry mix with a steadily declining share of the various growth industries. The high wage rates of the innovating area, quite consonant with the high skills needed in the beginning stages of the learning process, become excessive when the skill requirements decline and the industry, or parts of it, "filter down" to the smaller, less industrially sophisticated areas where the cheaper labor is now up to the lesser occupational demand. And presto! we have the small southern mill town, saddled with a low-wage, slow-growth, filtered-down industry.

To what extent can the various provocative Thompsonian hypotheses be substantiated? Combining forces with his colleague, John M. Mattila, Thompson has a go at a few of the associations he has developed between the industrial and demographic structures and the income and employment patterns of urban areas. They establish the significant impact on average family income and on income distribution of the educational level of the adults in the community, of the degree and type of specialization in manufacturing, of labor participation rates, and of a number of other variables. They find that local educational attainment had the most powerful influence on local income patterns, with a relatively large proportion of college-educated residents producing not only a relatively high average income, but a more equally distributed one as well. On the whole the findings support the largely deductive surmises of Thompson's *Preface*; and yet many of the most interesting and significant interrelationships in the ever changing dynamics of the open urban economy appear to escape detection. The data are too limited, our concepts too general, our methodologies too

9

crude. As Thompson and Mattila conclude, "Much more work and thought is called for on the interactions of the complex of equilibrating and disequilibrating forces barely suggested in this early effort."

Urbanization and Economic Growth

While Thompson has successfully lengthened the vista of urban economics beyond a simplistic short-term "export base" view to cover longer-run considerations, for the most part he takes the supply factors as essentially given. What about the genuinely long run? How and why do systems—or in this case, subsystems—develop, that is, change rather than merely get larger?

While recognizing the value of the contributions of theorists such as Von Thünen, Weber, Christaller, and Isard, Eric Lampard, as an economic historian, stresses the need for a "development" perspective on city-regions beyond those of the general theory of location and space economy and of macroeconomics. A critical limitation of the acquired theory of location and space economy is its dependence on a single-factor explanation, the variable cost of surmounting a distance under *ceteris paribus* general equilibrium conditions. It renders other output variables (labor, fuel, interest, taxes, topography, natural environment, political environment, and so on) devoid of spatial relevance and explains the ordering of activities almost wholly in terms of distance or transport inputs and transport rates.

Current "growth" theory has its own set of limitations, in Lampard's view. For example, the widely known Harrod-Domar formulation is grossly over-aggregated: saving and capital-output ratios (which supposedly govern the rates of growth of output and income) are the crudest of averages. The stability of the aggregate capital-output ratio, for example, is compatible with far-ranging shifts in industrial composition and levels of investment. The trouble is that the "macroeconomic apparatus is . . . designed to explain fluctuations in total income and product rather than the phenomenon of growth." Its main concern is with aggregate demand (within some prevailing limit of full-capacity output potential), whereas growth analysis must be concerned with the rate at which the upper limit of supply is changed over time.

Following the lead of Otis Dudley Duncan *et al.,*[4] Lampard urges that we will have to go to an "ecological" framework to be able to analyze the historical development of the system of cities. Basic to such an approach is the recognition that "the transformation of human settlement patterns involves the emergence and generalization of novelty

[4] *Metropolis and Region* (The Johns Hopkins Press, for Resources for the Future, 1960).

10

within the population concerned. . . ." The ecological framework allows the analysis of community systems "in terms of their position in the total ecosystem."

Urbanization (as well as industrialization), Lampard argues, should be regarded as a process in which productive factors, firms, and localities become increasingly specialized or more differentiated from each other. The "systematic" attributes of such a population system arise from the interactions of their specialized units and areas. The reinforcement of such transitive or input-output relations over time imparts a structure and therefore an *integral* character to the emerging system of division of labor.

Not only does specialization on increasingly large scales based on growing markets yield higher returns, but the large scale of operations at one stage in the production process creates opportunities for greater specialization at other stages through the backward and forward linkages that arise. The achievement of scale economies by some creates potential external economies which can be internalized by others. These often require clustering for their full realization, creating spatial specializations and specialized interdependence of town and country and, increasingly, of town and town, and of town and metropolis.

The decreasing costs associated with scale production at any particular urban site are subject, of course, to diminishing returns and will, at any time, be offset by rising transport and other distance-related costs of access to larger markets. Assuming relatively "free" conditions of entry, therefore, other entrepreneurs will introduce comparable production activities, where possible, at sites beyond the range of effective competition from the innovator. In this way, the localized specialty becomes more widely generalized throughout the space economy and contributes to the apparent convergence of industrial and income structures among the different regions and metropolitan centers that comprise the system.

Against this background it is possible to trace the improvements in quality of the labor force, for new grades of skills must be incorporated in new ratios with more complex and roundabout technologies; the increases in income with rising productivity per unit of labor and capital combined; and the drawing of populations to the cities. "It is in the interrelation of these residential, occupational, and socioeconomic attributes of the American population," Lampard concludes, "that the urban transformation and the evolving system of cities are most likely to be understood."

Thus, like Thompson, Lampard wants to rescue urban economics from the simplistic and narrow concepts that characterized its beginnings, such as central-place theory, as well as from the too formal, static, "least cost" partial equilibrium theory of plant location. He wants to bring it into the richer mainstream, looking for the roots of economic transformation in such concepts as Adam Smith's division of labor and Allyn A. Young's increasing returns to scale economies, by introducing the generally missing spatial dimension.

Finally, Lampard suggests that the traditional demographic concept of urbanization—involving principally the transfer of rural populations to points of urban concentration—is already obsolescent in an economically developed country such as the United States. The historical differential between rural and urban fertility has dramatically closed and the great reservoir of rural population no longer exists. Except for the migration of rural people from parts of the South into the national industrial-urban system, most contemporary movement is within the system of cities itself. In the future, concentration will be taking place, if at all, within the city size distribution and "attention will need to be focused on the characteristics of that phenomenon rather than on the migration of country people to the towns."

Urban-Regional Projections: The Cloudy Crystal Ball

The large role that policy concerns have played in developing the field of urban economics has from an early stage focused interest on urban-regional projections. Here, as elsewhere in the field, demand has led supply.

Public policy must, after all, be future-oriented. At a minimum, for policy decisions to be effective they must take into account what is likely to happen in the future. Sophisticated decision-makers want projections, the more explicit the better. Moreover, in some cases they will be concerned with consciously trying to "create" the future; if, that is, the policy-makers or planners are not happy about the projected trends, they might well try to change them. The anticipation of future conditions is, of course, also important for private businesses and other private groups. In fact, a whole consultant industry has grown up around the making of projections useful to business concerns for their production and location decisions. But here the question of "doing something about the future" does not generally arise; the businessman wants to know about probable future conditions so that he can make decisions with these as given.

The art of projection, according to one of its outstanding practitioners, Sidney Sonenblum, starts with an appreciation of the difference between trying to estimate what is likely to happen in the future and laying a foundation for influencing it. The first calls for a "predictive model" providing reasonable, quantitative estimates for selected variables in some future period. Such estimates can assist local urban government to anticipate public service needs, to establish priorities, and to evaluate the trade-offs that might be possible. They can assist private industry to appraise the relative size and stability of markets in various communities. Sonenblum suggests that the variables in which there is greatest interest are population, labor force, employment, government revenues and expenditures, consumer expenditures, income distribution, investment, and industrial output. Since these are the very variables that the technician usually projects with confidence, here supply may be creating the demand, rather than vice versa.

If the planner or policy maker wants to do something about emerging trends, he needs a different kind of projection, one designed to show the critical indirect structural relationships in which strategic variables can be manipulated. The planner's hope of influencing trends, so as to bring them more in line with highly valued objectives, depends on his identification of the instrumental variables and his understanding of the likely consequences of changes in these variables. A "planning model" is thus inevitably concerned with the behavioral characteristics of decision units as expressed by statistical approximations. Sonenblum is somewhat daunted by the difficulties in quantifying precisely the relationships that are strategic for urban planning purposes: quantification of key relationships needs to be quite accurate because of the multiplying consequence of each action sequence, but the requisite accuracy is difficult to achieve. Although we know quite a bit about how decision units respond to events, we know relatively little about the magnitude of the response and how long it takes. Thus, while the projections for planning purposes may be extremely helpful in suggesting where and perhaps when policy should be applied, the data may well lack reliability as long as magnitudes and time sequence are uncertain.

Urban-regional projections,[5] Sonenblum stresses, are essentially an extension of socioeconomic analysis of regional change. Since at the present time it is not possible to comprehend in a single analytical system all the relationships that are relevant to a region's change, or changes within all the regions taken together, the relevant relationships must be chosen. It is evident that regional change can be viewed from the national perspective, where national forces are taken as the primary determinants of the levels and growth rates of individual regions through their effects on the economic base of each region; or from the *local*

---

[5] The joint title is employed here because, in Sonenblum's view, the types of projection techniques he discusses are similar for the urban and larger regional scenes.

perspective, focusing on the local response to external forces.[6] The projection technique based on the national perspective involves first projecting those national changes that are of special relevance to metropolitan analysis: changes in population, employment, industry activity, income, productivity, investment, level and mix of demand, and federal policies and expenditures. Sonenblum thus makes it clear that those who do not have the capacity to evolve reasonable national projections, or to acquire them, had better stay out of the regional projection game. The prospective national changes can then be directly *allocated* to metropolitan areas according to anticipated deviations from the national average based largely on past trends, or to special characteristics in the area of location and trading relations.

When the perspective is from "inside out," the local area changes are seen to depend on the special characteristics of the individual community. The future can be said to be determined by the current size and structure of the community, or by the impact-multiplier which determines how its industries respond to challenges posed by the new developments, or by what happens to the factors of production in the area. The various perspectives from which future regional change can be viewed suggest that the projections can only be as sound as the analysis that lies beneath.

The fascinating aspect of urban-regional projections is their weighing of the knowledge provided by the field on a rather fine scale. Without intending it, Sonenblum's treatment of how one goes about making general economic regional projections or projections for selected key variables is an excellent summary of where the field of urban-regional economics stands. In making projections for a metropolitan area, for example, estimates of the occupational distribution of the labor force would be very useful, but they are very rare. Net migration information is better, but there are great gaps in our knowledge, which

---

[6] Harold J. Barnett, in commenting on the Sonenblum and Thompson papers at the Committee on Urban Economics conference, usefully sharpened the difference in emphasis on the relative importance of national and local factors in these two papers. (See the Barnett note at the end of Part I.)

The impact of national forces on the development of urban communities is everywhere evident. Does this mean that only national policies can hope to have any impact on what happens to cities around the country, that the individual community has its fate determined for it entirely from outside? It may be, in fact, that technological and other national forces have such a pervading influence that even national policies can only have a peripheral impact on the growth rate and change pattern of cities across the country.

Obviously, it would be tremendously helpful if we could weigh fairly accurately the scope and strength of the basically national forces at work, on one side, and the relative importance of internal structure and local policy within individual urban regions, on the other. Unfortunately, this is still beyond us.

Stolnitz in a separate paper identifies. In forecasting industrial activity, our inability to identify clearly the export component comes to the forefront. While comparative cost figures would be valuable, we are faced with the paucity of regional information (both statistical and analytical) on investment, capital stock, and productivity. Key sector estimates, therefore, necessarily have to be based on market studies rather than on comparative cost studies. We can anticipate better projections only to the extent that we can improve our data base and our basic concepts.

Human Resources in the City

In a vague and general sort of way, economists have always agreed with the admonition that mankind is the proper study of man. However, most of us have to concede surprise in discovering how much had been hidden from view until economists recently turned their attention to specific human resources considerations. It is natural that urban economics, coming late on the scene, would want to build this new-found concern into its theory, a purpose more easily stated than carried out. Convergence of two fledgling fields could hardly be expected to generate fast and easy intellectual payoffs; indeed, it calls for scholars of sturdy stuff.

Sensing this, George Stolnitz provides a carefully reasoned paper which says in effect: Come all ye Risk Takers, here is a fine challenge for you! Working materials are available; while large data gaps exist, there is enough solid information to satisfy researchers. Note the kind of story one can begin to piece together with such materials. It can permit us to distinguish the relatively novel from the long-standing— an important feature because "jumps" in the trends have different implications than do continuities for policy and research.

As Stolnitz points out, the growth in urban population is certainly long-standing: the recent urban-to-total ratios in numbers are nearly matched or exceeded by the ratios between 1900 and 1930. Many other seemingly new phenomena, such as suburbanization, have deep roots. Only in the changing racial composition of cities is something strikingly new encountered: the 1940–50 decennial change in the percentage of Negroes in central cities was over three times the largest shift of earlier decades, and the 1950–60 rise was about a third higher.

The important problem areas Stolnitz finds in the field of urban human resources meet three basic prerequisites that any sensible economist is likely to set up: research viability, clear relation to pressing policy issues, and close reciprocal linkages with mainstream economic theory. In Stolnitz' words, "Just as trade or capital theory contributes to and draws upon more general economic theory, so should an evolving human resource theory if it is to excite the interest of the next generation of economists."

There are many illustrations to choose from. One is the need to develop something like a "production function" approach to human resources problems of the city. There is need to develop solid information on inputs and outputs in order to arrive at a workable assessment of alternative methods for enhancing the employment, income, and productivity of significant individual components of the labor force. And there are fruitful possibilities in developing longitudinal studies that involve a "life cycle" approach to various groups in the society, tracing changes over time under different conditions. Similarly, if manpower movements could be related to regional and industrial changes— through manpower origin-destination matrices—we would know the industrial and occupational categories of labor as it is recruited for jobs in various parts of the country; movers could be compared with non-movers. A detailed view of "to" and "from" components would help us understand the gross manpower movements with their many ramifications, instead of relying on the more limited net movements which are now the main focus of attention.

Significant insights are also to be gained by regarding the neighborhood as a subsystem for economic analysis. In this way, the interrelationships between various forms of social pathology and labor characteristics might be studied, or the fiscal and real-resource constraints implicit in attempting various types of social solutions might be estimated. The city, Stolnitz suggests, is too aggregative a unit for many kinds of human resources analyses; a finer grain, such as that provided by the neighborhood, is necessary for a deeper understanding of both the producer-consumer and producer-social welfare interrelationships. On the policy side, Stolnitz points to the intimate bearing of personal, family, and neighborhood welfare conditions on the disadvantaged labor force. The threat of crime and delinquency to the provision of old and new ranges of urban amenities poses still broader policy issues, involving the quality of life of the entire urban community. "Given the enormous human and fiscal factors at stake," Stolnitz concludes, "it seems a plausible forecast that economic theory will again fulfill its traditional role of responding to unfamiliar problems when these become clearcut major occasions for socioeconomic policy."

II. INTRAMETROPOLITAN DEVELOPMENT

Extensive interest in the spatial organization of the urban economy, like much of urban economics, has been precipitated by a crescendo of policy problems, in this case associated with the orderly regulation of the land resources of the city, with the planning of its transportation and service systems, and with the long-range developmental problems and opportunities confronting urban planners and politicians.

Two generations of efforts to plan public facilities and to guide private developments in the directions implicit in local master or comprehensive plans had forced upon public officials and planners a realization that the internal organization of the city and the directions in which it tended to change were manifestations of powerful social and economic factors that determined land use patterns, the movement of goods and people, and the distribution of infrastructure. Some of these grew out of the relation of the city to the rest of the world. Others grew out of the optimizing behavior of local households and firms seeking the "best" or utility-maximizing location for their activities. Still others grew out of public or quasi-public decisions rendered on a technical basis. It was the outcome of this interplay of public-private, national-local, social-political-economic processes that in some complex way ordered in space that bundle of activities with their associated artifacts that we know as the city.

Intellectual Forebears

A generation ago it would have been difficult to add much to this description of the processes that make up the city. The experience of a good real estate broker could outweigh all of scholarly knowledge in understanding how the city was put together and how it was changing. As a matter of fact, it was the marriage of this experience of the urban real estate market with classical rent theory going back to David Ricardo that provided the first theoretical underpinnings to the commonsense descriptions of the organization in space of the city. It is not entirely accidental that the theoretical background for Haig and McCrea's study of the New York metropolitan region was preceded by almost a generation by the sophisticated analysis prepared by the New York mortgage banker, Richard M. Hurd.[7]

Contemporary with Haig's work, the Chicago school of urban ecologists led by Park, Burgess, and Wirth introduced the basic proposition that the social relations of the city were structured in space; that there were systematic relations between the activities that took place in the urban core and the character of the concentric zones that succeeded one another out into the hinterlands. A generation later their professional heirs were studying the ways in which economic groups distribute

[7] Hurd, *Principles of City Land Values* (New York: Real Estate Record and Guide, 1924.)

17

themselves in urban space; they were developing concepts to illuminate the crucial home-to-work relationships, which play such a significant role in urban organization.

The theory of industrial location, too, has been drawn upon in analyses of intrametropolitan development. Although location theory was evolved to explain the gross locational decisions of industries or their firms, it has provided a theoretical lever with which to view the locational behavior of business enterprises in the urban space as well. A corollary body of theory dealing with spatial competition and market area analysis completed the analytical equipment needs to tackle the explanation of the spatial structure and organization of the urban economy.

Thus, the economics of the urban spatial organization has arisen from the convergence of a number of conceptual themes. Rent theory has been joined to location theory to explain how urban structure comes about, while central-place theory and urban ecology and geography have provided us with macro-views of the way in which these structuring processes actually work themselves out as the city grows and changes. We now sense that we have the basic makings for a theory of urban growth and change as it is manifest in the spatial disposition of economic activities.

This is not to say that market processes and optimizing behavior explain everything about the internal organization of the city, but rather that, directly or indirectly, many of the behavioral processes of the city either have economic dimensions or work themselves out through the market mechanisms. Therefore, an understanding of these mechanisms can contribute to a better knowledge of those urban phenomena that are less specifically economic. The slum is an urban social phenomenon with powerful economic dimensions which can be made more intelligible through analysis of its economic referents. The seemingly inefficient pattern of urban scatteration, the bane of city planners the world over, can be seen to be a quite predictable consequence of the market interaction of a "new-housing" industry with a "residential site producing" industry. The physical blight of the "dark grey" areas of the city appears as a phenomenon of disinvestment associated with the changing profit expectations of owners of properties of different classes in different parts of the city. Indeed, most "urban" problems have market-locational dimensions which significantly condition the way in which—and the extent to which—public policy works toward solutions. And so, retrospectively, Edgar Hoover sees the principal thrust of his paper as having "attempted to provide some insights into the influences at work in shaping urban patterns, and the way in

18

which these influences account for the stresses and maladjustments that are only too evident today and [that] will continue to challenge our capacities for understanding and constructive action." This is perhaps too modest a view, for Hoover's paper in this volume carries the burden of capturing the state of knowledge about intrametropolitan development in 1967.

What Do We Know about Urban Structure?

Hoover pursues his responsibility here through a meticulous, thoughtful dissection of the urban organism, observing, to begin with, that it knows no ideal or equilibrium state: spatial structure "represents a snapshot of current states of mutual adjustment. Impacts of one change upon another, and spatial adjustments, take time, because of long-lived physical facilities, habits, social and business ties, and political commitments are entailed."

The basic issue is to understand how activities get located in the urban space, that is, to understand how the basic location factors influence households, businesses, and public agencies in deciding where and when to make their investments in the hardware core of their activities. For many activities, location is quite rigorously determined: customs warehouses belong near the waterfront dock area, airports are limited by topography and wind patterns, while many specialized distribution activities are tied to the region's point of maximum accessibility—the central business district—which, Hoover points out, is "a pretty stable datum, even though the extent and importance of its access advantage over other points can change radically." Still other activities are extremely sensitive to access considerations, that is, to the transportation costs of its linkage with other activities and to the frequency with which trips have to be made between them, such as the linkage of various kinds of retailing establishments with the residential locations of consumers.

The crucial point here is not so much the power of attraction of these activities but the extent to which the activity in question is concentrated in a relatively few (or many) points, that is, whether they tend to be diffused throughout the city or concentrated near its center. In addition, some activities tend to agglomerate in order to exploit some common advantages. All of these factors are modified in turn by their competition in the land market among the various activities seeking to exploit the differential advantages afforded by various locations.

The simplest kind of over-all descriptive measure of urban structure, Hoover points out, is the density gradient—the way in which average density varies with distance from the center of the city. A careful consideration of what we know about these gradients and what determines them leads quickly to his conclusion that "we still do not know very much in a quantitative way about demand functions in the multidimensional framework of space, access, income, and family structure, to say nothing of the other relevant socioeconomic variables." An elaboration of the gradient concept produces the central business district–concentric ring construct which can deal with the empirical richness of census data, and which is producing a substantial body of research on such matters as central city–suburban differentials in the socioeconomic characteristics of populations. At the same time economists have been theorizing about the economic determinants of the characteristic urban density gradient.

For most purposes, however, the density gradient is too gross a simplification of reality. Rather than being strongly focused on the center, activities and densities tend to be clumped in zones and subcenters throughout the urban region. Different kinds of economic activities have different access relations with households and with each other, so that a more detailed line of research has been opened up—largely by transportation studies—analyzing these relations in terms of access measures, through such general concepts as the "potential" and "intervening-opportunities" models, with considerable success. These studies emphasize the conclusions that subcentering and asymmetry of many activities are more descriptive of urban organization than the earlier radially symmetric constructs. Indeed, "an off-center concentration of some sizable activity can provide a nucleus . . . for cumulative development of a [new] focal access point . . . for other activities as well . . . ."

Turning to the dynamics of urban structure, Hoover points out that the major factors are easily identified—growth in size, aging, rising levels of income, and technological change. Demographic and economic growth are accompanied not only by physical growth upward and outward, but also by change in the "grain" of urban organization: size of urban areas is associated with a more elaborately differentiated pattern of land uses. The consequences of aging are difficult to assess. In part, aging reflects prior growth rates, but in part also the failure of the city to keep abreast of physical obsolescence and deterioration through appropriate maintenance outlays, so that its impact is not always distinguishable from growth. The influences of affluence and of technological change are equally difficult to predict, and frequently difficult to disentangle. The one depends on the income elasticities of demand for housing, transportation, recreation, and simple space. The other depends on the rate of adoption of productive and social overhead

20

innovations, which is to no small extent dependent on how well they can be afforded by the community. It may well be that the poor and the well-to-do will be no less segregated in the future, that the latter will continue to seek space and amenity while the former will exploit accessibility—generally with some difficulty—and the bare necessities of shelter in pursuing their locational preferences.

Finally, Hoover appraises some of the crucial problems arising from the spatial organization of the city. First, how can we adequately house the urban poor? A generation of housing legislation and of substantial public expenditures has scarcely touched the problem, for all of the now tarnished instruments of public housing, redevelopment, and renewal. The congestion of the city's media of interaction affords another unsolved problem in our inability to override the rising scale diseconomies of urban transportation systems. Neither new technology nor reorganization of the city have so far offered a way out of the problem. Finally, he points out, we don't really know how to exploit "the city's unique potential for maximum mass and diversity of contact, choice, and opportunity without unduly sacrificing other values."

The Role of Housing and Land Markets

In contrast to Hoover's broad overview of intrametropolitan development, Richard Muth brings to bear the analytical resources of the econometrician on some of the key unexplored areas in urban spatial structure. He begins with an examination of the evidence available about housing demand elasticities, production possibilities, and the conditions of factor supply, which lead him to conclude that the supply of urban land to the housing industry has an elasticity not greatly dissimilar from that of all urban land, which he estimates at about +1.2.

Strong economic forces can be seen to be associated with the density gradients of the urban region. Identifying distance from the center of the city with transportation costs, Muth has found a direct relationship between transportation costs and the median income of census tracts, but this relationship seems to be the result of strong negative correlations of both factors with the age of the dwelling unit: upper-income groups prefer new housing; lower-income groups can only afford the old housing left behind by the departing middle classes. Again, the gradient of transportation costs with respect to distance is paralleled by a decline in land costs resulting in a substitution of land for other factors in the production of new housing. Not only do the upper income groups seek more space in their housing services, but the gradient of land values assures that they will be able to maximize the realization of their preferences somewhere at a distance from the urban core.

21

There is, thus, a simple economic explanation for the spread of the metropolis with growth in population and increase in affluence. Ultimately, he reasons, the gradient of net population densities arises almost entirely from the decline in the value of housing produced per square mile with distance; and he hazards the opinion that gross population density gradients probably follow some negative exponential pattern with respect to distance.

The clustering of population densities, older dwellings, and low-income groups also proceeds from market forces reflecting attitudes and preferences. On the one hand, most of the perceptible market forces turn the upper-income housing consumer's attention toward the suburbs. At the other extreme, the low-income groups in the city are in many cases composed largely of Negroes. It is not the relative income disadvantage endured by the Negro that is the key factor as much as the fact of housing segregation, or, as he puts it, the fact that "whites have a greater aversion to living among Negroes than have some Negroes." The working out of market forces then leads to exclusiveness within the housing stocks occupied by the two groups. Further, he argues, there is some reason to believe that the excluded group is not disadvantaged in the cost of housing by this process.

Many would dispute Muth on these points. Anthony Downs points out that this analysis ignores the growing literature on race and housing and contradicts much scholarly opinion. Perhaps the issue really stems from the static character of Muth's analysis vis-à-vis the powerful growth and change aspects of urban development that have impressed other writers and analysts, as Downs suggests.

The quality of the urban housing stock is similarly subject to analysis by way of the market forces. External effects among classes of housing and among occupants having various income levels can be shown to be among the more significant factors. Demand factors also play a significant role: poor-quality housing has a strong negative correlation with income—"the principal reason for slum housing is the low incomes of its inhabitants!"

At this point, Downs finds himself taking issue with the narrowing of the problem implicit in the econometrician's formulations. Muth's paper "pays little attention to social factors, immobilities, market ignorance, and certain insights that might be obtained by using a broader perspective," he alleges. The housing market and housing policy are too complex and too important to be relegated exclusively to econometric analysis, to be sure; however, Muth's data and formulations are not too readily argued away. Clearly, both firmer concepts and better data will be required before these controversial issues can be fully resolved.

Finally, Muth turns his attention to the explanation of the phenomena of urban decentralization that have dominated American cities in recent years. The flight-from-blight effect, the differential local fiscal arrangements and levels of services, changes in the transportation and land value gradients, and land speculation are discarded for the conclusion that "increases in population and improvements in automobile transportation . . . are sufficient to account for most of the suburbanization of population and urban land area which occurred during the fifties."

The complexity of the issues exposed by Muth suggests that basic changes will not be brought about by policy solutions dictated by conventional wisdom without adequate regard for the market as well as the social processes involved. Racial segregation, suburban scatteration, the slum, and urban deterioration are the outcomes of allocational processes; solution of such problems will undoubtedly require changes in the processes themselves, as well as in the social-political environment in which they are carried out.

The City's Poor

In many ways the determinants of income are rooted in national rather than regional or local processes. While weekly wages vary widely from city to city, occupation- and industry-specific wage rates do not. A city's average weekly wage is thus an average which is influenced not only by the average weekly hours worked, but by the industrial and occupational composition of employment. The levels of poverty, then, must have roots in the way in which the local community participates in the national economy. Quite specifically, Oscar Ornati points out that "If we consider $4,000 to be the criterion of poverty, we find that the different incidences of poverty in different cities are related to their differing labor-capital coefficients and to the occupational (skilled-unskilled) ratios of their industries."

But the causes of urban poverty, according to Ornati, are not entirely to be found in industrial and occupational patterns, or even in employment as a whole. Part of the wide "band" of poverty can be attributed only to the prevalence of the elderly, the dependent, the unemployables and the less employables—like the urban unskilled Negro youth. Only part of the "band" is to be explained by the degree of prevalence of low-paying industries in the community.

Ornati looks at the city in terms of the organization and distribution of poverty that characterizes it. At the level of the system of cities, Ornati finds that the large concentration of the poor in the larger cities can lead to inappropriate conclusions if it is not recognized at the same time that the *incidence* of poverty is inversely associated with urban scale. Relatively fewer people fall below the poverty line in the major metropolitan areas than in middle-sized cities: "Not only is relative poverty more widespread in the smaller cities [than in larger cities] but the gap between small town and large city is widest at the lowest level of income." Small-town poverty, seen against the backdrop of the general economic decline of the small town in the American economy, presents a picture of hopelessness and futility which can only be matched by the more widely known picture of rural poverty. If you have to be poor, be poor in New York, or Chicago, or Los Angeles.

Poverty's more spectacular dimensions are to be seen in spatial terms. One way of characterizing the city is to disclose the contrast between the white, middle-class, child-oriented suburb and the Negro core of the central city with its aged poor, its dependent children, its working mothers. The slum, the quasi-slum, the declining grey area are "caused," according to Muth, by the poverty of their inhabitants; but in at least some cases, Ornati points out, their poverty is aggravated by the characteristics of the housing stock allocated to them by the market processes: the low-income condition of Watts in Los Angeles could be attributed, at least in part, to the lack of access of this part of the housing stock to employment opportunities.

Certain policy implications of urban poverty become readily apparent. The poor need much more basic support from public services than do the secure. Health, welfare, and public safety services are needed in far greater quantities than they are by the middle classes. Adequate public transportation is required for access to jobs. Public recreation is frequently the only kind available to the poverty strata. We have only recently come to understand the tremendously complex service needs of specific poverty groups which circumstances and the institutions of American society have locked into a permanent state of deprivation. Urban poverty, as Ornati so clearly points out, is not only a dimension of the urban economy, but has spatial aspects pregnant with policy implications. Somehow public policy must prevent urban poverty from evolving into a closed system.

Predicting the Future Form and Structure of the City

Do we know enough about the organizational processes at work in the city to predict at some level of reliability the future disposition of economic activities over the metropolitan landscape? Since the city is more than anything else a concentration of social and economic inter-action among persons and organizations, it is literally true that every-thing affects everything else. How can we replicate these complex systems? The development of intrametropolitan models has provided an intensive way of putting together the things that we know and for which we can find data, the things that we know but for which we must use indirect evidence, and the things that we don't know but can describe in sufficiently detailed terms to relate them to reality. If the model-builder has been sufficiently sensitive and clever, we will get some persuasive views of what is likely to happen to the distribution of urban activities and their channels of interaction in the future. Britton Harris' paper takes us deep into the methodological world of models of urban development where the issues raised by Hoover, Muth, and Ornati come to rest.

Harris provides us with an illuminating description of how the model-builder works with elements of theory, reality, and technique to deal with a characteristic problem of prediction—the location of retail trade activities. Beginning with the postulate that retail firms are profit maximizers, he examines the problems of classification of retail locaters, their spatial relationships to their clienteles as suggested by central-place theory, and the impacts of transportation costs on the behavior of the consumer. He illustrates the kinds of interesting theo-retical and practical problems the analyst must cope with. Where should one look for the behavioral parameters of the consumer as a shopper? How can one characterize the hierarchical aspects of the organization of retail trade? How can one introduce the implications of joint de-mand for retail goods and services? How can the sensitivity of retail trade to transportation considerations be tested? Finally, what are the normative implications of the spatial structure of retail activities? The answers to such questions are to be sought wherever leads are to be found, whether in the abstract formulations of scholars or the data sheets jammed in the desk drawers of practitioners.

Harris' discussion of the modeling of retail trade activities can, of course, be extended to the special problems of predicting the future distribution of the residences of various classes of households, to the location of industrial establishments, to the organization of business services, indeed, to the distribution of some classes of activities pro-ducing public services that are dependent on private locaters, such as schools. Not only does each of these classes have a locational logic of its own, but each takes its data from the critical characteristics of the distribution of the other classes of activities. Given the fact that every-thing depends on everything else, the art of model building consists in

25

large part in knowing what to omit and what is significant. In many ways the space economy of the city is more complex than that of the world because all of its subunits are so open, while the countries composing the world economy have at least some degree of closure with respect to the rest of the world. Thus, description alone is a task whose intricacy should challenge economic theory for years to come.

But such models have a purpose beyond describing the multitude of changes that are in process during each moment of the city's life. They are policy tools, and so contain explicit and implicit normative elements: "I take the view that the management of the scarce resource of space is a predominant problem in metropolitan development . . . that social welfare and economic development problems are strongly colored by spatial considerations . . . that the present tendencies of development in human settlement are far from optimal and, if allowed to continue, will produce unacceptable conditions," observes Harris. It follows, then, if the planners are going to realize their objectives, the model must be capable of describing likely future states of the city in space as they may be influenced by policies or plans which affect the structural conditions of the model and play some role in the identification of a "best scheme."

Harris points out that the model-builder encounters a gamut of issues to be resolved implicitly or explicitly. What kind of theory should be exploited as the basis for designing the principal features of the model? Since land-use, locational, and interaction aspects of these models are strongly identified with economic quantities or processes, it is clear that the main body of economic theory can be a basic source of analytical relations among them. Other kinds of theory are germane, also, and these are not confined to the social sciences. Should the model be constructed to represent all kinds of interaction, that is, should it be one large, highly integrated conceptual structure; or can it be built of smaller, partially independent units, each of which develops inputs for later stage submodels? A related question: where are the model's conceptual boundaries? Should it include political processes? Should it extend to the larger region? Should it deal with income classes? Answers depend on the kind of output sought, the quality and extent of the data available, and the degree of complexity that would seem to offer maximum payoff.

To what extent should the model be built up from the behavior of individual decision units—firms, agencies, persons—or from larger aggregations of units that behave similarly in terms that the model would distinguish? This is related to another issue: to what extent is it useful to employ probabilistic, as opposed to deterministic, statements in the model? Models based on individual decision units are likely to employ probability expressions to describe the choices of individual units among the alternatives offered by the model; more aggregated elements are likely to be treated as though their parameters behaved deterministically.

If the models are to be used to simulate the processes by which changes come about in the initial state of the model, then it will be necessary to define precisely how time enters into the model. What variables should be lagged? How should succeeding states of the model be related to their antecedent states? How do the model variables "age"? The issue of the extent to which dynamism is to be built into the model has implications for the time dimensions of the simulation exercise. Can the model be "solved" for various future states by simultaneous equations, or does it have to move forward in small steps or iterations that permit each successive stage to depend in large part on the unique events that made up the preceding stage?

Resolution of these issues takes place through successive compromises with theoretical postulates, the quality of available information, and the techniques accessible to the model-builder. This active process of compromise generates new insights into the nature of the urban spatial processes. Thus, while the initial—and still dominant—object of most such model-building activities is conditional prediction of future metropolitan spatial structure and associated elements, the exercise of trying to create artificially a process which acts like the complex processes of the city has a great potential in the enlargement of our understanding of the internal organization of the city. On the one hand, an increasing familiarity with the innate properties of the model elements can suggest new hypotheses about economic phenomena with which the model deals. On the other hand, the testing and calibration of the models with reality will provide a continuing refinement of existing knowledge about urban spatial organization. Finally, model-building is a learning process in which one can expect a progressive sophistication as the requirements for prediction and analysis converge. Advances in predictive precision and reliability depend on the breadth and depth of available knowledge about the spatial organization of the city. Thus, the social need to predict more effectively should provide a powerful social motivation for the increase of basic knowledge about space economy of the city.

Creating the Future

While Harris would expect model-building to provide valuable insights into future possibilities, should urban economics stop there? Responding to the first session of the Urban Economics Conference for which the papers in this volume were originally prepared, William Garrison salvaged a question that might otherwise have fallen between the topical chairs. "How," he asked, "could we develop *systems* of cities that are responsive to performance requirements that seem to be evolving in our society?"

Increasingly, he argued, we are developing the capability of creating whatever sizes and kinds of cities we want, to provide us with the kind of urban life that we value—rich in amenities and opportunities, efficient, productive. This is only true to the extent that it is known how cities of different sizes and organizations register meaningful differences in their roles as producers and in their "livability quotients" for their residents. (Barnett's comments about the diseconomies of large scale are particularly relevant here.) Thus, the decision to opt for a particular kind of system of cities must ultimately rest on knowledge of—and judgments about—those internal conditions of the city which determine the degree of amenity and efficiency achievable by various sizes and kinds of cities. Whatever the characteristics of the future economy of the United States, it is beyond doubt that the lion's share of the national economy will be located in its cities and more specifically in its metropolitan regions. Every change that Thompson would anticipate or Sonenblum and Harris predict with their models will have its impact within specific cities. In terms of over-all resources allocated to production, in terms of income generated, in terms of policy concern, the national economy and urban economy will become increasingly congruent, so that it is far from an idle question to ask what kinds of urban environments are most consistent with—or least hostile to—the future requirements of our economy and society. This surely is a core issue for urban economics.

Finally, the sociologist Donald Bogue urged economists to face up to the interdisciplinary dimensions of an urban civilization: "In my opinion, there are great opportunities today for collaboration among economists, sociologists, and members of the other social sciences in metropolitan research." By jointly working along the lines of the ten points listed below, he believes social scientists can accumulate deeper insight into the structure of metropolitan areas—how they are organized and how they will change in the future.

1) There should be a drive in urban economics to substitute direct observation for inferences from indirect data.

2) Certain sociological phenomena regarded as "natural" in economic analysis need to be given explicit economic evaluation.

28

3) The time has arrived for intensive longitudinal analysis for the explanation of urban change.

4) Much greater attention should be paid to the new urban sub-centers.

5) While we are engaging in macromodel-building, there is still ample room for microstudies of metropolitan structure.

6) Special economic attention should be paid to urban pathology.

7) A penetrating economic analysis of the urban slum housing industry is needed.

8) Economic regulation of the urban housing market is worth the attention of economists.

9) Economists should keep in mind that the assumption of un-limited or uninterrupted population growth is naïve and dangerous.

10) If we take what sociologists now know about the population that will be living in cities in future years, and carry out projections, we will get very different economic results from those we now antici-pate.

It is worth noting the role of a geographer and of a sociologist in broadening the scope and potential contribution of urban economics.

III. THE URBAN PUBLIC ECONOMY

In a book written almost a quarter of a century ago, which one of the editors of this volume co-authored,[8] some "basic maladjustments and deficiencies" were spelled out: "Urban communities, in general, suffer from the lack of over-all planning. Spreading blight, premature subdivision of land, decentralization, etc., confront local governments with many serious problems. . . . State and Local governments are faced with . . . limitations with respect to the taxes which can be employed and the rates which can be applied. . . . Local responsibili-ties to provide services are frequently not matched with adequate fiscal capacity. . . . An impressive number of communities throughout the nation are unable to supply services at anything resembling an ade-quate standard." The list is longer, and most of it still carries a familiar ring. This is partly due to our rising standards and aspirations, but there is also a remarkably large residue of unfinished business.

But if the problems of the urban public economy are of long stand-ing, serious intellectual concern with them—except only in the area of local taxation—is not. As Margolis points out, "the record of sophisti-cated analysis is not very long." Until the last few years, only a few

[8] A. H. Hansen and H. S. Perloff, *State and Local Finance in the National Economy* (W. W. Norton, 1944) pp. 11–12.

lonely scholars concerned themselves with these matters. An indication of the current situation is the fact that the book mentioned above, while seriously aged by postwar developments, remains the sole text in the field. But, fortunately, a new day is dawning; new interests, new approaches, and new tools are being introduced, and while few answers are as yet available about either the demand or supply of public services or about their financing, the questions, at least, are being seriously probed.

The Metropolitan Financial Picture

Dick Netzer's paper introduces us to the policy and research problems of the metropolitan public economy. It serves the valuable purpose of relating the traditional field of local public finance to the growing body of knowledge about the economic facts of metropolitan life. This happy conjunction permits the traditional field to pursue its central questions in a more fruitful context of policy and research issues. Thus, Netzer can open his discussion with an examination of the tax incidence issues with which local public finance has wrestled for many years; only this time he can raise the more general question of the over-all redistributive effects of the revenue and expenditure patterns which characterize the metropolitan area. Redistributive effects are localized, according to Netzer: *Within* any local jurisdiction the net consequences of revenues and expenditure policies tend to show perceptible redistributive effects, but *among* the local jurisdictions the situation is different. "The fiscal systems of the large metropolitan areas," Netzer concludes, "produce almost no redistribution between the central city poor and the suburban rich."

In the past, tax incidence and the economic impacts of the consumption of public goods have been studied independently. However, Netzer contends, the financing arrangements characteristic of modern metropolitan areas, with their fragmented jurisdictions, exert a substantial influence on what public services get produced and who consumes them. The result is a considerable divergence from optimality in the production of public goods. Thus he notes that tax rates and expenditure levels of local communities are negatively associated and that the richer communities provide superior services at lower tax rates. This is especially true of central city–suburb comparisons, and these disparities may be increasing. A larger stream of consequences flows from the sensitivity of some kinds of economic establishments to tax and service inequities. Influenced by these considerations, plants may be pulled away from their most efficient locations by caprices of tax policies and public service inadequacies, and so produce a spatial pattern of production that is more costly than it need be. However, he points out, the impact of local financial policies on the location decisions of plants is still something of a mystery. In general, he is forced to conclude, present fiscal arrangements appear to depress the output of public services and to generate land use and locational patterns that are substantially suboptimal.

What other arrangements are possible? De-emphasis of the property tax and greater exploitation of other sources of revenue are a logical step. Furthermore, there is an increasing need for arrangements that would permit levying taxes across the whole of the metropolitan base. The growing role of the state and federal governments in supporting urban services will be a significant factor making for equity among communities in the metropolitan area.

Already state and federal funds virtually support public welfare and highway services and make substantial contributions to other urban programs, an arrangement which could compensate in large degree for the spillover effects of local activities in these fields. More than this, the role of federal and state aid is frequently to encourage the production of additional services. Thus, the evidence suggests that direct state aid to local communities is likely to result in a higher output of services than actual production of those services by state agencies.

User charges, Netzer points out, will directly influence the output of public services, and have the further consequence of overcoming the political fragmentation problem. There is little doubt that there is "significant potential for greater and more sophisticated application of user-charge-type financing."

Netzer attempts to see what a model multilevel system for the financing of local, publicly produced services might look like. The differing capabilities of levels of government to play special roles in the financing of metropolitan services, he feels, should be exploited in developing the over-all system of metropolitan public finance. Its nationwide coverage uniquely suits the federal government to play a leading role in the output of activities concerned with redistribution and stabilization. For a similar reason, the states are in a position to make a contribution to these activities with distributive consequences. A multiplicity of local governments may provide the best response to the demand for other services that have no substantial geographic spillovers, while the spillover problem may best be handled by wider areas of government, including special-purpose units.

The achievement of this model system will have to take place through a series of deliberate steps, he maintains, and proceeds to examine metropolitan government, ad hoc regional agencies, and rearrangement of intergovernmental fiscal roles; only the latter survive the test of feasibility. Netzer then reconstructs, point by point, the division of responsibilities among the governmental levels, giving special attention to the tax-sharing proposals of which the Heller–Pechman plan is the archetype. Such programs offer the prospect of substantially increased output of urban services at the same time that the federal government would be carrying out its redistribution role in the total system.

Such a model system, it is argued, will accommodate a substantial amount of growth and change without attrition. Actually, the changes now under way in the urban organization of the nation will increasingly require the kind of governmental sharing of responsibility that Netzer suggests. Knowing this, we ought to move into it deliberately, if not "planfully."

While Netzer has given us an overview of the total process of metropolitan finance, its problems, its appropriate objectives, and its alternatives, Werner Hirsch and Julius Margolis take a close look at the economics of publicly produced services; the one taking up the conceptual and research problems on the supply side, the other examining the issues associated with the characteristics of demand.

The Supply of Urban Services

Hirsch sets out to examine urban services "as resource-using sets of activities . . . whose objective is to satisfy urbanites' wants and thus enhance their welfare." Immediately, a crucial problem is encountered: how to measure the output of public-service-producing activities. The ideal unit should be related to the way in which the consumer consumes it, the way in which his wants are satisfied; but it should also reflect in useful physical terms what the agency is actually producing. Both of these criteria are frequently difficult to satisfy, as the case of education attests. Associated with the output is the quality dimension, which is as responsive to changes in inputs as is the volume of output. Actually, the analytical problem is complicated by the fact that most services are produced at more than a single quality level and with substantially different characteristics. Hirsch illustrates the problems of measurement by looking at refuse collection as a typical public service.

The central difficulty in identifying the determinants of urban public service outputs is the formulation of the appropriate production functions, an essential step if the efficiency aspects of the urban public sector are to be dealt with. Hirsch sets up a conventional production function, and then examines its applicability to the public sector. He cites recent studies which give explicit recognition to the fact that public service

32

output is a combination of quantity and quality which can be traded off and is determined by inputs, service conditions, and technology.

The measurement of the input variables for the production function also presents some difficult choices. The treatment of capital, managerial efficiency, and physical resource inputs each presents unresolved conceptual problems. The choices between time series and cross-sectional data, and among statistical methods of estimation, provide other dimensions to be resolved by the investigator. Hirsch examines some empirical production functions to illustrate how these problems have been met by researchers looking at educational services.

Cost functions are crucial inputs to the decisions to produce urban public services, and these introduce other complications. What kinds of costs are incurred and by whom? Costs to the public constitute the principal concern of the budget-making operation, but segregable costs borne by individuals also influence the quality of the output, while tradeoffs between public and social costs may produce some special problems, as in waste disposal activities. However, the development of cost functions in public services follows closely on the procedures commonly applied in the private sector. To illustrate the development and application of cost functions in public services, Hirsch briefly analyzes some contemporary work in this area.

A class of research related to cost function studies Hirsch identifies as "expenditure determinant studies." Here the purpose is to specify socioeconomic variables closely associated with levels of output of public service. A substantial number of such studies have been carried out through multiple regression techniques which, while illuminating, have the basic defect of having little in the way of a solid base of rigorous theory. Nevertheless, they have provided insights and in some cases reasonably reliable predictive power.

Scale economies in the production of urban public services and their implications for government consolidation have been the source of a continuing public debate, and Hirsch's paper gives them proper recognition. He notes that "the conditions that help private industry to benefit from scale economies—lower factor costs, larger and more efficient plants, and induced circular and vertical integration—often do not appear to exist when local urban governments grow or consolidate." Speculating about the shape of the average unit cost function, Hirsch examines a number of studies of scale factors in public services for evidence of scale economies or diseconomies, finding that for single institutions scale economies appear to be significant, but that on a system-wide basis, for "horizontally integrated services no significant scale economies were found [in refuse collection] for communities of 200 to 865,000 residents. . . . Similar results were found for police protection and education, while fire protection showed some small economies of scale. . . ."

Also engaging Hirsch's attention are urban public service supply functions, with respect to which he finds an important research gap attributable in part to the fact that supply functions for the private sector do not shed much light on those for the public sector. Motivation for productive efficiency in government units is weak; monopoly elements dominate, and production costs have little to do with the pricing of the goods produced. The central feature of these functions is the public official who has a fixed budget and a fixed clientele; the quality of the service produced reflects the relationship between these.

All these considerations lead Hirsch to conclude that little improvement in the costs of government services is to be expected from scale economies, and hence from consolidation movements. Consistent with Netzer's conclusions, Hirsch places heavy emphasis on the need for new institutional arrangements that can enhance urban governments' incentive to perform their functions efficiently.

The Demand for Urban Services

Margolis begins his analysis of the demand side of urban public services with a review of the known facts about such services. He points out the large degree of variability among metropolitan and non-metropolitan areas in the expenditures for various classes of goods, but finds it not surprising, given the number of "determinants" involved in setting local levels of output. Among large metropolitan areas the variations are comparatively small because, in general, the characteristics of these large units are very similar. However, as one deals with the smaller units which make up these regions, the variability in the output of public services increases with the basic variability of social and economic characteristics of the subunits. Some of these dimensions vary systematically with spatial organization of the metropolitan region as well.

The existence of consumption and production externalities among urban services is well known. Geographic spillovers have occasioned sweeping pronouncements, especially with respect to issues concerned with quality of the environment and with education. Margolis argues for a much greater volume of analysis on these issues to provide a proper basis for production decisions with respect to the array of local public services and policies aimed at "internalizing" the geographic externalities. One should, he believes, move with caution in the direction of governmental reorganization based essentially on this objective.

Margolis initiates his discussion of the demand characteristics of urban public services with the observation that "the demand for an urban public service is not an unambiguous concept." No body of empirical study has accumulated on the subject, but some insights can be gained through literature that has developed around two lines of investigation: public goods and the economic theory of political decision, both of which focus on the mechanisms by which the normative conditions of the private economy might be realized.

"The perplexing feature of a public good is that it relies on individual preferences . . . but without an optimal mechanism to aggregate preferences," Margolis points out. As both Netzer and Hirsch suggest, many publicly supplied services are, in reality, essentially private goods. Merit goods produce other difficulties, because "society," not individuals, demands their production. The trend in analysis of the public sector is to treat merit goods as though they were public goods pure and simple, but such adaptations do not remedy the lack of any mechanism outside of the political processes to reveal preferences. One effect is that public goods are produced with at best a modest relation to individual preferences, which results in a lower output than the scale of preferences might indicate. Such an effect brings into play various rationing mechanisms—rents, congestion costs, administrative criteria—or may even induce private production of the goods where their costs can be related profitably to private activity.

The political processes provide another entree to the problem. Here voting and other political mechanisms are seen as the basis for preference-recording by an electorate which is a proxy for the consuming clienteles. In this format, migration among local government units is seen as one form of voting, since the migrant is choosing the bundle of advantages he most wants out of those offered by a number of localities in the same region. "It would be intriguing to explore the question whether voting both by ballot and by feet would solve the public goods problem and give rise to an optimal set of public services . . ." Margolis speculates. Several conceptual approaches have been used to relate political mechanisms to the market function: interpretation of political behavior in terms of postulates of welfare economics, study of the behavior of legislative bodies making production decisions, analysis of economic characteristics of political decisions in which socioeconomic aspects of the consumers are seen as crucial. In the end, it is clear that "the current state of our political models is not yet sufficiently advanced

35

to tell us how to estimate demand, nor can we be sure that they will ever be successful in that role."

Finally, Margolis turns his attention to benefit-cost analysis as a demand-connected set of constructs for the decision-maker. A crucial problem in its application at the local level is the importance of the distributional consequences of public services, which the original formulation of the approach tended to suppress in favor of the over-all impact on national income. Nevertheless, progress in the application of benefit-cost analysis to local production decisions has been quite remarkable, and its further development may considerably improve the effectiveness of public production decisions.

Netzer's overview of the public finance issues in the production of urban public services, Hirsch's careful unraveling of the issues of the production aspects of urban services, and Margolis' synthesis of the demand issues in the public economy provide a multidimensional view of the crucial conceptual and policy issue of the urban public economy. It remains only to relate these discussions to the policy problems of the urban economy at large.

Reflecting on these papers, Howard Schaller underlined the ambiguity of market concepts when they are adapted to the public economy. The concept of demand with respect to public services is an obvious case, but Schaller was more concerned with the output side of the market. Specifically, he wondered whether present information really made it possible to describe production functions for public services. Hirsch, he suggested, was too sanguine in this matter, notwithstanding his reservations. A persuasive identification of their products will have to be accompanied by a resolution of serious conceptual problems and information gaps on the production side before we can really feel confident that the production function for a public service is a meaningful concept.

IV. POLICY ISSUES

We have noted at the beginning of this Introduction the role policy concerns played in the development of urban economics. These concerns still are central and continue strongly to influence the selection of areas of research. The puzzling and complex problems revealed by the poverty program, for example, undoubtedly attracted economists to the study of human resources in an urban setting. Moreover, the availability of public funds for research in designated subjects is hardly a neutral factor in the choice of topics. Possibly even more pervasive is the indirect influence exerted by the presence or absence of usable data. Scholars have been drawn, for example, to the rich storehouse of data, beyond the means of individual scholars, produced through the transportation studies (at a cost of some $6 or $7 million in the case of the Penn-Jersey study and some $18 million in the study of transportation in the New York region). Even more to the point is the essentially applied nature of urban economics. Significant theoretical issues exist in every facet of the field, analysis of which will undoubtedly enrich the collective fund of economic theory. Nevertheless, the main task of the urban economist is to apply his economic theory and methodology in order to achieve a better understanding of the socially significant problems of urban economy and urban life.

Thus, in each of the papers in this volume, no matter how general or theoretical in form or tone it may be, the policy issues emerge as powerful magnets which draw concepts, methods, and data into their orbit, whether the question be how to maintain the economic growth of a great metropolis, whether to try to prevent "scatteration" in new construction in outlying areas, or how to maximize the efficiency of public services. None of this resulted from conference planning; yet each author, in trying to understand a special part of the urban reality, found that he had to come to grips with certain dominant urban policy issues. What the conference committee did plan was a session devoted entirely to policy issues. Alan Campbell, one of the rare breed of political scientists who understand the language of economists, and Jesse Burkhead, an economist firmly rooted in the rich traditions of political economy, undertook to review the full spectrum of urban policy issues.[9]

Wisely choosing to digest "this diffuse and inchoate area in three chunks," the authors first examine the large forces that shape the nature of urban policy. They find these in (1) the private market, (2) the metropolitan government structure, and (3) the political structure.

As to the first category, they point out that many of the "problems" often described purely in sociological terms are, in fact, the result of the operation of the market. Much of the difficulty stems from divergences between private cost and social cost where the difference is attributable to external costs that exceed external benefits. Uncompensated externalities abound.

In the second category, the dominant feature is functional and areal fragmentation of the metropolitan governmental structure (a triumph of the combined forces of administrative specialists and program spe-

[9] Two other papers, by Walter W. Heller and Richard Ruggles, dealing with federal block grants to states and localities, were presented at the conference. Because of their topical nature, these, together with extensive comments by Lyle C. Fitch, Carl S. Shoup, and Harvey E. Brazer, have been published separately in paperback form under the title *Revenue Sharing and the City*. (The Johns Hopkins Press, for Resources for the Future, 1968).

cialists, in the words of Robert Wood). This fragmentation, the authors suggest, greatly complicates the problem of controlling land uses and of providing—and financing—public services; particularly troubling is the difficulty of maintaining an adequate level of services in the central cities, with state aid biased in favor of suburban areas.

In the third category, the political arena, the authors stress the importance of the decline in strength of the politics of reform, the earlier coalition of farmers, small businessmen, and organized labor having been shattered. Yet if the conditions of urban existence—particularly for the disadvantaged—is to be improved, there must be a political base for reform, and it must have national as well as local dimensions.

The interplay among these three constellations of forces that shape policy in urban America gives rise to consequences which are at times exceedingly unpleasant, particularly in the continued pursuit of the "policy of racial containment" which destroys any sense of community responsibility for central city problems.

The authors examine policy responses to these major forces by looking in some detail at two "hardware" programs, urban renewal and transportation, and two "software" programs, education and anti-poverty. What is presented is a more or less impressionistic painting, displaying the workings of American economics and politics at the localized scale in all its rich and often puzzling complexity, as public and private activities and federal, state, and local policies and programs intertwine ever more closely. Policy changes are shown to be quite incremental, not sweeping; new directions are tried, but with caution. The demand for an overriding, unified federal urban policy, that could mesh specific programs into a meaningful framework, Campbell and Burkhead suggest, is not very realistic. "The difficulty with the demand is that it assumes agreement about what the problems are, their causes, and the kind of urban society desired. There is, in fact, no general agreement on any of these prerequisites to an urban policy . . . ."

But if a sweeping overriding national urban policy is not in the cards, broad-scale regional planning and publicly sponsored research and development might be helpful, particularly for the "hardware" programs. More troublesome are the problems of the "socially sick cities," the problems of the poor and disadvantaged. "The problems are so serious," say the authors, "that small-scale experimentation (as in the current poverty and education-aid programs) is insufficient. Massive undertakings are necessary. The politicians must be prepared for failures and they, in turn, must prepare the public. Thus far, no new generation of metropolitan leaders has appeared willing to take the kind of political risks implied." The political facts of life thus make it inevitable that urban policy leadership will have to continue to come from the federal level.

In each of the four programs outlined above, the authors bring to the forefront the contribution of the economists in providing concepts, methodologies, and data. Thus, the explanations that have been provided as to why under certain circumstances the market fails to halt physical deterioration and decay, calling urban renewal into being, are referenced, as are the discussions showing the large volume of externalities generated by an urban transportation system, the measurement of losses due to traffic congestion, the measurement of returns on investments in education, the workings of cost-benefit analysis in urban programs, and a number of other contributions helpful in understanding and guiding public policies and programs.

Consider urban renewal, for example. While fifteen years of experience have led to a great deal of demolition and new construction in the urban core, they have also left in their wake a considerable disillusionment about the complexity and costs of reconstituting our urban life. The authors' appraisal of the effectiveness of this complex program operating in an even more complex environment is simply "No balance sheet rendition is possible for urban renewal. To quote Abrams, 'Financial benefits cannot be offset against social costs nor an increase in revenues juxtaposed against the myriad peoples evicted from their homes.' "

Several basic disquietudes are warranted, according to the authors. The future form and function of the central city are not clear at this point in time. Is urban renewal, then, an appropriate area for federal intervention? It is likely that simpler, more direct means are available to deal with each of the conglomerate objectives implied by urban renewal programs. Nevertheless, urban renewal seems to have arrived as a permanent member of the federal government's urban policy kit. More sophisticated articulation of urban renewal with tangential programs, improvements in techniques, and a growing awareness of its limitations are proceeding simultaneously, the authors maintain. Furthermore, the economists have considerably enriched urban renewal analysis and decision-making, so that notwithstanding the unresolved conceptual problems, a broader rationality is possible throughout the program. Many crucial urban issues are left behind by urban renewal policies, certainly, but the future value of urban renewal may well emerge from the growing sensitivity of policy-makers to the fact it is an imperfect and limited tool in the urban revolution, but useful in an arsenal of policy weapons.

In like manner the authors tackle transportation, education, and the poverty program; description, analysis, and evaluation provide a critical mosaic of the federal-state-local policy interpenetration. Their approach argues, along with that of the authors of the papers in Part I of this book, that cities are integral parts of the nation, their policies so commingled with those of the nation as to defy the economists' facile dictum of independence, "all other things being equal."

As Campbell and Burkhead discuss the most critical issues in each of these programs, a disconcerting sense is experienced that perhaps the economists have only been nibbling at the edges: the core issues have simply not yielded to the traditional concepts and tools. Nevertheless, the benchmarks afforded by these papers evidence a beginning of sorts. The workings of the urban economy daily become more visible—and hence more intelligible. Already, economists have improved the context of decision-making by focusing attention on how much alternative solutions to a problem are likely to cost, and what kind and amount of benefits are likely to flow therefrom. A new generation of urban economists, building on the platform of method, theory, and information summarized in the pages that follow, can be expected to attack the complex and thorny issues which this book and its parent conference were designed to explore. The analysis and evaluation of the economies of urban scale, the role of the central business district in the economic health of the metropolitan region, the role of the urban slum in the exacerbation or perpetuation of poverty, the interdependence of land and capital markets with urban development policies—these and similar areas of economic ignorance are now ready for the economist's unique techniques of analysis, his capacity for quantification, and, most important of all, his special insights into the allocative processes of society. We hope that this volume urges him on.

PART I

THE URBAN COMMUNITY
WITHIN THE NATIONAL ECONOMY

*Wilbur R. Thompson**

INTERNAL AND EXTERNAL FACTORS IN THE DEVELOPMENT OF URBAN ECONOMIES

Urban-regional growth theory has subsisted since the uncertain date of initial systematic enquiry, sometime in the early twenties, on one simple but powerful idea, the export base concept. Because the history of this concept has been traced at length elsewhere,[1] as a prelude to the present discussion we need only remind ourselves of the concept's main characteristics and limitations as brought out through the years of debate.

THE LEGACY OF THE EXPORT BASE THEORY

From the beginning, economic geographers, economic historians, urban planners, and urban land economists have all seen the usefulness of distinguishing between those local industries which sell outside the "local economy" (later interpreted more precisely as the job commuting radius about the urban center) and those which sell within the "local labor market." The export industries clearly generate a net flow of income into the local economy from which the necessary imports can be financed. In this most immediate sense of current money flow, the export sector is basic and the local service sector is derivative in origin.

When, in the postwar period, economists began to take a more sustained interest in regional development, a parallel was seen between the export base concept and the export multiplier concept from Keynesian economics. The contributions of the economists here tended to reinforce the notion of the primacy of the export sector in the performance of the small-area, open economy because usually the economist was thinking in cyclical terms—of the expansion and contraction of output and employment within given export plant facilities. The direction of causation is clear as national cyclical change ebbs and flows through the portal of the local export sector and swirls about the passive stores and offices.

But the attempted marriage of the export multiplier and the export base theory was more than a little forced. Those with deeper and more sustained involvement with the city—urban planners especially—did

---

* Professor of Economics, Wayne State University.
[1] See especially the series of nine articles by Richard B. Andrews, in *Land Economics,* Vol. 29, No. 2 (May 1953)—Vol. 32, No. 1 (February 1956), and the writings of other early proponents and critics of the export base theory of regional growth, all reprinted in Ralph W. Pfouts, *The Techniques of Urban Economic Analysis* (Chandler-Davis, 1960).

43

not have in mind the direction of causation of variations in per capita income of a (nearly) fixed population and labor force over the business cycle. Urban planners care more about the lines of linkage in aggregate growth of total population over decades. Consequently they were interested in a very different kind of "multiplier" that defined locational linkages in the long run where new investment in plant and plant relocations attract other new plants and homes and stores.

Through the postwar period it has not always been clear when a given discussion was addressed to cyclical changes in local output, income, and employment of interest to, say, local public revenue and public assistance officials, or when long-run public investments in streets, utilities, schools or whatever were at issue. Both the projecting of next year's tax revenue and the pouring of cement are significant social questions, but the time horizons are, of course, quite distinct, as is also the relevant theory.

Understandably, some urban planners rebelled at the invidious comparison suggested by the terms "basic" and "local service," especially as these words implied a higher policy priority to the needs of the export sector. The export firms were more often than not those drab manufacturing plants on the edge of town, or currently moving there, while the local service sector was clustered in the more elegant high-rise buildings that dominated their favored downtown sites and symbolized "city" itself. Usually, the urban planner was not sophisticated enough in economics to defend well his intuition that in his world of the very long run (locational economics) it may well be the local service sector which is enduring (basic) and the manufacturing plant which is transitory.

As we move from local cycles to local development, we shift our interests from money flows, which clearly run from exports to local services, to concern for comparative costs relative to competing urban centers. The lines of causation are then turned inside out to the degree that comparative costs rest on the efficiency of local transportation systems, public utilities, banks and other financial institutions, schools and universities and other training and retraining centers, and a host of other critical supporting services. Such services are, moreover, likely to be more permanent than the particular factories of a given time period.

We begin to see more clearly the relationship between the time period and the lines of causation in urban change and development when we review more precisely the simplistic and somewhat tenuous dichotomy of export and local service. With time and the contributions of the economist, the concept of the export sector has been extended beyond direct exports to other regions to include local firms which supply intermediate products to local exporters. As one moves, however, from the more obvious "linked industries" (tire manufacturers in Detroit, for example) farther and farther back in the stages of production to trucking firms hauling inputs and outputs, to accounting, financial and promotional services, and even back to technical curricula in local schools, a near continuum of activity emerges. It becomes very difficult to dichotomize local activity, and the most basic work is indeed performed by the very same banks, schools, and utilities that service the households.

These complex lines of linkage among the many local activities can be, and were, brought out crisply and definitively in the many local input-output tables constructed around the country. But, again, the input-output tables quantify the flows among a given set of local industries and are most relevant to short-period variations, although some limited extension to growth paths is possible. We do not, however, have the full development equivalent, a locational matrix that tells us which industries follow a given industry to a locality and when. This is what the urban planners and economic geographers had in mind.

With greater urban size comes a tendency toward greater local self-sufficiency. More than a decade ago, critics of the early, more simplistic form of the export base theory noted the tendency for the base-to-service ratio to fall with increased size. While perhaps none of the early developers of the export base mechanism would have insisted, on being pressed, that the ratio of export to local service workers was fixed, they all too easily slipped into the habit of multiplying the change in the number of, say, manufacturing workers by some customary fixed coefficient to find the change in total employment and then remultiplying that employment figure by the (inverse of the) labor force participation rate to yield the change in total population of a community. Perhaps the number of retail food store clerks or barbers per thousand population is nearly constant across the spectrum of urban areas, but with larger size the threshold of economic local production for the local market is passed for one new activity after another. First come those activities with only modest economies of scale and high transportation costs (medical clinics, for example), and with great size even those activities with very large scale economies and low transportation costs (such as investment banking) come to be produced locally for local sale.

To hold the prime role for an export sector that accounts for a half of all local activity in an urban place of 10,000 population is a far cry from retaining that role when metropolitan areas reach one-half million and over and where the export sector may account for only one-quarter

45

of all activity. (And this applies even in cyclical analysis, where shifts in local investment and in the "local-consumption-of-local-production" function probably come to rival export multipliers in local cyclical impact.) Clearly, then, the relative roles of the export and local service sectors change with the relevant time period and the size of the urban region under analysis.

In the analyses to follow an all-embracing term will be used: the "local industry-mix." In static or very short-period analysis of a small urban area the distinctive and determining part of the local industry-mix is the current export mix, and the impact of the current local industrial specialties on local economic welfare will be traced through— on the pattern of income as well as the growth rate. But as we move through time and to larger size, the analysis will be directed to the process by which structural change takes place in the local industry-mix. The analyses will, therefore, begin with the export industry-mix and progress toward increasing involvement with the local service sector, especially those parts of it which facilitate adaptation to change and/or produce change itself.

URBAN-REGIONAL INCOME ANALYSIS

The easiest place for the economist to take hold of urban-regional growth and development is in the middle of the story, that is, at the present. As we come to understand better how a given—the current—industrial structure affects the performance of a local economy, even in static terms, we will come to see better the inexorable development of forces leading to change. The most conventional and powerful tools and skills of the economist can, moreover, be most quickly brought to bear in a static regional income analysis. Here we can begin simplistically by casting a local economy as a mere bundle of industries in space: Tell me your industries and I will tell your (immediate) fortune. How could a highly specialized economy fail to reflect in its level, distribution, and stability of income and growth rates its distinctive industry mix? Our analysis will, moreover, retain those traditional dimensions of economic welfare that follow from national income analysis.

The major point of departure will be that no attempt will be made to discuss the general level of income or the general degree of inequality or over-all national economic stability; only the pattern of regional deviations about the national average. Our charge in urban-regional economics is to determine why some urban areas are richer or more egalitarian or more unstable—or all three (as in the case of Flint, Michigan). Urban-regional economics, freed in the beginning from explaining the general state of the national economy, becomes the study of variations within the system of cities.[2]

While urban-regional income analysis is more than merely industrial analysis, it is intriguing and surprising to see how far one can go in explaining the level, distribution, and stability of local income as mere extensions of the local industry-mix. But because this has been done elsewhere at considerable length,[3] it should be sufficient here to summarize what seems, deductively, to be the more important lines of interaction between the local industrial structure and the local income pattern before pushing beyond into the much more difficult subject of change.

The Level of Income

The many subtle and interacting forces that operate to enrich a community may be factored into two generic determinants of the level of income: skill and power. We would expect, typically, to find above-average skill in local labor forces that are wrestling with the production of the newer products. Implicit here is some form of the "learning curve": new tasks tend to be the most demanding of intelligence and creativity, but in time the production process becomes rationalized and relatively routine. Not only are skilled workers more scarce and therefore higher paid, but skilled workers on new products tend to share the monopoly power of the early lead in a new industry; the high profit margins enjoyed, temporarily, by local innovators are passed on in part to local labor. Innovation, then, gives rise to both the skill needed to rationalize the new and strange and the price power of an early lead.

Other local economies producing older, slower-changing products may also profit from the weak competition that originates in pronounced internal economies of scale relative to the size of the market. Large investments in plant and equipment give rise to high fixed costs; the latter leads to substantially lower unit costs at very large outputs; this leads, in turn, to fewer plants (firms) and (implicit) collusion in pricing. Large investments reinforce this market power by impeding the entry of new firms as potential competitors. The price power of oligopoly is not enough, however, to enrich a community, especially if

[2] Worthy of attention at some other time and place is a careful investigation of the reverse side of the coin: the way in which a non-optimal system of cities depresses the national income.
[3] Wilbur R. Thompson, *A Preface to Urban Economics,* 1965, Chaps. 2–5; or for a revised but briefer version, Thompson, "Urban Economic Development, in Werner Z. Hirsch (ed.), *Regional Accounts for Policy Decisions,* 1966 (both books, The Johns Hopkins Press, for Resources for the Future).

the local plant is absentee-owned. Where there are large, multiplant corporations whose stockholders are scattered, oligopoly power in the local export sector can be translated into high wage rates and/or family incomes only when it is wedded to labor power. The necessary condition would seem to be an aggressive, industry-wide union only nominally resisted by a secure oligopoly that is able to support higher wages through higher prices.

Even a moderate degree of price elasticity in the demand for local labor in the oligopolistic export industry is not likely to constrain local income if the adverse employment effects of high wage rates can be worked off in an expanding market (in the form, perhaps, of a new or income-elastic product) or by easy out-migration. If the oligopolistic export industry is a growth industry, the community will enjoy the benefits of economic power to the fullest as the monopoly wage rate of the export sector "rolls-out" into the local service sector, enriching local teachers, bus drivers, and bankers by more than it deflates the money income of the export workers through increased local prices. Wage roll-out assumes that there is some appreciable labor mobility between the export and import sectors and some appreciable immobility of movement into the community from the outside, so that the high export wage largely benefits local residents. The effects of innovation, market power, and unionization on the level of income are summarized in Figure 1.

The Distribution of Income

Unions not only raise local wage rates and average family incomes; they also tend to reduce the degree of inequality. The frequent threat of skilled workers to break away and create their own union is indirect evidence either that "unionism" (ideology) or economic democracy (assuming majority rule and representative union government) is more egalitarian than the free competitive market. The lesser degree of (median family) income inequality exhibited by the more highly industrialized metropolitan areas is probably due in significant measure to the relatively narrow range of skills characteristic of manufacturing, especially branch plant, assembly operations. Still, the labor union would seem, a priori, to be an equalitarian force of comparable magnitude.

Some appreciation of the complexity of the forces determining the distribution of local income is gained by noting that the local labor markets that generate a large number of jobs for women tend to be among the most egalitarian of all. A high female labor force participation rate may come out of light manufacturing (as in a textile town),

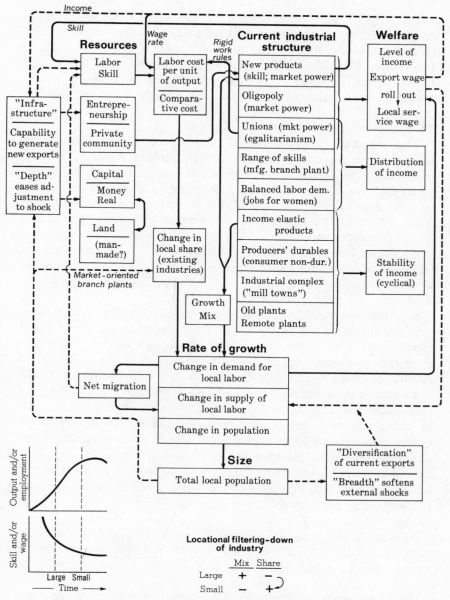

Figure 1. Patterns of urban-regional economic development.

but probably more often it is the commercial, financial, medical, educational, or governmental center which generates a balanced demand for labor.[4] Implicit here is the assumption, for which there is reasonably good supporting evidence, that working wives and other female second-income earners come more than proportionately from the lower-income households. Certainly, second-income earners also raise the average family income but their impact on the distribution of family income would seem to be more significant both quantitatively and socially.

The Stability of Income and Employment

Two standard concepts from "national economics" seem highly transferable in any attempt to trace through the lines of linkage between the local industrial structure and the relative severity of the local business cycle. Those areas specializing in producers' durable goods should be most unstable and those specializing in consumer non-durables most stable, following from the greater variation in investment expenditures than in consumer expenditures over the cycle and from the simple fact that durable goods can easily be made to last a little longer while the replacement of non-durables is less postponable. The early statistical evidence suggests, however, that an industry-mix explanation of the local cycle will not be sufficient.

Specialization in durables is not, for example, significantly correlated with the degree or rate of decline in employment during the 1957–58 recession. True, the census data do not permit sure and easy separation of *producers' durables* from consumer durables. Still, the tendency for durable goods to cluster (agglomerate in industrial complexes) while non-durables often stand alone as the sole support of the smaller place (the textile town, for example), may blur the sharp national contrast by posing industrial centers concentrating on *diversified* durable-goods against isolated towns concentrating on *specialized* non-durables. Any significant lead or lag in the timing of the industry cycle of any of the local durable industries softens the aggregate local fluctuation as the leading industry begins to fall while other local industries are still climbing, and begins to rise from its trough while the others are still falling.

Further, as we translate national economic concepts into regional economics, we must remember that a local economy is not only an atypical bundle of industries, it tends also to be a non-random, or a

[4] Since these non-manufacturing places tend to create more income inequality out of their wider ranges of occupations, their higher propensity to produce jobs for women tends only to make them less unequal than they would otherwise be, but still not as egalitarian as factory towns.

biased, sample of plants by age. The older industrial areas tend to have more of the older plants, and these tend to be the higher-cost facilities that are cut back first and brought back last over the cycle. To the degree, moreover, that the newer plants are more capital-intensive (automated), the higher ratio of fixed to variable (labor) cost should lower marginal cost and reinforce the tendency for the newer facilities to absorb more than their share of the smaller recession market and lesser share of the larger boom output.

Let us draw out the asymmetry of national and regional cycle analysis a little more by adding that most neglected facet: space. A locality may have relatively high-cost facilities not because of age but because of a more out-of-the-way location. Rarely do we incorporate the cost of transportation of either inputs or outputs into our cost curves. To do so, however, is to see clearly that remoteness from the market raises marginal delivered costs and amplifies output variations in response to demand and price fluctuations. Moreover, "remoteness" may have to be interpreted in the context of differential oscillation of regional markets. Products with high transportation cost are not ordinarily sold across the nation. Thus, a locality's cycle will tend to reflect the regional industry-mix as well as its own mix and its locational position in the region. There is little doubt that a paper-mill town in a region with a state capital and a large university would be in relatively good shape over the business cycle.

Growth and Income Patterns

By influencing the rate of growth of the local economy, local industrial characteristics also act indirectly to shape the local income pattern. A local export sector which emphasizes either new products or income-elastic products will tend to experience a greater than average expansion in output and in demand for labor. A steadily rising national per capita income acts directly to stimulate the growth of localities producing income-elastic products. Through increasing discretionary income more than proportionately, growing affluence also acts indirectly to stimulate the demand for new products. The buoyancy of a new-products economy comes not merely from the opportunity to exploit a new market unconstrained by depreciation rates and replacement schedules, but also from the eager search for variety—temporary enchantment with *a* new product becomes a persisting obsession for new products.

A greater than average increase in the demand for local labor interacts with an average increase in the supply of local labor (typical birth, death, and labor force participation rates) to create rising wage rates, overtime, upgrading, part-time jobs, relaxed job requirements, and other reflections of a tight labor market. A greater than average rate of growth in the demand for local labor should then lead to a relatively fast rising and, ultimately, a relatively high median family income, but even more surely should lead to a lessening of the degree of local income inequality. The marginal worker who finds a full-time job will, of course, experience the greatest rate of increase in income. Recent studies of income inequality have shown that it was the tight labor market of the war years which effected the great decrease in inequality and that there has been little or no reduction in interpersonal inequality since the end of World War II.[5]

Again, we distinguish between the national economy, which is a closed economy, and the local economy, which is open to the flow of people as well as goods. Classical economic theory would predict an increase in the supply of labor as the high wage rates, abundant jobs, and high welfare payments of this prosperous community attract the unemployed and unemployable. The seeming paradox of poverty amidst plenty in the booming locality is quite in conformance with classical theory. In the long run, growth industries do not make a locality richer, only bigger.

TOWARD A THEORY OF URBAN-REGIONAL GROWTH

Population Size

Since size is simply the cumulation of growth, those places which grow faster tend to get big more quickly and are at any given time larger. Growth creates size and size reacts to restructure the local economy so as virtually to ensure further growth at a near average rate —reacts, that is, to produce growth stability. The simplest, most dramatic and thus most widely appreciated structural change accompanying large size is toward a diversified mix of current exports. A large sample of exports, such as we find in Chicago or Philadelphia, is likely to include some very new, fast-growing industries, some middle-aged slow-growing ones, and even a few that are old and declining. Moreover, a large sample would be likely to mix income-elastic with income-inelastic products. Consequently, we would not expect to find the large, diversified export sector generating unusually rapid growth or very slow growth.[6]

[5] See for example, Herman P. Miller, *Income of the American People* (Wiley, 1955).
[6] The coefficient of variation ($\sigma/\bar{x}$) of the per cent change in population, 1950–60, for the twenty-two metropolitan areas with a million population or more was about one-half that of the smaller metropolitan areas. See Thompson, *A Preface to Urban Economics*, p. 192; or for a more extended treatment of

The very large metropolitan area is even more distinctive in its depth than in its breadth. The local social overhead—the infrastructure —that has been amassed is, more than export diversification, the source of local vitality and endurance. Stable growth over short periods of time, say up to a decade, is largely a matter of the number of different current exports on which employment and income are based. But all products wax and wane, and so the long-range viability of any area must rest ultimately on its capacity to invent and/or innovate or otherwise acquire new export bases.

The economic base of the larger metropolitan area is, then, the creativity of its universities and research parks, the sophistication of its engineering firms and financial institutions, the persuasiveness of its public relations and advertising agencies, the flexibility of its transportation networks and utility systems, and all the other dimensions of infrastructure that facilitate the quick and orderly transfer from old dying bases to new growing ones. A diversified set of current exports— "breadth"—softens the shock of exogenous change, while a rich infrastructure—"depth"—facilitates the adjustment to change by providing the socioeconomic institutions and physical facilities needed to initiate new enterprises, transfer capital from old to new forms, and retrain labor.

Impact of Size on Local Resources

Whatever may be the prime source of national economic development, entrepreneurship must be the heart of comparative regional growth in any system of open regions. The large urban area would seem to have a great advantage in the critical functions of invention, innovation, promotion, and rationalization of the new. The stabilization and even institutionalization of entrepreneurship may be the principal strength of the large urban area. In an earlier work, the argument was advanced that a large population operated to ensure a steady flow of gifted persons, native to the area. A population of 50,000 that gives birth to, say, only one commercial or industrial genius every decade might get caught between geniuses at a time of great economic trial such as the loss of a large employer, but in a population cluster of 5 million, with an average flow of ten per year, a serious and prolonged crisis in local economic leadership seems highly improbable.[7]

the effect of great size on stability, see Wilbur R. Thompson, "The Future of the Detroit Metropolitan Area," in W. Haber, W. A. Spivey, and M. R. Warshaw (eds.), *Michigan in the 1970's: An Economic Forecast* (University of Michigan, 1965).

[7] Thompson, *A Preface to Urban Economics.*

On further thought, the great viability of the large aggregate in a time of quick and sharp change seems to lie even more in the separate but co-ordinated institutionalization of the many entrepreneurial functions, especially invention, innovation, and quick adaptation to change. The very large metropolitan area typically hosts a large state university with well-developed programs in basic research and in graduate, professional, and continuing education. The main medical centers grow up to serve the nearby population, and the many advantages of scale draw medical research personnel and funds. As we become more of a service-oriented economy, the city itself becomes the very product that is being redesigned and re-engineered—becomes the experiment as well as the laboratory. Small wonder that the largest metropolitan areas can be so little concerned with promoting area industrial development, compared with the frantic activities of this kind conducted by the smaller areas.

When we turn to consider the co-operating factors of production, the case for the large urban area does not suffer. Money capital has long been recognized as the most spatially mobile factor, and is so handled both explicitly and implicitly in the locational analyses of Edgar Hoover and August Lösch. The advent of the modern large corporation, financing internally from depreciation reserves and retained earnings, and externally in a national money market, further weakens the locational influence of local capital supplies for the large, well-established, national-market business. But existing real capital is highly immobile—most often permanently fixed in space. The large urban area has by definition the largest and most varied supply of existing real capital—infrastructure—referred to above as the real economic base of the city. It is, in fact, difficult to define the boundaries between entrepreneurship and capital; consider the research laboratories of the large universities—a case where public capital spins off new products and new businesses.

Conversely, small business is often highly dependent on local capital supplies, both commercial credit for working capital and equity money. But the greatest proportion of small business is in local services, making such activity derivative from, not determinant of, regional growth, at least in the short run. To the extent, moreover, that local service activity does play a significant developmental role in the very long run, the large urban area is probably better able to finance this special group of small business which does depend on local capital supplies.

Turning to labor as a locational factor, the case for the large urban area is again reinforced. With the spread of unionism comes the spatially invariant wage, an indispensable concomitant of labor's bargaining power. An industry-wide wage rate in a given industry is a big step toward spatially invariant labor costs, although regional differences in productivity may remain owing to regional differences in skill and motivation. But probably, on net, increasingly automated production processes operate to reduce the opportunity for variations in worker skill or effort to a point where the quantity or quality of output is not significantly altered.

When workers quote the same wage for a given occupation at all places, they give up all influence on the location of work. If blue-collar, middle-income workers should happen to prefer small towns or medium-size cities as places that offer pleasant living and fishing, this is irrelevant as a locational factor. What could be most relevant is that the wives of the corporate managers prefer the theatre. Unionism acts to shift location from a production to a consumption decision and increasingly into the hands of management—urbane professionals.

Finally, let us consider land, which has always been a critical determinant of the locational pattern of economic activity. Most urban areas began by exploiting some natural resource or strategic position on the earth's surface; but for some time now, the share of activity accounted for by the extractive industries and raw-material-oriented processing industries has been declining. However, while on the production side the tie to land has loosened, increasing affluence has tightened it on the consumption side. With high incomes and greater leisure, land in the form of natural beauty and good climate retains significant locational power. But we must also recognize that more and more we live in a "man-made environment" where we fabricate lake-front lots and ski-slope snow, and where we can probably look forward to plastic trees and mountains. That is, capital becomes increasingly a substitute for land; capital is subject to economies of scale and is the magic wand of the entrepreneur-illusionist.

A Filtering-down Theory of Industry Location

If the larger urban areas are, in fact, more than proportionately places of creative entrepreneurship, then we might hazard a broad hypothesis on the nature of regional growth patterns—one that can be tested with available data.[8] Following current practice, let us factor regional growth into two major components: mix and share. An area may grow rapidly either because it has blended a mix of fast-growing industries (those of new products as in Los Angeles, or those with income-elastic demands as in Detroit), or because it is acquiring a

[8] U.S. Department of Commerce, *Growth Patterns in Employment by County, 1940–50 and 1950–60,* Vols. 1–8 (U.S. Government Printing Office, 1965).

larger share of the older, slow-growing ones (the movement of the textile industry to various North Carolina towns is such a case). The hypothesis offered is that the larger urban areas tend to combine a fast-growing mix with a steadily declining share of these growth industries. We modify here, then, the earlier position that the large urban area is highly diversified by suggesting that its rich mix is biased at least a little toward growth industries, but that its growth is dampened by the steady spinning-off of these industries. The result is typically a near-average growth rate.

The larger urban area is believed to invent, or at least innovate, to a more than proportionate degree and, therefore, to enjoy the rapid growth rate characteristic of the early stage of an industry's life cycle —one of exploitation of a new market. As the industry matures into a replacement market, the rate of job formation in that industry slows nationally and the local rate of job formation may slow even more if the maturing industry begins to decentralize—a likely development, especially in non-unionized industries, because with maturity the production process becomes rationalized and often routine. The high wage rates of the innovating area, quite consonant with the high skills needed in the beginning stages of the learning process, become excessive when the skill requirements decline and the industry, or parts of it, "filters-down" to the smaller, less industrially sophisticated areas where the cheaper labor is now up to the lesser occupational demands.

A filter-down theory of industrial location would go far toward explaining the southern small-towns' lament that they always get the slow-growing industries. Out-of-the-way towns like these find they must run to stand still, because their industrial catches come to them only to die. Meantime, these smaller industrial novices struggle to raise per capita income over the hurdle of industries which pay the lowest wage rates. Clearly, the characteristics of slow growth and low wage rates (low skills) might be viewed as two facets of the aging industry. The smaller, less industrially advanced area struggles to achieve an average rate of growth out of enlarging shares of slow-growth industries, originating as a by-product of the area's low wage rate attraction.

The larger, more sophisticated urban economics can continue to earn high wage rates only by continually performing the more difficult work. Consequently, they must always be prepared to pick up new work in the early stages of the learning curve—inventing, innovating, rationalizing, and then spinning off the work when it becomes routine. In its early stages an industry also generates high local incomes by establishing an early lead on competition. The quasi-rents of an early lead are in part lost to the local economy, as dividends to widely dispersed stockholders, but in part retained as high wage rates, especially if strong unions can exploit the temporarily high ability to pay. It would seem, then, that the larger industrial centers as well as the smaller areas must run to stand still (at the national average growth rate); but the larger areas do run for higher stakes.

In order to develop, it seems that the smaller, less favored urban area must attract each successive industry a little earlier in the industry's life cycle, while it still has substantial job-forming potential and, more important, while higher-skill work is required. Only by upgrading the labor force on the job and generating the higher incomes—hence the fiscal capacity—needed to finance better schools, can the area hope to break out of its underdevelopment trap. By moving up the learning curve to greater challenge and down the growth curve toward higher growth rates for a given industry, an area can encourage the tight and demanding type of local labor market that will keep the better young adults home, lure good new ones in, and upgrade the less able ones.

The Delicate Balance between
Equilibrating and Disequilibrating Forces

While we have much to learn from static regional analysis, it is necessary to move toward a more dynamic framework if we are ever to understand how the intricate interactions of development arise. A fully dynamic analysis is still far off, but a form of "stages" analysis provides the means of gaining new insights into the development process. At any given time the industrial structure of a local economy acts directly on the stock of local resources so as to alter their quantity or quality. Each process or stage of regional development leaves a legacy in the form of an altered stock of labor, capital, or entrepreneurship which acts to change the path of development. Only one illustration of a possible development sequence is offered here, but it is one which brings out the delicate balance between equilibrating and disequilibrating forces in regional development.

In the static, industrial-type analysis dealt with in the previous section, it was argued that a locality could parlay an oligopolistic export industry and a strong union into high wage rates and high incomes. A locality that transforms market power into local wage rates that exceed the relative productivity of its labor force will live well but dangerously on overpriced labor. As the relevant industry matures it will slow its rate of job formation, and especially the rate of *local* job formation, if substantial decentralization takes place with maturation, as is usually the case.[9] Confronted by a rate of local job formation inadequate to absorb the natural increase in the local labor force, the search for new industries is greatly hindered by its overpriced labor.

In the very long run local monopoly power may backfire in another way. Strong unions may set rigid work rules that become more binding and expensive as time passes and technology progresses. New processes which, with no greater effort than before, permit a worker to tend more spindles at one time or drill more holes in a given time period cannot be introduced locally. The new process must and will be innovated elsewhere, leaving the locality with a sharply declining share of what might still be a rapidly growing industry. In such a case, moreover, this high-cost labor market will tend also to become burdened with old plants and heavy cycles as well as slow growth. Thus the classic advantages of an early start—a pool of labor where "the skill is in the air" and bankers who know the industry and identify with it—all may be undone by rigid work rules in a world of rapid technological change.

The locality may have to go through a painful wage deflation before it can recover; in short, there may be a day of retribution. Then, again, there may not. If the beneficent oligopoly exhibits an extended stage of strong growth and is slow to decentralize, it could enrich its host area for a full generation or more, as in the case of the automobile industry and Detroit. That locality may come to acquire the education and skill which merits a relatively high local wage rate. Local affluence, however acquired, provides the private means and the tax base needed to build superior social overhead, and thereby to provide a wholly new local economic base to support new export bases. By the time the moment of truth arrives, the local labor force could have risen in education and skill to the point where it is no longer significantly overpriced, and has become, in fact, a scarce factor.

Thus, in this latter case, no equilibrating force would ever come into play. The original nexus of market power could lead instead to a set of disequilibrating forces, as power leads to affluence and affluence leads to education and skill and further affluence. Clearly, whether equilibrating or disequilibrating forces prevail is a matter of timing. The longer a locality holds market power the more likely it is that there will be no day of retribution.

Local rates of growth in employment, labor force, and population substantially different from the national average rate—or the local rate

[9] Even if we assume that the industry faces a nationwide union and a spatially invariant wage and, thereby, rule out relocation into lower-wage areas as operations become more routine, as argued under the filtering hypothesis above, decentralization to reduce transportation costs is a common pattern in maturing industries.

of natural increase—induce net migration flows, and thereby also create a tension between equilibrating and disequilibrating forces. Migration acts most simply to adjust the size of the local labor force and population to the level of economic activity and serves therefore as an equilibrating mechanism in the local labor market, with reference to both employment and per capita income. But migration also acts to change local population profiles to the extent that migrants differ from nonmigrants. If the more mobile (migratory) persons are the younger, more talented, more energetic or aggressive, then migration may serve to reduce the future economic potential of contracting or slowly growing areas, as it drains from them the next generation of professionals and entrepreneurs. Meanwhile, the more rapidly growing areas which receive the young migrants are building up a favorable age distribution of population, ensuring future growth. Migration, then, may begin as an equilibrating force but end as a disequilibrating one, as the rich become richer and the poor become poorer.

Next Steps

Clearly, we are now enmeshed in complex questions of timing. An oligopolistic export industry may die or leave before the community it enriches has time to grow up to its inflated wage, and thus the transition to a new industrial base becomes especially difficult. Or the beneficent industry may set in place an educated second generation before it slowly fades away. Again, net out-migration may relieve the pressure of a redundant labor supply long enough to allow the locality to transfer public funds from, say, public welfare to education and be born again. Or the net out-migration may become a "brain-drain" that leaves the community worse off after each "corrective adjustment" than it was before. We would profit greatly by turning here and now to good urban-regional time series data to test some of these hypotheses and to suggest new ones. But we lack such data. Still, the available census data do permit some preliminary inquiry that can provide a beginning in what will surely be a long search into the nature and causes of urban-regional economic development. A preliminary empirical inquiry of this nature is presented in the Appendix to this paper.

A NOTE ON THE GROWTH
OF THE LARGEST METROPOLITAN AREAS [10]

Any analysis of urban economic development that stresses, as this one has done, the relative cost of doing business in urban areas of

[10] This section results from comments made by Harold J. Barnett on an earlier version of this paper.

various size, is bound to be bullish on city size. The larger places have a clear and sizable advantage in such areas as cheaper and more flexible transportation and utility systems, better research and development facilities, a more skilled and varied labor supply, and better facilities for educating and retraining workers. Further, these economies of scale are captured by private business as lower private costs; at the same time private business is able to slough off on society various social costs that its presence imposes, such as its addition to traffic congestion and air pollution. If, then, the external diseconomies of business-created noise, dirt, congestion, and pollution are some increasing function of city size and/or density, factor market prices are biased in favor of larger urban areas and understate the true marginal costs of production in the metropolis. In the absence of sophisticated public policy and the even more sophisticated public management that would be needed to implement price reform, factor markets so biased promote urban growth and great size.

Effective limits to urban size would seem to have to originate in the household sector. Certainly, alarms of an urban crisis are almost invariably couched in the color words of amenities: congestion, pollution and other aspects of bigness, or at least poorly managed bigness. It is, in fact, not at all clear from this largely impressionistic (and frequently impassioned) literature whether the hypothesized rising costs and/or deteriorating quality of urban life with greater scale is due to some naturally scarce factor, such as fresh air or clean water, or due instead to the probable or demonstrated failure of urban public policy and management to apply the best technology and/or arrange the best combination of factors. It could be argued that urban public management is the scarce factor in the latter case, just as management has always been seen as the ultimate limit on firm size in neo-classical price theory. But the probabilities and strategies of relaxing natural resource constraints versus managerial constraints may be quite different. None of this is meant to minimize the difficulties involved in achieving better urban policy and management in our largest, most complex urban agglomerations.

To date, the most that can be made of these popular, if not classic, "problems" of great city size is that they have slowed slightly the growth of the largest urban areas: probably New York and less clearly Chicago. But, paradoxically, the loss of amenities with great size may redound to support the growth of the second echelon of metropolitan areas. Metropolitan areas with over a million population but less than Chicago's 8 million offer substantial infrastructure in support of modern business, although they do not rival New York and Chicago on this score. But then neither are their "problems" quite as big either—it is easier, if not quite as exciting, to live in these second echelon metropolitan areas.

We could argue that New York must wrestle with a somewhat more advanced form of each of the classic urban problems, or we could argue alternatively the equivalent: that New York must face each new problem in urban management first. Thus, New York was the first to have to learn how to handle 10 million people, and must soon be first to master the problems posed by 20 million. Each successively smaller city, roughly in its rank order, has one more example from which to profit, whether the examples be good or bad. If there is a downward sloping learning curve in urban public management and the challenges of the field are a function of size, Chicago finds the path a little easier because New York has gone before, and Detroit profits from the pioneering of both. Detroit, that is, should be able to offer in 1970 a better organized version of the 5-million population cluster, as a partial offset to the disadvantages it suffers living in the shadow of the greater choice and urbanity of Chicago.

A recent fifty-year projection of the Detroit metropolitan area, which assumed a zero rate of net migration, was criticized as being too optimistic because "the automobile industry is a maturing industry and will, of course, experience the typical slowing rate of growth." Certainly, the automobile industry will probably trace out its own variant of the classic growth curve. But to project the *long run* growth of an urban area from its current industry-mix would be to project the slowing growth and ultimate decline of all areas, as all existing industries are slowly dying. Who, in retrospect, would correlate the growth patterns from 1900 to 1950 of citrus fruits and Los Angeles, or buggies and Detroit? Why, then, must we link automobiles and Detroit for the next fifty years? Ten-year regional growth projections based on the local industry-mix may be defended, but for periods of two or more decades a static, fixed industry-mix technique is heroic if not naive.

Given the embryonic state of urban-regional growth theory, what fifty-year projection might we make for the Detroit metropolitan area? I would argue that Detroit is big enough to assemble the infrastructure necessary to: (a) support a rapidly advancing technology, (b) employ productively and creatively an increasingly educated labor force, and (c) serve an increasingly affluent and sophisticated set of households. From such a base, Detroit should grow at about an average ($\approx$ zero net migration) rate. At one end of the spectrum, the smaller metropolitan areas should about hold their current share of population in that the population of rural areas and small towns will soon be reduced to a bare minimum and the rural to urban migration cannot much longer feed these cities. At the other end, few would argue that New York and/or Chicago is likely to grow faster than its natural rate of increase and drain off growth from the second echelon areas. A zero net migration projection would, in fact, be an optimistic projection for either New York or Chicago, and even this high projection would not encroach on the future population growth of the Detroit economy.

Detroit's competition in the national system of cities would seem, then, to come largely from its peer group: Cleveland, Pittsburgh, Cincinnati, Milwaukee, and St. Louis. The question can be turned around from "Why project a zero net migration rate for Detroit?" to "Why not?" What cities will suck growth from these second echelon areas: the bigger ones with more problems? the smaller ones with less infrastructure? A good case can be made that each of the two dozen or so urban areas with a million to 5 million population will net out to about an average growth rate over the next fifty years, and more than double in size; New York and Chicago will pave the way, perhaps at a slowing rate (with therefore some convergence in size at the top). All this assumes, of course, the absence of national policy that would restrict the continued growth of big cities. And at this time and vantage point, it seems likely that our national policy will be directed more toward mastering the management of large population clusters than toward preventing their growth.

APPENDIX*

TOWARD AN ECONOMETRIC MODEL OF URBAN ECONOMIC DEVELOPMENT

Many of the hypotheses, explicit and implicit, in the main part of this paper can be tested with, or at least exposed to, the rich and readily accessible stock of census data. Much of the deductive work in the preceding pages was, in fact, stimulated by the many Censuses of Population and Manufactures available to the analyst over the past decade. To give no idea of the relative magnitudes of the many variables that are interwoven in the economic model developed above would leave the presentation incomplete, and would also leave unexplained what is a distinctive feature of modern economics: the attempt to quantify the phenomena under study. We turn, therefore, from economics to econometrics.

Because much census data are available only on the very infrequent basis of once every ten years, time series analysis is for the most part beyond our reach. Lacking data for a given place for many points in time, change through time can only be approached indirectly through a cross-section analysis which compares the change between two or three points in time for many places. Still, fresh insights can be gained into the regional growth process by using these infrequent data to test the many static associations between the industrial structure and the income and employment patterns of urban areas. And, to repeat the argument above, this is perhaps the easiest place from which to launch a more dynamic analysis.

We report here the early findings of a cross-section multiple correlation and regression analysis of 135 Standard Metropolitan Statistical Areas. This is less than the full number of 212 (in 1960) and 168 (in 1950), but it is the largest number for which certain critical data on manufacturing and income are available. Basically, this is the group of metropolitan areas that have 40,000 or more manufacturing employees. Admittedly, the early returns suggest that in many cases more was probably lost by dropping the smaller metropolitan areas (and even smaller urban places) than was gained by having access to the better

---

* This appendix is a progress report on a continuing cross-section multiple regression analysis of Standard Metropolitan Statistical Areas, which is supported by the Committee on Urban Economics of Resources for the Future, Inc. John M. Mattila is Professor of Economics, Wayne State University.

data for the bigger areas. Our work, therefore, suffers from being a model of medium- to very large-size urban areas, and an early extension to smaller places carries the highest priority.

We begin with three dependent variables that express important dimensions of the level and distribution of income: median family income (Y_M), the proportion of the population earning less than \$3,000 per year (Y_L), and an index of family income inequality, $\dfrac{Q_3 - Q_1}{Q_1 + Q_3}$ (Y_I). These are correlated with a wide variety of industrial, educational, and demographic variables. Next, preliminary probing behind some of the more important "independent" variables was attempted to get closer to the nature of regional development. The level of and distribution of education—median school years completed by persons twenty-five years old and over (E_M), per cent of population with less than six years of education (E_L), and educational inequality, the sum of the per cent of the population with less than six years and the per cent with more than one year of college (E_I)—entered the income equations as independent variables so frequently that these local educational characteristics were set up as dependent variables to be explained; that is, education was treated endogenously in the system of equations.

Median Family Income (Y_M)

We would be surprised if the local level of education were not the principal determinant of the level of income in the locality selected. We obtained a better fit by expressing educational level in terms of tails of the distribution of school years completed rather than the median value. A high median family income is associated with a low proportion of the adult population with less than six years of school. This variable (E_L) presumably measures quite directly, if imprecisely, general education, and also serves as a proxy for occupational skill and the general cultural environment of the locality. (Occupational variables, such as per cent craftsman and per cent clerical, are in the data deck and were allowed to enter but did not.) The complementary variable, per cent of adult population completing four or more years of college (E_{H4}) was directly associated with median family income. In that only about 4–12 per cent of the population fall in this class, we might infer that college graduates not only earn a high income on their own account but also supply the economic leadership, as entrepreneurs, managers and technologists, which raises the productivity and earnings of many others. Thus the presence of the most educated pulls up the median, a measure not mathematically responsive to the tails of a distribution, by favorably affecting the earnings of the great mass of workers.

The male labor force participation rate (L_M) is partly a demographic variable, rising with an age distribution heavily weighted with the earning age groups, and partly an economic variable, rising with the tightness of the local labor market. A tight labor market provides jobs for the elderly and the young, while heavy unemployment tends to discourage the marginal worker and prompts him to quit looking for work (i.e., drop out of the labor force) until prospects brighten. (An unemployment rate variable, per cent unemployed on March 15, 1960, is in the model but did not enter this equation.)

TABLE 1.

REGRESSION EQUATIONS FOR MEDIAN FAMILY INCOME (Y_M), PER CENT OF FAMILIES EARNING LESS THAN \$3,000 (Y_L) AND FAMILY INCOME INEQUALITY (Y_I) FOR 135 STANDARD METROPOLITAN STATISTICAL AREAS, 1960*

$$Y_M = 1155 \overset{(-.47)}{\underset{(5)}{-\,58E_L}} \overset{(.30)}{\underset{(7)}{+\,55F}} \overset{(.18)}{\underset{(8)}{+\,41L_M}} \overset{(.18)}{\underset{(18)}{+\,96M_{C/L}}} \overset{(.22)}{\underset{(4)}{+\,14M_{60}}} \overset{(.25)}{\underset{(14)}{+\,81E_{H4}}} \overset{(.14)}{\underset{(68)}{+\,272P_{60}}} \overset{(-.11)}{\underset{(16)}{-\,42L_S}}$$

$$\overset{(.14)}{\underset{(4)}{+\,10M_D}} \pm\, 271 \ R^2 = .87$$

$$Y_L = 44 \overset{(.55)}{\underset{(.04)}{+\,.57E_L}} \overset{(-.31)}{\underset{(.03)}{-\,.17M_{60}}} \overset{(-.31)}{\underset{(.06)}{-\,.48F}} \overset{(-.19)}{\underset{(.06)}{-\,.36L_M}} \overset{(-.11)}{\underset{(.15)}{-\,.50M_{C/L}}} \overset{(.12)}{\underset{(.13)}{+\,.39L_S}} \overset{(-.12)}{\underset{(.11)}{-\,.32E_{H4}}} \overset{(.10)}{\underset{(.03)}{+\,.06NW}}$$

$$\pm\, 2.2 \ R^2 = .88$$

$$Y_I = 52 \overset{(-.35)}{\underset{(.0003)}{-\,.003Y_M}} \overset{(.28)}{\underset{(.02)}{+\,.15NW}} \overset{(.29)}{\underset{(.04)}{+\,.27E_I}} \overset{(-.31)}{\underset{(.02)}{-\,.15M_{60}}} \overset{(-.08)}{\underset{(.04)}{-\,.12L_F}} \pm\, 1.8 \ R^2 = .89$$

* The coefficients were estimated by ordinary least squares method. Two-stage least squares estimates were made but did not differ significantly.

See list of variables at end of this section for definitions of independent variables.

Manufacturing specialization, as measured by the per cent of total unemployment engaged in manufacturing (M_{60}), is closely related to median family income probably due to some combination of: (a) a higher skill-mix in manufacturing than in services; or (b) more capital per worker and greater productivity, kept high at the margin by union control of labor supply; and (c) the combined product and factor price power of oligopolies and unions, more common in manufacturing than in services. Such a nexus of oligopoly, unions, and capital-intensive production is suggested by the complementary appearance of variables representing the capital-to-labor ratio $(M_{C/L})$ and the degree of specialization in durables (M_D), both rough proxies for "heavy industry," few firms, price power and difficult entry. On the negative side of this interpretation, an attempt was made to express market concentration as the weighted average per cent of the market accounted for by the four largest industries in the local manufacturing mix, but this more direct expression of the market power of the local export sector did not enter the equation. Perhaps concentration in expanding industries should be distinguished from concentration in declining ones, for the latter have little price power.

The appearance of population size (P_{60}) as a variable confirmed the many earlier findings that larger urban areas generate higher average money incomes than smaller ones, but size is a relatively weak variable here, in common with the findings of others. It is noteworthy, however, that population size does remain in as a minor explanatory factor even when a host of other factors intercorrelated with size are introduced. The negative association with the per cent of the labor force self-employed (L_S) is quite expected, as we recall the characteristically low earnings of small proprietors.

Perhaps the most subtle relationship of all is represented by the second most significant variable in the equation, foreign born as a per cent of total population (F). The interpretation could be quite direct: the foreign born have high occupational skills relative to their level of formal education, or they simply work harder, out of habit from the Old World or out of insecurity in the New World. In either case, this variable corrects for the overstatement of the formal education variable. Then, again, per cent foreign born may represent a special cultural milieu—a stimulating and productive interface of cultures? The foreign born variable intruded so persistently and powerfully throughout our work that we could not deny its existence for lack of a clear and satisfying rationale without an uncomfortable feeling that this variable was trying to tell us something.

The alternate form of the income level equation, per cent of the families receiving less than $3,000 per year ($Y_L$), is almost identical with the median family income equation with, of course, all the signs reversed. Two variables, in the median income form, population size (P_{60}) and specialization in durable goods (M_D), are replaced by per cent non-white (NW), but little should be read into this because of the very marginal role of all three variables.

Family Income Inequality (Y_I)

Family income inequality is closely associated with educational inequality, the sum of the per cents of the adult populations with less than six years of school and those with one or more years of college

(E_I). It could hardly be otherwise, as general education is a comprehensive proxy for basic productivity, adaptability to change, and general access to socioeconomic status and opportunity. We will explore education further below.

The second of the three leading variables, non-white as a per cent of total population (NW), is also quite expected and believable. Assuming that much of the lesser formal education of the non-white is picked up by the educational inequality variable (E_I), the non-white measure must be expressing added dimensions of the relative poverty of the non-white population, such as unequal work opportunity (job discrimination) or differentials in work motivation or both. Certainly this very simple summary ratio is wholly inadequate to the task of getting at the cultural complex it is vaguely reflecting; still, the implication seems clear: the greater the relative number of non-whites, the sharper the division in opportunity and motivation between races. Opportunity and motivation do, of course, interact to reinforce each other.

Less clear is the nature of the close inverse association between the level of income (Y_M) and income inequality. A plausible argument might be that an affluent community will tend to be a more equalitarian one simply because it can afford to be more magnanimous (*noblesse oblige*). Or, perhaps affluence leads to better social overhead; the role of government tends to increase with affluence, and it is on the public sector that we depend to equalize opportunity and to redistribute income.

Another possible interpretation is that the income-level variable is picking up some of the industry-mix effect. Local specialization in manufacturing is correlated with both a high level and a more equal distribution of income. Manufacturing employment as a per cent of total employment (M_{60}) does enter the income inequality equation, reflecting both the relatively narrow range of skills in manufacturing and the egalitarianism of labor unions, but only as a second-order variable (with a beta value about one-half those of the first three). Still, considering both its direct effect and indirect effect through income level, manufacturing specialization appears to rank right up with education, color, and affluence as a prime determinant of family income inequality.

The female labor force participation rate (L_F) is also a second order variable, but one which is clearly significant and one which expresses a highly plausible hypothesis. If working wives and other female second-income earners in the family come, more than proportionately, from low-income households, a higher female labor participation rate would tend to reduce family income inequality.

Median School Years Completed by Persons Twenty-five
Years Old and Over (E_M)

The average level of education in a locality at a given point in time, 1960 (E_M) is expressed in this equation as a function of the income level of the locality at a previous point in time, 1950 (Y_{M50}). High incomes provide both the means to have better schools and the means to stay in school longer. Further, the more advanced local economies that generate the higher incomes also create the higher occupations that demand higher education. The income most relevant is probably the family income at the time when the critical educational decisions are made—fifteen to twenty years of age. If this is so, 1950 family income would be relevant for only the younger members of the 1960 adult population, say, those in the twenty-five-to-thirty-year-old group. We should, then, have 1940 income for those who in 1960 were thirty-five to forty years old and perhaps also for those forty to forty-five years old, and so forth.

We need a distributed-lag model but we have no census income data prior to 1950. We run the risk here that 1950 income is so highly correlated with 1960 income $(r = .90)$ that the former becomes a proxy for the latter and we have a near circular relationship with 1950 (≈ 1960) income explaining 1960 educational level here and the 1960 educational level explaining 1960 income level in the first equation above. This could be acceptable if the two relationships were simultaneous but they are more likely sequential.

One of the more unexpected results was the association of manufacturing specialization with a low educational level. A high proportion of employment in manufacturing (M_{60}) is associated with a low median school year's figure (E_M) and with a high proportion of population with less than six years of schooling (E_L), with M_{60} taking second rank in the E_M equation. Integrating this finding with that above, we now characterize manufacturing areas as having low education but high income. This suggests either that general education is not a good proxy for productivity (income) due to on-the-job training, or that relative income is more a function of market power, achieved through oligopoly and union power, than of skill.

A high educational level is also found in metropolitan areas of greater vitality, whether measured by the rate of increase in median family income over the preceding decade (Y_G) or the previous decade's rate of growth in total population (P_G). Certainly, the direction of causation, if any, is unclear. A supporting interpretation would be that tightening local labor markets with rapidly rising incomes (Y_G), bringing a heavy net in-migration and a greater-than-average rate of increase

TABLE 2.

REGRESSION EQUATION FOR MEDIAN SCHOOL YEARS COMPLETED (E_M), PER CENT COMPLETING LESS THAN SIX YEARS (E_L) AND EDUCATIONAL INEQUALITY (E_I) OF THE ADULT POPULATION, FOR 135 STANDARD METROPOLITAN STATISTICAL AREAS, 1960*

$$E_M = 4.7 + \overset{(.14)}{\underset{(.0026)}{.0059P_G}} + \overset{(.76)}{\underset{(.01)}{.16Y_{M50}}} - \overset{(-.57)}{\underset{(.005)}{.046M_{60}}} + \overset{(.34)}{\underset{(.005)}{.028Y_G}} - \overset{(-.19)}{\underset{(.06)}{.212Y_{IG}}} \pm .53\ R^2 = .65$$

$$E_L = 60 - \overset{(-.67)}{\underset{(.0008)}{.0095Y_{M50}}} - \overset{(-.20)}{\underset{(0.8)}{2.6N\text{-}S}} + \overset{(.39)}{\underset{(.07)}{.59F}} - \overset{(-.08)}{\underset{(.018)}{.031MNM}} - \overset{(-.27)}{\underset{(.14)}{.77\phi}} - \overset{(-.27)}{\underset{(.03)}{.15Y_G}} + \overset{(.26)}{\underset{(.03)}{.14M_{60}}}$$

$$+ \overset{(.27)}{\underset{(.03)}{.16NW}} - \overset{(-.14)}{\underset{(.008)}{.026M_{D4L}}} \pm 2.6\ R^2 = .85$$

$$E_I = 53 - \overset{(-.27)}{\underset{(.65)}{3.3N\text{-}S}} - \overset{(-.40)}{\underset{(.27)}{2.6E_M}} + \overset{(.25)}{\underset{(.05)}{.21Y_{I50}}} - \overset{(-.45)}{\underset{(.15)}{1.2\phi}} + \overset{(.33)}{\underset{(.06)}{.48F}} - \overset{(-.25)}{\underset{(.03)}{.13M_D}} + \overset{(.12)}{\underset{(.031)}{.069NW}}$$

$$- \overset{(-.11)}{\underset{(.13)}{.29P_{G50/40}}} \pm 2.3\ R^2 = .85$$

* See Table 1.

in population (P_G), give rise to a relatively high educational level because the in-migrants are better-than-average educated. Young adults do tend to be both better educated and more mobile than their elders. (Since we are dealing here with metropolitan areas, such a pattern could be consistent with a substantial net in-migration of lower educated persons into the central cities of the growing metropolitan areas, if there is an even heavier in-migration of the highly educated into the suburbs of those areas.)

Finally, a low educational level is linked with a high degree of "intergovernmental income inequality" within the metropolitan area (Y_{IG}), as measured by the coefficient of variation ($\sigma/\bar{Y}_M$) of median incomes of the constituent municipalities of the metropolitan area. (A population-weighted standard deviation is used to reflect the dominant size of the central city.) This is a meaningful relationship if we permit the 1960 intergovernmental income inequality to stand for an earlier period, say 1950 or earlier. Clearly, political fragmentation of the larger metropolitan areas can and does divorce tax base (high-income families) from public service needs (low-income families) and threatens minimum public service levels, especially in education. Because there is clearly a lag of at least a decade between inequality in school tax base and over-all educational levels of the adult population, we must treat

1960 intergovernmental inequality as a proxy for 1950, until such time as we can establish the proper timing.

Educational Inequality: Sum of the Per Cents of the Adult Population with Less than Six Years of Education or More than One Year of College (E_I)

The dummy variable used to test for a North/South regional effect (N-S, with a metropolitan area in the North taking a value of 1 and one in the South taking a value of 0) was the first to enter the educational inequality equation, characterizing southern metropolitan areas as having greater inequality. This variable remained significant but declined rapidly in relative importance with the addition of other variables which picked up, more specifically and precisely, the characteristics that distinguish these two broad regions.

Demographic factors are very important in this equation. A high proportion of foreign-born (F) is understandably related to educational inequality. Given the almost unique emphasis on mass education in this country, the foreign-born tend to have relatively low levels of formal education and act to create comparatively great educational variation. The striking contrast—seeming paradox—of this finding with the ones above tying a large foreign-born share to a high median income (the Y_M equation) and a low per cent poor (the Y_I equation) suggests that the foreign-born came with or acquired here on the job high work skills, or they possess higher work motivation than the native born for any given level of formal education.

The role of the age-mix variable, per cent of total population over sixty-five years of age (ϕ), is less clear. A high proportion of elderly is correlated with greater educational equality and, while within this class educational differentials may well be relatively small because higher education was less stressed in their day, this is a small part of the total population and differs substantially from the mass in education, creating inequality between age classes. Our sample does not include the smaller urban places of more homogeneous education to which older persons often return on retirement, so we cannot speculate that a high proportion of elderly is a proxy for small urban places.

The association of a high proportion of employment in durables (M_D) with a low degree of educational inequality suggests that heavy industry and mass production may indeed constrain the range of occupations and therefore the education needed, as hypothesized in the first part. Certainly, the tie between per cent non-white (NW) and educational inequality is hardly surprising. Further, the association of high median education (E_M) with low inequality reinforces the earlier finding that high-income localities have more equal distributions of income. We seem to want and/or are able to afford—demand—a lessening of inequality with rising education and affluence.

Female Labor Participation Rate (L_F)

The female labor participation rate reflects the "discouragement effect" of a high rate of local unemployment (L_U), as females actively seek work when prospects are good in tight labor markets and drop out of the labor force when jobs are scarce. The marginal character of female employment is also shown by the inverse association between participation rates and average wage rates ($\overline{W}$). In those areas where wage rates are relatively high, there is less need for women to work and fewer do work. The income effect is also exhibited indirectly through the direct association between female participation and per cent non-white (NW). Negro households are not only poorer, and therefore more likely to send forth a second income earner, but probably even more significant here is the greater likelihood that the Negro household will be headed by a female who then becomes the sole support and must work.

TABLE 3.

REGRESSION EQUATION FOR LABOR FORCE PARTICIPATION RATES, FEMALE (L_F) AND MALE (L_M), FOR 135 STANDARD METROPOLITAN STATISTICAL AREAS, 1960*

$$
\begin{array}{c}
(-.48)\quad(-.26)\quad(.72)\quad(-.29)\quad(.34)\quad(.47)\quad(-.12) \\
L_F = 33.5 - 1.03L_U - .058M_{C2} + .25M_{60} - .10\overline{W} + .13NW + .40E_H - .058M_G \\
(0.15)\quad(0.012)\quad(.03)\quad(.03)\quad(.02)\quad(.08)\quad(.029)
\end{array}
$$

$$
\begin{array}{c}
(.25)\quad(.17)\quad(-.44) \\
+ .24F + .13M_{G50/40} - .16M_D \pm 2.1\ R^2 = .71 \\
(.06)\quad(.05)\quad(.03)
\end{array}
$$

$$
\begin{array}{c}
(-.95)\ (-.95)\ (-.39)\ (.37)\ (.48) \\
L_M = 102 - 1.5\phi - 0.54E_I - 0.73L_U + .30F + .26E_L \pm 1.8\ R^2 = .69 \\
(0.1)\quad(0.09)\quad(0.10)\quad(.05)\quad(.08)
\end{array}
$$

* See Table 1.

The complexity of the pattern of female employment is suggested by the higher participation rate in areas where the proportion of population with one or more years of college is relatively high (E_H). This may reflect either that educated females prefer "careers" to housework or that commercial-professional centers both attract the more educated and provide more jobs for women. The latter interpretation would seem to contradict the positive coefficient of the manufacturing specialization variable (M_{60}). A somewhat tortured reconciliation might be found in the integration of the *direct* association of all manufacturing and the *inverse* association of per cent in durables (M_D) and the capital-to-labor ratio variable (M_{C2}) with female participation. If the latter two are interpreted as proxies for "heavy industry," the three variables combine to express female labor participation as a direct function of specialization in "light industry," such as textiles, apparel, food processing and so forth. Clearly, much sharper reformulations of the relevant industry-mix variables are indicated.

A high female labor participation rate is also associated with a relatively rapid rate of manufacturing growth over the 1940–50 period ($M_{G50/40}$) and a relatively slow rate in the following decade, 1950–60 (M_G). The former could reflect greater introduction of women into factory work during World War II and the persistence of such work patterns through the ensuing years. On the other hand, a relatively slow current rate of growth in manufacturing could be a proxy for a relatively rapid rate of growth in services (not included in the data deck) and indicate growing job opportunities for women. But this may well be much too tortured an interpretation for such marginal variables—the lowest beta coefficients.

Male Labor Participation Rate (L_M)

The male labor participation rate is more difficult to explain than the female rate. This is not surprising because it varies much less between areas, with a coefficient of variation of 4.2 for males and of 10.5 for females; almost all men of working ages must and do work. Given this fact, the appearance of the demographic variable expressing the proportion of population sixty-five years old and over (ϕ) is not only understandable but partly definitional. An alternative would be to remove the older age group and work with the participation rate of the sixteen-to-sixty-five-year-old class. The male participation rate also reflects a "discouragement effect" as it varies inversely with the unemployment rate (L_U).

The remaining variables are hard to interpret. Why a low male participation rate should be associated with a high degree of educational inequality (E_I) and a low proportion of the population with less than a grade school education (E_L) is not clear. Why, that is, should a large proportion in the upper tail of education be associated with a low participation rate? The variable expressing foreign-born as a per cent of total population may be adjusting the old-age-group variable to reflect the higher propensity of foreign-born, older males to work, either due to a stronger work culture or due to their less frequent qualification for various retirement programs, such as social security.

Per Cent Change in Median Family Income, 1950–60 (Y_G)

The rate of increase in median family income from 1950 to 1960 was greater for the metropolitan areas which came out of a lower 1950 base (Y_{M50}). A tendency toward convergence in per capita income at the state level has been noted by many observers; the extension here of this pattern to the medium-size and larger metropolitan areas should not, however, be imputed to the smaller urban places, which too often lack the scale needed to catch up and instead slip into a downward spiral. A high rate of male net in-migration (MNM) is linked to a rapidly rising level of income and could be interpreted directly and causally if the migrants are above average in earning power. Perhaps more likely, the rate of net in-migration is almost the equivalent of the over-all population growth rate (P_G). In the latter case, we link two forms of growth: enlargement of mass and rise in per capita income. Growth industries and a tight labor market could produce both. The direct association of the male labor participation rate (L_M) with rising income seems also to say that a tight labor market is part of the growth syndrome.

TABLE 4.

REGRESSION EQUATIONS FOR GROWTH OF INCOME, EDUCATION AND POPULATION, FOR 135 STANDARD METROPOLITAN STATISTICAL AREAS, 1950–60*

$$\underset{(.002)}{Y_G} = 74 \underset{(.002)}{\overset{(-.65)}{-.016Y_{M50}}} + \underset{(.05)}{\overset{(.28)}{.21MNM}} + \underset{(.24)}{\overset{(.17)}{.55L_M}} + \underset{(1.9)}{\overset{(.40)}{8.9N\text{-}S}} + \underset{(.18)}{\overset{(.14)}{.29E_G}} + \underset{(.08)}{\overset{(.13)}{1.7GS}} + \underset{(0.6)}{\overset{(1.01)}{2.4E_H}}$$

$$\underset{(0.6)}{\overset{(-.89)}{-2.3E_{H50}}} \pm 7.8 \ R^2 = .50$$

$$\underset{(.31)}{E_G} = 32 \underset{(.31)}{\overset{(-.58)}{-2.8E_{M50}}} + \underset{(.04)}{\overset{(.14)}{.07NW}} + \underset{(.03)}{\overset{(.22)}{.11Y_G}} \underset{(.18)}{\overset{(-.17)}{-.41\phi}} \pm 3.5 \ R^2 = .54$$

$$\underset{(0.6)}{P_G} = -57 + \underset{(0.6)}{\overset{(.68)}{6.7P_{G50/40}}} + \underset{(.10)}{\overset{(.23)}{.46Y_G}} + \underset{(.003)}{\overset{(.16)}{.008Y_{M50}}} + \underset{(.021)}{\overset{(.11)}{.047M_{G50/40}}} + \underset{(.015)}{\overset{(.11)}{.029M_G}} \pm 11 \ R^2 = .72$$

$$\underset{\substack{\text{(alternate} \\ \text{form)}}}{P_G} = -134 + \underset{(.02)}{\overset{(.40)}{.11M_G}} + \underset{(0.3)}{\overset{(.25)}{1.3E_{H50}}} + \underset{(.39)}{\overset{(.20)}{1.3L_M}} + \underset{(.03)}{\overset{(.25)}{.10M_{G50/40}}} + \underset{(.11)}{\overset{(.14)}{.28Y_G}} \underset{(2.7)}{\overset{(-.19)}{-8.3N\text{-}S}} + \underset{(.12)}{\overset{(.15)}{.27\overline{W}}}$$

$$\pm 14 \ R^2 = .60$$

* See Table 1.

The North-South dummy variable $(N\text{-}S$, where $N = 1$ and $S = 0)$ seems to say that, having adjusted for the tendency toward interurban convergence in per capita income, northern urban areas tend to experience the greater rate of increase in median family income. The underdeveloped southern urban area may be gaining but apparently only slowly. The income-growth nexus is further defined and further complicated by the appearance in the equation of a "growth stability" variable (GS), defined as the 1950–60 per cent change in local population divided by the 1940–50 per cent change. A high value of this variable —accelerating growth—is, quite believably, associated with a rapidly rising median family income. Accelerating regional growth perhaps as much as rapid growth creates tight local labor markets and rising incomes. Further experimentation with combinations of the rate and rate of change in population growth is needed to clarify what is probably the most complex dependent variable of all.

The three educational variables seem to say, in concert, that the rate of increase in median family income is only weakly associated with a rapidly rising average education (E_G) but is strongly associated with the rate of growth of the college educated. A high rate of growth in the proportion of college educated is expressed indirectly by a negative coefficient for per cent with some college in 1950 (E_{H50}) and the positive coefficient for 1960 (E_H), that is, a relatively low point of origin in 1950 and a high terminal point in 1960. Again, our work indicates a very powerful and pervasive role for the most educated in generating regional economic development.

Per Cent Change in Median School Years of the Adult Population, 1950–60 (E_G)

The growth pattern of median adult education also shows substantial convergence, with the metropolitan areas exhibiting the lowest educational level in 1950 (E_{M50}) showing the most rapid rise. The interracial convergence that is occurring nationally probably underlies the direct relationship between per cent non-white (NW) and educational improvement. The rates of change of educational and income level are again linked. We would have much preferred to have used the rate of increase in income between 1940 and 1950 to explain educational change between 1950 and 1960, but census income data do not go back before 1950. It is doubtful that the 1950–60 change is a close enough proxy for 1940–50 change to override the tendency toward a reverse causation, income change (Y_G) as a function of educational change (E_G), already expressed above emphasizing higher education. Finally, an older population (ϕ) should and does show a smaller rise in median adult education because few in this group added any significant schooling during the preceding decade. Perhaps, also, a large proportion of elderly is serving to represent the older, slow areas engaged in more routine activities.

Per Cent Change in Population 1950–60 (P_G)

Two forms of the population growth equation are presented, one employing the rate of growth in the 1940–50 period ($P_{G50/40}$) to "explain" or better predict the rate of growth in the 1950–60 period, the other constructed with the preceding period growth rate blocked out. Building on the preceding growth rate produces not only a useful predictive device but this equation has analytical content as well: a kind of general empirical support for the arguments advanced in the text that significant forces generating cumulative disequilibrium build up in the regional growth process—leads become wider. In addition, population growth is linked to rising income (Y_G) "economic progress"—parallel to the income equation, where population growth was the independent variable, expressed by the male net in-migration rate (MNM). A small endogenous subsystem has formed in this set of equations.

A relatively high income at the beginning of the growth period, 1950 (Y_{M50}), leads, if not causes, rapid population growth—in-migration quite consistent with economic theory. Finally, rapid growth in manufacturing in the previous decade ($M_{G50/40}$) and in the current decade (M_G) is associated with rapid current population growth, suggesting a manufacturing export base "locational multiplier." This crude distributed-lags expression of the "filling-in" process, wherein the local service sector and total population follow manufacturing growth, is plausible and makes the whole equation seem quite sensible.

The second form of the population growth equation includes all of the variables in the first form, minus the rate of population growth in the preceding period ($P_{G50/40}$) which was blocked out, and plus a few new·ones. Median income growth (Y_G), current manufacturing growth (M_G), and prior manufacturing growth ($M_{G50/40}$) appear unchanged, and median family income at the beginning of the period (Y_{M50}) is replaced by a related variable, average wage in manufacturing (W). With 1940–50 population growth removed, urban areas with a high per cent of population with some college at the beginning of the growth period (E_{H50}) show more rapid population growth, quite consistent with the leadership role of the educated, repeatedly argued throughout both sections of the paper.

The southern metropolitan areas (N-S) exhibit greater population growth, probably reflecting the heavier agricultural orientation of that part of the country and the consequent heavier rural-to-urban movement during a period in which agriculture was experiencing a declining share of total employment. Finally, a tight labor market (L_M) is probably circularly associated with population growth, and we have yet to separate out the timing sequence.

SUMMARY

The principal relationships brought out by the system of equations discussed above are outlined in Figure 2. The level of family income

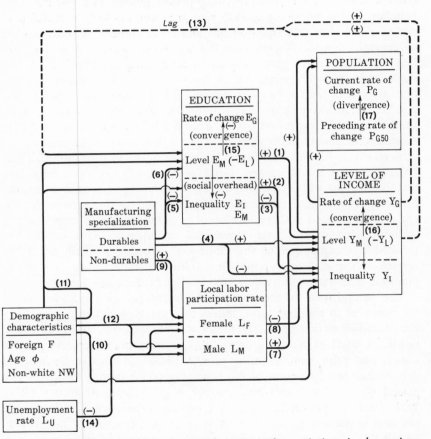

Figure 2. Schematic simplification of the principal associations in the various regressions.

and the degree of inequality in its distribution in an urban area are most closely associated with the educational level (1) and educational inequality (2) characteristic of the adult population of that locality. Especially noteworthy is the tendency for localities with a relatively large proportion of college-educated persons to exhibit a more equal distribution of income (3), representing perhaps a form of economic *noblesse oblige* or at least unplanned beneficial spillovers onto the less able.

Specialization in manufacturing also affects the local income patterns, tending to generate a relatively high level of family income and a more equal distribution of income, especially specialization in durables (4). Manufacturing also acts indirectly in a supporting way by tending to reduce educational inequality (5), and thereby to reduce income inequality, but in an offsetting way through its association with a low general level of education (6), and thereby a lower average income than otherwise.

A high male labor participation rate also raises median family income (7) and a high female participation rate tends to reduce the degree of income inequality (8). Specialization in non-durable goods manufacturing apparently acts indirectly to reduce income inequality by raising the female labor participation rate (9). Various demographic variables, treated as exogenous forces at this time, act directly on income (10) and indirectly by way of education (11) and labor participation rates (12). Finally, income appears to react back on education (13), with a lag of unknown timing. A tight labor market clearly raises labor participation rates (14) and thereby affects income patterns.

There is some evidence that equilibrating tendencies prevail with respect to interurban levels of education (15) and income (16), that is, a movement toward convergence was evident. There is, on the other hand, a suggestion of divergence in the rates of growth in total population (17) in this system of middle and large-size urban areas. Much more work and thought are called for on the interactions of the complex of equilibrating and disequilibrating forces barely suggested in this early effort.

LIST OF VARIABLES

Endogenous Variables

Y_M Median income of families, 1959.

Y_L Per cent of families with less than $3,000 income, 1959.

Y_I Income inequality ($Q_3 - Q_1/Q_3 + Q_1$), 1959.

E_M Median school years completed, 1960.

E_L Per cent with six or less years in school, 1960.

E_I Educational inequality (per cent with six or less years in school plus per cent with four or more years of college, 1960).

77

Y_G Per cent change in median income, 1950–60.
E_G Per cent change in median school years completed, 1950–60.
P_G Per cent change in population, 1950–60.
L_F Female, per cent in labor force, 1960.
L_M Male, per cent in labor force, 1960.

Exogenous (Explanatory) Variables

E_H Per cent with one or more years of college, 1960.
E_{H50} Per cent with one or more years of college, 1950.
E_{H4} Per cent with four or more years of college, 1960.
E_{M50} Median school years completed, 1950.
F Per cent foreign-born, 1950.
GS Growth stability $[(1 + P_G)/(1 + P_{G50/40}) - 1]$.
L_S Male, self-employed as per cent of total employment, 1960.
L_U Per cent unemployed, 1960.
$M_{C/L}$ Capital-to-labor ratio (total value added—all employees payroll/ total employment, 1960).
M_{4L} Degree of specialization within manufacturing (total employment in four largest industries/total manufacturing employment, 1960).
M_{C2} Capital-to-labor ratio (cumulative plant and equipment expenditures, 1958–60/number of production workers, 1960).
M_D Per cent employed in durable goods industries, 1960.
M_G Per cent change in manufacturing employment, 1950–60.
$M_{G50/40}$ Per cent change in manufacturing employment, 1940–50.
M_{60} Per cent employed in manufacturing, 1960.
MNM Male net migration rate, 1950–60.
$N\text{-}S$ North (1) or South (0).
NW Per cent non-white, 1960.
ϕ Per cent sixty-five years old and over, 1960.
P_{60} Logarithm of 1960 population.
$P_{G50/40}$ Per cent change in population, 1940–50.
$\overline{W}$ All employees payroll/total manufacturing employment, 1960.
Y_{IG} Intergovernmental inequality (population-weighted standard deviation of median incomes of political subdivisions, 1960).
Y_{I50} Income inequality $(Q_3 - Q_1/Q_3 + Q_1)$, 1949.
Y_{M50} Median income of families, 1949.

Note: All variables were derived from the various volumes of the *Census of Population* and *Census of Manufacturing* from the period 1940 to 1960.

SELECTED READINGS

Chinitz, Benjamin. "Contrasts in Agglomeration: New York and Pittsburgh," *American Economic Review*, Vol. 51, May 1961.

Committee for Economic Development. *Community Economic Development Efforts: Five Case Studies.* Supplemental Paper No. 18. New York, December 1964.

Dickinson, Robert E. *City, Region and Regionalism.* London: Kegan Paul, and New York: Oxford University Press, 1947.

Duncan, Otis Dudley, W. Richard Scott, Stanley Lieberson, Beverly Duncan, and Hal H. Winsborough. *Metropolis and Region.* Baltimore: The Johns Hopkins Press, for Resources for the Future, 1960.

Florence, P. S. "Economic Efficiency in the Metropolis," in *The Metropolis in Modern Life.* Garden City, N.Y.: Doubleday and Co., 1955.

Friedmann, John, and William Alonso (eds.). *Regional Development and Planning.* Cambridge: The M.I.T. Press, 1964.

Greenhut, Melvin L. *Plant Location in Theory and Practice.* Chapel Hill: The University of North Carolina Press, 1956.

Hanna, Frank A. *State Income Differentials.* Durham: Duke University Press, 1959.

Harvard University Graduate School of Public Administration for the Regional Plan Association. *New York Metropolitan Regional Study,* especially Robert M. Lichtenberg, *One-Tenth of a Nation.* Cambridge: Harvard University Press, 1960.

Hirsch, Werner Z. (ed.). *Regional Accounts for Policy Decisions.* Baltimore: The Johns Hopkins Press for Resources for the Future, 1966.

————. *Elements of Regional Accounts.* Baltimore: The Johns Hopkins Press for Resources for the Future, 1964.

Hochwald, Werner (ed.). *Design of Regional Accounts.* Baltimore: The Johns Hopkins Press for Resources for the Future, 1961.

Hoover, Edgar M. *Location of Economic Activity.* New York: McGraw-Hill Book Co., 1948.

Isard, Walter. *Location and Space-Economy.* New York: John Wiley and Sons, 1956.

————, et al. *Methods of Regional Analysis: an Introduction to Regional Science.* New York: John Wiley and Sons, 1960.

Lampard, Eric E. "The History of Cities in Economically Advanced Areas," *Economic Development and Cultural Change,* Vol. 3, January 1955.

Lösch, August. *The Economics of Location.* New Haven: Yale University Press, 1954.

Perloff, Harvey S., Edgar S. Dunn, Eric E. Lampard, and Richard F. Muth. *Regions, Resources, and Economic Growth.* Baltimore: The Johns Hopkins Press for Resources for the Future, 1960.

Pfouts, Ralph W. (ed.). *The Techniques of Urban Economic Analysis.* West Trenton, N.J.: Chandler-Davis Publishing Co., 1960.

Pittsburgh Regional Planning Association. *Economic Study of the Pittsburgh Region,* especially Volume I, *Region in Transition.* Pittsburgh: University of Pittsburgh Press, 1963.

Thompson, Wilbur R., and John M. Mattila. *An Econometric Model of Postwar State Industrial Development.* Detroit: Wayne State University Press, 1959.

Thompson, Wilbur R. *A Preface to Urban Economics.* Baltimore: The Johns Hopkins Press, for Resources for the Future, 1965.

Tiebout, Charles M. *The Community Economic Base Study.* Supplementary Paper No. 16. New York: Committee for Economic Development, December 1962.

*Eric E. Lampard**

THE EVOLVING SYSTEM OF CITIES IN THE UNITED STATES: Urbanization and Economic Development

ECONOMICS AND THE URBAN TRANSFORMATION

The urbanization of the U.S. population is a fundamental datum of social science. In 1790, some 95 per cent of the nearly four million inhabitants of the new nation were "rural" in residence and 85 per cent were occupied in "agriculture." Today, scarcely 5 per cent of the population of some two hundred million remain on farms and three out of four persons live in cities or suburbs. This urban transformation is held accountable by many social scientists for much that is novel and distinctive about present day life and livelihood in the United States; for virtually the entire social fabric has changed in the course of passage from farm to city.

But if some social scientists explain too much by a rather simplistic contrast of urban and rural "ways of life"—the generic properties of which have never been fully specified and tested—most economists still err in the opposite direction. The world of economic principles presents a largely spaceless system of production, consumption, and exchange in which countless buyers and sellers make marginal adjustments to changes in relative prices among various goods or between different points in time. Despite a general recognition of the growth in non-agricultural employments following the industrial revolution, and the association of this beneficent tendency with rising output and income, most economists in the English-speaking world have shown little or no interest in the urban transformation as such. Nowadays, to be sure, urban phenomena constitute important research salients in several branches of applied economics. With the emergence of a self-consciously "urban" economics over the past decade or so the city has become not only an economic and fiscal "problem," but a recognizable unit of microanalysis as well, comparable in power and significance to the industry or the firm. Most recently, in his path-breaking *A Preface to Urban Economics,* Thompson has broadened the scope of the field still further by linking the familiar macroeconomics of income, employment,

* Professor of History and Adjunct Professor of Urban and Regional Planning, University of Wisconsin.
This study draws heavily on published and unpublished writings by Beverly D. Duncan, Edgar S. Dunn, Jr., Joseph A. Swanson, Wilbur R. Thompson, and Jeffrey G. Williamson. None of these scholars, of course, is responsible for the uses and abuses of their suggestions and data in this paper.

81

and "growth" to the changing cyclical fortunes of hypothetical city-regions.[1] The present paper attempts another departure. It goes beyond both the microanalysis of urban efficiency and welfare, and the macroanalysis of income and employment, to explore the historical question of the urban transformation and its relation to national and regional economic development.

It is not the special task of urban economics, or indeed of any particular branch of social science, to explain the urban transformation in its entirety. Changes on the order of magnitude represented in Table 1 (p. 107), for example, could only yield their full import after prolonged and systematic inquiry from many different vantage points. Nevertheless, the power of urban-regional economics to enlarge our present understanding of the transformation should not be underestimated. First, its novelty is deceptive. There is an extensive tradition in the literature of economics that treats the location and size of urban "centers" in relation to the character of their productive activities.[2] Second, urban-regional analysis is already concerned with some of the short-run and cyclical aspects of the economic growth of localities in relation to aggregate growth. In what follows, these two salients will be reviewed with special reference to the growth and interaction of cities. Certain shortcomings of location and growth theories are then adduced and the case is made for a distinctive *development* perspective on the transformation of urban regions across the nation. Such a perspective is provided by a more explicitly behavioral-institutional formulation of the "functional-structural" hypothesis of differentiation. Finally the urban transformation is considered in some detail with reference to elements of structure and stability in the evolving "system of cities."

THE SPACE-ECONOMY AND THE SYSTEM OF CITIES

The taproot of the recent flowering of urban-regional analysis lies deep in the fertile soil of Johann Heinrich von Thünen's isolated plain with its single market center (1826). From Thünen's theory of aggregative agricultural locations stem two other branches of social-spatial theorizing that are the immediate sources for modern location analysis and for urban-regional economics:

1) the partial equilibrium, least-cost theory of industrial locations— an essentially microeconomic formulation which received its first comprehensive statement in the work of Alfred Weber (1909).

[1] Wilbur R. Thompson, *A Preface to Urban Economics* (The Johns Hopkins Press, for Resources for the Future, 1965).
[2] Brian J. L. Berry and Allan Pred, *Central Place Studies: A Bibliography of Theory and Applications* (Philadelphia: Regional Science Research Institute, 1961).

2) the central place theory of nodal settlements—given its first comprehensive formulation as a "theory of urban trades and institutions" by Walter Christaller (1933) and generalized into a theory of "the spatial order of the economy" by August Lösch (1940–44).[3]

Christaller saw his own theory of urban services complementing and rounding out Thünen's theory of agricultural locations and Weber's theory of industrial locations. Only in recent decades, however, have these distinctive stems in fact been grafted together by Isard in his construct of "the general theory relating to industrial location, market areas, land use, trade, and urban structure."

Isard's general theory of location and space-economy represents conventional Hicksian general equilibrium analysis as "a special case" in which transport costs are assumed to be zero and all inputs and outputs are viewed as perfectly divisible and mobile. Isard also treats the traditional theory of international trade as "a special case" of the general theory. His basic postulate is "that location and trade are as the two sides of the same coin. The forces determining one simultaneously determine the other." [4]

Agricultural Differentiation and the Structure of Industrial Locations

Thünen's celebrated model of differentiation in the cultivation of land areas postulated a uniformly flat plain with soil of equal fertility at all points. At the center of the plain was a town having uniform transport potential in all directions. Under such conditions, transport costs on farm produce were proportional to weight and distance and hence farm productions were distributed around the node in a pattern of concentric zones in accordance with the respective price and transport cost of each product cultivated. Given the demand of the town, the loci of different productions were determined by a combination of the *effort* involved in moving produce over unit distances to market and the *intensity* at which each unit area would yield the requisite output,

[3] Johann Heinrich von Thünen, *Der isolierte Staat in Beziehung auf Landwirtschaft und Nationalökonomie* (Hamburg: Fr. Perthes, 1826). Alfred Weber, *Über den Standort der Industrien* (Tübingen: J. C. B. Mohr, 1909) translated and edited by C. J. Friedrich as Alfred Weber's *Theory of the Location of Industries* (University of Chicago Press, 1928). Walter Christaller, *Die zentralen Orte in Süddeutschland* (Jena: G. Fischer, 1933); and August Lösch, *Die räumliche Ordnung der Wirtschaft* (2nd ed.; Jena: G. Fischer, 1944), translated as *The Economics of Location* (Yale University Press, 1954). Also, Peter Haggett, *Locational Analysis in Human Geography* (London: Arnold, 1965).

[4] Walter Isard, *Location and Space-Economy* (M.I.T. Press, 1956), p. 6. Also, Isard *et al.*, *Methods of Regional Analysis: An Introduction to Regional Science* (John Wiley, 1960).

subject to diminishing returns. Thünen showed thereby "that the controlling factor in the determination of land use is economic rent." [5]

By relaxing the assumptions, it is possible to allow for territorial specialization and exchange between physically distinctive land areas that are unevenly endowed with natural resources. Indeed, Isard has shown that it is possible to derive a whole array of products and services (including those with the multiple-input combinations typical of manufactures) with only minor modification of the Thünen model.[6] But for all the growth of manufactures, transport, and other services, further elaboration of the model does not adumbrate an industrial-urban transformation. The latter only occurs when technological advances, and the consequent expansion of manufactures, bring about such a voluminous and variegated output of minerals and other material inputs relative to the food requirements of the non-agricultural labor force that the locational tie of manufacturing and service activities to the agricultural population is finally broken.

Notwithstanding the preindustrial context in which Thünen established his isolated agrarian state, the model has a relevance to urban-regional economics. In all situations treated under Thünen-like assumptions, transport distances and their associated costs were fundamental to the territorial patterning of productive activities. While successive accommodations to reality may have modified the neat regularity of the zonal order (the distorting influence of scale economies, for example, in transport), the decisive role of transport distance in shaping the spatial order was never compromised. Given the initial market town on the plain it was, moreover, possible to derive other lesser clusters (of specialized non-agricultural activity) and a rudimentary system of interaction and dependence between partially differentiated land areas and their nodal centers.

The theory of industrial locations advanced by Weber was concerned with neither nucleated settlements nor a general system of interdependence, but rather with the locational "problem" of the firm and the industry. With his array of givens—fixed consumption, fixed sites of materials, a fixed territorial pattern of labor costs—the locational deci-

[5] Edgar S. Dunn, Jr., *The Location of Agricultural Production* (University of Florida Press, 1954), p. 99.

[6] Although zonal patterns would emerge around the centers of each additional product or service (depending on the numbers engaged in their output, the intensity of resulting land use in farm productions, and the width of product zones, all of which vary with distance from the original market center), the progressive articulation of a transport sector crossing the sets of agricultural zones would negate the equal unit-distance cost specification owing to scale economies in transport along main-traveled routes. Isard, *Location and Space-Economy*, pp. 3–9.

84

sion for the firm involved little more than the determination by technical empirical means of the point of *least* distance and weight of material inputs, as measured in "ton kilometers" to a given market. On the plane of industrial location, Weber allowed for a more complex interplay of three basic variables: transport cost, labor cost, and economies (diseconomies) of agglomeration. The comparison of differential transport and labor costs to a given market will determine the regional distributions of activity, while the tendency for industries to concentrate or scatter within a region will turn on the effects of agglomeration (or deglomeration) economies.[7] Weber did not analyze this agglomeration factor very deeply, but Hoover, among others, has underlined its relevance to urban growth by breaking it down into three facets: (1) large scale economies within the firm; (2) localization economies for all firms within an industry (from the increased output of the industry); and (3) urbanization economies for all firms regardless of industry consequent upon the increasing economic size of the city location.[8]

A notable advance on Weber came with Andreas Predöhl's translation of the partial equilibrium solution from physical "ton kilometers" into relative pricing terms. He did this, however, in the static framework of a Walras-Casselian general equilibrium of interdependent prices and quantities under conditions of perfect competition. Predöhl demonstrated that an optimal location could be determined by the *substitution* of lower cost combinations among alternative groupings of factors. By recourse to general equilibrium, he sought to determine the location of all economic activities. Since the optimal location (the one that yielded highest net revenue) was to be derived from the system of interdependent prices and quantities, it was logically inherent in the general equilibrium.[9]

Employment of the substitution principle was, nevertheless, critically weakened by its dependence on the general equilibrium condition of perfect competition. Such a requirement implies that all factors and

---

[7] These last might, for example, cause firms to move from their optimal transport or labor points, and concentrate together, if the extra costs incurred were offset by scale economies achieved by the industry generally upon the enlargement of its total output at the new location.

[8] Weber, *Location of Industries*, p. 138. Edgar M. Hoover, *The Location of Economic Activity* (McGraw-Hill, 1948), pp. 99–104 and 116–41. Also, William Alonso, "Location Theory," in John Friedmann and William Alonso (eds.), *Regional Development and Planning: A Reader* (M.I.T. Press, 1964).

[9] Andreas Predöhl, "Das Standortsproblem in Wirtschaftstheorie," *Weltwirtschaftliches Archiv*, Vol. 21 (1925). For Predöhl, relocation was merely the *substitution* of labor and capital outlays for spatial-occupancy (land-use) outlays or *vice versa*, depending on whether the enterprise moved away from or toward the central locus of consumption. Transport outlays, moreover, were merely a particular form of capital and labor outlays.

products are perfectly mobile and, consequently, that distance itself cannot be a major system variable. The unique locus of each activity at any time would merely be "a special case" of the distribution of productive factors in general "in terms of a one-point society." Yet it remains the fundamental premise of any spatial analysis since Thünen that cost of distance is *the* ordering element—the one wholly systematic factor—in the territorial distribution of economic activity.[10] Palander argued, moreover, that distance and related costs of transportation necessarily impose "local" prices upon otherwise identical goods and services, thus making it impossible to meet the requirement of large numbers of buyers and sellers in each market. He showed that buyers and sellers were, in fact, in relatively "monopolistic" situations depending on the respective advantages of their particular locations. Palander went on to affirm, furthermore, that Weber's "historical" evolutionary approach to the transformation of locational structures—involving the development of successive strata of secondary and tertiary populations over the primary agricultural (market) stratum—was superior on balance to the stasis inherent in the formal Walras-Casselian general equilibrium. He concluded that the problem of general location would be better handled both formally and empirically within a framework of the process of economic development.[11]

Central Place Hierarchy and the System of Cities

While a rudimentary system of interdependent nodes or "central places" might be derived from Thünen's theory of agricultural differentiation, the Weberian approach focused more narrowly on the comparative advantage of particular locations and the possibility of agglomeration economies at certain extractive or manufacturing sites. It remained for Christaller to contribute the theory of urban markets and services; a theory, so to speak, of the tertiary sector. This "central place" theory was later extended and refined by August Lösch in an attempt to specify the conditions of a general equilibrium model of the space economy under imperfect competition.

Although Christaller's theory was not a "system of cities" model in any explicit sense, it was nonetheless an attempt to explain the numbers, sizes, and spatial distribution of cities by a taxonomic ordering of their

[10] ". . . there are certain regularities in the variation of costs and prices over space . . . primarily because cost is a function of distance." Isard, *Location and Space-Economy*, pp. 35 and 79.

[11] Tord Palander, *Beiträge zur Standortstheorie* (Uppsala: Almqvist & Wicksell, 1935), pp. 273–85; Isard, *Location and Space-Economy*, pp. 42–43; Edward H. Chamberlin, *Theory of Monopolistic Competition* (3rd ed.; Harvard University Press, 1938), pp. 208–13.

different functions. Recognizing the pervasive influence of distance on human settlement patterns, Christaller hypothesized that towns are situated at the point of minimum aggregate travel vis-à-vis the population of a surrounding region (i.e., towns are located centrally to their areas of maximum profits). The smallest order of towns provides only everyday goods and services, and hence is distributed over the landscape at frequent and regular intervals. A town's "centrality" is, in fact, to be measured by the degree to which it serves a smaller or larger population area. The greater the centrality, the higher the order of goods and services it provides, the larger its complementary population-trade area, and the more infrequently spaced it will be in relation to others of the same order. Higher-order centers—altogether Christaller identified seven orders in southern Germany—offer all the goods and services of their inferiors in addition to their own more specialized functions.[12] Thus, numerous small centers come to be nested within the larger complementary regions of the higher-order centers or, in a somewhat different arrangement, along the main traffic routes that link the largest cities. Christaller's deductive method yields, therefore, a structure of hierarchically-ordered central places of different size. The system of cities, in this structural sense, comprises sets of functionally determined size-orders which are defined by the upper and lower limits of their respective ranges of central goods and services.

The Lösch model postulates the classic situation in which a producer on a flat, evenly populated, and uniformly endowed plain finds it profitable to enlarge his output beyond his immediate needs. In effect, he substitutes economies of larger-scale production for transport outlays in order to supply a surrounding trade area up to some radius distance where, notwithstanding scale economies, his product becomes too costly to ship. Ideally, of course, the resulting market area will be circular in shape around the central point of production. But competition from producers outside this trading circumference will compel those within to contract their intersecting circles into market areas of hexagonal shape. For each particular good and service, a "honeycomb" net of similarly shaped areas will cover the plain without leaving any corners or edges unexploited. Each consumer will accordingly have access to every product and every consumer will reside within the market area for each product.[13] There is no logical requirement, however, for the areas of

[12] Higher-order centers may actually have larger markets for lower-order goods than most lower-order centers, because shoppers coming in for the specialities will pick up many lower-order items at the same time owing to the convenience and economy of making one trip.

[13] There are *n* of these "honeycomb" nets for *n* products, each product having its own characteristic range of distribution according to the tension between its

any of the resulting honeycomb nets to coincide but, should they in fact do so, "neither the distances between points of coincidence, nor the number of production centers coinciding can be entirely accidental." This non-random nature of center distribution over the economic land-scape constitutes the core of the Löschian spatial system. To order the landscape systematically, Lösch groups his honeycomb nets for particular products and services by size of their respective market areas. He then proceeds to superimpose the set of nets and jiggle them about until as many production centers as possible coincide. At that moment the sum of distances between all points of production appears to be minimized, as are the total number of shipments and length of transportation routes.

The size distribution of Löschian cities thus depends on how many particular goods and services of what size markets coincide at any in-dividual central place. Where all goods and services are produced, there is a metropolis from which major transport routes radiate to other large centers. The resulting hierarchy of city sizes (and intervening routes) relates directly to the number of productions at any center and to the size of their dependent market regions. But cities of the same size do not necessarily produce the same order of goods and services, as in the Christaller case, nor do they appear to interact much with each other. The only function that all Löschian cities have in common, as Stolper remarks, "seems to be to reduce or minimize transport costs and to lead to the establishment of an efficient system of market areas." [14]

For all its rigor, the Löschian spatial order does not achieve general-ity. The ordering of production, for example, has yielded different-sized centers which, other regularities notwithstanding, are now difficult to square with the assumption on the demand side of an evenly distributed population. In the vicinity of the more populous cities, furthermore, the hexagonal market areas necessary for optimal output will be much smaller than they will be, say, out on the sparsely populated agricultural plain. What is more critical from the standpoint of historical develop-ment is that at no point does Lösch adequately cope with the phenom-enon of raw-material orientation which was so strong a feature of the Weberian tradition. Indeed, Lösch seems to deal only with those kinds of economic functions that utilize either ubiquitous raw materials or none.[15] Such categories would exclude most of the basic extractive and

optimal scale and the structure of transport rates. Wolfgang Stolper, "Spatial Order and the Economic Growth of Cities," in *Economic Development and Cultural Change*, Vol. 3 (January 1955).

[14] *Ibid.*

[15] Isard, *Location and Space-Economy*, pp. 251–53.

processing industries which, historically, have contributed so much to the spatial order and to the growth of national product.

The General Theory of Location and Space-Economy

Isard's wide-ranging theory is of concern here only insofar as it treats the locational problem in relation to interurban organization and structure. Ideally, every location decision is a matter of balancing anticipated costs and receipts under different degrees of uncertainty. When potential savings from a move outweigh the additional costs entailed, net revenue is enlarged and, other things being equal, the rational entrepreneur will make the move; he *substitutes* new sets of revenues and outlays for his previous sets, his new location for his old. Some costs are, nevertheless, more significant than others in their effects on the over-all spatial order. The differential advantages of possible locations at any time have their roots, broadly speaking, in three categories of costs:

1) *input costs:* labor, materials, fuel, water, taxes, insurance, weather conditions, political milieu, and so on (not all of which readily yield to the conventions of market pricing).
2) *transport costs:* the price of a composite input of services necessary to move labor, materials, equipment, and products.
3) *economies (and diseconomies) of agglomeration and deglomeration:* a set of relatively localized scale economies that may be (a) "internal" to the firm; (b) "external" to the industry at a particular location; or (c) "external" to the locality itself.

Among these sources of cost differentials, those having to do with distance are likely to be decisive in a spatial context. While all costs vary over time and space, only transport costs vary systematically with distance from any point, primarily because transport cost is some function of distance. Isard defines the critical transport input as "the movement of a unit of weight over a unit of distance" (for example, Weber's ton kilometers), the price of which is determined at any time by the interaction of demand and supply.[16] Fluctuation and disturbance notwithstanding, the space economy will accordingly tend toward equilibrium.

By granting paramount sway to transport outlays again, the general theory seeks finally to merge the hitherto disparate traditions of agricultural and non-agricultural location analysis. Cost differentials and substitution possibilities are shown to affect the location of farm enterprises

[16] *Ibid.,* pp. 77–90.

as much as they do the industrial plant. Differences in "rent" (the market price of the services of particular land) have, since Thünen, been recognized as the major factor determining the intensity of agricultural land use and hence the character of crop programs. But the rent differential in agriculture (or in other space-intensive functions), Isard argues, plays much the same locational role as fuel-cost differentials in fuel-intensive functions or labor cost in labor-intensive functions. In resolving whether to locate closer or further from his market, therefore, the farmer may substitute rent or transport outlays, the aluminum manufacturer may substitute power or transport outlays, and the textile producer, labor or transport outlays, and so on.[17]

There is one critical difference between locational change in agriculture and most non-agriculture that has important implications for an unfolding system of cities. The significant distinction would seem to be between the relatively unbroken, continuous, character of agricultural space and the fractured, discontinuous, and essentially punctiform character of most non-agricultural space. Even the highly graduated transport systems of today yield the entrepreneur only discrete areas of "accessible" space along the corridors of communication among major centers. Thus the limited radial character of trunk routes, the uneven distribution of terminal facilities and transshipment points, "discriminatory" rating conventions, agglomeration effects, and not least topographical features, are shown by Isard to produce a highly "punctured" transportation cost surface marked by "distortions and discontinuities." Substitution among transport inputs is, therefore, "not in the small but rather in the large . . . from one focal point to another."[18] Transport input substitutions outside of agriculture are, in fact, likely to entail quite radical interurban movements over expanses of intervening space.

The segmentary nature of the non-agricultural space continuum, if anything, tends to reinforce the hierarchical tendency of city size distributions. If city size is positively associated with (1) numbers of specialized functions carried on at a place, (2) the sizes of complementary market areas, and (3) if agglomerative scale-type economies rule out the presence of every function at each center, then cities of different sizes and degrees of "regional dominance" will necessarily appear. The larger the city in a system of cities—New York for example—the more likely that the trading orbits of its most specialized functions will embrace the entire system and the greater the interactive flows of goods, people, and communications (ton miles, passenger miles, message units,

[17] *Ibid.*, pp. 188–99. More generally, William Alonso, *Location and Land Use: Toward a General Theory of Rent* (Harvard University Press, 1964).

[18] Isard, *Location and Space-Economy*, pp. 251–53.

and so on) between it and lower ranking members of the hierarchy.

This is not to imply that the general theory of location now provides an "economic" explanation for the particular form of central-place hierarchy or the rank order of cities by size. Isard concluded that the universality and validity of such inferred or observed regularities was "a matter of individual opinion and judgement." [19] More recently, a searching comparative study by Berry of rank-size regularity and its hypothetical association with integrated systems of cities in advanced economies reached the conclusion that different city size distributions "are in no way related to the relative economic development of countries," nor to "the degree of urbanization of countries." Economic and social "maturity" are less the explanation of different city size distributions (which range all the way from simple primacy to lognormality) than "the number and complexity of forces" affecting the urban structure in each case.[20]

The structure of the central-place hierarchy is, nevertheless, affected by certain "indivisibilities" in productive operations and by economies of scale that inhere in the performance of production and marketing functions at nodal positions in the system. Beckmann has suggested a simple model.[21] Assume a rural population distributed uniformly over a plain. A first layer of centers is superimposed in the course of performing the most elemental production and distribution functions such that the size of center, c, is proportional to the population it serves (including its own). If r is the rural population in the marketing area, k the proportionality factor, and c the city size, then

$$c = k(r + c) \quad \text{or} \quad c = kr/1 - k,$$

so that $k/1 - k$ is "the effective 'urban multiplier.'" If s is a fixed number of lower-order centers served by any of the next higher order of centers, and k is the ratio of city size to population served, then

$$p_m = kP_m, \tag{1}$$

and

$$P_m = p_m + sP_{m-1}, \tag{2}$$

where p_m is the size of cities of each order m and P_m is the population served by them. Substituting (1) in (2) gives

$$P_m = s^{m-1}r/(1 - k)^m \tag{3}$$

and

$$p_m = ks^{m-1}r/(1 - k)^m, \tag{4}$$

[19] *Ibid.*, p. 57.

[20] Brian J. L. Berry, "City Size Distributions and the Distribution of City Size," in *Economic Development and Cultural Change*, Vol. 9 (July 1961), pp. 573–87.

[21] Martin J. Beckmann, "City Hierarchies and the Distribution of City Size," in *Economic Development and Cultural Change*, Vol. 6 (April 1958), pp. 243–48.

or, in other words, "both city size and population served increase exponentially with the level of the city in the hierarchy." Where m assumes its largest value, say, N ranks, then (3) describes the relation between total population P, the size of the smallest rural market area r and N the number of ranks in the city hierarchy, the total population P is given by

$$P_N = s^{m-1}r/(1-k)^N. \qquad (5)$$

Other relations can easily be derived, including that between total number of cities T, the number of ranks in the hierarchy N, and the number s of lower order satellites per city.

Beckmann also showed that the rank-size rule for cities, identified by Zipf, is also compatible with the hierarchy of central places and market areas.[22] In a recent formulation by Berry, the rule holds for any group of cities above a given size,

$$P_r{}^q = P_1/r, \qquad (6)$$

where P_1 is the population of the largest or first-ranking center, P_r is the population of the center of rank r, and q is a constant. Thus,

$$\text{Log } r = \log P_{1-q} \cdot \log P_r, \qquad (7)$$

such that "a plot of rank against size on double logarithmic paper should give a straight line with a slope of $-q$." In other words, the frequency distribution of centers by size is highly skewed in the form of a "reversed-J." A number of frequency distributions have a similar form through their skewness and each is evidently "the steady state distribution of the same simple stochastic process."[23] If the smallest class size of centers is continually being enlarged by new entrants, as is commonly the case, the steady state is that of the Yule distribution, which has a frequency function of the form

$$f(i) = ai^{-c}b^i.$$

[22] George K. Zipf, *Human Behavior and the Principle of Least Effort* (Cambridge, Mass.: Addison-Wesley, 1949), especially Chapters 9 and 10. See also, Figure 1 below, p. 127. Edgar M. Hoover, "The Concept of a System of Cities," in *Economic Development and Cultural Change*, Vol. 3 (January 1955), pp. 196–98, shows the essential identity of central-place hierarchy (median size rank of each order of center) and the rank-size rule as a form of the Pareto distribution.

[23] Brian J. L. Berry, "Cities as Systems within Systems of Cities," in Friedmann and Alonso (eds.), *Regional Development and Planning*, pp. 116–37. *Idem*, "Research Frontiers in Urban Geography," in Philip M. Hauser and Leo F. Schnore (eds.), *The Study of Urbanization* (John Wiley, 1965). Also R. E. Quandt, "Statistical Discrimination among Alternative Hypotheses and Some Economic Regularities," in *Journal of Regional Science*, Vol. 5 (1964).

The Need for a "Development" Perspective on Urban Regions

While the general theory does effectively unify the study of location and recast the theory of production in a spatial framework, it does not treat the income and aggregate demand side of equilibrium very fully. Nor does it formally confront the temporal problem of economic change and development. Notwithstanding Isard's live awareness of the industrial transformation "problem" throughout his *Location and Space-Economy,* the general theory is at most a theory of "morphostasis." In this regard, Thompson's contributions toward a broader definition of urban-regional economics represent a significant advance.

He is concerned with the economic performance of urban regions in the functional-spatial context of the national economy. Starting from Isard's general position, Thompson sets out to adapt the conventional macroeconomic apparatus—the factors and processes that affect the level, distribution, and stability of income and employment—to the study of the subnational small-area open economy: the urban region. By recourse to macro and micro concepts such as export and investment multipliers, price and income elasticities of demand, and the transport input substitution principle, Thompson explores the economic character of cities and their surrounding regions. He treats the performance of urban regions: (1) in the functional context of comparative advantage, the business cycle, and aggregate economic growth, and (2) in the functional-spatial context of a national system of cities. Finally he seeks to develop the implications of these "economist's questions" for the more particularistic and parochial problems posed by the planners and others concerned with what is called "urban managerial economics." [24]

If, in this manner, Thompson has gone too far afield from *intra*-urban problems—thought by some of his critics to be the "true" focus of urban economics[25]—an economic historian can only hail the departure as an important first step toward a resolution of the more general historical problem of the interrelation of urbanization and economic change: a problem at least as old as the writing of Adam Smith.

So far, however, Thompson's effort to involve urban economics more directly in the analysis of change has been confined to the first chapter of the *Preface* and to certain "growth-related" issues in the fifth chapter. In a more recent essay, he calls for a further updating of location theory to take more account of "the economic, technological, and in-

---

[24] Thompson, *Preface to Urban Economics,* pp. 1–7.
[25] For example, John F. Kain's review in *Journal of the American Institute of Planners,* Vol. 32 (May 1966), pp. 186–88.

stitutional facts of mid-twentieth century life." [26] Here he refers to the fact that the location literature is, by and large, still treating the one-plant, single-product, owner-controlled firm at a time when a growing share of output comes from multiproduct, multiplant, corporations "which are management controlled." The least-cost location for these latter organizations, he maintains, is at or near "a multiple node transportation center" which generally happens to be one of the nation's largest cities. Such large centers generate a volume of traffic along their channels of communication that leads to lower unit costs owing to the need to meet heavy fixed charges for transport and other facilities by ever-larger outputs. Competition for advantage among the larger cities, moreover, also reinforces the secular trend away from materials orientation toward market orientation for goods-and-services production in the expanding megalopolis. Although Thompson indicates the need to study long-run industrial relocations (as affected by rising mobility, and hence more uniform prices for labor and capital, or by the unequal distribution of tax burdens, and so on), he concedes that his own macroanalysis of urban-regional changes is essentially "a form of 'short run' economics which takes as given the local industry mix or export base and draws out its welfare implications . . . in terms of the level, distribution, and stability of income and employment." [27]

At virtually no point in the burgeoning urban-regional literature, nor in the older strand of location analysis, do economists yet come to grips with the secular process of urbanization itself. This is the process, nevertheless, that, from a demographic standpoint, forms the points of population concentration (peaks of population density) called "cities," and that, from an economic standpoint, registers the transfer of resources from the traditionally labor-intensive sector of husbandry into the more productive "modernizing" sectors. To be sure, urban-regional and location economists have not been concerned with the evolution of city systems as such nor with analysis of long-run economic transformations. However, were an investigator who was concerned with such phenomena to start from these two vantage points, he would shortly find himself proceeding under the severe constraints imposed by (1) the ahistorical micro-framework of the general theory of location and

[26] Thompson, *Preface to Urban Economics*, pp. 11–60 and 173–99. *Idem,* "Urban Economic Growth and Development in a National System of Cities," in Hauser and Schnore (eds.), *The Study of Urbanization*, pp. 431–90; *idem,* "Towards an Urban Economics," in Leo F. Schnore and Henry Fagin (eds.), *Urban Research and Policy Planning* (Beverly Hills, Calif.: Sage Publications, 1967).

[27] Thompson, "Towards an Urban Economics," in Schnore and Fagin (eds.), *Urban Research and Policy Planning*, p. 139.

space economy; and (2) the overly aggregated macro-framework of most theorizing about economic growth. For these and other reasons specified below, a different framework is required for the study of urbanization and economic development from that tentatively advanced by Thompson. What is at stake is not simply economic growth or rising gross national product per capita, but rather economic development and transformation: not merely the growth of cities or agglomeration, but the urbanization of society. There is the need, therefore, for a distinctive *developmental* perspective on the evolution of city-regions, a perspective that allows for greater disaggregation and, at the same time, yields generalizations of a somewhat lower order than those of formal theory.

Notwithstanding the valuable insights and experience represented by such concepts as comparative site advantage, scale economies in transportation or agglomeration, and the ordering effect of distance on the spatial distribution of activities, it is on operational grounds that the general theory of location and space economy is found wanting for the task at hand. The theory is intended to determine locations in a framework of general equilibrium; it requires optimal behavior by producers and consumers throughout the system.[28] But quite apart from the problem of handling so many complex interrelations, the outcome is still a static system that is not geared to the analysis of locational transformation. No doubt, while much can be inferred from resort to the method of "comparative statics" about shifts in structural parameters, there is no reason for admitting the assumption that all interim departures are "small in magnitude and quickly corrected by adaptive changes." Indeed, the long run might be defined as some extended period over which equilibrating conditions of continuity and stability do not obtain: a span during which the system is to a greater or lesser extent transformed by prevailing tendencies to disequilibrium. There are times and places in the course of the long run, to be sure, where conditions may approximate a static state and where much of a practical or policy interest might be learned from the assumption of "self correcting" deviations. But the dependence of the general theory on what, in last analysis, is virtually a single-factor explanation, namely the systematically variable cost of surmounting distance under *ceteris*

[28] A sharp critique of "models," "systems," and various locational taxonomies is given by Raymond Vernon and Edgar M. Hoover, "Economic Aspects of Urban Research," in Hauser and Schnore (eds.), *The Study of Urbanization,* pp. 191–207. The argument on pp. 195–202 is chiefly by Vernon. But see also, Robert L. Steiner, "Urban and Inter-Urban Economic Equilibrium," in First Annual Meeting of the Regional Science Association, *Papers and Proceedings,* Vol. 1 (Philadelphia, 1955).

paribus conditions, renders its particular solutions of little more than formal interest to the student of historical development. Nevertheless, as John Friedmann has suggested, "to a large extent, a dynamic location theory and a theory of economic development are one and the same." [29]

TRANSFORMATION OF LOCATIONAL STRUCTURES: GROWTH AND DEVELOPMENT

The introduction of concepts of economic growth and dynamics to urban-regional analysis by Thompson and others should, on the face of it, meet some of the more obvious objections to the static equilibrium framework in which most location economics has hitherto been cast. Problems of change can be specified with greater precision while the promise of the computer technology suggests that, given ample budgets for sufficient time, the tasks of analysis and measurement of social-spatial transformation are no longer insuperable.

For all its promise, however, growth theory remains one of the more artificial and fragile constructions in the macroeconomic repertory. The familiar Harrod-Domar model, for example, is grossly over-aggregated and altogether lacking in behavioral content. The saving and investment functions, and more especially the savings- and capital-output ratios (which govern rates of growth in output and income), are but the crudest averages. The stability of the aggregate capital-output ratio, in fact, is perfectly compatible with thoroughgoing shifts in the industrial composition and levels of investment. When disaggregated, moreover, the scores of individual ratios reveal highly unstable relationships, dependent on organizational and technological factors that affect the whole array of production methods from the extreme capital-intensive to the extreme labor-intensive.[30] Instability is further aggravated over time by cyclical changes in levels of income and no less by the variable performances of the workers engaged in maintaining capital goods.

The macroeconomic apparatus is, in fact, primarily designed to explain fluctuations in total income and product rather than the phenomenon of growth. Aggregate income and product at any time are normally dependent on aggregate demand within some prevailing "upper limit" of full-employment and capacity output. Hence the determination of

[29] John Friedmann, "Economy and Space: A Review Article," in *Economic Development and Cultural Change*, Vol. 6 (April 1958), p. 254.

[30] Albert Fishlow, "Empty Economic Stages," in *Economic Journal*, Vol. 75 (March 1965), pp. 112–25. More generally, F. H. Hahn and R. C. O. Mathews, "The Theory of Economic Growth; A Survey," in *Surveys of Economic Theory,* Vol. 2, *Growth and Development* (London and New York: Macmillan and St. Martins, 1965). These authors insist: "We want theories that can be used as plumbers use a spanner—not simply abstract systems."

aggregate income and product is largely the analysis of demand. Growth analysis, on the other hand, is concerned with that upper limit on supply and, more specifically, with the rate at which supply capacity changes over time. Growth is conceived, therefore, as a supply function—as an increase in an economy's capacity to meet some additional demand.[31]

Regardless of the empirical shortcomings, the concept of growth as a supply function has important implications for urban-regional economics. Relieved of any obligation to explain *general* states of the economy, the urban-regionalist concentrates—in Thompson's view—on the analysis of growth variations "within systems of cities." He is primarily concerned, therefore, with the changing supply capacities of the localities and the necessary investment activities involved. Shifts in the aggregate supply curve are, for the most part, treated as the sum of changing local capacities. By the same token, changes in aggregate investment are seen to have their effects on the "mix" of fast- and slow-growing industries locally and, thereby, on the rate of local economic growth.[32] Local growth, in turn, exerts an important influence on the changing patterns of local income. It is in these kinds of interactions of the system as a whole with its differentiated subsystems (in this case, urban-regions), that the possibility of growth *and* development ultimately resides.[33]

In the context of a system of cities, the distinction between growth and development takes on added importance. The concept of growth commonly employed in macroeconomics does not specify sufficiently the kind of change entailed by the industrial-urban transformation. For example, the increases in per capita incomes, which are at once a

[31] This is not to imply that determinants of aggregate demand are wholly unrelated to determinants of supply; changes in actual output to affect the rate of growth of potential output. But their relation involves the further concept of the "accelerator-multiplier" interaction, which usually has to do with the way in which entrepreneurial expectations concerning the future may ensure that total demand grows at the same rate as output potential.

[32] "The fundamental normative assumption here is that the local growth rate is a lever through which desirable changes in the level, distribution, and stability of income may be achieved. Much of what we label urban problems are, in fact, undesirable rates of local growth." Thompson, *Preface to Urban Economics,* p. 2.

[33] For present purposes, a system may be regarded as a complex of component *objects* (city-regions), possessing certain *attributes* as economic centers. The system is tied together by the *relationships* (interactions) among its components, whose attributes are thereby subjected to change and may, in turn, affect the system. See A. D. Hall and R. E. Fagen, "Definition of a System," in *General Systems,* Vol. 1 (1956). Also, Milton C. Marney and Nicholas M. Smith, "The Domain of Adaptive Systems: A Rudimentary Taxonomy," in *General Systems,* Vol. 9 (1964).

manifestation and a measure of growth, may stem from either absolute increases in the amounts of productive resources utilized per head of population, or increases in the relative efficiency with which given amounts of such resources are used. By either means, the per capita supply of resource inputs is enlarged, the supply capacity of the economy is enhanced, and to that extent output is potentially increased. Such a rise in output, however, might merely be additive: a succession of functionally continuous adjustments in existing modes of production. Growth may, in short, be merely more of the same. Changes that result in growth, on the other hand, may also lead to development.[34]

Growth would almost certainly involve development if, for example, the incremental outputs were sustained by secular declines in the ratios of input to output that followed upon innovations in productive organization and technique. Such productivity increments are the quantitative expression not only of additional inputs of labor and materials, but of less tangible inputs as well: new layouts of work, equipment, or plants; improved capacities of transport and communications systems; greater maturity of financial intermediaries; the application of new knowledge to productive ends; the emergence of a more liberal sociopolitical order, and so on. Where growth occurs through such interplay it is not a quantitative increase alone; it also involves a transformation of the modes of production and consumption into some state that is qualitatively different from its antecedents. No less striking than the rise in output per capita in the United States has been the change in the composition of total output; a change which reflects new patterns of spending and living by consumers as their average incomes rise. Here growth has involved development and ultimately transformation. While it is possible to describe the effects of such transformations in quantitative terms, such as rising dollar output per capita and higher levels of urbanization, the components of the measures do not provide their own explanation.[35]

If there is to be a rigorous model of the industrial-urban transformation, it will probably be a cybernetic one. Cybernetics—the study of control and communication in mechanical, biological, and social systems—is concerned, among other things, with determining conditions of equilibrium; cybernetic controls have hitherto been chiefly associated

[34] This distinction and its importance for regional economic analysis is given a highly original and provocative treatment in a manuscript in preparation by Edgar S. Dunn, Jr., "The Process of Social Change: As Related to Regional and National Development."

[35] See Eric E. Lampard, "Urbanization and Social Change," in Oscar Handlin and John Burchard (eds.), *The Historian and the City* (M.I.T. Press and Harvard University Press, 1963), pp. 233–38.

—in the contexts of engineering and social systems—with "self-regulating and equilibrating systems" such as thermostats or the market price mechanism. These processes are, in Maruyama's words, "studied under a general mathematical model of deviation-counteracting feedback networks" resulting in *morphostasis,* usually a most probable state under constraint.[36] Applied to the evolving system of cities, this concept is clearly incompatible with the notion of development or transformation sketched above, nor even with the idea of evolution, which implies an open-ended, information-generating process.

It is necessary to distinguish, therefore, between familiar equilibrium systems "that achieve stability under specific constant conditions and those that can learn or evolve new structures and behavior so as to remain stable under changing conditions" and "adapt to a fluctuating environment through a process of learning and innovation." [37] To this end, Maruyama draws attention to systems in which "mutual causal effects" stemming from an "initial kick," so far from counteracting all departures, "are deviation amplifying" and ultimately system transforming. The latter type of system does not lead by self-correction back to morphostasis but through deviation-amplifying processes, or *morphogenesis,* to an open-ended development with no evident tendency to entropy.

Maruyama returns, by way of example, to the flat, fertile plain from which even Thünen's single market center has been removed. From an initial kick given by one farmer anywhere on the plain, he then traces the unfolding of agriculture and the ramification of dependent service activities that give rise to a village concentration. The presence of the village reacts upon production and marketing subsystems whose mutual interaction and further ramification lead to manufactures, a city, and to increasing heterogeneity thereafter. The city grows in "deviation amplifying mutual feedback networks rather than in the initial condition or in the initial kick." [38]

Continuing interactions among the system, its differentiating subsystems, and their common surroundings generate entropy here and information there which together foster both "structuredness and unhomogeneity" through deviation counteracting and amplifying processes respectively. While one subsystem is becoming—through positive and

---

[36] Magoroh Maruyama, "The Second Cybernetics: Deviation Amplifying Mutual Causal Processes," in *American Scientist,* Vol. 51 (1963), pp. 164–69; reprinted in *General Systems,* Vol. 8 (1963), pp. 233–41.

[37] Mervyn L. Cadwallader, "The Cybernetic Analysis of Change in Complex Social Organizations," in *American Journal of Sociology,* Vol. 65 (September 1959), p. 155.

[38] Maruyama, "The Second Cybernetics."

negative feedbacks—structure generating and different, another is structurally stable and approximating its most probable state. Maruyama concludes with the notion that every system (including that of the cities) is made up of subsystems variously manifesting deviation correcting or amplifying processes whose prevalent effect will either tend to return the whole to morphostasis or to transform it by morphogenesis.

Differentiation and Development: the "Ecosystem" Framework

At the moment, for all its theoretical ingenuity, the operational significance of "the second cybernetics" to urban-regional economic history is marginal. Meanwhile, the principal thrust of this paper is away from "system" in the normative sense, toward the question of "process" in a behavioral sense—in particular the process of functional-structural differentiation. Differentiation has been a key concept in location analysis since Thünen and, doubtless, has close analogues in other branches of social science. It seems to underlie the use of terms such as "transaction," "interchange," "market," and even the talismanic word "system" itself. Nevertheless, division of labor—to give differentiation its classical name—has not excited much theoretical interest or sustained observation. Division of labor, to be sure, was central to Adam Smith's scheme for enlarging the wealth of nations and he devoted all of three or four pages to the topic. Since Smith there have been no more than half-a-dozen noteworthy discussions of the topic, of which Durkheim's remains, perhaps, the most thorough, perceptive, and justly celebrated.[39]

Industrial urbanization may be described in terms of the differentiation process. If we conceive of a preindustrial, low-productivity population as one in which factors, firms, and, to a large extent therefore, localities are relatively unspecialized and undifferentiated in space, industrialization and urbanization may be regarded as societal processes in which, among other things, factors, firms, and localities become increasingly specialized and, within their respective market areas, more differentiated from each other. Production sequences become more "prolongated" and "round about" in the sense that a growing volume of outputs represents specialized inputs for further processing or fabrication by other firms. So-called intermediate outputs become specialized

---

[39] Emile Durkheim, *On the Division of Labor in Society*, trans. George Simpson (Macmillan, 1933). Also, George J. Stigler, "The Division of Labor is Limited by the Extent of the Market," in *Journal of Political Economy*, Vol. 59 (June 1951), pp. 185–93; Eric E. Lampard, "The History of Cities in the Economically Advanced Areas," *Economic Development and Cultural Change*, Vol. 5 (January 1955), especially pp. 86–92; and Edward Ames and Nathan Rosenberg, "The Progressive Division of Labor and Specialization of Industries," in *Journal of Development Studies*, Vol. 1 (July 1965).

away from firms that formerly produced them for their own "internal" input and, as a consequence, proportionately fewer firms are making finished products for final consumption. The institutionally specialized production of certain capital goods occurs, for example, when manufacturers of final consumers' goods prefer to purchase certain inputs of equipment, say textile machinery or milling machines, rather than to produce them on their own account. A similar tendency holds for certain service inputs, for instance, warehousing or road haulage. The reinforcement and elaboration of such transitive relations over time impart a regular structure and integral character to the continuing reorganization of the division of labor. Such "systemic" attributes of a population are acquired in the course of progressive interaction among functionally specialized units and areas.

It remains to give a more explicit behavioral-institutional content to such departures, to determine the conditions for their subsequent generalization, and to seek explanations of why the process does or does not become arrested at any point. An important lead was given by Young as far back as 1928, in his paper "Increasing Returns and Economic Progress." [40] What he proposed was that unspecialized facets of a production process carried on *within* firms or by "multidextrous" jacks-of-all-trades can, so to speak, become differentiated "out," if they could be assured of a large enough market; that is, if the newly differentiated sequences in the process could be carried on by specialized business undertakings on a sufficiently large scale. The progressive division and specialization of industries would thus yield higher returns than were available previously to individuals, firms, or the economy at large. The necessary scale shift might be accomplished either by relocation of the new specialist in some area of localized industry that provides a large enough market for his product, or by achieving access to a larger market through transport innovations and the consequent reduction of the freight factor from his existing location.

[40] Allyn A. Young, "Increasing Returns and Economic Progress," in *Economic Journal*, Vol. 38 (December 1928). Economies from investment "are segregated and achieved by the operations of specialized undertakings which, taken together, constitute a new industry." Young's argument does not depend on "external economies" of urbanization. This latter form of scale economies remains as elusive as ever; see the rigorous analysis by Jeffrey G. Williamson and Joseph A. Swanson, "The Growth of Cities in the American Northeast, 1820–1870," in *Explorations in Entrepreneurial History*, Vol. 4 (2nd Series; 1966), pp. 44–67. Their use of size distribution data by itself tends to negate the urban economies hypothesis but "whenever scale variables are included in our model, the signs are always correct and the values of the parameters such that the optimum-sized city increases over time. Our disappointment arises when these coefficients fail to pass significance tests."

Specialized operations on a larger scale at one stage of the production process would create opportunities for innovation and specialization at other stages through the contingencies of backward and forward linkages. Returns to scale accruing "internally" to the firm or "externally" to the industry or locality are thus a fuller explanation of division of labor. But there is more to the specialization-differentiation process than simple, linear disintegration. Indeed, many rudimentary activities are already disintegrated and decentralized in respect of industrial process and organization (the putting-out system, merchant-employer system, and so on); industrialization often consists in their being "vertically reintegrated" on some more extensive scale of organization, in factories or other installations. This is commonly the case when mechanization or other special process considerations affecting scarce materials or skills are involved. The older, "un-integrated," decentralized modes of production can eventually no longer compete with the newer mode of organization which enjoys increasing returns—decreasing costs —to scale.

Not surprisingly, the introduction and generalization of power-driven machine processes in textile establishments became the enduring stereotype of industrial revolution in North America as well as in Europe. One unfortunate consequence of the stereotype was to focus attention on the technical conditions of quantity production to the neglect of the institutional prerequisites for the large scale *organization* of both production and distribution. Thus, when the specialized manufacture of textile machinery became differentiated in turn from units of textile production, it was because manufacture itself had become more localized and integrated in order to minimize the costs of operational and distance frictions in the increasingly complex flows of input-output dependency. Higher returns could not be secured until all specialized mechanical processes and their related inputs had been concentrated under single managements in the paleotechnic water- and steam-powered factory systems. In realizing the internal economies of scale, industrial organization created potential external (Marshallian) economies for the industry, part of which could be internalized (i.e., realized) by others such as the localized makers of machinery and machine tools. The special skills of the tool makers, furthermore, were not confined inexorably to that one industry or locality but rather their presence in the vicinity of textile mills meant that their craft—in some cases even the mechanical devices themselves—could be utilized to cheapen inputs in still other lines of manufacture. When generalized, such "technological convergences," as Nathan Rosenberg has aptly termed them, yield returns to scale that are reflected in the rising productivity of the entire space economy.[41]

Before the close of the nineteenth century, an analogous process of vertical integration was at work under the increasingly competitive conditions of large-scale production and distribution. By this time, the tendency involved not merely the concentration of specialized work processes in individual establishments or particular localities but the integration of hitherto separate and specialized business undertakings into larger and more unified systems of finance and control. Feeling the potentially lethal effects of intense competition, groups of entrepreneurs and financiers sought to heighten the degree of their control over independently organized material and transportation inputs or over the critical distribution channels for the sale of their products. The conduct of large-scale, technologically complex organizations, dependent as they were upon the commitment of vast aggregations of capital for indefinite periods under conditions of uncertainty, was meanwhile greatly facilitated by the adaptation of general laws permitting virtually unrestricted business incorporation. Until such times as "anti-trust" laws could be introduced to protect businesses from the more radical and "unfair" forms of competition, huge concentrations of capital were at stake and change in the structural morphology of business organization toward corporate control was in many instances not merely a convenience but also a strategy for economic survival. Thus, the impulse from returns to scale combined with a heightened sense of vulnerability to competition to induce managements into backward and forward integration on an interregional, and ultimately nationwide, scale.

The specializations of city and country and the resulting interdependence of small towns, cities, and metropolises are, likewise, manifestations of the same pervasive specialization-differentiation-reintegration tendency that yields increasing returns (decreasing costs) to scale. Notwithstanding different legal-institutional constraints, there is by analogy a similarly centralized mode of organization and control—the urban or metropolitan hierarchy—which seems to inhere in technological progress. Vertical reintegration of specialisms thus takes effect at three levels of functional organization, each of which has implications for spatial reorganization: in the integration of work processes, in business systems and structures, and in the system of city-regions itself.

[41] Nathan Rosenberg, "Technological Change in the Machine Tool Industry, 1840–1910," in *Journal of Economic History,* Vol. 23 (December 1963). Also H. A. Wooster, "A Forgotten Factor in American Industrial History," in *American Economic Review,* Vol. 16 (March 1926), pp. 14–27.

All three levels of integration, of course, are subject at any time to diminishing returns. The decreasing costs that are associated with larger-scale production at a given site will, all things being equal, eventually be offset by rising transport and other distance-related costs of distribution, along lines of the Löschian equilibrium of the firm under imperfect competition. Quasi-rents earned in the short run by innovators in knowledge, technique, or other critical input in temporarily inelastic supply will, assuming relatively "free" conditions of entry, encourage other entrepreneurial groups to undertake similar productions where possible at other sites beyond the range of effective competition from the original innovator. Needless to repeat, all constraints are themselves subject to revision and "relaxation" with further transformations of transportation and production functions. Somewhat paradoxically, therefore, a further effect of differentiation is to make plants, business organizations, and city-regions of the same approximate size functionally and structurally more alike. Innovations which, given increasing returns, prove profitable lead first to differentiation and then to generalization of the "novelty." This takes place more or less throughout the appropriate stratum of the space-economy. The ultimate outcome of the specialization-differentiation-reintegration-generalization tendencies is thus system transformation.

While the point should not be pressed too literally, it is true, nevertheless, that many plants already use specialized equipment to produce multiple products or seek multiple uses for the same product. Business systems, likewise, utilize their financial resources and organizational structures to diversify their outputs along a variety of lines. Cities that produce a "mix" of products and services for diverse markets near or far also seek to enhance their locational attraction, and thereby to achieve greater stability and well-being under conditions of technological progress. Amidst the welter of innovation, generalization, and convergence that is, in part, the outcome of uninhibited communication and movement, there remains the impulse to specialization and sufficient market imperfection for the innovator as well as the emulator to benefit therefrom. This helps counter whatever opposing tendency there might be toward system entropy.

One further point should be made concerning members of the population viewed as "human resources." With technological and organizational progress—the principal constituents of rising productivity—the quality of the labor force must also be improved in order to combine profitably with the improved equipment that is continually being substituted for the "inferior" but relatively high-priced labor inputs appropriate to older and obsolescent technologies. New grades of skill must therefore be developed in the population, then combined in novel ratios with more complex, "roundabout" technologies. The outcome of this heightened specialization is a division of labor between skillful men and "skilled" machines culminating in the phenomena of automation. Division of labor was not, in short, exhausted in the form of breakdown and simplification of linear tasks, exemplified by Adam Smith's pin-making operation, or John R. Commons' slaughterhouse production line. It is precisely the long-run tendency to employ more expertise in novel combinations with more complex and sophisticated technological systems that has negated Smith's fear that simplification and monotony of job tasks in division of labor would, for all its economic promise, render a growing proportion of the town populations "as stupid and ignorant as it is possible for a human creature to become." [42] Indeed, the requirement of greater knowledge-input has become a condition of rising productivity per unit of capital and labor combined in both town *and* country. It is this same requirement that transforms long-run economic growth into development.

The second and final thrust of this paper is to introduce the concept of the "ecosystem" as the most appropriate social-systems framework now available for the historical analysis of the role of differentiation in the evolving system of cities. For Duncan, who has done most in recent years to advance the study of human ecology:

the salient characteristic . . . of an ecological approach is its proclivity for analyzing human communities and economic systems in terms of their place in a total ecosystem, the major facets of which are populations adjusting to their environments by means of their technological equipment and patterns of social organization.

Thus, the space economy at any time is a special aspect of the prevailing human ecosystem.[43] It is not surprising that Isard, in view of his empirical studies of locational transformations, holds "societal development [to be] an historical process."

At any given point of time there exists an inherited physical structural framework . . . the evolutionary framework becomes critical as a locational factor, any pure substitutional theory which is not linked to specific regional structures is of severely limited significance.

[42] Adam Smith, *The Wealth of Nations* (Random House, 1937), pp. 734–35. Also, John R. Commons, "Labor Conditions in Meat Packing and the Recent Strike," in *Quarterly Journal of Economics,* Vol. 19 (November 1904).
[43] Otis Dudley Duncan *et al., Metropolis and Region* (The Johns Hopkins Press, for Resources for the Future, 1960), p. 3.

The concept of the ecosystem is readily adapted to the study of such cumulative historical developments, since it is grounded in the view (1) that the transformation of human settlement patterns (the evolving system of cities, for instance) involves the emergence and generalization of novelty within the population system concerned, and (2) that whatever is emergent at any time depends upon what happened earlier, in the sense that Boulding speaks of growth creating form "but form limits growth." It is significant that Abbott Payson Usher, a pioneer in North America of the study of the economics of invention and location, sought to understand "the broader aspects of the developing geographical patterns of population" and "the relations of these patterns to localized resources . . . under the technological conditions of each period." [44]

Such an approach is not likely to give rise to a deterministic model that includes all potentially relevant variables and "explains" the changing functions and locations of city-regions over time. The ecosystem method is unreservedly empirical, notwithstanding the scheme of conceptualization built up by the modern, "post-Chicago," school of human ecologists since 1950. The ecologist moves from the construction of pertinent data "to the classification of patterns in the data, and the investigation of empirical relations, seeking all the while to arrive at explanations of observed patterns and regularities by inductive means." [45] He proceeds, in short, from a direct examination of where cities are and what they do, toward a sequence of middle-ranging, comparatively low-level generalizations concerning the transformation of the system, its various attributes and relationships. The ecologist is not committed by a model to the premise that the system is an optimizing one, or that its successive adjustments will necessarily return it to a morphostatic equilibrium. For the moment, it is not necessary to go much beyond the observed fact that the system of city-regions is both *incremental* and *redistributional*. Marginal increments to its population and activity will be distributed unevenly and non-randomly throughout its territorial space with regard to both the "inertia" of inherited structures and the "force" of novel opportunities. [46]

[44] Isard, *Location and Space-Economy*, p. 180. Kenneth Boulding, "General Systems Theory—The Skeleton of a Science," in *Management Science*, Vol. 2 (1956). A. P. Usher, "A Dynamic Analysis of the Location of Economic Activity," unpublished manuscript, cited in Isard, *ibid.*, p. 31.

[45] Otis Dudley Duncan *et al.*, *Metropolis and Region*, p. 31. Also Duncan, "Social Organization and the Ecosystem," in Robert E. L. Faris (ed.), *Handbook of Modern Sociology* (Rand McNally, 1964), pp. 36–82. More generally, Amos H. Hawley, *Human Ecology: A Theory of Community Structure* (New York: Ronald Press, 1950).

[46] Apart from their substantive content, the results from such procedures often

THE URBAN TRANSFORMATION
IN THE UNITED STATES

The urbanization of population in the United States is a process as old as the history of the Republic. Every federal census since 1790 has reported a growing number of people living in cities, the numbers and sizes of which have likewise increased at every count. Table 1, column

TABLE 1.
NUMBERS OF CITIES ≥2,500, BY SIZE GROUPS, AND SIZE-GROUP SHARES
OF TOTAL U.S. POPULATION, 1790–1960

Date	All cities ≥2,500 (1)	U/P (2)	Cities 2,500–24,999 (3)	U/P (4)	Cities 25,000–249,999 (5)	U/P (6)	Cities 250,000+ (7)	U/P (8)
1790	24	5.1	22	3.5	2	1.6	–	–
1800	33	6.1	30	3.7	3	2.4	–	–
1810	46	7.3	42	4.1	4	3.2	–	–
1820	61	7.2	56	3.9	5	3.3	–	–
1830	90	8.8	83	4.7	7	4.1	–	–
1840	131	10.8	119	5.3	11	3.7	1	1.8
1850	236	15.3	210	6.4	25	6.7	1	2.2
1860	392	19.8	357	7.9	32	6.7	3	5.2
1870	663	25.7	611	10.5	45	7.0	7	8.2
1880	939	28.2	862	11.0	69	8.4	8 (1)	8.8 (2.4)
1890	1,348	35.1	1,224	12.9	113	11.2	11 (3)	11.0 (5.8)
1900	1,737	39.7	1,577	13.6	145	11.6	15 (3)	14.5 (8.5)
1910	2,262	45.7	2,034	14.7	209	14.2	19 (3)	16.8 (9.2)
1920	2,722	51.2	2,435	15.5	262	16.0	25 (3)	19.7 (9.6)
1930	3,165	56.2	2,789	16.1	339	16.6	37 (5)	23.5 (12.3)
1940	3,464	56.5	3,052	16.5	375	17.1	37 (5)	22.9 (12.1)
1950	4,054	59.6	3,534	17.3	479	19.2	41 (5)	23.1 (11.5)
1960	4,996	63.1	4,239	18.7	707	22.5	50 (5)	21.9 (9.8)

Note: Figures in italics are urban shares of total population.
Figures in parentheses, columns (7) and (8), are for the class of cities, ≥1,000,000, and their combined share of all U.S. population beginning in 1880. New York City and Brooklyn are separated before 1900; together they exceed one million by 1860.
Source: U.S. Census data.

(1), presents the growth of census cities, ≥2,500, from 1790 to 1960. The italicized column (2) indicates the proportion, U, of total population, P, that is concentrated in these cities at each decennial census date. Remaining columns in Table 1 show the increase in num-

---

resemble deductive hypotheses that require closer specification and testing in piecemeal fashion. Many social scientists may find conclusions reached by such means to be of greater historical interest than those obtained by more highly formalized operations on fragile data whose numerical form often lends a deceptive and unwarranted aura of specificity to a particular result.

bers of cities by certain size groups, and the share of urbanized population, U/P, that is resident in each of the size groups.

Scarcely less significant than the growth in numbers and sizes of cities has been their spread across the entire conterminous United States from the Atlantic to the Pacific oceans. Table 2 presents the levels of urbanization (proportion urbanized, U/P) at each census for the United States as a whole and for four major census regions which together make up the conterminous United States. Columns (6) and (7) exhibit the comparative levels of urbanization achieved by Rhode Island and Mississippi, the most and least urbanized of states since their respective admissions to the Union in 1790 and 1817. The exhibit at

TABLE 2.
URBANIZATION OF POPULATION, U/P, IN THE UNITED STATES, BY CENSUS REGIONS AND SELECTED STATES, 1790–1960

Date	U.S. (1)	Northeast (2)	South (3)	North Central (4)	West (5)	Rhode Island (6)	Mississippi (7)
1790	5.1	*8.1*	2.1	–	–	*19.0*	–
1800	6.1	*9.3*	3.0	–	–	*20.8*	–
1810	7.3	*10.9*	4.1	0.9	–	*23.4*	–
1820	7.2	*11.0*	4.6	1.1	–	*23.0*	–
1830	8.8	*14.2*	5.3	2.6	–	*31.2*	2.0
1840	10.8	*18.5*	6.7	3.9	–	*43.8*	1.0
1850	15.3	*26.5*	8.3	9.2	6.4	*55.6*	1.8
1860	19.8	*35.7*	9.6	13.9	16.0	*63.3*	2.6
1870	25.7	*44.3*	12.2	20.8	25.8	*74.6*	4.0
1880	28.2	*50.8*	12.2	24.2	30.2	*82.0*	3.1
1890	35.1	*59.0*	16.3	33.1	*37.0*	*85.3*	5.4
1900	39.7	*61.1*	18.0	38.6	*39.9*	*88.3*	7.7
1910	45.7	*71.8*	22.5	45.1	*47.9*	*91.0*	11.5
1920	51.2	*75.5*	28.1	*52.3*	*51.8*	*91.9*	13.4
1930	56.2	*77.6*	34.1	*57.9*	*58.4*	*92.4*	16.9
1940	56.5	*76.6*	36.7	*58.4*	*58.5*	*91.6*	19.8
1950	59.6	*75.4*	44.6	*61.1*	*59.9*	*87.0*	27.6
1960	63.1	*72.8*	52.7	*63.9*	*66.1*	*89.9*	36.2
EXHIBIT: NEW URBAN DEFINITION[a]							
1950	64.0	*79.5*	48.6	*64.1*	*69.5*	*84.3*	27.9
1960	69.9	*80.2*	58.5	*68.7*	*77.7*	*86.4*	37.7

[a] See text.

Notes: Figures in italics above the national average.

Northeast: Me., N.H., Vt., Mass., R.I., Conn., N.Y., N.J., Pa.

South: Del., Md., D.C., Va., W. Va., Ky., Tenn., N.C., S.C., Ga., Fla., Ala., Miss., Ark., La., Okla., Tex.

North Central: Ohio, Ind., Ill., Mich., Wis., Minn., Ia., Mo., N.D., S.D., Neb., Kans.

West: Mont., Ida., Wyo., Col., N.M., Ariz., Utah, Nev., Wash., Ore., Cal.

Source: U.S. Census data.

the base of Table 2 shows the effect of the new census definition of "urban" on levels of urbanization in the same territorial units. This definition was introduced in the 1950 census to include not only residents of incorporated places, $\geq 2,500$, but also those dwelling in the closely settled urban fringes surrounding cities, $\geq 50,000$.

Conceptualization and Measurement

The changes in levels of urbanization that result from the use of the new definition underscore the degree to which the empirical findings of social science depend on the concepts and measures employed. This dependence holds, of course, for all sciences but, owing to the vernacular usage of so many of his terms, the social scientist is particularly obligated to make his meanings clear. In this study "urbanization" is, for the most part, identified with the demographic process of population concentration, and "cities" with points of concentration (or peaks of population density).[47] There is no a priori reason why urbanization should not focus on a single concentration as in the models of Thünen and Maruyama. If urbanization is sustained, the concentration will grow in size, but there is again no necessity for the growth of concentrated population, U, to outstrip the growth of total population, P. The level of urbanization U/P, in short, need not rise. But, if city concentrations do grow in number as well as in size (Table 1), and if a majority of the population does come to reside in cities (as occurred in the United States by 1920), such features of urbanization are not to be explained by the process, for they define the process; other pertinent conditions apply.

For cities to increase in number and size, there must be not merely population and a spatial environment, but relevant social and cultural capacities as well. Such capacities are essentially *attributes* of the population and can exist in no other manner or form. What a population does with its sociophysical environment—following the ecosystem approach —depends largely on the patterns of social organization it assumes and the technological means at its disposal: in short, upon its cumulative capacity for adaptation.[48] The outcome of continuing adaptation, fur-

[47] This definition follows Hope Tisdale (Eldridge), "The Process of Urbanization," in *Social Forces,* Vol. 20 (March 1942). There is some danger in identifying urbanization with population concentration in space. Urban concentration may also take the form of urban population concentration *within the city size distribution:* for example, toward greater or lesser equality. See, Williamson and Swanson, "The Growth of Cities in the American Northeast 1820–1870," p. 94, note 6. Also Joseph A. Swanson, "More on Urban Concentration," unpublished (Graduate Program in Economic History, University of Wisconsin, 1967), which proposes a new measure of urban concentration.

[48] Eric E. Lampard, "Historical Aspects of Urbanization," in Hauser and

thermore, should in great part be observable in the populations' incremental and redistributional achievements.

Thus far, the phenomenon of urbanization has been characterized in terms of levels rather than of rates, since the former are more obvious and hence less difficult to measure and compare. Level of urbanization means simply the proportion of a total population that is concentrated in urban settlements (however defined) or, alternatively, the ratio that urban population bears to the total at any time, U_t/P_t.[49] Rate of urbanization might, therefore, mean a positive (or negative) change in that ratio, $\Delta(U/P)$, over a given period. This latter expression is simply a measure of the proportion of total population that has removed from non-urban to urban settlements during a given time interval. What it measures is the *absolute* change in the urbanization ratio, or the incremental share of population that has redistributed itself from non-urban to urban residence, as these categories are defined by the census authority. Clearly, the incremental population no less than the total population is composed of both urban and non-urban (usually rural) elements; hence, the rate of urbanization, $\Delta(U/P)$, is a function of changes in both components and, as a consequence, may be a highly ambiguous measure of the growth of cities and urban population per se.

While $\Delta(U/P)$ is the most common and, for certain economic purposes, important measure of the rate of urbanization, the mere quantification of absolute rural-to-urban "structural" change might be less significant for other purposes than a rate of urban population growth *relative* to total population growth, say $\Delta U/U/\Delta P/P$ or $\Delta U/\Delta P/(U/P)$, in any period. The latter, which can be expressed as $\Delta U_{t+1}/U_t/\Delta P_{t+1}/P_t$, relates what Jeffrey Williamson has termed the "marginal" urbanization rate of period $t + 1$ to the "average" urbanization rate. This measure is merely one of a small battery of alternatives (involving U and P) which, in contrast to $\Delta(U/P)$, will give a rate of urbanization variously standardized by a rate of population growth. A marginal rate

---

Schnore (eds.), *Study of Urbanization*. More generally, Richard L. Meier, *A Communications Theory of Urban Growth* (M.I.T. Press, 1962).

[49] This is the definition favored by Kingsley Davis in "The Urbanization of Human Population," *Scientific American*, Vol. 213 (September 1965). It lends itself, however, to the somewhat anomalous situation in which "cities can grow without any urbanization, provided that the rural population grows at an equal or greater rate." By the same token, numbers of urban residents may actually shrink and cities fall into decline; yet, if rural population were to fall at a faster rate, the urbanization ratio would *rise*. Such an ambiguous conception may actually obscure what is happening and is virtually useless for the study of preindustrial urbanization. See Leo F. Schnore and Eric E. Lampard, "Social Science and the City: A Survey of Research Needs," in Schnore and Fagin (eds.), *Urban Research and Policy Planning*, pp. 25–29.

of urbanization in this sense may be highly significant as a short-run indicator of socioeconomic change in an underdeveloped or preindustrial population, where all incremental urbanization is from the characteristically low U/P base of a predominantly agrarian order.[50] If attention were to be focused exclusively on the absolute rate, $\Delta(U/P)$, the critical period of urban acceleration might well be obscured.

The precise measurement of structural changes in a population is always complicated by the possibility of uncertain "gains" and "losses" incurred through migration across territorial boundaries. Migration across state lines, for example, may well account for the fluctuations in both rates and levels of urbanization in Mississippi before 1880 (Table 2, column 7), and for the same phenomenon more generally throughout the West South Central census division from 1810 through 1880. Such extreme oscillations, including instances of apparent de-concentration or "negative" urbanization, reflect the opening up of lands to agricultural settlement (or, before 1860, the heavy import of slaves from other states), which may have swamped the modest contemporary increases of urban population. By the same token, it is not inconceivable that migration of rural people from western New England, New York, and Pennsylvania during the early decades of westward movement of the nineteenth century may have raised those areas' U/P proportions at times beyond the levels warranted by the actual movement of people from the countryside to the towns. Given problems inherent in measures of structural change, the rate of urbanization will be most adequately measured for some purposes by the percentage increase in urban population itself, $\Delta U/U$, a rate which is independent of rural (and total) population growth. While this expression gives no indication whatever of rural-to-urban shift, it is (making due allowance for changes in definition and the incorporation of rural areas) the least ambiguous of all measures of city growth.

The Urbanization of Population

The urban transformation has already been outlined in terms of the levels of urbanization for the nation, four census regions, and two selected states (Tables 1 and 2). The differential effect of urbanization is illustrated by the fact that a state such as Rhode Island (and, incidentally, also Massachusetts) was more than half urbanized before 1850, the Northeast region as a whole by 1880, the North Central and Western regions, together with the nation, by 1920, with the South failing to reach that level before the mid-fifties. In terms of levels of urbanization,

[50] Jeffrey G. Williamson, "Ante Bellum Urbanization in the American Northeast," *Journal of Economic History,* Vol. 25 (October 1965).

therefore, some states in the deep South lag states in southern New England by more than a century. On the other hand, the lag between most Northeastern, North Central, and Western states in this regard is of much shorter span.

The rates of urbanization underlying the nationwide urban transformation are shown in Table 3. For comparative purposes, both the percentage rate, $\Delta U/U$, and the rate of rural-to-urban shift, $\Delta(U/P)$, expressed as percentage point increments by decades, 1790–1960 are given. Except for the two decades 1850–60 and 1860–70, the direction of the interdecadal pattern of rates is the same: rising rates of growth of urban population accompanying rising rates of rural-to-urban shift countrywide. But, whereas the increasing rate of rural-to-urban shift is

TABLE 3.

RATES OF URBANIZATION OF U.S. POPULATION, PERCENTAGE INCREASES AND INCREMENTAL URBAN SHIFTS, BY DECADES, 1790–1960

Rates	1790 –00	1800 –10	1810 –20	1820 –30	1830 –40	1840 –50	1850 –60	1860 –70	1870 –80
Per cent increase ($\Delta U/U$)	59.9	63.0	31.9	62.6	63.7	92.1	75.4	59.3	42.7
Incremental urban share $\Delta(U/P)$	1.0	1.2	−0.1	1.6	2.0	4.5	4.5	5.9	2.5

Rates	1880 –90	1890 –00	1900 –10	1910 –20	1920 –30	1930 –40	1940 –50	1950 –60	
Per cent increase ($\Delta U/U$)	56.5	36.4	39.3	29.0	27.3	7.9	20.6	25.4	
Incremental urban share $\Delta(U/P)$	6.9	4.6	6.0	5.5	5.0	0.3	3.1	3.5	

EXHIBIT: NEW URBAN DEFINITION, 1950–60.
Per cent increase, 29.3; Incremental urban share, 5.9

Source: U.S. Census data.

broadly sustained over the entire period 1820–70, the percentage rate of growth, which also rises after 1820, already subsides after 1850. From 1870 to 1950 the pattern of change in the percentage rate, $\Delta U/U$, is one of alternate fall and rise; after 1950 this pattern appears to have been interrupted, for the substantial rise of 1940–50 is sustained through 1950–60 (even by the old census "urban" definition). The decade 1920–30 also appears deviant, since its rate of increase fell below that of the preceding decade, 1910–20. A least squares straight line fitted to the percentage rate (Table 4) reveals, however, that the observed rates (Table 3) do fall alternately below and above the trend line and that, in fact, the decade 1920–30 is consistent with this pattern.[51] Thus, the failure of the rate of urban population increase to rise during 1920–30 is better interpreted as a retardation in the rate of fall away from the post-Civil War peak 1880–90 (Table 3) which, incidentally, was also the decade of greatest rural-to-urban structural shift in the entire history of the United States. Use of the percentage deviations from trend values (Table 4, column 4), reveals that inter-

TABLE 4.
TRENDS AND DEVIATIONS FROM TREND IN RATES OF CHANGE
OF U.S. URBAN POPULATION, 1870–1950

Decade (X)[a] 1870–80 = 0	Rate (Y) $\left(\dfrac{U_{t+1} - U_t}{U_t} \times \dfrac{100}{1}\right)$ (1)	Trend value (Yc) (2)	Deviations from trend	
			Amount $(Y - Yc)$ (3)	Percentage $\left(\dfrac{Y - Yc}{Yc} \times \dfrac{100}{1}\right)$ (4)
1870–80	42.7	50.8	−8.1	−16
1880–90	56.5	45.5	11.0	24
1890–00	36.4	40.2	−3.8	−9
1900–10	39.3	35.0	4.3	12
1910–20	29.0	29.7	−0.7	−2
1920–30	27.3	24.4	2.9	12
1930–40	7.9	19.1	−11.2	−59
1940–50	19.5	13.9	5.6	40

[a] For the formula $Yc = a + bX$, $a = 50.783$, $b = -5.274$.
Source: Adapted from Eldridge and Thomas, *Population Redistribution and Economic Growth*, Vol. 3, Table 1.61.

decadal fluctuations in rates of urban population increase were wider toward the beginning and the end of the period 1870–1950 than during the middle decades, 1890–1930.

Fluctuations in the rate of urban increase, $\Delta U/U$, during the period after 1870 reflect the changing contributions of different residential, nativity, and racial components of the national population. Over the successive decades between 1870 and 1910 foreign-born whites contributed 16.5, 23.5, 14.6, and 23.7 per cent respectively to decennial increases of urban population nationwide. During the decade 1910–20,

[51] Hope T. Eldridge and Dorothy S. Thomas, *Population Redistribution and Economic Growth, United States, 1870–1950*, Vol. 3 (Philadelphia: American Philosophical Society, 1964), pp. 216–26. Also, Leon B. Truesdell, "The Development of the Urban-Rural Classification in the United States, 1874 to 1949," Bureau of the Census, in *Current Population Reports, Population Characteristics Series P-23*, No. 1 (1949).

however, the foreign-born contribution fell off sharply to 6.8 per cent and, with greater legal restrictions on immigration, to 5.1 per cent, 1920–30.[52] Almost all urban increase thereafter was contributed by native-born elements (even more than in the first half of the nineteenth century), since the numbers of foreign-born urbanites fell *absolutely* after 1930–40. After 1910, migration to the cities was mostly from native rural elements, white and Negro. As a consequence, the incremental urban share, $\Delta(U/P)$, for the decade 1910–20—amounting to 5.5 percentage points—was somewhat greater than it would have been had migration from overseas maintained its previous rate of contribution to urban and total population growth.

One may infer from the character and timing of these rates of urban increase that, after the World War I decade, *all* urban measures derived from the federal census are increasingly inadequate down to 1950. Thus, after 1910–20 again, the long-run tendency for rural population to exhibit a falling rate of increase (as it had over every decade of the nineteenth century, except 1870–80) appears to have halted. During 1920–30 the rate of rural change, $\Delta R/R$, increased more markedly than in the previous decade (4.4 compared with 3.2 per cent) and it maintained a rising rate over ensuing decades to 1950 (6.4 and 7.9 per cent), when the census definition of "urban" was revised, as noted above, to take account of the changing—more "metropolitan"—form of urban concentration (Table 5). The phenomenon of rising rates of rural increase at this particular juncture suggests that, in fact, a rising share of urban population was redounding to the rural sector as a consequence of outmoded census categories. With the adoption of the new urban definition in 1950, the rising rate of rural increase was again arrested and, over the decade 1950–60, was converted to an absolute decrease (Table 5). Continued use of the old urban definition would have returned a positive rate of rural increase of 8.2 per cent instead of an absolute decrease of -0.9 per cent.

[52] Eldridge and Thomas, *Population Redistribution* . . . , p. 216. Other estimates on the climactic decade of immigrant contribution to urban increase 1900–10 are as follows:

Net Urban Increase	Alien Immigrants	Natural Increase	Native Rural	Incorporation
a) 11,826,000	41.0%	21.6%	29.8%	7.6%
b) 11,013,738	30.0–37.1%	27.3%	35.6–42.7%	–

Note: Line (a) is from J. M. Gillette and G. R. Davies, "Measure of Rural Migration and Other Factors of Urban Increase in the U.S.," in *Publications of the American Statistical Association,* Vol. 14 (September 1915), pp. 642–53; line (b) is from Earl Clark, "Contributions to Urban Growth," in *ibid.,* pp. 654–71.

The belated introduction of a new urban definition in 1950 had already been preceded by a concern for the larger urbanized populations of cities, suburbs, and certain "urban fringe" areas that mostly fell outside the old census urban classification. In 1910, the census had employed a category, "metropolitan district," that was designed to measure the entire urbanized agglomeration in an area rather than the population of the incorporated city alone. These districts were subsequently revised and extended as standard metropolitan areas (SMA's) and standard metropolitan statistical areas (SMSA's) in the censuses of 1950 and 1960.[53] Table 5 gives some indication of the degree to which

TABLE 5.
DECENNIAL RATES OF U.S. POPULATION GROWTH, 1900–60,
BY CENSUS CLASSIFICATION OF RESIDENCE

| Population area | (% increase) | | | | | | New def., |
| | 1900–10 | 1910–20 | 1920–30 | 1930–40 | 1940–50 | 1950–60 | 1950–60 |
(1)	(2)	(3)	(4)	(5)	(6)	(7)	(8)
United States	21.0	14.9	16.1	7.2	14.1	18.8	–
Rural	9.0	3.2	4.4	6.4	7.9	8.2	(−0.9)
Urban	39.3	29.0	27.3	7.9	20.6	22.6	(29.3)
SMSA	32.0	24.9	27.1	8.8	22.6	26.3	
Central city	37.1	27.7	24.3	5.6	14.7	10.7	
Outside	23.7	19.9	32.3	14.6	35.9	48.5	
Non-SMSA	13.1	6.5	5.4	5.4	3.7	7.9	
Number of metro-politan areas	44	58	97	140	168	224	

Source: U.S. Census data.

the old definitions of urban and rural had, by recent decades, come to understate the extent of the urban transformation and, by an equal amount, to exaggerate the size of rural populations (compare SMSA and census urban rates of growth since 1920–30 in Table 5). The adoption of the more inclusive definition in 1950 not only raised the decennial rate of urban population increase by more than a quarter but lifted the level or "proportion urban" by 4.4 and 7.8 percentage points respectively in 1950 and 1960 (Tables 5 and 2). Rates of rural increase

[53] 13th United States Census, 1910, Vol. 1, *Population: General Report and Analysis,* "Cities and Their Suburbs," pp. 73–77. W. S. Thompson, *The Growth of Metropolitan Districts in the U.S.: 1900–1940* (Government Printing Office, 1948), Table 6, estimates that the "new" urban definition applied to the metropolitan districts of 1910, 1920, and 1930 would have raised the urbanized metropolitan population by 8 per cent in 1910 and 1920, 11.5 per cent in 1930 and by 12.3 per cent in 1940.

accordingly were revised downward from an apparent rate of 8.2 per cent to a "true" negative rate of −0.9 per cent.

Use of the metropolitan classifications meanwhile has thrown new light on the character of the urban agglomeration process during the automobile age. While urban concentration continues countrywide with minor exceptions, a process of local deconcentration has been gathering momentum in and about the larger foci of concentration. Since 1920, the largely suburban "outside" populations of SMSA's have been growing at a faster rate *in the aggregate* than the populations of the corresponding central cities (Table 5). The proportion of all United States population resident in the "outside" rings of SMSA's grew between 1920 and 1960 from 17.6 per cent to around 30.0 per cent, while the population resident in the central cities barely held its own and, in the course of the fifties, actually went into decline.[54]

INDUSTRIAL URBANIZATION AND THE SYSTEM OF CITIES

In contrast to the demographic concept of urbanization treated above, the process of urbanization is sometimes viewed as a structural change affecting the patterned activities of the entire population. Where the patterning involved is that of the labor force or some other economic quantity, the urban transformation takes on an additionally significant dimension. Urbanization is said typically to entail the movement of population out of rural-agricultural communities and occupations into generally larger urban communities and non-agricultural occupations. Thus, the "structural" concept of urbanization gives primary recognition to the differential ordering of occupations and industries in space.

Urban-Industrial Development

The broad relation between urbanization of population and industrialization of the labor force (defined simply as shift into non-agricultural employments) is given in Tables 6 and 7. The former compares rates of incremental urbanization, $\Delta(U/P)$, and of industrialization of the labor force, $\Delta(NAL/L)$, by decades 1790–1960. It is noteworthy that the decades 1820–70 experienced rising rates of incremental ur-

---

[54] Amos H. Hawley, *The Changing Shape of Metropolitan America: Deconcentration since 1920* (Free Press, 1956) is the most complete demographic and economic analysis for the years 1900–1950. Deconcentration was already evident in some of the larger SMA's before 1890; see Leo F. Schnore, "The Timing of Metropolitan Decentralization," in *Journal of the American Institute of Planners,* Vol. 25 (November 1959), pp. 200–6. *Idem, The Urban Scene: Human Ecology and Demography* (Free Press, 1965), pp. 203–93, provides a timely caution against the use of national *aggregates* for describing socioeconomic and racial features of city and suburban populations in metropolitan areas.

TABLE 6.
INCREMENTAL URBANIZATION OF POPULATION AND INDUSTRIALIZATION
OF THE LABOR FORCE, UNITED STATES, 1790–1960

	1790 –00	1800 –10	1810 –20	1820 –30	1830 –40	1840 –50	1850 –60	1860 –70	1870 –80
$\Delta(U/P)$	1.0	1.2	−0.1	*1.6*	*2.0*	*4.5*	*4.5*	*5.9*	2.5
$\Delta(NAL/L)$		−10.0	*4.9*	*8.2*	7.5	8.3	1.9	0.4	*1.2*

	1880 –90	1890 –00	1900 –10	1910 –20	1920 –30	1930 –40	1940 –50	1950 –60
$\Delta(U/P)$	6.9	4.6	6.0	5.5	5.0	0.3	*3.1*	*3.5*
$\Delta(NAL/L)$	8.6	2.5	8.8	5.5	4.3	*4.6*	*5.0*	3.9

Note: Italicized figures are for successive decades of rising rates of increase.
Source: U.S. Census data. S. Lebergott, *Manpower in Economic Growth*, Table A-1.

banization (only through 1850 on a $\Delta U/U$ measure; see Table 3) in marked contrast to the fluctuating decadal rate of labor force industrialization; the latter only sustained rising rates of increment for more than a single decade in the periods 1810–30, 1870–90 and 1930–50. On the other hand, if the dampening down of the rate of interindustry shift from agriculture to non-agriculture during the decade 1830–40 is not allowed to negate the trend, there would appear to have been a massive

TABLE 7.
LEVELS OF URBANIZATION AND INDUSTRIALIZATION
IN THE UNITED STATES, 1800–90

Date	Urbanization level, U/P (1)	Non-agricultural labor force NAL/L (2)	Manufacturing mining and construction $MMCL/L$ (3)	Manufacturing in the non-agricultural labor force ML/NAL (4)
1800	6.1	26.3 (17.4)[a]	–	–
1810	7.3	16.2	(4.0)[b]	19.7
1820	7.2	21.2	–	–
1830	8.8	29.4	–	–
1840	10.8	36.9	14.5	23.9
1850	15.3	45.2	20.8	32.2
1860	19.8	47.1	20.0	29.3
1870	25.7	47.5	26.5	40.2
1880	28.2	48.7	25.7	38.8
1890	35.1	57.3	27.2	32.9

[a] Number in parentheses based on P. David, "Growth of Real Product in the U.S. before 1840," *Journal of Economic History* (1967), p. 166.
[b] Manufactures and mining only.
Source: S. Lebergott, *Manpower in Economic Growth*, Table A-1.

movement into non-agricultural pursuits over the entire period 1810–50 (which corresponds closely with the rising rate of urban increase, $\Delta U/U$, 1820–50). Nevertheless, allowing for changes in the age structure of the population and in labor force participation during every decade of the early nineteenth century, the discrepancies in timing and degree between the incremental urbanization and labor-force industrialization rates preclude the easy identification of the urbanization and industrialization processes (at least as conceived and measured in the present study).

The effects of differential rates of urbanization and industrialization on levels of urbanization and industrialization are shown in Table 7 for the period 1800–90. The twenties, forties, and eighties appear to have been decades of accelerated movement of labor out of agriculture (to a lesser extent 1810–20), the forties and sixties decades of accelerated commitment to manufactures; while the surge of industrialization in the eighties seemed unconnected with manufacture and more related to the growth of other non-agricultural activity.

By both population and labor-force measures, the decade of the twenties marked a critical departure. The twenties were a time of accelerated structural changes in both residential and occupational patterns, although sizable shifts out of agriculture were underway before 1820. The decade was one of quickened interindustry and interresidence movements, but whether the changes were altogether new, or merely a recovery and reassertion of tendencies previously interrupted by the Embargo and War of 1812, is not clear. From the twenties, however, there is the presumption that, whenever $\Delta(U/P)$ and $\Delta(NAL/L)$ are positive, some portion of the incremental shift in both cases represents the transfer of resources to a more productive (efficient) location or occupation.

If the years 1820–30 also marked the beginnings of a discernible upward movement in real farm product per worker, as indicated by Paul David, and if the intersectoral shift to non-agricultural employments represents an equal or greater rise in real non-farm product per worker (which is logical but by no means demonstrable as yet), then the incontestable advances of the forties in $\Delta U/U$, $\Delta(U/P)$, $\Delta(NAL/L)$, and $\Delta(ML/NAL)$, were but further increases in rates that, with the possible exception of the last, were evident from the twenties (Tables 3, 6, and 7).[55] The great era of accelerating structural change in the

[55] Paul David, "Growth of Real Product in the United States before 1840," in *Journal of Economic History*, Vol. 27 (June 1967); Williamson, "Ante Bellum Urbanization." Harder data for years after 1839 in terms of *value-added* by agriculture, mining, manufacturing, and construction (the last three comprising

labor force was clearly the span from 1820 to 1850, rather than the period from 1850 to 1880. But whereas the $\Delta U/U$ measure of urban increase accorded with this timing of accelerated industrialization, the structural measure of urban increment, $\Delta(U/P)$, while rising from 1820 to 1840, reached more massive proportions in the years 1840–70.

The differential effects of these urban-industrial processes upon regional industrial-urban structures and per capita incomes by 1840 are given in Table 8. Already the economic potential of the more industrially

TABLE 8.
REGIONAL DIFFERENTIATION IN THE UNITED STATES, 1840
(000's Population; $ current)

Regions	Population (P) (1)	Urbanization level (U/P) (2)	Non-agricultural labor force (NAL/L) (3)	Per capita income from commodity production and commerce (4)
United States	17,020	10.8	20.8	$64.8
New England	2,235	19.4	38.4	83.2
Middle Atlantic[a]	5,074	19.0	32.1	76.9
South Atlantic[a]	3,334	4.5	10.2	54.6
East South Central	2,575	2.1	8.0	55.1
West South Central[b]	450	23.4	14.2	103.6
East North Central	2,925	3.9	18.0	46.1
West North Central[c]	427	3.9	15.1	51.1

[a] MA includes (SA excludes) Md., Del., and D.C.
[b] La. and Ark. only.
[c] Ia. and Mo. only.
Source: H. S. Perloff *et al.*, *Regions, Resources, and Economic Growth*, Table 16.

urbanized regions of the Northeast was becoming apparent but, elsewhere, notwithstanding the sizable non-agricultural advantage of the

---

value-added by non-agricultural commodity production, in constant 1879 prices) are as follows:

Year	1839	1844	1849	1854	1859	1869
NAVA/TVA: (%)	28.1	31.3	40.3	43.2	44.5	47.4
5 Yr. Δ(NAVA/TVA):		+3.2	+9.0	+2.9	+1.3	
10 Yr. Δ(NAVA/TVA):			+12.2		+4.2	+2.9

Year	1874	1879	1884	1889	1894	1899
NAVA/TVA: (%)	54.0	51.0	58.9	62.6	68.1	66.7
5 Yr. Δ(NAVA/TVA):	+6.6	−3.0	+7.9	+3.7	+5.5	−1.4
10 Yr. Δ(NAVA/TVA):		+3.6		+11.6		+4.1

Source: Adapted from R. E. Gallman, "Commodity Output, 1839–1899," *Trends in the American Economy in the 19th Century; Studies in Income and Wealth,* Vol. 24 (National Bureau of Economic Research, 1960), Table A-1, Variant A, p. 43.

North Central states, per capita incomes from commodity production and commerce were still higher in all divisions of the South.[56] The extraordinary levels of income and urbanization in the West South Central division reflect the commercial importance of New Orleans and the Mississippi River system still at, or near, its peak relative to the growing Great Lakes navigation and the rapid expansion of West-East flows of trade.

TABLE 9.
INCREMENTAL URBANIZATION OF POPULATION IN THE UNITED STATES,
$\Delta(U/P)$, BY CENSUS DIVISIONS, 1790–1890

Region	1790 -00	1800 -10	1810 -20	1820 -30	1830 -40	1840 -50	1850 -60	1860 -70	1870 -80	1880 -90
U.S.	1.0	1.2	−0.1	1.6	2.0	4.5	4.5	5.9	2.5	6.9
NE	0.7	1.9	0.4	3.5	5.4	9.4	7.8	7.8	8.0	9.2
MA+	1.5	1.3	−0.2	2.9	3.9	7.4	9.9	8.8	6.0	7.8
SA	1.1	1.1	1.0	0.7	1.5	2.1	1.6	2.9	0.5	4.6
ESC			0.2	0.7	0.6	2.1	1.7	2.9	−0.4	4.3
ENC			0.3	1.3	1.4	5.1	5.1	7.5	5.9	10.4
WSC			−6.0	2.5	4.7	−8.3	−2.8	1.0	−0.8	2.6
WNC					0.4	6.4	3.1	5.5	−0.7	7.6
MT							3.9	2.2	9.3	7.7
PAC							12.0	13.7	3.1	6.7
MA−	3.6	2.7	2.5	5.0	5.6	7.8	9.6	4.5	5.1	4.6

Note: MA+ includes western Pennsylvania and northern New York. MA− excludes those areas. Italicized numbers above the national mean.
Source: U.S. Census data, and J. G. Williamson, "Ante Bellum Urbanization in the American Northeast," *Journal of Economic History* (1965), Table 1.

The association between urbanization, industrialization, and rising incomes seems to have become well established in the United States, and was indeed recognized during the second quarter of the nineteenth century. It likewise became a contemporary article of faith among the dominant business elements of many smaller and middle-sized cities that the future growth and enrichment of their communities were alike contingent upon the development of local manufactures. Subsequent effects of these tendencies on population distribution and industrial structures are sketched in the following pages.

Table 9 gives the rates of incremental rural-to-urban shift among the

[56] Richard A. Easterlin, "Interregional Differences in Per Capita Income, Population, and Total Income, 1840–1950," in *Trends in the American Economy in the 19th Century*, pp. 73–140. Also, Perloff *et al.*, *Regions, Resources, and Economic Growth* (The Johns Hopkins Press, for Resources for the Future, 1961), pp. 109–21.

populations of the United States and nine standard census divisions for the century 1790–1890. By the latter date, well over a third of the countrywide population was urbanized and the city had already become the focus of new opportunities. During much of that century span, the New England and Middle Atlantic states remained the most relentlessly urbanizing parts of the nation, to be joined after 1840 by the East North Central (Great Lakes) states and after mid-century by the Pacific states division of the West. Of special interest, from the standpoint of local and regional differentiation, however, is the varied performances of states in the Northeast, notably New York and Pennsylvania including and excluding certain counties of their northern and western divisions respectively.[57] It was, for example, the rapid rural settlement of western Pennsylvania, northern New York, and the great migration into the West South Central division (of the recently acquired Louisiana territories) that accounts for the one decade of "negative" urbanization in U.S. history, 1810–20. Without their western and northern counties, in fact, the two large Middle Atlantic states, along with New Jersey, comprised the most rapidly urbanizing division in the nation during that decade (see MA⁻, Table 9). In the 1860–90 period, on the other hand (when the Middle Atlantic division was still one of the most rapidly urbanizing parts of the country), it was the turn of "up-state" New York and, to a lesser extent, western Pennsylvania to sustain the rate of rural-to-urban shift. Urban development in the interior of the Middle Atlantic states coincided, of course, with the westward movement of rapid urbanization as the nation's industrial belt was enlarged by the incorporation of the western Great Lakes states and the upper Mississippi Valley after the middle of the century.

A closer examination of the interindustry shift that occurred in the nation's first urban-industrial belt, the Northeast, is presented in Table 10 for the two periods 1820–40 and 1870–90. The table compares levels of urbanization, U/P, industrialization, NAL/L, and manufacturing, ML/L, for each of nine states *relative* to the mean level for the Northeastern region as a whole. What is most noticeable, perhaps, is the structural diversity at any time between states of northern and southern New England, notwithstanding apparent convergence among the states before the middle of the century.[58] At all times, the structures

---

[57] Census reports in the early nineteenth century usually return New York, Pennsylvania, Virginia and a few other large states by "divisions." Actual counties included in the "divisions" for purposes of Table 9 and the related text are from Williamson, "Ante Bellum Urbanization," p. 598, note 13.

[58] Williamson, "Ante Bellum Urbanization," pp. 601–2, argues for convergence in state shares of *urban* population in the Northeast throughout the period 1790–1890.

TABLE 10.

RELATIVE URBANIZATION OF POPULATION, NON-AGRICULTURAL AND MANUFACTURING LABOR FORCE RELATIVES, NORTHEASTERN STATES, 1820–40 AND 1870–90
(Northeastern regional mean = 100)

Region	1820 U/P	1820 NAL/L	1820 ML/L	1840 U/P	1840 NAL/L	1840 ML/L	1870 U/P	1870 NAL/L	1870 ML/L	1890 U/P	1890 NAL/L	1890 ML/L
Northeast	*100*	*100*	*100*	*100*	*100*	*100*	*100*	*100*	*100*	*100*	*100*	*100*
Me.	26	81	49	42	75	59	47	78	74	48	77	77
N.H.	27	55	64	54	73	83	59	81	94	67	91	*104*
Vt.	–	53	65	–	49	55	7	51	53	16	59	58
Mass.	*207*	*167*	*124*	*205*	*166*	*149*	*151*	*125*	*134*	*139*	*119*	*124*
R.I.	*209*	*132*	*138*	*237*	*167*	*216*	*168*	*124*	*140*	*145*	*120*	*132*
Conn.	69	*108*	*116*	68	*107*	*112*	75	*107*	*114*	86	*107*	*117*
N.Y.	*106*	79	86	*105*	93	94	*113*	98	90	*110*	*103*	92
N.J.	25	*111*	*122*	57	*101*	*109*	99	*105*	100	*106*	*110*	*105*
Pa.	*118*	*117*	*131*	97	95	97	34	97	99	82	87	96

Note: Italicized figures above the regional mean.
Source: Urban data from U.S. Census. Labor force data: 1820 from J. G. Williamson, unpublished; 1840 from R. A. Easterlin, see fn 56 above; 1870 and 1890 from 9th and 11th U.S. Census, respectively.

of the census Middle Atlantic states seem to fall between the New England extremes and lie closer to the regional mean.

Scarcely less notable is the diversity with respect to the three measures at any time *within* the nine states. Only Massachusetts and Rhode Island, for example, are above the regional mean in all three measures at all four dates. The northern New England states, on the other hand, are far less urbanized than the region but have levels of manufacture and other non-agricultural activities much higher than their urban levels might lead one to expect. Vermont appears to have lacked urbanization altogether, in census terms, over the first half of the century, yet it obviously had manufacturing and services clustered in its small non-urban centers, places ≤2,500, even before 1820. The New Jersey situation is also notable in this regard. By 1840, its urban level was little more than half that of the region but, as far back as 1820, its level of manufactures and other non-agricultural employments exceeded the regional mean. Clearly the labor force in some of the Northeastern states was industrialized in the present sense without benefit of sustained urbanization and much of its market was, doubtless, to be found within the local agricultural stratum as well as in the towns of adjacent states.

More surprising, Pennsylvania had fallen below the regional mean by 1840 in all three measures and did not recover, except briefly in manufactures and non-agricultural activity around the middle of the century. Another peculiarity appears in the case of Massachusetts, which was second only to Rhode Island in the rapidity of its urban concentration. During ante-bellum years the Bay State's non-agricultural relative was always higher than its manufacturing relative, while in postwar years the reverse was true. By the nineties, only Vermont seems to have passed through the regional urban-industrial transformation without showing any strong tendency toward the structural convergence that was apparent on the state level elsewhere in the Northeast.

The cumulative effects of the urban-industrial processes upon nation-wide regional structures are shown in Table 11 for the date when the census first reported more than half the nation's population resident in

TABLE 11.
REGIONAL RELATIVES IN THE UNITED STATES, 1920 AND 1960
(U.S. mean level = 100)

Region	Personal income per capita (current $)	Urbanization level U/P		Manu-facturing in the labor force M/L	Agriculture in the labor force A/L	Mfg. and services in the labor force MS/L
		1920				
United States	$658.00	51.2		30.9	25.6	71.1
	100	100		100	100	100
Far West	*135.1*	*120.3*		93.5	71.5	*109.2*
Middle Atlantic	*133.7*	*145.9*		*130.7*	28.8	*125.1*
New England	*124.4*	*148.2*		*163.8*	27.0	*129.3*
Great Lakes	*107.9*	*118.7*		*121.0*	73.0	*110.1*
Mountain	*102.2*	77.5		60.5	*128.2*	83.6
Plains	86.7	73.6		68.0	*141.8*	86.6
Southwest	80.7	59.2		50.5	*175.1*	72.2
Southeast	56.4	46.8		59.5	*193.1*	66.0
		1960 New def. U/P	Old def. U/P			
United States	$2,230.00	69.9	63.1	26.9	6.6	92.0
	100	100	100	100	100	100
Far West	*118.6*	*116.7*	*108.1*	87.0	75.8	*102.1*
Middle Atlantic	*116.1*	*115.6*	*112.5*	*115.6*	31.8	*105.6*
New England	*110.0*	*109.0*	*119.0*	*135.7*	31.8	*105.8*
Great Lakes	*106.5*	*104.0*	*106.7*	*129.7*	77.3	*102.4*
Mountain	94.2	93.0	90.2	46.8	*150.0*	94.2
Plains	93.3	84.1	88.7	69.1	*242.4*	90.3
Southwest	86.1	*103.6*	*110.6*	54.2	*131.8*	95.2
Southeast	72.1	74.5	73.4	84.0	*157.6*	94.5

Note: Italicized figures are above the national mean.

Sources: 1920—Harvey S. Perloff *et al.*, *Regions, Resources, and Economic Growth*, Table 70; 1960—U.S. Department of Commerce and Census data.

cities. The economic potential of the new urban-industrial regions of 1840 (Table 8) has been realized notwithstanding the phenomenal rate of U.S. population increase (2 per cent per annum, 1840–1960) and the spread of settlement across the two-thirds of the conterminous area west of the Mississippi River. No less apparent in 1920 is the relative poverty persisting in the regions with low urbanization and low labor-force industrialization levels. The relative regional standings for 1960 are also presented in Table 11. No change is required in the order of regions by per capita personal incomes which, for present purposes, can be regarded as approximations of relative levels of living. Nevertheless, the Mountain region has fallen below the per capita income level of the nation and, for a period around 1950, New England appeared to have lost the third rank to the Great Lakes region (although it did not fall below the national average). The new census definition of "urban" appears to be a slightly better indicator of per capita personal income performance than the old definition. A notable exception is the Southwest, where urbanization in Texas and Oklahoma (by either definition) has not in itself sufficed to raise average income levels for the region, say, to those of the Plains (which, since 1950, has become "the most agricultural" region in the nation).[59] The fact that the Southeast (again by either definition) has not yet achieved the levels of urbanization generally prevailing on the Plains but has, nonetheless, greatly reduced the agricultural component of its labor force, indicates the significant role of out-migration in bringing southern structures into closer conformity with those of the nation. Finally, the manufacturing sector of the national labor force seems to have recovered a few percentage points from the low levels of 1940 and 1950, but the growth of service jobs rather than of blue-collar jobs has been the primary source of structural convergence in regional levels of non-agricultural activity.

A concise review of the urban transformation, temporally and spatially, is given in Table 12 by means of a relative urban distribution index (RUDI).[60] This measure compares changing regional shares of urban and total population countrywide. If the regional shares of urban and total population were to coincide, the relative urban distribution index number would be zero. Conversely, the higher the index number, the greater the differences in regional shares of urban and total popula-

---

[59] Perloff *et al., Regions, Resources, and Economic Growth,* pp. 122–283.

[60] RUDI is the result of summing absolute differences of the eight Perloff *et al.* regional shares of urban and total population and dividing by two. It is an extension of the measure used by Lowdon Wingo, Jr., "The Use of Urban Land: Past, Present, and Future," *Land Use Policy and Problems in the United States,* Proceedings of the Homestead Centennial Symposium, 1962 (Lincoln: University of Nebraska Press, 1963), p. 234.

TABLE 12.
RELATIVE URBAN DISTRIBUTION INDEX FOR THE UNITED STATES,
SELECTED INTERVALS, 1800–1960

1800	1840	1870	1910	1950	1960[a]
28.5	33.1	25.7	20.7	10.2	7.2

[a] Index for 1960 employs the new census "urban" definition. Regions used are those of Perloff *et al., Regions, Resources, and Economic Growth.*
Source: U.S. Census data.

tion. Apparently the westward movement of population during the first half of the nineteenth century brought about more uneven levels of urbanization among the different regions, but thereafter, and more especially since 1910, the distributions of urban and total population across the conterminous United States have become more alike. By 1950 the rapidly changing residential structure of the population was becoming more uniform countrywide, with the trend set toward urban-metropolitan location.

The Evolving System of Cities

The process of urbanization described in previous pages took the form of increases in the numbers and sizes of concentrations. By 1960, of 4,124 urban places, $\geq 2,500$, reported in the census for the conterminous United States, 1,891 centers had more than 10,000 inhabitants, 131 exceeded 100,000, and 5 surpassed the million mark. The entire array of central places, urban and non-urban $\geq 1,000$ is given in Table 13 by separate and cumulative size groupings. Of the

TABLE 13.
CENTRAL PLACES IN THE UNITED STATES, URBAN AND NON-URBAN,
BY POPULATION SIZE GROUPS, 1960

Size group (1)	Numbers of places (2)	Size group (3)	Numbers of places (4)
1,000,000 plus	5	$\geq 1,000,000$	5
100,000–999,999	126	$\geq 100,000$	131
10,000–99,999	1,760	$\geq 10,000$	1,891
1,000–9,999	8,237	$\geq 1,000$	10,128

Source: U.S. Census data.

1,891 cities with 10,000 and more residents in 1960, only 55 were in existence within or without the boundaries of United States territory in 1800. Of these 55, some 33 already exceeded 2,500 inhabitants, and, including Boston with 24,937 residents, 4 were 25,000 and over. New York City and Philadelphia vied for first place but, by either the incorporated limits of 1800 or those of 1960, New York was already the larger, having surpassed Philadelphia at some point between 1775 and 1790. By 1800, both could claim to exceed 50,000 inhabitants but, in fact, this was true for incorporated New York and only true for Philadelphia if the entire urbanized area were included.

In 1790, New York City and Philadelphia, the only cities ≥25,000, together contained well over a quarter of all U.S. urban population, while the twenty-two smaller centers, 2,500–24,999, contained the other 70-odd per cent. The five Atlantic seaports—New York, Philadelphia, Boston, Baltimore, and Charleston, S.C.—contained some 54 per cent of the nation's urbanized population. The next largest center, the port of Salem, Mass., was scarcely half the size of Charleston. For some time thereafter there was little in the day-to-day interchanges of commerce and communications or in the city size distribution itself to suggest the emergence of strong "systemic" relations among the centers, any more than in colonial times. The effective "system," if any, to which they all belonged was the larger North Atlantic trading system rather than that of the new nation. In contrast, the five largest centers of 1960—New York, Chicago, Los Angeles, Philadelphia, and Detroit, each with more than a million residents—were located across the continent from the Middle Atlantic shore, via the Great Lakes, to the coast of California and the Pacific Ocean. Together they contained less than 14 per cent of the nation's urbanized population.[61] The next largest agglomerations, Baltimore and Houston, Texas, reported nearly one million residents each. The "system of cities" concept implies that, owing to the growing preponderance of interchanges *among the centers themselves*, such transformations as those between the early nineteenth and the mid-twentieth centuries have not occurred independently of the total population system of which they are a part.

Carl H. Madden has found striking confirmation of this systemic interdependence among cities in the United States. He presents data on city growth (points of concentration) in a succession of frequency distributions for the entire array of cities, ≥10,000 in 1950, at every census date, 1790 through 1950. The results, summarized in Figure 1, show that for each of the seventeen censuses the populations of centers ranked by size follows approximately the same order of distribution,

[61] Table 1 (columns 7 and 8, figures in parentheses) above indicates that the share of U.S. population resident in the five cities, ≥1,000,000, has been declining since 1930. The share in cities, ≥250,000, also fell over the decade 1950–60 before which it had been roughly stable since 1930.

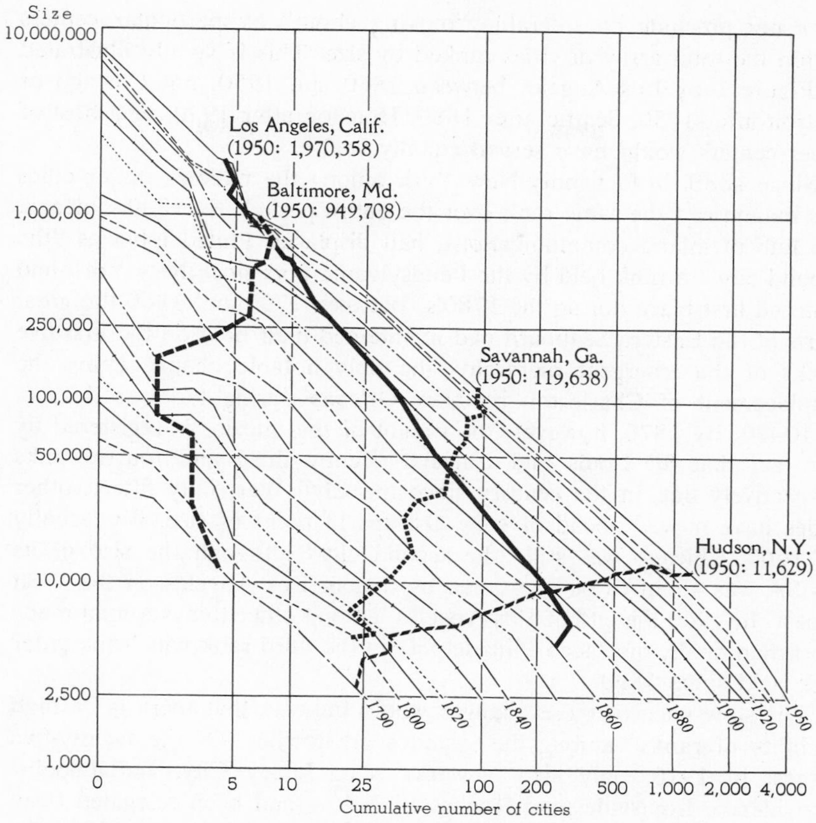

Figure 1. Population of urbanized areas ranked by size; and change in rank of four selected cities in ranking of cumulative number of places by size, 1790–1950. Source: *C. H. Madden, in* Economic Development and Cultural Change, *Vol. 4 (April 1956).*

although as changes in the respective positions of four selected cities (Los Angeles, Baltimore, Savannah, Ga., and Hudson, N.Y.) show, there are great divergences in the growth rates of individual places. Thus the form in which city growth occurs has shown remarkable stability "that may apparently be summarized by a simple empirical mathematical rule." [62] The steady state of the distribution, however,

[62] Carl H. Madden, "On Some Indicators of Stability in the Growth of Cities in the United States," in *Economic Development and Cultural Change,* Vol. 4 (April 1956). Madden suggests some form of Pareto cumulative "greater-than" frequency distribution but, according to Berry, 1965 (fn. 23 above), more likely a Yule distribution which takes account of the smallest size class being continuously enlarged by new city entrants.

does not preclude considerable "moving about" by particular centers within the total array of cities ranked by size. This is vividly illustrated in Figure 1 by Los Angeles between 1860 and 1950, but Chicago or Detroit after 1850, Seattle after 1880, Houston after 1920, or a host of other centers would have served equally well.

Since 1880, in fact, only New York among the nation's major cities has maintained the same rank over the entire period. By 1890 Chicago, the hub of inland communications, had displaced Philadelphia as "the second city," a rank held by the Pennsylvania port since New York had usurped first place during the 1780's. Between 1790 and 1860 the great ports of the Eastern Seaboard had maintained their hold on the first five ranks of the emergent hierarchy, the only notable change being the displacement of Charleston by New Orleans during the war decade, 1810–20. By 1870, however, the weight of the interior is registered by the fact that St. Louis and Chicago occupy third and fourth ranks respectively but, in the century since the Civil War, only fifteen other cities have moved ahead of New Orleans in point of size. As recently as 1960, Chicago was still "the second city" although the size of its SMSA was about to be overtaken by that of Los Angeles on the West Coast. In 1960 the city of Los Angeles, among other things a man-made port, had finally displaced Philadelphia in the third rank which the latter had held since 1890.

The slow pace of these changes would indicate that there is "a high stability of ranks" among the system's great cities. Of the twenty-five largest in 1910, only six—Newark, N.J., Jersey City, Indianapolis, Providence, Louisville, and Rochester, N.Y.—had been relegated from that league in course of the next half century of transformation. Of those cities that had entered the company of the top twenty-five during that interval, only Houston, Dallas, and San Antonio, Texas, together with Memphis, Denver, and Atlanta, remained in 1960. Denver, incidentally, had joined the league back in 1890 but had failed to maintain its size standing after 1900 until 1940. Hence, regularity and stability of city growth have been accompanied by "freedom to move up and down in ranking."

The spatial orientation of urban developments also manifests certain regularities. Growth of cities regionally since 1790 reveals a marked divergence of decennial rates of growth in different parts of the country. Rapidly growing or "new" regions are, not unexpectedly, characterized by an average of city growth rates that is high but also unstable, and eventual retardation of growth is a characteristic of average rates in every region. As the "tide of growth floods and ebbs" in the regions, the rates of growth of cities situated therein generally shift from the upper to the lower part of the national distribution of growth rates. By the decade 1870–80, no region of the country failed to contain cities in each quintile of the national distribution.[63]

Within the metropolitan "regions," Madden's data show that cities tend to grow on average at rates which decrease with distance from the metropolitan center, at least up to some "middle distance zone" of the region (45 to 64 miles out). Nevertheless, in each distance zone during any decade, there is a wide range of growth rates: some cities growing rapidly, others slowly, and a few even declining. The pattern of differences over decades, however, reveals that the largest cities are usually located nearest to the metropolitan center. Since 1870–80 cities in middle-distance zones have become and remained the next largest, while 65 miles and beyond cities have, on average, remained smallest. In the context of the historic westward movement of population, Madden concludes, that successive "new" regions to the West have experienced city growth rates which, on average, were high but unstable. There has been "freedom" of action for each city "to fail to grow."

The rise of new cities over-all appears to lead to a retardation of growth in older centers (much as Arthur F. Burns had found true for industries). Under conditions of technological progress cities appear to "compete" for new products and for rural-to-urban migratory streams (capital, too, presumably) within the general westward drift. According to Madden, the results of these forms of competition are reflected in the fact that "new industry is relatively frequently located in new cities and that such locations of new industry tend to produce declining rates of growth in older cities." [64]

Scrutiny of Figure 1 lends confirmation to at least part of Madden's thesis, while doubt remains about the rest. By 1860–70 Boston and Baltimore on the East Coast had been overtaken by St. Louis and Chicago, while Cincinnati held on to seventh rank, reflecting the growing weight of inland manufactures, transportation, and trade compared with all but the very greatest port centers on the East Coast. The last quarter of the century witnessed the rapid growth of newcomers beyond the Mississippi together with a slower maturation of the trans-Appalachian centers of heavy industry in the Ohio Valley and around the Great Lakes shores. Before 1880 San Francisco, the first of the major West Coast ports, and Pittsburgh, the first great heavy industrial agglomeration, had moved

[63] Madden, "Some Spatial Aspects of Urban Growth in the United States," in *Economic Development and Cultural Change,* Vol. 4 (July 1956).

[64] Madden, "Some Temporal Aspects of the Growth of Cities in the United States," *ibid.,* Vol. 6 (January 1958). Also, Arthur F. Burns, *Production Trends in the United States since 1870* (National Bureau of Economic Research, 1934).

into the top ten places ahead of New Orleans. During the eighties, Cleveland, Buffalo, Minneapolis–St. Paul and, in the last decade of the century, Detroit, Milwaukee, and Washington, D.C., epitomized the greater dependence of the national economy on the natural resource endowments and focal positions of the Great Lakes region and trans-Mississippi West. Washington, meanwhile, had begun to demonstrate the effect of its being the focus of a continent-wide political system, while New York City easily maintained its imperial position as the financial and organizational focus of the entire nation. Beverly Duncan has aptly described the period 1860–1900 as one of great regional or city-hinterland reorganization and of the emergence of "a system of cities." [65]

Since 1900, the countrywide system has been affected by both the science-based technology and the political-social transformation of society itself. The rapid introduction of new technologies of manufacture and communications, the sustained increases in average levels of living, together with the recurrent disturbances of wars and depression, have been accompanied by a greatly expanded role for public policy beyond its historic involvements in the public lands, internal improvements, tariffs, and interstate commerce. Nevertheless, the growth of metropolitan areas since 1900 has not, according to Beverly Duncan, resulted in the older centers losing their historic growth functions so much as in their failure to capture new functions when they have emerged. New Orleans, for example, was still in 1960—albeit in modernized form—much what it had been in 1860: a great commercial port, a collecting and warehousing center for raw materials and commodity productions of the interior, and a center for food processing. It was also becoming more of a center for tourism. New Orleans ranked sixteenth among the large city concentrations of 1960 but only twenty-eighth in 1964–65 among the nation's SMSA's.

The rapid growth entrants of the present century make their appearance in the following order: Los Angeles in the early 1900's and Kansas City during the decade of World War I. Between the wars the rank order of leading cities was not much disturbed, but the 1940's

[65] Beverly Duncan's unpublished data, which are drawn upon extensively in this section, will appear in revised form in Beverly Duncan and Stanley Lieberson, "Metropolis and Region in Transition" (tentative title), a sequel to Otis Dudley Duncan et al., Metropolis and Region. While it is true that the continent-wide system emerged after 1860, I have suggested that "regional" systems existed in the first half of the century and that by 1840 an "interregional" or "national" system had emerged over the territory then incorporated within the United States.

witnessed the rise of Houston, and the 1950's the rise of Dallas and Miami together with the somewhat less spectacular growth of Seattle-Everett. Duncan's analysis of the industrial growth profiles of the new twentieth century giants underlines the importance of both the oil industry and vegetable-orchard agriculture in the first ascent of Los Angeles, the maturation of Kansas City as a central place for large agricultural and ranch industries in the Plains region, and the role of the automobile and related activities in making Detroit the most conspicuous "rank jumper" among the established industrial cities. Since 1940 the apparent specializations of Houston point to petroleum rounded out by wholesaling, air and water transportation, and more recently the much publicized aerospace activities. The specializations of Dallas are also petroleum based, but are reinforced by commerce, trucking, air transportation, and the manufacture of aircraft and parts. Seattle is still a major center for the older lumber industry, but has also developed notable concentrations in aircraft manufacture, air transportation, hotels, and federal public administration. Miami, of course, reveals its reliance upon fine weather for the recreation and hotel-service industries, air transport, and radio-TV and, like Seattle, has recently developed a surprising amount of activity involving the armed forces.

The labor profiles of "new growth" centers in more recent decades also suggest aggregate trade, financial, and selective manufacturing functions on a scale comparable to, say, Kansas City, Cincinnati, Baltimore, Milwaukee, or Buffalo, but they do not show any sizable representation of the older sinews of industrial-urban concentration such as printing, metal-working, food-processing, or railroading. In regard to manufactures (which are by no means among the most buoyant sectors of labor force growth), Duncan designates a group of nine "twentieth century" growth industries—on the basis of their respective contributions to the growth of capital—and arbitrarily defines a 5 per cent localization of national employment in such industries as a "concentration." [66] In 1960 New York and Los Angeles, by this measure, each contained six concentrations, Chicago four, Detroit two, Philadelphia and Houston and Seattle one each. While these results are not wholly in accord with Madden's thesis, the inference was—so far as manufactures were concerned—that the older industrial centers of the Northeast (New York obviously excepted) do not compete, by and large, for any major seg-

---

[66] Beverly Duncan's provisional list of "twentieth century" growth industries included: automobile vehicles, aircraft and parts, plastics, synthetic fibers, most of office machinery and computers, electric machinery, rubber products, professional and photographic equipment, and petro chemicals and coal chemicals.

ment of the "air age" petroleum-based growth industries, nor are they likely to compete for the "atomic age" aerospace growth industries of the immediate future.

Meanwhile the manufacturing share of the growing labor force in most of the "upstarts" of the mid-nineteenth century has declined somewhat over the last eighty years or so. Among a select group of twenty-three older manufacturing centers in the Northeastern and North Central regions only four—Detroit, New Haven, Milwaukee, and Chicago—experienced net increases in the size of their manufacturing shares down to 1950 (Table 14). All but five of the remaining centers (Buffalo, Reading, St. Louis, Jersey City, and Cleveland) sustained sizable net reductions in their manufacturing labor force shares of from 5 to 27 percentage points.

TABLE 14.
MANUFACTURING IN THE LABOR FORCE OF SELECTED NORTHEASTERN
AND NORTH CENTRAL CITIES, 1870–1950

	1870		1950	
City (region)	Population (000's) (1)	M/L (2)	Population (000's) (3)	M/L (4)
1. Fall River N.E.	27	74.4 (1)	112	54.9
2. New Haven N.E.	51	35.4 (20)	164	47.8
3. Reading M.A.	50	49.6 (7)	109	47.5
4. Paterson M.A.	34	64.2 (2)	139	47.3
5. Detroit G.L.	80	20.3 (23)	1,850	46.0
6. Rochester M.A.	62	49.3 (8)	333	44.3
7. Dayton G.L.	31	51.4 (5)	244	43.2
8. Cleveland G.L.	93	46.0 (11)	915	42.4
9. Worcester N.E.	41	55.2 (4)	204	42.4
10. Milwaukee G.L.	71	40.3 (16)	607	42.4
11. Newark M.A.	105	60.8 (3)	439	38.8
12. Providence N.E.	68	46.4 (10)	249	38.5
13. Buffalo M.A.	118	39.8 (17)	580	37.3
14. Chicago G.L.	299	35.9 (19)	3,621	36.7
15. Philadelphia M.A.	674	48.8 (9)	2,072	35.2
16. Utica M.A.	29	50.0 (6)	102	34.3
17. St. Louis Pl.	311	35.1 (22)	859	33.9
18. Jersey City M.A.	83	35.2 (21)	299	32.8
19. Hartford N.E.	37	42.1 (13)	177	31.3
20. Pittsburgh M.A.	86	41.5 (14)	677	28.2
21. New York M.A.	1,478	41.3 (15)	7,892	28.0
22. Boston N.E.	251	38.0 (18)	801	23.7
23. Albany M.A.	69	43.9 (12)	135	16.3

Note: Figure in parenthesis in 1870 column (2) indicates rank in manufactures among the same twenty-three cities.
Source: U.S. Census data.

Because of their focal positions in the city hierarchy (among other factors), the New York, Chicago and, to a lesser extent, the Detroit and Philadelphia–New Jersey SMSA's may well continue to be highly competitive locations for sectors of even the most modern growth industries. Presumably many older centers will also continue to grow "with the country" from the accretion of trade and financial functions or from "planned" locations of manufacturing by major "defense" corporations and their government sponsors. Moreover, the older centers will not necessarily be excluded from participation in a wide range of style-based welfare-warfare state functions such as education, research and development, travel, and recreation. With important qualifications, therefore, Beverly Duncan's provisional conclusion resembles that of Madden: namely, that economic development in a system of cities comes about through a distribution of functions new to the economy rather than through a redistribution of the old.[67]

In a careful study of the growth and income characteristics of 212 SMSA's since 1950, Thompson showed that smaller areas manifested great variation in growth rates, ranging from decadal gains in excess of 100 per cent to absolute losses of up to 10 per cent. With metropolitan areas of greater size intermetropolitan variation in rates narrowed dramatically. Above the 500,000-inhabitants level all absolute decreases had been eliminated, except for Newark, N.J., while SMSA's ≥1,000,000 revealed least variation, ranging between 10 and 25 per cent increases for the decade 1950–60. The only exception was Los Angeles which, by Thompson's measure, exceeded 60 per cent. A comparison of growth rates of the fifties with those of the forties, moreover, showed a

[67] Madden, "Some Temporal Aspects of the Growth of Cities," pp. 162–68. Beverly Duncan's tentative conclusion, like that of Madden, differs in emphasis somewhat from Wilbur Thompson's notion that industrial innovations occur first in very large centers and only "spin off" to smaller centers after the "novelty" has demonstrated viability and maturity (*Preface to Urban Economics*, pp. 23–24, 37–38). Madden's data and citations refer primarily to the period before 1947; Duncan's data come down through 1960, but her choice of industries in this context refers only to "new" manufactures, not to all industry. On the enduring pre-eminence of New York as an innovator, on which all authorities seem agreed, see Raymond Vernon, in *Metropolis 1985* (Doubleday, 1960), pp. 35–62. Perloff *et al.*, in *Regions, Resources, and Economic Growth* (pp. 380–98), shows that almost 60 per cent of total net shift in manufacturing activity, 1939–54, was registered by the two states of California and Texas. This was mostly an "upward differential net shift" since the major part of "upward proportionality net shift" was located in the Great Lakes states which had registered less than 6 per cent of the *total* net shift. This terminology is explained (*ibid.*, pp. 70–74, 297–303). Nevertheless, the authors found "no positive correlation between increases in the proportion of workers within the 'growth industries' and relative increases in economic activity in general among the states" (*ibid.*, p. 68).

similar pattern of variation with size. With but two notable exceptions, the growth stability ratio varied only moderately for areas $\geq 500,000$.[68]

Thompson also compared the shares of local employment contributed by each of thirteen broad industrial categories for the fifteen largest SMSA's in 1950 and 1960. The standard deviation of the percentage shares in each industry for the fifteen areas was then divided by the mean of the percentages to yield a common measure of dispersion: the coefficient of dispersion. During 1950–60 this coefficient fell for eleven of the thirteen industrial categories; only "business and repair service" and "utilities" showed increasing variation among the fifteen areas. The coefficient for the fifteen manufacturing percentages in 1950 was 0.224 and in 1960 was 0.179, indicating thereby that manufactures (durables and non-durables alike) were becoming a more standardized component of the industrial structures of the larger SMSA's throughout the country.

Convergences in rates of growth and industrial structures among the largest SMSA's have also contributed in recent decades to a convergence in median family incomes. Thompson attributes this change to the beneficent effect of mixing high- and low-paying jobs. The only notable exceptions to this tendency were Pittsburgh, which suffered from unemployment in the 1950's and had failed to diversify, and Los Angeles which had a set of labor force characteristics unique to itself (involving "a tight labor market, in which overtime, second jobs, and second income earners in the family are prevalent"). The over-all trend in intermetropolitan variation in family income is summarized by a coefficient of variation falling from 0.69 to 0.57 during the 1950's. The convergence of large metropolitan industrial structures and family levels of living have also had the consequence of bringing about a closer degree of income inequality. Large SMSA populations have a broadly comparable mixture of "rich and poor" folk. Thompson computed the degree of family income inequality prevailing in the same SMSA's during 1950 and 1960 by means of first and third quartiles and first and ninth deciles (tenth and nineteenth percentiles). Ten of the fifteen SMSA's converged sharply; New York and Buffalo also converged but at much slower rates, while Minneapolis–St. Paul, Milwaukee and, to a lesser extent, Cleveland "break the pattern by starting low and falling still lower." The point, of course, is not that large SMSA's have a more equal distribution of incomes as the system of cities unfolds; only that they are all tending to exhibit about "the same degree of interfamily income inequality."[69]

[68] Wilbur R. Thompson, "The Future of the Detroit Metropolitan Area," in William Haber *et al.* (eds.), *Michigan in the 1970's: An Economic Forecast* (University of Michigan Graduate School of Business Administration, 1965).

[69] *Ibid.,* p. 221. As for future metropolitan growth, Jerome P. Pickard esti-

CONCLUSION

The incremental-distributional process sketched above suggests the working of "deviation amplifying processes" which have progressively led to system transformation. Innovation by individual and local specialization and subsequent distribution by generalization would be one way of describing how change occurs within an open space-economy without its becoming wholly disequilibrating and dysfunctional. By the selective generalization of novel behavior, and hence of structure, over time, the disequilibrating forces are counteracted by structure-stabilizing forces such that a convergence of behavior and structure ultimately ensues rather than a growing divergence and loss of cohesion. While there may have been some regional divergence of residential, labor force, and income structures at times during the first half of the nineteenth century, the third and, more assuredly, fourth quarters witnessed a gradual convergence. The present century has witnessed a more thoroughgoing convergence among the regions than at any previous time in U.S. history, notwithstanding the disturbing effects of continuous innovation and change (Tables 7, 10, 11, and 12).

The elements of structure and stability to be found in the evolving system of cities are broadly consistent with the notions of central place theory. Which of several patterns of city size regularity best fits and, *via* its assumptions, best "explains" the size distribution is only important perhaps to the regional scientist or statistical geographer. Once the stable form of the system has been identified, the phenomenon of "rank jumping" is potentially of greater interest but the study of system characteristics does not go far toward predicting or explaining the fates of individual system members. Historically, moreover, the small numbers of cities involved, say, before 1820 and the circumscribed nature of their hinterland trading regions (excepting perhaps Philadelphia, Baltimore, and New Orleans) lends little support to the notion that their mutual interactions were on a larger and more decisive scale than the relations of particular centers with "outside" areas.

Centrality or distance do not, however, account for all of "the variation in economic structure observed to be correlated with size of center." In *Metropolis and Region,* Duncan and associates proposed at least three principles supplementary to the notion that the larger cities specialize in economic functions which have broader market areas, in

---

mated that some two-thirds of a population of about 320 million at the close of this century will be located in four "urban regions": the Northeast, the Great Lakes, California, and Florida. Meanwhile, the fastest rates of metropolitan growth have been occurring in the West and South. (*Metropolitanization of the United States* [Washington: Urban Land Institute, 1959].)

135

order to account for the forms of service trade specialization for which the explanation from centrality does not hold:

1) Conditions of living in large cities generate certain "needs" or tastes not typical of life in small cities.
2) As city size increases, some services performed by businesses or households are demanded in sufficient quantity to support differentiation and specialization of units supplying them. Such "economies of scale" are *not* conditional on large non-local market areas.
3) As city size increases, some services hitherto performed by general units are taken over in part by units specialized in a restricted line of services. This local division of labor does not presuppose "either an increase in per capita volume of the particular service by all types of unit combined or an extension of the market area for the service—although both these may be concomitants, to be sure." [70]

Thus the demand for labor on which the size and character of the labor force and population depend is likewise not a simple function of centrality or distance. Central place theory—with its restrictive premises regarding areal topography, population-income size, and the employment multiplier—represents only one of a number of possible frameworks for comprehending a system of cities.

Although size of central place and market orientation (scale) do exert a nodal and, to some extent, hierarchical force upon the unfolding pattern of the industrial-urban system, there has also been a marked tendency for comparative site advantage (cost advantage) vis-à-vis other potential locations to determine: (1) the location and growth of firms in certain input-oriented industries, and (2) the intensive exploitation of "break-in-bulk" transport sites where the form of shipment of a good can be conveniently changed with the mode of conveyance. If such material (often fuel) or transport cost-saving loci continue to grow in the specialized service of the larger system, they will tend to acquire additional agglomerative "pull"—more on account of their size than of "centrality" as such—in the form of urbanization economies and enhanced attractiveness for market-oriented industries. In short, they become regional centers and "service exporters" in their own right along

[70] Otis Dudley Duncan *et al.,* in *Metropolis and Region,* pp. 79–81. Rutledge Vining, "A Description of Certain Spatial Aspects of an Economic System," in *Economic Development and Cultural Change,* Vol. 3 (January 1955), provides an empirical critique of central place theory and of "hierarchy" in particular.

the lines of Thompson's diagrammatic schema in *Preface to Urban Economics* (page 13). During the industrial era of U.S. history, therefore, Weberian principles of location can add much to the generalities of central place theory in explanation of the growth experiences at particular sites.[71] Since the 1930's, however, the decisions of government and government-oriented corporations must be invoked, along with the growing weight of market orientation, in order to account more fully for some of the achievements of the "rank jumpers."

Withal, the microeconomic principles of industrial location remain a potent and indispensable tool for the analysis of short-run urban-regional change. When applied in a framework of unorganized oligopolistic market systems (spatial oligopoly), such as that described by Greenhut, they take on the additionally satisfying aura of realism.[72] But on the question of a general equilibrium system again, it is hard to conceive of the enormous socioeconomic changes since 1790 as a process of adjustment to an endless series of most probable states of equilibrium for producers and consumers. Until the interesting notion of morphogenesis can be made operational, it is understandable that the historian might prefer the "input-output accessibility and multipliers" framework, adopted by Perloff and associates, as the most practical means of approaching the incremental-distributional transformation "problem" that long-run urban-regional growth and development represents.[73]

Meanwhile we conclude that the urban transformation contributed to the progressive unfolding of the industrial system in at least three spatially-structurally significant ways:

1) By converting the high fertility rural populations over time into the lower fertility town and city dwellers.
2) By transferring a rising share of the labor force over time out of

[71] See Eugene Smolensky and Donald Ratajczak, "The Conception of Cities," in *Explorations in Entrepreneurial History,* Vol. 2 (2nd Series; Winter 1965). This is a rigorous effort to apply location principles to the case history of one city, San Diego, California. See also Brian J. L. Berry and William L. Garrison, "Recent Developments of Central Place Theory," in *Papers and Proceedings, Regional Science Association,* Vol. 4 (1958). They use the two concepts of "threshold" (conditions of entry) and "range of good" (dimensions of retail trade area under spatial competition) to demonstrate the emergence of hierarchy regardless of the distribution of population and purchasing power. These concepts have recently been applied by Allan R. Pred to the historical geography of the United States. See *The Spatial Dynamics of U.S. Urban-Industrial Growth, 1800–1914, Interpretive and Theoretical Essays* (M.I.T. Press, 1966).

[72] Melvin L. Greenhut, *Microeconomics and the Space Economy: The Effectiveness of an Oligopolistic Market Economy* (Scott Foresman, 1963).

[73] For explanations of these concepts and related methods, see Perloff *et al.,* in *Regions, Resources, and Economic Growth,* pp. 63–106.

relatively unspecialized low-productivity occupations into more productive manufacturing and service sectors, leaving the country-sides for a renovated agriculture.

3) By forming a new socio-economic structure of urban population over time which is "middle" as well as "working" class. The social orientation and consumption styles of the newer professional, functionary, and white-collar categories are more "bourgeois" than those of many independent businessmen and property owners.[74]

But whereas nineteenth century urbanization was primarily rural-to-urban movement of population—an agricultural-to-non-agricultural shift in occupations and industries, with only slowly rising average levels of real income—the residential, industrial, and social mobilities of recent decades are increasingly brought about through urban-to-metropolitan and central city-to-suburban migrations: a new mode of urban concentration in the more fully urbanized ecosystem.

It is in the interrelation of these residential, occupational, and socio-economic attributes of the American population that the urban transformation and the evolving system of cities are most likely to be understood. But since the great reservoir of rural-agrarian population is rapidly drying up—except for some culturally "stranded" parts of the rural South—it is unlikely that a knowledge of any but the most recent experience of the urban transformation will be of much practical relevance to present and future "problem solving" activity in the nation's burgeoning cities. Clearly, the simple demographic concept of urbanization as population concentration, used throughout this paper, is already obsolescent. City growth henceforth will be taking place without much help from the process of urbanization in any of the more familiar uses of that term. In the future, concentration will be taking place, if at all, within the city size distribution itself, and attention will need to be focused on the characteristics of that phenomenon rather than on the migration of country people to the towns.

[74] In this paper I have dealt only with the second of these aspects. Taken together, the three "mobilities" form the subject of a larger study which is in preparation: "Urbanization and American Opportunity: Colonial Times to the Present." The "opportunity" considered refers to demographic, entrepreneurial, employment, and socioeconomic status changes.

SELECTED READINGS

Beckmann, Martin J. "City Hierarchies and the Distribution of City Size," in *Economic Development and Cultural Change,* Vol. 6, April 1958.

Berry, Brian J. L. "Cities as Systems within Systems of Cities," in John Friedmann and William Alonso (eds.), *Regional Development and Planning: A Reader.* Cambridge: M.I.T. Press, 1964.

Borchert, John R. "American Metropolitan Evolution," in *Geographical Review,* Vol. 57, July 1967.

Duncan, Otis Dudley *et al. Metropolis and Region.* Baltimore: The Johns Hopkins Press, for Resources for the Future, Inc., 1960.

Dunn, Edgar S., Jr. *The Location of Agricultural Production.* Gainesville: University of Florida Press, 1954.

Eldridge, Hope T., and Dorothy S. Thomas. *Population Redistribution and Economic Growth, United States, 1870–1950,* Vol. 3. Philadelphia: American Philosophical Society, 1964.

Isard, Walter. *Location and Space-Economy.* Cambridge: M.I.T. Press, 1956.

Lampard, Eric E. "The History of Cities in the Economically Advanced Areas," in *Economic Development and Cultural Change,* Vol. 5, January 1955.

Perloff, Harvey S. *et al. Regions, Resources, and Economic Growth.* Baltimore: The Johns Hopkins Press for Resources for the Future, Inc., 1960.

Pred, Allan R. *The Spatial Dynamics of U.S. Urban-Industrial Growth, 1800–1914, Interpretive and Theoretical Essays.* Cambridge: M.I.T. Press, 1966.

Smolensky, Eugene, and Donald Ratajczak. "The Conception of Cities," in *Explorations in Entrepreneurial History,* Vol. 2, 2nd Series; Winter 1965.

Thompson, Wilbur R. *A Preface to Urban Economics.* Baltimore: The Johns Hopkins Press for Resources for the Future, Inc., 1965.

Vernon, Raymond. *Metropolis 1985.* New York: Doubleday, 1960.

Williamson, Jeffrey G., and Joseph A. Swanson. "The Growth of Cities in the American Northeast, 1820–1870," in *Explorations in Entrepreneurial History,* Vol. 4, 2nd Series; 1966.

*Sidney Sonenblum**

THE USES AND DEVELOPMENT OF REGIONAL PROJECTIONS

Regional projections will be viewed here as an effort in the field of applied economics relating to (a) economic policy for multistate regions, states, and metropolitan areas; (b) physical planning in programs dealing with such concerns as land use, transportation, and spatial distribution of economic activity; and (c) human resource planning in programs dealing with income redistribution, training, and welfare. The emphasis, therefore, will be on the question of use of projections; particularly on the relationship between methodology and use. Increasingly projections, rather than past trends, have become the key indicators of economic and social change or in Biderman's felicitous phrase, "vindicators" of economic and social planning (57). But beyond this, the relationships spelled out in models that provide projections are themselves used in the planning process in order to mitigate trends considered to be undesirable, and to speed up desirable trends.

This suggests two broad classes of use for projections. First, they are used as "predictions" where the planner wants some idea of the size and shape of the future in order that his current decision can be responsive to that future environment. For example, water resource planning requires some idea of the future industry mix in order to determine the extent of likely pollution; educational planning requires some idea of the future age and ethnic distribution of the population in order to assess its "market"; welfare planning requires some idea of the future income distribution in order to evaluate the subsistence needs that are unlikely to be provided through the market mechanism.

The predictions should assist the planner in anticipating public service needs (we are not considering the private sector use of projections); should help him meet these needs in an efficient and timely manner; and should assist his evaluation of the priorities of needs and tradeoffs that may be required.

The predicted variable most needed for these purposes is the population, described by various characteristics such as age, occupation,

* Research Director, National Planning Association.

This paper has drawn considerably on research being conducted at the National Planning Association Center for Economic Projections. Particularly important have been the research results and critical comments of Joe Won Lee in the field of metropolitan projections, Ahmad Al-Samarrie in the field of state and income projections, and Peter Wagner in the field of location analysis.

ethnic composition, and income. Other variables that affect the population prediction and also are important indicators to the planner in their own right are employment, labor force, government revenues and expenditures, consumer expenditures, income distribution, investment, and industrial output.

The predictions should be reliable in the sense that they must be sufficiently close to the actual outcome of events that planning commitments can be based on the estimates. This means that the assumptions on which the projections are based should be the most probable ones. But the most probable assumptions require judgments about the likely decisions of policy-makers at the various levels of government; the attitudes of business managers and individuals as consumers, workers, and citizens; developments in international relations; and changes in technology. Such judgments are not entirely arbitrary, even though they are influenced only in part by factual observation about the past.

Because these judgments are required in the projection procedure it is sometimes desirable to provide conditional forecasts, or alternative projections as based on different sets of assumptions. This has the advantage of allowing the planner to decide which assumptions are most realistic or most desirable[1] for his specific purpose.

Usually, however, the planner is not interested in alternative projections, but in the projection based on the best possible judgments. He recognizes that the best judgment, at any given time, may not be the judgment vindicated by future events. Therefore, the planner will usually build control mechanisms into the planning process, which allows him to use projections that are not exact but only rough approximations of the actual outcome of events. As a consequence, the planner is usually more tolerant about the degree of "reliability" expected from projections than is the technician responsible for making the projections.

This difference between the perspective of the planner and that of the technician is a strategic one. The environmental conditions determining the tolerance of accuracy in the use of projections are not as stringent as the technical conditions determining the tolerance of accuracy in the making of projections. As a result, the allocation of projection research effort is often misguided, in the sense that for a few selected variables better projections are made than are "needed" while other potentially useful variables are ignored completely.

However, when we turn from projections used for predictive purposes to those used for planning that is concerned with identifying and quantifying strategic relationships, the above comments on reliability are not justified. In such a case the planner is interested less in reacting to some

---

[1] It is not necessarily the case that the most desirable assumption for planning purposes should always be the most likely assumption.

future environment than in trying to change trends that would occur in the absence of policy action. Thus he requires not only an approximate idea of the trends that would occur without a policy change, but also an idea of the instrumental variables that can and should be influenced by policy in order to achieve objectives.[2]

The planner's ability to change trends in order to bring them more in line with declared objectives depends on his identification of the instrumental variables and his understanding of the direct and indirect consequences of changes in these variables. In short, he needs an understanding of the key relationships that can bring about economic change.

In some cases the relationships are direct and simple. For example, in order to raise incomes of selected groups the planner can increase the benefit payments under public assistance or unemployment insurance. However, if his objective is not only to raise incomes but to reduce the incidence of poverty, it is by no means certain that income support would be effective. This is because there are many indirect relationships affecting the final outcome.

These effects have multiplying consequences; consequently, it is important that the relationships identified as important should be quantified as accurately as possible. To improve our stock of empirical knowledge about the relationships strategic for planning purposes it is useful to be aware of the following difficulties:

• While the relevant relationships in different regions generally involve the same kinds of variables, the parameters are likely to be quite different for the various regions.
• Over time, not only are the parameters of the relationships likely to be modified, but also the kinds of relationships that are strategic are likely to change.
• It is more difficult to obtain reliable marginal than reliable average relationships. For many planning purposes, the requirement of theory to work with relationships at the margin may have to be compromised by using empirical relationships at the average.

WHY IS REGIONAL INFORMATION NEEDED?

The Pursuit of National Objectives

At a very broad level of generalization, the nation's economic objectives are to maintain a reasonably full utilization of its resources; to improve the effectiveness of these resources so that an adequate pace of

---

[2] Both the "can" and the "should" will be influenced by the position of the planner—i.e., whether he is a federal, state, or local official.

economic growth is maintained; to achieve high levels of public and private demands; and to distribute the nation's output in some equitable manner so that hardship and social unrest are avoided.

Achievement of these objectives requires public actions that are politically acceptable and administratively feasible; it also requires effective production-consumption relationships among the "parts" of the nation. Traditionally, the parts of the nation considered relevant for analysis are households (as consumers and workers) and industries (as groups of establishments). When we consider the regional "parts" of the nation, we add a dimension of disaggregation which increases the opportunity for improving the efficient use of national resources. This is because there is a cost to overcoming distance; and reductions in this cost, without reducing resource use, will promote economic growth.

National policy might therefore be concerned with trying to achieve a more desirable spatial distribution of economic activity. Since regions are ordinarily not viewed as decision-making units, attempts at accomplishing these objectives tend to be indirect in the sense that they work through the effects of federal procurement policy on specific establishments or through offering financial and other inducements to households and business involved in making location decisions.

To improve the effectiveness of the national economy through influencing the spatial distribution of economic activity is an interesting problem in economic analysis, but it is probably not of urgent importance, because forces within the private sector (at least in the United States) tend to result in a reasonably efficient spatial distribution. Moreover, marginal improvements are likely to be costly as well as run counter to other preferences, such as the desire of households *not* to be relocated.

A more important part of the regional aspect of national policy is concerned with questions of equity rather than efficiency. Because some areas contain a disproportionate amount of problem groups—for example, large numbers of unemployed and underemployed as well as low-income and poorly educated persons, slow growth industries, etc.— it is sometimes easier for national policy to achieve equity objectives if it becomes concerned with encouraging structural changes in the region rather than attempting direct assistance for households, business, or other groups. So far as the regional policies of the federal government are concerned, this is probably the most crucial concern.

The Pursuit of Regional Objectives

The regional contribution to national economic objectives is probably less important as a policy concern than the pursuit of a region's own economic objectives.[3] These objectives, at the broad macro or economic development level of generalization, are the same as for the nation— reasonably full employment of resources, adequate economic growth, and equitable distribution for the region as a whole and among its parts —all within the constraint of political and administrative feasibility.

However, the effectiveness with which a region can pursue its macro-objectives is seriously limited by what is happening nationally and by the policy instruments it has available.

It is probably true that the regional macro-objectives cannot be achieved unless the national objectives are effectively pursued. If the nation is not on a path of full employment, individual regions will find it relatively difficult to be on such a path; if the nation is on a path of full employment individual regions will find it simpler than otherwise to stay on the same path.[4]

However, within these limits the individual regions can take actions (or the federal government can act for the region) that would relatively improve or deteriorate its position. To some extent these actions can be of a "beggar-my-neighbor" type. These, however, generally tend to be ineffective insofar as they relate to attempts by the region to attract (pirate) existing opportunities. The more significant competition among regions revolves around the attempt to attract increasing shares of the potential opportunities. It is how much of the increment to national growth a region is capable of attracting that determines whether it is doing relatively well or relatively badly.

The region has essentially two public policy instruments by which it can influence its over-all economic development—programs and persuasion. Persuasion can be applied to the federal government to adopt policies and programs that will benefit the region. Such persuasion has tended to concentrate on federal procurement policies to obtain federal installations or federal orders. Increasingly lobbying has been engaged in to persuade the federal government to adopt a mix of federal programs congenial to a region's own over-all growth. However, there is seldom a clear idea at the regional level as to the mix of federal activities conducive to the region's development; regional persuasion, therefore, tends to take the form of lobbying for grant formulae that will give a region its "fair share" of federal activities. Currently, this "fair share" argument is becoming significant in the context of untied bloc grants

---

[3] See article by Dykeman in (58); see also (2).

[4] The long period of national economic growth since the early 1960's seems to have been accompanied by growth in most regions and metropolitan areas. The groups bypassed by this growth have been occupationally and racially rather than regionally categorized.

versus program grants—with states lobbying for the former and cities for the latter. The persuasive abilities of governors as compared with mayors are likely to be critical in the struggle for federal funds, which apparently has developed. When it comes to attempts to influence broad (non-programmatic) federal monetary and fiscal policies, the regions can do relatively little.

Regional public bodies also attempt some persuasion of the private sector. The most obvious and least effective efforts are those that advertise and provide information in an attempt to attract business and households by extolling the virtues of an area. More important is the indirect approach implied by the development of an environment suitable to attracting business. The creation of this environment depends on the public programs the region pursues to improve its education and transportation systems, recreation facilities, air and water quality, tax structure, and so forth.

Thus, the major public tool for promoting a region's over-all economic development is the amount and mix of the money it spends on specific public programs. However, the major purpose of these programs is usually not to promote economic development, but rather to achieve the specific objectives (outputs) of the programs themselves. This is primarily the reason why a region appears to have little control over its general economic development. A region's leverage exists primarily as a by-product of its program activities, and relatively little is known about the relationships between specific programs and economic development.

DEFINING A REGION (44–47)

The preceding discussion has scrupulously avoided defining what is meant by a region. In some sense it suggests that a region represents an area about which public officials (regional or non-regional) are concerned. But this says very little about how to define a region. Regional economists are fond of saying that political jurisdictions are not appropriate regions for economic analysis, but they seem to have little difficulty in working with such regions; they are fond of saying that there is no natural set of economic regions but this doesn't prevent them from setting up criteria for regional definitions which would provide such a set.

In considering the problem of regional definitions we should distinguish between the attempts to disaggregate the nation into meaningful regions and the attempts to define the geographic boundaries of some given region. This distinction is analogous to that already drawn between the pursuit of national objectives and the pursuit of regional objectives. That is, we probably want to disaggregate the nation into regions because we are somehow concerned about the achievement of efficiency in the pursuit of the nationwide objectives; while we want to define the appropriate boundaries for a given region in order to effectively pursue the objectives of residents, business, and public bodies within the region.

If this is the case, then the national disaggregation process might try to define regions in such a way as to emphasize the differences among regions which would permit examinations of their *complementary* relations. For taking advantage of complementarities (regional specialization) is probably the most effective road to improving nationwide efficiency in the use of resources. Indeed, the early and crude regional groupings of the nation did precisely this—i.e., the farm areas vs. industrial areas vs. mining areas, the poor south vs. the richer north, urban vs. rural, etc. Furthermore, these kinds of regional groupings have proved very useful in regional economic analysis. However, as regions have begun to look more alike, and an industry location has become less natural resource based and more footloose, it has become more difficult to disaggregate into regions on the basis of complementarity criteria.

Recent attempts at regional disaggregation are concerned with establishing appropriate boundaries for each region which, in a sense, will "internalize" the common problems faced by the region and, if possible, also include the resources and institutions required to solve the problems. This seems to be the rationale behind the combined Census–Social Science Research Council effort to develop functional areas, the Commerce Department effort to develop county groupings as basic regions, and the Economic Development Administration effort to establish multistate development regions.

The difficulty with such an approach is that internalizing both problems and opportunities for given regions is likely to result in spatially overlapping regional boundaries—an inconvenient arrangement for both cartographers and data producers. The assumption is, however, that empirically this overlap can be made small; and that investigators of individual regions can always modify the standard classification to suit their own needs.

There is a difference between small area regionalization and large area regionalization. Small area boundaries are usually defined primarily by labor commuting characteristics, which means that metropolitan areas and their surroundings are the core of the regional classification. The problems that are internalized thus tend to be the familiar urban problems of land use, transportation, education, water quality, social welfare, etc. The larger region, however, tends to be concerned with issues of economic development where policy is required because the region is less developed, slow growing, over-specialized, etc. In such regions, state government is usually involved. Indeed, state government has a role to play not only in moving "upward" to multistate compacts, but also in moving "downward" to metropolitan areas and municipalities through setting objectives, reconciling conflicts, and providing financial assistance to localities.

Another way of viewing regional disaggregation is to think of the nation as a system of regions within regions—i.e., "vertical" rather than "horizontal" disaggregation. The advantage of such a system is that it allows common problems to be internalized within one set of boundaries while it permits additional opportunities for solving these problems to be bounded within the larger areas. In this way in seeking the solution of problems advantage can be taken of (a) complementary resources available within adjacent areas, e.g., rural land use or water supply for recreational purposes; (b) increasing potential market areas since the movement of goods is partly affected by distance; and (c) increasing governmental (financial and political) resources since the higher the level of government, the larger is the geographic area of responsibility. As changes occur over time or as different problems are being considered, the boundaries within boundaries can be changed— i.e., urban fringes can be brought within metropolitan area boundaries, adjacent metropolitan areas can be combined, small cities can become parts of larger urban complexes, etc.[5] For practical purposes such a "nesting" view of disaggregation should probably deal with central cities, metropolitan areas, states, multistate compact areas (which may or may not cover entire states), and the nation.

This last view of regionalization also has advantages for making projections as well as for problem solving. First, larger area projections can be used as control totals for allocating activities among smaller areas. Second, since the larger areas serve as a market or supply source for the small area, direct relationships can be drawn between the two areas which relate to considerations of comparative cost, factor mobility, export demand, and political persuasiveness. Third, observations can be made about the larger areas, which can be assumed to apply to smaller areas as well: sometimes the larger area observation is required as a proxy because sufficient data are not available for the small area; sometimes the larger area can be used as a "lead" sector in the sense that the smaller area in the future will tend to adopt the behavioral patterns already evident in the larger area. Fourth, some deci-

[5] This is exactly what is done by the U.S. Bureau of the Budget when it periodically revises its standard metropolitan area classification. Argument for this approach is provided in (24). See also fn. 8.

sions are made in the larger areas (e.g., federal budgetary decisions) whose impact can be traced through to the smaller area.

PERSPECTIVES FROM WHICH TO VIEW REGIONAL CHANGE

Economists tend to be concerned with two aspects of the process of regional change: the relationships among activities (variables) within the region, and the relationships between the region and the rest of the country. The interaction between the two sets of relationships determines the changes over time in the level of regional activities and future changes in the relationships among the activities.

It is not possible to comprehend in a single system all the relationships relevant to a region's change. There must be selection as to what relationships are important to describe as well as judgment about what causes change.

The diversity of metropolitan areas suggests that the activities and relationships that are important in one area may not be important in another; and even for the same area that which is important may vary for different time periods. Thus in one area it may be strategic to understand the relationship of the growth in job opportunities to the racial mix of the population; in a second area a critical factor may be the relation of manufacturing capacity to the defense budget; a third area may be concerned about the dependence of its prosperity on the national market for some given product or on the growth prospects for some specific other region; a fourth area might be alerted to the low level of public services provided or the fact that its residents import goods and services ordinarily produced within a community. And so forth.

But there are similarities among metropolitan areas as well as differences, which means that there are general and identifiable approaches to the analysis of the process of regional change. These general approaches are best conceived of as "perspectives" rather than models. They are related less to the statistical estimating procedures employed than to the analyst's view of how best to introduce those factors he believes are the primary determinants of regional change.

Changes in the supply and demand of productive factors in a region, changes in their efficiency, and changes in the goods and services they produce are significantly affected by geographic shifts in production and people. But the geographic shifts are themselves influenced by differences in the economic capabilities of regions. Here we have perhaps the most significant conflict of perspectives: Is the process of regional change best viewed as one where national forces are the primary determinants of the levels and growth rates of individual regions through their effects on the economic base of the region, or best viewed as a process whereby the internal structure of the individual region is the primary determinant of growth as it responds to external forces and even contributes to the development of those forces? [6]

Regional Changes Viewed from the National Perspective

What are the national forces that affect changes in a region? There are very few influences on the economy that can be identified as "national" in the sense that they have no regional origin; perhaps federal policy is the most significant. Other factors affecting or describing economic change, such as productivity, fertility, and labor participation, could be viewed as aggregates or averages of their regional values. What makes these factors national is that their consequences are nationwide rather than localized. A technology developed in Houston affects the productive capacity of Pittsburgh; a demand generated in Los Angeles influences employment in New York; a fertility decline in Mississippi influences population growth in Chicago.

It is reasonable, therefore, to start a metropolitan area analysis not with the geographic origin of influential factors but with the nationwide consequences of these factors; and then to go on to the specific geographic effects of these nationwide changes. That is, it is reasonable to start a metropolitan analysis with national projections. The national changes of particular relevance to metropolitan analyses relate to changes in population, employment, industry activity, income, productivity, investment, level and mix of demand, and federal policies and expenditures. [7]

Once the prospective national changes have been identified there are several ways by which they can be introduced into metropolitan analyses. The national change can be *allocated* to metropolitan areas. Thus, analysis can revolve around examination of the share of a national change that is likely to occur in each area. For example, if the nation's output of apparel products is expected to increase, how much of this increase is likely to occur in each area? Similarly, if the nation's labor

[6] I am grateful to Harold Barnett for his many constructive comments as a discussant of an earlier version of this paper. Mr. Barnett has correctly pointed out that while this paper emphasizes the attributes of the national perspective, the Thompson paper emphasizes the attributes of the local perspective. I acknowledge a prejudice in favor of the national perspective.

[7] The national and regional (multistate) projections which are cited in this report are those of the National Planning Association (6, 62).

participation is likely to change at a certain rate, what will be the deviation from this rate in a given metropolitan area?

The analysis, which has identified the factors responsible for the expected national change, then becomes relevant to the question of whether these factors operate in the same way, or are present to the same extent, in a given area to determine its deviation from or share of the national change.

Another way of introducing national changes into metropolitan analyses is to relate specific national changes to area characteristics. Two kinds of relations are particularly important: the *location* and the *trading* relations.

The location perspective is concerned with how expected national changes are likely to change the location of plants and of people. For example, if national income increases so as to encourage a shift in consumer expenditures for education, is this likely to mean more rapid migration to metropolitan areas that provide better education services? Similarly, if a technological change occurs which reduces the advantage of large scale production, will this mean that the location of capacity is likely to favor certain parts of the country rather than others?

The trading- or demand-perspective is concerned with how changes in the industrial and geographic mix of demand is likely to change production (and through production other variables) in specific metropolitan areas. For example, if industrial and consumer demands are growing faster in the Southwest than in New England, how will Dallas and Bridgeport be affected by these changes?

These three perspectives—allocation, location, and trading—are concerned with the same over-all problem of metropolitan area change, even though they select different aspects to emphasize. Let us now examine each perspective in somewhat more detail.

The Allocation Perspective (1–8). Allocation procedures are relatively easy to apply and probably result in the most reliable predictions. This is so because there are some trends applicable to a variety of areas, which are visible at the national level but cannot be identified at the regional level primarily because of inadequate data. These national trends can then be used as constraints on a given area's projection to make certain that the expected changes do not deviate by too much from the benchmark national trends. The major disadvantage of the allocation perspective is that areas that are at threshold points will deviate considerably from national trends and the allocation perspective is not likely to identify such areas.

151

The simplest allocation procedure is to project a given variable in an area in terms of the trend of its ratio to the comparable national (or some larger control total) variable. The ratio extrapolation implicitly builds in the effects of external events on the smaller regions which will cause future changes from past trends in the region. However, it fails to identify why the external events are occurring, and offers little opportunity for identifying how regions can plan for changing their response to the external event.

This same procedure can be made somewhat more comprehensive if all areas within the nation (or control area) are included. The advantage of working with all regions in the control area is that it permits comparisons of trends among regions so that each region can be projected in a balanced relation to other regions and to the total control area. This represents a short-cut, implicit method for handling interregional trade relations; also, the constraint imposed by allocating no more or no less than the control activity provides an opportunity to check the reasonableness of the control projection.

This kind of multi-area allocation approach requires a considerable amount of information about many areas; it is most useful when the intent is to provide projections for a variety of areas, rather than a depth analysis of a single area. The National Planning Association, which uses various versions of this procedure in its projections for each state and metropolitan area, suggests that these kinds of projections can be used for benchmark purposes by the in-depth studies of specific metropolitan areas. The procedure has been used in other studies and is being increasingly adopted for county projections which are made in the context of state control totals.

A significant refinement of the allocation procedure involves the use of shift analysis, which separates the "competitive" component of the ratio change from the "proportional" component and then analyzes the changing competitive shares for projection purposes. Although statistically appropriate for analysis of any variable, in practice shift analysis is usually applied to employment data.

When first introduced by Perloff and Dunn (63), it was used as an expository device for separating in quantitative terms the effects on an area's growth arising from two factors: the competitive effect, i.e., interregional competition within an industry; and the proportional effect, i.e., an area's advantage or disadvantage in being able to attract and retain rapid-growing and high-income industries as compared with slow-growing and low-income industries. Further research in this area, being pursued by the U.S. Commerce Department (22, 1) and by Mattila (4), is concentrating on analyzing the factors which determine the competitive component of the employment shift. Their approach offers the potential for combining traditional industry studies with area-wide indicators such as income, population, and labor force.

The allocation procedures gain empirical support from a general tendency for different parts of the country to become more similar, at least in their major characteristics. This tendency for convergence is apparent for the age distribution of population and labor force, labor participation rates, industry mix of employment, sources of income, and income distribution.

Part of the reason for convergence is that the less developed areas are industrializing rapidly and "moving up" to the national average. Also it seems to be the case that migrants adopt the behavioral characteristics of the area to which they move, which would make for convergence. Important but not measurable are the effects of improved education and rapid communication and transportation on reducing the geographic variation in economic behavior and activity. Probably there is also some effect from changes in technology and the growing population size of areas. That is, more and more areas are providing a large enough market to support efficient local enterprises, thus reducing the need for plants which sell in a nationwide market. Supporting this is the product-mix shift toward services which tend to be more efficient when production takes place within the market area. Finally, the increasing participation of state-local governments in economic affairs tends to generate a competition in providing amenities, which leads less to specialization and more to similarity.

Is this convergence trend likely eventually to reach the point where areas are all similar and all economically self-sufficient? This cannot be expected in a nation as dynamic as the United States. There will always be leading areas that are both innovating and obtaining maximum effectiveness from their economic base, while other areas respond to these changes. However, convergence does suggest a strong reason for giving substantial consideration to national forces in analyzing the prospects for economic change in regions.

What kind of story about metropolitan areas can be inferred from application of the allocation perspective? [8]

No matter what the growth in national population, there is a wide variation in the growth rates of different metropolitan areas. (Between

---

[8] Metropolitan area changes, as discussed in this paper, draw on (5) unless otherwise stated, and consider the metropolitan boundaries to be those defined in the year of observation. Other studies, and particularly federal data sources such as the Commerce Department income data, redefine the metropolitan boundaries in past years so as to conform with the most current definition.

1950–62 the annual population change of metropolitan areas ranged between minus 1.2% and 10.3%.) Nationally, over the long run, population and employment growth tend to move together with differences arising from changing labor participation and employment rates. In general, but not always, the metropolitan areas growing rapidly in population also grow rapidly in employment. The correspondence between metropolitan employment and population growth is not more exact because the proportion of the population which is employed will change at different rates among metropolitan areas, because of labor commuting, differences in the age composition, differences in the pattern of annexation as metropolitan areas increase their geographic boundaries, and changes in unemployment.

Natural increase (and particularly birth rates) explains most of the national population growth. Natural increase differences among metropolitan areas (particularly in fertility rather than death rates) explain only a small part of metropolitan areas' differences in population growth; differences in net migration explain the major part.

However, even though net migration explains differences in population growth among metropolitan areas, the projected level of growth of population for each metropolitan area depends significantly on the birth rate. The concept of a national fertility propensity is meaningful and applicable to given metropolitan areas (with, of course, area deviations). We are currently faced with great uncertainty about the future trend in births. The critical demographic question for the future of metropolitan areas, as well as the nation, is whether the recent declining trends to the currently low levels of birth rates are a short-term phenomenon and will begin to rise again, or whether they represent a long-term trend and will perhaps drop even further.

Even migration, which by definition is a place-to-place phenomenon, can be viewed in the context of nationwide propensities or attitudes. Thus, as Lowry has shown, outmigration from any area is largely a result of life cycle events—young people take jobs and leave parental households, people over sixty move after retirement, wives follow their husbands, and so on (52). Outmigration rates by age, color, and sex are remarkably similar among areas and seem to change only slowly over time. Outmigration is highest for the 20–24 age bracket and then becomes progressively lower—owing to job protection and attachment to an area, which seems to increase with age. Within each age bracket, however, outmigration is greater for the more educated and more skilled.

Gross inmigration to an area seems to be determined primarily by the presence of economic opportunities in the area which serve as an attraction for migrants from all other areas (52–54). However, some part of inmigration moves relatively independently of economic opportunity. The major group of inmigrants falls between those destination choices that are unmistakably oriented towards economic opportunity and those that are unmistakably not. This group moves primarily for economic reasons, but the actual choice of destination is determined by a selection among alternative economic opportunity areas which is based on secondary considerations involving amenities and other non-economic factors. According to some recent NPA research, non-white inmigration is less sensitive to job opportunities than white inmigration, apparently because non-whites have a greater propensity to migrate to areas where there are friends and relations. Also, it appears that not only the total of inmigration but also the inmigration of each age bracket can be reasonably well predicted by over-all job opportunities in an area. This suggests either that it is the condition of the area's total labor market, rather than the opportunities in specific occupations, which is relevant to inmigration, or that an area with growing job opportunities tends to provide opportunity for a variety of skills rather than concentrating opportunities in a few occupations.

Thus it appears that employment opportunities are the major determinant of metropolitan population growth—and an area's employment opportunities are influenced by nationwide employment changes. Metropolitan areas that can provide job opportunities are likely to grow particularly rapidly in regions having a relatively large non-metropolitan population. But in addition to the non-urban to urban shift, interurban migration also responds to economic opportunity, further affecting the differential growth among metropolitan areas.

Changing labor participation also affects a metropolitan area's population growth, primarily because it affects the potential for migration to the area. Labor participation in metropolitan areas is higher than in non-metropolitan areas, largely because of the high participation rates for women. It is also the differences in female labor participation which to a large extent explain interarea differences in over-all labor participation, just as it is changes in female labor participation which have a significant effect on the over-all labor participation and growth in the labor supply of the nation. Area differences in labor participation are probably narrowing partly because of the rural-to-urban movement, partly because of a narrowing of income differentials, and partly because non-white female participation is moving closer to the average for whites.

Just as for the nation, labor participation of women, non-white males, and younger persons in metropolitan areas is likely to be higher at rapid rates of economic growth than at slow rates. Thus the simple view of migration as the balancing mechanism for bringing labor supply and demand in an area closer to equilibrium must be modified, at least to the extent of allowing labor participation changes to contribute to the balancing process.

Nationally, there are profound changes occurring in the industry-mix of production, which accompany the long-run changes in technology, income, and consumer and public demands. While these latter changes do not seem to be related to over-all changes in population growth, the industry-mix itself does seem to be directly related to the population growth of a metropolitan area. Thus, in the past, differences in population growth among metropolitan areas have been closely related to differences in growth of manufacturing employment. This relationship is likely to weaken in the future as metropolitan growth becomes more closely related to employment in non-commodity sectors. This is because of the rising significance of tertiary activities, and implies that metropolitan growth will become more responsive to internal pressures within a given area than to nationwide markets for commodities.

Compared with non-metropolitan areas, metropolitan areas not only have a smaller share of their employment in agriculture and mining but also in government while having larger shares in manufacturing, construction, and tertiary-type industries. However, these differences are diminishing, particularly for manufacturing, trade, finance and insurance, transportation and utilities, and federal government. Also, the industry-mix of metropolitan areas located in different regions of the country is tending to become more similar as the less urbanized regions become urbanized and as each of the metropolitan areas becomes increasingly dependent on non-commodity activities. In spite of the move towards similarity, some differences are likely to persist: manufacturing employment will continue to comprise a relatively higher share of employment in those metropolitan areas located in regions that are more highly urbanized than the average.

The relation between a metropolitan area's growth and the broad region of the country in which it is located depends on two factors. First, fast-growing metropolitan areas tend to be located in regions with a high proportion of non-metropolitan population because they absorb a substantial portion of the rural-to-urban population shift. But the pace of a region's over-all growth is determined not by the rural-to-urban movement so much as by interurban movements. Thus a region will grow fast when its metropolitan areas, which are the major locus of the nation's economic activity, are growing fast. It is metropolitan

156

area growth which determines a broad region's growth, and not the reverse.

As a result of rising employment and increased productivity, the nation's personal income (in constant prices) has doubled in the past two decades, while its per capita income has increased by 50 per cent. Still faster increases for the nation can be expected in the future. Metropolitan areas, however, need not follow national trends. Because of the rural-to-urban shift, total personal income in metropolitan areas increases faster than in the nation as a whole, while per capita income increases slower in metropolitan areas than in the nation. These differences can be expected to be reduced along with an expected slow-down in the rate of urbanization.

Reasonably reliable metropolitan area income data have only recently begun to become available.[9] These data suggest that differences in per capita income levels among metropolitan areas—with per capita incomes being relatively low in metropolitan areas located in the less urbanized regions—are related to differences in industry-mix, area productivity and size, and also to differences in the share of the population that is employed, which tends to be low in the less urbanized areas.[10] These same kinds of factors affect the nation's per capita income growth over time.

Personal income has grown more slowly in the non-metropolitan parts of the country, but per capita income has grown faster, reflecting the rural-to-urban population shift. Although per capita income outside metropolitan areas is converging toward the metropolitan level in proportionate terms, in absolute dollar terms the gap is widening. The largest difference and fastest convergence between metropolitan and non-metropolitan per capita income levels are found in the less urbanized or generally low-income regions of the country.

Wages and salaries are a relatively more important component of personal income in metropolitan areas than in non-metropolitan areas, while the reverse is true for proprietors' income. These differences, how-

[9] The NPA has prepared income estimates for 224 metropolitan areas for selected historical and projected years; the Commerce Department has published income data in greater component detail for 97 metropolitan areas (and the remainder to be published soon) for selected historical years (26). Unfortunately, definitional differences (see fn. 8) not only make comparisons difficult but also result in some difference in analytical conclusions about metropolitan area income trends.

[10] Commerce Department data show that per capita income differences among metropolitan areas are diminishing over time. NPA data, however, show that the interarea differences (e.g., as measured by the coefficient of variation) remain constant.

ever, are diminishing. As measured by industrial source, income changes in manufacturing and government have been most important to income growth in metropolitan areas, although for the slow-growing areas changes in mining income have also been important (26).

There is very little direct information on metropolitan area productivity. However, inferences from national and state data would indicate that metropolitan productivity (net output per employee) is roughly related to metropolitan per capita income (6, 43). The areas having an over-all high productivity relative to other areas tend to have a relatively high productivity in each of the major producing sectors, while the reverse is probably true for the low productivity areas. This tentative observation that differential product mix is not the significant factor in over-all productivity differences among metropolitan areas may simply be a reflection of wage roll-outs in the area since the value of net output is dominated by the payroll component.

The Locational Perspective (9–15). While the allocation procedure is concerned with geographically distributing national aggregates, the locational perspective is concerned with the geographic distribution of factors that determine the location of industrial capacity. The allocation perspective tends to emphasize how the present geographic pattern of economic activity came to be and how it is likely to change; the locational perspective tends to emphasize the decisions of firms as to why and how they should select one location in preference to another when initiating or expanding capacity.

Individual firms within an industry will tend to consider the same set of factors as important in their location decisions. But different industries will tend to assign different degrees of importance to the various factors entering into location decisions. Also different areas will be capable of providing the critical factors in varying degrees.

Thus the process of geographic distribution of economic activity involves an interplay between industry and area. Factors important to specific industries and factor endowments in specific areas will change over time. Indeed, as industry relocates, the relative factor endowments among areas will change as a consequence; and areas will attempt to adjust their factor endowments specifically to meet the requirements of industry.

Because of progress in technology, improvements in income, and changes in industry-mix, location factors important to an area's development have tended to become more amenable to public and private policy influences. For example, in earlier days natural resources were critical location factors. However, the location factors important to

158

today's industries include such things as appropriate labor skills, ready access to fast transportation, adequate public services, good educational systems, and a diversified industrial and commercial base affording opportunities for external economies.

These factors tend to be characterized by a high degree of mobility potential. That is, they can be and are provided in a large number of areas. Two implications result from this. First, industry is increasingly more footloose in the sense that it can consider location in many areas rather than just a few areas where some specific location factor is available. Second, important location factors often can be relatively easily moved to or developed in areas where industry wants to locate, rather than requiring industry to move to areas where the location factors are already available in abundance.

The location decision, it should be noted, is important not only to new plant locations but, even more, to expansion of capacity at existing sites. Most firms expand capacity at their present locations either because these locations continue to provide satisfactory locational advantages, or because the advantages provided in other areas are generally not strong enough to balance the costs involved in overcoming inertia and locating in a new untried area. This, in turn, suggests that the factors affecting the initial location of an industry might be quite different from the factors influencing the industry to remain where it is.

Usually an area has location problems not so much because industries and firms pick up and leave the area entirely (although this does occur in some cases), but rather because, instead of undertaking local additions and plant extensions, firms chose to expand in some other area. This may be due to a variety of factors such as a cheaper or more plentiful labor supply elsewhere, restrictive labor regulations imposed by unions, the growth of new or expanding markets in other places, or simply a desire by multi-plant firms to achieve a more uniform spread geographically. For some firms, such factors as subsidized financing, subsidized rents, or abatement of taxes may be of locational importance.

Factors affecting location will usually have both positive and negative influences on capacity change in specific metropolitan areas. These conflicting influences partly explain the difficulty in introducing location criteria into empirical models of regional growth. Without attempting to be exhaustive, some significant aspects relating to industry location might be suggested.

The availability, characteristics, skills, attitudes, and wages of the work force are among the important factors in location decisions for most manufacturing industries. Most but not all capacity expansions will be based on an expectation that there is already an adequate and

159

available work force in the area, rather than the expectation that the increased activity will be able to attract or train the needed labor. Sometimes, plants will be attracted to a tight labor market confident that they can bid away the required labor from other establishments; often labor, particularly management and technical labor, will come from other plants in the firm. Large firms will often limit their capacity expansion so as to require only a small share (say 5 to 10 per cent) of the total work force in the labor market area. This limits the effects on the community of fluctuations in their business, and also reduces the firm's dependence on what happens in a specific labor market.

Although the importance of a supply of low-skilled, low-wage labor is diminishing as a location factor it is still significant to many industries in both manufacturing and services. Somewhat paradoxically, incomes can be most easily upgraded in metropolitan areas that provide opportunities for the low skilled. There is some evidence, for example, that areas growing most rapidly are those growing in a "balanced" fashion, i.e., those providing opportunities for a variety of skills and industries.

The significance of highly skilled and managerial labor as a locational factor is influenced by their mobility. Thus, they can move to locations which provide jobs; or, because of strong preferences as to where they choose to reside, the establishment location can be influenced by the residence preferences. To some extent the increasing tendency toward separation of headquarters, research, engineering, and operating functions of a firm is influenced by these kinds of residentiary preferences.

The positive effects of improved efficiency and expanded markets derived from agglomeration factors may be offset by the increased costs resulting from congestion in metropolitan areas. On balance, the positive factors seem to outweigh the negative factors even in the larger metropolitan areas, as establishments try to retain the advantages and reduce the disadvantages through a spatial reallocation of economic activity within the metropolitan area.

When location factors are viewed as inputs to the production and marketing functions, their actual or implied comparative costs should be considered as a locational influence. However, because of data difficulties cost measurements have tended to be restricted to labor costs, transportation costs, taxes, land costs, and capital costs as they apply primarily to manufacturing industries. This suggests the possibility that location analyses give an undeserved importance to those factors that are measurable.

Federal policy has a significant influence on the location of capacity, but usually this influence is unintended rather than intended.[11]

[11] Under the Employment Act of 1946 the federal government was given spe-

Federal procurement (essentially defense) tends to favor the high-income areas which have the "capability to perform." [12] Direct federal installations probably favor the low-income areas, on balance. Federal domestic grant and transfer programs (which are primarily directed towards households and not industry) have a significant indirect effect on the quality of labor in an area, and this, on balance, probably serves to dampen the geographic redistribution of capacity.

The Trading Perspective (16–21). From this perspective, economic growth in a region is made dependent on a region's trading relations with other areas. The region's growth, therefore, depends on the growth of markets in its trading partners' areas and the change in the share of those markets that are satisfied by the region's production.

Usually in these kinds of models the growth in the market areas is taken as exogenous stipulation very often based on national allocation techniques; the regional analysis is then concerned with anticipating changes in the trading coefficients as they are affected by such considerations as price and wage differentials, distance costs, scale economies, and other comparative advantage factors.

The trading perspective, of course, emphasizes the view of the nation as a system of commodity flows. Its relevance is based largely on the same kinds of arguments which underlie international trade theory. However, as commodities become less important in the national economy, the commodity flow may also become relatively less important to metropolitan area growth.

When presented in terms of input-output tables, the trading perspective provides a framework for spelling out specific relationships among industries and between regions. It can show how the sources of a region's change might originate in external markets, in local markets, and in market "shares." It can be very useful to marketing decisions of business and can be used for public planning both as a projection device and as an optimization tool with the application of linear programming.

The great difficulty with the trading perspective is that there are very few data available on trading relations. About the only generalization

---

cific legislative responsibility for fostering economic growth and for promoting the full utilization of the nation's economic resources. However, the Act is not interpreted as requiring the federal government to foster growth and full utilization of resources in each area of the country. The Economic Development Administration, however, seems to interpret its mission in this latter context.

[12] Vannevar Bush seems to be the first to have propounded this doctrine when he announced in 1942 that the Department of the Army would place its research contracts "wherever the talent was."

we can make is that there seems to be some kind of direct relationship between commodity flow and distance—but even this does not seem to be true for some industries.

The two potentially useful sources of commodity flow data—the Census of Transportation and ICC waybills—have both proven inadequate because of their small sample size. Some data on trading relations are generated on an ad hoc basis through surveys of establishments, which are conducted in connection with specific studies made for selected areas. But the results, to date, are meager.

The absence of direct data on trading relations has led to attempts to infer trading relations indirectly. A "taxonomic" approach tries to classify industries as to the extent to which they enter interregional trade on the basis of the characteristics of the products produced by the industry—for example, the interregional trade of bulky or perishable commodities tends to be limited (21). A "location coefficient" approach compares the per capita production of a commodity in a region against some "normal" per capita production to determine whether there is a need for import or export—for example, the high volume of financial activities relative to population in New York means an export of financial services. A "balancing" approach tries to match the geographic distribution of production against the geographic distribution of demand with the differences representing the goods and services entering into interregional trade (20). These calculations can take a very sophisticated form involving the determination of regional demands through the use of interindustry tables, which spell out production requirements by industry; comparing these demands with industrial production in the region; then using gravity formulations to determine the regional origin and destination of the commodities that show a regional imbalance in production and demand.

The great difficulty with these approaches is that they tend to assume two kinds of relationships, which have yet to be proven accurate: first, that production input coefficients for given industries tend to be similar among regions; and, second, that the costs of overcoming distance can be functionally related to the volume of commodity traffic between producer and buyer.

Another kind of trading perspective is found in the concept of nodal regions (17). From this perspective, a growth center is identified as the economic core of some larger region. The growth of the areas outside the core is then made dependent on changes in the core, since the outside areas sell labor, services, and light manufacturing products to the core industries.

The nodal concept is basic to the current area development planning of the Economic Development Administration, and is also important when considering the establishment of "new towns." It is a perspective which appears particularly well suited for making state projections. The reasoning is that since a state is generally not an economic region, and since the basic economic analysis should be done in terms of economic regions, then projections should first be made for the nodal or growth area, and the state projection then based on these nodal expectations. (Note that this also has some specific planning implications in the sense that state planning is dependent on planning for the nodes.) The nodal areas, in effect, will turn out to be metropolitan areas, so that we can see a clear relationship between metropolitan and statewide projections.[13]

[13] While there are few data on geographic trading *relations* there is considerable information on production and other activities by region. Some highlights of the expected regional trends would provide some substantive content for the application of the various national perspectives (6).

In terms of regional population, employment, labor force, and income growth, there is a persistent shift from the Northeast, Great Lakes, Plains, and Southeast (excluding Florida) to the Southwest, Rocky Mountain, and Far West states.

Employment in the New England, Great Lakes, and Middle Atlantic regions has been increasing but is expected to continue to increase at a relatively slow rate due chiefly to the failure of these regions to attract growing capacity in specific industries. In fact, the net downward employment "shift" would have been much larger in these regions were they not favored by those industries which have been growing rapidly at the national level—i.e., the "growth" industries.

In contrast, the relatively slow growth expected for the Plains states is explained by both an unfavorable industrial structure and a weak competitive position in almost all industries (except agriculture and transportation equipment).

Growth of employment in the southeastern states (exclusive of Florida) will be slowed down by their specialization in industries that have been declining or slow-growing nationally. Except for agriculture, the Southeast has shown a strong competitive performance in almost all industries, especially in trade, services, and non-durable manufacturing.

The very rapid growth in employment of the Far West is attributed to both a favorable industrial structure and a competitive advantage in specific industries.

The relatively rapid growth of employment expected in the Southwest and Mountain states results from a favorable competitive advantage in specific industries overbalancing an unfavorable mix.

It can be noted that except for areas where the decline in agriculture has its maximum impact (the Plains states and parts of the Southeast and Mountain regions), a region's competitive performance in specific industries is generally much more important than its industry composition in influencing the rate of over-all employment change.

The Middle Atlantic, Southeast, and Far West states account for three-fourths of the nation's personal income. Following population and employment growth, income in the Far West, Southeast, and Southwest states can be expected to grow

Regional Changes Viewed from the Local Perspective

The three perspectives discussed—the allocation, location, and trading perspectives—have been identified as "national" because the analysis of metropolitan area growth is viewed as starting with something which happens outside the area. The other side of the coin is to view a local area, in a paraphrase of Wilbur Thompson, as a bundle of activities in space (see his paper in this volume). There are three perspectives from which this "bundle" can be viewed: *stages, impact-multiplier,* and *production-function* perspectives.

In the stages perspective the area is viewed as an entity whose future changes are determined by its current size and structure. In the impact-multiplier perspective the area is viewed as an entity whose industries are responding to meet the challenges imposed by some major new event. In the production-function perspective the area is viewed as a production entity whose future changes depend on what happens to the factors of production in the area.

The Stages Perspective (22–27). The simplest view of stages of growth is simply that regions get bigger. Thus the economic structure and resources of an area are measured for some recent intervals and their past trends are extrapolated as a function of time. These kinds of economic base studies extended into the future are very often used for small area projections. When used, they are neither reliable as predictions nor do they explain any events. However, they are easy to apply and they satisfy the requirements for regional economic studies,

---

relatively rapidly, while the New England, Middle Atlantic and Great Lakes incomes grow slowly.

The rate of growth in per capita income is expected to be faster in the low-income southern states than for the high income states in the Northeast and Great Lakes. However, this convergence in per capita incomes is not so rapid that we can expect similarity among states' per capita income levels; indeed, the gap between high- and low-income states is so large that in spite of the relatively slow percentage growth in the high-income states, the absolute dollar difference in per capita income levels is likely to widen. It should also be noted that the relatively slow growth of high-income states does not necessarily mean that the income of current residents is growing slowly but could mean that migrants into the high regions tend to have lower earnings.

The income size distribution also varies fairly significantly among states, primarily as related to differences in the average per capita income levels. The richer, more industrialized states have a more equal distribution of income than the low-per-capita-income states. Also affecting both the per capita income and income distribution differences among states are the per cent of families headed by non-whites, the per cent of the population employed, the level of education of adult persons, and the per cent of families headed by skilled and white-collar workers. Because there is an interstate convergence in these factors we can expect an interstate convergence in income distributions.

which are sometimes imposed as a condition for obtaining public funds.

The traditional view that regional change follows a process of moving through various stages of development emphasized the process of resource depletion and discovery on the one hand, and shifts in demand and technology on the other hand—and was usually applied to broad regions. More recently this kind of perspective is being applied to metropolitan areas or county groupings. Using cross-section data, the attempt is made to relate the size of an area to its industrial mix in order to arrive at an idea of the "functions" served by different sized areas. City-hierarchy classifications (23) and some of the applications of "shift analysis" (22) to employment data reflect attempts to implement the stages concepts. If an area's industrial mix can be shown to be related to its size, then it becomes possible to envision a dynamic analytical process which projects the industrial mix from an area's current size and then projects the later size of the area from the expected industrial mix.

Some data indicate that a metropolitan area's size, its growth, and its industry-mix are related. Thompson, for example, points out that when a metropolitan area reaches a certain size its further growth cannot be stopped essentially because the infrastructure in the area is too valuable to permit its obsolescence. This is supported by the Borts-Stein view of the regional investment process which suggests that new investment goes where the old investments have been made (39). Jonathan Lindley, on the other hand, finds that the rapidly growing counties are medium-sized areas, that is, between 50,000 and 500,000 people, essentially because the small areas have lost their economic function as agricultural distribution centers and because large areas have created costs of congestion and diseconomies of scale which discourage people and industry (27). Commerce Department data indicate that there has been a strong inverse relationship since 1929 between the population size of a metropolitan area on the one hand and on the other hand growth rates of personal income, population, and per capita income (26). Dunn has suggested that areas move through four stages of development, which are defined by relating the size of the area to the kinds and volume of its exports and imports (25). (Because it becomes more difficult to advance from one stage to the next as an area moves up the hierarchy, some areas will not go through the whole development process.)

As opposed to these views, some data developed by the National Planning Association indicate that in recent decades there is no consistent relation between the size of a metropolitan area and its growth (although, as has been cited earlier, there is a relationship between industry mix and growth) (5). Neither the assumed congestion in larger areas nor the lack of viability in smaller areas puts them at a growth disadvantage with respect to medium-sized areas. Indeed, the NPA data show a remarkable consistency over time in the size distribution of metropolitan areas. Using the standard Budget Bureau definition of metropolitan areas in the year of observation (thus allowing for annexation of surrounding counties to existing areas and the addition of new areas as they qualify), NPA data indicate that in each benchmark year since 1950 metropolitan areas with less than 200,000 people comprise about 45 per cent of the total number of metropolitan areas and include 10 per cent of the total metropolitan population; corresponding percentages for metropolitan areas between 200,000 and 1,000,000 people are 45 per cent of the number of metropolitan areas and 35 per cent of the total metropolitan population; while for areas over 1,000,000 in population size the percentages are 10 per cent and 55 per cent, respectively. This kind of constancy in a Lorenz distribution is similar to what has already been observed for household income distribution: it allows for individual areas to move up in size-class but over-all the size relationships among metropolitan areas (i.e., their skewness) remains the same in spite of the rapid growth in urban population.

The Impact-Multiplier Perspective (28–37). In this view some major event is assumed to occur within a region which will so dominate future developments that the region's change can be anticipated by measuring the consequences of the event and the needs that it generates.

The most obvious application of this kind of view relates to the introduction of a major investment program or facility. Planning in undeveloped nations very often follows this approach. However, it is also used for advanced country planning, particularly for small area planning in the United States; for example, measurement of area development and benefits resulting from new recreational facilities was a favorite study of the Area Redevelopment Administration, and measuring the consequences of public investments (e.g., roads) is important in the Appalachian program. Measuring the depressing consequences of natural resource depletion was once quite common; the more modern form of this perspective is to measure the growth consequences of R&D, technical, and educational resources. The most common marketing kind of impact measured relates to defense budget changes—usually a disarmament assumption (31). Here the national defense change is translated into its direct regional impact, and the consequences on the area are then traced out—almost invariably through input-output tables.

The impact-multiplier perspective is most useful in short-term forecasting. There is nothing implicit in the perspective which facilitates the identification of long-run structural changes that might occur as a result of the impact. Also, since there are other events than the impact which are usually affecting the community at the same time, the reliability of impact projections is reduced.

However, the relationships that are made explicit in the impact-multiplier context are very valuable for program planning. Since most urban planning is concerned with overcoming *current* deficiencies in public services, the failure to introduce long-run structural changes may not be important to the planner. Also, since the approach is suited to alternative stipulations of hypothetical impacts, the planner can obtain useful information about how a suggested policy is likely to affect the levels and kinds of activities in the area.

The multiplier relationships are the critical aspects of this perspective. These relationships are usually spelled out in interindustry terms. The kinds of input-output tables that have been developed for regions vary considerably: some have very detailed industrial sectors; most, however, are very aggregative. Most measure value flows, although employment flows are also measured (35). Some emphasize a "from-to" table—i.e., the flows between regions—while others emphasize the flows between industries (28), and still others try to detail the geographic and industry flows simultaneously (32). Some try to show the area's imports and exports in great detail (33), while most will show them as aggregates. Some try to use local banking data as their basic source of information, while others will conduct special local establishment surveys and supplement these with national input-output information (35). Beyond these kinds of differences among the empirical efforts made, there is also a continuing debate about what accounting "conventions" are appropriate to adopt, particularly with respect to the treatment of the local government, investment, and household sectors (59).

What generalizations are possible from all these data? Clearly, a community multiplier will depend on its industry mix, on what it produces at "home," and on what it imports as well as on the kind of impact assumed (36). The export multiplier (excluding induced investment and consumer effects) seems to vary between 1.3 and 2.0 for metropolitan areas. It is not clear whether there is a trend for the multiplier ratio to increase or decrease with time; nor is it clear whether the multiplier is smaller or larger depending on the size of the metropolitan area or its location (34).

The Production-Function Perspective (38–43). "The conceptual and empirical basis for believing in the existence of a simple and stable relationship between a measure of aggregate input and a measure of aggregate output is uncertain at best. And yet an aggregate production function is a very convenient tool for theoretically exploring some of the determinants of economic growth, and it has served as a framework for some interesting empirical studies of long run economic change. Moreover, in an attempt to assess the growth prospects for an economy, to identify the variables that are likely to determine the growth rate, and to examine the policies affecting growth, the explicit or implicit use of an aggregate production function is almost indispensable." (42)

In writing this paragraph, Nelson had in mind the national economy. In principle, it should be applicable to a metropolitan area's or region's economy as well. But, in reality, it is not. There are no theoretical explorations of a region's aggregate production function.[14] There are no empirical studies using regional production functions as a tool for analysis—indeed there is only slight interest in even obtaining empirical measures of regional output (38, 43). There are no attempts to use an aggregate production function for identifying the variables and policies that influence a region's growth.

Has the regional economist overlooked an important area of research, or is he justified in his neglect?

The production function approach provides capacity projections in the sense that it is interested in measuring the expected change in the supply of productive factors available and changes in their efficiency.[15] These capacity changes need not be measures of the largest technologically possible capacity changes but can be constrained by a whole set of social, economic, and political factors, such as labor participation rates, work hours, spending habits of consumers and government, etc.

At the national level, the production function is powerful because it is assumed that the supply of the productive factors (labor and capital) can be reasonably well disentangled from their efficiency; the effects of each on output can be isolated; and the influences affecting the

---

[14] There are some studies of specific regional industry production functions; however, these are used in a cross-section sense to develop production functions for the nationwide industry rather than for purposes of regional analysis (40).

[15] The implicit assumption, of course, is that resources available in the projected year will be reasonably fully utilized. This assumption is reasonable not because it is supposed that serious cyclical movements can now be controlled by public policy (although to some extent this is true), but rather because the change in economic activity over, say, a ten-year period will be substantially greater than any possible variation in activity due to the economy's cyclical position in a given year.

supply of the productive factors (particularly the labor input) can be stipulated from outside the production function itself.

Let us look at a simple Cobb-Douglas production function as formulated by Nelson.[16]

$$\Delta O/O = \Delta A/A + b\,\Delta L/L + (1 - b)\,\Delta K/K \qquad (1)$$

To use equations (1) or (2) for regional projection purposes, we could obtain measures of factor productivity change ($\Delta A/A$ or $\Delta A^*/A^*$), factor shares (b), and quality of inputs (λ) from a regression equation relating the change in output to the change in the supply of capital and labor (assuming the historical data are available).

Nelson points out that for the national regression equation the results would be heavily influenced by the time period chosen for observation, since the capital stock and productivity changes are interdependent while the productivity change and capital quality change are undoubtedly not constants. But these kinds of difficulties would be much more significant for the regional equation than the national equation. For example, on the interdependency issue, capital stock changes rather than productivity changes could be calculated as the "residual" in the regional regression on the grounds that comparative productivity among regions determines the rates of investment. Also, on the constancy of the parameters issue, the region's technological improvement constant would be significantly affected by technological improvements made elsewhere and the pattern of geographic diffusion; interpretation of the factor share constant would be difficult because of net labor and property transfers to and from the region; and the capital quality improvement constant would be significantly affected by differences in extent of plant obsolescence among regions.

So for the regional production function even more than for the national production function, it would be necessary to go behind a regression equation to identify how and why technological improvement

---

[16] O = output; L = labor; K = capital stock; A = total factor productivity; b and $1 - b$ equal the elasticities of output with respect to labor and capital, respectively, which under competititive assumptions represent proportionate payments (factor shares) to labor and capital.

Nelson's extended version of the Cobb-Douglas, where changes in the "quality" of labor and capital are embodied in L and K, is as follows:

$$\Delta O/O = [\Delta A^*/A^* + b\lambda_L + (1 - b)\lambda_K - (1 - b)\lambda_K \Delta \bar{a}] + b\Delta L/L + \\ (1 - b)\Delta K/K \qquad (2)$$

Thus the bracketed term in equation (2) $= \Delta A/A$ where $\Delta A^*/A^*$ represents a closer approximation to a true technological change than $\Delta A/A$, since λ_L and λ_K represent changes in the quality of labor and capital and $\Delta \bar{a}$ equals the age of capital.

169

and the quality of capital and factor shares might be different in the future than they have been in the past.

But suppose this could be done for the region by drawing on what we know from other sources. Presumably, we could introduce this knowledge so as to have a regional production function which reflects the future rather than the past. Would there still be difficulties in applying this production function for projection purposes?

Application of the national production function seems to depend on the proposition that changes in the supply of labor and its quality are relatively more constant than the other variables, or, at least, can be stipulated with relatively more reliability. This, of course, is not true at the regional level because of migration. Migration will not only account for sharp shifts in the regional labor supply, but also in its quality, since migrants need not have the same education and skills as the non-migrants. Thus, it turns out that changes in the region's labor supply cannot be stipulated independently of changes in the region's capital stock or changes in its productivity. If we were to assume that migration could be independently stipulated, we would in effect be incorrectly assuming that capital stock changes in a region are determined by migration, or, in other words, that industry location follows residential preferences.

It is primarily for this last reason that production function analysis does not seem applicable to regional projections; namely, that we require some important factor in the regional production function whose change is reasonably constant—or which can be reasonably reliably predicted—and we don't know what that factor is.

Regional analyses suggest some factors which deserve attention from this perspective—although it is difficult to see how they would fit into a production function or even to have any confidence that they could be reasonably reliably predicted. Included are: entrepreneurship, natural increase in the labor force, equity capital, relative profits, non-economic oriented migration, public policy, and land availability. These factors have certain characteristics of "regional attachment" which might serve to influence changes in the productivity, labor, and capital stock variables of the production function.

PROJECTION OF SELECTED VARIABLES

The preceding sections have discussed different ways of viewing the over-all process of regional change. These different perspectives are often in competition with each other in the sense that different aspects of the regional economy are selected for emphasis and different relationships are judged as critical for determining the process of regional change. They are also complementary, however, in the sense that there are several important variables viewed as key indicators of economic progress in each of the perspectives. These include population, labor force, employment, industry activity, and income. These same indicators are also viewed as critical by regional planners who require projections of these variables for program planning or who are interested in directly influencing future changes in the variables.

This concluding section describes specific projection techniques that relate to each of the variables. These techniques can be applied independently of one's over-all perspective of regional change. Also if desired, they can be incorporated as sub-models within more comprehensive model formulations. Finally, by pointing to some specific factors leading to change in the variables, description of the projection techniques can be of direct use to planners.

Regional Population Forecasting (52–55)

There are many examples in which population is forecast by a trend extrapolation or as an extrapolation of the region's relation to some control area. Usually, this is done for small areas such as counties, where there is little interest in what is likely to happen to other variables in the area. Essentially some very rough measure of size of the area is wanted and this inexpensive approach is considered adequate. Population projections for metropolitan areas rarely are done in this way.

The more sophisticated methods will try to introduce consideration of the interrelationship between economic and demographic factors. This usually means a combination of survival cohort and migration analysis. A population calculation is made in terms of fertility and death rates over the projected interval, which is then modified by expectations about migration into or out of the area (55). Most metropolitan areas will be growing in population (because of some continuation of rural to urban movements as well as because of natural increase). In rough orders of magnitude, if less than half of the population increase is attributable to natural increase, the metropolitan area will be a rapid growing area.

In applying the survival-cohort technique for an area, five-year age brackets are easily used with readily available computer programs. The death rates, by age bracket, can usually be the same for a region or metropolitan area as for the national average, since there is little difference among regions. If population by color is required, separate (national) death rates for whites and non-whites will have a slightly improved effect on the results.

Fertility rates do display some regional differences, even if standardization for income, color, and rural–non-rural characteristics are applied. This is particularly the case for small areas such as counties, but less so for larger areas. However, outweighing the effect of regionally differential fertility rates on the area's population projection will be the (intuitive) judgment as to whether the already low nationwide fertility rate is likely to decline further or perhaps move back to the levels of a few years ago. Therefore, expectations about national fertility rates are strategic to regional population forecasting.

In some cases the migration component of population change is a trended value of past net migration. This procedure, however, is not adequate, partly because there is not much reliable historical data on migration and partly because the net migration data we do have appear to be highly volatile over time. Improved migration analyses are usually based on cross-section analyses over areas during some given time interval, which relate the flow of migrants to the availability of economic opportunities (52). Employment opportunities seem to be more powerful than wage rates as a determining variable. The projection procedure can be implemented by allowing employment to serve as a "lead" variable—although there is not much evidence as to what the appropriate lead time should be.

Net migration can also be obtained by a somewhat more elaborate procedure than regressing it against employment. Projected job opportunities (labor demand) can be compared with the projected labor force implied by a cohort-survival growth in population (labor supply). Differences between labor supply and demand can then be reduced by assuming that migration responds to this difference. This approach is most effective when it involves a series of successive approximations in which adjustments are made to initial estimates of labor participation, unemployment, and the proportion of jobs held by women, as well as adjustments to migration in order to reduce the labor imbalance.

It has been pointed out that, irrespective of time and place, gross outmigration from a metropolitan area can be reliably predicted by the age distribution of the population in the area; while gross inmigration is determined by the relative job opportunities among areas. This suggests that, for predictive purposes, migration analyses can by-pass extensive consideration of place-to-place flows and the effect of distance on migration.

However, separate calculations of gross inmigration and gross outmigration to arrive at a net migration estimate can considerably improve results.

Outmigration can be based on outmigration rates (i.e., the share of outmigration in each age, sex, color cohort- population), which are approximately the same in each metropolitan area and for different intervals of time. Inmigration can be calculated on the assumption that the destination choice of outmigrants is primarily determined by economic opportunities in the area relative to economic opportunities elsewhere. The migration of population cohorts who select a destination partly independently of economic opportunity—for example, the elderly, college students, armed forces, family dependents—can be determined on the basis of specific characteristics influencing their choice, or can be related to the labor force migrant flow.

Regional Labor Force and Employment Forecasting (49–50)

At the national level the difference between total labor force and total employment is strategic because it highlights the question of unemployment, which is one of the significant issues for economic policy. At the regional level, however, issues of unemployment are not particularly illuminated by the labor-force–employment difference, partly because net commuting is a part of this difference, but primarily because it throws no light on the relation of migration to unemployment.

Thus for long-run purposes, the planner is often indifferent as to whether he has labor force or employment projections and is sometimes even unaware as to which he has. However, whether total labor force or total employment is being projected does have significance for how the process of regional change is being viewed. The labor-force projection tends to emphasize a demographic and "top down" process while the employment projection emphasizes an economic and "bottom up" approach.

The labor-force projection is demographic because it usually starts with population projections (by age, sex cohorts and, if possible, by color), applies labor participation rates by appropriate cohort group, and then adds considerations of net migration—which may or may not depend on consideration of job opportunities or employment demand in the region.

The critical aspect of this approach is what happens to labor participation rates. The labor participation rates in individual metropolitan areas tend to follow the same pattern of change as in the nation as a whole: the rate for women is increasing; the rate for older men is declining because of earlier retirement; the rate for young people is declining because of more schooling and possibly because of slow growth in job opportunities; and non-white women have a relatively high rate while non-white men have a low rate.

Although the individual metropolitan areas follow this pattern generally, there are differences in the over-all participation rate among

173

metropolitan areas, which are quantitatively important. For this reason it is preferable to work with area-specific participation rates rather than the national average. The differences among metropolitan areas are, in part, attributable to age-mix and job-opportunity differences (it can be shown that lack of job opportunities decreases labor participation particularly for the young, the Negroes, and women). But there are probably some other reasons, as well, which involve social attitudes. There is some evidence of convergence in the participation rates of metropolitan areas; also, there appears to be some evidence that migrants, particularly women and non-whites, adopt the participation patterns of the area to which they move.

The labor-force emphasis is a "top down" approach because after the total labor force is projected it is possible to decompose this total into specific occupational and industrial groupings, which are usually the indicators relevant to planning. The decomposition procedures have three major variants: the first is to project the area's trend in its "structural" relationships (that is, in its mix of industries or occupations); the second is to project the relationship between the area's structure and the national (or some other control region) structure; and the third is to make interarea comparison studies that permit the determination of a relationship between an area's size and its structure.

The employment projection is economic because it is concerned primarily with forecasting the area's demand for jobs and specifying the factors in job change. Since this is best done as an analysis of change in specific industries, it is a "bottom up" approach in the sense that the total employment is derived as a summation of the individual industry projections. Techniques for industry employment projections are considered in the next section, below. Also, a detailed review of industry and occupational projection techniques is available in (49).

There are two reasons why the best projection procedures are those which combine the demographic (top down) and economic (bottom up) approaches. First is the issue of substitutability. If industry demands are separately projected, the capability of labor (and other factors) to shift from one industry to another tends to be ignored. For example, if some industry's past growth in an area is expected to slow down, will this slack be taken up by some other industry; would California, in other words, have grown almost as rapidly in the past decade even in the absence of a large defense budget? The answer is probably yes, since California would have adapted its resources to whatever national markets required. Conversely, if some industry's growth speeds up in an area, would this be in addition to the growth of other industries, or partly at their expense? For example, would industrialization in the Southeast have occurred at the same pace if agriculture had not been a declining employment industry? The answer is probably no, since adequate resources would probably not have been available. Thus the industry demand approach tends to assume that migration can provide whatever adjustments are required by the changing demands on the area.

But, this is possible only within limits, so that it is necessary to impose area-wide considerations on the separate industry demands, which in effect means that area-wide considerations will influence the changing level of specific industry demands. At the same time, if only area-wide considerations were applied—for example, only considerations of the natural increase in the labor force—then the role of migration would be underemphasized and industry demand would be too much responsive to only local factors. Two techniques have been suggested for integrating the demographic and economic approaches: to adopt an analytical process which feeds back between considerations of area size and structure; and to adopt an analytical process which feeds back between consideration of labor force supply and employment demand.

The second reason for wanting to combine the demographic and economic approaches relates to the kinds of detail required for planning. Although industry employment detail has some planning relevance (primarily as it relates to attempts to attract industry), public planning seems more concerned with estimates of the occupational, age, sex, and color distribution of the labor force, as they relate to issues of training, welfare, education, housing, etc. Partly because of data availability and partly because of firmer theoretical grounds, it seems easier to project industry employment directly than to project occupational employment directly. That is, it seems more reasonable to determine occupational requirements in an area on an industry-by-industry basis after having determined industry employment requirements, rather than doing the reverse. But industry employment estimates will provide very little "starting" information for projecting age, sex, and color, even though some industries can be distinguished by the extent to which they tend to employ selected age, sex, and color groups. Thus projections of the cohort groups must be approached with a heavy emphasis on the demographic aspect.

Apart from questions of relative emphasis, both planning requirements and projection reliability require that labor force and employment, area and industry, occupation and industry, cohort group and occupation—in short, people and economics—each be paired in the analysis of regional change.

175

Regional Industrial Activity Forecasting (56, 60, 61, 64, 67)

The core of most economic projection models is in their treatment of industrial activity. The measure of industrial activity is usually either output (net or gross) or employment. Whether the output or the employment measure is used seems to depend on issues of data availability, since conversion from one to the other can be accomplished by use of employment to output relationships.

In some simple models individual industries in a region are projected independently of their relationship to other industry activities in the region. In most models the interrelationship among industries is of vital importance. Even when considering a system of industries, however, it is usually necessary to emphasize some key sectors in the economy and then relate other sectors to developments in the key sectors. In the terminology previously used, the key sector analysis provides some measure of the scale or size the area is likely to be, while the analysis of the other sectors becomes the structural description of the area. The techniques for projecting key sectors are different from those for projecting related activities.

The key sectors will usually be those which include a relatively large share of the region's industrial activity, new industries or installations likely to generate a large volume of indirect effects, special industries such as defense, subject to non-market influences, and export industries (i.e., goods and services sold outside the region). Except for the export industry group, it is usually easy to identify a region's key sectors. However, export industries are difficult to identify because most industries will produce products for both local and non-local markets. Location quotients are sometimes used to obtain an indication of export sectors, but extreme care must be taken in the interpretation of whether or not a large location coefficient implies an export activity. Direct survey of enterprises and the Transportation Census commodity flow data are also sometimes used to identify export activities. In spite of the recognition of the need for improved empirical observations on export activities, most models that use an export procedure will identify commodity production as the critical export activity, and then modify this by some of the more obvious exceptions.

The key sector projections are usually made in micro terms, i.e., market studies of the industry. Sometimes the industry's activity in the nation (or some other "control" area) is projected and then the region's deviation from this change is determined. This deviation can be obtained by consideration of growth in the markets which the region is likely to serve, or consideration of comparative cost which will influence the opportunities that a region has to serve various markets.

Although specific consideration of comparative cost factors should be of great importance in industry studies, they are not generally introduced systematically. The reason for this is that there are usually a large number of areas which meet the necessary and sufficient conditions for a plant to newly locate or expand capacity, so that the actual location decision often hinges on marginal factors difficult to identify or generalize from. This situation is not improved by the paucity of regional information on investment, capital stock, and productivity.

Usually, therefore, key sector studies are market studies rather than comparative costs studies, where it is assumed that comparative costs among regions will, in the absence of some obvious information, change in about the same way as it has in the past. The differential shift approach to industry projection is conveniently used in this way—where the historical differential shift can be modified by ad hoc considerations incorporated in the projection model (21).

In determining the industrial repercussions on regional production of the key sector activity an "industry complex analysis" is often used, which determines the satellite or supplier industries that congregate near the key sectors for technological or other reasons. Or, more elaborately, an interindustry apparatus can be used for the same purpose.

However, more important than how satellite industries respond to the key sector changes is how the industries tending to serve the local population are related to the key sectors. The key sectors, of course, create employment, profits, household income, and public revenue, which are an important source of local demands, through a multiplier process. This process can be used to develop estimates of the local serving industries by a simple multiplier ratio; or estimation equations can be developed for each of the local industries separately, which will relate the industry's activity to, say, total income or total employment in the region. Conceptually, this presents no problem since the income generated by the local industries themselves can be solved in a simultaneous system with the income created by the key sectors and income earned from non-local sources. The difficulty arises because the parameters of the regression equations are likely to change over time as a result of relative changes in productivity and consumer purchase habits, as a result of changes in the size and density of a region, and as a result of changes in the extent to which local type goods and services are imported from outside the region.

Another difficulty is that some local population-serving industries seem to lead developments in export industries rather than the reverse. For example, changes in construction and finance-insurance activities seem to occur before changes in export activities. While these specific illustrations probably represent trivial statistical observations, a much more sophisticated understanding is needed of the process by which growth in industry employment (markets) attracts people who require services and facilities which induce further increases in appropriate supplies of labor and facilities that then attract further industrial capacities. The point is that even more than for national growth models, regional growth models inadequately describe the process of leads and lags which brings about economic change.

This is perhaps why the use of interindustry models in regional analysis does not seem to add much to our understanding, even though the models represent a significant data contribution. The use of linear programming models and gravity models (which usually deal with interindustry relations) do offer potential for increased understanding of the regional growth process, even though they operate under very severe constraints (65).

The role technology should play in making regional projections also deserves careful consideration. R&D activities, as an employer of high-income resources, are usually sought after. But does such activity improve the productivity of a region? Certainly, it develops and attracts a highly skilled labor force and to that extent improves productivity. On the other hand, probably more often than not, the technological improvements developed in one region have their major impact on production activities in other regions. It may be for this reason that technological improvements tend to be introduced into regional models as a nationwide phenomenon affecting national industries, while regional industry productivity improvements are then seen as deviations from the national industry trend.

Regional Income Forecasting (48, 51)

The simple procedure for projecting personal income in a region is to trend per capita income changes, usually in relation to national changes which would thereby build in over-all productivity improvements and increased government transfer payments.

Another aggregative approach can be adopted if there are regional net output projections available, since the major part of net output produced in a region is also a part of personal income received. The chief differences between output and income arise from the income earned by commuting labor, the net interregional flows of property income, and transfer payments by the federal government.[17] In order to obtain per-

[17] Personal income tends to be about 80 per cent of net output with a range among states of about 70 per cent to 90 per cent in 1960.

sonal income projections the relationship between personal income and net output can then be projected.

More reliable projections, as well as greater detail for planning purposes, will be provided if the industrial sources and components of personal income are analyzed separately. These detailed data have been available for states and are becoming available for metropolitan areas through the U.S. Department of Commerce. Labor and proprietor income (earned income) per employee in each industry can be calculated; allowance can be made for productivity improvements in each industry either by evaluating the regional industry trend or relating it to the national productivity projection; then the productivity improvement factor and an industry employment projection can be combined with the base-period earned-income-per-employee estimate to derive the labor component of income produced. An adjustment for labor commuting, which would be required for most metropolitan areas but only some states, would then have to be made to arrive at the labor component of income received.

Property income (interest, rents, dividends), although a small component of personal income, is most difficult to project because ownership is not geographically distributed in the same way as industry activity. This is reflected in the interstate variations in the ratio of property income to personal income, the high per capita income states tending to have a relatively high share. The most practical approach for projecting property income is to use these kinds of variations as the basis for judgments as to how the geographic distribution of property income is likely to differ from the geographic distribution of population or labor income.

Projection of the transfer payment component of personal income depends on expectations about the Federal government's policy with respect to raising average beneficiary payments particularly for social security and unemployment insurance. The best judgment in this area is probably that over the long run such increases will at least equal price-plus-productivity increases in the private economy. Area deviations from these national average beneficiary payments can then be calculated (probably on the basis of a more rapid rise for low-income areas) and applied to projected estimates of the number of beneficiaries, which can be largely estimated from demographic analyses.

Per capita income and total income projections by area are important to business planning, particularly in the context of marketing and plant location decisions. However, for public planning purposes projections of the household income distribution are important. This is not only because public revenues will vary with the income distribution as well as with total income, but more significantly because of the requirement to identify the need for public services by low-income groups.

Lack of data seriously limits the potential for income distribution analysis. The decennial census provides the only comprehensive set of information; the Bureau of Labor Statistics has recently begun to provide some annual data whose sample size seems too small as a basis for analysis; also, the Office of Economic Opportunity has sponsored some selected ad hoc studies concentrating on the lower end of the income spectrum.

In view of the data difficulties perhaps the best assumption is that the projected income-size distribution in an area has the same Lorenz curve as it had in the most recent census year. By this it is meant that the percentage of families at any given point in the income distribution in the base year is equal to the percentage at that point in the projected year times a constant, the constant being the ratio of average income per family in the base year to the average income in the projected year. General stability in an area's Lorenz curve is to some extent borne out by census data.

Stability in the Lorenz curve does not mean that the income distribution is the same among areas. There is some evidence that high-income areas and low-income areas tend to have a more unequal distribution than the middle-income areas—explained perhaps by the effect of property income on the income distribution. Also, there is some evidence that migration has an effect in making the income distribution look more alike among regions. If this is true, then it would seem that low-income migrants are improving their own economic position even though it results in a reduction of the average income in the area to which they move. Similarly it suggests that the "rich" areas are likely to continue to be faced with public budget problems at least as serious as those of "poor" areas.

SELECTED READINGS

(The references are grouped to conform with major sections of the paper. This grouping is often arbitrary since the reports cited will usually cover a wider range than suggested by some specific subject-matter heading.)

Allocation Perspective

1. Ashby, Lowell D. "Regional Change in a National Setting," *Staff Working Paper in Economics and Statistics, No. 7.* Washington: U.S. Department of Commerce, April 1964.
2. Chinitz, Benjamin. "The Regional Dimension of National Economic Growth." University of Pittsburgh, Center for Regional Economic Studies, April 1964.
3. Little, Arthur D., Inc. *Projective Economic Study of the Ohio River Basin,* Appendix B, Ohio River Basin Comprehensive Survey: prepared for the Corps of Engineers, U.S. Army Engineer Division, Ohio River. Washington: U.S. Government Printing Office, August 1964.
4. Mattila, John M. *A Study of Long-Run Regional Employment Growth,* Working Paper No. 10. Lansing, Michigan: State Resource Planning Program, Michigan Department of Commerce, December 1966.
5. National Planning Association, Center for Economic Projections, "Metropolitan Areas—Industry Employment in 224 Metropolitan Areas, Vol. I." *Regional Economic Projections Series,* Report No. 67-R-1, Washington, May 1967.
6. ————. "State Projections to 1975: Quantitative Analysis of Economic and Demographic Changes," *Regional Economic Projections Series,* Report No. 65-III. Washington, 1965.
7. Perloff, Harvey S. "Relative Regional Economic Growth: An Approach to Regional Accounts," *Design of Regional Accounts.* Baltimore: The Johns Hopkins Press, for Resources for the Future, Inc., 1961.
8. Suits, Daniel B. *Econometric Model of Michigan.* Research Seminar in Quantitative Economics, The University of Michigan, June 1965.

Location Perspective

9. Chinitz, Benjamin, and Raymond Vernon. "Changing Forces in Industrial Location," *Harvard Business Review.* Vol. 38, No. 1, January-February, 1960.
10. Eisenmenger, Robert W. *The Dynamics of Growth in New England's Economy, 1870–1964.* Middletown, Conn.: Wesleyan University Press, 1967.

181

11. Greenhut, M. L., and Marshall R. Colberg. *Factors in the Location of Florida Industry.* Tallahassee: Florida State University, 1962.

12. Perloff, Harvey S., and Lowdon Wingo, Jr. "Natural Resource Endowment and Regional Economic Growth," in Joseph Spengler (ed.), *Natural Resources and Economic Growth.* Washington: Resources for the Future, 1961.

13. Real Estate Research Program Staff. *Industrial Location Bibliography.* Los Angeles: University of California, Graduate School of Business Administration, July 1959.

14. Thompson, James H. "Methods of Plant Site Selection Available to Small Manufacturing Firms." Small Business Management Research Report, *West Virginia University Bulletin,* Series 62, September 1961.

15. Wonnacott, Ronald J. *Manufacturing Costs and the Comparative Advantage of United States Regions.* Upper Midwest Economic Study, Study Paper No. 9, Minneapolis: University of Minnesota, April 1963.

Trading Perspective

16. Arnold, Robert K., *et al. The California Economy, 1947–1980.* Menlo Park, Calif.: Stanford Research Institute, December 1960.

17. Berry, Brian J. L., and William L. Garrison. "The Functional Bases of the Central Place Hierarchy," in *Readings in Urban Geography,* ed. by Harold M. Mayer and Clyde F. Kohn. Chicago: University of Chicago Press, 1959.

18. Hamilton, H. R., *et al. A Dynamic Model of the Economy of the Susquehanna River Basin.* Columbus, Ohio: Battelle Memorial Institute, November 13, 1964.

19. Henderson, James M., and Anne O. Krueger. *National Growth and Economic Change in the Upper Midwest.* Minneapolis: The University of Minnesota Press, 1965.

20. Leontief, Wassily. "Multiregional Input-Output Analysis," in *Structural Interdependence and Economic Development.* New York: Macmillan and Co., 1963.

21. National Planning Association, Center for Economic Projections, "Economic Base Study, Upper Mississippi River Basin." Report to U.S. Army Corps of Engineers. Washington, 1967.

Stages Perspective

22. Ashby, Lowell D. *Regional Structural Displacement and Its Relation to Growth.* Washington: U.S. Department of Commerce, October 1963.

23. Berry, Brian J. L. "Cities as Systems Within Systems of Cities," in *Papers of the Regional Science Association,* Vol. 10, 1964.

24. Davis, Kingsley, and Eleanor Langlois. *Future Demographic Growth of the San Francisco Bay Area.* Berkeley: Institute of Governmental Studies, University of California, 1963.

25. Dunn, Edgar S., Jr. "The Transition and Stability Characteristics of U.S. Regions." Southern Economic Association Meeting, November 1965.

26. Graham, Robert E., Jr., and Edwin J. Coleman. *Personal Income in Metropolitan Areas: A New Series, Survey of Current Business.* Washington: U.S. Department of Commerce, Office of Business Economics, May 1967.

27. Lindley, Jonathan. "The Economic Environment and Urban Development," in *Proceedings of the Eighth Annual Conference of the Center for Economic Projections.* Washington: National Planning Association, 1967.

Impact-Multiplier and Interindustry Perspective

28. Berman, Barbara R., *et al. Projection of a Metropolis: Technical Supplement to the New York Metropolitan Region Study.* Cambridge: Harvard University Press, 1961.

29. Isard, Walter, and Eugene Smolensky. "Application of Input-Output Techniques to Regional Science," *Structural Interdependence and Economic Development,* Proceedings of the International Conference on Input-Output Techniques, Geneva, 1961. New York: St. Martin's Press, 1963.

30. Little, Arthur D., Inc. *The Metropolitan Stockton Economy: Analysis and Forecast.* Stockton, Calif.: Department of City Planning, 1964.

31. Leontief, Wassily, *et al.* "The Economic Impact—Industrial and Regional—of an Arms Cut," *Review of Economics and Statistics,* Vol. XLVII, No. 3, August 1965.

32. Moses, Leon N. "A General Equilibrium Model of Production, Interregional Trade and Location of Industry," *Review of Economics and Statistics,* Vol. 42, 1960.

33. Hochwald, W., S. Sonenblum, and H. E. Striner, *Local Impact of Foreign Trade.* Washington: National Planning Association, 1960.

34. Thomas, Morgan D. "The Export Base and Development Stages Theories of Regional Economic Growth: An Appraisal," *Land Economics,* Vol. XL, No. 4, November 1964.

35. Tiebout, Charles M. *The Community Economic Base Study,* Supplementary Paper No. 16. New York: Committee for Economic Development, 1962.

36. ———. "Community Income Multipliers: A Population Growth Model," *Journal of Regional Science,* Vol. II, Spring 1960.

37. Weiss, Steven, and Edwin C. Gooding. *Estimation of Differential Employment Multipliers in a Small Regional Economy,* Research Report to the Federal Reserve Bank of Boston, No. 37, November 1966.

Production-Function Perspective

38. Borts, George H. "The Estimation of Produced Income by State and Region," in *The Behavior of Income Shares. Studies in Income and*

Wealth, Vol. 27. National Bureau of Economic Research. Princeton: Princeton University Press, 1964.

39. Borts, G. H., and J. L. Stein. *Regional Growth and Maturity in the United States, A Study of Regional Structural Change.* Providence, R.I.: Brown University, 1962.

40. Hildebrand, George H., and Ta-Chung Liu. *Manufacturing Production Functions in the United States, 1957: An Interindustry and Interstate Comparison of Productivity.* Ithaca: New York State School of Industrial and Labor Relations, Cornell University, 1965.

41. Marcus, M. "Capital Labor Substitution Among States: Some Empirical Evidence," *Review of Economics and Statistics,* Vol. 46, No. 4, November 1964.

42. Nelson, Richard R. *Aggregate Production Functions and Medium-Range Growth Projections.* Santa Monica, Calif.: The RAND Corporation, December 1963.

43. Romans, Thomas J. *Capital Exports and Growth Among U.S. Regions.* Middletown, Conn.: Wesleyan University Press, 1965.

Defining Regions

44. Berry, Brian J. L. "An Inductive Approach to the Regionalization of Economic Development," *Papers and Proceedings of the Regional Science Association,* Vol. 6, 1960.

45. Bogue, Donald J. and Calvin L. Beale. *Economic Areas of the United States.* Glencoe: The Free Press, 1961.

46. Duncan, Otis D., *et al. Statistical Geography: Problems in Analyzing Area Data.* New York: The Free Press of Glencoe, 1961.

47. Gilpatrick, Eleanor. *Suggested Economic Regions in Illinois by County.* Springfield, Ill.: Division of State and Local Planning of the Board of Economic Development, March 12, 1965.

Selected Variables

48. Easterlin, R. A. "Long Term Regional Income Changes; Some Suggested Factors." *Papers and Proceedings of the Regional Science Association,* Vol. 4, 1958.

49. Fishman, Leslie, *et al. Methodology for Projection of Occupational Trends in the Denver Standard Metropolitan Statistical Area.* Boulder: Bureau of Economic Research, Institute of Behavioral Science, University of Colorado, March 1966.

50. Harms, Louis T., *et al. Projective Models of Employment by Industry and by Occupation for Small Areas: A Case Study.* Philadelphia: Temple University, March 1966.

51. Hochwald, Werner. *Interregional Income Flows and the South.* Chapel Hill: University of North Carolina Press. (Reprinted from *Essays in Southern Economic Development.*)

52. Lowry, Ira S. *Migration and Metropolitan Growth.* San Francisco: Chandler Publishing Co., 1966.

53. Olsson, Gunnar. *Distance and Human Interaction.* Philadelphia: Regional Science Research Institute, 1965.

54. U.S. Department of Commerce, Area Redevelopment Administration. *The Geographic Mobility of Labor: A Summary Report.* Washington: U.S. Government Printing Office, September 1964.

55. U.S. Department of Commerce, Bureau of the Census. "Illustrative Projections of the Population of States: 1970 to 1985," Population Estimates, *Current Population Reports,* Series P-25, No. 326. Washington: U.S. Government Printing Office, February 7, 1966.

General

56. Artle, Roland. "External Trade, Industrial Structure, Employment Mix, and the Distribution of Incomes: A Simple Model of Planning and Growth." Reprinted from *Swedish Journal of Economics,* February 1965.

57. Bauer, Raymond A., ed. *Social Indicators.* Cambridge: The M.I.T. Press, 1966.

58. Friedman, J., ed. *Journal of American Institute of Planners,* Vol. 30, No. 2, May 1964.

59. Hochwald, Werner, ed. *Design of Regional Accounts,* and Werner Hirsch, ed. *Regional Accounts for Policy Decisions.* The Johns Hopkins Press, for Resources for the Future, Inc., 1966.

60. Hoover, Edgar M. *Spatial Economies: The Partial Equilibrium Approach.* University of Pittsburgh, Center for Regional Economic Studies, May 1964.

61. Hoover, Edgar M., and Raymond Vernon. *Anatomy of a Metropolis.* Cambridge: Harvard University Press, 1959.

62. National Planning Association. "National Economic Projections to 1976/77," *National Economic Projections Series,* Report No.66-N-1. Washington: September 1966.

63. Perloff, Harvey S. *et al. Regions, Resources, and Economic Growth.* Baltimore: The Johns Hopkins Press for Resources for the Future, 1960.

64. Petersen, James W. *Regional Economic Forecasting: A Survey of Available Techniques.* Report prepared for the National Aeronautics and Space Administration under Contract Number NASW-1086, September 1964.

65. Spiegelman, R. G. *Review of Techniques of Regional Analysis.* Menlo Park, Calif.: Stanford Research Institute, June 1962.

66. Spiegelman, R. G., *et al. Application of Activity Analysis to Regional Development Planning: A Case Study of Economic Planning in Rural South Central Kentucky.* U.S. Department of Agriculture, Resource Development Economics Division, Economic Research Service, Technical Bulletin No. 1339. Washington: U.S. Government Printing Office, 1965.

67. U.S. Department of Commerce, Bureau of the Census. *Directory of Federal Statistics for Local Areas: A Guide to Sources 1966.* Washington: U.S. Government Printing Office, 1966.

*George J. Stolnitz**

THE CHANGING PROFILE OF OUR URBAN HUMAN RESOURCES

This paper has two main purposes: first, to review some salient features of the empirical backdrop against which our mounting national concern with urban population dynamics and human resources has been evolving, and, second, to review some leading needs and opportunities for advancing the economic theory of human resources. The emphasis in Section I is on historical perspectives in addition to immediate facts. A longer-run view is worth while both for its own sake and for helping us distinguish the relatively novel from the long-standing. "Jumps" in the trends have different implications for policy and research than do continuities. The general conclusion reached here is that the recent upsurge of attention to the population and human resource problems of the city bears no clear relation to the aggregate trends, whether these are regarded period by period or in terms of their cumulative effects. Rather, a greatly altered scale of political tolerances and a new depth of social aspirations seem at play. Structural problems of the urban labor force and population have assumed a prominence which an earlier era might have assigned to aggregative tendencies only.

Nor is it enough to equate urban structural issues with national ones on grounds of the sheer weight of urban numbers—some two-thirds to three-fourths of the national population, depending on definitions. The urban human resource problems now most in the public eye have their own distinctive character. Distinctions between the large city, smaller agglomerations, and the rural sector are often essential. Within the large urban or metropolitan community itself, internal distribution and population composition by race have become central occasions for policy and research attention alike. Almost certainly, such attention will be disproportionately concerned, relative to numbers, with the structurally underprivileged parts of the urban population and labor force, spatial location and race being especially prominent elements. A far more extensive review than the one attempted here would focus on central city and other parts of the metropolitan community, along with race, income, and employment, as a minimum set of orienting cross-classifications. Indeed, as suggested in Section II, an emerging economic theory of urban human resources might well have to include the neighborhood as a significant unit among its primary spatial variables.

* Professor of Economics, Indiana University.

Theoretical work by the economist has been laggard in the human resource field at the national level, and conspicuously so in urban matters. Nothing like an established subdiscipline of mainstream economic theory exists which might be recognized by its provision of tested relationships, established strategic variables, or basic parameters. We have mountains of data, innumerable cross-classifications, and a sophisticated statistical methodology for description and summarization. But we lack conceptual frameworks for shaping the data to deeper-reaching uses, say corresponding in scope and organizing power to the consumption function, multiplier-accelerator models, or balance-of-payments adjustment theory.

Not surprisingly, the converse is also largely true. The data that the theoretical economist is likely to require for his own special versions of growth and efficiency are typically lacking in the case of human resources. Neither the input nor output data needed to analyze alternative "production possibilities" for upgrading manpower development are known beyond the barest of indications. And until such data become available, cost-benefit approaches to the main problems of the city concerned with human resource development must remain largely stultified. Longitudinal forms of information, which alone would permit needed analytical approaches to problems of urban structural underemployment and its sociodemographic concomitants, are generously described as cursory. Our current research inadequacies in these regards are not only a matter of informational constraints but also of extremely limited models and conceptual tools.

The broad classes of theoretical research areas identified below have been selected with an eye to three main prerequisites: research viability, clear relation to the empirical or institutional facts as well as to pressing policy issues and, finally, close reciprocal linkages with mainstream economic theory. Just as trade or capital analysis contributes to and draws upon more general economic theory, so should an evolving human resource theory if it is to excite the interest of the next generation of economists.

That my attempt in these directions is tentative will be too obvious to merit elaboration. It will be enough if the discussion assists in hastening recognition of a long-standing gap in the capacity of economic theory to serve the pressing empirical problems of the day.

As final preliminary, it should be noted that the empirical part of the paper leads up to the theoretical in a number of ways. First, it suggests that many of our main current concerns with urban human resource questions reflect new political orientations to old problems. Our policy targets with respect to urban human resources and manpower in general, and their disadvantaged components in particular, have become much more demanding than they were only a decade ago. Most of Section II centers about the theme that an economic theory of human resources which is responsive to the facts and policy issues should be development- and micro-oriented simultaneously. Second and more specifically, the special problems of the Negro documented in Section I are presupposed in the section on dual-sector models in Section II. Third, the statistical definitions and limitations pointed up in the empirical context of Section I form a necessary backdrop for the references to new data needs for theoretical research, which are encountered throughout the last part of the paper.

I. THE URBAN POPULATION PROFILE:
SOME HISTORICAL PERSPECTIVES

The trends of the times are not always close guides to the issues of the day. Our recent upsurge of concern with human resource problems in the city may be clearly related to some of the main facts, but not to numerous others of comparable prominence. Many of the trends cited today as justifying or requiring new policies go back decades in time and some have actually slackened rather than become more pronounced during the last generation. The contributions of social and economic change to evolving political goals are never straightforward or complete, but I would venture that the origins of our current concern with urban human resource problems are as much in the political realm as in the socioeconomic: civil rights rather than income differences, the right to equal opportunity rather than lagging shifts in the occupational structure. If the gap between public aspirations and social attainment has been widening, the reasons seem to me to be found in an autonomous forward movement of our felt needs rather than in the novelty of the needs themselves.

The present review of the empirical setting of our urban human resource problems focuses on population and labor force. Income and poverty along with social-welfare issues as such are not treated since these are covered in other papers. Where longer-run series exist, much of the emphasis below is on variations in trends, their accelerations or decelerations, in addition to the trends themselves or current levels. This is particularly the case for a number of demographic characteristics.

A longer-run point of view seems to have been comparatively neglected in the study of urban populations and their human resource dynamics, perhaps because of rather severe limitations in the data. Thus long-run series of as primary a variable as total urban numbers are either difficult to obtain or to interpret, owing to variable statistical and political definitions. The most consistent series at hand on urban population and the one used below relies on a pre-1950 definition.[1]

The available series on metropolitan areas are perhaps even more difficult to handle, given the rising numbers of entire areas or county components that have become statistically eligible for metropolitan status over time. One can achieve geographic consistency in various ways, but none is entirely satisfactory. The series for 1960 metropolitan counties, used below, has decreasing metropolitan or urban relevance for earlier periods. An available alternative, the corresponding series for 1900 metropolitan counties, would be increasingly incomplete the more recent the decade.[2]

Turning from numbers to the components of population change, we again find formidable gaps and limitations. For intercensal years, owing to the absence of population estimates, only absolute numbers of births and deaths are available. Only at the time of the census can urban and metropolitan birth rates or other current fertility measures be documented with any degree of completeness. A similar situation holds for mortality, for the same reason.[3] The situation with respect to internal migration, the main determinant of growth in many individual areas, is still more ad hoc; even for census years, use of the existing data is beset by major gaps and definitional inadequacies.[4]

[1] The population difference under current and pre-1950 definitions came to 12–13 million in 1960, some 10 per cent of the census figure for that year. (U.S. Bureau of the Census, *U.S. Census of Population: 1960,* Vol. I, *Characteristics of the Population,* Part 1, U.S. Summary, 1964, Tables E and 3.) For 1950 the corresponding difference was 7–8 million as originally published and cited well into the subsequent decade (see, for example, Conrad Taeuber and Irene B. Taeuber, *The Changing Population of the United States* [Wiley, 1958], p. 118), but 6–7 million as revised in the 1960 census. (*U.S. Census of Population: 1960,* Vol. I, Table 3.)

Annexations, another factor clouding the use of urban definitions, become especially important both for interpreting over-all urban trends and for distinguishing between the central city and "ring" parts of metropolitan areas. In 1960, nearly 9 million persons were living in places annexed during the previous decade by incorporated places of 2,500 population or more as of 1950. The central cities of metropolitan areas accounted for somewhat over half of this number. (*Ibid.,* pp. xx–xxiv.)

[2] Moreover, however the question of counties might be resolved, the metropolitan community as defined statistically may contain both rural and urban parts outside its central city. Attempts have been made in the census since 1950 to document the "outside urban" part more closely under an "urbanized areas" concept. In 1960 the "outside urban" population came to 10–11 million, accounting for the bulk of the population difference cited earlier between the old and new definitions of "urban" (*ibid.,* Table E); most of this group consists of persons living in high-density, unincorporated residential clusters near central cities.

[3] U.S. Public Health Service, *Vital Statistics of the United States,* annual reports.

[4] See section on internal migration, below.

Total Numbers

The ambivalences suggested between current political goals centering on urban population and their relation to factual concomitants are perhaps nowhere more evident than in the trends of total numbers. Even by an earlier, relatively conservative definition of "urban," the U.S. population had reached a 50 per cent urban level by 1920. Moreover, each decade between 1900 and 1930 saw a greater rise in the per cent urban than has been true in either of the decades since 1940.[5] The upturn in the urban growth rate between the 1940's and 1950's (from about 21 to 25 per cent) marks no novel range of trend, therefore, though it is somewhat surprising in view of the saturation effects to be expected from our already high urban-to-total population ratio.

In terms of public and policy attention alike, the "crisis of our cities" has been mainly identified with the larger or largest agglomerations. Often the population growth or sheer size of such agglomerations, relative to the nation, is made to appear at the heart of the matter. "Crisis" interpretations are innumerable, of course, but at least this particular version ought to be quickly laid to rest.

Contrary to frequent opinion, the national percentage living in cities of more than a million population has been falling over the past generation; in 1960 it reached a level not encountered since 1920. Similarly, within the urban sector itself, the 1960 percentage of people living in cities of over 250,000 was less than in any census of this century.

Turning to growth patterns, these reveal corresponding discrepancies between public impression and statistical fact. It is true that urban population has grown at a more rapid rate than national numbers during each of the last two decades, but such differences were far higher in each decade between 1900 and 1930. Urban places of 250,000 or more grew at only half the over-all urban rate in the 1950's and three-quarters the latter rate in the 1940's; these mark a sharp reversal of the comparative rates since the turn of the century.

"Urban" to now has referred to the variable areas identified by a

---

[5] U.S. Bureau of the Census, *Population Trends in the United States: 1900 to 1960* (Technical Paper No. 10, by Irene B. Taeuber, 1964), Table 1.

The 1930's, a period best ignored as a depression "freak" for purposes of trend analysis, showed practically no rise. The series being discussed relate essentially to incorporated places of 2,500 population and over plus some high-density areas added under so-called "special rules." Partly because these data are so closely bound to incorporation definitions, the trends for metropolitan areas will also be discussed occasionally. Although these have their own limitations, being oriented about larger cities only, they do include urban-style residential concentrations in unincorporated places within metropolitan counties, in addition to their incorporated places.

uniform definition. As an alternative we may consider the counties identified as metropolitan in 1960, a geographically invariant set of areas but also one of diminishingly urban character on the whole as we move back in time. Despite these differences in definition, much the same patterns emerge. The aggregate population of the 1960 metropolitan counties reached the halfway mark relative to national numbers as far back as 1920, the corresponding percentages have increased steadily since 1900 (again excluding the 1930's) but have not accelerated, and the decennial growth rates during 1900–30 have tended to exceed those since 1940.[6]

A corollary growth process, the heavy concentration of national population growth within urban or metropolitan areas, again shows no novel recent tendencies when compared with earlier decades. In 1950–60 the urban sector (pre-1950 definition as before) accounted for nearly four-fifths of the national rise while the corresponding numbers for 1940–50 imply very nearly the same relative contribution, though considerably smaller in absolute amounts. The same order of contribution has again held for 1960–66, using the metropolitan counties reported for this period by the Bureau of the Census.[7] Nevertheless, such contributions are not outstandingly high compared with those of earlier decades, when the much lesser (relative or absolute) size of the urban sector might have been expected to depress its share in over-all growth. The recent urban-to-total ratios of growth in numbers are nearly matched or exceeded by the ratios in each decade between 1900 and 1930.[8] For the 1960 metropolitan counties, comparison of the de-

[6] *U.S. Census of Population: 1960,* Vol. I, Table 2.
The particular choice of metropolitan counties is of limited importance in these respects. For example, both the counties classified as metropolitan in 1950 and those so identified as of 1900 show higher decennial growth rates before 1930 than in the 1940's. (Conrad Taeuber and Irene B. Taeuber, *The Changing Population of the United States* [Wiley, 1958], Table 42.) As indicated earlier, no long-run series exists for the urban population defined according to the current definition.
The Northeast and North Central regions conform closely to the above national norms while the South and West deviate in several important ways, whether we consider the urban or metropolitan series.
[7] U.S. Bureau of the Census, *Current Population Reports,* Series P-20, No. 157 (December 16, 1966).
[8] *U.S. Census of Population: 1960,* Vol. I, Table 1.
Since the 1950–60 urban population rise under current definitions exceeded the total national rise, the conclusions of this paragraph may be misleading. I am unable to judge what a long-term, "current definition" series would show if one could be estimated. Possibly, if the facts were known, the patterns just cited might have to be interpreted more conservatively, as referring to the urban sector less some of its most recently settled parts.

cennial contributions to national growth between 1940–60 and 1910–30 lead to a similar conclusion. The 1900–10 contribution was a good deal lower, but even then amounted to about three-fifths.

Here again total numbers alone—at least some of the most important ones—do not explain in any clearcut fashion our current alarmed sense of urban issues. Other possible bearings of urban population dynamics on our accelerating concern with the city are considered next. These center about compositional rather than aggregative demographic elements, starting with the internal spatial distribution of the urban population and proceeding to its associated variations by race.

Internal Distribution

Postwar suburbanization tendencies, a second leading theme in the recent rapid rise of public attention to urban problems, are also viewed usefully in historical terms.[9] It is true that some of the main issues arousing concern appear at first glance only to be underscored by a longer-run view. Between 1900 and the interwar years the central-city component of the 1960 metropolitan counties accounted for a slowly rising proportion of their total population, one which reached approximately two-thirds at its peak. In contrast, the proportion since 1940 has declined at an accelerating rate, to little more than 50 per cent in 1960 and about 47 per cent in early 1966.[10] Similarly with respect to growth rates, where the central-city component of today's metropolitan areas grew more rapidly than their ring component between 1900 and 1920, the situation reversed itself sharply thereafter.

Today the cumulative effects of these reversals have reached the point where, but for annexations, central cities in the aggregate face early population declines. Although such cities grew by about 10 per cent during the 1950's, compared with nearly 50 per cent for the remaining parts of the metropolitan areas, the corresponding percentage rates with annexation effects excluded would have been under 2 and over 60, respectively.[11] The 1960–66 growth of central cities, reported by the Bureau of the Census in a recent survey, was only 2 per cent,

[9] For useful discussions of relevant concepts and their relation to the available statistics, see Otis D. Duncan and Albert J. Reiss, Jr., *Social Characteristics of Urban and Rural Communities, 1950* (Wiley, 1956), pp. 5–8, 117–19; *The Changing Population of the United States*, pp. 118–20; and *U.S. Census of Population: 1960*, Vol. I, especially pp. xviii–xx, xxii–xxiii, xxvi–xxvii, xxix–xxxv.

[10] *Population Trends in the United States: 1900 to 1960*, Table 2; *Current Population Reports, Series P-20*, No. 157.

[11] *U.S. Census of Population: 1960*, Vol. I, Table Q.

and allowance for annexations might well convert the apparent increase into a decline.[12]

If the force of these trends seems clear enough, their usefulness as indicators of recent versus earlier rates of suburbanization is not. In particular, dividing the metropolitan area into only two parts—central city and other—may be too crude for adequate interpretation. If we consider the so-called urban and rural parts of metropolitan areas outside their central cities, we find that the population growth problems associated with rapid suburbanization—far from being a new major phenomenon—have been with us on a large and mounting scale for over a half-century. Data available for the 1950 metropolitan counties show that their "outside urban" parts grew much more rapidly in numbers than either their central cities or rural parts during every decade between 1900 and 1930.[13] The fact that, since 1930, the so-called rural parts of metropolitan areas took the lead in growth rates appears to signal mainly a longer-distance aspect of more recent suburbanization phenomena rather than the birth of a new kind of trend.[14]

Viewed in this light, the fiscal and service burdens which rapid suburbanization places on the central city are seen to be much more a chronic or secular problem than a sudden occasion for municipal crisis. It is possible, of course, that the process of cumulative suburbanization has reached a critical threshold level fairly recently, but if this is the case it would be extremely useful to see the proposition verified.

The seeming newness of mass suburbanization tendencies should perhaps be qualified in another respect, though it would be difficult to document the point statistically. Residential moves to the outlying parts of the central city rather than across its boundaries must have taken place on a substantial scale in earlier decades. It also seems likely that such moves tended to be "suburb-seeking" much as now. For academic and perhaps policy purposes, it would be useful to know the extent to which these earlier forms of suburbanization phenomena reflected ethnic differences or "social distance" between movers and non-movers.

[12] *Current Population Reports,* Series P-20, No. 157.
Essentially the same growth-rate comparisons to at least the 1950's would appear to hold if we used either the 1950 or 1900 metropolitan counties. (*The Changing Population of the United States,* Table 42.)
[13] *Ibid.*
[14] A partial check on this interpretation is provided by the relatively long-settled metropolitan areas as of 1900, which show the same patterns. (*Ibid.*)

Race

Compared with any of the population trends considered previously, the changing color composition of our urban and metropolitan areas gives the greatest sign of deviating from the past. Between 1960 and 1966, possibly for the first time over a period of this length, the central cities of metropolitan areas experienced a decline in absolute size of their white population—somewhat more than a million persons or over 2 per cent.[15] Even here, however, some historical perspectives are useful. An absolute decline, though dramatic, may have been long foreshadowed by the trends, while other parts of the picture are by no means straightforward or in line with prevailing impressions.

Among the 1960 metropolitan counties as a whole, the ratio of Negro to total population moved irregularly and within a narrow range between 1900 and 1930, being practically the same at the end of the period as at the start. Although the ratio has increased in every census since 1930, the largest decennial rise has only been some 1.5 percentage points, and this occurred during the war decade of the 1940's rather than in the 1950's. The same maximum may also exceed the upward shift of the 1960's, according to current rates of change.[16] Moreover, the percentage that is Negro living in the parts of (1960) metropolitan counties outside their central cities has also moved upward historically, both in the 1900–20 and the 1940–60 periods. The 1920–30 rise exceeded the 1940–60 uptrend, though it may recently have been equaled by the 1940–66 increase.

For a sense of "something strikingly new," therefore, we have to look at the central city. Although the percentage that is Negro here has not only been increasing but as a rule accelerating since the early part of this century, the pace of the acceleration would have been difficult to foretell in 1940. The 1940–50 change in percentage was over three times the largest shift of any earlier decade since 1900, and the 1950–60 rise exceeded the 1940–50 increase by about one-third.[17] Ironically, the recent decline of white population in central cities may have been associated with a halt to the historical acceleration of their percentage Negro; since 1960 the latter has risen at about the same decennial rate as in the 1950's.

[15] *Current Population Reports,* Series P-20, No. 157.

[16] *Population Trends in the United States: 1900 to 1960,* Table 2; *Current Population Reports,* Series P-20, No. 157. The available statistics on race sometimes refer to Negroes and sometimes to the non-white population, a distinction which can be overlooked for present purposes. Nationally, Negroes constituted over 90 per cent of the non-white population in 1960. The distinction might be essential for some regions, however; in the western states Negroes were less numerous than other non-whites.

[17] *The Changing Population of the United States,* Table 2.

The growth-rate analogues of these trends provide their own mixture of long-run stabilities and reversals. Again taking the 1960 metropolitan areas as a whole, the ratio of Negro to white rates of growth moved from about two-thirds in 1900–10 to equality during the following decade. Since then the ratio has varied between about 1.5 to somewhat over 2. Although the ratio for the 1950's was not far above that for a generation earlier, the 1960–66 ratio has been the highest on record during this century, about 2.3. As a result, the metropolitan component of the national Negro population has just gone over the two-thirds mark, somewhat above the corresponding proportion for whites.[18]

Outside the central city the Negro growth rate between 1900 and 1960 not only tended to increase over time but in relation to the white rate. Neither of these points has received its due attention, possibly because there has been a marked slackening in both respects since 1960. The 1960–66 growth rate for Negroes has been well under half the corresponding changes of the previous two decades and also far below the ratio-to-white levels of that period. It would be important to know whether the recent slowdown stems mainly from the urban or the rural parts of metropolitan areas outside their central cities. If the former or urban component is involved, the slowdown could indicate that policies attempting to equalize Negro housing opportunities throughout the metropolitan community are encountering new ranges of obstacles. A reduced growth rate in the rural part could have an almost opposite meaning, possibly that the Negro is more able than in the past to depart for places of residence he prefers.

Finally, within the central city itself the recent decline of the white population has been a fairly straightforward extension of trends already well under way decades earlier. If we again exclude the unique 1930's, the decennial growth rate for whites has been falling sharply throughout this century, from about a one-third level in 1900–10 to one-fourth in the 1920's, one-tenth in the 1940's and half this or about one-twentieth in the 1950's. Similarly the high growth rate of central-city Negroes in recent years, some 40 per cent on a decennial basis since 1960, is well in line with historical tendencies. Rates of this magnitude or more were the rule not only in 1940–60 but also much earlier, in 1910–30. The rate for 1900–10 was only somewhat smaller, about one-third.

In short, not all but many of the main recent trends relating to the color composition of our metropolitan areas are nothing new. The

---

[18] For urban areas (current definition) the recent fractions are higher but in the same direction, nearly 75 per cent for Negroes and 70 per cent for whites in 1960. (*Population Trends in the United States: 1900 to 1960*, Table 3.)

trends often preserve the direction and even the magnitudes of processes set in motion decades ago. Their heightened reflection in recent policies is perhaps more a kind of threshold effect, determined by the weight of current numbers, than a matter of their pace as such.

A closer look at this hypothesis would require review of the patterns by region and, perhaps even more, by individual cities. Over 90 per cent of the Negro populations in the Northeast, North Central and West groups of states were concentrated in metropolitan areas in 1960, compared with under 50 per cent in the South.[19] Among the ten largest cities the Negro accounted for about 15 per cent of total population in two instances (New York and Los Angeles) and from nearly 25 to over 50 per cent in the other eight. The extent to which our big-city human resource problems revolve about the Negro can be initially gauged by these facts, provided a generous additional allowance is made for the factor of disadvantaged status. And, conversely, the extent to which our main Negro human resource issues nationally are big-city problems can be underscored by the recognition that one-third of the Negro population lives in our twenty-five largest cities and over half in the central cities of metropolitan areas.[20]

Internal Migration

Consistent time series of internal migration patterns involving urban or metropolitan areas are almost impossible to obtain. The census first included a question on recent migration in 1940, shifted its definition of "recent" in 1950, and returned to its original definition in 1960.[21] In principle, the primary data could be used to document movements between individual pairs of small areas such as individual counties. In practice, nearly all of the available census tabulations indicate previous residence by "Yes–No" types of categories only, such as same or

[19] *Ibid.*, Table 2.
[20] Ben J. Wattenberg with Richard M. Scammon, *This U.S.A.* (Doubleday, 1965), pp. 271–73.
[21] The 1940 and 1960 questions related to residence five years earlier, the 1950 question to one year earlier. The much longer census series available on lifetime migration involve state of birth as minimum spatial units, hence provide urban information only for current residence.
As illustrations of these sources, using 1960 data, about half the population over 5 living in cities of 250,000 or more had resided in the same house in 1955, another third had changed residence within the same county, 5 per cent had come from another county in the same state, and somewhat under 10 per cent had come from another state. Of the total population in the same group of cities, between 50 and 60 per cent were born in the same state, one-quarter were born in another state and one-tenth were foreign born. (*U.S. Census of Population: 1960*, Vol. I, Tables 304 and 305.) Statistics analogous to these are published for a large variety of areas of current residence.

different house, county, state, or larger region. Short of going back to unpublished sources, therefore, the metropolitan–non-metropolitan origins of migrants can be only partly identified. Even less can be ascertained about the urban-rural status of previous residence. All of these statistical problems surrounding migration proper become amplified in time series analysis by the further factor of variable urban and metropolitan area definitions.

A notable attempt to overcome a number of these limitations has been made by Ann R. Miller in a study of all metropolitan areas with cities of 250,000 or more population in 1960.[22] The study provides estimates of decennial net migration—by sex, age, color, nativity and individual area—for each decade between 1930 and 1960, using 1960 metropolitan counties throughout. For both 1940–50 and 1950–60, corresponding estimates are also given for the central-city and "ring" parts of each area, with the effects of changing central-city boundaries removed. The study areas combined contained about four-fifths of the national metropolitan population and half of the total population in 1960. Because a survival method of estimation was employed, the net migration measures all relate to persons aged ten and over at the end of each decade.

Miller's findings are quite possibly the first longer-run migration series in depth for a well-defined, large set of U.S. metropolitan or other urban areas. They suggest that 7 to 8 million white persons in net migrated to the cited areas over the entire three-decade period. About half as many Negroes were similarly involved, a far higher proportion in relative terms. The former movements accounted for about one-quarter of the total rise in the white population of the study areas during the depressed 1930's, three-fifths in the 1940's and two-fifths in the 1950's. For Negroes the corresponding contributions were about six-sevenths in the first two decades and two-thirds in the last. By far the largest rates of migration were in the young adult ages of twenty to thirty-five, a standard result which in this case helps explain the drop in the relative importance of net migration between the last two decades. Miller traces this drop in good part to the declining national number of young adults during the 1950's, the outcome of low birth rates during the 1930's. To an extent, therefore, the drop can be attributed to national "population supply" factors rather than to the changing "demand" or attractiveness of the areas for newcomers.

The data also serve to bring out the very sharp internal-migration

[22] Ann R. Miller, *Net Intercensal Migration to Large Urban Areas of the United States: 1930–40, 1940–50, 1950–60,* Analysis and Technical Reports No. 4 (University of Pennsylvania Population Studies Center, 1964).

contrasts between the central cities and rings of large metropolitan areas since 1950. The combined central cities under study tended to contribute almost as much to the heavy net in-migration of their rings through their own net out-migration as did the "rest of the world" combined, assuming that those leaving the central city went to the suburbs of the same metropolitan area in the main. No doubt something like this was the case in fact, but here again, as with so many internal-migration issues, origins information would be needed to answer the question decisively. What does seem clear is that the internal-migration feedbacks between central cities and rings changed drastically about 1950. Miller's estimates for the 1940's show a small net inflow for the cities compared with a net outflow some ten times larger during the 1950's, along with a volume of net in-migration for rings about half that of the following decade. These marked compositional variations were accompanied by approximately equal volumes of net in-migration for the metropolitan areas as a whole during the last two decades.[23]

The differences by race revealed by the data are equally noteworthy. For whites, the aggregate migration loss from central cities during the 1950's was over half the gain in the rings, hence also exceeded the net gain for the metropolitan areas as a whole. For Negroes, both central cities and rings show a gain in the aggregate, the former by over a three-to-one margin. An analogous pattern of net internal counter-movements again occurred in the 1940's within large metropolitan areas, on a much smaller numerical scale for whites and in approximately the same numbers for Negroes.

These last patterns suggest a more general point. Since internal migration tends to be much like an iceberg phenomenon, with net magnitudes typically constituting limited fractions of total movements, documentation of its underlying structure requires an extended statistical framework. Not only are the magnitudes of in- and out-movements important for many purposes, but also their determinants often appear to require separate systems of interpretation.[24] Origin-destination or "from-to" matrices are needed to portray such two-way population flows, both among and within individual metropolitan areas (or groups of areas) as well as between metropolitan and non-metropolitan sectors. Although some of the basic data required for such matrices already exist, very little work has been undertaken in this direction.

Turning from the finer structure of migration movements to more aggregative effects, the contribution of net migration to total metropolitan area growth in the United States appears to have been diminishing

[23] *Ibid.*, Tables 10, 11.
[24] Ira S. Lowry, *Migration and Metropolitan Growth* (Chandler, 1966).

rapidly in recent decades. The decline of the contribution between the 1940's and 1950's, from over two-fifths to one-third for all metropolitan counties combined, may be attributed in good part to the special war-time circumstances of the earlier decade.[25] But the same trend has apparently also continued or even accelerated in the 1960's. According to as yet unpublished estimates by the Bureau of the Census, net internal migration to metropolitan areas (defined as of beginning 1967) accounted for little more than one-fifth of their aggregate population change during 1960–65.

Moreover the absolute volume of such migration has also declined substantially. To rough orders of magnitude, the 1960–65 total is about one-third of the volume for 1940–50 and closer to one-fourth that for 1950–60. Preliminary indications are that the slowdown has been especially marked in the metropolitan areas of industrial regions and states. The possible effects of the slowdown on the internal distribution and racial composition of the metropolitan community are still to be documented and may not be known until the 1970 census is completed.

Mortality and Fertility

The sharp uptrend since the war of the natural-increase component (births minus deaths) of metropolitan population growth is demonstrated by the downtrend of its complement, the net-migration component, as just discussed.

With respect to the underlying mortality and fertility patterns themselves, it is necessary to be brief. The problems of limited data and variable area definitions cited earlier would make the reconstruction of meaningful long-run series a formidable undertaking at best; such information does not, in fact, exist. And even for recent periods a variety of limitations in the data makes over-all summary in depth hazardous.[26] Rather than attempt any original or extensive elaboration of the data, it is best to stick to a few highlights.

[25] U.S. Bureau of the Census, *Current Population Reports,* Series P-23, No. 7 (November 1962), Tables 2, 6.

[26] In the case of mortality, for example, the first life tables ever prepared for metropolitan and non-metropolitan areas cover the period 1959–61 and await future publication. The closest analogues to be found in the past are the urban-rural life tables for 1939, published almost a quarter-century ago. Statistics on crude death rates for urban or metropolitan areas are only somewhat more available, as a rule for census years alone, and are of limited value for comparative purposes. Such rates may be greatly affected by age composition, thereby distorting the way in which they summarize mortality proper. Thus, in 1960 the crude rate for metropolitan areas was about 7 per cent lower than the rate for non-metropolitan areas. After adjustment for variable age composition (using the 1940 national age distribution for both areas, the conventional procedure utilized today in government statistics) the rates fall by under 20 and

One is that it is often important to distinguish carefully between urban-rural and metropolitan–non-metropolitan differences in studying their demographic patterns. Thus, rural mortality today continues to be significantly lower than urban mortality, as apparently has held true since the beginning of vital records in this country. For recent years the same point can also be documented within the urban and rural parts of metropolitan and non-metropolitan areas alike. In both groups of areas the rural component shows consistently lower death rates than the urban, as well as lower infant mortality.[27] As a further indication, estimates of 1960 age-adjusted (standardized) death rates show that the rate for metropolitan counties containing central cities was 10 per cent higher than the rate for other metropolitan counties.[28]

In contrast, at least in recent years, mortality in the metropolitan sector as a whole (which includes a sizable rural component) and the non-metropolitan sector (with an even larger urban component) appears to be nearly the same. Age-adjusted death rates for 1960 are practically identical in both groups of areas, by sex and color as well as for the total population. Unadjusted rates for 1950 again indicate a near equality, though these may be somewhat biased by age-composition factors in favor of the metropolitan sector.[29]

The need for a similar urban-metropolitan distinction is again evident in examining fertility. Rural-urban differences in fertility have been high historically and remain so today, as indicated by any of numerous measures.[30] On the other hand, the analogous metropolitan–non-met-

---

over 25 per cent, respectively, to the point where the metropolitan rate becomes higher, by 4 per cent. A main virtue of the life table is that it avoids such distortions.

Fertility statistics present analogous or other difficulties. Crude birth rates for urban or metropolitan areas are similarly infrequent and entail their own scale of distortions in comparisons. More refined measures of fertility, on the other hand, often differ in areas covered (more frequently urban-rural areas in previous periods and metropolitan–non-metropolitan areas in recent years) or in nature (general and total fertility rates, gross and net reproduction rates, children ever born per woman or ever-married woman in any of various reproductive age groups, child-woman ratios with similar variability in the age intervals utilized), depending on the source.

[27] U.S. Public Health Service, *Vital Statistics of the United States: 1960,* Vol. II, *Part A—Mortality,* 1963, Table 1-0; U.S. Public Health Service, *Infant Fetal, and Maternal Mortality: United States—1963,* Series 20, No. 3 (September 1966), Table 11.

[28] References in this section to standardized death rates are from data kindly provided by the National Center for Health Statistics.

[29] *Vital Statistics of the United States: 1960,* Vol. II, Table 1-N.

[30] *U.S. Census of Population: 1960,* Vol. I, Table 81; *The Changing Population of the United States,* pp. 250–53, 262–63; Wilson H. Grabill, Clyde V. Kiser, and Pascal K. Whelpton, *The Fertility of American Women* (Wiley, 1958), Tables 7, 23.

ropolitan differences are found to be considerably smaller as a rule—
well under 10 per cent in the case of some measures though higher
for others—during the relatively recent period for which official statistics are available.[31]

In short, there is no simple way of splicing past urban-rural fertility
measures with the metropolitan–non-metropolitan data being increasingly emphasized by the national vital statistics system. The great value
of metropolitan area units for analytical purposes does not include as
yet the power to discriminate closely among urban style-of-life factors
affecting fertility. Pending a major-scale reconstruction of consistent
series, the "urban" economist or demographer must continue to make
shift with distressingly diffuse and erratic combinations of basic materials.

A second key generalization concerns the much higher mortality and
fertility of Negroes compared with whites. The very large declines of
Negro-white differences in national life expectancy over the past half-
century make it clear that mortality differences in urban and metropolitan areas must also have come down sharply. Nevertheless, the
differences in these areas remain substantial, as they do nationally.
With age composition held constant, the metropolitan death rate in
1960 for Negroes was about 40 per cent higher than for whites,[32] while
Negro infant mortality was approximately twice that for whites in
metropolitan and urban areas alike.[33] The difference in life expectancy,
a much more conservative measure in making proportionate comparisons, may have come to about 10 per cent. Moreover, as Rashi Fein
points out with respect to national trends, the declines of Negro mortality in recent periods have been slower in some respects than the
corresponding earlier declines among whites.[34]

The corresponding fertility comparisons tend to be more stable, in
view of the larger absolute values of the measures involved.[35] Never-

[31] U.S. Public Health Service, *Natality Statistics Analysis: United States—
1964*, Series 21, No. 11 (February 1967), pp. 20–22; U.S. Public Health
Service, *Vital Statistics of the United States: 1960*, Vol. I, *Natality*, pp. 1–15
and Table 1-AD.

[32] Here again, crude death rates are of little use for purposes of cross-sectional
comparisons. The 1960 Negro crude rate was only slightly above that for whites
in metropolitan areas and no higher in urban areas. Since the crude-rate differences in 1950 were rather substantial, however, their near-disappearance by
1960 suggests that a significant degree of convergence would be found if more
precise measures were available for both of these years.

[33] U.S. Public Health Service, *Infant, Fetal, and Maternal Mortality: United
States—1963*, Table 11.

[34] Rashi Fein, "An Economic and Social Profile of the Negro American,"
Daedalus, Vol. 94, No. 4 (Fall 1965).

[35] George J. Stolnitz, "Uses of Crude Vital Rates in the Analysis of Repro-

theless, they are equally or even more striking. Nationally, Negro fertility has shown the same broad temporal swings over the past half-century as is found for whites, while remaining consistently at higher to much higher levels.[36] In 1960 the metropolitan difference in current fertility rates between whites and non-whites was of an order of magnitude of one-third.[37] Since metropolitan and national measures are not far apart for either group, the national (and non-metropolitan) differences were similar.

The continuing high fertility of the American Negro in the city (and nationally) has far-reaching implications. Not only does the Negro family face lower income and employment chances than does the general population, but it also has more mouths to feed. And not only do deep-seated forces of family and social disorganization beset the Negro today and foreseeably, but the fact that so large a part of his number is especially vulnerable to the intergenerational effects of such forces clouds his future further. Implicitly or explicitly, the consequences of these demographic factors permeate much of the subject matter of this volume.

Labor Force

Although American labor-force statistics today rank with the very best in the world, the student of the urban sector faces numerous and often overwhelming data limitations. Even for the country as a whole, current definitions for the main manpower categories date back only to 1940 while series for many subgroups of major interest, in particular the structurally disadvantaged or "special problem" parts of the work force, tend to be much more recent. The excellent monthly surveys of the national labor force are apparently too small for providing urban-rural or metropolitan–non-metropolitan data; in any event such information is not published. Supplementary surveys, designed to document subgroups of special interest, are being taken on a rapidly expanding scale, but here again for national or broad regional areas rather than for urban-metropolitan categories. As a rule, too, the larger the size of survey and the greater its potential usefulness for disaggregation, the longer is the period before results become known. All of the non-census series which can be applied at subnational levels of investigation are either seriously incomplete in scope or serve spe-

---

ductivity," *Journal of the American Statistical Association,* Vol. 50 (December 1955).

[36] *Natality Statistics Analysis: United States—1964,* pp. 11–13; *Vital Statistics of the United States: 1960,* Vol. I, pp. 1–3, Tables 1-A–1-F; *U.S. Census of Population: 1960,* Vol. I, Table 81.

[37] *Vital Statistics of the United States: 1960,* Vol. I, Table 1-AD.

cial administrative purposes; none provides more than extremely limited information on personal characteristics.[38]

In short, to treat the American urban or metropolitan labor force with any adequate attention to completeness or socioeconomic depth, it is still necessary to await the decennial census. If we further consider the changing census definitions of "urban" or the variable inclusiveness over time of "metropolitan areas," we find that little of a consistent over-all nature can be said about any period before 1950 or even 1960 in many instances. Retrospective reconstruction of some major aggregate series is possible to an extent, say for the 1960 metropolitan counties since 1940, but such has apparently not been undertaken or at least published. Accordingly, the discussion here is essentially concerned with some main census-documented changes since 1950.

Participation Rates. In 1960 the urban labor force came to 51 million, a participation rate of 57 per cent relative to the urban population aged 14 and over and one higher by some 2 percentage points than both the 1960 national rate and the 1950 urban rate.[39] In both 1960

---

[38] The main examples are the Bureau of Labor Statistics series on employment and earnings, the Bureau of Employment Security series on the insured unemployed, and the labor-market area surveys conducted by the latter agency. In the case of the first, a valuable long-term compilation is now available on numbers by industry for state and metropolitan areas, but the task of converting these to meaningful rates remains to be done. No information is provided on sex-age-color components. (U.S. Bureau of Labor Statistics, *Employment and Earnings Statistics for States and Areas 1939–65*, Bulletin 1370–3, June 1966.) The insured unemployed series covers industry and state categories only, with no urban or metropolitan information and again with no demographic detail for any area. The labor-market area surveys, which are taken on a regular basis for standard metropolitan areas or for smaller areas with an urban core, constitute the most current information we have of any kind for something like a nationwide urban sector. The data from this source are too partial in scope and coverage, however, to warrant discussion here. (U.S. Bureau of Employment Security, *Area Trends in Employment and Unemployment*, monthly reports.)

[39] U.S. Bureau of the Census, *U.S. Census of Population: 1950*, Vol. II, *Characteristics of the Population*, Part 1, U.S. Summary, 1953, Table 50; *U.S. Census of Population: 1960*, Vol. I, Table 82.

The actual urban uptrend may have been somewhat larger with area held more constant. It is curious in this connection that at least the 1960 census volumes do not show a single table with comparative 1950 and 1960 data for the urban labor force; every table presenting urban-rural classifications is for 1960 only and every table giving time-series information is for area categories other than urban-rural. The same seems also to have been true of the 1950 publications.

The 1960 census count of labor force in metropolitan areas was lower by about 5 million than that for urban areas, but with very nearly the same aggregate participation rate (higher for males and lower for females by about one-half percentage point) and with a practically identical unemployment rate and 1950, urban rates exceeded national levels for each of the four sex-color groups.

As a result the dependency ratio (persons not in the labor force relative to labor force) has been perceptibly lower for the urban population than in the nation, in rounded terms about 1.45 and 1.55, respectively, for 1960. The corresponding differential for non-whites was twice as large, 1.55 compared with 1.75, or a difference of 0.20 compared with 0.10.

The white–non-white comparisons indicated by these figures mark a major point of impact of the fertility differences noted earlier. Moreover, the contrasts (and implicit social-welfare problems they reflect) would be far sharper if meaningful comparisons of dependency could be documented by sex. The above white–non-white differences in dependency ratios would be significantly larger but for the very high participation rate of non-white working mothers with young children. Among urban women with own children under six, the percentage in the labor force was only twenty for whites compared with over thirty-five for non-whites.[40] The Negro woman faced with a possible conflict between economic necessity and child-care responsibilities is about twice as likely as the white woman to resolve it in favor of the former.

All of the intercensal 1950–60 rise in the over-all urban participation rate was the result of entry of females into the labor force. While the rates for urban males (both white and non-white) declined, those for females increased and by substantially larger margins. Nevertheless, females contributed less to labor-force growth in the city than in the national economy. Although they comprised about one-third of the total labor force at both national and urban levels as of 1960, they accounted for somewhat under half of the urban growth in labor force during 1950–60 compared with three-fifths nationally.[41]

The 1950–60 increase of urban labor force accounted for all of the national rise, not only for combined races but also among non-whites alone. The contribution of non-whites to growth of total urban labor force came to about one-sixth, or far above their relative size (roughly 10 per cent) in either year.

Occupation. The data on this subject, although voluminous, provide a classic illustration of many of the statistical limitations cited earlier and of the scale of efforts needed to overcome them. Urban occupa-

---

(*ibid.,* Table 101). Since the data for urban areas are somewhat more convenient and detailed (for example by color) as well as more meaningful for 1950–60 comparisons, they will be used in most of this section.

[40] *Ibid.,* Table 82.

[41] *Ibid.; U.S. Census of Population: 1950,* Table 50.

tional patterns by sex can be documented adequately from a number of recent censuses, but only for 1960 by color as well. The valuable historical series for 1900–50 reconstructed by Kaplan and Casey[42] provides an added measure of intertemporal consistency compared with the original census data but are national only, continue to reflect some major differences in census definitions over time, and contain no information by age or color. With respect to metropolitan areas, many of the main tabulations for 1960 are essentially starting points of series still to develop in the future.[43]

For these reasons and for brevity, it is best to focus the present discussion on white-collar differentials by color and sex. Not only can many of the leading recent tendencies and policy issues surrounding urban occupational patterns be handled in this manner, but it is also possible to do so without undue attention to details.

The 1960 urban percentage of white-collar workers in the employed labor force exceeded the national percentage by somewhat over 5 points for males and 3 for females. For males this represented a marked decline from the 1950 differential of some 8 points; for females the direction of change was similar but its magnitude minimal, a drop in differential of less than a single point.[44]

Despite rather widespread impressions to the contrary, the urban percentage in white-collar occupations appears to have risen slowly during the 1950's, not much above one point for either sex. The main source of the increase for males was in the "professional, technical, and kindred workers" classification, and for females in the "clerical" category. The other two white-collar categories ("managers, officials, and proprietors excluding farm" and "sales workers") tended to show small increases or declines for both sexes. Unfortunately, there is no reliable way of gauging urban changes since 1960 from the available national trends, given the possibility of shifting urban-national differentials for either or both sexes.[45]

The broad issue of white-collar differentials between whites and nonwhites encompasses many of the details of our rapidly changing policy

[42] U.S. Bureau of the Census, *Occupational Trends in the United States: 1900 to 1950* (Working Paper No. 5, by David L. Kaplan and M. Claire Casey, 1958).

[43] U.S. Bureau of the Census, *U.S. Census of Population: 1960, Selected Area Reports, Standard Metropolitan Statistical Areas* (Final Report PC (3)-1D, 1963).

[44] *U.S. Census of Population: 1960*, Vol. I, Part 1, Table 87; *U.S. Census of Population: 1950*, Vol. II, Tables 124, 126.

[45] Approximately, it appears that the 1960–65 uptrend in the national percentage of white-collar workers has been at a rate little different from the 1950's. (U.S. Bureau of Labor Statistics, *Monthly Report on the Labor Force*, December 1965, p. 14.)

orientation toward human resource problems at urban and national levels alike. The 1960 urban percentage of white-collar workers for either sex was three times higher among whites than among non-whites.[46] Nationally, the contrasts were comparable. Moreover within the white-collar group itself, the largest contrasts for males were in the "professional," "managers," and "sales" categories, the first two of which are its most prestigious and generally best-paid parts. For females, the smallest contrast was in the "professional" category, but only because this group contains a high concentration of teachers among non-whites.

Within metropolitan areas the 1960 male and female percentages of "professional," "clerical," and "sales" labor force who were white were all well over 90 for the areas as a whole and reached 95 to 99 for persons living outside their central cities. The central-city–outside-residence distribution of persons working in these occupations ranged from near equality among white inhabitants to an approximately 5 to 1 ratio among non-whites.[47] The situation for the "managers" group is not given by the census.

As to more recent years, survey data indicate that the national fraction of white-collar workers in the Negro labor force has risen appreciably since 1960, especially among females.[48] For either sex, the annual rate of change in the fraction ranks well within the upper range of intercensal shifts found during this century for the work force as a whole.[49] Hence, very nearly the same comparisons must apply with respect to the numerically preponderant white component of the work force, for which specific trend values are unavailable. Finally, although the above national uptrends for Negroes in the 1960's have apparently been far larger than the ones for whites in recent years, we will probably have to wait for the 1970 census to learn what has happened in the urban or metropolitan sectors proper.

Unemployment. As indicated earlier the decennial census is still our best or only source for dealing with most aspects of urban unemployment, despite its sometimes large and highly variable margins of

[46] *U.S. Census of Population: 1960*, Vol. I, Table 88.
[47] *U.S. Census of Population: 1960, Selected Area Reports . . .* , Table 3.
[48] The fractions for 1960 and 1966, according to the April surveys of the labor force for these years, were 13.7 and 17.1, respectively, for non-white males, 18.0, and 25.7 for females. (U.S. Department of Labor, *Employment and Earnings*, Vol. 6, No. 11 [May 1960], Table A-11; U.S. Bureau of Labor Statistics, *Employment and Earnings and Monthly Report on the Labor Force*, Vol. 12, No. 11 [May 1966], Table A-23.)
[49] *Occupational Trends in the United States: 1900 to 1950*, Table 2.

207

error.[50] At a minimum, benchmark comparisons between decennial urban data and continuous national series are needed to establish whether the latter can serve as proxies for the former during intercensal periods.

Answers from the last two censuses to the benchmark question turn out to be mixed. Urban unemployment rates in 1960 were practically identical with the corresponding national values among all sex-color groups; the largest discrepancy, for non-white males, came to only one-half percentage point. However, in 1950 the differences tend to be larger, consistently so for non-whites, and are sometimes in the opposite direction. As a result, the 1950–60 changes in unemployment rates shown by the national series prove unreliable indicators of the urban shifts, whether in the aggregate or for sex-color groups.[51] It is true that the 1950 and 1960 unemployment rates were generally similar, both nationally and in the urban sector, so that a different conclusion might be warranted for years with sharply contrasting unemployment. But it seems reasonable to hypothesize that national data may well be unreliable barometers of urban movements in most situations calling for labor-force analysis and policy decisions. Much the same conclusion seems indicated for sex differentials and for essentially the same reasons.

Unemployment-rate differences by color present a more promising possibility in these regards. The familiar fact, shown by monthly labor-force surveys, that national Negro unemployment has been approximately double the white rate for over a decade is also to be seen in the urban and national statistics of the last two censuses. A substantial change in the relationship according to continuous national series would therefore appear to warrant a generally similar conclusion for the urban labor force. Even here, however, caution may be in order. Thus, where the 1950 and 1960 censuses show a rise of a full percentage point in the unemployment-rate difference by color for males in the nation, they suggest a slight decline in the city. Variations of this magnitude are likely to exceed political tolerances for some major purposes of policy and interpretation. This would be particularly so in periods of

---

[50] Thus the 1960 national census count of unemployed was 4 per cent lower than the more accurate labor-force survey figure for the same part of the year; in 1950 the relative undercount, similarly defined, was 19 per cent. A variety of checks undertaken by the Bureau of the Census shows that unequal errors for different parts of the labor force, along with variable errors over time, have been typical. (See, for example, U.S. Bureau of the Census, *Evaluation and Research Program of the U.S. Censuses of Population and Housing, 1960: Accuracy of Data on Population Characteristics as Measured by CPS-Census Match* [Series ER 60, No. 5, 1964], and *The Employer-Record Check* [Series ER 60, No. 6, 1965]; also *U.S. Census of Population: 1960,* Vol. I, pp. lxii–lxiv.)

[51] *Ibid.,* Table 82; *U.S. Census of Population: 1950,* Vol. II, Table 50.

possible transition, when even rather small changes need to be regarded closely for signs of longer-run tendencies.

Unfortunately, little or nothing can be said about the host of other structural problems that characterize the urban labor force and command major policy and research interest today. Individual case studies apart, a statistical blackout persists for the urban section with respect to such questions as unemployment by occupation and industry, duration of unemployment and the long-term unemployed, persons working part time for non-economic or "involuntary" reasons, the special problems of the young and non-white labor force, working mothers and numerous others. Even first comparisons between urban and national patterns are precluded in all of these instances. Since the urban labor force is so large a proportion of the national total (about 70 per cent in 1960), it seems reasonable to assume that large structural changes or differentials in the one would be reflected in the other. But we are still in the stage of very general hypothesis on this matter, particularly for the smaller components of the labor force which are often involved.

II. APPROACHES TO AN ECONOMIC THEORY OF URBAN HUMAN RESOURCES

The present section seeks to describe some major theoretical thrusts which might characterize a rapidly evolving field of economic research in urban human resources. It deals with some main sets of theoretical issues that would seem both central to urban human resource questions yet unanswerable in the absence of the economist's special skills. That there will be mounting "external" pressures on the economist to enter the field, at least at empirical-descriptive levels, can be taken for granted. Hence, the emphasis here is on challenges to the theoretical-minded economist over the next decade or so. Can we point to research needs and opportunities that would define urban human resource economics as (1) a distinguishable subdiscipline of economic theory, drawing upon and contributing to its mainstream modes of analysis, and (2) also a theory faithful to the main institutional and policy issues?

The broad answer to this question may seem as clearly negative to some as positive to others. The pessimist may well point to the past, arguing that the very limited or fragmentary interfaces we find to exist today between mainstream economic analysis and the study of urban human resource problems are no accident. Certainly, nothing like a body of theory, models, and key parameters exists that could be compared with standard micro- or macro-analysis, international trade economics, or even growth and development analysis. The optimist may grant all this yet pin his faith on the future, relying on the promise that economic theory follows "the big problems."

The approach taken here is that a closer look is preferable to guessing in the large. Neither of the above views can be pushed very far without attention to subject matter. The five broad subject areas examined below seem to me to rank high on several counts: analytical needs, theoretical challenge, comparative neglect to now, relevance to practical applications, ready points of contact with mainstream economic theory.

The first section, "Some Basic Raw Materials," deals with the need for evolving a production-function store of knowledge concerning problems of manpower upgrading and development, as comprehensive and fundamental in its way as the corresponding body of analysis for commodities. The correlative need for a longitudinal approach to many central aspects of human resource development is the subject of the second section. Here again, striking analogues and dissimilarities with established economic theory will be apparent, in this case with respect to capital theory. The third section deals with an almost entirely new area of research which could be opened up if data became available on manpower movements between industries, occupations, and regions. The fourth section reflects the consensus among informed observers that many of our most difficult economic problems on the urban human resource scene—and with these some key challenges to policy—are interwoven all along the line with non-economic issues, labeled here briefly "Social Welfare and Disorganization." The fifth section takes up a number of the salient "tradeoff" questions confronting ambitious policy efforts to induce convergence between Negro human resource characteristics and those of the general population. A dual-sector development framework seems called for, one which should eventually encompass several interrelated components: initial economic differentials and their social correlates, of the kind illustrated in Section I, as boundary or starting-point conditions; caste-type obstacles to convergence in addition to more conventional immobilities; the relevant benefit-cost calculations implicit in alternative tradeoff possibilities and their associated policy instruments. Such calculations are the subject of much of what follows.

It is hardly necessary to emphasize limitations. Large margins of error and unavoidable vagueness are the hallmarks of any attempt to look into the future of "a possible major new area of research." The discussion below is clearly no more than an initial sounding board, selective in what it includes and preliminary in what it says. The five broad subject fields singled out focus on primarily development issues rather than human resource problems as a whole. Largely omitted are questions associated with the urban or metropolitan area as a labor market; for example, the supply-demand determinants of wages by industry, industry mix itself, or the impacts of an urban area's labor-market dimensions on its income level, spatial organization, and service performance. In part such questions are covered elsewhere in this volume (see the Thompson-Mattila, Hoover, and Hirsch papers). In part, too, such questions are already well established in urban economic analysis. Our concern here is with human resource development issues in research that have been relatively neglected, rather than the forms of static or industry-based studies conventionally encountered in urban wage and employment analysis.

Other limitations will be equally apparent. Thus even if the selected subject areas are viewed in their own terms, the overlaps will be seen to be large. Only suggestive definitions of either the areas or their principal components have been attempted, while urban and non-urban applications are often intermingled. Although all of the general and individual topics to be cited appear integral to the urban sector, many could apply as readily to national or non-urban human resource questions. This last would not be a limitation in itself, of course, but it does suggest the further need for a finer structure of discussion than the one presented. Distinctions between size of place are ignored, though large-city–smaller-city distinctions would appear central at numerous points.

Nevertheless, with all due qualifications, I would expect that an evolving, powerful economic theory of urban human resources might well be characterized at its core by something like the selected general aspects to be discussed. At least the cited problem areas seem ample to constitute a sufficient, if not necessary, basis for fashioning a distinctive, yet integrated subdiscipline within over-all economic theory.

Some Basic Raw Materials

It seems obvious that the financial and real-resource inputs and outputs of manpower educational, training, and development processes must be at the heart of the economist's contribution to the human resource area, whether urban or general. The thrust of the recent and still evolving research on "investment in human capital" and "the economics of education" reflects a more general point. If human resource economics is to proceed much beyond historical description or ad hoc responses to administrative needs, it will require the conceptual tools common to economic theory at large: a sense of opportunity costs, methods to evaluate alternative pathways to preassigned policy goals or the instrumental prerequisites of new goals, optimization in

211

the use of scarce resources for achieving competing ends, a sense of both the direct and indirect costs and benefits resulting from market forces or social policies. It is indicative that the first major entry point in the human resource area by analytical rather than institutional economists deals with education as an investment factor in economic growth. Nor is it accidental that such research has been so largely focused on measurable costs and returns, a necessary condition for making theory operational.

An evaluative review of the literature on the "economics of education" is not necessary here, since the subject has been widely discussed elsewhere.[52] It is enough for present purposes to say that research in this general area has been too aggregative in some respects and too circumscribed in others. Thus it tends to deal with national rather than urban or individual-city populations, combined races rather than components of the labor force or population by color, formal schooling to the relative neglect of other educational and manpower training possibilities.

Even a cursory review of outstanding manpower and human resource policy questions makes it clear that these omissions are a primary next challenge to research. Something like an entire body of *production function* analysis will have to be evolved, similar to what we find in industrial economics, if economists are to make much headway toward a theory which is both recognizably within their discipline and realistic. Concepts, models, and cumulative information on the order of magnitude of a system will be required—similar in scale to production analysis for commodities while distinctive in content—if we are to arrive at workable assessments of the main manpower development problems confronting us on the urban scene. Fundamentally, this is to say that the economist must cope with the distinctive development problems of individual parts of the labor force just as he does for automobiles and textiles. Moreover, the analogy with commodities takes us only part of the way. The inputs and outputs of human resource development processes must be formulated in their own distinctive terms.

Refinement of definition need not be pursued, but it is instructive to indicate some intended points of emphasis. A first point is the one just indicated of contrast with the aggregative-growth orientations of

[52] See, for example, T. W. Schultz, "Investment in Human Capital," *American Economic Review*, Vol. 51, No. 1 (March 1961); Gary S. Becker, *Human Capital: A Theoretical and Empirical Analysis, with Special Reference to Education*, National Bureau of Economic Research General Series, No. 80 (Columbia University Press, 1964); C. Arnold Anderson and Mary J. Bowman (eds.), *Education and Economic Development* (Aldine, 1965).

212

recent research on the economics of education. The focus here is on the urban labor force and especially its low-income, unskilled, and non-white components (although much the same could be said for the rural labor force, the farm-to-city migrant or any other group singled out for policy or analytical attention). At the same time, growth need not be the sole or even a relevant criterion in orienting the proposed research. Major programs to foster urban manpower development may have primarily social or political rather than economic purposes, with only small or conceivably negative bearing on the aggregate growth rate.

A second point of emphasis is that the objectives or outputs of our main production possibilities for upgrading manpower are often long-run or something like life-cycle in nature, rather than short-run or immediate. This is in sharp contrast with standard production analysis, which stops at the point of product availability or sale; some contrasts on the input side will be noted shortly. Conventional capital theory provides a much closer analogy, with its concept of a discounted stream of returns, but falls short in other ways. Appropriate rates of discount, if any, may be very different in human resource applications; perhaps more important, the risks of non-utilization ("unemployment") play no central role in capital analysis but may be crucial to manpower problems. Thus in vocational training of a twenty-year-old, his employability one or two decades later may have to be taken centrally into account along with his job chances immediately after graduation. We know very little about the scope for tradeoffs between short-run and long-run returns within low-skill or otherwise disadvantaged parts of the labor force. Only if short-run optimization always entailed a corresponding long-run condition—say if the job most immediately available were also the optimum pathway to job security and earning power a decade from now—could the problem be ignored.

The presumption that this is not the case is of course entrenched deeply within much of our educational philosophy and social legislation. For the disadvantaged parts of the labor force it is probable that employment, income, and output in successive periods are in especially erratic relationship with each other. We can expect the same to be true of younger groups not yet in the labor force. Our knowledge of such relationships is still embryonic, not only for the disadvantaged but also for the average or advantaged labor force. Life-cycle analysis of spending patterns, perhaps the closest approximation we have in economics, has been concerned with description rather than with optimization. And conversely, recent research in growth theory on optimal time paths of development has been oriented to successive time periods rather than to cohorts moving over time and in any event to variables other than labor force. A cohort or longitudinal approach to optimization questions in manpower development would therefore signal a clearly differentiable body—and style—of analysis, as is discussed more fully below.

Third, and in keeping with conventional production economics, information on a fairly full range of input possibilities, at least the main ones, needs to be accumulated for assessing manpower development alternatives. Formal schooling or years of school completed, the variables most commonly used until now in investigations of the growth contributions from education, represent only a subset of the prominent possibilities when juxtaposed with our main human resource problems in the city. Vocational schooling and a large variety of special, ad hoc or compensatory programs for the undereducated, disadvantaged, or technologically displaced adult labor force also need to be examined in input-output terms. Collectively these alternatives will involve many billions of dollars in the next decade, with probably many more billions contingent on our evolving evaluation of their effectiveness. To guide rational choice among possible alternatives, the distinction between short-term and life-cycle or longitudinal effects is likely to be especially relevant as well as troublesome.

Fourth, both the input and output aspects of manpower development processes and policies are likely to entail sharp distinctions by demographic variables, such as sex, age, and color. Sociological and economic distinctions in addition to demographic ones may be equally relevant: for example, marital status, prior formal education, or previous employment experience. So far as I can see, the need for such distinctions has no close counterpart either in conventional production or optimization analysis. The underlying theoretical complication is that the direct beneficiaries of manpower development on the output side are also controlling parts of the materials mix on the input side, not only determining the nature of the "product" but also the probability of its appearance. Formal schooling apart, therefore, a balanced choice among appropriate compensatory, special or remedial production possibilities affecting manpower potential may have to be varied according to the characteristics of the beneficiary, and in central rather than merely marginal ways.

Thus, for an adult head of family an effective upgrading program may require a guaranteed income component in addition to training inputs proper if dropouts and recidivism are not to become excessive. Retraining of working mothers who are heads of families may require special child-care facilities to avoid similar setbacks. For the under-

214

privileged teenager living in a smaller city, an optimal approach to long-term upgrading may be to assure that he complete high school or attend junior college in order to meet expected large-city demands for his services. For the hard-core school dropout coming from a broken home in a large city, the best approach may be to provide intensive vocational training for meeting occupational demands in a smaller city.

In short, adequate knowledge of manpower "production possibilities" may well entail very large batteries of processes rather than a relatively few. Recent experience under the Manpower Development and Training Act, to cite only one empirical touchstone, makes the point abundantly clear.[53] In dealing with manpower development, the economist may have to make as many individual case studies as he does of industries.

A final point involves a further contrast with conventional production analysis. Industrial information on input costs and mixes can be typically obtained from the plant manager, engineer, and accountant, who must be expert in these questions as parts of their daily job. No comparable source of information can be expected from the manpower development practitioner, who generally comes from the ranks of political administrators, educators, social workers, applied sociologists, or persons with similar non-economic background. Although the latter would have to supply most of the needed input information, the economist is likely to have to reshape such materials to a significantly greater extent than in the case of industry analysis. The contrast on the output side is even sharper. Where the uses of commodities beyond the productive or distributive unit tend to become a datum to the economist, the tracing through of a manpower development program in terms of its consequences for job stability, productive capacity, or earning power calls inherently for the economist's attention. In part, too, some significant externalities may have to be brought into the picture at this point, for example, in the form of labor-force–social-welfare interrelations of the kind elaborated below.

A Longitudinal Style of Analysis

As already suggested, a rounded economic theory of manpower development requires for many purposes a life-cycle or longitudinal approach to analysis, in which actual groups would be traced over time. Implicitly or explicitly, most instruments and objectives of our human resource policies are directed to improving the cumulative job and

---

[53] *Manpower Report of the President and a Report on Manpower Requirements, Resources, Utilization, and Training by the U.S. Department of Labor,* March 1966.

income experience of individual components of the labor force. Such experience cannot be extracted from conventional time series, for example, of unemployment, since these aggregate the temporary or random experience of the "relatively advantaged" with that of the "disadvantaged." At best, even when highly disaggregated, such series only identify the persons in any given category at successive points of time, not the actual movements over time of given groups of individuals. An intertemporal, "continuous register" form of documentation is needed for the last, whether the "disadvantaged" or any other selectively defined group of the labor force is being singled out.

No series is presently available which would combine these needed features of disaggregation and continuity. Although longitudinal information on labor force is being increasingly compiled through special surveys, it remains extremely scattered and occasional; much or most of it can only be applied to national labor-force groups or subgroups. Incredible as it may seem today, not a single series exists in the United States for documenting job mobility between industries or occupations. Although some fairly broad bodies of data could in principle be assembled for this purpose, using existing records systems, all such possibilities would be beset by important gaps. And even these limited possibilities have been virtually ignored.

The last indicates that the fault is not only with the absence of basic data. Active research interests, particularly if associated with pressing policy needs, tend to lead quickly to the generation of prerequisite statistics in the United States. Moreover, even if large bodies of longitudinal information were already in existence, we would still need to develop conceptual models for summarizing them from a great variety of policy and research viewpoints.

The case for such models is easily illustrated. Current unemployment is often a major determinant of future chances of unemployment. Sustained unemployment or highly erratic employment may lead to unemployability, while the latter may well imply social disorganization in a variety of forms. The extension of these examples to human resource development processes in general seems clear. Future manpower potential is closely conditioned by the past, perhaps uniquely so when compared with other major classes of economic phenomena. The future, roughly forty-year positioning of the twenty-five-year-old is very typically predetermined by his initial main labor-force characteristics—relative skill level and earning power, broad occupational experience and even industry of work—unless strong countervailing forces intervene. Other leading explanatory elements are such background factors as demographic characteristics, residential origins, past migration, education and previous or current instabilities of employment.

Longitudinal models of an "iterative" type would seem clearly needed here, in which the cumulative background characteristics of a given manpower "stock" would predetermine its probabilities for future labor-force flows. To repeat, the stocks of greatest interest are often relatively limited and specific parts of the total labor force, in particular its most disadvantaged components. For these or other groups the same methodological approach would hold, whether such models were intended to project future manpower prospects in the absence of policy intervention or to guide the selection of adequate policy instruments.

Operational models which could assist in selecting relevant explanatory variables and in identifying their major effects are far from being developed as of now. We know little about either the intertemporal causal mechanisms at play or the magnitudes of the suggested interrelationships. At a minimum and even at a descriptive level, the summary measures and parametric concepts most relevant for interpreting longitudinal labor-force statistics have yet to be identified adequately. In demography, where longitudinal data have been studied much more intensively, the answers to these questions are still at a formative stage.

The familiar concept of a working life table is a useful framework for illustrations. Consider a cohort type of table, which describes the progression of a fixed group aging over time; this is to be distinguished from the more usual or period type, which synthesizes the experience of different age groups (cohorts) in a fixed period. Assume also that cohort-defined information were available for one or more of such characteristics as unemployment, income, migration, industrial mobility, occupational background, skill levels and the like, in addition to labor-force participation rates. Given the data, well-established methods and theory exist for documenting in life-table fashion a variety of shifts in labor-force status, for example, between unemployment and employment, or between occupations, industries or regions. The usual procedure of dealing only with movements into and out of the labor force is conventional rather than inherent in the theory. Thus within an expanded life-table framework one could derive such descriptive parameters as: the cumulative fraction of unemployed to total man-years in the labor force; probabilities of re-entering the labor force or of shifting between its employed and unemployed components; the ratio of underemployed to total man-years according to selected criteria of underemployment; the near-term or long-term consequences of inter-

217

regional or interindustrial movements compared with no movement; the comparative probabilities of subsequent unemployment among persons in different labor-force categories at an earlier time in the cohort's work history. Monetary counterparts to many of these questions could also be readily formulated, in which the man-years spent in a given labor-force category would be weighted by income earned or foregone according to the case.

It is important to observe that such life tables could be truncated, covering only a part of a cohort's history. There is no need to await a full history before usefully researching its parts. Each of the various measures just cited could be in relation to a sub-range of a cohort's work years rather than all years. Five-, ten-, or twenty-year histories might well be enough for many purposes. In addition, direct documentation for parts of a given history could be combined with estimates or projections for other parts.

The cohorts to be studied could be of many kinds: for example national birth-sex-color groups, the erratically employed identified in a given city or region as of a given initial date, enrollees in a compensatory education or manpower upgrading program, and so on. Tables for successive or alternatively defined cohorts would permit time series and comparative analyses. Quantitative identification, in cohort terms, of cyclical and structural factors affecting manpower utilization and development would be of special interest at this point if sufficiently fine disaggregation were possible. Comparisons between synthetic and longitudinal bodies of information would provide a way of defining and measuring period *versus* cohort effects, perhaps in much the same ways as have been utilized effectively in demographic research. The parameters found in a body of tables could serve as dependent or explanatory variables in a variety of predictive and structural regression systems.

Data analysis along these or cognate lines would have to be accompanied by new approaches to data collection. The statistical difficulties surrounding a cohort or analogous time-path approach should not be underrated. Longitudinal surveys of selected labor-force groups are expensive, even if the groups are small, and are beset by numerous problems of attrition because of mortality, migration, and other reasons. The census, which alone would permit access to groups defined for smaller areas or for desirably detailed combinations of socioeconomic characteristics, could only provide a limited amount of longitudinal information through retrospective inquiries. A related approach, to identify a given group in successive censuses, would be feasible only if matching of individual records could be achieved; such matching possibilities are still extremely limited. Administrative records provided by the Social Security system could constitute a mine of information on earnings, location of work, within-year and longer-term movements between employers, areas, and industry, all by sex-age-color components of the insured work force. At the same time such records have problems of their own, such as lack of closure, use of counties as minimum spatial units, and limited background information on socioeconomic characteristics. Tax records might turn out to be a comparably useful source but after a good deal of testing and innovation.

Possibly, too, the difficulties would prove to be as much political as statistical. The collection and use of cohort data from census and administrative sources may be highly circumscribed by confidentiality constraints.

If the difficulties are forbidding, the pressures arising from policy, administrative, and academic sources to overcome them are not minor either. It is already clear that longitudinal data on labor force will be compiled increasingly over the years, if only on a partial and occasional basis. Hence the point of the foregoing comments is not that the difficulties are insuperable. Rather it is that something like a revolution in statistical methodology may be needed to support an emerging economics of human resources, possibly no less thoroughgoing than the one required for national-income purposes a generation ago.

Manpower Mobility Analysis

Because of the absence of any basic series on industrial or occupational mobility, as mentioned earlier, economists have no adequate way of relating manpower movements to regional or industrial change. Although the census presents current labor-force characteristics by migration status (even these are only partially documented in the published statistics), no information is collected on previous industry or occupation. Hence, while the population origin-destination matrices cited in Section I are at least obtainable in principle, the corresponding matrices for manpower categories are ruled out from the start. To provide the necessary information the census would have to include a question on previous industry and occupation, in addition to the one on previous residence.

Manpower origin-destination matrices would have numerous important uses if made available, particularly if past industry and occupation were cross-classified with region of previous residence. They would document for the first time the sources of manpower recruitment by industrial and occupational categories. Shifts within regions according to these categories could be compared—in terms of volumes, demo-

219

graphic characteristics, and economic determinants—with shifts between regions. Movers could be similarly compared with non-movers, whether with respect to industry and occupation, region, or both. Gross manpower movements according to any of these categories are likely to be large multiples of net movements, probably requiring separate identification of the main causal factors affecting their "to" and "from" components. Such information can only be attained from matrix-type classifications of data. In turn, gross or net movements of labor force by industry and region could thereby be tied directly with shifts in regional income, regional employment, and industrial output.

Correlating manpower-movement matrices with the housing characteristics ascertained by the census would provide the first significant documentation ever made available in this country on the residentiary impacts of labor-force mobility. Such matrices could also add an important dimension to the types of longitudinal studies discussed above.

Among other possible major uses one in particular is worth citing. This is that the joint availability of migration and manpower "from-to" matrices would permit our first examination of the numerical associations between population movements and labor-force mobility. As of now this primary aspect of economic change has eluded analysis.

Social Welfare and Disorganization: The Neighborhood as an Urban Subsystem

The commonplace that human resources are ends in themselves, not merely or even primarily factors of production, was probably never a sufficient reason for the comparative neglect of labor-force–social-welfare interrelations in mainstream economic theory. Whatever the reasons for such neglect in the past, however, the need for major-scale analytical breakthroughs to encompass the subject seem almost self-evident today. On the policy side, the intimate bearing of personal, family, and neighborhood welfare conditions on the disadvantaged labor force and on structural manpower issues in general has become increasingly apparent. The growing threat of crime and delinquency to the provision of old and new ranges of urban amenities poses still broader policy issues, involving the quality of life of the entire urban community. Given the enormous human and fiscal factors at stake, it seems a plausible forecast that economic theory will again fulfill its traditional role of responding to unfamiliar problems when these become clearcut major occasions for socioeconomic policy. On the analytical side, the time seems equally ripe. Economists are no longer reluctant to apply pricing methods to nonmarket problems of a primarily social-cost nature. Feedback models, featuring ramified long-run interrelations among households, productive sectors, and government under highly variable institutional settings, are increasingly encountered in development analysis. Statistical and computing capacities for applying analogous models to urban problems are expanding enormously. Externalities arising from urban clustering, agglomeration effects, producer-consumer feedbacks, or amenity issues are universally recognized to be at the heart of much of present-day urban economics.

It can be expected, therefore, that the economist will be increasingly impelled—both for internal or professional reasons as well as by policy pressures—to apply his theoretical tools to the "social pathologies" of the city. Crime, juvenile delinquency, illegitimacy, urban hazards to mental and physical health, slum housing, underemployment and underemployability, the child-care needs of low-income working mothers, family instability and disorganization—these and others provide an abundant array of substantive topics under this general heading.

The economist's special skills can make a severalfold contribution in this broad area. First, the fiscal implications of attempted policy solutions to the problems of urban social disorganization need to be made far more precise and refined than has been the case to now. As a rough but probably useful benchmark of the dimensions of the task, contemporary fiscal analysis relating to employment policy took something like a decade to a generation of cumulative experience to reach a developed state. A similar period, accompanied by equally intensive high-level research, may well be required before we can achieve a comparable expertise in the areas of urban social policies and their labor-force concomitants. Certainly the numerous pronouncements one hears today about the "cost of saving our cities" seem better designed for shock effect than for informed decision-making.

Second, there is a vast need for new principles and methods to help identify the appropriate limits of social policies at each of several margins. Whatever the specific catalogue of priority urban social problems, the fiscal and real-resource inputs implicit in attempting solutions encounter constraints on several fronts: the competition for support among the social-problem areas themselves within the same city, the competitive demands of other policy needs within the city and, when state or national funds are involved, the corresponding demands from other cities. In all of these respects, the generic economic problem is the classical one of adapting needs to the constraints of scarce resources.

Although policy efforts to meet social problems often appear as a political "given," their relative expansion or contraction at any relevant margin is not. Once their respective ranges of "absolute necessity," if any, have been exceeded, the need arises for choice and allocation. It follows that some form of cost-benefit calculus is requisite if fiscal or other economic adjustments at the margin are to be rational rather than haphazard. This is so whether the policy objectives are almost exclusively "social" (i.e., non-economic), both social and economic, or predominantly economic.

Third, if today's social pathologies seem the obvious forerunners of many of tomorrow's problems affecting the structurally disadvantaged labor force, the nature of the linkages—in part intergenerational—and the policy levers sufficient for their remedy have remained comparatively unexplored. Novel, longitudinal-type models of costs and benefits may well be indispensable here, as suggested earlier in other connections. Hopefully, such models could eventually encompass two-way systems of linkages, from social-problem causes to structural labor-force effects in one direction and from labor-force causes to social-problem effects in the opposite direction.

The numerous interfaces suggested by the facts between the pressing problems of social disorganization and those of the structurally disadvantaged labor force may well have an important micro-spatial dimension in addition to the intertemporal ones just cited. Urban economists have not typically recognized the neighborhood as either a useful or researchable unit for dealing with main variables other than housing. However, a closer look at today's major human resource problems in the city suggests that this may be a mistake. Recent attempts to identify "poverty areas" support the hypothesis that the low-income or "social problem" neighborhoods of large cities may have their own "fine structure," not only in relation to the rest of the community but among themselves. Some Negro neighborhoods, for example, are found to experience rapid economic advance while others suffer stagnation or deterioration. Accordingly, for analyzing main reciprocal spillovers between depressed economic conditions and disadvantaged social background, such spatial units as the central city or even the so-called "ghetto" may be much too aggregative.

Increased research focus on the neighborhood as a form of socioeconomic subsystem may have a number of payoffs over and above its practical uses for administrative purposes. For example, suppose it were found that the main "problem areas" of the large city tend to exhibit predictable differentials in the size or trend of welfare loads, required public services, employment potentials within and outside the neighborhood, or responses to neighborhood-improving and manpower development policies. Such differentials would then point the way to causes, hence to new sources of remedial policies. As another example, the city transportation planner tends to assume that "people need to move to the jobs." From human resource and social planning viewpoints, however, a more perceptive approach might also call for "jobs to come to the people." There may be an important need to so accommodate the circumstances of secondary workers and the especially disadvantaged, for example, female heads of low-income families, students seeking nearby part-time work, the extremely illiterate, those too poor to afford cross-town travel and the like. Aid in starting small businesses to serve neighborhood markets could be another step in this direction. If service industry and even factory places of work could be intermingled with residences in a manner acceptable from both business and amenities viewpoints, a broader part of the labor force could be similarly accommodated.[54]

Analysis of the neighborhood as a locus of labor-force–social-welfare interrelations would require the collation of data from varied and novel combinations of sources—social agencies, public police records, and censuses of business, to name a few. Fortunately, a rich store of benchmark cross-classifications on social, economic, demographic, and housing characteristics can soon be expected for area units as fine as city blocks, if current plans for the 1970 population and housing censuses materialize as expected. Here, as often, the major impetus for ever-finer geographic data has come from the administrator, market researcher, and other local-area users. If the foregoing suggestions are warranted the social scientist will find, not for the first time, that his next analytical challenges have been foreshadowed by the practitioner.

Dual-development Approaches

Viewed as an economic development issue, many human resource problems of the urban Negro population in this country exhibit striking similarities with the dual-economy dilemmas often confronting low-income nations. In both cases the underlying economic problem is to "close the gap" between an advanced and a lagging component of the population, by promoting especially rapid growth within the economically "backward" sector. A political consensus exists that a self-sustaining trend toward sectoral equalization of income and productive capacity must be achieved "at all reasonable costs"—even if the professed outreaches the proffered as a rule. In the American city, much as in low-income nations everywhere, some salient social factors—conflicting value structures, discrimination, caste-type inhibitions to cross-

[54] Harvey S. Perloff, "Common Goals and the Linking of Physical and Social Planning," in *Planning 1965* (American Society of Planning Officials, 1965), pp. 11–12.

overs between leading and lagging sectors among others—are obstacles to development of the disadvantaged. Although the American Negro forms a minor fraction of the national population when compared with the numerical preponderance of the lagging sector in most dual economies, the difference becomes considerably smaller and is shrinking rapidly in our main central cities—undoubtedly the critical locus of the Negro "development problem" in the United States during the next generation.

A special class of dual-sector models would be needed to encompass the full combination of these elements. The specific nature of such models is difficult to predict but at least three general features might be especially prominent.

One feature would center about the appropriate mix of aggregate and structural policies affecting the Negro in the urban (or total) economy. At a 6 per cent over-all unemployment level, for example, the structural disadvantages of the Negro labor force might well become secondary to the needs of aggregate employment policy, even if development targets affecting the Negro remained fixed. Policy efforts favoring the Negro might be made subordinate under such circumstances to optimization targets for the entire population. With 4 per cent unemployment or less, the appropriate policy mix might veer greatly toward the structural, again in relative terms. Or it might be, if operationalized models could show it, that longer-run economic factors or priority social goals appeared overwhelmingly predominant compared with shorter-run factors. In this event the best policy would presumably be to adhere to given suboptimization targets for the Negro on a more or less autonomous basis. Our knowledge of these questions is still textbookish compared with our relative sophistication in other policy-mix issues—for example, the co-ordination of monetary and fiscal policies against recession, or the respective roles of tariffs and devaluation in tight balance-of-payments situations.

A second main use of the envisaged models would be to clarify the tradeoff relations, in fiscal and real-resource terms, which hold between suboptimization goals for the Negro and more general goals. (In principle, of course, the structurally disadvantaged white population could also be singled out for explicit attention, though the added analytical demands imposed by moving from binary to trinary sets of interrelations are often major. Possibly, too, the structurally "average" or advantaged Negro subpopulation should be excluded from special consideration to the extent that data permitted.) In particular, the investment costs and expected returns arising from structural policies favoring the Negro would be explicitly balanced against alternative investment needs and opportunities, whether for enhancing aggregate growth or for achieving other structural targets. At a quite different level, dual-sector macro models could explore the interrelations between tight aggregate-employment policies, their effectiveness for reducing Negro unemployment and their associated risks of inflation.

It is not necessary to enter into the specific nature of the above interrelations: for example, whether investments favoring Negro development and those aimed at aggregate growth are more likely to be competitive than complementary. Methodologically in either case, a conceptual-statistical framework adequate for the task should illuminate the nature, magnitudes, and sources of the main balancing items. The use of cost-benefit estimates for individual structural policies, of the kind illustrated earlier, would presumably enter at this point. Such estimates would be needed as raw materials, to be fed into the dual-sector framework in the form of parametric inputs. About all to be said here about feasibility is to repeat the hope that workable estimates could be obtained fairly soon with sufficient research attention. Unless suboptimization policies on behalf of the Negro are simply taken as political invariants or unless economic analysis of such policies is simply too difficult to attempt, the needs of fairly rational decision-making will have to be met by some such kind of dual-sector analysis.

The above sets of policy-mix and tradeoff issues, particularly the second, would seem unavoidably imbedded in a dual-sector approach to Negro human resource problems. A third set of analytical possibilities worth citing would center on the impact of total-population or larger-area policies on the Negro population in specific urban areas. Unlike the previous two sets, this third would be comparatively optional. There is ample room for research scrutiny of dual-development patterns and policies at the national or regional level. Yet it would be enormously useful if the analysis could be advanced a step further, toward an individual-city scale of observation. The difficulties which would confront such spatial-demographic pinpointing are well known. Although national and state outlays for human resource development purposes are partly earmarked by city, in good part they are not. Moreover, even the earmarked portions of such outlays raise substantial problems in identifying eventual effects, in view of such spillover factors as internal migration. Inherently, the unearmarked parts raise allocation and identification problems from the start.

On the sides of both inputs and effects, therefore, reasonably sensitive and powerful "trace-through" techniques are needed if an adequate focus on the individual city or similar area is to be achieved. Such "trace-through" problems are not peculiar to the human resource field

225

or to its Negro aspects, of course, but here again the latter point to some relatively distinctive yet central needs for rounding out a basic part of urban economics.

The foregoing discussion has been a highly constrained survey of the urban human resource field. Methodology and unresolved theoretical needs—both long-standing and evolving—have been its main concern, not the specific social and policy issues which have given the subject a fresh importance in recent years. The five problem areas just described seem natural meeting-grounds between the skills and professional inclinations of the economic theorist, on the one hand, and many of the major needs for theoretical guidance called for by administrators, planners, and other social scientists, on the other. However, whether these or other such grounds will become researchable terrain is still to be seen. The consensus among most urban economists that this has not been the case on any significant scale should be sufficient precaution in itself against optimistic prediction.

As to the subject areas themselves, the breadth and flexibility of the ones singled out are neither sufficient assurance against major omissions nor a necessary condition for uncovering viable research strategies. Research designs have been suggested but not devised. Similarly on the empirical side, nothing like an adequate citation or even listing of practical issues and institutional factors has been attempted. Social-welfare goals and problems have been treated only as inputs to economic research problems, rather than for their own sake. Although the role of multidisciplinary approaches should be explored in a fuller exposition, this important aspect of the subject has been essentially ignored.

Since these limitations are so apparent, a final and rather grandiose speculation can do no harm. It may be, if intuition or hope more than informed judgment can serve, that a "post-Beveridge revolution" in economic theory is in the making, not too dissimilar in scope, intellectual challenge, and potential usefulness from its Keynesian predecessors. Should it occur, the main impetus would again come from the force of events—in this case our new political tolerances and objectives relating to the city and its human resource development problems.

SELECTED READINGS

Anderson, Charles Arnold, and Mary Jean Bowman (eds.). *Education and Economic Development.* Chicago: Aldine Pub. Co., 1965.

Becker, Gary S. *Human Capital: A Theoretical and Empirical Analysis, with Special Reference to Education.* (National Bureau of Economic Research General Series, No. 80.) New York: Columbia University Press, 1964.

Duncan, Otis D., and Albert J. Reiss, Jr. *Social Characteristics of Urban and Rural Communities, 1950.* New York: Wiley & Sons, 1956.

Lowry, Ira S. *Migration and Metropolitan Growth.* San Francisco: Chandler Pub. Co., 1966.

Miller, Ann R. *Net Intercensal Migration to Large Urban Areas of the United States: 1930–40, 1940–50, 1950–60.* (Analysis and Technical Reports No. 4.) Philadelphia: University of Pennsylvania Population Studies Center, 1964.

Perlman, Mark (ed.). *Human Resources in the Urban Economy.* Washington: Resources for the Future, 1963.

Schultz, T. W. "Investment in Human Capital," *American Economic Review,* Vol. 51, March 1961.

Taeuber, Conrad, and Irene B. Taeuber. *The Changing Population of the United States.* New York: Wiley & Sons, 1958.

Taeuber, Irene B. *Population Trends in the United States: 1900 to 1960.* U.S. Bureau of the Census, Technical Paper No. 10. Washington: U.S. Government Printing Office, 1964.

Thompson, Wilbur R. *A Preface to Urban Economics.* Baltimore: The Johns Hopkins Press, for Resources for the Future, 1965.

U.S. Department of Labor. *Manpower Report of the President and a Report on Manpower Requirements, Resources, Utilization, and Training.* Washington: U.S. Government Printing Office, March 1966.

Vernon, Raymond. *The Myth and Reality of Our Urban Problems.* Cambridge: Harvard University Press, 1966.

DISCUSSION OF PART I

COMMENTS BY HAROLD J. BARNETT*

Sidney Sonenblum's paper seems to be looking toward a textbook on projections. It has textbook virtues. It is very clear and orderly. It is exhaustive and painstaking in taxonomy, and patient in concern for methodology. It has textbook defects. It becomes a bit exhausting and painful to the impatient reader, in its extended taxonomy and methodology. Also as in a text, Sonenblum invents new terms and labels in need to identify and give life to some of the cells he has conceived. These are sometimes aptly descriptive—for example, "impact-multiplier," "stages-of-growth," and "production-function" models. Infrequently, the terms are less well conceived.

But this is quibbling. Sonenblum is the world's leading expert in regional projections activity. His paper is an important contribution to the art of projection. I will turn to some of the substantive points in Sonenblum's paper in a moment, after characterizing Wilbur Thompson's.

Thompson begins deceptively by saying or showing that differences in industrial composition explain regional differences in level, distribution, and stability of income, and in growth rates. Sonenblum also made this point. But then it becomes apparent that Thompson is dissatisfied with industry accounts as the measures of difference among regions. He wants to know why and how the regions got their industrial composition, why they change, how growth occurs or does not occur —the laws of urban growth, in effect. He is characteristically imaginative and energetic. In a person less obviously devoted to research and discovery and less motivated for the sake of intellect and social welfare, the level of ambition could be too long a reach. The many major economic relationships, like a troop of tumblers, dive and somersault and leapfrog on and over each other as they come on stage, several at a time. I could not grasp the whole act. But once I accepted this, I could follow selected individuals of the troop, with pleasure and interest. This is the general character of Thompson's paper.

Internal vs. External Dynamics

I now make a more substantive comment by comparing the two papers in a major respect. Both the Sonenblum and the Thompson

* Professor of Economics, Washington University.

229

paper involve hypotheses on strategic variables in relation to regional economic levels and growth. I think these two experts are, to a degree, at significant variance. In general, Sonenblum finds *national* forces to be the primary determinant of the levels and growth of the individual regions. The growth rates of the several industries are determined nationally, and the individual region's industrial activity tends to reflect the extent to which those industries are resident and related to the industries at the national level. In similar vein, he says: "A technology developed in Houston affects the productive capacity of Pittsburgh; a demand generated in Los Angeles influences employment in New York; a fertility decline in Mississippi influences population growth in Chicago."

Sonenblum also states that he has found no relationship between the initial size of an area's population or employment and its subsequent growth rate and that, due to a tendency toward similar industrial structures, growth differentials among metropolitan areas are narrowing.

Thompson, on the other hand, emphasizes the importance of the internal structures and growth processes of the individual regions. For example: "The very large metropolitan area is even more distinctive in its depth than in its breadth. The local social overhead—the infrastructure—that has been amassed is, more than export diversification, the source of local vitality and endurance. . . . The economic base of the larger metropolitan area is, then, the creativity of its universities and research parks, the sophistication of its engineering firms and financial institutions, the persuasiveness of its public relations and advertising agencies, the flexibility of its transportation networks and utility systems, and all the other dimensions of infrastructure that facilitate the quick and orderly transfer from old dying bases to new growing ones. A diversified set of current exports—'breadth'—softens the shock of exogenous change, while a rich infrastructure—'depth'—facilitates the adjustment to change by providing the socioeconomic institutions and physical facilities needed to initiate new enterprises, transfer capital from old to new forms, and retrain labor."

At various points Thompson refers to other advantages of size exhibited by the larger metropolitan areas—typically, the large state university with its research centers, the major medical centers, the flexibility of transportation networks and utility systems, the innovative propensities, and so on. In summary, as Thompson sees it, "Product and income may be measured at the national level but they are produced at the local level, more or less efficiently, depending on the form and functioning of our cities."

The foregoing bi-polarization I have presented is an overstatement:

Sonenblum knows that cities have insides, and Thompson is aware of the thrust of national economic variables, and both authors have qualified the statements in their papers. But there are important differences in their basic judgments concerning regional economic levels and growth.

Size of Metropolitan Region

I should like to contribute a comment on one aspect of the influence of size of metropolitan area population and government on scale economies, to which Thompson assigns such major importance. The question involves "economies of social scale" of metropolitan regions, and my particular comment concerns *diseconomies* which may arise if the regions become very large and monolithic metropolitan governments develop.

The literature of the day emphasizes inefficiency due to small size of urban communities and the absence of metropolitan governments. We less often think of the diseconomies of very large social scale. Yet Werner Hirsch states in his paper that public sector activities, such as education, police and fire protection, and refuse collection, do not experience economies from social scale in the larger metropolitan regions, even though industrial goods, such as electricity and gas, do. Moreover, I observe that important new types of size diseconomies have appeared—pollution, congestion, bureaucracy in government, and deterioration of such public services as street safety, schools, and access to countryside. The diseconomies that are reflected in lessening qualities of public goods and other amenities may indeed be more important than a measure of increasing costs as such. Some years ago Nicholas Kaldor reflected on why a firm's cost per unit of output should ever turn up if all factors were variable. He concluded that one factor, the central management, was an indivisible factor of production by definition of the firm, and it would eventually become overloaded as size of firm increased. Analogously for metropolitan areas, we can think of overextended central government as a comparable fixed factor and a major reason for eventually increasing costs and declining qualities of public goods and amenities.

White Migration

I now move to a related question, and speculate about migration, extending the comments of Sonenblum and, to a lesser extent, Thompson. Sonenblum points out, using Ira Lowry's data, that out-migration from metropolitan areas is a direct function of income and age, and in-migration varies directly with job opportunities. We know that income is steadily growing and that we are unsteadily progressing toward persistent full employment—that is, job opportunities in almost all metropolitan areas. Let us assume the society is, as Galbraith has suggested, economically affluent and secure. To what places will the increasing flow of migrants go (to what places would we go?) if regional differences in job opportunities and in real private incomes were not influential? A major possibility is that the migrants would flow to places where the real income of public services and of other amenities was substantially greater. Subject to lags, populations would flow to places which were rich in the "urban assets" which Hirsch, Perloff, and Leven have been concerned to measure—such amenities as climate, public services, good government, higher education facilities, public spirit, cultural facilities, medical centers, and recreation facilities. But we will not all move to California or New York. These population flows, if rapid and continued long enough, would eventually reduce the amenity levels. They would overburden the government and the public services; produce congestion and pollution; and diminish the value of private, public, and free goods, as well as psychic income from residence and citizenship. Thereupon the attractiveness of these urban centers to new population would decline, due to diseconomy of social scale.

These speculations, if they have merit, are different from but companions to Thompson's. He emphasizes the infrastructure of large places as it relates to cost, productivity, and market control. I have been describing infrastructure as it relates to consumer preference and citizen amenities. Interurban migration is the key to future population and employment growth of the metropolitan regions. Except as it is caused by job opportunity, a declining cause except for non-whites, it seems to me interurban migration will increasingly reflect citizen preference for public goods and other amenities, quality as well as volume.[1]

Negro Migration

The foregoing treats only of white migration. George Stolnitz, in his paper, contributes an important discussion of Negro migration. I should

[1] I have seen a projection by Jerome Pickard that at the end of this century two-thirds of the population will be in the Northeast, Great Lakes, California, and Florida. Perhaps such projection does not give weight to the possible "diseconomy" of very large scale which I have suggested. Perhaps, however, I am underestimating the persistence of the favorable influence of city size and job opportunities on in-migration. In studies completed after my preparation of these comments, several of my graduate students have found just these variables to be major determinants of white adult migration in the period 1955–60. See "Three Studies of the Quality of Urban Environments," by Ault, Campbell, and Witt (St. Louis: Washington University, Institute of Urban and Regional Studies, November 1967).

like to extend this a bit by noting briefly the magnitudes and implications of the Negro migration from the South to the North and West.

The Negroes' migration is toward better jobs, and in hope of freedom and equality. They migrate from southern farms and cities to northern and western cities, in large numbers. From 1950 to 1960, these cities absorbed almost a million southern Negroes—or tried to. Since World War II, immigrant Negroes have become a significant fraction of these city populations; there have been serious problems of accommodation. But, contrary to popular belief, the major problems are only barely present. The needed social adaptations of northern and western cities to the inflow are only just beginning. Two facts are worth mentioning.

Negroes in the South (fourteen states and the District of Columbia as defined by the Census) comprised about 68 per cent of the U.S. Negro population in 1950, and 60 per cent in 1960. This is a large percentage decline in a decade—a tenth. But the high rate of migration to northern and western cities is likely to continue for decades before the flow moderates. In 1960 there were still 11 million Negroes in the South, where they were one-quarter of the region's population. There were less than 8 million Negroes in the rest of the country, where they were only one-sixteenth of the population. Though the Negro migration from the South may appear rapid to the northern and western cities, it has not even begun to reduce the level at its source. Southern Negro population numbered 9.9 million in 1940, 10.2 million in 1950, and 11.3 million in 1960.

As we fix in mind the fact of a continued flood of southern Negro migrants to northern cities, implications begin to emerge. One is that ghettos will not only continue, they will become larger and more numerous. Against the chill of the "new land," the migrant Negro will desire, as former immigrant groups did, the warmth of his own culture, ethos, and color. Since ghettos will persist on a very large scale, we must transform them into decent places to live and work. The ghetto schools must be fit for educating the children for urban culture and society.

A second implication, beyond continuation of urban ghetto societies for at least first-generation migrants, is that at the same time there will be a major and continuing spread of the Negroes who have adapted throughout the urban society. The children of migrants, if we are successful, will want to disperse. Hopefully, they will have opportunities for integration by residence, school, marriage, and profession. This means that integration of a partially dispersed Negro population must be accommodated by urban society.

A third major implication concerns employment. The Negroes in the ghettos will be, as they are now, the least desirable of the labor force in the eyes of educated, polite society—uneducated, unskilled, poorly spoken, and uncultured. As now, the workings of the private economy and minimum wage laws will yield major unemployment among them, even in a so-called full employment society. Contrary to what we have now, public employment or subsidized employment measures must be designed to provide jobs for all who need but cannot find them. There will be more ghettos and more unemployed to accommodate than there are now.

Innovations in Theory

In Section II of his paper, "Approaches to an Economic Theory of Urban Human Resources," Stolnitz makes a powerful plea for major innovations in economic theory. At first I thought that his plea for new theory was for more extensive applications of general economic theory to human resources, particularly in urban economies. By analogy, applications of price theory, with a bit of macro, cycles, and growth analyses, have yielded us the applied fields of industrial organization, agricultural economics, and international trade. But he means far more. In addition to improved applications of conventional theory, he really is calling for new and greatly improved and revised theory. This theory would include political and social psychological variables; would be dynamic and long term with respect to education and training; would handle indirect costs and benefits of market forces and social policies; would comprehend neighborhood institutional and spatial parameters; and would include a life-cycle or longitudinal system of analysis for groups.

I really don't know how to comment. Earlier I said that Thompson was rather ambitious in his paper, but Stolnitz's stated desire is at least an order of magnitude more so. One is tempted to think that this is the stuff of dreams. And yet people *are* working on the components. Orcutt is devotedly working on a microanalytical model with resemblance to Stolnitz' longitudinal system. Dahl and Lindblom, and McKean, Maas, Margolis, and others are trying to include political variables. McClelland has proposed a radical hypothesis for training innovators and alleges it has been somewhat successful. Galbraith and Hagen have argued that our conventional models of development are wrong, and have proposed revised psychological parameters. Stolnitz is apparently not alone.

PART II

INTRAMETROPOLITAN DEVELOPMENT

*Edgar M. Hoover**

THE EVOLVING FORM AND ORGANIZATION OF THE METROPOLIS

It is a truism that socioeconomic organizations involve primarily mutual interrelations among decision units rather than the conveniently simple one-way impacts and sequential effects that we like to use whenever possible in building explanatory theories. And spatial organization in the urban setting presents this aspect of mutual interdependence of everything on everything to an especially notable degree, precisely because the very raison d'être of a city is that it puts enormous numbers of diverse households, business firms, and other decision units cheek by jowl so that they may interact in fruitful and efficient ways.

So when we try to construct a conceptual model of how various residential and non-residential activities are spatially distributed in an urban area, we find a vast web of interdependence. Shopping centers locate primarily on the basis of access to consumers; people like to live close to their work, schools, shopping areas, and other types of facilities that they have occasion to use. Business firms of various types are attracted by access to labor supply, other related firms, or transportation facilities. In many kinds of urban activities, like seeks like. There are strong pressures for neighborhood homogeneity as such, as illustrated by the exclusive suburb, the garment district, and the automobile row. Every user of space has also to consider its price, and that will depend on how desirable the site is to other users.

Picturing all this even in greatly simplified terms as an equilibrium or dynamic system, the model builder or other theoretician trying to encompass the whole is likely to find himself hopelessly engulfed in myriad simultaneous equations in futile search of a useful solution or any solution. He has long since abandoned any attempt to elucidate by diagrams, since every important relationship seems to have many more than the graphically manageable two or three dimensions.

The situation is perhaps not quite as hopeless as this may imply. In tracing what determines what and how, there are a few welcome entries to and exits from the otherwise endless pretzel of causation. In the first place, some of the locations in an urban area can be regarded as determined exogenously and not just in response to the rest of the local pattern. Perhaps the most obvious example is a port and waterfront area, which is primarily determined by natural locational advantages.

* University Professor (Economics), University of Pittsburgh.

In the second place, it is clear that the actual spatial structure does not represent or even closely resemble a static equilibrium of the locating forces. Rather, it represents a snapshot of current states of mutual adjustment. Impacts of one change upon another, and spatial adjustments, take time, because long-lived physical facilities, habits, social and business ties, and political commitments are entailed. Consequently, at any given juncture a great many of the locations and locational shifts can pragmatically be viewed in terms of one-way, rather than reciprocal, impact. Actual decisions, even some planning decisions over substantial periods of time, can therefore take most of the current setting as given, and ignore a large part of the conceivable ultimate "feedback" effect.

It remains true that heroic and ingenious simplification of reality is necessary for any comprehensible image of the spatial structure. Throughout this paper, therefore, runs the question of how we can boil down facts and concepts and still have something nutritious left at the bottom of the kettle.

In this paper I shall try to describe the current state of understanding of economic forces affecting the spatial pattern of activities in urban areas. A vast amount of effort in recent years has been devoted to measuring those spatial distributions and their shifts, and constructing more sophisticated theories and quantitative models to interpret them. This effort, essential to any insight into coming problems and opportunities and to any co-ordinated planning and public policy, has been productive. We know a great deal more now about how the parts of urban areas fit together, about the processes of adjustment to changed conditions, and about the not-so-obvious effects of such specific major undertakings as freeway construction and urban renewal. Unfortunately, the problems also are growing and proliferating. It is not quite so clear that we have come much closer, in terms of knowing what should be done—to say nothing of actually doing it—toward real mastery of our urban destiny.

To the best of my knowledge this paper contains no new ideas. The most that it attempts to do is to bring together in some useful integration the key concepts and empirical findings that are at our disposal in understanding the changing spatial structure of the urban area, with particular reference to American cities and their suburbs and fringes. No attempt is made here to construct a rigorous theory of urban locations and their shifts, or to catalogue the literature. Although it will be convenient here and there to refer to various types of operational and semi-operational econometric models that have been developed, their assumptions, and what we know about the main parameters involved, this paper does not go into the design and construction of such models or their postnatal feeding and care. Professor Harris deals with those questions elsewhere in this volume, and this paper may be regarded as complementary to his.

This paper is organized in four main sections. The first identifies basic location factors affecting the placement of activities in an urban setting, with some attention to ways in which these factors can be measured and expressed in operational terms for analytical models. Section II takes stock of some useful empirical findings on typical spatial patterns in urban areas, and observed trends in those patterns; it indicates the extent to which these observed characteristics can be rationalized in terms of the location factors previously identified. Section III is more specifically addressed to changes and the adjustment problems they raise. Some basic sources of spatial change are identified and their effects traced. The paper concludes with a few observations on what all this analysis may suggest in terms of policy issues and useful lines of further urban research.

I. PRINCIPAL LOCATION FACTORS

The first step in building a useful conceptual framework for understanding urban spatial patterns is to sort out the multifarious location factors that influence the preferences and placement of specific activities or types of decision units. What is suggested below is a logical way of reducing these factors to a manageably small number of groups.

"Given" Locations

As already intimated, there are some kinds of locations within an urban area which are not determined primarily by where the other activities of the area are. Actually there are two distinct bases for exogenous determination of locations in an urban area.

For some kinds of activities, certain topographical or other natural site features are essential, which means that the lay of the land narrows down the choice to one or a very small number of locations. Ports for water traffic illustrate this, and there are some urban areas where the topography limits jet airport sites almost as drastically. In the past, defense considerations played a major part in locating the center of the city and the city itself. Localized recreational features such as beaches also illustrate this kind of factor, and in a few urban areas extractive industries (mainly mining) occur and are, of course, limited to certain special sites.

There is a further type of exogenously-determined location where the independent influence arises not from site features so much as from

239

the fact that the activity in question is primarily concerned with contact with the outside world. Not just water ports but all kinds of terminal and interarea transport activities come under this head. Since there are great economies of scale in interregional transport and in terminal handling of goods, the urban area's gateways to and from the outside world constitute a set of focal points whose locations within the area help to determine—rather than just being determined by—the other activities of the area. This does not, of course, mean that such terminal locations (unless constrained by natural site features) are absolutely and permanently unresponsive to the changing pattern of other activities in the area served: such terminals are from time to time shifted to improve local accessibility or to make way for more insistent claimants for space. But the terminal locations do, in dynamic terms, play a primarily active role in shaping the pattern, and are to be viewed as part of the basic framework around which other activities are fitted.

Finally, in practice, we can generally take as given the focus of *maximum over-all accessibility* within the urban area. If we think of that as, for example, the place at which all the people of the area could assemble with the least total man-miles of travel, it is simply the median center of population, depending upon where all of the various types of residence are located. But travel is cheaper and faster along developed routes, and the cost and layout of these are affected by scale (traffic volume) and topography. So, evaluated in terms of travel cost and time, the focal maximum-access point can be regarded as a quite stable datum, even though the extent and importance of its access advantage over other points can change radically. We find in major American urban areas that, despite great over-all growth and far-reaching change and redistribution of activities, the focal point in this sense has usually shifted only a relatively short distance over periods measured in decades and generations, and that the earlier central foci are well within what we currently recognize as the central business district.

This concept of a single, most central focal point in an urban area is then significant and useful in developing simplified bases for understanding the over-all pattern. Obviously it has limitations, some of which will be discussed later in this paper. In the first place, there is in principle a variety of distinguishable central points of this sort, depending on what kinds of people or things we are imagining to be assembled with a minimum of total expense or effort. The employed workers of the area are not distributed in quite the same pattern as the total population, the shopping population, the school-attending population, the office workers, the industrial blue-collar workers, the theater-going or the library-using population; there might be a different optimum

240

location from the standpoint of access for each of these types of people. Where goods rather than people are moving (as for example in the case of wholesale activity or production serving local needs such as daily newspapers or bread) the transport conditions are different and this may again mean a different optimum-access point. Finally, we have to recognize that, in varying degrees, the concept of one single point serving as the origin or destination for all flows of a specified type may be unrealistic and defensible only as a convenient fiction. Thus, if we identify some central point as having best access to the homes of the entire clerical office force of an urban area, this does not imply that all offices should logically be concentrated there. What it does imply is that, solely from the standpoint of commuting access for the clerical workers and ignoring claims of alternative space uses, it would make sense for the density of clerical employment to peak at that point. The significance of the focal point is determined, then, by the extent to which the activity involved is dependent upon (1) concentration in a single small district, and (2) access to the flow in question.

Access Linkages

Since the function of an urban concentration is to facilitate contacts, the most important class of location factors shaping in the spatial pattern involves the advantage of physical proximity as measured by the money and/or time saved. This applies to cases in which such costs are substantially increased by added distance. Where they are not, they have nothing to do with urban concentration. For example, information in a widening sense (now including not only the printed word but sounds and computer signals and various types of pictures) can now be transmitted electronically over long distances just as quickly as over short distances, and sometimes just as cheaply to the user. This kind of contact, then, does not in itself depend upon, nor help to maintain or explain, intra-urban concentration.

Most relevant to the urban pattern are kinds of access for which costs are high and increase very rapidly with distance within the intra-urban range of distances (ranging from next door to a few dozen miles). Access involving human travel belongs par excellence to this category. Human beings require more elaborate and expensive vehicles (in dollars per ton of freight) than almost anything else. And, in particular, the time cost becomes generally even more important than the actual transport cost.

For people and things alike, the time cost to the passenger or the owner of the cargo is essentially an "opportunity cost," measured in terms of what useful services the person or thing being transported might

241

otherwise be yielding. For commodities, we can measure this crudely in terms of interest on the investment represented by the value of the goods tied up in transit. For human beings, a commonly used yardstick is the rate of earnings while at work.[1] Thus, a man who earns $5.00 an hour would consider the time cost of a half-hour trip to be $2.50. This rate of time cost equals the accrual of interest (at 5 per cent per annum) on an investment of about $880,000. So, calculated on that basis, human freight carries a time cost equivalent to that of a commodity worth at least $300 an ounce—perhaps not "more precious than rubies," but somewhere in the range between gold and diamonds.

The locational importance of an access linkage—i.e., the economic advantage of proximity—depends not only on how much the trip costs but also on how often the trip is made. Access to one's regular work place is likely to be a weighty consideration because it generally involves at least five round trips a week. It becomes somewhat less important if one shifts from a six day to a five day or shorter working week.

In the case of shopping trips, the costs of the trip should be related to the amount of the purchase in order to get a measure of the proximity advantage. Thus, if ten minutes' additional travel in each direction (twenty minutes round trip) is valued at, say, $1.50, it would be worthwhile making the extra travel in order to save $1.50. That is 15 per cent on the purchase of $10 worth of groceries, but only 1½ per cent on the purchase of a $100 television set. We could infer that it is logical to travel ten times as far to shop for television sets as to shop for groceries, if the amounts of purchases stated are representative and if the price differentials among shopping places are about the same for both types of goods. Here again, only time costs are considered; but this illustration illustrates the wide variations in the strength of the proximity incentive, even within the limits of one category of relationship, like retail trade.

The various kinds of access linkage that tie together the urban complex can be meaningfully classified in a good many ways: for example, by mode of transport or communication, or according to whether the incentive toward proximity is thought to influence predominantly the location of the sender or that of the receiver of whatever is being transported. Perhaps as useful a classification as any other can be based on the distinction between households and other decision units—i.e., between residential and non-residential activities.

---

[1] This way of evaluating time cost is used for lack of anything better. We need more information on what value people of various sorts place upon time spent in transit under various circumstances.

Access among non-residential activities. This involves in part inter-industry transactions such as those recorded in an input-output table. Business firms have an incentive to locate with good access to their local suppliers and their local business customers. To that extent, an interindustry transactions table gives us an idea of the relative volume and importance of the flows of goods and services between establishments[2] of the same and different industries, though this does not go very far toward measuring the relative strengths of locational attraction. Nor do these input-output figures take account of some strong business proximity ties that do not directly involve transactions at all. Thus, local branch offices or outlets of a firm are presumably located with an eye to maintaining good access to the main local office, while at the same time avoiding overlap of the sublocal territories served by the branches (for example, the individual supermarkets of a chain or branch offices of a bank). There are strong access ties between the central office of a corporation and its main research laboratory, in-volving the frequent going and coming of highly paid personnel, but no entries in the input-output tables.[3]

Access among residential activities (interhousehold). A significant proportion of journeys from homes are to the homes of others. Such trips are by nature almost exclusively social and thus involve people linked by family ties or closely similar tastes and interests. This suggests that the value of "interhousehold access" can also be expressed fairly accurately in terms of homogeneity preference—like seeks like. As we shall see later, however, the pressures toward neighborhood or "microspatial" homogeneity include a good many other factors in addition to simple access.

Access between residential and non-residential activities. This type of access is far and away the most conspicuous in the urban flow pattern. The entire labor force, with insignificant exceptions, is con-

[2] Although interindustry transaction (input-output) tables are organized in cross-tabulations of *industries,* the basic unit is the industrial plant or other *establishment,* and interestablishment transactions within the same industry are shown in the diagonal cells of the table.

[3] It would be useful, I think, to try to construct tables showing the transport and communication charges incurred in the transaction flows between each pair of industries. This could lead to a still more useful cross-tabulation in which such charges were expressed as coefficients on a per-mile, per-unit-of-output basis. These coefficients would roughly measure the strength of spatial attraction between pairs of industries attributable to transport and communication costs. On this point, as on many others in the present paper, I am indebted to my colleague Professor David Houston for stimulating comments and discussion.

243

cerned with making the daily journey to work as quick and painless as possible. Such trips are much the largest single class of personal journeys within any urban area.[4] In addition, the distribution of goods and services at retail makes mutual proximity an advantage for both the distributors and the customers; some attention has already been paid here to the factors determining the relative strength of the attraction in the case of different types of goods and services. Trips to school, and for cultural and recreational purposes, make up most of the rest of the personal trip pattern. There is mutual advantage of proximity throughout: the non-residential activities dealing with households are most advantageously placed when they are close to concentrations of population, and at the same time residential sites are preferred (other things being equal) when they are in convenient access to jobs, shopping districts, schools, and other destinations.

The way in which these mutual attractions shape the locational pattern of activities within the urban area depends not so much on the strength of the attraction as on the degree to which the non-residential activity in question is concentrated at relatively few points (since almost any such activity is much less evenly diffused over the area than residence is). At one extreme, there are non-residential activities that need access to a large fraction of the households of the urban area, but that are confined to one location, and perhaps one establishment or facility. Thus, a visit to a large department store or some kind of specialty shop, or to a main library, or to the opera, or to attend university classes may mean, in many urban areas, a visit to one specific location, without alternatives. All such trips within the area have a single common destination focus and the attraction, from the household side, is centripetal, or at least monocentric. From the standpoint of the non-residential activity in question, optimum access means the choice of a point of minimum total travel time for all of the interested households in the area.

At the opposite extreme are activities not subject to any compelling scale economies or other economics of concentration, which can therefore have a dispersed or many-centered pattern. Drugstores, barbershops, branch banking offices, and the like are basically neighborhood-serving rather than catering to a broad citywide clientele. A good loca-

4 For relevant reference material, see J. R. Meyer, J. F. Kain, and M. Wohl, *The Urban Transportation Problem* (Harvard University Press, 1965), and Louis K. Loewenstein, *The Location of Residences and Work Places in Urban Areas* (The Scarecrow Press, Inc., 1965). Also, for a primarily bibliographical survey of the whole question of access, see Gunnar Olsson, *Distance and Human Interaction: A Review and Bibliography* (Bibliography Series, No. 2, Philadelphia: Regional Science Research Institute, 1965).

tion is simply one in which there is a sufficient amount of business within a short distance. And the attraction of such activities to the householder is within rather than between neighborhoods, being measured in blocks rather than in miles. The gradient of access advantage is a local one, replicated many times over in all parts of the area, rather than a single one peaking at some one point.

Agglomerative Factors

Access considerations involve a mutual attraction between complementary parties: stores and customers, employees and firms, pupils and schools. But there are also economic incentives favoring the concentration and clustering of identical or similar units of activity. The simplest case of this is perhaps that of scale economies. A large electric power plant is more efficient than a smaller one. A large store can, in addition to possible cost savings, provide more variety and thus enhance its attractiveness to buyers. As already suggested, some kinds of activities (such as opera performances) are subject to scale economies to the extent that only in the largest cities can more than one establishment be supported. Business corporations as a rule find that they can best concentrate their research laboratories at one location, and the same applies somewhat more obviously to their central offices.

A different and more subtle case involves the basis for clustering of many similar business firms or institutions. The classic case is the mid-Manhattan garment center, but analogous complexes are found in every city, such as "automobile rows," the financial district, and various types of specialized wholesale districts.[5]

If we inquire more deeply into the reasons for these clusterings we find that the establishments in the cluster are sharing some common advantage that is generally a pool of especially suitable labor, a variety of specialized business services, or the congregation of customers seeking to compare a variety of offerings. Sometimes two or all three of these kinds of external economy are involved. If the individual small firms in the cluster have good enough access to these external advantages, they themselves can specialize narrowly in functions not requiring large-scale operation, while at the same time having passed on to them the economies of a large labor market, a large concentration of buyers, and specialized business services produced on an efficiently large scale.

It appears, then, that these external economies of certain clustered

[5] Cf. Robert M. Lichtenberg, *One-Tenth of a Nation* (New York Metropolitan Regional Study, Harvard University Press, 1960) for a penetrating analysis of the "external-economy" industries in New York.

245

activities are really based on two factors previously discussed: access, and economies of scale. What is new is the extension of the concept of scale economies to labor markets and shopping comparison markets as operating mechanisms.

Finally, the clustering of like activities can reflect immediate environmental interdependence. A site has value according to its access but also according to its physical features and to the character of its immediate surroundings. Neighborhood character in terms of cleanliness, smells, noise, traffic congestion, public safety, variety interest, and general appearance is important in attracting some kinds of use and repelling others. Prestige types of residence or business are of course particularly sensitive to this kind of advantage, which often is more important than any access consideration as such. A high-income householder may be willing to lengthen his work journey greatly for the sake of agreeable surroundings.

As has been suggested earlier, the usual effect of this type of consideration is to make neighborhoods more homogeneous within themselves, and more unlike other neighborhoods—a tendency toward areal specialization by uses, or segregation in the broad sense. With few exceptions, a given type of activity finds advantage in being in a neighborhood devoted to reasonably similar kinds of uses, and disadvantage in being in violent contrast to the neighborhood pattern. Zoning controls and planned street layouts play a part in reinforcing this tendency.

Competition for Space: the Cost of Sites

I have cataloged above the various kinds of locational pulls and pushes that affect activities in an urban area. Most of the relationships mentioned are pulls—they involve a mutual locational attraction among complementary or similar units of activity. This reflects the underlying rationale of a city as a device effecting close contact and interaction on a grand scale.

But every land use needs some space or elbow room on which to operate, and the sites with best access or environmental features command a high scarcity value. The market mechanism works (albeit imperfectly like most markets) to allocate locations to uses and users who can exploit them to best advantage as measured by what they are willing to bid for their use.

Simplification and Synthesis

The various determinants of location in an urban area have been discussed above. In a really complex analysis, each could be broken

246

down much further. But we seek simplification. It appears that basically there are just three kinds of considerations that determine the relative desirability of locations for particular decision units such as households or business establishments. These are (1) access, (2) environmental characteristics, and (3) cost. They reflect the fact that the user of a site is really involved with it in three different ways. He occupies it, as resident or producer, and is thus concerned with its site and neighborhood, or immediate environmental qualities. He and other persons and goods and services move between this site and others; he is therefore concerned with its convenience of access to other places. Finally, he has to pay for its use and is therefore concerned with its cost.

Ruthless simplification along these lines makes possible the useful step of building a conceptual model of the spatial structure of an urban economy. For example, in such a model we can reduce the complex factor of access to the simple form of access to a single given focal point, as if all intra-urban journeys were to or from downtown and all shipments of goods also passed through downtown. We can in the interests of maximum simplicity even assume that the cost of transportation within the urban area is directly proportional to airline distance. Access is then measured simply in radial distance from the center.

We can assume away all differentiation of sites with respect to topography, amenity, and environmental advantage. These two simplifications also imply ignoring the manifold types of external-economy effects and environmental attractions and repulsions that have been discussed. In effect, we envisage each type of activity as *independently* attracted (by access considerations) toward the urban center; the only interdependence among the locations of the various activities arises, then, from the fact that they are bidding against one another for space.

It is also appropriate to develop a condensed classification of activities. No two households, factories, or other decision units are exactly alike in their location preferences, but they can be grouped into more or less homogeneous classes on the basis of similarity in access/space trade-off. Among households, for example, it appears from empirical studies that income level and family structure (presence or absence of young children) are the principal determinants of this trade-off.

With the above types of simplification as well as with others, it is possible to develop more or less systematic theories or frameworks of analysis for urban spatial patterns. Some of these patterns will be taken up here; Professor Harris' paper, elsewhere in this volume, is more specifically directed to this question. It is sufficient here to note that most such models are partial in the sense that they attempt to explain or predict the location of one type of activity in terms of its adjust-

247

ment to given or assumed locations of the other activities, including transportation services. Thus, a retailing location model may analyze the way in which retail stores locate in response to the advantages of access to the homes of consumers, a residential location model may analyze the way in which residences locate in response to the desire to shorten the journey to work, and so on.

II. APPLIED THEORY AND EMPIRICAL KNOWLEDGE

So far, we have merely cataloged the location factors at work in urban areas and suggested some ways in which they can be conceptually combined. But what do we know about actual urban patterns, their changes, and the strengths of the determining forces that have been identified?

Monocentric Gradients

Taking stock of what we know about urban spatial patterns may well start with the simplest kind of descriptive measure of such a pattern—a density gradient. Implicit here is the concept of a city as a multitude of space-occupying activity units seeking close contact. If these activity units are affected by more or less the same kind of access attraction (for example, households are affected by the desire to shorten the journey to work), and have some leeway in the amount of space they occupy, we should expect their density (intensity of space use) to be at a peak at the center (the point of optimum total access) and to fall off in all directions with increasing distance from the center. Such a tendency can be described by a density gradient, where density is a negative function of radial distance.

In this simple scheme the decline of density with distance depends on two things: (1) the rate at which the area's non-central activity units (households, in a purely residential journey-to-work model) are willing to trade off spaciousness of home sites against a quicker or cheaper journey to the center; and (2) the time and money cost of transport. Obviously, a variety of circumstances—such as better transport in some directions than in others, and variations in site quality—can complicate this neat symmetrical picture; but it remains quite recognizable in the real world.

As Colin Clark demonstrated, the gradient of population density with respect to radial distance, in a wide selection of large modern cities, has a consistent shape, identifiable as an exponential function. In any specified city, residential density tends to fall by a uniform percentage (b) with each unit increase in distance from the center. Any such gradient can therefore be specified by two parameters: D_0,

248

the peak density at the center, and b, a slope factor, in the following formula:

$$D_x = D_0 e^{-bx}$$

where x represents radial distance.[6]

Since this particular conformation describes residential density, it fits only in those parts of the urban area that are primarily residential. The peaking of residential densities resembles not so much a sharp conical mountain peak as a volcano, with a crater of lower gross density in the innermost zone pre-empted mainly by non-residential activities. The D_0 parameter in the gradient formula is thus fictional, representing an extrapolation to what the gross residential density would theoretically be at the center if non-residential uses did not pre-empt that location. Alternatively, it is possible (though more difficult in terms of data availability) to construct the gradient on the basis of *net* residential density (i.e., excluding streets and all other land not actually in residential lots).[7] Such gradients still fit the same type of formula but show, as would be expected, much less pronounced "cratering." One might surmise that if hotels were classed with residential uses, a true peak of net density would appear at the center.

Clark noted that the slope of the density gradient (b) varied considerably from one city to another, and showed a consistent downward time trend for any given city. It was not clear, however, whether this reflected increasing size or increasing age, or some combination of the two.

More recent analysis by Berry, Muth, Alonso, and others has verified the prevalence of the exponential form of residential density gradient,[8] and has developed and begun to test useful explanatory hypotheses about

[6] Colin Clark, "Urban Population Densities," *Journal of the Royal Statistical Society*, Series A, Vol. 114, 1951, pp. 490–96.

[7] It has been shown that in the Chicago area the fit of the gradient formula is better for net than for gross residential density. Carol Kramer, "Population Density Patterns," *CATS* (*Chicago Area Transportation Study*) *Research News*, Vol. 2, 1958; and *Chicago Area Transportation Study* (*Final Reports*), Vols. 1–2, 1959–60.

[8] For a comprehensive survey of the literature up to 1963, see Brian J. L. Berry, J. W. Simmons, and R. J. Tennant, "Urban Population Densities: Structure and Change," *The Geographical Review*, Vol. 53 (July 1963). Still more recent work by Bruce Newling, not yet published at the time of this writing, involves a more sophisticated gradient formula in which the logarithm of density is a *quadratic* rather than linear function of radial distance. This model provides for the characteristic "cratering" at the center and lends itself well to cases in which the zone of peak density for a specific type of land use makes radial concentric shifts over time, as, for example, in the Burgess and related types of zonal land use models discussed later in this paper.

its determinants, so that more reasoned projections of changes in density patterns can be made.

In brief, it appears that:

1. Larger cities have, in addition to higher central densities, lower (flatter) slope coefficients.

2. In developed countries, a city's gradient slope declines as the city grows.[9]

3. The central density is largely determined by conditions (such as transport, communication, production technology, income levels, and occupation structure) during the period when the city became established as such. Once set, the basic form of the city (particularly in the central area where investment in structures is heaviest) is subject to considerable inertia. At any given time, then, the age of a city (definable in terms of the date at which it attained some specified minimum size such as 50,000) is highly correlated with its central density. The familiar dichotomy between newer American "auto-oriented" cities like Phoenix and older "pre-automobile" cities recognizes this effect. Berry concludes, "Knowing the population of a city and its age, it is possible to predict fairly closely the pattern of population densities within it."

4. The central density in specific cities has generally been declining in this century, presumably showing response to some of the same factors that explain flattening of the gradient slopes, and suggesting that those factors have, in the period covered, outweighed the density-increasing effects of growth per se.

The most intensive statistical analysis of the urban density gradients has been done by Richard Muth.[10] After a series of tests of fit and linearity applied to density figures for forty-six U.S. cities in 1950 on the basis of samples of twenty-five census tracts in each city, he concluded that the negative exponential function would seem to be the best simple approximation to the pattern of population density decline with distance from the city center in urban areas. This was true despite the fact that there were numerous deviations from regularity and that, over all, the

[9] For example, the parameters of the residential density gradient for the Chicago urbanized area are presented for all decennial years, 1860–1950, in Berry, Simmons, and Tennant, *op. cit.,* p. 399. The "central density" rose to a peak in 1900 and 1910 and thereafter declined; the "slope" parameter showed an uninterrupted decline from 0.91 in 1960 to 0.18 in 1930. Clark, *op. cit.,* traces the steady flattening of the London density gradient from 1801 to 1941, with central density showing signs of a decline in the more recent decades.

[10] Cf. two papers by Richard F. Muth: "The Spatial Structure of the Urban Housing Market," *Papers and Proceedings of the Regional Science Association,* Vol. 7 (1961), pp. 207–20; and "The Distribution of Population within Urban Areas," in Universities-National Bureau for Economic Research, *Determinants of Investment Behavior* (National Bureau of Economic Research, 1967).

exponential formula as a regression equation "accounted for" only about half of the observed intracity variation of densities.

Comparing the fitted gradients of different cities with respect to their slopes and central densities, Muth tries out a number of possible explanatory factors. On the basis of his investigations, those factors with some claim to established significance include the following (signs indicate whether the gradient is steeper [+] or flatter [−] with higher values of the specified variable):

Automobile ownership (−)
Age (+)
Recent growth rate (−)
Quality of housing in the central city (+)
Income level (−)
Degree to which the manufacturing employment of the metropolitan
    area is concentrated in the central city as against the suburbs (+)
Size (−)

It is significant that in the latter of the two papers cited, Muth concluded on the basis of an expanded empirical investigation that "The distribution of population between the central city and its suburbs and the land occupied by an urban area are to an important extent, though not solely, explainable by the same forces that affect the spread of population within the central city." [11]

Various empirical investigations have brought to light similar fairly consistent density gradients for other important categories of land use in addition to residence. Duncan, for example, presents a gradient of

[11] Muth, "The Distribution of Population within Urban Areas," *op. cit.*, p. 296. Only two qualifications to this general statement appeared. First, an influx of lower-income persons into the central city is apparently associated with a greater degree of suburbanization of population, whereas within the limits of the central city the income effect seems to be in the other direction (a steeper density gradient with lower income level). This, as Muth suggests, makes sense in view of the fact that the central city is a separate fiscal unit and the presence of a larger low-income group tends to make the tax burden heavier for the upper-income groups, whose incentive to escape to other jurisdictions is thereby increased. Secondly, Muth's results imply that the central city population and, to a lesser extent, the land area occupied by the central city and its suburbs tend to respond less than would be anticipated to factors which reduce the relative rate of population density decline within the central city. He suggests (*ibid.*, p. 298) that "such a result might follow from a long-run disequilibrium in 1950 in urbanized area population distribution which could have resulted from the depression of the thirties and the war and post-war adjustments of the forties." If so, this would imply that some further suburbanization is to be expected just for catching up to what the basic determinants already would have called for.

manufacturing employees per thousand square feet of land occupied (i.e., net manufacturing employment density) for Chicago in 1951, showing a reasonably good fit to the exponential formula and with a slope substantially flatter than that of the typical residential density gradient.[12] Daytime population likewise shows the same kind of gradient. In this case the slope is much steeper, and the central density much higher, than for residential population.

Finally, there is enough evidence to establish that the gradient of land values in urban areas also follows the same general exponential form. There are not yet enough data to support very specific statements on intercity differentials and trends in the gradients of manufacturing employment density, daytime population density, or land values. It seems almost certain, however, that all three have been flattening out during recent decades.

Analysis of the behavioral factors underlying these gradient patterns poses many complications. If all households could be assumed alike in preferences and place of work, the form of the gradients of residential densities and rents could be read as representing the individual household's trade-off between more space and quicker access. But it is not so simple. We know that this trade-off depends on income level, for one thing, because (as long ago noted by Burgess in respect to American cities) higher-income families tend to live farther from the central city than lower-income families, particularly if allowance is made for presence or absence of young children. This means that the observed over-all residential density and land-value gradients represent in part the gradation of trade-offs; the analysis of residential distributions involves an additional dimension. Similarly for manufacturing employment density, in the case of the employment-density gradient referred to earlier, a breakdown of manufacturing into twenty-five industry groups disclosed that they displayed very different degrees of centrality, associated with employment density. A still finer breakdown would of course show the same kind of differentiation within an industry group.

Though rapid progress is being made in the accumulation of relevant data and further insight into determining factors in this simplified framework of the monocentric gradient, it is clear that we still do not know very much in a quantitative way about demand functions in the multidimensional framework of space, access, income, and family structure, to say nothing of the other relevant socioeconomic variables. For example, it is not yet clear that the observed strong negative correlation

[12] Otis Dudley Duncan, "Population Distribution and Community Structure," in *Population Studies,* Cold Spring Harbor Symposia on Quantitative Biology, Vol. 22 (1957).

of city size with residential density gradient slope really implies a causal relationship involving size per se, or merely covers up the influence of a number of other variables (for example, income) which are correlated with size. And although it seems quite evident that higher-income households have a stronger preference for space relative to access than do lower-income households, we do not know precisely how much or why.[13] To the extent that people's valuation of travel time costs reflects their earning level, it might seem that the demand for access should have a rather strong, positive income elasticity. Muth speculates, however, that the "income elasticity of marginal transport costs" is low compared with the income elasticity of housing demand, and that there is a high income elasticity of preference for *new* housing. Moreover, automobile ownership is positively related to income, and this would help to diminish the onerousness of transport for wealthier households.

Broad Quasi-concentric Zones

The analysis of urban spatial patterns in terms of continuous gradients of density or other characteristics related to radial distance is rather severely constrained by lack of available data. Information about the characteristics of very small neighborhood areas that can be arranged by radial distance is mainly confined to Census of Population tract and block data and the data collected in connection with transportation studies. In both cases, only a limited number of urban areas and characteristics are covered, and the data do not go back very far in time. Wider and deeper coverage is obtained by sacrificing the distance detail and considering the metropolitan or urbanized area as broken down into a crudely concentric series of zones: the central business district, the rest of the central city, and the ring of suburban areas constituting the rest of the Standard Metropolitan Statistical Area (SMSA).[14] Mention has already been made of Muth's finding that the central city/ ring differentials appear to reflect more or less the same factors as those associated with distance differentials within central cities, and are simply extended over a wider range.

Aside from the loss of distance detail, one disadvantage of the central city/suburbs dichotomy is that the results depend on the politi-

[13] Alonso has presented what purports to be a rationalization of this phenomenon and it has been widely cited and accepted. I am not persuaded of its validity. Cf. William Alonso, "A Theory of the Urban Land Market," in *Papers and Proceedings of the Regional Science Association,* Vol. 6 (1960), p. 156.

[14] Data available in recent censuses make possible a further split which has been used in a number of studies. The "suburban area" can be defined as territory outside the central city but within the officially designated "urbanized area," while the "fringe" is territory outside the urbanized area but within the SMSA.

253

cally determined factor of where the municipal boundaries lie.[15] On the other hand, it is clear that political boundaries per se are among the relevant determinants of location choice since they are associated with important differentials in taxes and public services.[16]

As an illustration, one of the most recent quantitative investigations along these lines is that of Schnore and Pinkerton[17] on urban area characteristics associated with changes (1950–60) in city/ring differentials in educational level. Educational levels in this period improved generally; in most cases they improved more in the ring than in the central city; and the extent to which a ring improved relative to its central city was positively correlated with both the size and the age of the metropolitan or quasi-metropolitan area involved.

This extends the conclusions of earlier work which had indicated that the relative socioeconomic status of suburbs compared with central cities (as measured by income, education, occupational mix, and other characteristics) is significantly higher in older and larger U.S. metropolitan areas than it is in younger and smaller ones.[18]

Differentiation by Activities

It is clear that to get much beyond a few elementary explanations as the foregoing, some explicit attention has to be paid to the heterogeneity of both residential and non-residential land uses in a less simple conceptual scheme.

[15] For an analysis of the extent to which central city annexations (1950) affect the apparent comparative rates of population growth of central cities and their suburban rings, see Leo F. Schnore, *The Urban Scene: Human Ecology and Demography* (The Free Press, 1965), Ch. 6. The SMSA's also are of course subject to the same imputation of semi-arbitrary demarcation. Cf. Allan G. Feldt, "The Metropolitan Area Concept: An Evaluation of the 1950 SMA's," *Journal of the American Statistical Association*, Vol. 60 (June 1965), pp. 617–36, for a discussion and some measures of the extent to which specific metropolitan areas can be regarded as "under-bounded" or "over-bounded."

[16] The importance of the desire of suburban communities to retain control over their public service patterns and other aspects of their style of life is brought out with exceptional clarity and conviction (in the context of a discussion of intrametropolitan differentiation and the incentives for and against governmental consolidation) in Oliver P. Williams, Harold Herman, Charles S. Liebman, and Thomas R. Dye, *Suburban Differences and Metropolitan Policies: A Philadelphia Story* (University of Pennsylvania Press, 1965).

[17] Leo F. Schnore and James R. Pinkerton, "Residential Redistribution of Socioeconomic Strata in Metropolitan Areas," *Demography*, Vol. 3, No. 2 (1966).

[18] Cf. for example, Leo F. Schnore, "The Socio-Economic Status of Cities and Suburbs," *American Sociological Review*, Vol. 28 (1963), and (for an illuminating contrast with another cultural type) Leo F. Schnore, "On the Spatial Structure of Cities in the Two Americas," in Philip M. Hauser and Leo F. Schnore (eds.), *The Study of Urbanization* (John Wiley & Sons, 1965), pp. 347–98.

254

That is not at all inconsistent with the picture of urban spatial structure in terms of symmetrical, monocentric gradients of density and other characteristics. We simply recognize the fact that there are different kinds of households and other activity units which have different access /space trade-off preferences and therefore would concentrate in different zones even if access for all groups were measured simply in terms of distance from the same central focal point.

The well-known Burgess zonal hypothesis is an early example of a schematic model developed along these lines more than forty years ago.[19] Its kinship with Von Thünen's much older zonal model of rural land uses around an urban focal point is obvious.

Activities are grouped on the basis of the congregation in successive distance zones from the center outward, viz.:

1. Central business district activities: department stores and specialty shops, office buildings, clubs, banks, hotels, theaters, museums, organization headquarters
2. Wholesaling
3. Slum dwellings (in a zone of blight invaded from the center by business and light manufacturing)
4. Middle-income industrial workers' residences
5. Upper-income single-family residence
6. Upper-income suburban commuters

It should be noted that this schema was based on empirical observation of patterns prevailing at the time, and also that it was put forward as a simplified *dynamic* model. The Burgess hypothesis was that these various types of uses preserve their sequence, but that as the city grows each zone must spread and move outward, encroaching on the next one and creating zones of transition and "land use successions." The transitional problem thus created in the third (blighted) zone was emphasized.

We have in the Burgess model an elementary classification of urban land uses by locational types which is still useful as a starting point. Downtown uses, light manufacturing, wholesaling, and three or four levels of residence characterized by income level are singled out as

---

[19] For a brief account of the genesis and nature of the "concentric zones," "sectors," and "multiple nuclei" approaches to analysis of urban form, and some references to the original primary sources, see Chauncy D. Harris and Edward L. Ullman, "The Nature of Cities," in Harold M. Mayer and Clyde F. Kuhn (eds.), *Readings in Urban Geography* (University of Chicago Press, 1959), pp. 282–86. Sectoral and subcenter patterns will be discussed in greater detail later in this paper.

significantly different and important locational types. Finally, heavy industry is not in the Burgess model at all, which makes sense in the light of the location factors we have discussed earlier. Heavy industry requires large level sites with good transport to and from the outside world, and access to the urban "center of gravity" is of little relevance since most of the inputs (except labor) and outputs are non-local.

The development of more sophisticated models has subsequently proceeded along several rather distinct lines. Thirty years ago (a decade after Burgess), Homer Hoyt presented a schematic model emphasizing the differentiation of urban land uses according to directional sectors rather than simply radial distance, and found sufficient empirical evidence and rationale to support this approach as at least an important complement to the radial distance schema. Others have developed models that emphasize the fact that there is, conceptually and empirically, more than a single "focus" of advantage for the location of specific types of uses. Operational models recently developed in association with intra-urban transportation and planning studies relate each important class of activity to its own set of trip destinations. But at the same time, a considerable advance in sophistication and empirical knowledge has been made on the basis of the original simple mono-centric conception. Two main contributors along this line, Lowdon Wingo and Richard Muth,[20] have worked out theories of the location of residences according to distance from a central urban focus. These theories incorporate in a highly sophisticated and relatively complete way the elements of consumer (householder) demand and the economics of transportation. A further step—on which progress but no conclusive break-through has been made—is to introduce disaggregation of the population according to a few such characteristics as income, family size, color, and occupation, into a similarly sophisticated model, and to derive from empirical analysis the behavior parameters that full quantitative analysis of the disaggregated residential pattern requires. We have little useful material as yet, for example, on just what the access/space trade-off elasticity is for specific kinds of households, and how it varies with income, family structure, and time. Nor do we have adequate quantitative analysis of the factors underlying the tendency toward neighborhood homogeneity as such. (Professor Harris' paper elsewhere in this volume discusses more specifically the problems involved and the progress being made in this line of empirical analysis.)

[20] Muth, "The Spatial Structure of the Urban Housing Market," op. cit.; "The Distribution of Population within Urban Areas," op. cit.; Wingo, Transportation and Urban Land (Resources for the Future, 1961).

256

Residential Location with Multiple Access

In the most radically simplified sort of model of urban spatial structure, access is measured by the cost of a journey from an outlying point to a specified central point. This simple notion seems adequate so long as we are comparing the relative access advantage of various non-central points. Things become more complicated when we take the inverse standpoint and try to evaluate the relative access advantages of alternative central points. If equal importance is attached to proximity to every non-central point, then the "best" (or "most central") focal point is presumably the one for which the total costs of transport from all other points are least. But this offends realism by ignoring any possible attenuation of interaction with greater distances; an economist would object on the score that it assumes a completely inelastic demand for contact or the necessary transport. In the real world, if a desired destination becomes harder to reach, more thought is given to "economizing" by going there less often or by substituting some more convenient alternative destination.

The "gravity-and-potential" approach to interaction over distance is an empirically based attempt to introduce a greater degree of realism here. The value of access to a point varies positively with the desirable contacts or opportunities present there (e.g., the number of jobs available in a center of employment). It will vary negatively with distance or transport costs. The "alternative opportunities" approach, taking explicit cognizance of a choice of destinations, in effect measures transport cost partly in opportunity-cost terms.[21]

Urban transportation studies in recent years have piled up a vast body of statistical material on the way in which people respond to access opportunities in their choice of travel paths. To a much smaller extent, these data throw some light on the more basic question of how residential development patterns can be expected to respond to changes in transport facilities and in the locations of work places and other trip destinations.

For example, in the potential measure of the work-access advantage of various residential locations, a key question is how heavily the various job locations are to be "discounted for distance." Do 1,000 jobs ten miles away have the same attraction as 500 jobs five miles away? Or only 250? Does the attraction attenuate in proportion to distance (or travel time), or in proportion to the square of the distance, or some other function of distance?

J. Douglas Carroll, Jr., and others (mainly in connection with intra-

[21] For a comprehensive view of these and related approaches, see Olsson, *op. cit.*

metropolitan transportation studies) have provided many answers to this question. When the whole pattern of point-to-point travel flows is ascertained in such a survey, it can be compared with what the pattern of flows would be on an "expected" basis (i.e., if travel time made no difference, and the mix of destinations were the same for every point of origin). When the deviations of the actual from the expected trip frequencies are regressed against travel time between points, we have an empirical measure of the inhibiting effect of travel time upon interchange. This differs according to trip purpose and type of traveler, and mode of transport; but in general, for any specified kind of trips, the effect can be roughly expressed by a power function. That is, other things being equal, the number of trips between two points varies inversely as some power of the travel time. The exponent attached to travel time in this formula can be regarded, then, as a meaningful index of the importance attached to access for that particular kind of interchange.

It follows that if we want to map the relative work-access advantage of various residential areas for a specified kind of people, a "work-access potential" index for each residential area can be constructed by dividing the number of jobs at each employment center[22] by the travel time to that center from the area in question, raised to the indicated power, and summing for all employment centers within maximum commuting range. A comparison of the access potential maps for different population groups shows the urban pattern of comparative advantage in terms of access. To the extent that access and the cost of space determine residential location, we should expect to find each population group predominantly concentrated in those parts of the urban area in which its comparative advantage of access is the highest.

The consensus of the studies thus far available is the following:

1. For the kind of measurement just described, simple airline distance is a reasonably adequate substitute for travel time.
2. The exponent attached to distance (or travel time) varies significantly according to type of person, trip purpose, and type of destination.
3. The exponent is relatively low for:
   a) trips to the central business district, for any purpose, as compared with trips to other destinations within the urban area;

---

[22] We ignore here a further refinement by which the attraction of an employment center may be treated as not simply proportional to the number of jobs, but, say, to some power of the number of jobs, introducing a scale factor.

    b) higher-status, white-collar workers, particularly in the professional and managerial category;

    c) social-recreational trips compared to work trips.

4. The exponent is relatively high for:

    a) trips to destinations outside the central business district;

    b) lower-status, blue-collar workers;

    c) women;

    d) trips to school (elementary and secondary), as compared to work journeys.

This kind of analysis of travel patterns and residential area differentiation has some value in describing and predicting transportation demands, residential development patterns, and locational choice for consumer-oriented activities (retail trade and services). But it needs to be stressed that all we really get is a description of how people have reacted to an existing set of choices of destinations and residential areas. The access formulas are not demand functions in a proper sense but describe the interaction of both demand and supply conditions.

Thus, we cannot conclude from such evidence that the top-echelon business executive really has a weaker preference for access than the supermarket checker. One reason that the executive lives farther from his work is that his work opportunities are mainly concentrated in one place—the non-residential central business district—while the supermarket employee may find a job in any of a hundred locations widely scattered over the whole area and close to residential neighborhoods. One reason that journeys to school show a high exponent (implying strong access influence and a relatively short journey) is of course that schools are widely dispersed and, in fact, explicitly oriented to residential neighborhoods. Also omitted from consideration are factors of imposed segregation (we know relatively little about the residence preferences of Negroes) and neighborhood amenity (some styles of life are simply not feasible at any price in high-density neighborhoods). The upshot is that a great deal more analysis would be needed in order to develop a more basic understanding of what people really prefer and why.

We need such an understanding in order to assess the impact and the desirability of programs and changes that affect the range of choices available: e.g., provision of modern housing in close-in areas, provision of suburban "office centers," loosening of racial segregation constraints, provision of convenient and speedy mass transit. The danger in models based simply on existing origin-destination patterns, "trip desire lines" and utilization of existing public versus private transport modes is that they tend to make the status quo into the ideal. This is objectionable if we believe that "the status is nothing to quo about."

Classification of Activities

A crucial problem for operational analysis of urban spatial patterns in general is the devising of classification systems that group the various urban activities or land uses into a manageably small number of locationally homogeneous categories. We know already that if any very useful analytical results are to be expected, the biggest land use category, residence, needs to be subdivided into at least a few groups according to income level, color, and household structure (basically, numbers of children and labor-force participants in the household). This subdivision is essentially because the characteristics markedly affect the relative preference and effective demand for location within the urban area. We know, too, that there is a hierarchy of consumer-oriented or household-serving activities loosely describable as "retail trade and consumer services" which can be logically subdivided according to the trade-off between scale and consumer access.[23] At one end of this gamut are big-league ball parks, opera houses, Tiffany's, and major art museums; at the other the "Ma and Pa" corner grocery; in between, the groupings making up the subhierarchy of neighborhood and regional shopping centers.

A vast amount of descriptive material exists on the relative amounts of intra-urban central concentration of different types of retail and consumer service activities, and the larger chain-store firms and shopping center developers have developed highly sophisticated market and cost analysis procedures to guide their choice of location.[24] Data in terms of classes of stores, for example, such as those reported in the Census of Business, are less basic here than those in terms of commodity or service purchases, since the mix of products or services for any class of outlet is flexible. An example of the latter approach is a study (based on Greater Boston survey data) which developed a three-way classification of various merchandise lines according to the percentage of suburbanites' purchases which are made downtown. It is

[23] For a suggested "hierarchy of CBD land uses and land values," identifying a series of specific business activities and the ranges of land values that they can support, see Larry Smith, "Space for the CBD's Functions," in *Journal of the American Institute of Planners,* Vol. 27, No. 1 (February 1961), Table 4, p. 38.
[24] For an up-to-date picture of the "state of the art" in this type of work, see Bernard J. Kane, Jr., *A Systematic Guide to Supermarket Location Analysis* (New York: Fairchild Publications, 1966).

reported that consumers in the "outer fringe" shop downtown for a major proportion of their needs in a list of "high-ticket fashion goods" including fur coats, fine jewelry, furniture, and so on; for about half of their needs in a list of "middle-ticket shopping goods" including shoes, men's shirts, pressure cookers, and so on; and for lower proportions of their needs for "radios, television sets, hard white goods, children's wear, and low-ticket women's wear." [25]

It would seem that a still more penetrating analysis of the factors underlying changes in the location of retail and consumer service functions relative to consumers would pay off. Some application of factor analysis might help to develop more locationally homogeneous and stable groupings of commodity and service lines and store types. The relationships suggested earlier in this paper between size and frequency of purchase, variety of goods, transportability of customer and product, scale economies in distribution, and location could be worked out more fully in quantitative terms to give a basis for explanation, prediction, and planning along more than purely extrapolative and empirical lines. An eminently logical and promising conceptual approach is that involved in the application of central-place theory to intra-urban, market-oriented activities, since that theory is designed specifically to explain location when the main factors involved are (1) scale or other agglomeration economies and (2) access to a highly diffused or continuous market. Until very recently, central-place analysis had been applied only on a more macro scale, in reference to the functions of small and large urban centers in a system of cities. [26]

For a consumer-oriented activity at any given level in the intra-urban central-place hierarchy, an index of customer access potential is a useful guide to an optimum choice of locations. This method is illustrated in a study of shopping centers in the Baltimore metropolitan area. [27] It was found that the actual sales at the various centers (or in

[25] John P. Alevizos and A. E. Beckwith, "Downtown Dilemma," *Harvard Business Review,* Vol. 32, January–February 1954, p. 117.

[26] ". . . the aggregative [central-place] model and the attendant inequalities are applicable not simply to systems of urban centers, but also to systems of business centers within cities. The same basic relationships repeat themselves . . . referring to streetcorner, neighborhood, and community centers, respectively." Brian J. L. Berry, "Research Frontiers in Urban Geography," in Hauser and Schnore, *op. cit.,* pp. 407–8. Berry's article cites (pp. 424–30) recent literature on both interurban and intra-urban applications of central-place analysis.

[27] T. R. Lakshmanan and Walter G. Hansen, "Analysis of Market Potential for a Set of Urban Retail Centers," a paper prepared for presentation at 20th International Geographical Congress Symposium, Nottingham, England, July 1964 (mimeo.). See also Lakshmanan and Hansen, "A Retail Market Potential Model," *Journal of the American Institute of Planners,* Vol. 31, Special Issue on "Urban Development Models: New Tools for Planning (May 1965).

some cases, the number of shopping trips to those centers, from transportation survey data) corresponded rather closely to what would be predicted on the basis of an index of access to the homes of consumers (weighted by their total retail expenditures). Every point in the urban area has some value on the access index. It should be noted that the access index in this case tells us neither how many shopping centers there should be nor where. It does, however, evaluate the relative market possibilities or locational advantage of each of a specified set of shopping center locations. The number of viable centers of a given hierarchy level is presumably dependent on the importance of scale economies in the production function, and the preferred location in any specific part of the urban area would be suggested (with sufficiently fine-grained data) by "local peaks" in the access index.

Subcenters

Although a city or metropolis generally has one identifiable main center, there are subordinate centers as well. Spatially an urban area is multinuclear, and some models of urban spatial structure particularly stress the development of subcenters. Current and foreseeable trends, entailing the rapid sprawl and coalescence of originally discrete cities and towns into metropolitan and megalopolitan complexes, bring this multinuclear aspect increasingly into prominence as a basic characteristic of the urban pattern. Los Angeles today and the Boston-Washington megalopolis tomorrow are striking examples. So are the numerous "Twin Cities," "Tri-Cities" and even "Quad-Cities."

The central-place principle already discussed is the key to part of this phenomenon. Any consumer-serving activity that can attain its economies of scale and agglomeration without having to serve the entire urban area from a single center will increase its proximity to consumers by more or less dispersion into shopping centers, each of which serves a part of the whole area. And each shopping center is in turn a concentration of employment activity, a focal point for access for work, shopping, and recreational trips. The basic concentric patterns of access advantage, centripetal movement of people, and centrifugal movement of goods and services, is replicated in each part of the urban area, albeit for a more restricted range of central-place functions than those represented downtown. Gradients of residential density, land values, and intensity of land use appear around each of these subcentral points, like hillocks on the shoulders of a major peak.

But this explanation in terms of central-place functions only goes part way. It does not explain why subcenters of activity are functionally differentiated in some ways that have nothing to do with their relative size or their standing in the central-place hierarchy.

The logic of this further subcenter basis is evident as soon as we recognize that, among the types of activity which usually do agglomerate in one place within an urban area, there are many for which the central business district is not an economic location. These activities are highly concentrated, but typically off-center.

For some, the basic reason is inherent in their production functions: they simply do not use space intensively enough to afford downtown land. Let us revert for a moment to the initial model, in which each kind of activity occupies one of a series of concentric annular zones. Suppose that (in the absence of any economies of scale) some particular activity would be optimally located in a ring five miles out from the center, and that this activity uses a million square feet of land. If the ring goes all the way around, it would be only six feet wide! In the real world, a more compact shape would certainly commend itself. A location can be found where the entire million square feet could be in one compact tract, with the access potential to the whole urban area a little less than the five mile radius ring would have, and/or the cost of the space per square foot a little higher than it would be in that ring. These access and price penalties would in practice be more than offset by the convenience and economy that the activity would gain by substituting an off-center blob for a thin ring as its site. Examples of this are everywhere. Art museums, ball fields, airports, and universities are all activities generally occupying only a single location in an urban area, but a definitely off-center location, for the reasons already suggested.

In the examples just cited, blob is preferred to doughnut because the activity in question is subject to some economies of agglomeration which tend to be increasingly difficult to achieve in a ring distribution the farther out the ring is. These economies of agglomeration can reflect either scale economies for individual units, or establishments (such as an airport or a university), or access advantages from close clustering of many individual units of the same type (as in the case of automobile showrooms). Two further points should be noted here, however.

First, an exception. The innovation of circumferential freeways has made it more feasible for some kinds of activities (for example, electronics and similar light and technologically oriented industries) to assume a distribution along at least a sizable arc, i.e., part of a doughnut. Boston's Route 128 is a case in point.

Secondly, the tendency toward concentration at the expense of symmetry is found in specific types of residential land use as well, reflecting among other things the previously mentioned preference for neighborhood homogeneity which acts like an agglomerative force for any particular class of residence (e.g., very high-income, single-family houses), even where low densities are involved.

A still further basis for off-center concentration appears in situations where the activity in question serves a market that is itself lopsidedly distributed in relation to the over-all area. For example, if residential areas that are occupied by higher-income and educational groups are predominantly northwest of the city center, trade and service activities catering especially to those groups will find the point of maximum market access potential somewhere northwest of the city center.

Finally, special topographical or other site features may make a particular off-center location optimal even though it does not have the best access. The availability of a large level tract amid generally hilly topography may well be the decisive factor for such uses as airports or major industrial developments.

Whatever the basis, an off-center concentration of some sizable activity can provide a nucleus (through employment opportunity and other considerations) for cumulative development of a focal access point (a local peak of access potential) for other activities as well, including residence.

Sectors

Some approaches to the explanation of urban spatial patterns have stressed tendencies of differentiation according to direction rather than distance from the center. The sector theory is associated especially with Hoyt, and has been stated as follows: ". . . growth along a particular axis of transportation usually consists of similar types of land use. The entire city is considered as a circle and the various areas as sectors radiating out from the center of that circle; similar types of land use originate near the center of the circle and migrate outward toward the periphery." [28]

In terms of the pattern existing at any given time in an urban area, it is easy to explain sectoral differentiation on the basis of such factors as (1) topographical and other natural variation, (2) the presence of

[28] Homer Hoyt, *The Structure and Growth of Residential Neighborhoods in American Cities*, U.S. Federal Housing Administration (U.S. Government Printing Office, 1939). The quotation is from Chauncy D. Harris and Edward L. Ullman, *op. cit.*, in *Readings in Urban Geography*, p. 283. Cf. also, in the same volume, Homer Hoyt, "The Pattern of Movement of Residential Rental Neighborhoods," pp. 499–510.

a limited number of important radial transport routes, and (3) the previously discussed incentives toward a greater concentration of any one activity than a symmetrical concentric ring layout would afford. But the Hoyt hypothesis is couched primarily in dynamic terms, as an explanation of persistent sectoral differences in the character of development. And in that context, it introduces two further useful concepts.

One is that of succession of uses of a given site or neighborhood area. Except at the outer fringe of urban settlement, each type of land use as it expands is taking over from an earlier use; by and large, the growth process involves (as described earlier in the concept of the simple monocentric model) an outward encroachment by each type of activity into the next zone. Some such transitions are cheaper or easier than others, and the extension tends to be in the direction of easiest transition. Thus, obsolete mansions are conveniently converted into funeral homes; row houses and apartments are easily converted, subdivided, and downgraded into low-income tenements; and obsolete factory space is easily used for wholesaling and storage. The well-known "filtering" theory of succession of uses in the urban housing market implies gradual and continuous, rather than abrupt, change in residential neighborhood character.

The other useful concept might be called "minimum displacement." The growth process uproots all kinds of housing and business activities in the zones of transition, forcing them to seek new locations. Copious empirical evidence bears out the reasonable presumption that when these moves are made by householders or small and neighborhood-serving businesses, there is a very strong preference for remaining as close as possible to the old location. This cohesion, or inertia, which is quite rational in the light of both economic and social considerations, of course tends to perpetuate a sectoral differentiation and to cause a particular activity to move gradually outward along the line of least resistance rather than into another sector.

III. GROWTH AND CHANGE

The remainder of this paper will focus on the dynamics of urban spatial structure, which up to this point has come in for only incidental attention. Most of our real problems involve dislocations (imperfect adjustments) which arise because of some change. Urban areas grow in size, they age, their populations achieve higher living standards and changed consumption patterns, the technology of production, transport, and exchange develops, and public action plays new roles.

We can start off by trying to isolate the effects of certain sources of change that seem relatively simple, one-dimensional, and predictable.

265

One of these is growth in size, with the related phenomenon of aging. Another is rising income levels as such, also a trend that we have become accustomed to taking for granted.

Growth

Some kinds of changes in spatial patterns in an urban area stem simply from increased size, independent of higher levels of income or technology. One appropriate way to shed light on the structural implications of pure size is to make cross-sectional comparisons among urban areas of different populations in the same country at the same time.

What differences, then, do we find associated with larger city size as such? Some of the most obvious ones can be rationalized in terms of the basic density gradient model of an urban area. Increased total size has both intensive and extensive impacts: the central densities or other measures of peak central intensity rise; in other parts of the area the intensity of land use increases. Residential densities in any given zone increase, except that the central non-residential crater expands. Increases in density are greatest, percentage-wise, at the outer fringe of urban development.

We also envisage (as impacts of growth per se) the successive pushing out and widening of the various more or less concentric zones of activity, already discussed in the context of the original Burgess model. An increase in the length of all types of journeys and hauls of goods is likewise to be expected.

But as such journeys and shipments become lengthier and more expensive with expansion of the area, there are partially compensatory adjustments, representing responses to the increased incentive to keep travel time and cost from being excessive. Subcenters for various single activities or groups of activities play an increasing role in a larger urban area, because the total market in the area, for more and more kinds of goods and services, comes to be big enough to support two or more separate production or service centers at an efficient scale rather than just one. This is clearly pictured in the intra-urban central-place schema. Thus, the hierarchy of central places in a small town consists of just a single order of activities, all concentrated on Main Street. In a larger place there may be two levels in the central-place hierarchy: downtown activities and neighborhood subcenters. In a still larger urban area there will be more levels: some kinds of activity being replicated in dozens or even hundreds of individual neighborhoods, others being replicated in a handful of big shopping centers serving a whole sector of the area, and still others serving the whole area from a single location

266

(which, in the simplified central-place schema, is, of course, the central business district).[29]

It would appear, then, that growth as such helps to account for the flattening of density gradients that has characteristically shown up as a trend in our cities—though there are, of course, other and perhaps even more important reasons as well. And this growth impact, involving the development of more and more kinds of subcenters of non-residential activity, comes in response to the enlarged total market in the area as a whole and the desire to keep length of journeys from increasing too much.

Finally, the larger size of the area, with its expanded and more variegated manpower, services, materials, and markets, provides the basis for an increasing number of non-central-place subcenters as well —i.e., off-center concentrations of non-residential activity that are not simply oriented to the neighborhood consumer market but may serve the whole area and outside markets as well.

Thus, the picture of changing patterns in an urban area that is simply getting more populous, assuming no changes in the state of technology or level of income, is this: Development proceeds both vertically (i.e., in terms of more intensive use of space) and horizontally (in terms of use of more space). Each specialized zone of activities widens and moves outward, encroaching on its outer neighbor and giving way to its inner neighbor. New types of central-place activities arise in the central area. The variety of types of activity and occupancy increases. Off-center foci of both central-place type and other activities increase in number, size, diversity, and importance. The gradient of residential densities becomes higher but flatter. The average length of journeys and total amount of travel and internal goods transfer increases, but not as much as it would if all non-residential activity remained as highly concentrated at the center as it was originally. The pattern of transport flows becomes much more complex, with more criss-crossing and more non-radial traffic.

With the increased variety of activities, occupations, and styles of life represented in a larger area, and the proliferation of more and more orders and types of subcenters, it is clear that size of an urban

[29] There is plenty of empirical verification of the smaller relative importance of the central business district as a travel destination in larger cities. It appears further that the effect is more pronounced for non-work journeys than for journeys to work. Cf. for example, Richard B. Andrews, *Urban Growth and Development* (Simmons-Boardman, 1962), Ch. 3, citing relevant evidence from U.S. Bureau of Public Roads, *Parking Guide for Cities* (U.S. Government Printing Office, 1956). Table 26, p. 29; D. L. Foley, "The Daily Movement of Population into Central Business Districts," *American Sociological Review,* Vol. 17 (October 1952), p. 541; and U.S. Census of Business.

area is associated with a more elaborately differentiated pattern of land uses: more spatial division of labor and specialization of functions. This increased heterogeneity in the whole fosters, somewhat paradoxically at first sight, increased homogeneity within individual neighborhoods and other subareas, or segregation in the broad sense of the term. We have considered earlier the various pressures for micro-scale homogeneity within urban areas, and these pressures can operate to a much greater degree in the framework of a larger and more varied community complex. One manifestation of this is the magnitude of the problem of de facto racial segregation of schools (i.e., reflecting neighborhood composition) in larger cities. Another is the problem (again, most in evidence in the larger cities) of accommodating intensely cohesive specialized business concentrations such as the Manhattan garment district and urban wholesale produce markets which are highly resistant to piecemeal moving or adjustment. A third manifestation is the problem (also more in evidence in the largest metropolitan areas) of political and economic conflict between the main central city and surrounding suburbs and the resistance of the latter to merger or basic co-ordination with the central city or with one another.

Thus, it appears that many of the most pressing problems of our larger urban areas today, ranging from traffic congestion to racial discord, city/suburb conflict, and the fiscal crises of central cities, can be traced in some part to sheer size. They are implicit in even the extremely simplified models of urban structure already discussed in this paper. Still more broadly, it is clear that larger agglomerations, as such, raise increasingly challenging problems of divergence of private from social (and local from over-all) costs and benefits, in view of the intensified proximity impacts involving scarcity of space, pollution of water and air, environmental nuisances, and generally increased interdependence of interests. These problems are part of the quid pro quo for the economic and social advantages of greater diversity of contact and opportunity: the rationale of the city.

This hypothetical and mainly deductive picture of trends of change in a single growing area conforms very closely, as would be expected, with what we observe empirically in a cross-sectional comparison of urban areas of different sizes in one country at one time. Moreover, we recognize in the picture a great many familiar features corresponding to observed historical and current trends. We can infer that simple growth plays a part in accounting for them and can be expected to exert a similar influence in the future.

But in some ways the picture does not fit. Conspicuously unrealistic in relation to observed trends, for example, is the implied rise in the central density parameter of the residential density gradient. As we have seen, this figure has characteristically fallen off in the present century, at least in urban areas in the more developed countries. Influences other than growth per se must account for that phenomenon and for a great many other features of the actual evolution of urban spatial patterns.

Aging

The relative age of urban settlements, urban populations, neighborhoods, and structures is always identified as a significant factor accounting for different spatial patterns of development and a wide range of urban problems, in both empirical and theoretical analyses. As noted earlier, Berry, Muth, Schnore, and other research leaders in this field assign the aging factor a prominent role. It has been shown that significant further insights into differences observed in cross-sectional comparisons can be gained when the relative ages of the areas compared are introduced as an explanatory variable, and reasons have been put forward for this effect.

Aging in the literal sense implies simply the effect of the passage of time upon something (e.g., a person, a firm, a building, a city) that retains its identity. This is not so simple a variable as might at first sight appear. The age of a person is of course reckoned from his birth, and that of a structure from its construction. But structures can be modified and renovated. Mark Twain used to refer to his favorite "old" jackknife, which had had several new blades and several new handles. And how old is a city?

Pragmatically, the age of a city has been measured by arbitrarily assigning as its date of birth the date at which it attained some specified minimum population, such as 50,000. If, at the same time, we are considering the current population of the area as an independent variable, the relation between the two, of course, reflects the average rate of growth per annum since the assigned "birth date." In other words, size, growth, and age are rather tightly interdependent; we have really two variables rather than three.

In the case of a region's population, the age structure reflects not the age of the region but essentially the previous rate of growth. A fast-growing urban area almost inevitably has a relatively young population, whether the growth comes from high birth rates or from net in-migration, and a slow-growing area is characterized by a relatively old population.[30]

[30] Some qualifications must be noted here. Mortality differentials among areas are ignored, and there is also the special case of the fast-growing "Senior Citi-

There is a somewhat less direct relationship between the previous or current growth rate of an urban area and the degree to which its physical and human resources are "behind the times" or overage in an economic sense. The latter depends on the extent to which renewal has failed to keep pace with changing needs and conditions. Growth and change have a dual effect on obsolescence in this context. They influence both (1) the need and incentive, and (2) the economic capabilities for renewal and expansion.

This is well brought out in Ira S. Lowry's penetrating critique of the filter-down theory of the housing market.[31] That theory assumes or implies that housing depreciates inexorably with the sheer passage of time. Under that hypothesis, if the upper income groups who can afford it indulge a preference for new housing, the same units will then over the course of time be passed on, at ever lower prices, to occupants with lower and lower income levels, and each stratum of urban society except the top will have access to the housing given up by the stratum above. Something like this appears to occur in the used car market, and Lowry's contention is that the analogy has been unwarrantedly assumed to apply to the housing market as well. The filter-down process does not actually operate very effectively in housing, he shows, because housing quality deterioration is not by any means so closely related to age as is the case with automobiles. Instead, it depends primarily on maintenance, the structure itself being almost indefinitely lasting if adequately maintained. Unless the owner can afford maintenance, the housing rather quickly loses both habitability and economic value.

Affluence

We complacently assume, in looking to the future, that we shall be ever more numerous and also ever richer. The latter effect has been shown to be mainly contingent on continuous advances in technology rather than the mere accumulation of a larger stock of capital per man;[32] but barring world holocaust we feel that such advance is now built in and dependable in the more fortunate developed nations, if not elsewhere. Certain kinds of technological change we shall have to discuss later in terms of their specific effects on the urban spatial pat-

---

zens" communities so common in Florida and the Southwest. It remains true, however, that the average age of an area's work force is inversely related to the previous rate of growth of employment in the area.

[31] Ira S. Lowry, "Filtering and Housing Standards: A Conceptual Analysis," in *Land Economics,* Vol. 36, No. 4 (November 1960), pp. 362–70.

[32] Cf. Edward F. Denison, *The Sources of Economic Growth* (New York: Committee for Economic Development, 1962).

tern; but some observations can be made on the effects on that pattern stemming from rising levels of economic well-being as such.

A higher family income in real terms means more to spend on both living space and transportation, two kinds of expenditure that we have already identified as peculiarly significant in shaping urban residential patterns. It means also more to spend on a wider variety of other goods and services (including public services), and finally the opportunity to take some of the gains in the form of leisure and in a broad range of pursuits that combine both consumption and "investment in human capital" aspects, such as education and cultural activity. Which of these avenues of increased benefit will be emphasized (i.e., the relative income elasticities of different kinds of expenditure plus leisure) is largely culturally determined; it has to be gauged from empirical evidence on actual behavior, and can change greatly.

Mention has been made of the fact that cross-sectional evidence (comparing the behavior of the poor and the rich at any one time) strongly suggests that rising income levels will go into the purchase or rental of more residential space and more daily travel in such a way that lot sizes and the length of intra-urban journeys will continue to increase while residential densities and slopes of density gradients will continue to fall in our urban areas.[33]

The extent to which this trend will continue, however, cannot be predicted with confidence. Some of the outward movement of upper-income groups may be associated with the income difference as such, though (as suggested earlier) we do not seem to have any convincing deductive demonstration that this should be so. Some is without doubt due to greater automobile ownership, and in that respect we may expect differentials among income groups will diminish. Some reflects a preference for new housing against old, and that factor might con-

[33] This empirically substantiated phenomenon is sometimes characterized as showing that "access is an inferior good"; i.e., as people get richer, they buy less access rather than more, because they prefer to spend their added incomes on something else; just as a Southern farmer might be expected to buy less grits, molasses, and corn liquor (and more beefsteak and bonded bourbon) if he struck oil on his land. The analogy is slippery and a bit misleading, however. What does buying more access mean in the urban context? If it means investing in a car that will quicken or ease or cheapen the journey to work, then it is clear that the income elasticity is strongly positive, not negative. Automobiles are not yet an "inferior good" as the term is used in economic analysis. If buying more access means moving closer to the work place, then it really means *reducing* transport cost and time and either reducing residential space or paying more for it. A further complication in integrating the access/space trade-off into rigorous analysis in terms of price and income elasticities is that access has to be conceived as some kind of inverse (perhaps a reciprocal of travel cost), of which one very important component (time) is appropriately imputed at a price depending on income.

ceivably change with a shift in tastes or in refurbishment technology. And some reflects a flight from proximity of low-income (particularly Negro) newcomers to the central city, who have so far been rather tightly concentrated there by sociopolitical as well as economic barriers. Arrest and substantial redress of the threatening drift toward a contrast of slum cities and all-white suburbs might well have cumulative equalizing effects in the long run. So might a sufficiently drastic enhancing of downtown amenities, that might make the central area something more than a destination for necessary work and special shopping trips.

It is pretty clear that a partial cause of the relative decline of the central areas of cities is the trend toward increased leisure, at least as embodied in the prevalence of the five-day work week and longer vacations. It is generally assumed that still further reduction of work hours will, on balance, heighten people's appetite for spacious home sites and neighborhoods, if only because they can spend more time around home. Here again, there is a conceivable offset in the possibility that the central areas of cities will offer more tempting recreational, cultural, and other off-hours opportunities than they do now. But the only conclusion that has a really firm presumptive basis is that increased leisure will continue to mean a greater number and diversity of non-work trips, probably averaging longer in distance and time. One may surmise that access to the central areas of cities is likely to diminish in importance relative to other access, though perhaps not nearly as rapidly as has happened in the past few decades.

Technological Progress

It is both difficult and artificial to make any sharp separation between the impact of affluence and the impact of technological change upon ways of life and the urban spatial pattern. Greater affluence comes from technological change, and at the same time this change provides new kinds of goods and services for the more affluent society to buy.[34]

Specific attention needs to be given, however, to technological

[34] For what is perhaps the best recent discussion of the role of technology and rising income levels in reshaping urban spatial patterns, with some predictions of future developments, the reader is referred to Meyer, Kain, and Wohl, *op. cit.*, Ch. 2. The authors emphasize that, although transport and communications development, and particularly the private automobile, have played a leading role in the relative decline of urban central areas, a number of other factors have also been in part responsible. These include (in addition to the effects of more income and leisure already discussed here) new technologies in materials handling and distribution that have radically changed factory and store layouts, mechanized and automated data processing, and television as a means of both entertainment and communication.

changes in transport and communication in view of their direct relation to change in spatial patterns. Indeed, the impact of mass ownership of automobiles (particularly in suburbanization of industry and population) has been so evident and so copiously analyzed that there would be little point in belaboring it here. Quasi-universal car ownership is indeed a fait accompli, and perhaps we should devote more attention to the future implications of a termination of the changeover rather than to the fairly long-standing experience of the changeover itself. More positively, we need to conjecture as to the nature and spatial impacts of whatever is the next step in urban transport progress. Innovations have a way of responding to persistent economic pressure, and some of the pressures are already clear. Chief of these is the more and more obvious conflict between effective realization of the access advantages of individualized transport in terms of flexibility and convenience, and the high space requirements of such transport in its present form. Despite (or might we better say, because of?) the zeal of public parking authorities and freeway promoters, and the persistence of use of curb space for parking at quite nominal fees, the private automobile has, in at least some cities, worn its welcome to the center pretty thin. The possible implications of a more efficient system for bringing large numbers of people into close contact in agreeable surroundings appear large in terms of revitalization of the urban mechanism at its most vital spot.

Much has been made, in some speculations about the urban future, of the idea that with improved facilities for transport and particularly communication, distance means less and less, and people's contacts and access cease to be closely associated with space or location.[35] It is clear that the typical household and business has had and will find it increasingly easy to develop and maintain ties with households and firms in other regions, and that such contacts will continue to increase. It is less clear, however, that this really has much bearing on the future of intra-urban spatial patterns with which we are concerned. A more likely presumption is that these growing external contacts are simply in addition to, and not substitutes for, local contacts, which are likewise becoming more numerous, convenient, and multifarious. And there is no reason to expect a radical change in space relations unless

[35] For a discussion that emphasizes the potential effects of reduced transport and communication costs in terms of diminished rationale for concentration, lower land values, and substitution of amenity for access as the major location factor, see Melvin M. Webber, "Order in Diversity: Community Without Propinquity," in Lowdon Wingo, Jr. (ed.), *Cities and Space: The Future Use of Urban Land* (The Johns Hopkins Press for Resources for the Future, 1963), pp. 23–56.

and until some essentially distance-free communication obviates the necessity for existing important access desires that do depend on distance. The telephone did not do away with either the business office or the shopping trip, and it is doubtful that it diminished social travel. It is not easy to envisage any other device doing so in the foreseeable future.

IV. SOME IMPLICATIONS FOR URBAN PLANNING AND ANALYSIS

Some Problems

This paper is not meant to survey the whole range of current urban problems or to prescribe solutions.[36] It has, however, attempted to provide some insights into the influences at work in shaping urban patterns, and the way in which these influences account for the stresses and maladjustments that are only too evident today and will continue to challenge our capacities for understanding and constructive action. It is appropriate to conclude, then, with a few observations on some of the most basic unsolved problems which should be high on the urban economist's agenda.

Slums. Among these challenges is the old maxim, "the poor always ye have with you." A quite sizable proportion of our urban populations —and in absolute terms perhaps an increasing number of persons and households—are, in this most affluent of nations, simply unable to afford what the consensus prescribes as decent housing. The problem is not new, of course; what is most disquieting is that a rising gross national product does not make it go away. The question of where and how to house the urban poor is basically unsolved, and mainly met by palliative subsidy or by evasion. Disillusionment with redevelopment programs that merely shove the slums from one neighborhood to another is by now nearly universal, but it is not clear just what we should try next.

One clearly basic step toward a solution that would enable nearly everyone to afford decent housing is, of course, the enhancement of the income earning capacity of the lowest-income groups. Along with a greater capacity to afford housing, this presumably also confers greater capacity to contribute to the economic and social level of the community and a greater degree of acceptability as neighbors, and thus greater occupational and spatial mobility. For this we have to rely

---

[36] The best effort in that direction to date is the overmodestly-titled work by Wilbur R. Thompson, *A Preface to Urban Economics* (The Johns Hopkins Press for Resources for the Future, 1965).

mainly on intensified and more effective programs of education and training for both jobs and citizenship. The realization has been slow in coming that the poorer neighborhoods will require superior facilities and programs of a more intensive and extensive nature. This conviction is still far from being generally shared and expressed in actual policy decisions.

It is also reasonable to expect that an important contribution must come from the side of technological progress in the housing industry (in the broadest sense) if we are to close the gap between present minimum standards and what the poor can afford. There are three distinct aspects to this: more efficient and cheaper construction designs and methods, more efficient and cheaper ways of adapting existing structures and neighborhoods to low-income occupancy, and more realistic and purposeful adaptation of the standards themselves (which are still subject to a variety of anachronistic and irrational constraints imposed by legal codes, tradition, and restrictive practice in the industry). Have there been any intensive expert efforts (e.g., stimulated by design competitions or research contracts) to specify just what kinds of housing could, with best use of current know-how, really be provided on a no-subsidy basis, and just how vitally these would fall short of a tolerable minimum? [37] This might provide some useful guidance to the features in which technological advance is most crucial.

More directly relevant to the question of urban spatial patterns is the growing acceptance of the idea that the most effective attack on slums will involve both improving and diluting them, i.e., providing better living conditions and more jobs in the slums, and at the same time removing barriers to out-migration. A given aggregate amount of poverty and ignorance, according to this idea, is socially less serious and more quickly curable if it is scattered than if it makes up a solid mass.

Development of a slum is a syndrome involving particularly the deterioration of housing and private community facilities on the one hand, and the growing predominance of very low-income residents on the other. These tend to interact in a cumulative way. Lessinger and others have shown that the economics of property ownership in such an area discourages individual upkeep, modernization, and replacement of substandard buildings, and that this is particularly true in large, continuous, homogeneous slum areas with no vacant land or newer development nearby. Drastic surgery in the form of massive urban renewal, with displacement of populations and other disadvantages, has

[37] This suggestion should not be misinterpreted as a condemnation of public subsidies to low-income housing.

been the principal remedy applied thus far, and it must be regarded as costly and less than satisfactory to all concerned.

In a recent provocative article,[38] Lessinger argues that "compaction" in development—meaning the full build-up of large residential areas all at one time, so that the dwellings are homogeneous as to age—is the main source of our slum problem, and that urban land use and transport planning should aim instead at "scatteration." This means the encouragement of "leapfrogging" in developing new residential areas, with plenty of intervening land left for later development and consequently a greater ultimate degree of variation in age of housing among neighborhoods.

This suggestion raises two questions. To what extent does it conflict with what we have identified as a basic preference for neighborhood homogeneity, and to what extent does it conflict with the aim of an efficient urban layout in terms of quick, cheap, and easy transport?

The first of these questions does not seem serious, if we can assume that the homogeneity people really value is in terms of quite small neighborhood areas, and that they are relatively indifferent as to who lives a mile or so away. The really intractable slum and ghetto problems, both in terms of their social effects and the economic problems of motivating maintenance and modernization, are those that involve areas much larger than anything that could reasonably be called a neighborhood.

Grounds for controversy really arise, however, when we consider the relationship of scatteration to transport planning. Lessinger appears to conclude that the benefits of scatteration are likely to outweigh any additions to transport costs entailed by increasing the number of gaps in settlement, and that a development design involving radial corridors with rapid transit is fated to produce nothing but finger-like slums. Accordingly, among the many policies for discouraging compaction, he suggests indefinite postponement of such transit projects and continued reliance on private automobiles.

This conclusion will not go unchallenged. To the extent that access is a controlling factor on the timing of development of urban areas, the pattern will depend on how travel time is related to airline distance. Transport modes in which time is closely related to distance in any direction (involving a smooth continuous "transport surface" and a very fine-grained network of possible routes of travel with free access)

[38] Jack Lessinger, "The Case for Scatteration," in *Journal of the American Institute of Planners*, Vol. 28 (August 1962), pp. 159–69. The author emphasizes that compaction and scatteration are quite independent of, and not necessarily at all correlated with, density.

should produce a relatively solid, continuous wave of development, of which a prototype might be found in the patterns of cities when nearly all travel was by foot or horse-drawn vehicle. At the opposite extreme, transport modes in which there are a limited number of relatively fast routes, and in which stops along those routes are also limited in number, should be expected to lead to development patterns highly uneven in density, with separated local clusters around the stops. Possible prototypes of this are the commuter suburbs that developed around fairly widely separated stations on commuter rail lines, and also the newer developments that are occurring around the interchanges of limited-access highways outside of and between our cities.

Thus, if we are looking for urban transport policies and plans that facilitate scatteration, we should try to make the transport surface discontinuous. This can be done by stressing channelized and limited-access modes of transport, including rapid transit with much greater extension and more widely spaced stops than conventional subway systems, rather than relying exclusively on modes in which travel time is closely related to distance in a fine-grained, unlimited-access network of highways and streets.

Downtown. A second complaint is that our urban areas are being to various degrees "strangled" and "turned inside out" by traffic congestion. The former refers to the reduction in functional effectiveness of the central areas, while the latter refers to one of the responses to that pressure: the flight of many kinds of activities to less-congested outlying areas, with some reversals in land value gradients, sequence of land uses, and travel flows. It is understood that these manifestations are due largely to the newest major forms of transport for people and goods, now accounting for most of both internal and interurban carriage. These are the private automobile and the airplane, both of which require very large amounts of elbow room, particularly at terminal points, in relation to what they carry. The rise of these two modes to major status has inevitably produced major difficulties of adjustment in urban areas.

Here, once again, we need to keep in mind that the raison d'être of an urban concentration is provision for close, easy, and multifarious interpersonal contact. From that standpoint, an urban layout is efficient when there is a focal point for concentration of as many as possible of those activities which require access to a high proportion of the firms and households of the urban area and which (because of scale economies or external economies of close agglomeration) are most efficiently confined to one location in the area.

Among such activities that are logical candidates for central location on the basis of their access and agglomeration requirements, terminals for interregional passenger transport are certainly included. Yet airports, in the present state of air transport technology, are obviously far too space consuming and noisy to be eligible for anything like a central location, and are in general far removed. If the interurban public transport of the future can be designed to be compact and in other respects compatible with intensive development in its terminal area, it will be entirely logical to expect cities to have their main external-transport terminals integrated with the main focus of their internal circulation system at the core, as it was a generation ago.[39] Current and foreseeable developments in fast interurban ground transport (e.g., proposals for the Northeast Corridor) suggest considerable promise in this direction. Prospects for relocating air terminals to city centers seem much more conjectural. But it is not unlikely that at some future time urban historians will consider as a curious temporary aberration the mid-twentieth-century period in which interurban transport did not go directly from one city center to another.

Perhaps the most fundamental urban problem involves the search for ways of exploiting the city's unique potential for maximum mass and diversity of contact, choice, and opportunity without unduly sacrificing other values. For one thing, we need to understand a great deal more (and in more specific and quantitative terms) about just what it is that urbanism does contribute to economic and social progress through its contact opportunities. A recent and valuable multidisciplinary survey[40] has illuminated the question from many angles, some of them new. But it would seem that until now, urban economists have made less headway than some other kinds of "urbanists" in developing adequate operational knowledge on the external economies associated with urban concentration and, more specifically, with intra-urban concentration. There is room for a great deal more empirical analysis as well as for amplification of the theories of location and regional development to cover complex spatial relations involving contact and time as major parameters. A host of suggestive hypotheses still awaits verification.[41]

The problem of advantages of concentration and how to exploit them comes to a head in the central business district. It is there that

[39] This paragraph is included simply as provocative speculation. Meyer, Kain, and Wohl, op. cit., Chap. 2, expect freight terminals to move to beltway junction locations, and I should not dispute the reasonableness of that projection.

[40] Hauser and Schnore, op. cit.

[41] See, for example, Robert M. Lichtenberg, op. cit., for a penetrating discussion of external economies of intra-urban agglomeration, with a substantial amount of relevant empirical evidence; and Benjamin Chinitz, "Contrasts in Agglomeration: New York and Pittsburgh," in American Economic Review, Vol. 51 (May 1961), pp. 279–89, for some suggestive hypotheses.

the potential contact opportunities are highest and the conflict with space requirements the most serious. A basic challenge to the ingenuity of urbanists is to devise ways of improving downtown areas in all of the three relevant aspects: making them *easy to get to, easy to get around in,* and *attractive and effective* as places to work or visit.

As yet, we do not know very much about the possible effectiveness of various ways of increasing the realized contact potential of central business districts. The efforts in that direction in the United States have been rather fragmentary and often mutually conflicting, and there has been some reluctance to regard experience in foreign cities (such as Rotterdam or even Toronto) as applicable to American cities. Pedestrian malls have been tiny and tentative. New downtown "amenities" have been mostly in the form of wider streets, parking garages, convention halls, and shiny skyscrapers. Radical modernization of mass transit, integrated with adequate parking and transfer facilities at the other end, and adequate intra-downtown facilities (such as mini-buses, moving sidewalks, and so on) has not really been given fair trial. Policies of various public authorities on transport have quite generally been both conflicting and self-defeating.[42] But it seems clear, despite the dearth of experimental evidence, that imaginative and consistent transport planning is basic to any improvement, or even maintenance, of the functional effectiveness of downtown areas.[43] At the same time it is clear that transport is not the whole story.

The central business district is, of course, only one key feature in the urban spatial structure. Rational planning requires not only finding out what activities can appropriately be concentrated at the center, but also what the rest of the pattern could or should look like. Urban designers continue, with increasing sophistication, to come up with a variety of alternative kinds of basic framework for systematic urban development. Economists have been slow to join forces with them in design and evaluation: for example, in making rational specifications about the specific types of activities that belong in various zones and subcenters, and in developing the traffic flow implications of the alternatives. A few major urban land use and transportation planning studies have

[42] For a critique of prevailing public policies in this regard, see E. M. Hoover, "Motor Metropolis: Some Observations on Urban Transportation in America," in *The Journal of Industrial Economics,* Vol. 13, No. 3 (June 1965).

[43] It appears that even the present relatively antiquated types of rail commuter service aid downtown activity. See, for example, John R. Meyer, "Knocking Down the Straw Men," in *Challenge, The Magazine of Economic Affairs,* Vol. 10 (December 1962), pp. 7–11, for data showing that central business district retail sales held up consistently better in relation to total SMSA sales in 1948–54 in metropolitan areas served by rail rapid transit than they did in metropolitan areas without such service.

279

attempted a genuine evaluation of this type. But there should be room for some parallel regional analysis of a generalized type, constructing and testing alternative spatial models to evolve some useful design principles that would have a sounder economic foundation. I suggest that such schematic studies, with reasonably realistic parameters derived from detailed studies in specific urban areas, may well be the quickest way to clarify or to resolve some fundamental disputes about the merits of different basic designs conceived by urban planners. There is, for example, the basic question of scatteration versus compaction already mentioned in connection with an important article by Lessinger.[44]

It seems likely that intra-urban central-place analysis will offer a useful approach, but certainly not to the exclusion of other tools in the urban/regional economist's kit. For example, a good deal of attention has been paid in recent years, in connection with planning for the development of depressed or underdeveloped regions, to the concept of growth points or growth poles. The idea is to identify, and to concentrate direct stimulus on, certain strategic locations where economic improvement will both respond strongly to encouragement and spread rapidly to surrounding areas. It would seem reasonable to apply an analogous selection process on a micro scale, to locations within urban areas. For this we need to find out how to measure both potential response and potential diffusion of impact.

Some General Guidelines

Goals tend to be taken for granted, and this paper has been no exception. The various alternative prospects that planners and projectors sketch for us appeal in different ways to different people, and this is inevitable in view of the variety of vested interests and preferences regarding such matters as space, access, mode of transport, privacy, level of public services, and the like. One answer is that the available alternatives should be spelled out as fully and fairly as possible and presented for basic decisions by the voters. Any realistically attainable degree of informed democratic consensus is, of course, likely to fall well short of that ideal. Should the urban economist simply offer no judgment, or boost his own personal preferences as such?

Perhaps he need not retreat quite that far. As an economist, he is, of course, indoctrinated to seeing that efficiency is recognized as a consideration. He will have some difficulty in really measuring efficiency in a broad way, but this criterion will help in rejecting some demon-

---

[44] For a view opposed to Lessinger's, see M. Mason Gaffney, "Containment Policies for Urban Sprawl," in Richard L. Stauber (ed.), *Approaches to the Study of Urbanization*, "Governmental Research Series," No. 27, (University of Kansas Publications, 1964), pp. 115–33.

strably self-defeating or inconsistent combinations of policies. More positively, though, he can with some justice plug for flexibility and for variety as goals of an ultimate or quasi-ultimate nature.[45]

There is no space in this paper to develop the importance of these objectives in a comprehensive way; I propose to conclude by simply putting forward a few illustrative implications.

Recognition of the value of flexibility involves merely recognition that an urban economy is a live organism. Any systematic plan of centers and subcenters and zones (such as has been suggested might be evolved in a rather sophisticated way with central-place analysis) should be challenged with the question of what happens in response to the forces of change discussed earlier in this paper: growth, aging, economic improvement, and the imperfectly foreseeable variety of changes in technology. No design can be judged until pictured in a state of adjustment; our most acute distresses, and our most intriguing opportunities, are accompaniments of adjustment.

Partly distinct from flexibility, but also a fundamental urban value, is variety. A recurrent theme in this discourse has been that the prime function of a city is to provide opportunities for the widest possible variety of contacts. The employer wants to be able to tap a labor market and find, at short notice, just the right skills and aptitudes; the job-seeker wants to find a job that fits his abilities, interests, and personal preferences; the business firm wants to be able to choose from a wide range of technical, advisory, transport, and marketing services; the home-seeker wants to find a neighborhood and a house tailored to his needs; and so on and on. Wide freedom of choice in these and other respects is unquestionably both desired and conducive to the best utilization of the community's resources, quite aside from any other merits or demerits cities have.

As noted earlier, sheer size is associated with increased latitude of choice. A larger city contains not merely *more* of each kind of activity and opportunity, but *more kinds,* permitting a closer and more efficient fit of supply to demand.

But size is not the only determinant of variety. It is a characteristic which can vary rather widely among cities of a given size, and one which can be enhanced or impaired by technological change or other factors. Let us merely note here a few points on the ways in which urban variety of choice relates to the spatial pattern.

A conscious policy of fostering variety of opportunity and choice will entail efforts to increase interoccupational, interindustry, and

[45] For a good statement of the value of wide choice in this context, see Webb S. Fiser, *Mastery of the Metropolis* (Prentice-Hall, 1962), pp. 160 ff.

spatial mobility. Our programs of education, training and retraining, and improved placement organization are directed this way. These developments, in addition to greater spatial mobility, more effective communication, and progress in softening racial and other discriminatory barriers, should widen effective job choice. This makes urban labor markets less imperfect as markets, while at the same time increasing interregional mobility and choice as well.

The spatial factors principally involved in regard to widening of job choice are two: residential segregation and transportation. Both are especially applicable to low-income, low-skilled, and non-white members of the labor force; these are the people *for* whom and *from* whom the greatest economic benefits will accrue in the widening of urban residential and work choice and the fuller utilization of manpower resources that this makes possible.

The above suggests that intra-urban transportation (private and/or public) has a case for subsidy (though not necessarily an ever-increasing amount of subsidy).[46] On the basis of the general virtues of widened choice, one could argue for preserving and developing a wide range of densities of development and a wide range of *modes* of intra-urban transport. High-density, high-speed transit services on special rights-of-way go with a strong core and radial configuration, in contrast to an over-all pattern that emphasizes more even dispersion and replicated subcenters while de-emphasizing any central core or stem.

One thing that makes comparative evaluation difficult is that, in terms of return on the transport investment, each of the schemes tends to be somewhat self-justifying. That is, a well-developed rapid transit system fosters the kind of settlement pattern that gives such a system good business, while reliance on highways fosters the kind of settlement pattern that can least economically be served by anything but the private automobile. Obvious though this feedback effect may seem, it has still not been given real recognition in most planning and transportation studies.[47]

---

[46] On the rationale for subsidy to *public* transport in urban areas, see Benjamin Chinitz (ed.), *City and Suburb* (Prentice-Hall, 1964), pp. 35–41.

[47] ". . . the entire metropolitan land use configuration is a direct function of our transportation system's design. . . . Yet, transportation planning is still dominated by the idea that transportation facilities are to be designed to serve existing and projected demand for traffic service."

"The value neutrality of transportation planning is clearly impossible. . . . The effect of a transportation system . . . is to create its own traffic demand. The only way out of this causal circle is to impose, from the outside, a policy decision—i.e., a political decision—at least about the desired patterns of land use and traffic movement." Melvin M. Webber, "Transportation Planning Models," in *Traffic Quarterly,* Vol. 15 (July 1961), pp. 380, 382.

In deciding on the relative merits of contrasting layout alternatives, such as those described, it is both appropriate and important to note that the "radial corridor" type of layout embraces a full range of development densities, concentrations of access potential, and traffic densities, while the alternative, more uniformly dispersed pattern embraces a much smaller range in each of these respects. What the latter excludes is the highest range of intensities and densities; perhaps this throws away a unique economic advantage of urban agglomeration. But we have as yet no way of gauging this effect quantitatively. No one really can say what advantages Los Angeles is missing through not having the kind of compact center that an auto-dominated metropolis must forego, and what it gains in return. But in the absence of adequate knowledge, it would appear good strategy to rely on the principle that a wide choice of types of environment, contact densities, and transport modes is desirable per se, and hence to lean toward the incorporation of at least a basic framework of really fast and really compact public transport as part of any major urban structure.

Another aspect of variety in the urban pattern is variety in levels and styles of public services. Reference has already been made to the strong desires of small suburban municipalities to preserve independence in this regard, which is related to but not identical with their desire to preserve homogeneity in such characteristics as race, income, or religion. We cannot consistently condemn their resistance to annexation or metropolitan government while still recognizing the value of keeping the latitude of choice of environments as wide as possible. The difficulty, and the challenge to administrative ingenuity, come in reconciling diversity and local pride with a suitable degree of co-ordination on basic services of common importance to the whole metropolitan area such as water resources, health services, higher education, and transport.[48]

On this, we are still groping for an answer. Apparently what a large urban area ought to have, for optimum functional efficiency and satisfaction, is great heterogeneity and diversity on a macrospatial scale, but at the same time this is associated in practice with homogeneity on a microspatial scale. I am not aware that we have any kind of systematic theory ready to apply to this problem.

[48] It is appropriate to refer again here to the excellent analysis of the suburban-independence question in Oliver P. Williams *et al., op. cit.*

SELECTED READINGS

Gaffney, Mason. "Containment Policies for Urban Sprawl," in Richard L. Stauber, ed. *Approaches to the Study of Urbanization.* Governmental Research Series No. 27, Lawrence, Kansas: University of Kansas Publications, 1964.

Hauser, Philip M., and Schnore, Leo F., eds. *The Study of Urbanization* (particularly the articles by Harold M. Mayer and Brian J. L. Berry). New York: John Wiley & Sons, 1965.

Hoover, Edgar M. "Motor Metropolis: Some Observations on Urban Transportation in America," *Journal of Industrial Economics,* Vol. 13, June 1964.

————, and Raymond Vernon. *Anatomy of a Metropolis.* Cambridge: Harvard University Press, 1959.

Lessinger, Jack. "The Case for Scatteration," *Journal of the American Institute of Planners,* Vol. 28, August 1962.

Lichtenberg, Robert M. *One-Tenth of a Nation.* Cambridge: Harvard University Press, 1960.

Meyer, John R., J. F. Kain, and M. Wohl. *The Urban Transportation Problem.* Cambridge: Harvard University Press, 1965.

Olsson, Gunnar. *Distance and Human Interaction: A Review and Bibliography.* Philadelphia: Regional Science Research Institute, 1965.

Schnore, Leo F. *The Urban Scene: Human Ecology and Demography.* New York: The Free Press, 1965.

Thompson, Wilbur R. *A Preface to Urban Economics.* Baltimore: The Johns Hopkins Press, for Resources for the Future, Inc., 1965.

Vernon, Raymond. *Metropolis 1985.* Cambridge; Harvard University Press, 1960.

Williams, Oliver P., Harold Herman, Charles S. Liebman, and Thomas R. Dye. *Suburban Differences and Metropolitan Policies: A Philadelphia Story.* Philadelphia: The University of Pennsylvania Press, 1965.

Wingo, Lowdon, Jr., ed. *Cities and Space: The Future Use of Urban Land.* Baltimore: The Johns Hopkins Press, for Resources for the Future, Inc., 1963.

————. *Transportation and Urban Land.* Washington, D.C.: Resources for the Future, Inc., 1961.

*Richard F. Muth**

URBAN RESIDENTIAL LAND AND HOUSING MARKETS

Economics is concerned primarily with the study of markets. Prices established on these markets play a crucial role in the allocation of resources to different uses and in determining the resulting level of the national income. The markets for residential land and for housing are among the quantitatively most important of all urban markets. According to one estimate, about three-fourths of privately developed land is devoted to residential use in urban areas,[1] and consumers typically spend around one-fifth of their disposable incomes on housing. Most urban problems are related in one way or another to the operation of urban land and housing markets, and many—such as urban decentralization, poor-quality housing, and the residential segregation of Negroes— are more intimately related to them than to any other markets. Despite their importance, however, until lately urban residential land and housing markets have received little attention from professional economists. Because of the insistent claims of other problems, relating to depression, inflation, and economic growth, economists have tended to concentrate on these. With the increasing intensification of urban problems over the past ten or fifteen years, however, economists have devoted more and more attention to the study of urban residential land and housing markets.

In this paper I summarize some recent work on this subject. The first section is concerned principally with the aggregate demand and supply relations for residential land and housing in the urban area as a whole. In the second and most of the third sections, I shall consider the interrelations among the residential land and housing markets which exist in different parts of an urban area. The final part of Section III is concerned with the reasons for the existence of separate markets for white and Negro housing and their interdependence, while Section IV examines the market for slum versus good-quality housing. The final section examines the increasing decentralization of urban areas over time, especially during the decade of the fifties.

* Professor of Economics, Washington University.
[1] Harland Bartholomew, *Land Uses in American Cities* (Harvard University Press, 1955), especially p. 121.

285

I. THE AGGREGATE DEMAND FOR AND SUPPLY OF URBAN HOUSING AND LAND

The supply of urban housing depends upon both production possibilities and the supply of productive factors, including land, to the housing industry.[2] Similarly, the demand for all urban or for urban residential land may be viewed as derived from the demand for the commodity it helps to produce, production possibilities, and the supply of other productive factors. As an alternative to estimating the structural equations of an econometric model embodying the above-noted relationships (data for which would be quite difficult to obtain), a great deal can be said about the probable magnitudes of housing supply and land demand elasticities based upon theoretical knowledge and bits and pieces of empirical evidence. In this section, then, I will first summarize the best information known to me about housing demand elasticities, production possibilities, and conditions of factor supply. I will then consider the implications of this information for the supply elasticities of housing and demand elasticities for urban land.

The demand for housing services, as distinguished from the asset or stock demand, in any area depends primarily upon total population, per capita or per family disposable income, and, to a lesser extent, the relative price of housing services. Apart from any changes in average family sizes or other demographic characteristics, one would, of course, expect housing demand to vary proportionally with population. Traditionally, it has been believed that, as a "necessity," housing demand is inelastic with respect to income. Many statistical investigations would seem to support this belief. However, the recent work of Reid[3] and myself[4] suggests that the income elasticity of housing demand is at least $+1$ and may be as large as $+2$. My comparisons of the rate of new residential construction over time and certain other comparisons in the work cited above suggest that the real-income–constant price elasticity of housing demand is about -1, though it too may be even larger numerically. I have since made other comparisons of the varia-

---

[2] As the above statement suggests, by housing I mean that bundle of services produced both by structures and the land they occupy. The consumer demands for structures and for land are almost certainly closely interrelated, and treating land and structures as inputs into the production of a commodity called housing is a convenient way of handling their interrelationships. In addition, treating residential land as an input into production for final demand rather than as an item of final demand is more in accord with the usual treatment of other classes of land (for example, agricultural).

[3] Margaret G. Reid, *Housing and Income* (University of Chicago Press, 1962).

[4] Richard F. Muth, "The Demand for Non-Farm Housing," in Arnold C. Harberger (ed.), *The Demand for Durable Goods* (University of Chicago Press, 1960).

tion of housing expenditures among different parts of a city and among various cities. In the former case, the price of housing services varies because of variations in transport costs (this is discussed in greater detail in Section II); in the latter, the price varies with variations in construction costs. The comparisons also suggest that the relative price elasticity of housing demand is about unity.[5] Since interest costs are about one-half of the costs of housing services, a unit price elasticity would imply an interest rate elasticity of demand for housing services of approximately −0.5. (This is discussed in greater detail in Section II.)

Information on production possibilities can be summarized by relative factor shares, i.e., total payments to a factor divided by the total value of output, and the elasticity of substitution in production of one factor for others (at least if one is willing to assume constant returns to scale in the production of housing). From 1946 to 1960, the proportion of site to total property value for new FHA-insured houses rose from 11.5 to 16.6 per cent.[6] Since the costs of improvements to land may easily equal or exceed raw land costs, and interest costs plus property taxes are about three-fourths of the total costs of providing housing services, land costs are probably of the order of 5 per cent of the costs of housing services. Based upon weights typically used in residential construction cost indexes, labor and materials each account for approximately 45 per cent of the cost of structures or not quite 43 per cent of the cost of housing services. The rise in the share of land in the cost of providing housing in the postwar period, along with increasing land rentals, suggests a less than unit elasticity of substitution of land for structures in housing production. Indeed, the FHA reports that from 1946 to 1960, land costs increased by 180 per cent or more,[7] while during the same period construction costs rose by around 77 per cent.[8] Elsewhere, I have shown that the above-noted price changes and land shares imply an elasticity of substitution of about 0.75.[9]

Even for the nation as a whole, it appears that the long-run supply schedule for structures is highly elastic. In my study of changes in the rate of residential construction in the period between the two world

[5] These are discussed in detail in a monograph I am now preparing, entitled "The Spatial Pattern of Residential Land Use in Cities." For an example, however, see Appendix Table A.2.

[6] U.S. Housing and Home Finance Agency, *Fourteenth Annual Report* (U.S. Government Printing Office, 1961), Table III-35, p. 110.

[7] *Ibid.,* p. 109.

[8] As measured by the U.S. Department of Commerce implicit residential nonfarm deflator.

[9] Richard F. Muth, "The Derived Demand Curve for a Productive Factor and the Industry Supply Curve for a Productive Factor and the Industry Supply Curve," *Oxford Economic Papers,* Vol. 16 (July 1964), especially pp. 229 ff.

wars, I found little or no tendency for building material prices or wage rates paid construction labor to vary with the rate of new residential construction.[10] The evidence I was able to examine suggests there is a high rate of mobility of firms into and out of the housebuilding industry, and there was little apparent tendency for fluctuations in the incomes of construction firms to be associated with significant fluctuations in

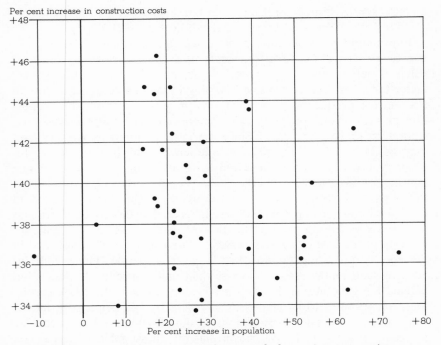

Figure 1. Relation of change in population and change in construction costs, by city, 1950–60.

housing prices. Maisel has found that large-tract builders in the postwar period have approximately 10 per cent lower costs than do the smallest housebuilders.[11] But so long as other builders exist in significant numbers, his findings merely imply that the large-tract builders will earn a rent attributable to their special advantages. I would expect the supply of structures to be even more elastic for any given urban area than for the nation as a whole, because, in the long run, building materials and

[10] Muth, "The Demand for Non-Farm Housing," pp. 42–46.
[11] Sherman J. Maisel, *Housebuilding in Transition* (University of California Press, 1953), pp. 189 ff.

288

probably construction workers and firms would shift among urban areas in response to differential changes in their prices or earnings. In this regard, the comparison of the change in urbanized area population and in construction costs for forty-one U.S. cities during the fifties, shown in Figure 1, indicates little if any association between them.[12]

Since the total amount of land in any area is essentially fixed, the supply curve of urban land is this fixed amount less the agricultural demand curve for land. It follows immediately that the elasticity of urban land supply is the negative of the agricultural demand elasticity for land. Most agricultural products are sold in national markets, and the output of the agricultural industry surrounding an urban area is, in most cases, only a small fraction of the output coming into the national market. For this reason, one would expect the demand curve for the output of local agricultural firms to be highly elastic. Under these conditions I have shown elsewhere[13] that the demand elasticity for agricultural land, λ, is given by

$$\lambda = -\frac{\sigma + \rho_L e_N}{\rho_N}, \text{ where} \tag{1}$$

σ = elasticity of substitution of land, L, for non-land, N for factors in production,

ρ_L = land's share, and

e_N = the elasticity of supply of non-land factors.

Recent work by Griliches suggests that $\sigma = 1$ for agriculture and, indeed, that the production function for agriculture can be closely approximated by a logarithmically linear, or Cobb-Douglas, function.[14] Since about 15 per cent of the value of agricultural output is paid out to land,[15] equation (1) suggests that in the short-run—when $e_N = 0$— the supply elasticity for urban land is about +1.2. In the long-run, except for agricultural labor the supply of non-land factors to the industry, consisting of agricultural firms surrounding an urban area, is likely to be very high. If one thinks of agricultural labor and all other non-land factors as being inputs into the production of all non-land

[12] The population data are from U.S. Bureau of the Census, *U.S. Census of Population: 1960*, Final Report PC(1)-1A (1961), Table 22. The measure of construction costs used is the (unpublished) Boeckh residential brick structures index, 1926 U.S. average = 100, for cities.

[13] Muth, "The Derived Demand Curve . . . ," p. 227.

[14] Zvi Griliches, "Research Expenditures, Education, and the Aggregate Agricultural Production Function," *American Economic Review*, Vol. 54 (December 1964), pp. 962–64.

[15] Using Griliches' coefficient for land and buildings. See, *ibid.*, Table 2, p. 966.

factors,[16] then, for an infinitely elastic supply of non-land agricultural factors,[17]

$$e_N = \frac{\rho_{NW}\sigma_N + e_W}{\rho_W}, \text{ where} \tag{2}$$

σ_N = elasticity of substitution of agricultural labor, W, for non-land, non-labor factors in producing non-land $= 1$,

ρ_W = labor's share relative to the shares of all non-land factors, and

e_W = elasticity of labor supply to local agriculture.

Since Griliches' results suggest that $\rho_W \simeq 0.53$, for $e_W \geq 0$ $e_N \geq 0.89$. Hence, in the long run, equation (1) implies that the elasticity of urban land supply, $-\lambda$, is at least equal to $+1.3$. An easy calculation shows that each three-unit increment in e_W adds one unit to $-\lambda$, so that, while far from being inelastic, the supply schedule of all urban land is, at most, moderately elastic.

The supply curve of urban residential land can, of course, be analyzed in a fashion similar to the above. The elasticity of urban residential land supply is the elasticity of the total urban land supply minus the elasticity of demand for urban non-residential uses. The latter parameter can also be analyzed, qualitatively at least, in terms of Marshall's four determinants. Since the supply of non-land factors is likely to be high, the derived demand elasticities for any particular urban user, λ', is given approximately by[18]

$$\lambda' = -\rho_N\sigma + \rho_L\eta, \tag{3}$$

where, in addition to the symbols defined in connection with equation (1), η is the final product demand elasticity. Since, for most private, non-residential users of urban land, the relative share of a firm's receipts paid out to land is probably still smaller than for housing, λ' will depend mainly upon the elasticity of substitution of land for non-land factors in producing housing.[19] Since, for most private, non-residential users of urban land, it would seem that ratio of land to total property value is higher toward the city center where rentals per unit

[16] Since $Q = \prod_{i=1}^{n} A_i^{a_i}$, Q can be written as $Q = A_1^{a_1} R^{a_R}$, where $R = \prod_{i=2}^{n} A_i^{a_i,R}$, $a_i,R = a_i/a_R$, and $a_R = \sum_{i=2}^{n} a_i$.

[17] Muth, "The Derived Demand Curve . . . ," p. 227.

[18] See Muth, "The Derived Demand Curve . . . . , p. 227."

[19] Note, however, that for firms selling only a small part of the total output coming onto some national market, η is likely to be very high numerically. The statement in the text would not hold for these firms.

of land are higher, σ is probably less than 1 for non-residential as well as for residential users of land. If so, the urban non-residential demand for land is likely to be inelastic, and the elasticity of land supply to the housing industry would depend mainly upon the supply elasticity for all urban land.

The above inferences enable one to establish the values of the supply elasticity of urban housing services and residential demand curve for land closely enough for most practical applications. Making the appropriate change in subscripts in equation (2), a $\sigma = 0.75$ and $\rho_L \simeq 0.05$ implies an elasticity of housing supply per unit of residential land of about $+14$. Hence, even if the supply of residential land were perfectly inelastic, changes in housing prices are likely to result mostly from shifts in the supply schedule for housing. The above values for σ and ρ_L together with $\eta = -1$ by equation (3) likewise imply that the elasticity of demand for residential land is about -0.75. A less-than-unit elasticity of demand for residential as well as for non-residential urban land would account for the tendency for aggregate urban land rentals to decline with improvements in transportation, which, in effect, increase the supply of urban land.

II. THE INFLUENCE OF ACCESSIBILITY ON THE INTENSITY OF RESIDENTIAL LAND USE

Even to the casual observer, it is obvious that land tends to be most intensively used nearest the central business district (CBD) of cities and that land use intensity typically declines as one moves outward to their edges. Empirical studies by Clark[20] and by me[21] have demonstrated that for a wide range of times and places urban gross population densities tend to decline at a roughly constant relative rate from the city center. In this section I first consider the effect of differences in transport costs to the center upon the prices consumers will pay for housing of given quality in different parts of a city. Next, I consider the effect of variation in housing prices on the variation in rentals of, and the value of, housing produced per square mile of urban residential land. I then discuss the determinants of the fraction of land used for residential purposes. In closing the section, the extent to which the above-noted factors influence the behavior of gross population densities is discussed.

Consider a household with utility function $U = U(x,q)$, where q

[20] Colin Clark, "Urban Population Densities," *Journal of the Royal Statistical Society*, Series A, Vol. 114 (Part IV, 1951), pp. 490–96.
[21] Richard F. Muth, "The Spatial Structure of the Housing Market," *Papers and Proceedings of the Regional Science Association*, Vol. 7 (1961), pp. 207–20.

is the quantity of housing services purchased per unit of time, and x is its expenditures on all other commodities except transportation but including leisure.[22] The household is subject to the budget constraint $C = x + p(k)q + T(k,y) - y \leq 0$, where p, the price per unit of housing service, and T, the household's expenditure on transportation, are functions of the distance, k, of its location from the CBD. Since T is assumed to include the value of time spent in travel, it is also a function of money income, y, defined to include the money value of travel

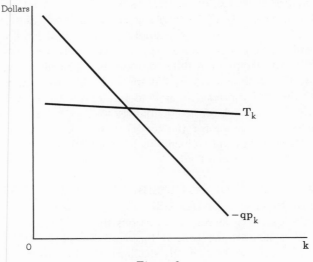

Figure 2.

and leisure time. Differentiating the LaGrangian function $G = U - \mu C$ with respect to x and q, yields the following well-known proposition: to maximize its utility, the household consumes housing and all other commodities in such proportions that the marginal utility per dollar spent is the same for both. Differentiating with respect to k, one finds

$$-qp_k - T_k = 0 \quad \text{or} \quad \left(\frac{-p_k}{p}\right) = \left(\frac{T_k}{pq}\right). \tag{4}$$

The first form of (4) states that, at its equilibrium location, the savings on the quantity of housing purchased there by a short move must be exactly balanced by the change in total transportation expenditure made. The condition stated in (4) is illustrated in Figure 2.

---

[22] In this paper, I treat owner-occupiers of housing as though they, as tenants, purchase housing services from themselves as landlords or producers of housing services.

Equation (4) has several implications of interest. First, a positive marginal transport expenditure with respect to distance implies that the price per unit of housing services must decline with distance. Second, by differentiating (4) with respect to k and remembering that the household's real income is constant in the neighborhood of its equilibrium location, a sufficient condition for the location implied by (4) to be a utility maximizing one is that

$$\left(\frac{p_{kk}}{p_k}\right) \leq -E_c(q,p)\left(\frac{p_k}{p}\right) + \left(\frac{T_{kk}}{T_k}\right), \tag{5}$$

where $E_c(q,p)$ is the income-compensated or real income-constant price elasticity of housing demand. If (5) did not hold—that is, if the $-qp_k$ curve in Figure 2 had a slope which exceeded that of the T_k curve—the household could continue to increase its real income by moving farther away from the CBD, and no city would exist. Provided, as seems sensible, $T_{kk} \leq 0$, housing prices must decline by decreasing absolute amounts with distance; in fact, for $E_c(q,p) \leq -1$, housing prices must decline at a non-increasing relative rate with distance. Third, as seen from the second form of equation (4), anything which increases expenditures for housing services relative to marginal transport expenditure will reduce the price gradient $\left(\frac{-p_k}{p}\right)$. In the same vein, the stability condition (5) implies that the equilibrium location for households whose housing expenditures are higher relative to their marginal transportation expenditures will be at greater distances from the CBD.

Because of the great variation among households in income levels at a given time and the fact that, at annual growth rates of 2 to 3 per cent per year, average income for a city as a whole can increase by from 22 to 35 per cent in a decade, the effect of a household's income on its equilibrium location is a question of substantial quantitative significance. Now, the greater a household's income the greater its expenditures on housing tend to be. Hence, the smaller must be the price gradient at the CBD, while the greater is the distance from the CBD of its equilibrium location. However, household income difference occurs largely because of differences in the hourly earning opportunities of its members and, consequently, the value they would be expected to place upon their travel time. Thus, one would expect both of the curves shown in Figure 2 to shift upward with an increase in a household's income, and the impact of an income change on equilibrium location depends upon which shift is the greater. In Appendix Table

A.6, it is demonstrated that there is in fact a strong tendency for the median income level of census tracts to increase with distance from the CBD; the simple regression coefficients (not shown) for the six cities examined there indicate that median income tends to increase by about 8 per cent per mile, or more than doubles over a ten-mile range. But when a variable representing the age of dwelling units in a tract is added to the equation, the association between income and distance disappears, while the partial correlation between income and age of dwelling is rather strongly negative.

Empirically, then, it would seem clear that most of the tendency for average income to increase with distance is due to the intercorrelation of both variables with age of dwelling. The failure of average reported money income to increase with distance apart from the increase associated with newer dwellings may result from the fact that the income elasticities of housing expenditure and marginal transport expenditures are the same. Beesley's work, though, suggests an income elasticity of marginal transport expenditure no more than unity,[23] while the estimates described in the first section suggest an income elasticity of housing demand of unity or more. The failure of census-reported average money income to rise with distance when the effects of dwelling unit age are eliminated might still be consistent with an income elasticity of housing demand in excess of unity, however. In addition to workers employed in the CBD, one usually finds substantial numbers of workers throughout the city who are employed so close to their work places that transport costs for their work trips are negligible when compared to those borne by CBD workers. Since for locally employed workers, too, housing prices decline with distance from the CBD, their money wage incomes must decline with distance as well. This decline in their money income, in turn, would tend to offset the increase in money incomes of CBD workers when data for both groups are combined, as in the census reports.

I now wish to consider the effects of the decline in housing prices on urban residential land rentals with distance, and the value of housing produced per square mile of residential land. If firms producing housing —all of whom are presumed to have the same production functions— are to earn the same incomes regardless of their locations, the decline

[23] M. E. Beesley, "The Value of Time Spent in Travelling: Some New Evidence," *Economica,* New Series, Vol. 32 (May 1965), pp. 174–85, found that both clerical and executive officers employed by the British Ministry of Transport apparently valued their travel time at a rate equal to about one-third of their average earnings, although their annual incomes averaged £650 and £850, respectively.

in housing prices with distance means that land rentals must likewise decline. Elsewhere,[24] I have shown that this decline is given by

$$r_k = \left(\frac{Q}{L}\right) p_k \quad \text{or} \quad \left(\frac{r_k}{r}\right) = \frac{1}{\rho_L}\left(\frac{p_k}{p}\right), \text{ where} \tag{6}$$

Q = output of housing produced per firm,

L = land used per firm,

r = rental per unit of land, and

ρ_L = land's relative share in the value of housing output.

Since, as was indicated in Section I, land's share is of the order of 0.05, the rental gradient $(-r_k/r)$ is of the order of twenty times the price gradient. Since the preceding discussion of household equilibrium suggests that the price gradient will tend to be smaller at greater distances from the city center, equation (6) implies that the rental gradient must decline with distance on this account. However, the discussion in Section I suggests that, because of a less-than-unit elasticity of substitution of land for other factors in producing housing, land's relative share would tend to decline with distance. This decline would mean that at greater distances from the center the elasticity of residential land rentals with respect to housing prices would be higher. The latter effect tends to offset the tendency for the rental gradient to decline because of a declining price gradient with distance.

The decline in land rentals, in turn, leads producers of housing to substitute land for other features of housing at progressively greater distances from the city center. While elevator apartment buildings might tend to predominate in areas close to the center, at progressively greater distances one finds that first walk-up apartments, then row-houses, duplexes, and finally single-family, detached houses become the predominant type of structure. Given the decline in residential land rentals, one easily finds from equation (2), with appropriate changes in subscripts, that[25]

$$\frac{d\ln}{dk}\left(\frac{pQ}{L}\right) = \left(1 + \frac{\rho_N}{\rho_L}\sigma\right)\left(\frac{p_k}{p}\right). \tag{7}$$

From the parameters described in the first section, the elasticity of the value of housing with respect to price—the first term in the right mem-

[24] Richard F. Muth, "Economic Change and Rural-Urban Land Conversions," *Econometrica*, Vol. 29 (January 1961).

[25] The supply elasticity of land per unit of land is, of course, zero, while the 1 is added since variations in values, not quantities, of housing produced are being considered.

ber of (7)—is of the order of $+15$. Now, as shown by the coefficients in the last column of Table 1, the relative decline per mile in the value

TABLE 1.
PARTIAL REGRESSION COEFFICIENTS OF DISCBD
HOLDING AGEDUS AND INCOME CONSTANT

City	Dependent variable	
	VALHOU	VALAND
LARGE CITIES		
Houston, Texas	−.085†	−.48*
Milwaukee, Wisconsin	.074†	−.17*
MEDIUM CITIES		
Memphis, Tennessee	−.042	−.19*
San Diego, California	−.094†	−.66*
SMALL CITIES		
Dayton, Ohio	.053	.30
Syracuse, New York	−.11	−.54*

* Significant at the 1-tail 0.10 level.
† Significant at the 2-tail 0.10 level.
Note. See Appendix.

of housing produced per square mile is, on the average, about equal to $+0.3$. The latter figure, in turn, implies that housing prices decline at the relative rate of about 0.02 per mile with distance from the CBD. By the second form of equation (4), since housing expenditures are about one-fifth of income, and earnings are about 0.8 of income (as usually defined), the marginal costs of transport per mile are about 0.5 per cent of earnings for the same time period, say, per day. Assuming people work eight hours and make two trips per working day, T_k per mile per trip is about 0.02 times their hourly earnings rate, or, at an average speed of 25 miles per hour, T_k per hour is about half the workers' hourly earnings rate.

Like land rentals, the relative change in the value of housing produced per mile at different distances is subject to two forces. First, because the price gradient tends to decline with distance from the CBD, the slope of the curve relating the value of housing produced per square mile of residential land tends to become numerically smaller at greater distances from the CBD. Secondly, however, because of the less-than-unit elasticity of substitution of land for other factors in producing housing, (ρ_N/ρ_L) declines with distance, and the value of housing produced per square mile becomes more responsive to any given price changes. Empirically it appears to me that these two forces just about balance, so that the value of housing produced per square mile of land declines at roughly a constant relative rate.[26]

The greater responsiveness of housing output at greater distances from the CBD has another important implication. With an increase in housing demand, whether from increased population, disposable income per family, or, perhaps, subsidies to housing, the price per unit of housing services will tend to increase everywhere. With a unit price elasticity of housing demand, the increase in price per unit will leave expenditures per household unchanged, so by the second form of equation (4) housing prices will rise by the same relative amount everywhere. But the value of housing produced is more responsive to price changes at greater distances from the CBD. It can be shown that, using the parameter values already described, the elasticity of the value of housing produced per unit of land would vary from about 7.5 to 22.5 over a ten-mile range. Thus, with an increase in housing demand, the output of housing and population would tend to grow more rapidly at greater distances from the CBD.

Since the total amount of land at any location within a city is fixed, the supply of land to the housing industry is again this fixed total less the non-residential demand for land. To the extent that the transportation system is radial (streets or highways, say), a given width with a given capacity would require a larger fraction of the available total land area closer to the CBD, and the required capacity for the intracity transportation system would be greater closer to the CBD.[27] Furthermore, if private, non-residential users find locations next to railroads or major highways especially desirable, the fraction of total land they use would decline with distance from the CBD. For these reasons one might expect the fraction of total land area which is used for residential purposes to increase with distance from the CBD. Since this fraction is bounded from above, however, it would have to increase at a decreasing relative rate after some point.

With the growth of the city and, thus, housing demand, changes in the fraction of land area used for residential purposes depend partly on the elasticity of supply of land to the housing industry. The latter, of

[26] For the south side of Chicago, I concluded that a quadratic term in distance added little to the explanation of variations in the value of housing per square mile of residential land. See Richard F. Muth, "The Variation of Population Density and Its Components in South Chicago," *Papers and Proceedings of the Regional Science Association,* Vol. 11 (1964).

[27] Cf. Edwin S. Mills, "An Aggregative Model of Resource Allocation in a Metropolitan Area," *American Economic Review,* Vol. 57 (May 1967), pp. 197 ff.

course, is the negative of the elasticity of demand for land on the part of non-residential users. Since firms for whom the relative importance of land is small have a comparative advantage in locating where land rentals are high, one would expect the relative share of land for non-residential firms to increase with distance from the city center. As can readily be seen from equation (3), however, the latter will cause the non-residential demand elasticity to increase numerically with distance only if the elasticity of final product demand is numerically larger than the elasticity of substitution. To the extent that firms in a given local industry sell only a small part of the output coming into some nation-wide—or even worldwide—market, the local industry's demand elasticity would be high and the above-noted condition would hold. If, on the other hand, a local industry is the sole supplier of a regional—or even citywide—market, its demand elasticity for land might grow numerically smaller with distance from the CBD.

Systematic differences in demand elasticities for non-residential land might also arise because of differences in final product demand elasticities. Firms whose market area is the whole of the city tend to locate near the center in order to maximize accessibility to their market. Because there are fewer substitutes for their products than for the products of firms in the outer part of the city, the final product demand elasticities for firms near the center would tend to be numerically smaller. Both for this reason and the increasing relative importance of land noted in the preceding paragraph, there is a weak presumption that the non-residential demand elasticity for land increases numerically with distance from the CBD. If so, with an increase in population and housing demand, one might expect the fraction of urban land in residential use to grow more rapidly in the outer parts of cities. Of course, the fraction of land used for residential purposes is also affected by shifts in the demand for non-residential land. If, as an urban area grows, population tends to grow more rapidly in outer parts of cities, so would the demand for many types of retail and service outputs produced at widely scattered points throughout the city. In addition, the land used for transportation would tend to grow more rapidly at greater distances from the CBD. Such changes would tend to increase the non-residential demand for land relatively more in the outer parts of cities and to offset the previously noted tendency for the fraction of urban land used for housing to grow more rapidly there.

I shall now summarize the analysis of this section by considering its implications for the pattern of population densities in urban areas. Since population per unit of land used for residential purposes, or net population density, D, is

$$D = \frac{P}{L} = \frac{\left(\frac{pQ}{L}\right) \times \frac{P}{H}}{(pq)}, \text{ where} \tag{8}$$

P = population,

H = number of households, and

q = quantity of housing services consumed per household,

$$\frac{d\ln D}{dk} = \frac{d\ln}{dk}\left(\frac{pQ}{L}\right) + \frac{d\ln}{dk}\left(\frac{P}{H}\right) - \frac{d\ln(pq)}{dk}. \tag{9}$$

It is frequently argued that larger families, especially those with young children, tend to locate in the outer parts of cities. While I have found a tendency for the average size of family to increase with distance from the CBD, the average change per mile—about 1 to 3 per cent—is quite small compared to the average change in population density—about 30 per cent per mile.[28] As noted earlier in this section, apart from the association with age of dwellings, there is little or no tendency for the average income level of an area to increase with k. Furthermore, a unit elastic demand for housing would suggest that expenditures on housing per household would be unaffected by variations in housing prices, so purely on locational grounds the third term of the right member of (9) is also small.

Apart from the effects of the age of dwellings on the location of households by income, then, the tendency for net population densities to decline with distance from the CBD would result almost wholly from the decline in the value of housing produced per square mile with distance. It might be argued, of course, that the decline in (pQ/L) also reflects the effects of age of dwellings, but Appendix Table A.7 suggests that this is not the case. (I shall comment further on this point in the following section.) Furthermore, it was suggested earlier that there are two effects upon the size of $\dfrac{d\ln}{dk}\dfrac{pQ}{L}$ and, hence, the relative change in net population density at different distances that tend roughly to offset each other. First, stability of locational equilibrium for any individual household requires that the price gradient decline with distance. Secondly, though, the decline in land's relative share with distance means that the value of housing produced per square mile of residential land becomes more responsive to any given price change. Thus, net population densities tend to decline at a roughly constant relative rate with distance from the CBD.

Gross population density, or population per unit of total land area,

[28] Muth, "The Spatial Pattern . . . ," Chap. 8.

depends upon the fraction of total land area used for urban purposes as well as upon net population density. If, as I suggested above, the fraction of land that is residential increases at a declining relative rate, gross population densities would decline at a smaller relative rate than net densities and the relative rate of decline would become numerically greater at greater distances from the CBD.[29] In my examination of data for south Chicago in 1960, however, I fail to find any appreciable variation in the fraction of land that is residential with distance from the CBD or with any other measure of accessibility; gross and net population densities respond in very much the same way to variations in these accessibility measures.[30] In addition, in my examination of the pattern of gross population densities in forty-six U.S. cities for 1950, I fail to find any significant tendency for gross population densities to decline at numerically increasing relative rates.[31] Thus, it appears to me that a negative exponential pattern of gross population densities in relation to distance is as good an approximation to actual patterns as any other.

III. OTHER FACTORS INFLUENCING THE CONSUMPTION AND PRODUCTION OF HOUSING IN DIFFERENT PARTS OF A CITY

Until quite recently, most writings on urban residential land and housing tended to neglect accessibility. They emphasized instead the dynamic effects of a city's past development upon current conditions, and preferences of different households for housing in different locations, especially as they are influenced by income. In this section I want to discuss some of the a priori reasons why population densities might be directly related to the age of dwellings and inversely related to the income of the inhabitants of an area. I also want to point out some of the empirical findings bearing on these relationships, which are described more fully in the Appendix. Finally, I will consider some of the reasons for the residential segregation of Negroes and whether Negroes pay higher prices for housing of given quality.

Because the marginal costs of transport to workers commuting to the CBD were almost certainly greater prior to the automobile and expenditures on housing per household were smaller (since incomes were lower),

[29] This follows easily from the fact that the log of gross population density is the sum of the logs of net population density and the fraction of total land that is residential.

[30] Muth, "The Variation of Population Density . . . ," pp. 178–79.

[31] Muth, "The Spatial Structure of the Housing Market," pp. 213–14. Of course, one might find gross population densities declining at a roughly constant relative rate if net density declined at a numerically decreasing relative rate and the fraction of land that is residential increased at a declining relative rate.

it would be anticipated on the basis of equation (4) that the housing price gradient was larger. Thus, everything else being the same, housing prices would have been higher in areas close to the city center and lower in those parts of it near the edges. For this reason the output of housing per square mile was probably greater than its equilibrium for the auto era near the city center, while the converse was true in its outer parts. Hoover and Vernon have argued that, once an area has been initially developed, "neighborhood density patterns . . . have been rather stubbornly resistant to change." [32] They also note that zoning restrictions typically place an upper limit on population densities, and that these restrictions have grown up only after about 1920.[33] For these reasons one might expect that population densities and the output of housing per square mile would tend to be greater than they would otherwise be in those parts of the city developed prior to 1920.

When one examines population density and measures of the output of housing per unit of land in relation to distance from the CBD, the proportion of dwellings built prior to 1920, and the median income of a census tract, one does find some confirmation of this hypothesis. While adding age and income somewhat weakens the partial correlation between gross population density and distance, these correlations remain significantly negative. Surprisingly, though, while the partial correlation between population density and age (Appendix Table A.1) is positive in four of the six cities examined for the year 1950, it is significantly positive at the 0.10 level in only two of the cities. As measured by the proportion of dwellings which are in single-family structures, there appears to be a strong tendency for the physical output of housing per square mile to be above average the higher the proportion built prior to 1920. But in only one of the six cities does one find a significantly greater value of housing produced per square mile in older parts of the city. I suspect that the reason for the apparent contradiction is the lower prices per unit of housing service in older areas.

Population densities might also vary between older and newer areas because of differences in per capita expenditures on housing. With a unit elasticity housing demand, lower housing prices in older areas would not affect expenditures for housing. As was noted in the previous section, however, there is a strong tendency for higher-income households to inhabit newer housing. The best explanation for this tendency, I believe, is that older housing is more cheaply converted to occupancy by lower-income households, though it amounts to very much the same

[32] Edgar M. Hoover and Raymond Vernon, *Anatomy of a Metropolis* (Harvard University Press, 1959), p. 132.
[33] *Ibid.*, p. 133.

thing to say instead that higher-income households have stronger preferences for newer housing than have lower-income ones. In any event, because of the negative association between age and income one would expect to find a smaller average expenditure on housing per household in the older areas. In addition, in Appendix Table A.2, one notes a negative partial association between age and the per-family expenditure on housing when income is held constant. The latter might result from the fact that households with weaker preferences for housing tend to locate in older areas where the quantity of housing per dwelling is smaller.

There are several reasons why higher-income households might seek out locations in the outer parts of cities. One of the most obvious possibilities is that higher-income households have stronger preferences for space and privacy relative to structural features of housing. As Hoover and Vernon put it, "higher income people use their superior purchasing power to buy lower density," and "rising incomes and leisure are the basis for a demand for newer houses as such, and in general for more spaciously sited homes." [34] Also, the fraction who are homeowners typically increases with income, and, for a variety of reasons, most homeowners live in single-family, detached houses. The latter, of course, tend to be cheaper in the outer parts of cities, where land rentals are lower relative to construction costs. Finally, federal mortgage programs and the federal income tax advantage of home ownership[35] tend to reduce the relative price of housing to homeowners and increase their expenditures on housing inclusive of the subsidy. Because they consume more housing, higher income households have a greater incentive to take advantage of these subsidies. As was shown in Section II, the increased expenditures on housing lead the families affected by these subsidies to locate greater distances from the CBD where the price gradient is smaller. For these reasons one might expect population densities to be lower in census tracts where the average income level is higher. One might also expect part of the decline in population density with distance from the CBD to be due to the association between density and income.

Quite surprisingly, however, in Appendix Table A.1, one finds little partial relationship between population density and income. While the partial correlation coefficient is negative for four of the six cities examined, it is significant at the 1-tail 10 per cent level only for one. In view

[34] *Ibid.*, pp. 169, 222.
[35] For a discussion of this subsidy, see Richard Goode, "Imputed Rent of Owner-Occupied Dwellings under the Income Tax," *Journal of Finance*, Vol. 15 (December 1960), pp. 504–30.

of the strong positive relationship between income and expenditures on housing per household, this can be the case only if the value of housing output per square mile tends to increase with income. The latter relationship is indeed found in Appendix Table A.7, where the partial correlation coefficient is positive in all cities, rather strongly so in four of them. Even more puzzling, in Appendix Table A.8 one finds little partial correlation between income and the proportion of dwellings in single-family structures, which I interpret as varying inversely with the physical output of housing per square mile of land. To me, the best explanation for this apparent contradiction is as follows: because of favorable neighborhood effects, the price per unit of housing, and thus land rentals, tends to be greater in higher income areas, offsetting any tendency for higher-income households to live at lower population densities but producing a higher value of housing output per unit of land.

The residential segregation of Negroes has become one of the most important political and social issues of the day. There are several possible reasons for this segregation, or residential separation. Because Negroes tend to have lower incomes and different occupations than whites, one might suspect their segregation would result from these factors rather than from race itself. However, Taeuber has shown that little of the Negro segregation vis-à-vis the white population can be attributed to income and occupational differences.[36] Similar conclusions were reached by Pascal.[37] In the popular mind, the residential segregation of Negroes is felt to be due to a unique aversion—not shared by the rest of the community—on the part of landlords and real estate agents for dealing with Negroes. Such a hypothesis cannot account for many other forms of segregation, such as segregation in churches and fraternal organizations or the residential segregation of many other groups without apparent coercion. More importantly, if landlords, say, fail to rent to Negroes because of their own aversion, they will have a higher average level of vacancies and lower incomes than others. It would then be in their interests to sell out to others who do not possess the same aversions.

A much more satisfying explanation for racial segregation in housing is Becker's, namely that whites have a greater aversion to living among

[36] Karl E. Taeuber, "Negro Residential Segregation, 1940–60: Changing Trends in the Large Cities of the United States" (Paper read at the annual meetings of the American Sociological Association, 1962); see also Karl E. Taeuber and Alma F. Taeuber, *Negroes in Cities, Residential Segregation and Neighborhood Change* (Aldine Publishing Co.: 1965).

[37] Anthony H. Pascal, "The Economics of Housing Segregation," *Abstracts of Papers Presented at the December 1965 Meetings* (New York: Econometric Society), p. 2.

Negroes than have other Negroes.[38] Thus, the two groups would tend to inhabit disjoint residential areas, since some white households would be willing to offer more for the occupancy rights to a dwelling in an area occupied largely by other white households than would a Negro resident. Not only is Becker's explanation consistent with most other forms of segregation, but it readily explains the failure of landlords or real estate agents to deal with Negroes. By so doing the landlords would be faced with either decreased rentals from white tenants or a higher vacancy rate, the real estate agents with a loss of future business from some white residents of an area.

As Becker points out, residential segregation need not imply discrimination, or higher housing prices relative to marginal costs of housing for Negroes.[39] Rather, the level of housing prices in the interior[40] of the Negro area relative to the white area depends upon the relative rate of growth of housing demand in the two areas as compared with the rate of change in their size. Indeed, Bailey has demonstrated that, under the conditions postulated by Becker, the only possible long-run equilibrium position under diverse ownership of properties is one in which prices in the interior of the Negro area are lower than in the interior of the white area.[41] The latter is the case because, given equality of prices in the interiors of the two areas, prices will be lower on the white side of the boundary separating the two areas than on the Negro side. For this reason, owners of occupancy rights on the white side of the boundary will have the incentive to sell them to Negroes, and with the expansion of the Negro area relative to the white area housing prices will fall in the former and rise in the latter. Of course, if Negro, relative to white, housing demand were growing fast enough for a long enough period relative to the growth of the Negro area, housing prices in the interior of the Negro area could rise above those in the interior of the white area.[42]

Census data on housing expenditures indicate that at a given money income level expenditures for housing by non-whites are as much as a third or more greater than expenditures by whites.[43] Such comparisons

[38] Gary S. Becker, *The Economics of Discrimination* (University of Chicago Press, 1957), p. 59.

[39] *Ibid.*

[40] That is, far enough from the boundary separating Negro and white residential areas so that prices are not affected by the presence of the other group.

[41] Martin J. Bailey, "Note on the Economics of Residential Zoning and Urban Renewal," *Land Economics,* Vol. 35 (August 1959), pp. 288–90.

[42] Becker, *op. cit.,* appears to have believed that housing prices in Negro areas were in fact higher than those in white areas, and offered essentially this explanation for the differential.

[43] For example, see Muth, "The Variation of Population Density . . . ," p. 176.

are frequently interpreted as demonstrating that Negroes pay higher prices per unit for housing. However, census data on contract rent include, in addition to space rent, expenditures for any furnishings and utilities included in the rental payment agreed upon, and a higher proportion of non-whites than whites inhabit rental housing. For a variety of possible reasons, the costs of supplying housing to Negroes may be higher. Most important, though, with a unit or elastic housing demand with respect to price, higher prices per unit would leave unchanged or reduce expenditures for housing, not increase them. If, however, one examines physical indicators that one would expect to reflect price variations, such as population densities, crowding, and the proportion of dwellings that are in single-family structures, the differences between Negro and white areas are small.[44] Furthermore, in a recently published study of the sales prices of single-family houses in the Hyde Park area of Chicago, Bailey actually finds lower prices in Negro areas.[45] Thus, it is far from clear that the residential segregation does in fact lead to higher housing prices for equivalent quality for Negroes.

IV. FACTORS AFFECTING THE CONDITION OF URBAN HOUSING

Two of the most important urban problems of today are those popularly described as urban blight and suburban sprawl. The former, of course, refers to the poor, and perhaps deteriorating, condition of the central city housing stock, the latter to the striking tendency in recent years for population to grow at more rapid rates in the suburban parts of urban areas than in their older, more centrally located parts. It is widely believed that the two phenomena are intimately related, indeed, that urban blight is to a very great extent responsible for suburban sprawl. In this section I shall discuss various factors affecting the quality of a city's housing stock and some empirical evidence which sheds light on their relative importance. The next and final section considers the question of urban decentralization.

Most explanations for the growth of slum or poor-quality housing in recent years are based upon factors that influence its supply schedule. In many, the increase in the supply of poor-quality housing results from a decline in the demand for good-quality housing. A variety of reasons, such as the development of automobile transportation, physical obsolescence, poor initial planning, and failure of local governments to sup-

---

[44] *Ibid.*, p. 182.

[45] Martin J. Bailey, "Effects of Race and Other Demographic Factors on the Values of Single-Family Houses," *Land Economics*, Vol. 42 (May 1966), pp. 215–20.

ply a proper level of municipal services, have been suggested for the initial decline in the demand for good-quality housing. Whatever the reason for it, though, the decline in demand would lead to a fall in housing prices in the affected areas and thus to the returns to investment in residential real estate. For this reason landlords have reduced their expenditures for maintenance and allowed their properties to deteriorate in quality.

Another group of forces which might tend to increase the supply of poor-quality housing might be lumped under the heading of market imperfections and external economies. It is frequently asserted that capital market imperfections prevent property owners from undertaking expenditures on existing residential real estate in the older parts of cities that would otherwise be privately profitable or socially desirable. If such were the case, however, I would expect that, say, insurance companies would find it profitable to buy, rehabilitate, and resell large parcels of residential real estate in cities. Their failure to do so might be explained by imperfections in the market for existing dwellings, especially by the costs of assembling large tracts now under diverse ownership where any individual owner might try to hold out for a higher price than he might otherwise obtain if he suspects the assembler's intentions. Several features of our tax system are also said to increase the supply of slums. The accelerated depreciation provisions of the federal income tax laws keep older structures in use longer than they might be otherwise. To the extent that age of structure itself tends to reduce housing quality, these tax provisions would increase the proportion of the housing stock that is of poor quality. Property taxation may tend to reduce improvements to sites and their existing structures. In addition, if poor-quality units are taxed at lower effective rates than others, perhaps because assessments are based upon factors other than the income the property produced, the supply of slums will be increased.[46]

There are several kinds of external effects which might lead to too much poor-quality housing relative to the demand for it. Planners and others have long felt that non-residential land uses tend to reduce the values of surrounding residential properties. Such effects would, of course, provide a rationale for zoning regulations which limit the uses to which land may be put in different areas of a city. Davis and Whinston have recently argued that a single property owner's expenditure for improvement of a structure tends to make the immediately surrounding properties more desirable. Thus, owners of surrounding properties ben-

[46] The forces noted in this paragraph are stressed by Jerome Rothenberg, "Urban Renewal Programs," in Robert Dorfman (ed.), *Measuring Benefits of Government Investments* (The Brookings Institution, 1965), pp. 303–4.

efit, too, and are discouraged from making improvements in their own properties. In this way, from the social viewpoint, too little has been spent on improvement.[47] While such effects might be expected in all areas of the city, by limiting expenditures on existing dwellings they would tend to lower the average quality of the existing housing stock and increase the proportion below any given quality level. The Davis-Whinston effect provides a rationale for various building and occupancy codes which set minimum standards for different features of what we call housing, though not necessarily for codes which, in effect, attempt to impose middle-class standards on lower-income housing.

The same facts that bring about segregation of Negro and white residential areas hold true for lower-income and higher-income residential areas.[48] Thus, similarly, where the price per unit of housing is the same in the interior of the two areas, at the boundary separating them, prices per unit will be higher on the poor-quality side. Unlike the case of racial segregation, however, costs of conversion from good-quality to poor-quality use are likely to be of significant practical importance. These may take the form of expenditure in converting existing dwelling units to smaller ones or from the delay in recovering one's invested capital through deferral of maintenance and repair expenditures. In long-run equilibrium the price per unit of housing services in the interior of the poor-quality area, because of conversion costs, may be greater than in the interior of the good-quality area. But the boundary price differential implies that in long-run equilibrium, too large a portion of the existing stock of dwellings will be devoted to producing poor-quality housing. The Bailey boundary effect provides a rationale for zoning to prevent the poor-quality residential area from expanding too far, or, if it already has, for renewal of the area.

The expansion of the area occupied by poor-quality housing might also result from increases in the demand for such housing. The condition of dwellings inhabited, as well as the amount of space per person and other features, may be viewed as inputs into the production of a commodity called housing. Hence, anything which reduces the quantity of housing demanded, such as a fall in income per family, or a rise in the relative price of housing services, might be expected to reduce the derived demands for housing quality and for space. As a consequence, one would expect that dwellings would decline in quality and that more persons would occupy a given floor space or number of rooms. Along

[47] Otto A. Davis and Andrew B. Whinston, "The Economics of Urban Renewal," *Law and Contemporary Problems*, Vol. 26 (Winter 1961), pp. 105–17; also Rothenberg, *op. cit.*, pp. 299–301.

[48] See Bailey, "Note on the Economics of Residential Zoning and Urban Renewal," *op. cit.*

307

these same lines, if Negroes paid higher prices per unit of housing, one would expect their consumption of housing to be smaller. A higher proportion of Negro households at a given income level would thus occupy poor-quality units, and the fraction of Negro households with more than, say, one person per room would be higher than for whites.[49]

It is not difficult to account for an increase in the demand for poor-quality housing in the central cities of urban areas on the hypothesis that it is but one aspect of a low consumption of housing per household. During the first half of this century the per capita stock of non-farm housing showed relatively little increase in the United States, mostly, I believe, because the relative price of housing rose greatly.[50] Low-income migrants to the United States have tended to congregate in cities, and large-scale migration of lower-income persons from the rural South to cities has occurred, especially during the forties. Also, the lower-income population has had a higher rate of natural increase than the higher-income population. Because of the Bailey effect described earlier, whatever the reason for their initial establishment in the older parts of the urban area, one would expect poor-quality housing areas to grow outward from their edges rather than for new concentrations to be established. It is quite likely, then, that the consumption of housing per household in the central cities of our metropolitan areas actually declined prior to 1950, and with it the demand for poor-quality housing increased. Now, if existing structures differ in their cost of conversion from good-quality to poor-quality housing—in particular, one might expect older dwellings and dwellings in multi-unit structures to be more cheaply converted than others—one would expect the relative price of poor-quality housing to rise as the demand for poor-quality housing increases. At the same time, the increase in demand would increase the returns to previously existing poor-quality dwellings.

In my opinion, there is strong evidence that differences in the fraction of the housing stock which is substandard [51] can best be accounted for by variations in the demand for poor-quality housing.[52] As is shown

[49] Closely related to the above are the arguments that residential segregation restricts Negroes to areas of the poorest housing quality or that, through ignorance, recent immigrant and racial minority groups, especially Negroes, tend to inhabit poorer housing than do others. On the latter point, see Rothenberg, *op. cit.,* p. 302.
[50] For a fuller discussion, see Muth, "The Demand for Non-Farm Housing," pp. 73–74.
[51] That is, dilapidated and/or without private bath.
[52] I summarized this evidence and presented the more important empirical results in "Slums and Poverty" (paper read at the International Economics Association Conference on the Economic Problems of Housing, 1965). A more detailed empirical investigation is described in Muth, "The Spatial Pattern . . . ."

in Appendix Table A.3, in five of the six cities examined there is a strongly negative partial correlation between the proportion of substandard and median-income dwellings. Appendix Table A.4 indicates that similar results are found when crowding[53] is compared with income. The income elasticities of the proportion that is substandard and of crowding shown in Appendix Table A.5 are quite similar, as would be expected if quality and space per person were inputs into the production of housing. These elasticities average about −2.5. In comparisons made among census tracts in south Chicago for 1950 and 1960, and in comparisons among various U.S. cities in 1950, I likewise find that the proportion that is substandard is strongly and negatively related to income. In these latter comparisons, in which many more variables are included than in those shown in the Appendix, the elasticity of the proportion of dwellings that are substandard with respect to income was about −3.5. Furthermore, when separate partial repression coefficients of the proportion substandard on income are fitted for the lower and upper halves of the south Chicago tracts by median income, the differences are negligible. If ignorance of housing opportunities operated with greater force among the lowest-income groups, I would expect the response of housing quality to income differences to be greater in the lower half of the income distribution.

In view of the great variation of median family income among the census tracts of most cities, an elasticity of the magnitude noted above can account for great variations in the proportion substandard. In south Chicago in 1960, for example, median tract incomes range from a low of about $3,000 per family to a high of around $10,000; according to my estimates the proportion substandard would be only 0.5 per cent as great in the highest-income tracts as in the lowest. In addition, in my intercity comparison I find an elasticity of the proportion of dwellings that are substandard with respect to construction costs that is about the same numerically as the income elasticity. This would be expected, of course, if poor housing quality were symptomatic of a low consumption of housing per household, since the estimates noted in Section I suggest that the price and income elasticities of housing demand are about the same order of magnitude.

While there is strong evidence that variations in the proportion of substandard dwellings reflect variations in demand, there is little evidence that this proportion is affected by variations in supply. The comparisons shown in Appendix Table A.3 give little evidence of a negative partial correlation of the substandard proportion and distance from the CBD, as would be anticipated if an automobile-induced de-

---

[53] The proportion of dwellings with more than one person per room.

cline in demand had led to quality deterioration. My more detailed examination of data for south Chicago leads to the same conclusion. Appendix Table A.3 shows a marked tendency for a higher proportion of dwellings to be substandard in areas of older housing as do my south Chicago comparisons for 1950. In 1960, however, no such tendency is apparent in the south Chicago data. The south Chicago data also show a strong tendency for a higher substandard proportion in census tracts with an above-average rate of population turnover in 1950 but not in 1960. I am inclined to attribute the effects observed for 1950 to the lingering effects of rent control.[54]

My south Chicago and intercity comparisons gave little evidence that crowding leads to a deterioration of housing quality, while the proportion substandard was actually lower the higher the rate of population growth. The latter finding is directly contrary to the belief that diseconomies associated with rapid population growth lead to slum formation. Nor do I generally find a higher proportion of substandard dwellings in the areas adjacent to manufacturing or retail centers as would be expected from external diseconomies associated with surrounding uses of land. In this last connection, another recent study finds little or no tendency for housing values to vary inversely with the presence of non-residential land uses.[55] In my south Chicago comparisons, there is likewise no apparent tendency for a higher proportion of substandard dwellings in Negro tracts when this is evaluated separately from such factors as income differences. The last is contrary to what would be expected if residential segregation resulted in higher housing prices to Negroes or restricted them to areas of the worst housing quality.

Most important of all, perhaps, for appraising the increase-in-the-supply-of-slums hypothesis, is the suggestion in the south Chicago data that the effect of dwelling unit condition upon income is quite small. I estimated the elasticity of median tract income with respect to dwelling unit condition to be -0.07 in 1950, and -0.04 or even less for 1960. If dwelling unit condition has a negligible effect upon the location of households by income, or on the incomes of given households through the disabilities which result from inhabiting poor-

[54] Since rent controls reduce the profitability of investment in structures whose rentals are controlled, landlords reduced their expenditures for maintenance and repair. Such a reduction could well lead to a more rapid rate of deterioration in older structures. This is particularly true in areas of rapid population turnover.

[55] John P. Crecine, Otto A. Davis, and John E. Jackson, "Externalities in Urban Property Markets: Some Empirical Results and Their Implications for the Phenomenon of Municipal Zoning" (paper read at the annual meetings of the Southern Economics Association, 1966).

quality housing, then the increased supply hypotheses cannot account for the negative association between housing quality and income.

One of the most striking pieces of evidence bearing on the reasons for the expansion of slums is the great decline in the proportion of dwellings substandard in the fifties. Estimates made by Duncan and Hauser indicate that, of the six Standard Metropolitan Statistical Areas (SMSA's) they studied, only in New York did the number of substandard dwellings increase during the period 1950–56.[56] And here, rent controls are still in existence. In the five other SMSA's and in the cities of Chicago and Philadelphia the number of substandard dwellings declined by one-third in six years. Furthermore, around 90 per cent of this decline was due to the improved quality of given units. Now, none of the increased-supply theories can account for such an improvement, and on many one would anticipate a further decline in quality. Quality improvement is quite readily explainable on the demand hypothesis, however. Unlike the first half of the century, a substantial increase in housing consumption appears to have taken place during this period. Goldsmith's estimate of the value of the stock of private non-farm housekeeping units (including land) in 1947–49 prices, for example, increased by 23 per cent from the end of 1949 to the end of 1955,[57] while population increased only 12 per cent. While the absolute size of the low-income population of urban areas and the land area they occupy has continued to increase, and some dwellings have deteriorated as a result, increased consumption of housing per family implies a decline in the demand for housing below any given quality level. In fact, the rate of quality improvement noted by Duncan and Hauser is quite consistent with the income and price elasticities of the substandard proportion I have estimated from cross-section data. During the fifties, median family income in real terms grew at a rate of about 3 per cent per year and real construction costs by 1 per cent per year. Given elasticities numerically equal to 3.5, such changes would imply a reduction in the substandard proportion of about 7 per cent per year or just slightly over one-third in six years' time.

Evidence on the price per unit of housing services is relevant both for appraising alternative theories of the spread of slums, and for judging whether, from the social viewpoint, too much poor-quality housing

[56] Beverly Duncan and Philip M. Hauser, *Housing a Metropolis—Chicago* (The Free Press, 1960), pp. 56–58. The data used were from the 1950 Census of Housing and the 1956 National Housing Inventory, which employed identical definitions of housing condition.

[57] Raymond W. Goldsmith, *The National Wealth of the United States in the Postwar Period* (Princeton University Press, 1962), Table B-12, p. 253.

is being produced relative to the low-income demand for it. Direct data about the price of housing in slum versus other areas are quite difficult to obtain. Martin Bailey's study of the sales prices of single-family houses in the Hyde Park area of Chicago suggests that prices are lower in slum areas than in otherwise comparable good-quality housing areas.[58] In my study of south Chicago data for 1960, however, I found that net population density, the value of housing output per square mile of residential land, and crowding all tended to be significantly higher in areas where the proportion of substandard dwellings was higher, while the proportion of dwellings in one-unit structures was lower.[59] These findings suggest that the price per unit of housing service is higher in slum than in other areas. Even more striking, perhaps, is the fact that in urban renewal projects site acquisition costs typically exceed the resale value of the cleared land. From data developed by Anderson, it would appear that through the end of 1962 site acquisition costs cumulated to slightly more than $2 billion, while expected proceeds from the sale of cleared land amounted to just under $1 billion.[60] If slum housing were less expensive per unit than better housing, such a difference could arise only if renewal has been premature, or poorly planned and executed.

It is clear, therefore, that the principal reason for slum housing is the low income of its inhabitants. Demolition, as in urban renewal, or programs such as stricter code enforcement, that raise the cost of producing poor-quality as contrasted with good-quality housing, do virtually nothing to attack the basic cause of slums. While these programs reduce the fraction of poor-quality housing, they also raise the price of housing for lower-income households. It appears that not only has the private market not produced too much poor-quality housing relative to the demand for it, but also that the private market has clearly responded to rising incomes by upgrading the average quality of the existing housing stock. Thus, it seems to me that measures taken to raise the incomes of lower-income groups offer the best prospect of solving the problem of poor-quality housing.

V. FACTORS AFFECTING THE SPREAD OF URBAN AREAS AND SUBURBANIZATION

Since the end of World War II, the suburban parts of an area have tended to grow more rapidly than the central city and, indeed, in many

[58] Bailey, "Effects of Race and Other Demographic Factors on the Values of Single-Family Houses," *op. cit.*
[59] Muth, "The Variation of Population Density . . . ," p. 183.
[60] Martin Anderson, *The Federal Bulldozer* (The M.I.T. Press, 1964), Table 2.1, p. 21, and Table A.1, p. 231.

cases the population of the latter has actually declined. In popular discussion, this decentralization of urban populations is often viewed as a "flight from blight," an attempt to escape the undesirable physical and social conditions of central cities. This section will discuss the various reasons for decentralization in some detail, and present empirical evidence relevant for appraising them.

The preceding section discussed the growth of the poor-quality housing area in the central city. Even though this growth is more likely to have stemmed from an increase in low-income population than from the physical factors which lead directly to a decline in good-quality housing demand, it might still be responsible for an increase in good-quality housing demand in the outer parts of the urbanized area. Similar effects might result from the expansion of the Negro population of the central city.

Least obvious, perhaps, is the stimulus to suburbanization provided by current municipal fiscal arrangements. In our society some of the most significant redistribution of income and wealth is probably that provided by municipal governments through the provision of public education, health services and hospitals, and many welfare programs. Historically, municipal governments have been dependent primarily upon taxes levied within their own boundaries for funds to finance expenditures for these purposes. Even if middle- and upper-income households had no aversion to living among lower-income or minority groups, a growth in the lower-income population of the central city would probably tend to increase expenditures for municipal services relative to tax collections at previously existing rates. As a result, the tax burden on higher-income households and business firms in the central city would tend to increase. Since the resulting increase in taxes could not be escaped merely by moving to the outer part of the central city, higher-income households and business firms would have an incentive to move beyond the boundaries of the central city.

Then, too, the distribution of population between the central city and its suburbs could be influenced by many of the forces affecting population density gradients, discussed in Section II. One of the most obvious of these is improvements in transportation, which, by equation (4), would reduce the price gradient. As a result, the price of housing in the central part of the urban area would decline, while in the outer part it would rise. The latter would, in turn, increase the rental value of residential land in the outer parts of cities and lead to a conversion of land from agricultural to urban residential use. At the same time the output per unit of residential land would rise in the outer parts of cities, by a relation quite similar to equation (7), and population would be redistributed from the central to the outer parts of the area. Indirectly, the greater population growth in the outer part of the urban area might stimulate a higher proportion of business firms to locate in the outer part of the area to be nearer either their customers or workers. Directly, improvements in intracity transportation might reduce the relative costs of central city versus suburban locations for many nonresidential land users.

Either population or income growth per family would lead to an increase in the demand for housing and for the products of most other users of land as well. In consequence, I would expect land to be converted to urban uses and the total land area of the urbanized area would increase. In Section II, I argued that, because land's relative share is lower in the production of housing and probably other urban commodities as well, the value of housing produced is more responsive to price increases in the outer parts of urban areas. Hence, as the demand and therefore the price for housing services increases, both the value of the housing produced and the growth of population increase relatively more rapidly in the outer part of the urban area. The effect of this differential growth would, of course, be especially strong in the suburbs. Sections II and III also suggested several other reasons why, with rising incomes, the demand for housing in the outer parts of the urbanized area will grow relatively. In Section II, I argued that, if anything, the income elasticity of housing demand is likely to exceed that of the marginal costs of transport, so that with an increase in income the housing price gradient would decline. Secondly, if rising incomes increase the demand for newer structures, population would tend to grow relatively more rapidly in the outer parts of the urban area, which typically are newer. Finally, similar effects would result if higher-income households showed stronger preferences for space relative to structural features of housing, or for home ownership as such. The desire to take advantage of federal income tax advantages to home ownership and the federal mortgage programs available as their incomes increase also positively affect the demand for newer housing.

The urban decentralization of recent years is sometimes attributed to land speculation. Regardless of the reason, if land within the borders of an urban area is held vacant or in less-developed use than current conditions alone might justify, then the boundary of the urban area will tend to be further from the CBD than would otherwise be the case. It should be noted, though, that the failure to develop land currently is perfectly rational and need not be wasteful if the additional returns from doing so are less than the increased future conversion costs. In its vulgar form, the land speculation hypothesis claims that because the future rate of growth of an urban area, and especially its outer zones, is overestimated, or because individuals mistakenly believe that anticipated development will be concentrated in a particular direction, too much land is held for future development.

A more sensible reason that too much land might be withheld from its best use, based upon current conditions alone, is provided by the capital gains provisions of federal income taxation. The fact that the return from holding land for future use is taxed as a capital gain encourages more land to be held for future conversion than would otherwise be the case. If this were the only factor at work, one would expect the returns from landholding to be about equal to those from common stocks, which from recent work would appear to be of the order of 9 to 12 per cent. However, the holding of land for future development is a very risky undertaking, and the Friedman-Savage expected utility hypothesis[61] suggests persons may be willing to accept a lower average return for the small chance of a large gain. If so, the appropriate rates of return with which to compare the returns to holding land would be those on highly risky investments, perhaps uranium stocks.

In another paper I have empirically examined the determinants of the spread of population within urban areas, especially its distribution between the central city and its suburbs, and the amount of land used for urban purposes.[62] Based on these results I would argue that increases in population and improvements in automobile transportation, as reflected in car registrations per capita, are sufficient to account for most of the suburbanization of population and change in land area which occurred during the fifties. During this period urbanized area population increased by about 30 per cent, and such an increase would, according to my estimates, cause the central city density gradient to decline by 15 per cent, or from 0.30 to just over 0.25. The growth in urbanized area population would also have caused its land area to increase by around 30 per cent and the central city population by 27 per cent. The effects of increased car registrations per capita, from 0.26 to 0.35—almost a 35 per cent increase—are much more dramatic. By itself, this factor would cause the central city density gradient to fall from 0.30 to about 0.13, central city population to fall by about

[61] Milton Friedman and L. J. Savage, "The Utility Analysis of Choices Involving Risk," in *Journal of Political Economy*, Vol. 56 (August 1948).

[62] Richard F. Muth, "The Distribution of Population within Urban Areas" in Universities—National Bureau of Economic Research, *Determinants of Investment Behavior* (National Bureau of Economic Research, 1967). These results for the year 1950, plus additional ones for 1960, are included in Muth, "The Spatial Structure. . . ."

14 per cent, and land area to increase by 47 per cent. The decline in the fraction of SMSA manufacturing employment inside the central city from 0.71 to 0.62 would reduce the density gradient by about 7 per cent and the central city population by slightly less than 4 per cent, but it would have a negligible effect upon land area. The increase in income over the decade would have reduced the density gradient by about 20 per cent. But the average central city and suburban incomes grew by about equal amounts, and changes in them have a roughly equal but opposite effect on central city population and urbanized area land.

There appears to be little evidence that urban decentralization has been a flight from blight. With one exception, none of the physical characteristics of the central city appeared to have any appreciable effect upon the distribution of an urbanized area's population. There is some evidence that a high proportion of either substandard dwellings or Negro population leads to a greater relative demand for housing in the outer part of a central city relative to its inner zones. But my comparisons give little reason to believe that these factors have had much impact upon the suburbanization of population or on the total land area used for urban purposes. Indeed, for the forty-six cities I studied, the proportion of substandard dwellings fell from 0.20 to 0.11 during the fifties, so a deterioration of the central city housing stock during the period could hardly have led to further decentralization in any case. It does appear to me, though, that where the income level of the central city is low relative to that of the whole urban area, there is a higher degree of suburbanization of population and more urban land than I would otherwise expect. This finding may reflect the municipal fiscal problem described earlier.

On the whole, it does not appear to me that urban decentralization has been carried too far. During the fifties, for the areas I studied, the increase in central city population averaged about 9 per cent and land area 81 per cent. In total, the effects discussed two paragraphs above imply increases of 9 per cent and 77 per cent respectively. For both 1950 and 1960, the fraction of the population living in the suburban parts of urban areas tended to be somewhat smaller and to respond much less to changes in urban area population and to factors affecting the central city density gradient than would be expected if population distribution in the suburbs were simply an extension of that in the central city. Finally, the preliminary findings of the only study I know of dealing with this matter show the returns from holding land subsequently put to residential or commercial use in the Philadelphia area

316

to be about the same as the average for all common stocks.[63] There would not seem, then, to be any rationale for those governmental programs which seek to halt or reverse the decentralization of urban areas.

[63] F. Gerard Adams, Grace Milgram, Edward W. Green, and Christine Mansfield, "The Time Path of Undeveloped Land Prices During Urbanization: A Micro-Empirical Study," Discussion Paper No. 24, Department of Economics, University of Pennsylvania (processed, July 1966).

APPENDIX

THE RELATION OF POPULATION DENSITY TO ACCESSIBILITY, AGE OF DWELLINGS, AND INCOME

The major purpose of this Appendix is to determine the extent to which the association between population density and distance from the central business district results from the intercorrelation of the latter with the age of dwelling units and the incomes of their inhabitants. To do so, regressions were run for six of the cities for which I had previously estimated density gradients.[64] The forty-six cities studied were divided into three approximately equal groups on the basis of urbanized area population, and two cities were chosen at random from each of these groups. The cities chosen from the largest third by urbanized area population were Houston and Milwaukee. Memphis and San Diego were selected from the middle third, and Dayton and Syracuse from the smallest third by size. In each case but one, the same twenty-five randomly selected census tracts previously used in estimating population density functions were used for the multiple regressions.[65]

The three principal dependent variables used are gross population density, GRODEN, and its two major components, housing expenditures per household, VALHOU, and the value of housing produced per square mile, VALAND. GRODEN is the same measure used previously.[66] Using census data,[67] the total value of housing produced and consumed in dollars per month in a census tract was estimated as the sum of the number of units reporting contract rents, multiplied by average contract rent, and the number of units reporting values multiplied by 1/100th of the average value of one-unit, owner-occupied dwellings.[68] VALHOU was then obtained by dividing the total value

[64] Muth, "The Spatial Structure of the Housing Market," Table 1.
[65] For one of the Syracuse tracts most of the population was institutional, so this tract was eliminated from comparisons. Hence, for Syracuse, the comparisons are based on twenty-four tracts only, instead of twenty-five, as for the other five cities.
[66] Muth, "The Spatial Structure of the Housing Market."
[67] From U.S. Bureau of the Census, *United States Census of Housing: 1950*, Vol. V, Table 2.
[68] It is commonly believed by real estate appraisers that the monthly rental value of single-family houses is about 1/100th of the value of the house.

318

of housing as defined above by the sum of the units reporting contract rents and values. Similarly, VALAND is the total value of housing per tract divided by the total land area of the tract in square miles. If the proportion of units with furnishings and utilities included in contract rents declines with distance or if the income elasticity of demand for furnishings and utilities is less than that for space, the measure of VALHOU is likely to underestimate the true increase in per household expenditures with distance. This underestimation tends to be offset, though, if the effect of rent control tends to decline with distance, as seems likely for several reasons. The measure of the total value of housing produced relates to total land area rather than to residential land alone, as would be more desirable. It almost certainly under-estimates the true value because of the omission of non-reporting units, but the latter's effect on the change in VALHOU with distance or other variables is less certain. The natural logs of all three of these variables were used.

In addition to the above dependent variables, three others were used in the analysis. For comparison of the value measure of housing con-sumption, two physical measures reported by the census were used. These are the proportion of dwelling units reporting substandard con-ditions (dilapidated and/or without private bath), SUBSTD, and the proportion of dwelling units reporting persons per room with more than one person per room, PEROOM (a measure of crowding).[69] Natural logarithms of both of these variables were used. Certainly, the average consumption of housing per household will vary inversely with these variables. But since substandard condition or crowding as defined above is at best indicative only of an amount of housing consumption less than a certain level, the relation between quantity of housing con-sumed per household and either SUBSTD or PEROOM need not be a strictly linear one. In addition, both of these measures refer strictly to consumption of structural features of housing rather than the structural features plus the land. This is because it is conceptually possible for households living in substandard housing and/or under crowded condi-tions to occupy relatively large amounts of land, though it is empirically unlikely. The condition of dwelling units also, of course, reflects the in-centive of owners to maintain their properties, and thus it may be influ-enced by variables not directly related to the per household consumption of housing. The third additional dependent variable, the proportion of dwelling units which were in single-family structures (ONEFAM) was

[69] The data used are from U.S. Bureau of the Census, *United States Census of Population: 1950*, Vol. III, Table 3.

used as a measure of the physical output of housing per unit of land.[70] Since one-unit structures generally use more land per structure than other housing types, the physical intensity of residential land use most probably varies inversely with ONEFAM; but, of course, the relation here need not be a strictly linear one either. The natural rather than logarithmic form of this variable seemed the better form on purely statistical grounds.

In each of the regressions, distance to the CBD in miles (DISCBD), was used as an independent variable.[71] In a second regression, the proportion of dwelling units built prior to 1920 that reported age (AGE-DUS) was included as a measure of age of dwellings and neighborhood, and the median income of families and unrelated individuals for the tract in dollars per year (INCOME), was the income measure used.[72] From scattered diagrams plotted for each of the cities, the various simple relationships appeared to be roughly linear and homoscedastic if DISCBD and AGEDUS were used in natural form and income in logarithmic.

Simple correlation coefficients between GRODEN and DISCBD and partial correlation coefficients between GRODEN and DISCBD, AGE-DUS, and INCOME are shown in Appendix Table A.1. (Since close-ness of association is my principal concern here, these rather than regression coefficients and their standard errors are reported for most of the relationships investigated. Where the regression coefficients themselves or elasticities are of interest, they are shown separately.) In all six of the cities gross population densities show a significant tendency to decline with distance from CBD, and the simple correlation coefficient is numerically about equal to 0.7 or more in five of these. When AGEDUS and INCOME are added, as shown in the second line for each city, the partial correlation coefficients are distinctly smaller for all of the cities except Houston and San Diego; they are still significantly less than zero in four cities, and almost so for Syracuse. Only in the case of Dayton, moreover, is a substantially larger fraction of the variance among tracts explained by adding AGEDUS and IN-COME, as shown by the R^2's in the last column of Appendix Table A.1. The partial correlation of AGEDUS is positive in four cases, and significantly so in two, while the partial correlation coefficients of IN-COME are generally quite small and significantly negative only for

[70] More exactly, the proportion of dwelling units in one-unit detached (including trailers), one-unit attached and one- and two-unit semi-detached structures, from *ibid*.

[71] As described in Muth, "The Spatial Structure of the Housing Market."

[72] The data for these are from *United States Census of Population: 1950, op. cit.*, Tables 3 and 1, respectively.

TABLE A.1.
SIMPLE AND PARTIAL CORRELATION COEFFICIENTS OF GRODEN WITH
DISCBD, AGEDUS, AND INCOME

City	Explanatory variables			R^2
	DISCBD	AGEDUS	INCOME	
LARGE CITIES				
Houston, Texas	−.76*	—	—	.58
	−.76*	−.35	−.18	.63
Milwaukee, Wisconsin	−.84*	—	—	.70
	−.47*	.49*	−.021	.78
MEDIUM CITIES				
Memphis, Tennessee	−.68*	—	—	.46
	−.31*	.20	−.0072	.48
San Diego, California	−.78*	—	—	.62
	−.74*	−.17	.12	.66
SMALL CITIES				
Dayton, Ohio	−.47*	—	—	.22
	.11	.48*	.10	.42
Syracuse, New York	−.71*	—	—	.50
	−.27	.22	−.30*	.59

* Significant at the 1-tail 0.10 level.

Syracuse. Thus, it would appear that the simple association between distance and GRODEN is indeed partly the result of the interrelationship of DISCBD and AGEDUS. But even when age and income are held constant there remains a strong negative relationship between GRODEN and DISCBD. It would appear, indeed, that among comparably located tracts, densities tend to be positively associated with age of dwellings, but that the association between GRODEN and AGEDUS is not as strong as between density and distance. Finally, the partial association between density and income is quite weak, and the one significant negative relationship observed could easily result from sampling variability.[73]

Turning now to variations in the value of housing consumed per household, Appendix Table A.2 shows a distinct tendency for VAL-

[73] The probability of obtaining one or more significant results at the 0.10 level from six independent samples purely by chance is about 0.47. The probability of two more such results, however, is only about 0.11, while four or more such results would occur in only about one out of a thousand cases. Thus, I would think it too unlikely for chance variation to be responsible for two or more significant results; four or more would be highly significant. Considering only the signs of the coefficients, the probability of obtaining four or more plus signs if there is no relationship (or plus and minus signs are equally probable), is about 0.34, while the probability of five or more plus signs is only about 0.11. Hence, the presence of four agreements in sign is not especially convincing evidence for a particular hypothesis, but the presence of five or more is.

TABLE A.2.

SIMPLE AND PARTIAL CORRELATION COEFFICIENTS OF VALHOU AND
DISCBD, AGEDUS, AND INCOME

City	Explanatory variables			R^2
	DISCBD	AGEDUS	INCOME	
LARGE CITIES				
Houston, Texas	.11	—	—	.012
	−.60†	−.17	.85*	.32
Milwaukee, Wisconsin	.83†	—	—	.69
	.43†	−.61*	−.12	.80
MEDIUM CITIES				
Memphis, Tennessee	.30	—	—	.091
	−.21	−.25	.85*	.79
San Diego, California	.000	—	—	.000
	−.40	.079	.61*	.50
SMALL CITIES				
Dayton, Ohio	.56†	—	—	.32
	.18	−.22	.76*	.80
Syracuse, New York	.67†	—	—	.44
	−.28	−.50*	.77*	.84

* Significant at the 1-tail 0.10 level.
† Significant at the 2-tail 0.10 level.

HOU to increase with DISCBD, the simple correlation coefficient being significantly different from zero at the 0.10 level in three cases and positive in two others. As suggested in the second section, however, this is due mostly to the increase in income with distance. For, when AGEDUS and INCOME are added, the partial correlation of VALHOU with DISCBD is negative in all cases but Milwaukee. The partial correlation coefficients of income, however, are quite high for all cities except Milwaukee and, except for San Diego, about 80 per cent of the variation among tracts in the consumption of housing per household is accounted for. For five of the cities, AGEDUS is negatively associated with VALHOU, and this association is significant in two cases. The last result suggests that less housing per dwelling unit is contained in older buildings, since with a housing demand elasticity of −1, lower prices per unit for older dwellings would not affect the per household expenditure on housing. A smaller quantity per unit, in turn, might reflect depreciation or the fact that older units were designed and built for the lower incomes of their original inhabitants. In either case, households with weaker preferences for housing and which purchase less of it at any given level of income may tend to locate in areas of older housing with smaller quantities per dwelling unit.

Appendix Tables A.3 and A.4 indicate that the results are quite simi-

TABLE A.3.
SIMPLE AND PARTIAL CORRELATION COEFFICIENTS OF SUBSTD AND
DISCBD, AGEDUS, AND INCOME

City	Explanatory variables			R^2
	DISCBD	AGEDUS	INCOME	
LARGE CITIES				
Houston, Texas	.000	—	—	.000
	.77	.35*	−.88*	.86
Milwaukee, Wisconsin	−.84*	—	—	.70
	−.46*	.48*	−.064	.77
MEDIUM CITIES				
Memphis, Tennessee	−.24	—	—	.056
	.092	.066	−.76*	.63
San Diego, California	−.48*	—	—	.23
	.23	.24	−.62*	.74
SMALL CITIES				
Dayton, Ohio	−.57*	—	—	.32
	.19	.63*	−.67*	.84
Syracuse, New York	−.75*	—	—	.57
	−.092	.73*	−.64*	.88

* Significant at the 1-tail 0.10 level.

TABLE A.4.
SIMPLE AND PARTIAL CORRELATION COEFFICIENTS OF PEROOM AND
DISCBD, AGEDUS, AND INCOME

City	Explanatory variables			R^2
	DISCBD	AGEDUS	INCOME	
LARGE CITIES				
Houston, Texas	.046	—	—	.022
	.72	.18	−.85*	.81
Milwaukee, Wisconsin	−.53*	—	—	.28
	−.46*	−.17	.050	.31
MEDIUM CITIES				
Memphis, Tennessee	−.24	—	—	.056
	−.046	−.078	−.71*	.54
San Diego, California	.26	—	—	.067
	.54	.039	−.48*	.44
SMALL CITIES				
Dayton, Ohio	−.45*	—	—	.20
	.022	.24	−.70*	.72
Syracuse, New York	−.62*	—	—	.39
	.25	.15	−.75*	.77

* Significant at the 1-tail 0.10 level.

lar when SUBSTD and PEROOM are used as measures of the consumption of housing per household. SUBSTD shows a significant negative association with distance in four cases and PEROOM in three, but when income is added, the partial association disappears for all cities except Milwaukee. Again, there is a strong negative partial correlation with income for all cities but Milwaukee, and the R^2's tend to be quite high, especially for SUBSTD, despite obvious shortcomings in the data used.

The major difference between the results in Tables A.3 and A.4 is that AGEDUS is significantly related to SUBSTD in four cities and positive in the other two, while the partial association between PEROOM and AGEDUS is quite weak. This last result suggests that the smaller quantity of housing per dwelling in older buildings may take the form of poorer quality, but not less space per person. The association of age and condition of dwelling unit with income held constant lends some support to those theories of slum formation that attribute poor housing quality to the decline in demand for housing in older neighborhoods. The lack of any substantial negative association between SUBSTD and DISCBD when age and income are included, however, casts doubt on the hypothesis that the decline in demand for housing in older parts of the city, which accompanied the lowering of marginal transport costs by the automobile, has led to slum formation. For if this were the case, the decline in demand, and hence in housing prices and the incentive to maintain housing in good condition, would have been relatively greater the nearer the CBD. However, if in response to such declining demands some old housing had already been replaced by 1950, the age variable might partly reflect the effects of automobile-induced slum formation.

Since SUBSTD and PEROOM are physical, rather than value, measures of housing consumption, one might expect a negative partial association between them and DISCBD if housing prices decline with distance from the CBD. There are two reasons, however, why this effect might not show up. First, as noted above, both variables are strictly measures of the consumption of structural features only, and not of land. If housing prices and hence land rentals tend to decline with distance, the former leads to more consumption of structural features—which are related to non-land factor inputs—but the decline in land rentals tends to reduce the consumption of structural features. The strength of the former effect depends upon the price elasticity of housing demand and that of the latter upon the elasticity of substitution in production. The values suggested earlier are about -1 and 0.75, respectively, so these two effects may tend roughly to cancel out. And second, especially in view of the above, SUBSTD and PEROOM may be too crude as physical measures of housing consumption to capture the effects of declining housing prices at the rate of less than 2 per cent per mile, which was the rate suggested in Section II.

The partial income elasticities of the various measures of housing consumption for the six cities are shown in Appendix Table A.5. The elasticities of VALHOU tend to cluster around a value just slightly greater than +1. This value is consistent with my earlier finding using time-series data for the nation as a whole,[74] but is somewhat smaller than those found by Margaret Reid for a variety of comparisons.[75] The VALHOU elasticities in Appendix Table A.5 may tend to be somewhat too low because of the inclusion of furnishings and utilities in contract rent, though rent control effects may tend to offset this and, because part of the intertract variation in income, is of a transitory rather than a permanent nature. However, the agreement of the elasticities in the first column of Appendix Table A.5 with previous esti-

TABLE A.5.
PARTIAL INCOME ELASTICITIES OF MEASURES OF HOUSING
CONSUMPTION PER HOUSEHOLD

City	Dependent variable		
	VALHOU	SUBSTD	PEROOM
LARGE CITIES			
Houston, Texas	1.15	−3.74	−2.76
Milwaukee, Wisconsin	−.056*	−.18*	.10*
MEDIUM CITIES			
Memphis, Tennessee	1.18	−1.89	−1.51
San Diego, California	1.71	−3.76	−2.77
SMALL CITIES			
Dayton, Ohio	1.16	−2.94	−2.35
Syracuse, New York	.99	−1.77	−2.23

* Not significant at the 1-tail 0.10 level.

mates is quite encouraging in view of the obvious crudeness in VAL-HOU as a measure of average expenditures on housing. The partial elasticities of SUBSTD and PEROOM with respect to income, shown in the second and third columns of Appendix Table A.5, are sub-

[74] Muth, "The Demand for Non-Farm Housing."
[75] Reid, *op. cit.*, pp. 176–81. Reid found elasticities of owner-occupied housing value only with respect to income, using the latter as independent, for census tracts, carefully selected to remove most of the differences in household type to which value and income data refer. These elasticities of housing value averaged about +1.5 for seven large cities.

stantially larger numerically than those of VALHOU, averaging about −2.5. The estimated elasticities of PEROOM agree quite closely with those found by Reid using data for different metropolitan areas.[76] In view of the fact that both SUBSTD and PEROOM refer to housing of the poorest quality, elasticities of this magnitude are not surprising. The fact that the estimated income elasticities of SUBSTD and PEROOM are so nearly the same bears out the suggestion I made in Section III that condition and crowding are but closely related aspects of housing consumption and respond in a similar fashion to the latter's determinants.

Having seen that the principal source of variation in the consumption of housing is in income, it is of interest to examine the factors associated with variation in income within cities. As shown in the first column of Appendix Table A.6, the simple correlation coefficient between income and distance is significantly positive in all six cities, although in

TABLE A.6.
SIMPLE AND PARTIAL CORRELATION COEFFICIENTS OF INCOME, DISCBD, AND SUBSTD

| City | Explanatory variables | | R^2 |
	DISCBD	AGEDUS	
LARGE CITIES			
Houston, Texas	.47*	—	.22
	.10	−.55*	.45
Milwaukee, Wisconsin	.48*	—	.23
	.22	−.12	.24
MEDIUM CITIES			
Memphis, Tennessee	.35*	—	.12
	−.069	−.32*	.21
San Diego, California	.62*	—	.38
	−.071	−.70*	.68
SMALL CITIES			
Dayton, Ohio	.39*	—	.15
	−.22	−.55*	.41
Syracuse, New York	.80*	—	.63
	.66*	−.34*	.68

* Significant at the 1-tail 0.10 level.

only one of these does distance explain more than two-fifths of the intracity variance of income. But when AGEDUS is added to the regressions, as shown in the second line for each city, the partial correlation between INCOME and DISCBD is negative in three cities and significantly positive only for Syracuse. The partial correlation coeffi-

[76] *Ibid.*, especially pp. 326–27.

cient between INCOME and AGEDUS is negative for all six cities, significantly so in five of them. This result suggests that it is the inter-correlation of DISCBD and AGEDUS rather than distance itself which accounts for the increase in income, and hence the consumption of housing per household with distance from CBD.

I now wish to consider the other major component of population density—the value of housing output per square mile of land. Simple and partial correlation coefficients for VALAND are shown in Appendix Table A.7. The simple correlation of DISCBD is significantly

TABLE A.7.
SIMPLE AND PARTIAL CORRELATION COEFFICIENTS OF VALAND AND DISCBD, AGEDUS, AND INCOME

City	Explanatory variables			R^2
	DISCBD	AGEDUS	INCOME	
LARGE CITIES				
Houston, Texas	−.60*	—	—	.36
	−.84*	−.42	.55	.73
Milwaukee, Wisconsin	−.65*	—	—	.42
	−.28*	.25	.046	.45
MEDIUM CITIES				
Memphis, Tennessee	−.41*	—	—	.17
	−.32*	.095	.54	.41
San Diego, California	−.66*	—	—	.44
	−.72*	.0096	.37	.61
SMALL CITIES				
Dayton, Ohio	−.22	—	—	.050
	.25	.54*	.51	.36
Syracuse, New York	−.54*	—	—	.29
	−.32*	.097	.0052	.30

* Significant at the 1-tail 0.10 level.

negative in five of the six cities, and, when AGEDUS and INCOME are added, the partial correlation coefficients for these five cities remain so. But, rather surprisingly, the association between AGEDUS and VALAND appears to be quite weak. Though five of the partial correlation coefficients in the second column of Appendix Table A.7 are positive, only that for Dayton is significantly so. Even more surprising is the fact that all of the partial correlation coefficients of INCOME and VALAND are positive and three are greater than 0.5. This last result suggests that, if anything, the intensity of the value of housing output per unit of land is greater in higher-income neighborhoods, rather than the reverse as has been frequently suggested, if the effects of differences in location are removed.

327

Some insight into the reasons for these unexpected results can be found by examining the proportion of dwellings in one-unit structures, ONEFAM, which I would interpret as a physical rather than a value measure of housing output per unit of land. Appendix Table A.8 shows

TABLE A.8.

SIMPLE AND PARTIAL CORRELATION COEFFICIENTS OF ONEFAM AND DISCBD, AGEDUS, AND INCOME

City	Explanatory variables			R^2
	DISCBD	AGEDUS	INCOME	
LARGE CITIES				
Houston, Texas	.69*	—	—	.47
	.69*	−.076	−.37	.56
Milwaukee, Wisconsin	.56*	—	—	.31
	−.12	−.59*	.001	.55
MEDIUM CITIES				
Memphis, Tennessee	.66*	—	—	.44
	.28*	−.32*	−.34	.53
San Diego, California	.31*	—	—	.094
	−.29	−.40*	.10	.40
SMALL CITIES				
Dayton, Ohio	.79*	—	—	.62
	.57*	−.035	.21	.65
Syracuse, New York	.81*	—	—	.66
	.35*	−.73*	.60*	.90

* Significant at the 1-tail 0.10 level.

that the simple correlation coefficients of ONEFAM with DISCBD are significantly positive in all six cities, while the partials are significantly positive in four, indicating again a decline in the output of housing per square mile with distance from the city center. As contrasted with the results for VALAND in Appendix Table A.7, the partials of ONEFAM and AGEDUS in Appendix Table A.8 are all negative— significantly so for four of the cities, indicating a greater physical output of housing per unit of land in older neighborhoods apart from differences in location. Also quite different from the results of Appendix Table A.7 are the partials of ONEFAM and INCOME in the third column of Appendix Table A.8. There is little association between land use intensity and income, for, while four of the partials are positive, only one is significant.

Taken together, the partials of AGEDUS in Appendix Tables A.7 and A.8 would seem to imply that, in line with the decline in demand theories of slum formation, the price per unit of housing in older neighborhoods is lower than in newer ones. The positive association in Appendix Table A.8 suggests that the physical output of housing per unit of land is indeed greater in older neighborhoods of comparable location, but the weak association in Appendix Table A.7 indicates the price times quantity per unit of land is little different as between the two kinds of areas. Alternatively, the effects of depreciation, which is associated with age, may be to reduce the number of units of housing of given quality per dwelling and thus the value of output per unit of land. ONEFAM, however, relates to original intensity of output rather than to this intensity currently. Either of these interpretations is consistent with the higher proportion of substandard dwellings in older neighborhoods noted in Appendix Table A.3. Another interpretation of the conflicting results might be that a larger fraction of total land area in census tracts in older areas of the city is used for non-residential purposes. If so, the value of housing output per square mile of total land area would be reduced, but ONEFAM would not be so affected since it more nearly approximates output per unit of land actually used for residential purposes. Still another possibility is that older areas were more strongly affected by rent controls, and hence the value of housing output was more greatly underestimated in these areas.

On the other hand, the partials of INCOME in Appendix Tables A.7 and A.8 may indicate that the price per unit of comparable housing, and hence land rentals, is higher in higher-income neighborhoods because of favorable "neighborhood effects." If higher-income households had stronger preferences for space versus structural features of housing they would tend to live in areas of lower output of housing per unit of land on this account. But higher land rents resulting from more desirable surroundings would work in the opposite direction. Then, if the output of housing per unit of land were about the same in higher- and lower-income neighborhoods but price per unit of housing were higher in the former, the value of housing output per unit of land would be greater in the higher-income neighborhoods.

Differences in the effects of rent control and the fraction of total land area used for residential purposes might also help account for these results. It is possible that rent controls had less impact on higher-income neighborhoods, so that the market equilibrium value of housing output is less underestimated in these areas. Or, persons whose incomes had risen during the period of rent control, and who might normally have moved to single-family dwellings because of this increase, might have chosen to remain in multifamily units because of their low, controlled rentals. It is also possible that higher-income households have an aversion to living in areas of mixed land uses and so locate in areas remote from commercial and industrial uses. If this

329

were the case, the fraction of land used for residential purposes, and hence the total value of housing, would be greater per square mile of total land area in the higher-income neighborhoods, but ONEFAM would not be.

Whatever the reasons for the associations of AGEDUS and IN-COME with VALAND and ONEFAM, it appears quite clear from Appendix Tables A.7 and A.8 that variations in the output of housing per unit of land with distance from the city center are not primarily the result of factors correlated with distance. When AGEDUS and IN-COME are introduced the partial correlation coefficients generally remain statistically significant and of correct sign, and the regression coefficients of VALAND on DISCBD (not shown) give little evidence of decline on the average for the six cities examined. Whatever effect age and income together have on the decline of population density with distance operates mostly through their effects on housing consumption rather than output. If anything, it would appear that average household expenditures on housing are lower in older areas, and population densities therefore higher, since the value of housing output per unit of land appears to be about the same in older areas as in newer ones. The effects of income differences on the two principal components of population density tend to cancel each other, however; expenditures for housing per household tend to be greater in higher-income areas, and thus densities lower, but this is largely balanced by the greater value of housing output per square mile in the higher-income areas.

SELECTED READINGS

Adams, F. Gerard, Grace Milgram, Edward W. Green, and Christine Mansfield. "The Time Path of Undeveloped Land Prices During Urbanization: A Micro-Empirical Study." Discussion Paper No. 24, Department of Economics, University of Pennsylvania (processed), July 1966.

Alberts, William W. "Business Cycles, Residential Construction Cycles, and The Mortgage Market," *Journal of Political Economy,* Vol. 70, June 1962.

Alonso, William. *Location and Land Use; Toward a General Theory of Land Rent.* Cambridge: Harvard University Press, 1964.

Anderson, Martin. *The Federal Bulldozer.* Cambridge: The M.I.T. Press, 1964.

Bailey, Martin, J. "Effects of Race and Other Demographic Factors on the Values of Single-Family Houses," *Land Economics,* Vol. 42, May 1966.

————. "Note on the Economics of Residential Zoning and Urban Renewal," *Land Economics,* Vol. 35, August 1959.

Becker, Gary S. *The Economics of Discrimination.* Chicago: University of Chicago Press, 1957.

Beesley, M. E. "The Value of Time Spent in Travelling: Some New Evidence," *Economica,* New Series, Vol. 32, May 1965.

Clark, Colin. "Urban Population Densities," *Journal of the Royal Statistical Society,* Series A, Vol. 115, Part IV, 1951.

Crecine, John P., Otto A. Davis, and John E. Jackson. "Externalities in Urban Property Markets: Some Empirical Results and Their Implications for the Phenomenon of Municipal Zoning." Paper read at the annual meetings of the Southern Economics Association, 1966.

Davis, Otto A. "A Pure Theory of Urban Renewal," *Land Economics,* Vol. 36, May 1960.

———— and Andrew B. Whinston. "The Economics of Urban Renewal," *Law and Contemporary Problems,* Vol. 26 (Winter, 1961).

Duncan, Beverly, and Philip M. Hauser. *Housing a Metropolis—Chicago.* Glencoe, Ill.: The Free Press, 1960.

Goode, Richard. "Imputed Rent of Owner-Occupied Dwellings under the Income Tax," *Journal of Finance,* Vol. 15, December 1960.

Hoover, Edgar M., and Raymond Vernon. *Anatomy of a Metropolis.* Cambridge: Harvard University Press, 1959.

Hoyt, Homer. *One Hundred Years of Land Values in Chicago.* Chicago: University of Chicago Libraries, 1933.

Hurd, Richard M. *Principles of City Land Values.* New York: The Record and Guide, 1924.

331

Kain, John F. "The Journey-to-Work as a Determinant of Residential Location," *Papers and Proceedings of the Regional Science Association,* Vol. 9 (1962).

Laurenti, Luigi. *Property Values and Race; Studies in Seven Cities.* Berkeley: University of California Press, 1960.

Maisel, Sherman J. "Fluctuations in Residential Construction Starts," *American Economic Review,* Vol. 53, June 1963.

―――. *Housebuilding in Transition.* Berkeley: University of California Press, 1953.

Meyer, John R., J. F. Kain, and M. Wohl. *The Urban Transportation Problem.* Cambridge: Harvard University Press, 1965.

Mills, Edwin S. "An Aggregative Model of Resource Allocation in a Metropolitan Area," *American Economic Review,* Vol. 57, May 1967.

Mohring, Herbert. "Land Values and the Measurement of Highway Benefits," *Journal of Political Economy,* Vol. 69, June 1961.

Muth, Richard F. "The Demand for Non-Farm Housing," Arnold C. Harberger, ed. *The Demand for Durable Goods.* Chicago: University of Chicago Press, 1960.

―――. "The Distribution of Population within Urban Areas," Robert Ferber, ed. *Determinants of Investment Behavior.* New York: National Bureau of Economic Research, 1967.

―――. "Economic Change and Rural-Urban Land Conversions," *Econometrica,* Vol. 29, January 1961.

―――. "Slums and Poverty," Adela Adam Nevitt, ed., *The Economic Problems of Housing.* London: Macmillan, 1967.

―――. "The Spatial Structure of the Housing Market," *Papers and Proceedings of the Regional Science Association,* Vol. 7, 1961.

―――. "The Variation of Population Density and Its Components in South Chicago," *Papers and Proceedings of the Regional Science Association,* Vol. 11, 1964.

Nourse, Hugh O. "The Effect of Public Housing on Property Values in St. Louis," *Land Economics,* Vol. 39, November 1963.

Oi, Walter Y., and Paul W. Shuldiner. *An Analysis of Urban Travel Demands.* Evanston, Ill.: Northwestern University Press for the Transportation Center at Northwestern University, 1962.

Pascal, Anthony H. "The Economics of Housing Segregation," *Abstracts of Papers Presented at the December 1965 Meetings.* New York: Econometric Society, 1965.

Rapkin, Chester, Louis Winnick, and David M. Blank. *Housing Market Analysis.* Washington: U.S. Government Printing Office, 1953.

Reid, Margaret G. *Housing and Income.* Chicago: University of Chicago Press, 1962.

Rothenberg, Jerome. "Urban Renewal Programs," Robert Dorfman, ed., *Measuring Benefits of Government Investments.* Washington: The Brookings Institution, 1965.

Taeuber, Karl E., and Alma F. Taeuber. *Negroes in Cities, Residential Segregation and Neighborhood Change.* Chicago: Aldine Publishing Co., 1965.

Turvey, Ralph. *The Economics of Real Property.* London: George Allen and Unwin, Ltd., 1957.

Wingo, Lowdon, Jr. *Transportation and Urban Land.* Washington: Resources for the Future, Inc., 1961.

*Oscar A. Ornati**

POVERTY IN THE CITIES

A number of conceptual and methodological problems confront the economist concerned with the study of poverty. Indeed, in spite of the fact that almost all economists at one point or another have indicated awareness of the existence of poverty, the application of economic analysis to the study of poverty is in its beginnings.

There is no fully developed analytical framework within which the economist may elaborate his work on poverty. The concepts of the classical economists present some insights, but their relevance is limited to extreme conditions. Ricardo's iron law of wages hovers in the background as we note that some of the regularly employed are still defined as poor. The Malthusian precepts linger about as we note the poverty proneness of families with more than six children age 18 or less. Yet surely average wages are well above current poverty definitions and gains in per capita incomes have not been dissipated on larger families. Walrasian macroeconomic general equilibrium analysis, given market imperfections, might be consistent with unemployment and poverty but poverty in the cities needs explanation precisely because of persistent high levels of employment in most industries and in most occupational classifications in the United States.

Since the beginning of this decade much has been written about poverty and a good deal has been learned. But most of what is known is definitional and taxonomical. We know that certain population groups have a greater poverty proneness than others. Poverty-linked characteristics overlap and converge.[1] We also know that there are significant links between the poverty of certain individuals and their education, their father's education and their "levels of aspiration."[2] But there are no truly integrated causal analyses, few verified hypotheses, and no ascertained constancy of quantifiable phenomena.[3]

* Professor of Economics and Director, Project Labor Market, Graduate School of Business Administration, New York University.
[1] Oscar A. Ornati, *Poverty Amid Affluence* (Twentieth Century Fund, 1966), pp. 37–53.
[2] J. N. Morgan, M. H. David, *et al., Income and Welfare in the United States* (McGraw-Hill, 1962), pp. 387–404.
[3] For a statement of criteria on progress in any of the social sciences, see the illuminating essay by Fritz Machlup, "Are the Social Sciences Really Inferior?" in M. Natanson (ed.), *Philosophy of the Social Sciences* (Random House, 1963).

Poverty, to the extent that its causes can be suggested, would seem to be the result of insufficient personal assets, limited economic growth, insufficient productivity. It is also a problem of the quality of human resources of some population groups; specifically, of the imbalances between existing human resource qualities and the quality of human resources demanded by the market. Market imperfections contribute, as does lagging economic growth in certain communities. Poverty is also the result of the closed, discriminating or "antagonistic-to-the-poor" nature of our society.

The spur for studying poverty in the cities is to be found in policy needs; the "greatly altered scale of political tolerances and a new depth of social aspirations" is what goads our concern in the study of poverty as it does for the study of most urban problems.[4] The dynamic for studying poverty in the cities is generated by the fact that they are the place of residence of most of the nation's poor, strengthened by the widespread call for anti-poverty action, and nourished by the availability of governmental funds for anti-poverty and urban-betterment activities.

The resolution of the policy issues that arise from the presence of the cities' numerous poor calls for two types of interrelated strategies: activities aimed at improving the poor's present and future condition— what Musgrave has called the fulfilling of "meritorious" wants[5]—and activities aimed at using and mobilizing the existing and future resource potential of the poor population. The first set of strategies involves primarily issues of "equity," the second, issues of "efficiency."

DEFINITIONS AND MEASUREMENTS
IN POLICY ANALYSIS

In choosing among different strategies, definitional and measurements problems must be considered first. Priorities among programs and among areas must be set in the face of limited resources. This is not easy as governmental allocations of funds are necessarily carried out within value and political parameters. Beliefs about where the poor live are deeply imbedded in American folklore. Some stem from where people used to live. Beliefs about the cities are equally intertwined in various strands of American folklore often based on preconceptions about where the "virtuous" poor and non-poor live or lived. Some are myths readily contradicted by census data; other data, because of the way they are collected, are used to reinforce on-going myths. Fact and fancy have become so blurred by this mixture of emo-

[4] See the paper by George Stolnitz in this volume, p. 187–227.
[5] R. A. Musgrave, *The Theory of Public Finance* (McGraw-Hill, 1959), pp. 9, 10.

tion, ignorance, and history that they often appear indistinguishable. But what people think does affect policy, so fact and fiction must be severed with the surgery of analysis. Data must be organized to serve the decision makers and to justify their actions.

The Poverty Line

Poverty is defined as the gap between income and certain minimal standards of life. These are "relative," as socially determined standards vary with the nation's income, its distribution, and the social and political values of the period.[6] Yearly dollar equivalents for four-person families (and *their* equivalents for unattached individuals and different size families) are selected through the establishment of ideal budgets which identify certain life standards and styles. Those falling below them are called poor. The three thousand dollar level (on occasion updated for changes in the Consumers' Price Index since 1960) is most commonly used for administrative purposes. It is from this level that the number of the poor and the proportion of the poor in the cities is calculated. The datum is static, incomplete, and with a plethora of implied values and causations. Yet it defines a universe, a "clientele," and permits the establishment of rough policy priorities for the disbursement of funds. (In such a ranking, New York City, for example, becomes entitled to very large funds just because it is the city with the largest number of poor people, even though its proportion of poor in the population is low.)

The isolation of poverty and the consequent ranking that follows from such a "cutoff line" in the income distribution continuum has many limitations. By remaining mute as to intracity differences in the income distribution below $3,000, it ignores the cities' poverty "intensity." Calculating the intensity of poverty—and this can be done because frequency distributions of income by city are easily available in units of at least $1,000—as well as the number and the proportion of the poor below the poverty cutoff line, permits the construction of a single allocative mechanism more responsive to the "income need" dimension. When the measure of intensity of poverty is added to the simple count of the poor, the position of New York does not change, but Cincinnati, for example, moves from nineteenth to sixteenth place. Adding the intensity measure changes the count ranking of most cities.

The Poverty Band

More important as a limitation to policy is the selection of the $3,000 level itself. It is obvious that $3,000 represents different

6 Ornati, *op. cit.*, pp. 7–13.

amounts of purchasing power in different cities and in different parts of the nation. Life styles will be viewed as different and there is discussion of differences in poverty that results from applying the $3,000 cutoff both in Washington, D.C. and in Royal Oak, Michigan; "subjective poverty" and feeling of "impoverishment" will obviously differ in the various cities. This last problem need not deter us since policy-making cannot readily be based on perceptions and images. After all, the sixties are the age of the economist and not of the psychologist! Whereas the $3,000 cutoff line stands for different life styles among different cities, in any given community there are definite and determinable differences between the real value of $3,000 and $4,000 or $5,000.[7]

Different dollar cutoff points define the problem in essentially different terms. They are not simply representations of different life styles and different sizes of poor populations. The differences relate crucially to the "causes" of poverty. The anti-poverty programs and the resource development programs to be carried out in each city should be tailored to such causes. Illustrations as to how different dollar cutoff points affect different cities in different manners will be presented further down the line. Before doing so it is important to digress and comment briefly on the availability of data—particularly to note how poverty statistics can be applied to the formulation of urban anti-poverty policies.

The Limitation and Organization of Available Data

Census statistics are the major source of data for the study of poverty in the cities. In general the study of poverty is handicapped by limitations in the data, since it is only recently that statistics have been collected with a view to their usefulness in the study of poverty. Some of the lack of data stems from well-meaning, albeit misconstrued, legislation or administrative decisions forbidding their collection.[8]

More serious than the lack of data is the problem of getting hold of them. Many communities have now, for a goodly number of years, been collecting statistics on their own poor. Private philanthropic groups, and the various local welfare councils, are in possession of useful and detailed information that is hard to get at and basically non-comparable. In addition, particularly since 1964, a number of

[7] For a lengthier discussion of the problems and methodology in the definition of poverty and for the policy advantages of using a "poverty band" over a "poverty line," see Ornati, op. cit.
[8] See, for example, C. L. Erhardt, "Race or Color in Vital Records: Why Confidential?" in American Journal of Public Health and the Nation's Health, Vol. 52, No. 4 (April 1962).

community and neighborhood organizations have—primarily to justify federal grants for community action programs—been conducting "household surveys" containing valuable sociodemographic data. These, although very uneven in character, deserve the student's attention.

Others in this volume have noted the importance of intergenerational or longitudinal analyses.[9] For these, Old-Age, Survivors, and Disability Insurance data appear to provide the best source. Data about recipients of federal categorical assistance (such as Old Age Assistance, Aid to the Blind, Aid for Dependent Children), often mentioned as sources of data for such studies, are of limited use as most of them are collected primarily for fiscal and operational purposes. The crucial information that these programs generate lies in the folders of the case workers.

The bulk of the work on poverty conducted so far has been based on Census statistics. In almost all of the "counting of the poor" the data have been organized in terms of "composition" and "incidence."

The isolation of poverty that follows from the selection of any cutoff point ($3,000, $4,000, and $5,000 or "subsistence," "adequacy," and "comfort") in the income distribution continuum permits the construction of statistics of *poverty composition,* which indicate how the population below given levels of income is made up in terms of socioeconomic and demographic characteristics. We know for each city how many of the poor are white, aged, females, employed, and so on.

Any cutoff point permits also the construction of statistics of *poverty incidence.* These indicate the number and proportion of poor within the population of each city's socioeconomic and demographic group. We know for each city how many of its Negroes, its youth, its men, and its unemployed are below given levels of income.

The Policy Use of the Poverty Band with Composition and Incidence Analysis

While they may not reveal the "causes" of poverty, composition and incidence data, on a city-by-city basis, at each of the three levels of the poverty band can shed light on some of the many corollaries of poverty. For example, neither being over sixty-five nor being a "female head of family" is in itself a necessary cause of poverty, yet these phenomena are associated with poverty. Cities with a disproportionate number of aged and unmarried mothers will, most probably, have a disproportionate number of poor. Specific anti-poverty programs may benefit, in the first instance, one group of poor more than another and

[9] See Stolnitz, *op. cit.,* p. 215.

consequently, according to the composition of its poverty, one city more than another.

Liberalizations in income tax deductions—by the way of added aggregate demand and employment—would help some cities more than others, depending upon the number of poor in each demographic category and on the proportion of the poor in the labor force. The negative income tax (as currently proposed, with its $3,000 criterion) will primarily affect the population that is not in the labor force. The poor, aged, and infirm recipients of social security and pensions would be unaffected by the liberalization of income tax deductions, but would benefit from the negative income tax. By contrast, the Negro unskilled laborer, father of three, employed and earning about $3,000, would be almost unaffected by the negative income tax, but would benefit somewhat from income tax reductions. He would be a major beneficiary of a children's allowance subsidy system. National strategies aimed at ameliorating the condition of the poor will have a different impact on different cities according to the demographic characteristics of their "poor" even if the "size" and the "intensity" of their poverty were equal.

The different bands of a city's poverty are reflected also in the housing available to the poor. It goes without saying that the worst slums house the poorest poor. What does seem to need saying, however, is that without improvement in a family's income the *opportunity of a city* to obtain better housing for its poor varies considerably according to the level of poverty that is considered.

The situation becomes clear when we represent the different levels of poverty by (illustrative) dollar amounts reflecting cost of housing per room. Assuming the traditional symbolic family of four, living, as required by most budgets, in four rooms, spending a quarter of its annual income on rent, yields a band of spending for rent from about $15 per month per room at the bottom of the range, to about $20 for the family with $4,000, to $26 or perhaps a little more for the family with $5,000. The $5,000-income family has considerably more "leeway" than the $3,000-income family. With a little "encouragement," possibly financial subsidy, private industry can build housing to rent for amounts ranging between $25 and $30 per room. But we cannot presume, no matter how high the national rate of growth or how liberal the interest rates, that private industry will be able to build housing to rent at $15 per room.

Thus, even with a willingness to subsidize the construction of all low-income housing, the city finds that the provision of adequate housing for those living in the worst slums cannot proceed along the same lines as the provision of adequate housing for those living in the "better" slums. The construction of homes for the latter requires a one-time subsidy; but continuing expenditures would be required for housing adequately the poorest poor because, with a $15-per-room monthly rental, city housing, no matter how financed, cannot break even.

Consideration of different levels of poverty suggests also different programs regarding transportation. Consider Los Angeles, with its excellent freeways and its very limited public transportation: the worker earning the equivalent of $4,500 family income or more somehow manages to buy a jalopy, which may make him free to take a job anywhere in the sprawled-out city. At the $3,000 level, there is simply no money available with which to purchase a car or even to maintain one if it were donated. Consequently, unless the $3,000 earner were to receive a windfall, his geographic mobility and thus his employment opportunities are severely restricted. Were California to make deductible the costs of traveling to work, the $4,500 earner would be benefited but the $3,000 earner would not. The provision of more public transportation, on the other hand, would aid the $3,000 earner substantially more than the $4,500 earner. Housing and transportation are, of course, interrelated. It has also been shown[10] that residential segregation by race affects travel behavior and reduces employment opportunities for non-whites. In most large cities significant disequilibria between residential and job locations are acerbated by disequilibria between public transportation and job location. This affects the poor, whether white or non-white. These topics are discussed by others in this volume and later in this essay. They are mentioned here only to note the extent to which policy considerations bearing on the poor in the city are obscured by a definition of poverty that is limited to a single dollar level.

Data on poverty incidence at the three levels of the band throw light also on the merit of the claims of groups lobbying for activities from which they benefit. A simple ranking of the incidence of poverty by socioeconomic groups and by cities, documents, *inter alia,* what common sense does not necessarily suggest. That is, that reduction of poverty in the cities of the North is achieved more by programs aimed at the reduction of racial discrimination (often viewed as a problem of the South), while in some cities in the South, more is achieved in programs that alleviate the poverty of the aged, who are represented primarily by northern and western lobbies.

[10] See J. R. Meyer, J. F. Kain and M. Wohl, *The Transportation Problem* (Harvard University Press, 1965), and numerous papers by Kain, including "Postwar Metropolitan Development: Housing Preferences and Auto Ownership," presented at meetings of the American Economic Association, December 1966.

To sum up, in view of the multiplicity of the corollaries of poverty, the reduction of the size, and future probable size, of the poverty populations of American cities calls for different programs geared to different potential beneficiaries at different dollar levels of income.

A City's "Risk of Poverty"

In the study on poverty carried out at the New School for Social Research in New York, "the risk of poverty," defined as the degree of attachment between the possession of a given characteristic and incomes below poverty, was calculated for a number of sociodemographic groups for the nation as a whole.[11] It measures the average probability of poverty of various groups, and the data permit extrapolation into the future; we learned from this that the probability of poverty among teenagers will increase and that of non-white teenagers will increase even faster. The measure is akin to the Weberian notion of the individual's "life chances." It is clearly a very limited device and covers only a part of the problem.

The city's risk of poverty, in relation to its distribution of populations with poverty-linked characteristics, can be calculated in the same fashion. The limitations of this measure for cities are even greater than for demographic groups. It throws light on very simple derived propositions that go beyond what is learned from the composition statistic alone. The approach suggests, for example, that a city with a large non-white population will have a greater present and future risk of poverty. Verification, by inspection, of the usefulness of this risk measure points to the reasons for its limitation.

Approximate calculations of the comparable risk of poverty of Washington, D.C. and of St. Louis yield a significantly higher level of poverty for Washington on the grounds that it has almost twice as many Negroes. In fact, the proportion of Washington families earning less than $3,000 a year is almost half that of St. Louis. This, of course, is due to the fact that a city's demographic profile is determined by the level and character of its demand for labor, the city's rate of growth, and the tightness of its ghetto. On all these grounds, Washington has better scores than St. Louis.

KNOWN CHARACTERISTICS OF THE SPATIAL DISTRIBUTION OF POVERTY

The old canard that poverty is a rural problem persists because of confusion between rates and levels. Indeed, in rural farm areas a larger *proportion* of the population is poor. In terms of numbers the opposite

[11] Ornati, *op. cit.*, pp. 37–50.

is the case and, almost irrespective of definition, there are more poor in the cities than in rural areas. In spite of this, however, there is a net economic advantage to living in the city, for poor as well as non-poor, and city poverty can be best understood in a context which highlights this fact. In this context the dynamics of poverty reduction are clearest.

Urban Advantage and Size of City

The nature of urban advantage was studied in detail by comparing the incidence of poverty in urban areas, in rural farm, and in rural non-farm areas in 1949 and 1959.[12] It was found that: (1) Well over half of the families with incomes below $1,000 in 1949 lived outside urban areas and were either rural farm or rural non-farm. The same situation held in 1958 for families in an income category (below $1,500) approximately equivalent in purchasing power. (2) In the next category of income ($2,000 per year in 1949 and $2,500 in 1958), again more than half of the families were rural residents. (3) But in the third income class ($3,500 per year in 1949 and $4,500 for 1958), a clear numerical majority of the families lived in the cities. To this one must add the fact that more of the "unattached" in each low income class were in cities in these two years. Thus, in terms of numbers in both years, the majority of those classifiable as poor lived in cities.

A smaller percentage of city than of rural families were poor, however. Let us look at the year 1958, for instance. In that year, 6.7 per cent of urban families were under $1,500 income contrasted with 27.1 per cent of rural farm and 8.5 per cent of rural non-farm families. Similar relationships obtained in the other categories of low income. *While more poor families live in cities, city families have less chance of being poor.* For the unattached individual this is even clearer. The chance of the "loner" being poor in the city is much less than in the hinterlands. Since 1959, these existing trends have continued.

The advantage that urban areas have when contrasted with non-urban ones holds also in terms of size within the urban categories. In large cities the fall in the incidence of poverty, however defined, is as clear as is the rise in median income. Although poverty declines in successively larger urban groupings, the rate of change is uneven. The most marked and dramatic change takes place at the very top. Cities of more than a million show a substantially lower incidence of poverty than cities of 250,000 to one million; the decrease is more marked here than among the four other usual classifications of urban size. Thus, not only is there an inverse relationship between size of a metropolis and

[12] *Ibid.*, p. 54.

the proportion of its families who are its destitutes, but the link of poverty is weakest precisely at the point where urban population exceeds one million. The income distribution pattern of unattached individuals is similar to that of families. For 1960, and proportionately thereafter, individual median income falls steadily from $2,548 in the largest cities to $1,408 in the smallest towns, broken only by the unexpectedly higher incomes of unattached individuals in cities of 25 thousand to 50 thousand. Indeed, census data paint a dreary picture of small town poverty for "the loners." In 1960, nearly two out of five had incomes under $1,000 and about three-quarters lived on less than $3,000 per year. Clearly, an unmarried person in small-town America who is not beset with financial trouble is, at best, a rarity. It almost seems as though prosperity travels on a highway that passes through the Main Streets of America, scarcely touching those living there alone.

Poverty's "Incidence" and "Composition" by Size of City and Cycle

Census data organized along the criteria discussed so far provide a number of insights, all of which need further analysis and refinement. When the concentrations of extreme income groups—the very rich and the very poor—are surveyed according to the size of city, and when relative poverty is studied rather than any one poverty line, we discover that large inequalities of wealth are more characteristic of smaller than of larger cities. Indeed, not only is relative poverty more widespread in the smaller cities but the gap between small town and large city is widest at the lowest level of income. Dollar differences between low income and high income increase monotonically as size of city decreases.[13] The coexistence of the very rich and the very poor—at least as these terms are reflected by income—does not occur as much in places such as Los Angeles and Chicago as it does in Montgomery, Alabama, and Rome, New York. Thus, to the extent that one can link the recent turbulence of our larger cities to the frustration of poverty, explanations that go beyond the simple income differentials must be invoked. It is probable that, as is the case with all political unrest, protest germinates precisely when a given group's conditions begin to improve—which happens faster and sooner in the large cities. It is the confrontation between this group and that whose income is just visibly higher that creates conflict.

[13] This phenomenon is in fact more complicated. A greater proportion of America's small cities are located in the South and therefore the data reflect also the greater poverty of the South as a region. The phenomenon is most marked in southern states with the lowest economic growth rates. It is here, in our own area of underdevelopment, that the well-known polarization of income and status of the emerging nations finds its best parallels.

Incidence statistics by size of city also illustrate the dynamics of income and population. Youth's greater aspirations and the way they escape the economic dead ends show up in census data. The young man going west in 1960 may skip over the towns only slightly larger than the one he left behind; instead work is sought in Los Angeles, San Francisco, San Diego, or Seattle—where wages are higher and job alternatives more numerous. The aged, of course, move less. The incidence of poverty of the aged in smaller cities is thus higher simply because they are left behind.

Data on income distribution and size of urban place are available for a number of postwar years and permit cyclical comparisons. Such comparisons are, however, difficult. First, the postwar cycles have been mild; second, the data are not adjusted to account for in- and out-migration. Reduction in the proportion of low-income units in a particular size urban place cannot therefore be assumed to be the result of an improvement in the economic condition. It may, instead, be a reflection of a worsening of conditions which led to out-migration of the lowest-income units. Despite these hazards, some of the impact of cyclical factors can be identified at least for 1957, a year of high employment and general prosperity, and 1958, a year of relatively high unemployment and recession.

First, it should be noted that the findings for 1960 are not unique. The same inverse relationship between size of urban place and proportion of low-income units existed in earlier years. The relationship appears in both "good" and "bad" times. There are, however, internal changes worthy of note: the proportion of family units with low income in the largest and smallest urban places seems quite stable between 1957 and 1958. Yet in 1958 and in 1960, the most significant increases in the proportion of low income units took place between the largest and second-largest urban places. On the other hand, in 1957, a more prosperous year than either 1958 or 1960, the second-largest urban areas were relatively better off and the widest gap in proportion of low-income units was between places ranking second and third.

The relationship between the proportion of low-income units and size of urban place for individuals shows a somewhat different pattern over the 1957–58 downswing. The inverse relationship is present in both years but there is no perceptible change between the largest and next-largest urban place as in the case of families. Instead, a change in the proportion of low-income units in the smallest-size place (2,500 to 25,000) can be observed. Here again, the sensitivity to the cycle varies along the band of poverty. Correlations between changes in business conditions and changes in the number of families earning less than

345

$5,000 a year are high and significant. At the $3,000 level no change appears.

Intracity Location of the Poor

Analysis of census data indicates that the central city is the repository of the population living below the minimum subsistence level. This results from the accelerated influx of Negroes into the great urban centers, from the absolute and relative decline of population of the large cities despite the burgeoning of urban populations, and from the continued movement of the higher-income populations to the urban fringe.

Non-white over-representation in central cities is typical of urbanized areas in general. By 1960, fewer than five out of every one hundred residents of the fringes of urbanized areas were non-whites, while in the central cities themselves, nearly one in five was non-white. In 1960, already half of the non-white population of the country lived in these central cities, but only every third white person.[14]

The different urban and suburban population compositions go a long way to offset intracity income distribution patterns.

A family who lives in a central city of the nation's 213 urbanized areas has nearly twice as much chance of receiving less than $3,000 annual income than families in the same 213 areas who live outside the city limits. Furthermore, in most of the sixteen largest urbanized areas the city limits contain anywhere from about one and one-half to three times as high a ratio of families making under $3,000 as the urban fringes. Typically, one-tenth of suburban families but more than one-sixth of central city families receive less than $3,000 yearly income.

The central city as the repository of the very poor is attested to also by other measures. In the central city, the poverty extends to educational attainment, and the gap between inner and outer urban core is wide. About 51 per cent of those over twenty-five who live on the urban fringes have completed at least four years of high school; only 41 per cent of those over twenty-five in the city itself are high school graduates. In some areas, the educational gulf is even greater. In Chicago and its central cities, only 35 per cent of adults over twenty-five have the equivalent of a high school education. In Chicago's suburbs, about 54 per cent have at least a high school education. The ratio varies in different cities but the city always lags behind the suburb.

If the suburb is the land of the child, the central city is the land of the aged poor. The "over sixty-five" population of the sixteen major

---

[14] U.S. Bureau of the Census, *U.S. Census of Population: 1960,* Vol. I, Characteristics of the Population, Part 1, *United States Summary* (1964), Table 100, p. 233.

central cities ranged from 5.4 per cent in youthful Houston to more than 12 per cent in five major central cities. In fourteen out of the sixteen major central cities the proportion over sixty-five was as high or higher than the national ratio of 9.1 per cent for the urban population in general. Without exception, in each major central city there was a greater proportion of the aged than in its urbanized areas as a whole. For example, the 65-and-older group are 13 per cent of the city of Pittsburgh and only 9.6 per cent of the urbanized area; they are 13.4 per cent of the population of Minneapolis and 9.3 per cent of the Minneapolis urbanized area. The differences would be even more striking if the city and only the urban fringe were compared, since the ratio for the urbanized area is raised by inclusion of the inner core and its elderly.

Predictably, concentration of the very poor in the central city is evidenced in statistics on the locational distribution of recipients of federal welfare programs. Just over half of the families receiving Aid for Dependent Children (ADC)—51.4 per cent—lived in urbanized areas, compared to only 6.8 per cent in the urban fringe.

The ADC recipient rate in central cities—63 per 1,000 child residents under 18 years old—was nearly four times the rate outside the central cities but within standard metropolitan statistical areas.[15]

The majority of Old Age Assistance payments still go to non-metropolitan counties. However, within metropolitan counties payments have been increasing while the proportion of the OAA caseload living in cities of under 10,000 population has been declining concurrently with the increasing proportion of caseloads in the larger cities.[16]

Intracity Differences at Various Levels of Poverty

When the locations of the poor above "minimum subsistence" within the city are analyzed, in other words when we reintroduce the notion of the band of poverty, the concentration of the poor is much less marked.

The various caveats about monocentric gradients discussed elsewhere in this volume by Hoover apply, of course, to poverty location factors, as they do to density, location of manufacturing employment, residential location, and so forth. Some of the variations in the pattern of cen-

---

[15] Robert H. Mugge, "Aid to Families with Dependent Children: Initial Findings of the 1961 Report on the Characteristics of Recipients," in *Social Security Bulletin,* Vol. 25 (March 1963), pp. 4 and 5.

[16] Bureau of Public Assistance, Department of Health, Education, and Welfare, *Characteristics and Financial Circumstances of Recipients of Old Age Assistance, 1960,* Part I, *National Data,* Public Assistance Report No. 48 (August 1961), p. 11.

tralization described above are due simply to size; indeed, increases in the number of poverty centers correlate positively and closely with increases in the size of urbanized areas. Other variations in the patterns of residence of the poverty populations are the result of "leapfrogging" development patterns; others follow from the scattering of job locations in turn due to changes in technology and the characteristics of demand.

When we study the location of the population within the band of poverty we find that the scattering increases as higher levels of incomes are considered. The proportion of the poor outside the central city increases. In the larger urbanized areas we find significant subcenters of poverty, extending into the suburbs, which may or may not be linked to discriminatory housing patterns. Cities with significant non-white populations have suburban subcenters of poverty populations of greater density. All suburban subcenters are characterized by the presence of many aged and unattached individuals.

Neighborhood Poverty

Harlem, Bedford-Stuyvesant, and South Jamaica in New York City; Watts, East Los Angeles, and Florence in Los Angeles; Woodlawn and Lawndale in Chicago; Hough in Cleveland and so on, are poverty neighborhoods. They are clusters of low-income residents that cross the boundaries of the central city or of the Central Business District. They cut across "census tracts" and "health districts." Here, populations with poverty-linked characteristics congregate and many indices of social pathology are at their highest. Here also unemployment rates, underemployment, and dependency are high.[17] They are often referred to as the "ghettoes" due to the high proportion of Negroes living there. Because of the recent emphasis upon community-based programs of social renewal, neighborhoods are units about which statistical data are becoming increasingly available.[18] This suggests the possibility of research on poverty within boundaries not so far tackled by the urban economist. At this point, it is unclear how fruitful this would be. On the one hand, it can be argued that a poverty neighborhood is no more than a temporary clustering of poor people and that it can be no further identified; it can be argued that the neighborhood is organized to carry out social rather than economic activities, that it delineates no market, that it has no trade to speak of and, in general, that it is economically so dependent upon the rest of the city as to have no economic life of its

[17] U.S. Department of Labor, *A Sharper Look at Unemployment in U.S. Cities and Slums,* A Special Report, GPO 956-413, February 1967.

[18] See, for example, U.S. Bureau of the Census, *Characteristics of the South and East Los Angeles Areas,* Series P-23, No. 18 (June 1966).

own. On the other hand there are a number of policy suggestions coming forth of late, and strands of analysis which suggest that the "poverty neighborhood" is viewed as a submetropolitan entity in its own right. Causes of neighborhood poverty are suggested, for example, in the work of Thompson,[19] in a number of discussions of urban renewal and in proposals for community development corporations.[20]

Actually, one need not resolve the issue of whether a neighborhood is or is not a meaningful economic parameter to argue that more research of a quantitative-descriptive type about poverty neighborhoods is useful. Here, it suffices to list a few questions—for which we have no answers: Does the cost of providing urban services—having corrected for density and quality—differ in poverty and non-poverty neighborhoods? Are urban services of the non-welfare or ameliorative type provided in the same proportion in poor and non-poor neighborhoods? How significant in the persistence of poverty neighborhoods is the fact that the poor pay more? [21]

TYPOLOGIES, ANALYTICAL MODELS, AND POVERTY

What accounts for the fact that cities of equal size differ in poverty intensity? What accounts for the negative relationship between size of place and incidence of poverty? What causes different patterns of intracity locations of poverty? For these and similar questions we have only broad answers. In the sections above we have only summarized what has been learned in the last five or so years in terms of identifications of the dimensions of poverty and suggested ways in which the data can be organized to be of greater use to policy makers. Occasional observations about existing relationships noted so far are mostly formal and do not probe causality. Little is known and much research is needed about causation.

Typologies of economic and social activities are the traditional tools of analysis of urban studies. As such studies progress and become more refined we add to them certain behavioral propositions. From such analyses we make inferences about poverty.

Employment and Poverty in the Cities

The analysis of poverty in the cities always begins with the study of the cities' employment characteristics. The number of available jobs,

[19] Wilbur R. Thompson, *A Preface to Urban Economics* (The Johns Hopkins Press, for Resources for the Future, Inc., 1965), pp. 223 and 376.

[20] U.S. Senate, Committee on Government Operations, *Federal Role in Urban Affairs,* Hearings before the Subcommittee on Executive Reorganization, 89th Cong., 2nd Sess. (August–December 1966).

[21] D. Caplovitz, *The Poor Pay More* (The Free Press, 1963).

349

their industrial and occupational characteristics, the average number of hours worked, the extent of the mix of industries are all viewed as determining the poverty levels of cities.

Thus, cities of roughly equal size will have more or fewer poor according to their industries' labor-capital coefficients and according to their industries' skill mix. Big cities have more jobs than small cities and therefore big cities have a lesser proportion of poor people: in fact, big cities have, relative to smaller towns, more jobs or a greater proportion of high-paying jobs. Furthermore—with some exceptions such as Detroit and Pittsburgh—the bigger the city the greater the diversity of jobs. In the bigger city, the low-skilled worker is relatively likely to be able to obtain an equivalent job in another industry should his employer leave the area; thus, industrial diversity makes for employment stability. Stability maintains income levels, which tend to attract new industries, which in turn tend to keep wages high. Further, the opportunities for mobility encourage the acquisition of skills and industriousness on the part of the labor force.[22]

The pertinence to poverty analysis of the cities' aggregate employment profile or of the cities' economic activities is indirect. Both types of analysis operate by the way of insights as to median income levels and do not provide us with information as to the income distribution. Models of urban economic development in most cases[23] use median family income as the dependent variable. But analyses based on the median are, as we know, not mathematically responsive to the tails of the income distribution. Thus, urban growth models that help explain why certain cities have higher median income than others, or higher employment levels than others, do not predict that these may also be cities of high poverty concentration in terms of either income or employment. The employment profile model, furthermore, implicitly assumes that the labor market is more or less citywide. While this assumption does little if any violence to derived propositions about growth, it is inappropriate to an analysis of poverty inasmuch as the poor operate in smaller and closer labor markets.

Probably the most that can be done by linking the cities' industrial profiles to poverty analysis is to identify very broadly types of causes

[22] These and related propositions have actually been long known to the labor economist who stumbled over them in his search for explanation of interarea employment and wage differentials. In some cases, they have been set in a specific urban context; see, for example, M. Segal, *Wages in the Metropolis* (Doubleday, 1960), and most recently systematized in the context of urban economics by Wilbur R. Thompson. See his paper in this volume.

[23] An exception to this is the study by John M. Mattila and Wilbur R. Thompson who, in addition to median family income, use a measure of family-income inequality. (See pp. 62 ff.)

with different levels within the band of poverty and note that: (1) If we consider $5,000 to be the criterion of poverty, we see that much "poverty" is explained by the presence of low-paying industries. (2) If we consider $4,000 to be the criterion of poverty, we find that the different incidences of poverty in different cities are related to their differing labor-capital coefficients and to the occupational (skilled-unskilled) ratios of their industries. (3) If we consider $3,000 to be the criterion of poverty, then the different incidences of poverty among cities may be better explained by demographic composition. In this case, wage rates, labor intensivity, or occupation have little direct influence.

Economic Change, the Labor Market, and Poverty

That "too fast" or "too slow" change brings about disequilibria that contribute to poverty is obvious. Yet our knowledge of the causes of poverty in cities would be enriched were we to look at some implications of various rates of economic change in greater detail.

Poor people who are employed have low-wage, low-skill jobs. Low-income jobs are heavily concentrated in (a) goods-handling in consumer trades and services, and (b) heavily competitive lines of manufacturing. Trends over the last decade seem to suggest, generally, that the (a) industries are declining industries, while the (b) industries are moving away from the cities. This explains some metropolitan poverty.

The optimum location for a new industry, or even for an industry with a changed input "mix," is likely not to be in the communities or in the neighborhoods from which major industry has recently moved. As plants move, there will naturally be changes in geographical patterns of labor demand. Obviously there are population movements concurrent with industrial movements—but we have only the vaguest idea of *who* moves out of a town or out of the old neighborhood when his employer leaves and *who* moves into a city when a new employer settles there. Similarly, we know that some cities have been successful in evading reductions in median family income when a major employer has left by succeeding in attracting other employers (often from different industries). But we have made little attempt to study the effects of this upon income distribution.

Presumably the experiences of specific cities are useful both to those facing similar challenges and to planners in the communities to which the unemployed might be expected to move. The basic questions regarding labor-force participation of the poor, lack of employment opportunities, and relatively unproductive employment (i.e., low-paying jobs) surely call for analysis of mobility/migration patterns *even more than* of the cities' industrial structure. This must be so for the simple reason

351

that the income distribution of the employed population is the result of a balance of supply and demand that involves the *quality* of the labor force as well as level. The demand for labor is a derived demand and low-skill industries attract individuals with low skills. The character of in-migration is thus crucial and cities will, of necessity, account for different proportions of populations with poverty-linked characteristics according to the peculiarities of available employment.

Technological change and change in the pattern of demand affect the cities' poor in other ways as well. New industries locate in the cities' newer areas if not in the suburbs; the poor live in older neighborhoods. These displaced poor were linked to the old jobs by public transportation systems as well as by well-worn labor market information networks. The new jobs are located outside the areas reached by the existing transportation networks; even when this does not deny to the poor access to the jobs, it does raise significantly their cost of going to work. In addition, at times with an assist from urban renewal programs, housing available to the poor also tends to shift away from the existing public transportation networks which are geared primarily to feeding the central business districts where the poor find less employment opportunities. Shifts in jobs and in residence generally do not offset each other, on the contrary they tend to have a cumulative impact.

New industries bring with them newer and more formalized hiring practices, generally tend to require higher levels of education, and hire through newspaper advertising and private employment agencies. The poor suffer from all these developments as, in addition to limited formal education, they are less prone to use information channels that will lead them to the new employers. Studies that look at the economic and institutional peculiarities of the labor market of the poor thus appear to hold large promise. As there has so far been no research on the causes of intracity location of the poor, such labor market studies could usefully be integrated around hypotheses that test the proposition that the scatteration of the poor away from the center of the city is related to cities' growth rates.

Policy action, particularly in terms of the allocation of federal funds among various cities, need not and should not wait for the results of research of the type suggested here. In the policy context the simpler the identification of the city employment and economic profile the better. Probably the most appropriate categorization is the one developed by Nelson.[24] For each of eleven economic sectors of the national economy, using census data for employment in each of the sectors by

[24] See H. J. Nelson, "A Service Classification of American Cities," in *Economic Geography*, Vol. 31 (July 1955).

city, Nelson determined the proportion of the city's employment which is the average for all cities in the group with that population size. Then he computed for each city separately the deviation of the employment proportion in each sector from the employment-proportion which is the average for that sector for cities in its size group. Each city is consequently classified by the sectors in which a relatively large proportion of its labor force is employed.

Cities' occupational profiles, to the extent to which they could be constructed by a technique similar to that used by Nelson,[25] are probably useful. A preliminary hypothesis that deserves testing is the positing of a high and negative correlation between the cities' poverty measure and white-collar employment. This seems to be so even though there appears to be no relationship between the cities occupational mix and median family income.

In-migration and Poverty

The "newcomers" have always been America's "huddled masses." They also make up a significant proportion of the cities' poor. But here again, we must distinguish between "incidence" and "composition." We do not know how many of the "newcomers" are poor and how many of the poor are "newcomers." Also, the newcomers must be distinguished between foreign-born and internal in-migrants; on the latter group, research is frustrated by an almost complete lack of data. Historians of the immigrants from foreign shores rarely bring to their study the tools of the labor market analyst. The relative success of the various groups is thus explained as though jobs did not matter in terms of time, the rate of acculturation, national traits, economic conditions at the time of arrival, and the prejudices of the people in the receiving areas. In studying the incidence of poverty among the non-native born the data suggest that the size of the group—as a proportion of city population—is substitutable for time. The relationship of the efficiency of the labor market information system with the size of the group deserves careful study.

Labor economists, long concerned with the problems of mobility in the framework of interfirm, interindustry, and regional wage differentials, have not yet turned to a close analysis of the question of the extent to which the cities' pockets of poverty are due to the level and characteristics of migration. We know that the poverty of the depressed

---

[25] Most of the job possibilities open to the poorer populations are lumped in the extremely broad existing categories—skilled, semi-skilled, unskilled. City occupational profiles that can be constructed would be based on these categories, which have not been revised since their inception prior to the turn of the century. Their usefulness, therefore, would be extremely limited.

areas is, to a large extent, a corollary of the out-migration of the more productive elements of their population. This helps our understanding of the poverty of some of the cities of the depressed areas and, in particular, of the smaller cities in Appalachia. Not much more is known that bears directly on the relationship between in-migration and the cities' poverty beyond the fact that the in-migrants are more responsive to the availability of jobs than to their pay level.

We do not know, with enough precision, the way in which rural in-migrants are absorbed into the urban labor market, nor what are the adjustment problems that they face. There are hints that their labor market behavior is different from that of the bulk of the labor force in terms of job searching patterns and that they tend to move in fixed patterns.[26]

Greater knowledge about in-migration in terms of labor market behavior, and rates and characteristics of in-migrants is undoubtedly necessary as there are increasing indications that the persistence of poverty in the cities, even during the recent part of the prosperous sixties, is due to continued in-migration of the rural poor.[27]

Investment in Human Beings

The policy thrust that sees poverty as primarily a matter of inadequacy in the endowment of particular population groups responds to the allegedly new concern with "investment in human capital." [28] Advocates of more education, better health, more housing, and so on, as the way to do away with poverty, derive their position from a set of interdependent hypotheses which move us towards establishing some of the elements of a theory of poverty.

The central hypotheses are two. First, that differences in income distribution are fundamentally only the reflection of differences in the distribution of assets; this for the majority of the population means individual, personal, human assets. Second, that spatial differences in in-

[26] See M. Lurie and E. Rayack, "Racial Differences in Migration and Job Search," in *Southern Economics Journal,* Vol. 32 (July 1966); and J. S. and L. D. MacDonald, "Chain Migration, Ethnic Neighborhood Formation and Social Networks," in *The Milbank Memorial Fund Quarterly,* January 1964.

[27] See, for example, U.S. Department of the Census, *Changes in Economic Level in Nine Neighborhoods in Cleveland: 1960–1965,* Series P-23, No. 20. The same conclusion is suggested also by some unpublished data prepared for the Office of Economic Opportunity by the Department of the Census, which compares 1964 and 1965 in terms of percentages of families and unrelated individuals below poverty level, by selected characteristics, for the U.S. as a whole. See also the discussion of Project SCANCAP below.

[28] G. S. Becker, *Human Capital* (National Bureau of Economic Research, 1964).

come distribution reflect the fact that public investment in human capital is inversely correlated to poverty incidence.

Much valuable work is being done in studying the impact of investment in human beings and preliminary conclusions on the relative yield, to the individual and the nation, of a dollar spent in such areas as education and health, are becoming available.[29] Almost no work is being done on the yield on investment in human beings in a spatial context. This, at least in part, is because there is a large number of conceptual problems in testing the second of the two hypotheses above. First, there are time lag problems. Second, there is the problem of isolating the influence of varied growth rates and *their* impact on poverty in terms of the employment effect. Third, there is the problem of in-migration and out-migration to which reference has already been made.

The preliminary conclusion in the work of Thompson and Mattila that ". . . the degree of inequality in [family income] distribution in an urban area [is] most closely associated with the educational level and educational inequality characteristic of the adult population of that locality"[30] is important. They further suggest that the tendency of localities with large proportions of college-educated persons to be associated with more equal distribution of income represents "perhaps a form of economic *noblesse oblige* or, at least unplanned beneficial spillovers onto the less able." I interpret this to mean that the presence of the educated in a city leads to greater investment in human capital, but whether this is actually due to their "greater education" we do not know because of the known intercorrelation between income and education.

Studies directed at the corollaries, rather than the causes, of poverty also throw some light on the proposition that investments in human capital are inversely correlated to poverty. Among these, worthy of note—and incidentally an object lesson in the proposition that urban economists must scurry all over to find material—is a careful and able study by Dentler and Warshauer[31] on "dropout rates" in 142 cities. Dentler finds that differences in levels of high school withdrawals and in adult functional illiteracy are functions of the communities' total

[29] See, for example, Becker, *op. cit.*; "Investment in Human Beings," a special issue of *The Journal of Political Economy,* Vol. 70, No. 5, Part 2 (October 1962); and T. W. Schultz, "Investing in Poor People: An Economist's View," in *American Economic Review,* Vol. 55 (May 1965).

[30] See John M. Mattila, and W. R. Thompson, p. 76 of this volume.

[31] See R. A. Dentler and M. E. Warshauer, *Big City Dropouts* (Center for Urban Education, 1965), p. 35.

environment: the size and change in size of population, of differences in occupational structure, personal income, and local employment conditions. What is significant is the additional finding that "departures of cities from expected levels of high school withdrawal, *given* their social and economic conditions, are related in large part to *per capita* welfare, health and educational program expenditures."

Again the verification of the link of investment in human beings to poverty in the spatial context is indirect. It is nevertheless helpful, particularly since the investment factors were found to exert different influences on white and non-white withdrawals, which permits more precise policy inferences. It should be noted that the Dentler study did not conclude with recommending greater educational expenditures. It is cited here only as one among the few studies that probes, in a spatial context, the relationship with which we are concerned.

Continued study of the relationship between investment in human beings and poverty on a city-by-city basis is, in my judgment, of paramount importance. Through such study one can obtain guidance for policy both for intracity allocations in terms of amelioration in the conditions of the poor, and in terms of a better utilization of human resources.

Whatever the findings about investment in human beings, problems of implementation of anti-poverty policy on a city-by-city basis remain. For this purpose, I will briefly detour to report upon an Office of Economic Opportunity contracted evaluation study aimed at assessing the impact of community action programs and of other programs aimed at the restructuring of the cities.

Impact of Community Action Programs
The identification of the consequences, both direct and indirect, of community action efforts with a specified program or with a mix of programs was evaluated by computer simulation of fifteen years in the life of CAPSBURG.[32] Not an evaluation in the sense of a detailed study of ongoing programs, and contracted primarily to establish whether a System for Comparative Analysis of Community Action

---

[32] CAPSBURG is a synthetic urban center of less than 50,000 people with many traits common to older north central American cities. In addition to reflecting the data of the 1960 Census in its over-all features, the typical internal wide spectrum of economic and housing conditions of most cities is picked up in seven hypothetical neighborhoods of varying degrees of poverty and deterioration. CAPSBURG was programmed through over 105 parameters to which exogenous variables and the variables relating to the community action programs or their absence were added. The simulation runs which moved CAPSBURG through time assumed different program mixes, different levels of funding, and different levels of economic activity.

Programs was feasible, project SCANCAP [33] established that computerized simulation can indeed give some quantitative content to at least certain consequences of public policy. Not all of the consequences of public action were found to be quantifiable with high levels of reliability: "Our knowledge and understanding of first order effects and direct relationships is substantially better than our ability to disentangle the effects of second, third and higher orders which evolve from any particular action or event." [34] But computer simulation traces into the future the consequences of specified programs (provided, of course, the inputs are meaningful and the GIGO principle[35] is respected) in a fashion that no pencil and paper analysis permits.

The various computer "runs" that were made can be grouped as to whether the major program emphasis was on employment and manpower training, or on education. The simulation yielded the following, albeit tentative, findings:

1) The direct effects of manpower projects have short time lags, immediate effect on individual incomes, and bring about no *fundamental changes in population attributes.* At the end of fifteen years the occupational distribution of employment in the slum neighborhoods tends to remain unchanged and the children of low-income families continue to enter the labor market unskilled. Youth unemployment appears to remain roughly constant.
2) The direct effects of educational programs are delayed in their income effects while the skill and occupational distribution of the population as a whole is more deeply and more lastingly affected.
3) Significant population movements take place over the estimated period of time which was simulated. There is a major shift of population from the poorer neighborhoods to other areas of the city, particularly marked for the non-whites and associated primarily with program mixes which emphasize education. There is a significant net out-migration of whites from CAPSBURG while the total population of CAPSBURG increases.
4) In spite of the presence of community action programs, and related *inversely to the level of funding,* is the continued poverty of CAPSBURG's poor neighborhoods. Indeed, at the end of the period under analysis, the sociodemographic characteristics of the slum neighborhoods are little different from what they were at the be-

[33] Project SCANCAP, by Operations Research and Planning, Philco Tech. Rep. Division, Fort Washington, Pennsylvania, May 1966.

[34] *Ibid.,* p. 1.

[35] The GIGO principle establishes that in computers if you put Garbage In you get Garbage Out.

357

ginning. This is more marked with computer runs that assume growth in employment than with those that do not. In-migration, of course, is the offsetting variable.

Some of SCANCAP's findings, as well as many other statements about the continued future poverty of the cities, stem from unwarranted assumptions about rates of population growth. The significantly lower birth rates of the sixties, the narrowing in the differentials in rural and urban birth rates, the decreased proportion of urban residents who are of rural origin, all suggest that future city poverty will decrease. Most probably the problem of youth unemployment—but not of the poverty of the teenage population of the sixties—will not be as serious in the second half of the seventies. Of course, all discussions of the future of poverty in the cities presume a continuance of at least the rates of economic growth of the sixties.

SCANCAP provides no conclusive evidence. It highlights two questions. The first is whether the impact of anti-poverty programs in the cities can ever be tested by measuring the number of the poor in the city; indeed, if anything, it (with Dentler) almost suggests an inverse relationship between a city's successful anti-poverty program and the number of its poor. The second question points at the relationship between the community's ability to accept and act upon anti-poverty programs or urban restructuring programs and their success. A number of scholars are busy trying to establish sociopolitical typologies to throw light on this problem.[36]

Anti-Poverty Action at the Neighborhood Level

The continued concentration of poverty in certain neighborhoods and the political pressure to do something about it, have led to a number of proposals for their economic rehabilitation. In terms of current political and social values, the fact that the city is a sort of "sausage factory" at one end of which the poor enter and where, at the other end, many of them leave poor no more is not enough. Something will have to be done to regenerate the neighborhood itself so that it will change as the people themselves change.

There is no well-developed theory for doing so. All one can do at this point is to spell out a possible economic rationale for policy action: In the first instance, a model for economic redevelopment at the neighborhood level assumes a degree of homogeneity of behavior among

[36] See, for example, J. O. Greenstone and P. Peterson, "Reformers, Machines and the War on Poverty," *Proceedings of 1966 American Political Science Association;* and J. Dryfoos, *An Exercise in Socio-Cultural Ecology,* unpublished Master's essay, Sarah Lawrence College, 1966.

the residents, at least as far as purchasing is concerned, which exceeds that observed as holding for the residents of other neighborhoods. It further assumes the possibility of adopting essentially "protectionist" policies aimed at reducing the money flows out of the neighborhood. It also assumes the existence of significant unused cash and labor resources. On the basis of such assumptions one can argue the advantages of banding neighborhood people together in a variety of co-operative type ventures aimed at physical rehabilitation of the area, at the creation of locally based, small enterprises, and eventually at the development of increased employment and incomes within the neighborhood itself. The paradigm, of course, is the efforts of underdeveloped countries with autarchic development policies with loans or grants from abroad.

The model has much to recommend it. Indeed, it is as possible to organize the neighborhood residents for constructive co-operative action as to fight City Hall. It is also true that poverty neighborhoods have a good deal of cohesiveness and, on occasion, an *élan vital* absent in neighborhoods of higher income. Certainly labor resources are underutilized. It is possible to assume that either through community involvement or because of the presence of charismatic leaders, such labor resources would be forthcoming for communal activity within the neighborhood even though the supply price of many unemployed workers is higher than that which the larger city labor market is now ready to pay, given their existing skill levels.

Poverty neighborhoods also have significant internal cash flows stemming from sources other than employment: welfare payments, the number rackets, sales from pilferage, car thefts, sales of pipes from dilapidated buildings, all make for a traffic and an "economy" essentially unrecognized and untapped.[37] Neighborhood rehabilitation assumes the rechanneling of some of these funds and of much of the energies involved. Neighborhood rehabilitation requires also the provision from outside of technical knowledge and of managerial abilities now absent.

It is difficult to say whether such plans for neighborhood rehabilitation would in fact succeed; certainly the knowledge of the urban economist is not enough to forecast their outcome. There is little doubt that urban economists concerned with poverty will learn much by studying pilot neighborhood rehabilitation projects. What deserves particular study is the policy presumption, specifically or implicitly presented by advocates of neighborhood-based anti-poverty actions, that the cost-yield ratios of such ventures are higher than those of citywide activities.

[37] This point was suggested by Anthony Downs. See his comments in this volume, pp. 419–29.

Indeed, the presumption is that there are significant trade-offs between expenditures for the encouragement of neighborhood-based activities and the cost of such citywide expenditures as police, fire prevention, and welfare.

SUMMARY

The definition of poverty and its measurement presents numerous difficulties. For purposes of policy, measurement of a "band of poverty" and of the "intensity" of poverty below it are both useful and feasible. Analyses of the "composition," "incidence" and "risk" of poverty are important to policy formulation as they help the allocation of scarce funds among cities as among programs.

The characteristics of the spatial distribution of poverty are fairly well known, both in terms of relationship to size of city and on an intra-city basis. Our knowledge of the latter, though, is limited to poverty defined as "minimum subsistence."

More work is required on the causes of poverty. Urban typologies and urban development models do not tell much about intercity poverty differentials (a) because they are concerned primarily with income averages and not income distribution, (b) because the "growth-poverty" relationship and the "employment-poverty" relationship is unclear, and (c) because not much is known about migration and the possibilities of internally generated neighborhood renewal.

Investment in human capital is an area of study of much promise. The central hypothesis, that investment in human capital is inversely correlated to poverty incidence, needs verification. While none is so far available, studies aiming at it are enlarging our knowledge of poverty policy significantly.

Governmental spending to increase the rate of investment in human beings will continue, whatever the fate of the current War on Poverty. Such spending is bound to make for less unequal patterns of income distribution in the future. If that is not achieved it will at least reduce somewhat the proportion of individuals in that part of the income distribution that we call poor. Pinpointed increases in investment in human beings will make for a more efficient allocation of human resources as well as for greater equity.

In a broader prospective, concern with investment in human beings is the continuation of a long pattern of change in the role of government. The enlargement of the governmental role in socioeconomic matters had been forecast as the necessary result of the democratic mechanism by analysts of capitalist development such as Schumpeter and Strachey. All forecasts involved the eventual socialization of investments. But the prophecies, of the older as well as of the newer critics, are coming into being in forms the prophets never imagined. The millennium had always been described as the redistribution of physical assets, the socialization of investment implied the government investing where the private sector saw no profit-making possibilities.[38]

As far as the poor are concerned both the changes that have occurred and those that the evolution of capitalism would bring about affects them only indirectly. Socialization of investment in human capital is more direct, seems more equitable and appears more effective.

Poverty in the city is serious and it needs to be reduced if we are to come closer to having the ideal urban polity. But not all of the cities' problems are problems of poverty, even though the solution of many of its problems—housing, transportation, education, health, justice— might help the condition of the poor. Much can be done in the restructuring of cities' institutions and organization that will prevent future poverty. Yet one thing must not be lost sight of: The city is not now, never was, nor will ever be, essentially characterized by poverty. The contrary is the case: it is best characterized by its wealth.

[38] See John Strachey, *Contemporary Capitalism* (Random House, 1956), p. 259.

SELECTED READINGS

Becker, G. S. *Human Capital*. New York: National Bureau of Economic Research, 1964.

Caplovitz, D. *The Poor Pay More*. New York: The Free Press, 1963.

Gordon, M. S., ed. *Poverty in America*. Proceedings of a Conference at the University of California. San Francisco: Chandler Publishing Co., 1965.

Hoover, E. M., and R. Vernon. *Anatomy of a Metropolis*. Cambridge: Harvard University Press, 1959.

Investment in Human Beings. A special issue of *The Journal of Political Economy*, Vol. 70, No. 5, Part 2, October 1962.

Morgan, J. N., M. D. David, *et al. Income and Welfare in the United States*. New York: McGraw-Hill, 1962.

Ornati, O. A. *Poverty Amid Affluence*. New York: The Twentieth Century Fund, 1966.

Orshansky, M. "Counting the Poor." Various reports in *Social Security Bulletin*, 1964, 1965, 1966.

Pearl, A., and F. Reissman. *New Careers for the Poor*. New York: The Free Press, 1965.

Schultz, T. W. "Investing in Poor People: An Economist's View," *American Economic Review*, Vol. 55, May 1965.

Thompson, W. R. *A Preface to Urban Economics*. Baltimore: The Johns Hopkins Press, for Resources for the Future, Inc., 1965.

U.S. Senate, Committee on Government Operations. *Federal Role in Urban Affairs*, Hearings before the Subcommittee on Executive Reorganization. 89th Cong. 2nd Sess., August–December 1966.

*Britton Harris**

QUANTITATIVE MODELS OF URBAN DEVELOPMENT: THEIR ROLE IN METROPOLITAN POLICY-MAKING

Decision-makers and social scientists have a common interest in understanding the quantitative dimensions of metropolitan development and its functional processes. This identity of interest is expressed by the fact that each, from his own point of view, is interested in conditional predictions regarding function and development. The scientist makes use of conditional prediction as a method of testing theories. The decision-maker or the planner uses conditional predictions in a much more practical and immediate sense. He is interested in evaluating the putative consequences of innovations and changes in policy designed to affect urban processes. These evaluative forecasts are conditional predictions in identically the same sense as those made by the social scientist for the testing of theories. The difference between the approaches in these two different contexts arises not out of the formal content of the methods, but out of the selection of variables and of measurements of consequences, that is, the selection of inputs to and outputs from the predictions, which are made by means of these experiments.

Without further systematic elaboration, I will therefore assume this formal identity of interest throughout the balance of the discussion. I will bear in mind and occasionally illustrate possible divergences of focus between the social scientist and the policy-maker.

THE NATURE OF MODELS

The current vehicle for conditional prediction regarding metropolitan growth and development in this broad context is a computerized mathematical model or group of models. For purposes of this discussion, I wish to restrict the use of the term "model"; thus I find it necessary to define three distinct ways in which the term "model" is used and to focus on one of them.

Generally, a model is a representation of reality, and therefore the act of setting forth a model represents a commitment (however temporary) to a theory. For example, physicists may speak of "the Bohr model of the atom." Note, in this connection, that the model in question is carefully designed to correspond with some conception of reality; this correspondence and the intent of the scientist in identifying it clearly define such a model as a theory.

* Professor of City and Regional Planning, University of Pennsylvania.

363

A second and very different application of the term "model" is to a purely mathematical formulation without regard to content. Some people thus speak of linear programming and dynamic programming models or of a linear regression model, with the main focus on the mathematical structure. These mathematical models are viewed as some sort of general forms with lives and identities of their own. It is perhaps not often enough remembered that these models represent no more than purely formal relationships until we specify variables, constraints, and so on —that is, until we assert that real-world phenomena have a certain mathematical form. The point is subtle but important that a model must be "of" something, and hence that a mathematical model is not a model but a form. The model or theory consists in a statement that real-world phenomena are isomorphic to or can be well represented by a particular form. The really serious difficulty here is that available mathematical forms frequently do not fit real-world phenomena, and that new forms must be invented in order to establish an isomorphism.

In order to distinguish between theories and operating models, I prefer to reserve the term "model" for an operational concept, and to suggest the substitution of the term "theory" for "model" wherever this substitution is needed, as in the case of the Bohr model above. Given this assumption, I can reiterate my earlier definition: "A model is an experimental design based on a theory." [1] This definition is certainly far from perfect, but it tends to emphasize two aspects of models that I consider to be of major importance. First, it stresses the connection between models and theories, while at the same time admitting models to be frequently truncated theories, sacrificing richness and completeness for operational purposes. It may be that a few descriptive models escape this definition because very little can be said about their related theory. Second, the definition emphasizes the experimental content of the theory, by which I mean that a model is an experimental means of putting the theory into contact with the real world. This contact of experimentalism may take a number of different forms.

It may be noted that the term "model" as defined has no mathematical or computer references, and I suppose it is possible to imagine and even to construct a model that is logical rather than mathematical, that is in fact expressed verbally, but that can nonetheless be used for experimental purposes. To continue the definition, therefore, a mathematical model is an experimental design based on a theory, in which

---

[1] Britton Harris, "The Uses of Theory in the Simulation of Urban Phenomena," *Journal of the American Institute of Planners,* Vol. 32, No. 5 (September 1966) and *Highway Research Record No. 126: Land Use Forecasting Concepts* (Highway Research Board, National Council—National Academy of Sciences, 1966).

relationships are expressed in functional form and interactions are subject to manipulation. In general, the functional relationships assumed for a model are quantitative in the sense that they imply the use of ratio scales, but this is not necessarily true, for the functional forms implied may be defined by the model design, but not by the theory. Thus, the experimental use of models tests not only the congruence of the theory with reality, but also the congruence of the model with the same reality. It is sometimes important to remember that overthrowing the latter does not necessarily overthrow the former.

THE POLICY-MAKING PROCESS

Having laid the groundwork for my discussion of models, I would like to make a few comments on the process of metropolitan policy-making. I view this process from the standpoint of a planner and, to a considerable degree, from a standpoint of a space planner. I first of all take the view that the management of the scarce resource of space is a predominant problem in metropolitan development and that social welfare and economic development problems are strongly colored by spatial considerations. Secondly, I consider that the present tendencies of development in human settlement are far from optimal and, if allowed to continue, will produce unacceptable conditions. In the light of the complexities of spatial organization, a piecemeal and problem-oriented attack on these trends is not likely to be successful. I therefore see the need for planning, which is future-oriented decision-making, and for planning which considers the total urban metropolitan system. Thirdly, since metropolitan areas change slowly, and since human artifacts in the urban environment endure for many decades, I think that our orientation to the future must have a fairly long-range view. Finally, I think that the decision-making process must contain a strong drive toward social optimality. This drive will probably not be wholly successful, but it is clear that we need to produce a much better urban environment, even if it is somewhat short of being the "best possible." To summarize, therefore, I will concentrate hereafter on optimal, long-range, metropolitan planning, with some considerable emphasis on its spatial aspects.

The planning and public decision-making process has three essential phases for purposes of the present discussion. These phases are design (or invention), prediction, and evaluation. Although the phases are encountered in that order in practice, the process is a cyclic one and can be entered at any point. Quite clearly, in particular, the general form of the criteria on which putative decisions will be evaluated must be known in advance, or the process of design may be abortive. Still

365

further, the selection of useful policy measures, or design features, depends on some prior knowledge (however fragmentary) of the effects predicted for them.

It is conceivable that in certain contexts, this three-stage process can be collapsed into a single operation. Thus, for example, we can imagine an optimizing model of warehouse location which essentially creates successive "designs" of patterns of location, predicts their costs, and determines whether this is the best pattern or, if not, how it can be improved. At the conclusion of this process, a design has been generated whose effects are known and which is evaluated as the best achievable.[2] For this process to be readily feasible in this form, a number of conditions must be met. First, the policy design space must be tractable under systematic exploration, and consequently is desirably both continuous and unimodal. Second, the effects must be easily predicted, and either the effects themselves or their evaluation or both should be analytically derivable. Finally, the evaluative criterion must be one-dimensional, well defined, and readily calculable. In addition, it must be arrived at by a transformation which is the same function as is used in the optimum-seeking procedures themselves. These requirements, taken together, are very stringent and not easily satisfied in practice, and for this reason the actual process must usually be divided into at least the three phases discussed above. This ideal process, however, is worthwhile as a goal and as a guide to model-building.[3]

THE DIMENSIONS OF MODELING

The variety and depth of the discussion in other papers in this volume make it unnecessary for me to review in detail the history of our knowledge of the urban environment and of our attempts to extend this understanding. While there are many problems related to modeling that might bear careful scrutiny, I have chosen to limit myself to two major aspects of the problem. In the immediately following sections, I shall develop a sequence of dichotomies or antinomies which define some of the major dimensions of the strategy of model-building. In the sections following this discussion, I shall examine in some detail some

[2] An example of this procedure is the solution to the generalized Weber problem (Alfred Weber, *Theory of the Location of Industry*, translated by C. Freidrich [U. of Chicago Press, 1929]) and the warehouse location problem which are discussed in some detail by Leon Cooper, "Solutions of Generalized Locational Equilibrium Models," *Journal of Regional Science*, Vol. 7, No. 1 (Summer 1967).

[3] For a more detailed discussion of this problem, see my paper, "The City of the Future: The Problem of Optimal Design," *Papers and Proceedings of the Regional Science Association, 1966* (in press).

of the theoretical and practical problems that have arisen in actual model construction in the general framework of land use prediction.

We may usefully define five or six dimensions of difference between various models. The following list suggests the nature of these dimensions:

1) descriptive versus analytic,
2) holistic versus partial,
3) macro versus micro,
4) static versus dynamic,
5) deterministic versus probabilistic,
6) simultaneous versus sequential.

We might also classify models in various ways according to the extent to which they deal explicitly or implicitly with each of the three major phases of the planning process. However, the six dimensions outlined here are centered on, but not exclusively related to, the prediction or simulation phase of planning. This is the phase of the planning process in which the economist should be particularly interested, since it deals with the representation of real-world phenomena, in the context of the behavior of individuals and firms allocating scarce resources. This view can be expanded, partly in an economic context, to consider all of those benefits and utilities that ultimately depend on public decisions.

The dimensions under consideration interact strongly with each other, and cannot usefully be considered in isolation except for purposes of discussion. The interrelations between dimensions are strong enough so that they are not perfectly orthogonal, but I do not believe that the correlation of any pair is so strong that we could usefully eliminate one of them. The variation along dimensions is not usually dichotomous, so that we could in principle generate from these six dimensions a very extensive typology. Considering only the polar extremes, we have a possible sixty-four types of models, of which perhaps only a score of types contain useful examples. Even so, it is more economical to discuss the typology in terms of its dimensions than it is to attempt to present a complete classification and discussion of a large number of models or to attempt to draw the typology itself out of this discussion.

Descriptive versus Analytic Models

The distinction between descriptive and analytic models is of special interest to those who take an economic view of urban metropolitan development. One might reclassify this dimension as expressing the antinomy between induction and deduction. One is forced, of course,

367

to recognize that each of these logical and scientific approaches has its own important role, and to recognize that frequently the strategy of investigation and the development of theory lead to a controlled interaction of the two modes of procedure. Clearly, however, the inductive or descriptive approach represents an exploratory investigation into the types of covariation which appear likely to sustain efforts toward theoretical analysis, precise formulation of relationships, and the testing of theories. The analytic or deductive approach can scarcely be undertaken without more or less detailed statements of universal relationships which one hopes will stand up against rigorous comparisons with the real world. Although the spectrum of possible approaches is more or less continuous, it would appear that the analytic approach necessarily has to make statements about cause and effect which are quite specific and which are possibly testable at both the aggregated level and at the level of individual actors in the processes under study.

It is relatively easy to adduce examples both from general economics and from urban locational theory to illustrate these ideas. Much of the earliest writing in general economics was inductive and descriptive in nature, and this tradition has even continued into modern times in some treatments of business cycles and of short-range economic forecasting. Clearly, however, much more rigor has been introduced into this science by the specification of functional and causal relationships. Some of these are aggregative, as in econometric models of the national economy, while in other fields, such as the theory of the firm, the focus is on individual decision-making entities and the causes for their actions.

In coming to grips with the urban functional and developmental system, similar disparate approaches can be recognized. On the one hand, for example, in another paper at this conference, Hoover refers to the negative exponential relationship of density and distance as one of the major observed regularities in metropolitan arrangements. On the other hand, Muth's paper analyzes a large number of more or less behavioral postulates regarding housing supply and demand, and attempts to relate these both to economic theory and to observed data. While there is obviously some connection between these ideas, it is plain that the density law is purely descriptive, since it is not derived from any detailed specification of cause and effect, while the detailed examination of the behavior of aggregates of households has yet to be integrated into a complete analysis of urban function and development. Earlier efforts to carry out this integration by Muth and others seem to me so far to require too strong assumptions,[4] while the theoretical inte-

[4] Richard F. Muth, "The Spatial Structure of the Housing Market," *Papers*

gration by Alonso, Wingo, and others has not yet been adequately tested empirically.[5]

It seems likely that if we examine the continuum from largely descriptive to highly analytical models, we can obtain some clues as to the general requisites for adequate performance and satisfactory content. Insofar as the analysis treats of economic quantities, these should be present in the model and the analysis. For example, it seems somewhat captious to analyze the economic aspects of location and development without specifically dealing with land values, housing values, and rents. These data, however, are often omitted or represented by proxy variables because they are difficult to obtain. On the other hand, some models which contain these price variables when dealing with housing do not really contain any quantity variables. That is, the quantity of housing is taken to be one dwelling unit, regardless of size or condition. In dealing with locational aspects as these influence the space market, we frequently find that no real economic variables regarding transportation costs and times are entered into the model, but that these in turn are proxied by various distance measures.

It is also evident that locational choices are influenced by factors that affect household utilities and business profits in indirect ways difficult to measure. On the household side, these influences may include amenities, health, safety, educational opportunities, and desires for social segregation or integration. For businesses, the influences may include forms of access to the market and to factors of production through interactions which are rarely recorded and difficult of measurement. Not only the measurement, but also the conceptual treatment of variables of this type are rather difficult to approach with existing economic theory and techniques.

Another economic concept worth some exploration is the full extent of the relation between supply and demand. Most theories and models of locational behavior concentrate principally on the demand for land

---

and Proceedings of the Regional Science Association, Vol. 7 (1961); and David R. Seidman, "An Operational Model of the Residential Land Market," paper presented at Seminar on Models of Land Use Development, Institute for Environmental Studies, University of Pennsylvania, October 1964 (mimeo).

[5] William Alonso, *Location and Land Use—Toward a General Theory of Land Rent* (Harvard University Press, 1964); and Lowdon Wingo, Jr., *Transportation and Urban Land* (Resources for the Future, 1961). See also the first steps towards an empirical investigation of these matters in John Herbert and Benjamin H. Stevens, *A Model for the Distribution of Residential Activities in Urban Areas,* PJ Paper No. 2 (Penn-Jersey Transportation Study, Pennsylvania State Department of Highways), abridged in *Journal of Regional Science,* Vol. 2, No. 2 (1960); and my unpublished paper, "Basic Assumptions for a Simulation of the Urban Residential Housing and Land Market," Institute for Environmental Studies, University of Pennsylvania, July 1966.

and structures. Supply models have tended to deal mainly with the supply of additions to the stock of structures, something that is not, of course, equivalent to the supply of services, which must be equilibrated with demand. Owing to the existence of large and relatively unconvertible stocks of capital, this supply of services in a metropolitan area is relatively fixed at any point in time, but the modes by which it changes would repay more intensive study than it has yet received. The supply of land in the metropolitan area is largely fixed, but the supply function that helps to determine rates of development is probably very complex, resulting from the interaction of personal, institutional, and business factors, and containing dynamic elements related to speculation, anticipations, and knowledge of the market.

In view of these difficulties and omissions in the practical construction of models and testing of theories, it is not surprising that there tends to be a substantial gap between the most precise economic formulations of locational behavior and the practice of empirical investigation and model construction. It appears that the complete information demands for the construction of adequate models from the analytic point of view are most severe, and that some compromise is inevitable. There is, however, one compromise which seems likely to be counterproductive and which I should recommend be avoided: this is a concentration on comparative studies among cities. Such studies are useful in a limited context to provide a classificatory system for cities which are to be studied in more detail, and to indicate the types and ranges of variation which must be accounted for in any complete theory. Beyond this, however, the available data for any sizable set of urban areas turns out to be so sparse that a very large number of significant economic variables must be represented in the model by proxies. These investigations are thus robbed of much real analytical content.

We can drive this point home by asking a relatively simple question. In any particular metropolitan area, how useful would the results of a comparative analysis be in predicting the future population of center-city neighborhoods and surburban municipalities? Quite clearly, predictability would tend to be rather poor. The converse of this proposition, however, has not been tested, and I believe it very likely that properly designed models, developed and tested for a particular city, would have considerable validity and predictive accuracy when adapted to other cities.

The detailed specific metropolitan model therefore offers three advantages over comparative metropolitan studies of a descriptive nature. First, for single metropolitan areas, detailed data may be more easily acquired, and the model may be made to correspond more precisely with an analytical concept or theory of metropolitan relationships. Second, within the metropolitan area a specific model of this type will probably have greater predictive power. And third, the application of such a model in a new context provides more powerful and satisfactory means of testing theories than do the usual statistical measures of goodness of fit.

Holistic versus Partial Models

The distinction between holistic and partial models, our second dimension, tends to point most sharply to a parallel distinction between policy-making and academic analysis. In establishing urban metropolitan development policy for a long time horizon, the decision-maker is ultimately forced to consider not only the total environment, but the totality of ultimate effects, both direct and indirect, of given policies. He is thus implicitly concerned with a holistic approach to the analysis of the metropolis. The academician, on the other hand, and especially the discipline-oriented academician, can in many instances afford to hold the environment constant and examine its impact on a subsystem of the metropolitan area. This is the approach of partial equilibrium economic analysis.

The obvious economies of partial analysis of metropolitan problems, and its strong support from the discipline orientation and from the practice of past academic research, argue strongly for a partial analysis strategy, and quite correctly so. Holistic models will thus be built up out of partial models, communicating with each other and interacting in a computer, much as the subsystems of the metropolitan area interact in the real world.

There are two or three problems inherent in this approach, which can be overcome by careful planning. First, it seems likely that the actual communication between subsystems is much more complex and diverse than at first appears to be the case. The implication for research is that models of subsystems and of partial equilibrium must contain a larger number of variables or a larger number of functional connections with the "constant" environment; these models must be "richer" than in the past. This injunction raises some statistical problems, since the tendency is to reduce rather than to increase the number of independent variables, and since these variables in the metropolitan sphere are apt to be collinear in consequence of the long-term operation of locational processes. A second difficulty arises from the fact that partial models are apt to use variables not ordinarily predicted by any other partial model. Thus, for example, the analysis of residential location would wisely make use of the variable, rents. In

371

this case, however, a collection of models designed to be holistic and to be used for predictive purposes would have to include a model of the housing market which generates rents, since this is a given of the residential location model. In special cases, through the use of equilibrium concepts, prices and locations can sometimes be generated by the same model. A third and obvious difficulty in the application of partial analysis arises from the need to ensure that the division of the total problem into subproblems is not only exhaustive, but also realistic in the over-all system sense. This realism dictates that the hypothetical interaction between subsystems be minimized insofar as possible. Nonetheless, because of technological or administrative considerations, subsystems with high levels of interaction with other subsystems —transportation, for example—be separately treated.

There is another sense, and a more troublesome one, in which we may view the dichotomy between holistic and partial models. We can imagine a model or a system of models which deals realistically with space utilization, location, and some of their costs and benefits. To what extent should this model be expanded to include aspects of social interaction, education, health, and other important problem areas in metropolitan development? The inclusion of these factors would presumably increase the problems of model construction by an order of magnitude, yet these areas of public policy compete for budgets and provide utilities to the population that are of great and perhaps overriding importance. Still further, should this model be expanded to include aspects of regional economic development, competition with other regions, and feedbacks due to improved or deteriorating local public services? Finally, could the model be expanded to include all or part of the political and planning process, predicting not only the direct effects, but also the political acceptance and implementation effectiveness of various policies?

If we thus proceed stepwise in expanding the number of variables and processes that are endogenous to our model system and reducing the number that are exogenous, we shall wind up with a holistic model that represents the totality of human social development. I am by no means opposed to or disheartened by the prospect of attempting to construct such models, but I think we must recognize a hierarchy of problems and of competencies, and for practical reasons stop this process short of the ultimate goal at this time. I do believe, however, that there is an important need to begin work on integrating the effects of social and educational policies into models dealing with space use and spatial distributions in the metropolitan area.

Macro- versus Micro-Models

There is a widespread latent dispute in the field of locational theory and modeling over the relative fruitfulness of macro- and micro-models. This therefore is our third dimension of variation among models. Similar controversies arise in the field of economics. I shall merely touch on some of the seemingly more important aspects of this difference.

First of all, let us recognize that basically many aspects of the final results we wish to predict are aggregated, or macro-results. We are interested in total population (possibly by groups), total transportation system utilization (by mode and by hour of the day), total community facility utilization (by location and by class of user), and so on. We are even interested in total, over-all, benefit versus cost calculations. On the other hand, it is equally clear, first, that the impacts of metropolitan conditions fall on individuals, families, and organizations, and must be evaluated in terms of their welfare, and, second, that these same entities make a large number of the decisions which help determine the levels of the aggregate variables in which we are interested. Thus it would appear that the interests of prediction for decision-making might be well served by aggregative models, but that analytical completeness and accuracy would be better served by disaggregated models, possibly based on the simulation of the behavior of individual decision units.

This distinction, however, is clouded. Any theory and model can be more or less analytical. Even highly aggregated models of economic behavior, such as econometric national forecasting models, make use of hypothetical or observed relations derived from the theory of the firm. Here, some considerable sectoral disaggregation has been undertaken and clear distinctions are made between production and money-flows which respond to different rules of behavior. In metropolitan modeling, similar extensive disaggregation by types of entities and by aspects of their behavior within broad locator classes has frequently been found desirable. This desirability is recognized equally by more sophisticated decision-makers or those concerned with very specific problems, and by academicians interested in theoretical and predictive accuracy. Even those, such as Lowry, who most strongly favor the use of aggregative models[6] recognize the interest, utility, and importance of extensive *areal* disaggregation. In any event, most of the aggregated metropolitan models make more or less use of theories, concepts, introspection, and observation regarding behavior at the micro level.

[6] Ira S. Lowry, "A Short Course in Model Design," *Journal of the American Institute of Planners,* Vol. 31, No. 2 (May 1965).

The central issue regarding the relationship between models of the process of individual decision-making (or behavior) and aggregative models is probably the question of rules of aggregation. This question, however, takes two forms. In the first instance, if the behavior of individual units within an aggregated group may be expected to vary, there may be both mathematical and statistical difficulties in predicting the appropriate average behavior for the group as a whole. Second, important instances may exist in which the behavior or response of a particular aggregate differs from any simple function of the response of its constituent individuals. This might be true of neighborhoods and subcommunities within the metropolitan area. It would seem likely that neither case can be adequately studied without microanalytical research on the behavior of decision units in the metropolis, which may ultimately provide a sound basis for finding and using the appropriate levels of disaggregation.

It is perfectly obvious that the construction of holistic, analytic, and disaggregated systems of models is at the present stage very difficult, because adequate data are not available to sustain the necessary research. Since it seems unlikely that a complete range of necessary data will ever be available for an entire metropolis (or that there would ever be assembled a research staff capable of using it in time), it necessarily follows, I believe, that while piecemeal research on specific topics will proceed at the microanalytical level, most functioning models will be more or less aggregative. Note, however, the discussion which follows regarding deterministic versus probabilistic models. It is also evident that presently available data will not in general sustain very sophisticated microanalysis. Lowry appears to take the position that macro-models, in any event, may be more satisfactory than micro-models; I take his view to reflect, at least in part, the fact that, given presently available data, the assumptions and finagling which are necessary to achieve greater disaggregation are counter-productive and may indeed be unsound.

I cannot, however, pursue this argument to the point where it may be contended that aggregative models are apt to be intrinsically more accurate than disaggregative models. This may in fact be the case if the measure of accuracy is taken as the fit for an observed situation in the present or recent past. If, however, we take the view that one of the major sources of future change will be changes in mix of the underlying population, then the dangers of overaggregation in relation to prediction become apparent. The process of aggregation itself, especially where the proper rules of aggregation would be nonlinear or discontinuous, effectively debars the model from adjusting properly to future changes in mix. The use of aggregative models therefore inevitably freezes some portions of the present mix of population attributes and behaviors. Dis-aggregation tends to reduce this mix and its attendant dangers, and microanalytical models might completely eliminate it except insofar as the mixture is inherent in the behavior of decision units themselves.

Static versus Dynamic Models

Urban analysis and decision-making deal implicitly with change and with trends of development, and consequently require the use of models which are in some sense dynamic. On the other hand, questions of optimization are more easily approached through considerations of static equilibrium. This antinomy is the basis for our discussion of the fourth dimension of variation among models.

Urban planning has traditionally been oriented not only toward the future, but also toward the prefigurement of future states. These states take the form not only of architectural and city planning utopias such as the garden city and the *Ville Radieuse,* but of exploratory devices like the sketch planning for the year 2000 in Washington, D.C.,[7] and finally of action-oriented detailed targets such as may be summarized in a comprehensive plan. While these views of the future of the city or the metropolis tend to cut through or ignore most of the problems of implementation and developmental paths, I believe that they have serious significance. I also believe that their implications can fruitfully be explored through the use of economic and quasi-economic equi-librium concepts. These concepts imply, together with equilibrium, an optimum condition which may or may not coincide with the social wel-fare optimum as defined in the decision process. Indeed, this is one of the main difficulties in the use of economic models for optimizing. The other is the character of the policy space, which is discontinuous, unbounded, and has many local optima.

Analytically, there are other serious difficulties with optimizing and equilibrium concepts. One of these has to do with the fact that in the real world most locators are never in equilibrium, and therefore the observation of their equilibrium tendencies may be more or less diffi-cult. This difficulty is of varying importance as between one class of locators and the next. Retail trade probably reaches an equilibrium of sorts rather rapidly. Residential location is far from being at a general equilibrium, but during any year a very large number of locational decisions could be observed from which strong and valid implications about equilibrium tendencies might be drawn. Large institutions such as

[7] U.S., National Capital Regional Planning Council, *Year 2000 Policies Plan,* 1963.

hospitals and universities, medium and large-size manufacturing establishments, and collections of establishments with large agglomerative economies, such as a garment center, are generally very far from equilibrium. In these latter cases, the costs of moving are so great that very substantial locational diseconomies would be incurred. Since the entities involved are large and diverse in nature, the frequency of entry of new entities able to make optimal locational decisions is very low, and may not provide an adequate observational basis for the determination of the true equilibrium conditions or tendencies.

A second and converse analytical difficulty may arise in certain cases where a system or subsystem is, in fact, tending to equilibrium. If the equilibrium in some sense represents a balance between two opposing forces (such as density and accessibility), then the variables representing these forces may become increasingly collinear. In this situation, the statistical observation of the equilibrating process becomes very difficult. We must be careful to distinguish this case (which I believe to be real, important, and intractable) from a more elementary, but still troublesome situation. This more primitive case arises when the analyst uses a large number of variables in an experimental framework and creates collinearity by using variables or groups of variables which, in fact, measure the same phenomenon. In this case, the reduction of the variable set is reasonable and legitimate. However, in the case where the collinearity arises out of an approach to equilibrium, the elimination of variables demolishes the representation of the real-world phenomena.

These analytical difficulties merely serve to emphasize the fact that the system of scientific interest is a dynamic one which ought, at least in some aspects, to be the subject of dynamic theories and modeling. At the same time, many of the real decision problems faced in metropolitan areas are related to the dynamic characteristics of the metropolis rather than to static optimal conditions. As a consequence of these joint considerations, a large proportion of all modeling effort is directed towards the construction of models that are in some sense dynamic. In principle, a dynamic model can be formulated as a system of differential equations or difference equations. The latter formulation corresponds formally to the use of lagged variables in the familiar econometric models of economic growth and cyclical fluctuation. It is in general somewhat unusual to find a model explicitly formulated in one of these manners, owing to the analytic complexity of metropolitan relationships. We find, instead, the use of recursive sets of models in which the changes taking place in a given period depend on the state of the system at the beginning of this period, and hence indirectly on the changes of the preceding periods and the states at earlier times. This formulation is well suited to linked sets of partial models, and corresponds precisely in a fundamental sense with the basic characteristics of a difference equation formulation.

The critical problems in the construction of dynamic metropolitan models have to do with the manner in which the influence of time is entered into the system, and concomitantly with the manner in which dynamic influences are measured and analyzed. Here one must inject a note of caution, pointing out that, for metropolitan areas, the available time series data are very sparse, non-comparable, and incomplete in the areas of interest. For this reason, many standard econometric strategies fail badly, leading to ever more aggregative, generalized, and uninformative analyses and models. For purposes of the theory and experimental modeling of metropolitan dynamics, time is first of all injected by introducing exogenous changes into the model, such as economic growth, population migration, and income change. These important variables are, as a practical matter, frequently analyzed and projected under the same roof as the work of intrametropolitan modeling, but they are conceptually distinct and belong in the realm of interregional and national economic projections. The dynamic behavior of locators and developers, which properly belongs within an intra-metropolitan model, can be analyzed with some difficulty on a sector-by-sector and disaggregated basis. The dynamic and time-dependent behavior of these parts of the metropolis requires careful attention over an adequate time span, together with a design of analysis which attempts to isolate the invariant aspects of behavior and to "partial out" a multitude of environmental influences. For these reasons, the "spectrum" of manufacturing location may cover thirty years or more; of retail trade location, five to ten years; and of residential location, five to fifty years, depending on our view of the processes involved.

Thus, even if we take a generalized view of location, a fixed ten-year intercensal period is a Procrustean bed for analysis. We may usefully attempt to sidestep this issue by assuming that, over a short period of time, we can sample the spectra of a number of different classes of locators; such a sample could be cross-sectional with respect to the populations, but longitudinal with respect to their behaviors. The problem then becomes one of sample size, and is much more satisfactorily resolved with respect to residential locators and "mom-and-pop" stores than it is with respect to shopping centers and large manufacturers.

Reference to economic "models" of the first type, or theories, suggests that any truly dynamic, intrametropolitan, locational model contains implicit in its structure conditions regarding stability and steady-

377

state equilibrium; I have yet to see these matters adequately explored. Such an exploration could be a two-edged sword (or should I say a Wilkinson-Occam's razor?) which would dissect, on the one hand, the inherent characteristics of the model and, on the other hand, policy implications for sustained adequate adjustments within the metropolitan area.

Probabilistic Models

The manifold uncertainties, both real and apparent, surrounding metropolitan development and human behavior give rise in some quarters to a hankering after probabilistic rather than deterministic models of urban metropolitan development. If I correctly understand the thrust of this desire and the characteristics of models of different types, then it would appear that most emphases on probabilistic models are misplaced and counterproductive. There are probably in principle only one or two important and useful applications.

We must clearly recognize that there will always be a probabilistic element in the simulation of metropolitan phenomena, based on the fact that individual behaviors do indeed contain elements of free will and of social and personal history which are inaccessible to us for analysis and prediction. Thus, in a particular defined group of the population, some will buy books and others will buy TV; some will drive to work and others will take the bus. When we assign proportions to these behaviors, we are dealing in probability, and their analysis is subtle and complex. But the construction of models in which these proportions are deterministically calculated does not fall within the class of probabilistic models for this discussion.

There is a large class of uncertain events that impinge to a greater or less extent on any projection model. These include most particularly unpredictable cultural and technological changes of major magnitudes. They also include, perhaps, selected major intrametropolitan decisions such as, say, the relocation of a large factory, hospital, office, or university. In analyzing the implications of these uncertainties, a probabilistic model which internally generates the random events is surely inappropriate. These events and their effects, if important enough to be examined, should be under the control of the investigator, and should be entered as inputs to runs of the model.

There is perhaps an intermediate scale of uncertain decisions whose variational impact on metropolitan development is worth examination through probabilistic models. A class of such decisions might be the decisions by small developers over a relatively short period of time, say five to ten years. The object of this type of experimentation would be to discover the range of variation to be expected from constrained random decisions in the over-all pattern of metropolitan development. The general experience of simulation in situations with fairly large numbers of actors has been that the range of variation resulting from successive runs is relatively small, and that the outcomes are highly peaked to their central tendency. This peakedness increases with the length of the runs and the number of actors. Thus, the area of appropriate investigation is circumscribed to a rather narrow intermediate range.

This range almost certainly does not include individual household decisions and the decisions of small establishments. While it may be entirely appropriate to conduct research on the basis of observations on these entities, there appears to be no compelling necessity for probabilistic simulation with random behavior programmed within the model. The work of Orcutt and others suggests, however, one important exception to this dictum.[8] If it is determined, for example, that the number of significant dimensions of variation between households is very large, then the cross-classification of these dimensions may create an exorbitant number of behaviorally distinct household classes. This is serious enough in a static model, but additionally in a dynamic model the transfer of households from one class to another may itself be probabilistic according to very complex rules. In these situations, a probabilistic simulation may be conducted by creating a very large sample of the population of households, and allowing their attribution to classes to arise naturally out of their defined characteristics and their transitions from one state to another. In this case, the probabilistic treatment of households represents a solution method to a very difficult computational problem. It is to be expected, however, that the random distribution of outcomes will be of little or no interest in itself. In fact, the expense and difficulty of running a model of this type is great enough to preclude any deep exploration of such randomness.

Simultaneous versus Sequential Simulation

The final dimension along which we may classify models is on the basis of whether their treatment of different groups of locators is simultaneous or sequential. This distinction is not a very profound or troublesome one, and is included mainly for the sake of completeness and clarity.

It is generally recognized that many metropolitan locational and development decisions are made in a manner which is in principle

---

[8] Guy Orcutt, John Korbel, Alice M. Rivlin, and Martin Greenberger, *A Microanalysis of Socio-Economic Systems: A Simulation Study* (Harper, 1961).

simultaneous. In practice, most models must deal with mathematically intractable locational relationships which do not lend themselves to analytic solutions, and which are therefore solved by iteration. The fact that iteration has the appearance of a process in the actual operation of a model should not be taken to belie the fact of simultaneity. Simultaneous solutions are inherently required by static models, since variables are not lagged and the history of the system does not determine any aspect of the locational pattern. But simultaneous systems of mutual locational determination have two difficult operating characteristics. First, the fewer the exogenous spatially distributed inputs (such as fixed transportation facilities or fixed unique locators), the more sensitive and less rapidly convergent is the iteration process. In the extreme case, with no fixed facilities and an unbounded plane, the location pattern may be indeterminate and the iterations may not converge. The second and more troublesome difficulty arises from a different kind of indeterminacy. Given non-linear interactions between locators, the iteration process may converge only to a local equilibrium, and there may be many such. In these cases, the final solution depends on the starting values used in the iterative process, and this in turn may open up opportunities either for injecting normative decisions or for taking account of the history of the system.

Even in a dynamic model it is possible to achieve simultaneity, if this is desired, by iterative solution of the successive steps in the recursive locational model, or by other specific features of the initial model design. The iterative procedures are so cumbersome, however, that it has become customary to operate sectoral locational models sequentially within each recursive step. In this case, successive recursions are thought of as providing an opportunity, if one is needed, to replace iterations and to take account of the interactions between locators. Alternatively, and more popularly, the succession of locational models is represented as having some relationship to the sequence in which actual development takes place and to the lags which are observed in the real world. Thus, for example, residential location may be regarded as a price-setting activity in the suburban fringe, even leading the rest of the model through speculation. If manufacturing location is then made to depend in part on the price of land, it can usefully follow residential location in the recursive operation of the model. This may in fact, of course, result in a geographical lead on the part of manufacturing, which could be forced further toward the periphery in its search for cheap and sizable tracts of developable land.

Quite clearly, considerations of simultaneity versus sequence present a troublesome and perhaps damaging set of problems when we are dealing with static models. In the case of dynamic models, however, and especially dynamic model systems, an exploration of these questions can be a fruitful source of insight into the true behavior of metropolitan growth patterns.

APPLICATIONS OF THE DIMENSIONS OF MODELING

I have now concluded a basic review of the dimensions along which models may be classified. Perhaps a close reading of what I have said will reveal my own prejudices, but these are better stated directly and with appropriate qualification. I uncompromisingly favor the analytic approach to theorizing and model construction, enlightened by an adequate inductive understanding of the phenomena which we are examining. Analysis must almost certainly proceed on a partial basis, but I believe that we shall be able to construct increasingly satisfactory holistic models by plugging partial models into a total system. Our models must, I feel, deal with aggregates of the population, of land, of structures, and of public monies. But these aggregates must be defined in a realistic sense, and the rules of aggregation of decision units must be well explored and clearly understood. This implies many studies and much theory at the micro level, well related to the construction of macro-models. I see different roles for static and dynamic models, and I suggest that the related equilibrium aspects of each are an important unexplored area for theoretical and empirical research. In the construction of dynamic models, I recommend especially scrupulous attention to the definition and measurement of the dynamic elements (state changes and decisions) by which the operation of time is introduced into the model. I foresee that the most efficient and economical models will be deterministic in nature, although they may assign probabilities to various categories of decision-makers. The success of this approach, however, will depend on whether we can efficiently classify decision-makers into a very limited number of groups, failing which stochastic models must be used as a solution method. I favor systematic rather than random exploration of the uncertainties of our projection procedures. My choice between simultaneous and sequential models is largely one of convenience.

In the following portion of the discussion, I present critiques of a number of models of metropolitan development which are of current interest and applicability. These critiques will be fairly general, covering, insofar as possible within the confines of this paper, the general conceptual form of the model with its advantages and disadvantages, data requirements, tests of reliability, and usefulness in the planning process.

I approach the job of a critical evaluation of models work in a somewhat ambivalent frame of mind. On the one hand, I may perhaps urge the pursuit of some forms of conceptual precision with what amounts to moral fervor. On the other hand, I am quite aware that both in my own work and in many other practical efforts, this type of precision must frequently be sacrificed to operating exigencies, including data availability and the allocation of time and funds. In what follows, therefore, I hope that I may view the work of others with the same charitable indulgence which I grant myself when faced with practical problems. In principle, I wish to give them full credit for the efforts they have exerted and the useful ideas they have brought forward. At the same time, it is clearly necessary for the progress of the modeling field that some conclusions be drawn from these efforts as to the difficulties and pitfalls which the user might expect to encounter and, even more important, as to the shortcomings that might be considered and possibly overcome in the design of other locational models. It goes without saying that my own conclusions in this regard are debatable, and I hope that such a debate will ensue to the general benefit of the field.

A brief digression on the subject of statistical objectives in relation to models is also in order. It seems to me that, in explaining aggregated areal phenomena at about the level of the traffic zone or census tract, it should in principle be possible to achieve coefficients of determination in the vicinity of .95 to .99. These levels imply roughly that the relative error of estimate may exceed 20 per cent or 10 per cent in more than one-third of the cases. Coefficients of determination at this high level are apt to appear unreasonable to the statistician or the experienced worker in model formulation, but the errors associated even with estimates of this precision are apt to seem unreasonable to the average planning director who critically examines the results of a modeling experiment. In certain cases, the source of the error may be identified as a point at which the model identifies unrealized trends and thus in a sense predicts better than the real world. This can be a useful feature. In other cases, however, one must look for a reduction in error either through improved or more relevant data, or through a more realistic specification of the model.

Where the objective of the model is to derive parameters from micro data pertaining to individuals or households, coefficients of determination of .20 may be very good, and coefficients as high as .50 are rarely if ever achieved in practice. Here, in my opinion, the coefficient of determination is not a guide to the accuracy or reliability of the model. Such microanalyses are, however, frequently used as a basis for aggregated projections, and applied to some base period an estimate of reliability can be obtained.

Still another contrast in this area must be mentioned. There is a general impression that adding variables or functional forms makes it almost certain that R^2's in the vicinity of one can be readily obtained. This is in fact not the case, and many phenomena, even on an aggregated basis, are extremely resistant to full "explanation." In general, therefore, I do not automatically decry a failure to obtain the high levels of explanation that I believe to be desirable. The obverse situation may also obtain: very high levels of the coefficient of determination do not necessarily imply that a projection model will be wholly successful. Here the situation is somewhat more difficult to analyze, since, as noted above, we have no easy way to apply the model to a base that is very different from the data to which it was fitted. In order to determine the projection implications of a particular model, we must therefore scrupulously examine not merely the statistical measures applied to its calibration, but the structure of the model itself and any possible inconsistencies and contradictions which it may contain. It is even conceivable that, by reformulating a model, we may lower the R^2 for the period of calibration, yet on theoretical grounds increase our confidence in its predictive accuracy.

Retail Trade Location

An illustrative discussion of the use of models for predicting the behavior of a particular class of locators can well be based on the location of retail trade and services. This problem has been intensively studied in theory and in practice, with reasonably successful results. The present state of modeling therefore illuminates some of the modeling procedures which may be followed and, more particularly, the relationships between models and theories.

Fundamental theoretical considerations affecting the patterns of retail trade location are rather simple, but, as in the case of many other urban phenomena, the interplay of these considerations with each other and with the environment gives rise to a fairly rich variety and complexity. In the first instance, retail trade location, like much of the location of a variety of economic activities, can be regarded as a problem in profit maximization. Unlike the case of industrial location, however, transportation considerations related to inputs and outputs are a minor consideration, and the Weberian concepts of industrial location do not directly apply. The primary requirement for profit maximization in retail trade and services is the attraction of customers, which is in itself in many ways more location-sensitive than the movement of goods—since the transportation of people is more expensive and since the entities transported have "free will."

In consequence of the sensitivity of profits to the attraction of customers and also, within limits, as a consequence of the freedom of entry of firms into retail trade and services, two important operational characteristics of the location pattern may be distinguished. First, sites at which customers may be readily attracted are valued very highly by retail trade locators, and therefore competition for the allocation of land with other sectors scarcely needs to be considered; retail trade can and does outbid most other land uses. Secondly, the fixed investment in buildings and equipment required for retail trade location is relatively small in relation to the volume of business, and especially small in relation to the advantages which accrue from the exploitation of a superior site. In consequence, retail trade, considered as a whole, can and must adjust rapidly to changes in the location of demand. With certain qualifications, therefore, at any point in time the location of retail trade activity can be considered to be in equilibrium in response to market forces. Changes which subsequently occur may be regarded as adjustments to changes in demand and in the technology of supply, and not in any major part as an adjustment to pre-existing disequilibrium.

In addition to these salient characteristics, certain other features of retail trade location require some comment. Particularly, the various branches of retail trade and services each have a unique internal structure which is based on economies of scale to the establishment and sometimes to the corporation. In the extreme case, the internal economies of scale dictate a minimum size of establishment. Both minimum sizes and scale economies have been secularly sensitive to the technology of retail trade, to the levels of income and hence of demand of the customers, and to the technology of assembling customers. Similar considerations also apply to agglomeration economies. In the department store, some of these economies are internalized by horizontal integration, but more commonly they are realized by a tendency for retail trade establishments to form clusters or centers. These are based in the first instance on ease of access, or the location of a daytime population of working customers, or both (as in the central business district). In the second instance, however, the existence of a substantial agglomeration of shopping opportunities partly generates its own reason for existence in that the customers for one type of establishment become accessible to other types of establishments. This phenomenon is of course expressed in the existence of community shopping centers

384

and in the creation of new large regional or district shopping centers.

Four broad lines of approach may be distinguished in relation to attempts to model the phenomena which we believe arise out of the foregoing theoretical considerations. These approaches may be considered essentially on the basis of the extent to which they take into account the postulated interactions between supply and demand, on the one hand, and between retail trade locators as influenced by considerations of scale and agglomeration, on the other hand.

The simplest types of retail trade location models explicitly or implicitly assume that the volume of retail trade (as measured by employment, floor space, or annual sales) is directly related to the ambient purchasing power. This purchasing power can be measured in principle either by the density of income or by the accessibility to income, or to respective strata of the population. This concept is implicit in the methods by which the Hill EMPIRIC model accounts for the growth of retail trade activity in response to the changing accessibility and density of classes of the resident population and of other sectors of the employed labor force.[9] Similar concepts in a static equilibrium context rather than a growth context will be found in Lowry's *Model of a Metropolis,* where retail trade demand is distributed from place of residence by formulas for interaction as a declining function of distance.[10] In the Lowry model, minimum size constraints for various lines of activity take into account in a rudimentary way some economies of scale and lead in practice to some agglomeration. It may be objected in principle to both of these examples and to all models of this simple structure that they do not adequately account for the known tendency of retail trade centers to "peak" in selected locations and that they therefore predict an excessively uniform distribution. On the other hand, they are or can be made responsive not only to changes in the location of demand, but also to the state of the transportation system.

A second and to some extent equally unsatisfactory approach to retail trade location is based on a contrary set of considerations. Given that the location of retail establishments in a metropolitan area is non-homogeneous, considerable interest attaches to a study of the statistical properties of their spatial distribution. This type of analysis has been suggested by Vining[11] and conducted in some areas by Dacey.[12] In rela-

[9] Donald M. Hill, "A Growth Allocation Model for the Boston Region," *Journal of the American Institute of Planners,* Vol. 31, No. 2 (May 1965).

[10] Ira S. Lowry, *A Model of Metropolis,* Memorandum RM-4035-RC (The RAND Corporation, August 1964).

[11] R. Vining, "A Description of Certain Spatial Aspects of an Economic System," *Economic Development and Cultural Change,* Vol. 4 (January 1955).

[12] M. F. Dacey, "Two-Dimensional Random Point Patterns: A Review and an

tion to retail trade, a major contribution of this type was made by Rogers.[13] Properly considered, such studies can examine in greater or less detail the statistical aspects of sizes, thresholds, and agglomeration tendencies in different lines of retail trade, but their predictive ability is weak. They do not ordinarily contain any specific reference to market demand or consumer behavior, and consequently do not lead either to a prediction of levels of retail trade in various parts of the metropolis, or to the prediction of specific locations of larger clusters.

It is fairly obvious that the descriptive aspects of the two classes of approaches just discussed could fruitfully be used in combination, but I am not aware of any serious efforts to do so. The basic concepts are, however, combined in two other closely related approaches which give more complete and more theoretically satisfying bases for approaching the problem.

The general theoretical concepts developed above have long been integrated in the general view of the location of retail trade and services which is in principle more satisfactory than either of the two general approaches so far discussed. This integration provides, in fact, a fundamental basis for central place theory, and has been developed in the context of modern models by economic geographers, notably Berry and his associates.[14] The key postulates of central place theory have to do: first, with the willingness of customers to travel to satisfy their needs; second, with the effect of minimum-size thresholds on the distribution of different lines of trade; and, third, with the agglomerative tendencies of these activities. The first and second postulates are necessary and sufficient to define "the range of a good," and thus to establish market areas for retail trade centers. The third postulate is necessary to explain the existence of centers rather than individually uniform but mutually unrelated distributions of distinct activities. In connection with the second postulate, it leads by extension to the definition of hierarchies of centers, with each higher class in the hierarchy containing a larger number of activities, some of whose ranges are larger than the ranges of any goods supplied in lower orders of the hierarchy, and whose

---

Interpretation," *Papers and Proceedings of the Regional Science Association,* Vol. 13 (1964); and "A Stochastic Model of Economic Regions," Discussion Paper No. 4 (Department of Geography, Northwestern University, 1965).

[13] Andrei Rogers, "A Stochastic Analysis of the Spatial Clustering of Retail Establishments," *Journal of the American Statistical Association,* Vol. 60 (December 1965).

[14] Brian J. L. Berry, "The Retail Component of the Urban Model," *Journal of the American Institute of Planners,"* Vol. 31, No. 2 (May 1965), and *Commercial Structure and Commercial Blight,* Department of Geography Research Paper No. 85 (University of Chicago, 1963).

market areas are, at least in these respects, larger than those of smaller centers.

The applicability of these concepts and of the conclusions which may be drawn from them have been investigated in detail for the city of Chicago by Berry. He has found an admirable fit between these concepts and the observed phenomena on the basis of extremely detailed activity and land use data. When market areas are properly defined and when account is taken of the differences between new and old types of shopping centers, a submetropolitan hierarchy of central places emerges and indicators of size, such as total floor area, numbers of establishments, and numbers of lines of business, fall into a distinctive and striking pattern.

It may, I believe, properly be objected that this model is to some extent descriptive and retrospective, even though it is based on a generally sound and powerful theory. Particularly, since the analysis requires the predefinition of market areas, its predictive power is weak, and it would be in general very difficult to use the model to predict the future location of shopping centers. It is conceivable that this problem might be attacked head-on by the use of Leon Cooper's formulation of the "generalized Weber problem." [15] This approach attempts to optimize the location of a fixed number of "warehouses" supplying a predefined "demand." The minimand is transportation cost, which is analogous to the consumer inconvenience which is minimized by the hierarchical structure of central place theory. Cooper's algorithms would, in their present state, have to be applied once for each level of the hierarchy, and this application would probably bring to light one of the more troublesome difficulties of central place theory, the fact that there is no a priori coincidence between centers at different levels in the hierarchy.

The predictive problems regarding the location of new centers are in any event compounded when we consider the use of this and the next group of models in a growth situation. At any point in time, the equilibrium size and location of shopping centers may not coincide with past or anticipated optima. Yet despite the earlier mention of the mobility of retail trade, investments in large shopping centers are relatively immobile. In an application, therefore, of shopping center locational models, it may be necessary to inject some of the anticipatory behavior of center developers, thus broadening the definition of equilibrium and making the retail location problem dependent not only on the state of development of the rest of the region, but also on its probable future development and perhaps on entrepreneurial behavior.

[15] Cooper, *op. cit.*

387

Because of the difficulties in applying Berry's central place model to projections, and because a certain real or fancied unrealism of its assumptions, a growing body of modeling practice with regard to retail trade is pursuing a different line of attack. This line of attack is heavily dependent on various concepts developed by transportation studies in modeling human travel behavior, and at first glance it appears distinct from and even antithetical to central place theory. In fact, however, it may be argued that the ideas are similar, if not identical.

The basic concepts of accessibility models of retail trade location originate in the idea of attenuation of interaction over distance, and more particularly in the gravity formulation that interaction is inversely proportional to some power of the spatial separation of supply and demand. This widely used transportation concept actually had its origin in the description of retail trade behavior with Reilly's law of retail gravitation.[16] These ideas were developed for transportation applications by Voorhees.[17] At about the same time, Carroll used the same concepts experimentally to delimit market areas in the Flint metropolitan area.[18] This delimitation was based on the concept of a line of equal probability of interaction with two separate market centers; this line shifts in relation to the gravitational constant used in Reilly's formula, and the empirically established locus of equiprobable interaction can be used to choose the appropriate constant. This formulation illuminates the basic difference with central place theory: it is here assumed that non-overlapping and exclusive market areas do not exist, but that every consumer has some probability, however small, of interacting with every shopping center. In practice, this distinction is mainly of theoretical interest, since outside the boundaries of a particular market area, the probabilities fall off very rapidly.

Further exploratory development of these ideas was undertaken by Huff,[19] and fully developed models were applied to Baltimore by Lakshmanan and Hansen,[20] to Philadelphia by Harris,[21] and to the

[16] W. J. Reilly, *The Law of Retail Gravitation* (W. J. Reilly Co., 1931).

[17] Alan M. Voorhees, "A General Theory of Traffic Movement," The 1955 Past Presidents' Award Paper (Institute of Traffic Engineers, New Haven, Conn.).

[18] J. Douglas Carroll, Jr., "Spatial Interaction and the Urban-Metropolitan Description," *Papers and Proceedings of the Regional Science Association,* Vol. 1 (1955); also in *Traffic Quarterly,* Vol. 9, No. 2 (April 1955).

[19] David L. Huff, *Determination of Intra-Urban Retail Trade Areas,* Real Estate Research Program, Graduate School of Business Administration, Division of Research, University of California, Los Angeles, 1966.

[20] T. R. Lakshmanan and Walter G. Hansen, "A Retail Market Potential Model," *Journal of the American Institute of Planners,* Vol. 31, No. 2 (May 1965).

[21] Britton Harris, "A Model of Locational Equilibrium for Retail Trade," paper

Buffalo region by Fidler (following exploratory work by Ferguson).[22]

The basic operational features of this group of models may be briefly described. A model of consumer behavior with regard to shopping travel is formulated by analogy with trip-making behavior. The future location of purchasing power is projected. The future state of the transportation system is defined in terms compatible with the consumer behavior definition. In some prespecified manner, a set of shopping center locations is chosen, and the interaction of consumers with these centers is examined. In the event that "arrivals" exceed "opportunities," the size of the center is expanded or new centers are introduced, and, conversely, the size of the center may be contracted or it may be deleted. At equilibrium there is a rough balance between the demands of the predicted population and the location of future shopping centers, which is believed to provide a locational pattern in some sense optimal. Several interesting questions arise as to the development and application of these models.

One such question is the origin of the behavioral parameters. Lakshmanan and Hansen (and in a related case, Lowry) derive these parameters from actual trip-making behavior for one or more shopping purposes. Fidler and Harris, on the other hand, looked for one or more parameters which would optimize the match between opportunities and arrivals in an existing pattern. In these cases, actual travel behavior was implicit rather than explicit, and thus not directly analyzed.

A second question revolves around the hierarchical structure of retail trade. A treatment of this issue requires the use of information regarding the location of trade by a number of categories, usually at the three- or four-digit Standard Industrial Classification (SIC) level. Such data are not generally available, and have been used, so far as I know, only in the Berry studies. A two-digit classification yields some discrimination, and it turns out that the differing characteristics of retail locators can be entered into the model both by way of the behavioral patterns of their patrons and by way of minimum scale constraints. This problem has not been thoroughly researched in connection with models of this type. Both the Lakshmanan-Hansen and Fidler models, for example, handle these thresholds and scale economies essentially by dealing only with shopping centers of a certain minimum size. The Harris model contains a specific provision to vary consumer behavior

---

presented at a Seminar on Models of Land Use Development, Institute for Urban Studies, University of Pennsylvania, October 1964 (mimeo).

[22] Jere Fidler, "Commercial Activity Location Model," Publication TPOO-332-01, Subdivision of Transportation Planning and Programming, New York State Department of Public Works, Albany (January 1967).

in accordance with density of opportunities, but this provision has not been well implemented in relation to shopping center foci within larger areal units. In the Harris model, this behavior can in principle be made to vary not only by line of retail trade, but also by class of demander.

A third question of interest is the treatment of joint demand for retail facilities by different classes of the population and by the population based at home and based at place of work. The Lakshmanan-Hansen and Fidler models consider only one type of demand, residentially based. The Harris model, on the other hand, can accommodate a number of demand strata, and has produced interesting results using as demanders the residentially-located population and employment-located jobs.

The sensitivity of the models to transportation considerations is still another aspect of importance. These models are implicitly transportation sensitive, and, indeed, a number of difficult questions arise as to whether one should use transit networks, auto networks, or some mixture of the two in their implementation; still further, this mix might change in a predictive use of the models. It is of interest to note that wide variations in future retail and related location resulted from applications of the Harris model with different transportation systems, and similarly in applications of the EMPIRIC model in the Boston region. The Penn-Jersey applications were particularly responsive to changes in the terminal charges for automobile storage in the central business district.

A final question of interest, requiring some considerable future investigation, is the optimality implications of these models. The clearest indication in this direction comes from the finding of the Lakshmanan-Hansen study that the most nearly "balanced" distribution of shopping centers also corresponded with the minimum expenditure of travel effort by shoppers, given the alternatives studied. Of course, in a more developed model circumstances might arise in which consumers would trade off additional travel effort for a greater variety of shopping opportunities. A detailed study of this question would require more sophisticated analysis and better data than have been used heretofore in studying these problems.

A general summary of retail trade location models suggests a number of broad conclusions. What we have reviewed here is a group of models in the public domain, the last set of which corresponds in principle with a certain amount of private practice conducted by retail chains and their consultants. These studies collectively suggest that transportation considerations are indeed important in shopping center location, that the location of demand and the behavioral preferences of consumers are also important, and that there is a broad correspondence between the principles of central place theory and the actually observed locational tendencies. Questions not settled extend to a number of issues. It is not known how sensitive these models are to various areal systems. It is not known how much disaggregation of shopping by lines of activity is necessary to generate realistic definitions of the hierarchical structure of location. The complete pattern of consumer behavior in shopping has not been fully investigated, and especially it has not been expressed in fundamental terms that might be expected to be invariant under a very different set of future conditions. Similar remarks might be made regarding the entrepreneurial behavior and technological organization of retail trade itself. Thus, while the analysis and projection of retail trade location appears to be on the right track and be capable of dealing with these problems at several levels of complexity, there probably remains a substantial amount of work to be done, even if the ultimate effect of that work in some cases may be to shut the door of further elaboration of models in certain directions.

Residential Location

In the preceding discussion, we have seen, not unexpectedly, that the location of trade depends to a very considerable degree on the location of consumer demand. This, of course, is but one illustration of the key importance of residential location in modeling metropolitan arrangements and development over time. Residentially developed land occupies more than 50 per cent of all urbanized land in metropolitan areas, and when we consider the provision of streets, shops, parks, and other community facilities, this proportion is undoubtedly considerably higher. In a very real sense, the demand for residential land is the price-setting demand in most parts of the metropolitan area.

The location of residences creates the basic demand for community facilities and services, and since most person-trips in the metropolis have either their origin or destination at home, residential location plays a determining role in shaping the demand for transportation. Finally, since the average citizen spends about two-thirds of his time at home (although half of this time he is asleep), the cost and amenity of residential facilities are a major target for planning control. The use of models for predicting residential location is therefore a central focus of interest in the development of land use models.

The general environment of ideas out of which modeling of residential activity has grown is well known and widely understood. At the simplest level, it is apparent that land prices and residential densities increase towards the centers of metropolitan areas and towards the subcenters with remarkable regularity, in the manner discussed in Hoover's paper in this volume.[23] The general features of this rent and density gradient may be used in a descriptive fashion for a variety of modeling purposes. One of the first relatively sophisticated models of land development, used by the Chicago Area Transportation Study,[24] discriminated between gradients along different sectors and took into account the two aspects of over-all density: net density and proportion of development. The concepts of density gradient over the whole metropolitan area were developed in a more sophisticated and dynamic context by Blumenfeld and Jurkat.[25] Two recent models of residential development use a similar descriptive technique based on concepts of the decay of interaction with distance: Lowry's *Model of a Metropolis* and the Hamburg-Lathrop model developed for the Transportation Planning and Programming Subdivision of the New York State Department of Public Works.[26] These two models differ in that Lowry uses a modified gravity formulation, while Hamburg and Lathrop use an opportunity formulation, and in that Lowry explicitly recognizes trip origins at all places of work, while in the Hamburg-Lathrop model, the selection of central origins is arbitrary, but may include any number. There is a feedback in the Lowry model between shopping and residential location which does not exist in the other model.

The basic point to be considered in relation to these models is their essentially descriptive character. Despite the fact that the description is based on a well defined real-world process, what actually happens is that the models equate two processes which are not necessarily, or even probably, the same, and what has been observed is a correlation rather than a cause and effect relationship. The undoubted fact utilized in both models is that the journey from work to home declines in relative frequency with distance. Furthermore, the functional form of that decline has a strong resemblance with the observed negative exponential decline of density from the center of the city. It is somewhat difficult to imagine, however, any process by which this matching of home and workplace can occur as a function either of distance or of opportunity considered as a single variable. For this reason, the supposed equivalence

[23] See pp. 237–84.

[24] John R. Hamburg and Roger L. Creighton, "Predicting Chicago's Land Use Pattern," *Journal of the American Institute of Planners,* Vol. 25, No. 2 (May 1959).

[25] Hans Blumenfeld, "Are Land Use Patterns Predictable?" and Arthur Row and Ernest Jurkat, "The Economic Forces Shaping Land Use Patterns," both in *ibid.*

[26] George T. Lathrop and John R. Hamburg, "An Opportunity-Accessibility Model for Allocating Regional Growth," *Journal of the American Institute of Planners,* Vol. 31, No. 2 (May 1965).

of the two processes must be said to be descriptive rather than explanatory.

There is, however, the well known theoretical development, best summarized by Alonso and Wingo, which derives from agricultural rent theory and provides a transportation-based explanation for the observed rent gradients.[27] These models in their theoretical form are more simplistic than the Lowry model in that they assume only a single center of employment, and this simplifying assumption greatly clarifies the theoretical development of individual preferences in the housing market. By virtue of this assumption and their theoretical analyses, Alonso and Wingo strongly suggest that the rent and density gradients observed in metropolitan areas are a function of preferences in the housing market and of command over resources by different socio-economic groups rather than functions of some form of travel behavior per se. At the simplest levels, these two views of the problem can, in fact, only be reconciled if we can assume a single employment center and the travel decay function which reflects a distribution of space preferences in the population rather than a distribution of travel preferences.

Before we turn to a realistic consideration of the interaction between the two views, I should like to make a digression on the state of the Alonso and Wingo theories pure and simple. These theories rest rather heavily upon speculations regarding consumer preferences for increased space versus the convenience of shortened travel. These speculations are almost wholly unsupported by careful empirical studies. We could, in fact, make three alternative assumptions about tastes, each of which might equally well explain the observed phenomena in the context of the Alonso model. Our first hypothesis following Alonso directly would be that the rent structure and distribution of densities is determined under American conditions by a general preference for low residential densities which the well-to-do are progressively better able to satisfy than are the poor. This hypothesis supports the simplest type of model.

It is, however, equally reasonable to advance the second hypothesis, that the preferences of the American public extend not only, and possibly not primarily, to low density, but rather to good housing conditions, neighborhood cleanliness, and possibly to novelty or non-obsolescence of the housing stock. As a matter of historical accident, American cities that have grown rapidly under changing technical conditions exhibit a coincidence between age, deterioration, and obsolescence on the one hand and high densities on the other. The presumed space preference of the population is therefore a reflection of

[27] See footnote 5.

393

historical accident, and masks an altogether different preference. This hypothesis might be taken to be more general in that it would explain more adequately the differing location patterns in the slower-growing and better-maintained cities of Europe and Latin America.

Still a third hypothesis might be advanced which is specifically excluded from Alonso's theory by his efforts to avoid considering externalities. This is that the higher-income and higher-status groups in the American population are anxious to segregate themselves socially and geographically from lower-status groups. This leads to a situation in which lower-income groups expand their occupancy of urban areas in those sections that are adjacent to the obsolescent and deteriorating housing they already occupy. The higher-status groups retreat from this incursion in ever expanding waves outward from the center of the city. The basic phenomenon, it might therefore be contended, rests on social preferences rather than on either of the two preceding hypotheses regarding consumption.

I think that we can legitimately make three major points regarding this digression. In the first place, it is now evident that what at first glance appears to be a complete and fully developed theory may in fact contain large gaps which require further theoretical and analytical exploration. In the second place, owing to the very high correlation between density, blight, obsolescence, and social status in American metropolises, it is going to be extremely difficult to distinguish by critical tests between these three hypotheses. This statement can indeed be generalized to many other disputed points regarding metropolitan development. Finally, however, this case makes it abundantly clear that alternative hypotheses deal with very real social issues which vitally affect policy determinations regarding the future development of our cities. In this example, unless we can disentangle the relative importance of these three or more possible causes for residential choice, we shall have difficulty in charting the future optimum development of the American metropolis.

I return now to the main line of development, contrasting those models that explain residential choice on the basis of housing preferences with those that explain it on the basis of the relationship between home and workplace. Once we abandon the assumption that an overwhelming majority of jobs are centrally located, these two explanatory forces become hopelessly intermingled, and no simple solution exists which will permit us to treat them jointly and simultaneously. One way out of this dilemma, which has been implemented, at least in part, by Steger and others for the Pittsburgh Community Renewal Program, would be to disaggregate the employment in major centers by associated levels of income and to make a Lowry-type distribution from place of work to residential facilities of different qualities. With this procedure in the general model, the reconciliation of the demand and assumed supply of residential space becomes somewhat difficult. An alternative solution on which I am now working was first proposed by Herbert and Stevens in 1961, and simulates the housing market on the basis of consumer preferences and a linear programming market model. In this case, the actual connections of home to workplace must be disregarded, but partial account can be taken of these connections by the calculation of accessibility measures.

A more general solution to the whole problem would be to classify households not only by family type, as suggested by Herbert and Stevens,[28] but also by location of workplace. This solution would lead to an enormous linear programming market model which is not at present computationally feasible. It may also be remarked that any attempt to combine these two views of the problem, and indeed, the Lowry model itself, runs up against the difficulty that employment and wages are measured with respect to individuals, whereas residential location and family income are measured by households. These two phenomena cannot be independently treated; a young secretary may form a small household in independent quarters near the central business district, while a housewife may take a job as a checker in the nearby supermarket.

One of the main advantages of a programming type of market simulation model based on a genuine preference analysis and on market-clearing concepts, like the Herbert-Stevens model, is the output of values of the dual variables which gauge the intensity of demand for land and provide inputs to other submodels dealing with industrial and commercial location and with public policy determinations. Equally important, the dual variables applying to household types may be interpreted as needed adjustments in their preference anticipations in the current market and thus provide a basis for comparing the benefits conveyed under different plans. In the more extended suggested application of this model, the dual variables for household types would vary with place of work, and these variations might provide a further basis for analyzing the locational advantages of different sites from the point of view of these sites' attraction to the employed work force. All of these measures have the incomparable advantage of being expressed directly in dollar terms.

Practical efforts to model residential location do not in general follow either in detail or in principle the foregoing suggested outline.

[28] See footnote 5.

One of the main obstacles to moving in this direction is the extreme difficulty in estimating household preferences realistically, a difficulty which is beset by both data limitations and theoretical dilemmas. I am currently engaged in research attempting to unravel some of these problems, dealing with issues which were implicitly raised but not resolved in the original Herbert-Stevens formulation.

In the absence of a completely integrated and economics-based residential location model, the practice in transportation studies has been to rely on descriptive methods, some of which have been discussed above. As Lowry points out in a recent paper, such descriptive models tend to fall into two classes: those which predict what happens to the occupancy and composition of areas, and those which focus on the distribution of locator groups.[29] The original Chicago Area Transportation Study model, work by Hansen,[30] and the Lowry model, tend to fall in the first class. A purely demographic model, by Chevan,[31] utilized for preliminary purposes by the Penn-Jersey Transportation Study and widely circulated, also falls in this class and develops a more detailed projection of the population composition of areas than do the more aggregated models. Models of the second class, which deal with the redistribution of population groups, include the final Penn-Jersey Residential Locational Model,[32] and, with qualifications, the Hill EMPIRIC model.[33] Because the latter model uses a simultaneous equation estimating procedure, it may be imagined that the competition between residential classes for location is taken into account; to this extent the model partakes of some characteristics of both classes.

An alternative approach toward a somewhat disaggregated locational projection is common in various forms in planning studies and urban renewal programming; perhaps surprisingly, this approach seems to have more explicit economic content than the descriptive procedures so prevalent in transportation studies. Recognizing the difficulties of a

[29] Ira S. Lowry, *Seven Models of Urban Development: A Structural Comparison* P3673 (The RAND Corp., September 1967).

[30] Willard Hansen, "An Approach to the Analysis of Metropolitan Residential Extension," *Journal of Regional Science*, Vol. 3, No. 1 (Summer 1961).

[31] Albert Chevan, "Population Projection System," Technical Report No. 3, Penn-Jersey Transportation Study (Delaware Valley Regional Planning Commission, Philadelphia, 1965).

[32] The basic structure of this model is discussed in David R. Seidman, *A Linear Interaction Model for Manufacturing Location*, Penn-Jersey Transportation Study (Delaware Valley Regional Planning Commission, Philadelphia, 1964). A further and more complete discussion will be found in the forthcoming Technical Report No. 1 of the DVRPC about September, 1967; this report has not yet been titled, but will deal with the general subject of the "Methodology of the Activities Allocation Model."

[33] Hill, *op. cit.*

realistic preference analysis, the procedures under consideration generally attempt to preclassify the present and future stock of housing and to preclassify the residential locators into classes of households, following this by a matching procedure which assigns one class of locator to one or more types of housing. This matching procedure contains a large element of economic realism in that there do in fact exist submarkets for housing on both the supply and demand sides. Operationally, the application of this method requires heroic assumptions and presents in particular two rather vexing difficulties. Even given the assumptions, it is in practice somewhat difficult to establish a reasonable set of allocation rules which will deal realistically with the situation in which housing supply and demand in submarkets do not match exactly. Perhaps even more troublesome is the fact that with changes in income and in size and composition of demand over a whole metropolitan area, the interaction between preferences and the market will inevitably tend to shift the manifest preferences of locators. In this case, the assumptions underlying the matching process become very arbitrary indeed.

An effort to rationalize this matching process and to move at least partway in the direction of preference analysis has recently been suggested by Ellis, a student at Northwestern University.[34] His model was based on the analysis of actual data for Tucson, Arizona. While the approach appears promising, it would also seem that the claim of adaptability of the model to changed future conditions is somewhat exaggerated.

I have so far limited myself almost entirely to the demand side of residential location, although it is clear that some features of supply are subsumed in the operation of a number of descriptive models. For example, if the population of a built-up residential area is found to increase under the operation of a particular model, it is evident that there must be an implied process of conversion of dwelling units or of redevelopment of land. For more accurate modeling, and particularly for modeling directed at the exploration of urban housing policy, it is evident that the supply side of the housing market must receive much more explicit and detailed consideration.

Some indications as to the way in which this detailed consideration might be given to supply considerations for the existing stock of structures may be found in the Arthur D. Little model prepared under the direction of Ira Robinson for the San Francisco Community Renewal

[34] Raymond H. Ellis, "Modeling of Household Location: A Statistical Approach," prepared for presentation at the 46th Annual Meeting of the Highway Research Board, Washington, D.C., January 1967.

Program.[35] Here a detailed theory and model are developed as to the response of appropriate owners to changing market conditions, and their consequent actions in maintaining, remodeling, and redeveloping structures. This behavior is expressed in a form which renders it directly modifiable by changes in policy regarding taxes, inspection, rehabilitation, and so on by public agencies. The demand side of this model consists of a relatively simple matching type of submarket analysis of the kind discussed above.

The work of Chapin and his associates at the University of North Carolina has examined in a disaggregated fashion both the supply and demand sides of the market, and most particularly of the market for new housing.[36] This work focuses jointly on the activity patterns of households and the relationship of these activity patterns to residential choice, and on the behavior of developers, including their response to private demand and to public facilities and policies. Some of this work also exhibits the only genuinely stochastic approach to residential locational behavior. Despite their many interesting features and their insights into consumer and entrepreneurial behavior, these efforts have not attempted to provide a model or group of models which could be used for long-term projections and for complete market simulation.

Market models of the development of new housing might be expected to be derivable from the host of studies of urban fringe development which have been conducted over the past twenty years. To the best of my knowledge, however, these studies have been so fragmentary as to provide a very shaky basis for the construction of a complete theory and the implementation of adequate models. We still do not know the answer to a number of key questions in this area. Examples of such questions might be the following: To what extent do the practices of developers and the economics of their operation directly influence the supply of new housing, and to what extent is the developer an intermediary who converts land into housing in direct response to market demand? To what extent and in what circumstances does zoning really affect densities of development, and to what extent is it in the long run a reflection of the pressures of demand? What systematic theory is available to provide a sound explanation for the

[35] Ira M. Robinson, Harry B. Wolfe, and Robert L. Barringer, "A Simulation Model for Renewal Programming," *Journal of the American Institute of Planners,* Vol. 31, No. 2 (May 1965).

[36] F. Stuart Chapin, Jr., and Shirley F. Weiss, *Factors Influencing Land Development,* August 1962; Chapin, Thomas G. Donnelly, and Weiss, *A Probabilistic Model for Residential Growth,* May 1964; and Chapin and Weiss, *Some Input Refinements for a Residential Model,* July 1965, all published by the Institute for Research in Social Science, University of North Carolina, in cooperation with the Bureau of Public Roads, U.S. Department of Commerce.

patchy and leapfrog nature of metropolitan development; in other words, why do not whole contiguous areas of the metropolis get systematically developed in a short period of time in response to demand? It may readily be seen that, while the answers to these sticky questions are quite essential to the development of sound metropolitan policies, providing them involves very difficult analysis of institutional and behavioral characteristics of the supply side of the housing market which we are not yet in a position to complete.

In principle, there seems to be no obstacle to the marriage of demand models and supply models provided that each can be couched in such terms as will provide as outputs the necessary inputs to the other. It is already clear, however, that this communication probably must proceed in economic terms, thus underlining the desirability of explanatory rather than purely descriptive residential location models.

Manufacturing Location

Models for the location of manufacturing industry in the metropolis exhibit another and different paradox. As recently as ten years ago, economists and regional scientists inclined to the belief that the interregional industrial location problem was substantially solved and that this solution could be extended to intrametropolitan analysis.[37] The proposed solutions were based upon classical considerations of transportation and land costs, and were most frequently formulated in a linear programming framework. The general belief in the tractability of this problem was to some extent reinforced by the existence of a wealth of data extending as far back as 1920 in many metropolitan areas and collated on a county basis in the national Censuses of Manufactures and in County Business Patterns. Some aspects of manufacturing location, as exhibited by this wealth of data, appeared to display relatively stable trends.

Recent developments in manufacturing location, changes in interregional location patterns, theoretical considerations, and practical difficulties seem to have shaken somewhat this earlier confidence in a ready solution to this problem. The abrupt changes in the fifties in the rate of growth of total manufacturing employment, in the composition of manufacturing industries, in interregional location, and in suburban versus central city location have brought into question the reliability of trend projections. An examination of these changes in the

---

[37] For an example of an over-optimistic and non-operational approach of this kind, see Benjamin H. Stevens and Robert E. Coughlin, "A Note on Inter-Areal Linear Programming for a Metropolitan Region," *Journal of Regional Science*, Vol. 1, No. 2 (Spring 1959).

era of automation and rapid technological shifts has at the same time suggested the possible inappropriateness of classical locational theory and its implementation by equilibrium models of a linear programming variety. It is especially apparent that in a technological environment with increasingly skilled labor inputs and with a high degree of fabrication, the relative importance of labor force assembly is increasing by comparison with the transportation costs of inputs and outputs, and even in relation to site costs.

It would therefore appear that a reconsideration of the theory of manufacturing location is required, based upon the emergence of new and imperfectly understood conditions governing the choice of optimal locations. At the same time, it must continue to be recognized that whatever tendencies may exist within manufacturing industry for a movement toward an optimum, this movement is or may be severely restrained by the existence of sunk costs in present locations—costs which are perhaps an order of magnitude larger than the related costs for retail trade establishments. Since both the sunk costs and the advantages of a new location are extremely difficult to measure, a projection model that is dependent on rates of change becomes very difficult to define and calibrate. This difficulty is compounded by the fact that within manufacturing there exists a wide variety of locational requirements by differing three- and four-digit industries, and that even within these industries the requirements vary by size of firm and financial resources. Thus, while the problem is complex and multidimensional, the number of observations on which to base an analysis is severely limited.

In the Lowry model, this problem is evaded altogether, since the location of manufacturing and of certain other activities to be discussed below are taken as given and input to the model rather than being output from it. For the Pittsburgh economy, with its large-scale site-oriented manufacturing industries, this assumption is not unreasonable, but in many other metropolitan areas it would be. The EMPIRIC model as used in Boston, however, makes manufacturing location endogenous to the model. Here all manufacturing is treated as a single homogeneous industry and the response of increases and decreases in manufacturing location between 1950 and 1960 is related to the densities and accessibilities existing in 1950. The competition of other land uses during this period of relocation is taken account of by a process of simultaneous estimation of parameters. Similar but not identical procedures, specifically omitting simultaneous determination, were used in the Penn-Jersey Transportation Study.[38] In the calibration phase, the

[38] See footnote 32.

Boston experiments yielded higher correlation coefficients than the Philadelphia study, and in the projection phase, the results were noticeably more sensitive to alternative transportation inputs. Both of these models suffer from an obvious difficulty in that the changes taking place from 1950 to 1960 may depend heavily on the mix of changes affecting the whole metropolitan area during that period. If, therefore, a new set of over-all changes affects the growth or decline of industry in the future, it will not be reflected in the operation of these aggregated projection models.

An additional difficulty in this analysis arises from the fact that industrial location may in selected instances be sensitive to public policies. Many central cities are increasingly aware of the putative importance of retaining manufacturing industry, and some cities attempt to shape their redevelopment and zoning policies accordingly. This situation introduces the possibility that manufacturing location may in part be removed from the modeling effort and placed in the realm of policy inputs. Many land use projection studies have indeed taken zoned industrial land as a basis for the projection of future locational patterns. It is my own belief that this solution is compounded, in roughly equal parts, of a realistic assessment of the role of policy and of desperation over the inadequacy of present models.

It seems likely that slow progress will continue to be made in this field, partly on the basis of firm-by-firm studies of relocation, expansion, and the establishment of new businesses, and partly on the basis of the development of models which are perhaps partly stochastic in nature owing to the diverse nature of the locating universe. An example of an inadequately exploited firm-by-firm study is my own work on the Philadelphia area, completed over ten years ago in collaboration with Robert Sparks,[39] while the most interesting and useful example of the stochastic locational process is to be found in the work of Stephen Putman of CONSAD Research Corporation for the Pittsburgh Community Renewal Program.[40] This stochastic model was designed to remedy the basic deficiency of the Lowry model, discussed above, in respect to the location of a relatively narrow class of industry within the city of Pittsburgh itself. The generalization of this model to a whole metropolitan area, to all of manufacturing industry, and to long-term projections would prove arduous.

[39] Britton Harris, *Industrial Land and Facilities for Philadelphia—A Report to the Philadelphia City Planning Commission* (Institute for Urban Studies, University of Pennsylvania, 1956).

[40] Stephen H. Putman, "Intra-Urban Industrial Location Model: Design and Implementation," paper presented at Thirteenth U.S. Annual Meeting, Regional Science Association, St. Louis, Mo., November 1966.

One additional note of caution must be struck in this area. It is already obvious that a thorough analysis of manufacturing location and relocation will require the co-ordination of the results of a number of disparate studies which already exist, and the initiation of carefully designed new studies. Hopefully the data for some of these studies may ultimately be derived not from ad hoc interviews, but from state and national administrative data collection activities. In addition, however, we must note that the operation of a disaggregated industrial location model for projections, which seems to be required by the nature of the problem, will in its turn require disaggregated inputs. This would imply that for a projection model of a complete nature, it would be necessary to predict future industry mix by two- and three-digit industries and by size of firm—surely a most difficult undertaking.

Other Activities and Land Uses

The requirement of completeness in most metropolitan simulation models has the effect of exposing the academic tendency to focus on a few areas of interest and to sweep many other problems under the rug. Thus our extended discussion above of the location of retail trade and services, residences, and manufacturing employment has completely neglected many other large urban land users and traffic generators whose location and requirements are of major importance in metropolitan planning. The paragraphs that follow give a brief and impressionistic review of these other land users in order to convey an idea of the magnitude of the modeling problem and to indicate some directions for its solution.

Most conveniently, this review might follow a systematic tour through the remaining five or six SIC one-digit industries. These industries, in the Hill model, are grouped as of other employment (except for wholesale trade, which is combined with retail for data reasons), and in the Lowry model are divided between basic industry whose location is exogenous and retail trade. Such a guided tour of the SIC's would, however, neglect certain important considerations which will be discussed first.

Initially, we may note that certain important land users are not employers, and consequently have to be accommodated outside of any activity location models. The most important of these categories is "streets and highways," part of which are planned as major facilities and part regarded as a kind of developmental overhead. This overhead has been systematically estimated for various types of development by many studies, including the Penn-Jersey Transportation

Study.[41] Another important land user is public open space, the distribution of which is usually regarded as a policy decision exogenous to the model. It is conceivable, however, that the allocation of land to public open space might be pre-established under policy guidelines which are implemented within the model in consequence of and following upon other locational decisions, such as residential development. In all probability, future models will have a mixed mode of operation in this regard.

The whole question of the disposition of land involves two important issues central to modeling the whole metropolitan area but peripheral to the examination of any particular activity location pattern. These questions are the density at which development takes place, and the extent to which land in any particular area at any particular point in time is or is not developed in urban uses. These two issues involve complex questions of land pricing, speculation, and entrepreneurial behavior, in addition to questions of public policy, land reservation, and subdivision control, which have been very inadequately explored and for which no satisfactory models exist.

Our tour of the remaining SIC's can in part be accomplished by an enumeration of major groups and in part by pointing to certain difficulties which arise in using the SIC classification system. These difficulties revolve largely around the geographical separation of functions within SIC groups, so that goods-handling and other functions are frequently found in separate locations. Perhaps the most important facet of this separability of functions within SIC categories has to do with the separation of central offices from other operations. More strictly, we can perhaps define the related functions of management and of information processing which have somewhat different characteristics and which may be separated both from direct productive activities and from each other. These central office functions partake of the nature of business services and of governmental and institutional activities which are in part discussed briefly below. They reflect the growing importance in our economy of service functions by contrast with primary and secondary activities. The growth of service functions, both in their own right and as a differentiated and separable function within other activity classifications, poses a large group of planning and projection problems.

---

[41] Analysis of these problems at the Penn-Jersey Transportation Study was conducted under the general heading of a group of models called "SPACEC" models. Existing descriptions of these are fragmentary, but a full discussion will be found in the Delaware Valley Regional Planning Commission Technical Report No. 1 (see footnote 32).

In the latter case, these problems are exacerbated, at least at the level of analysis, by the incompleteness of the SIC classification and of state Bureau of Employment Security records regarding the function discharged by establishments. It is evident that considerable research regarding the central office function, its future growth potential, and its locational characteristics will be required before this activity can adequately be modeled and before its needs and influences can adequately be dealt with in planning activities.[42]

Now to resume our tour:

The location of agriculture and of the extractive industries in metropolitan areas is in general a matter of diminishing importance and concern, and will not be further treated here.

The location of the construction industries, which in many cities is a very substantial employer, is at present very poorly modeled. In particular, proper data as to the actual location of employment in this industry are difficult to acquire because the employment is generally reported from a home office, while the actual place of work is on site. If the employment were properly located, it seems likely that it could be related at any point in time to changes which are occurring in total employment and residential population by small area—since these imply new construction for possible establishments, residences, and public facilities. I have not, however, seen models or analyses which take adequate account of these phenomena. The use of these concepts clearly implies a dynamic projection, from which "accelerator" properties may be derived.

In the analysis and projection of the location of public utilities employment and transportation employment, we are again confronted, first, with inadequate data and, second, with inadequate theories and analysis. A part of these industries is located in relation to sites, most of which have become entrenched by the sunk costs of private and public investment (piers, railway marshaling yards, airports, generating stations, etc.). The projection of this part of these activities can be handled externally to the modeling effort. A second part of this employment represents central office and clerical functions. Still a third part (local offices, branch exchanges, repair services, etc.) are distributed in relation to demand as modulated by economies of scale. These parts could in principle be handled like retail trade.

Wholesale trade divides into two main branches, with and without stocks. The former is one of the remaining transportation and site-oriented activities which might well be analyzed with reference to

[42] S. M. Robbins and N. E. Terleckyj, *Money Metropolis*, New York Metropolitan Region Study (Harvard University Press, 1960).

classical theory, taking into account a changing technology and the anticipation of management regarding future changes in the environment. Wholesaling without stocks is essentially a business service.

Finance insurance and real estate, business services, non-profit institutions, legal services, medical services, and government exhaust the remaining SIC's. Broadly considered, they share a number of characteristics with utilities and transportation services. A certain number of establishments are unique locators whose growth and possible relocation need to be considered outside the model because of their unique characteristics and possible large sunk costs. These include, for example, major seats of government, hospitals, prisons, insane asylums, universities, and similar institutions. This group in certain cases is almost indistinguishable from the larger business services, in which one might include, for instance, not only the principal offices of banks, but also the main post office and (say) a large research laboratory. Finally, once again, all of these activities have a large component which is distributed in relation to demand, partly from private households and partly from businesses, once again with due regard for economies of scale and agglomeration.

It may indeed be suggested that the scope of models dealing with retail trade and services might be broadly expanded to deal in part with the whole service sector of the economy, public and private. This expansion was attempted, using the Harris model, at the Penn-Jersey Transportation Study with quite considerable success.[43] Its initial advantage lies in the fact that the influences of business demand and household demand are implicitly determined and do not require an examination of the functions of each individual establishment. A second advantage appeared in an unanticipated way when, for certain SIC's, the failure of the model to achieve a good fit was directly traceable to particular establishments located in specific zones. These establishments proved, in fact, to be unique locators, whose institutional characteristics, site requirements, or sunk costs had not been previously identified. The disadvantage of the application of these models is that they assume a constant mix of the services supplied by a given SIC to different sectors of demand. Thus, for example, no shifts between business and residential services would be imputed to the future development of the banking industry unless specific provisions were made for them. Such projections would be difficult to relate to the performance of the model in its present form.

---

[43] These results are discussed in the Delaware Valley Regional Planning Commission Technical Report No. 1 (see footnote 32).

MAJOR ISSUES IN MODELING

We may now pose, on the basis of the salient characteristics of models and our sketch of current practice, a number of related questions regarding the utility and accuracy of models for both scientific and decision-making purposes.

One of the central issues revolves around the so-called validation and testing of models and theories. Owing to the great lack of time-series data, we must customarily find that dynamic models are validated by the goodness of fit to the data from which they have been originally developed. An important class of exceptions may be noted in the case of the Lowry model and the Lakshmanan-Hansen model of retail trade, where locational patterns depend on trip-making behavior and where, therefore, the reproduction of phenomena is in part independent of the fitting of parameters. Similar conditions will apply to a developed form of the Herbert-Stevens model, when and if it is completed.

Even these cases of indirect validation are not strong enough for my taste, and I should like to see stronger tests devised for the predictive capability of models. It is out of the question to wait ten or twenty years for new data to be generated for such tests. Very rarely, it might be possible to test a model for a given city on the decade 1940–50, having fitted it to the decade 1950–60. Tests on the decade 1960–70 will be possible within about five years. Meanwhile, I would seriously suggest that a far more potent and generally available test would be to apply models and parameters developed for, say, Chicago to, say, Minneapolis–St. Paul. The mere contemplation of such a test imposes on the theorist and the model-builder the responsibility for a general analytic framework which is transferable to very different situations, and for the derivation of relatively invariant parameters. But when projection models are designed for use in cities which will have, within the period of projection, twice the population and twice the income per capita, I do not think that it is unreasonable to seek such a level of generality.

Another route for exploring the performance of models used for projections is to examine in detail, as suggested above, some of their inherent dynamic and equilibrium properties. This line of investigation is properly used in the model design stage. It is probably even more difficult and subtle than I imagine, and I repeatedly call attention to it partly because it has almost totally been neglected.

Dynamic and static equilibrium also probably have strong implications for optimization, and hence for welfare. They are thus related directly or indirectly to the evaluation stage of the planning process.

406

In a general sense, we may suggest that a static equilibrium may be implicitly defined in an analytic model by the achievement of optimal conditions (given competition and the environment) by each of a large number of groups of locators. In a dynamic model, movement and change are activated by a striving toward a similar optimal status. It is, of course, possible that the second-order conditions for equilibrium or a neglect of externalities influencing behavior may lead to a situation, like the Prisoners' Dilemma, in which individual optimum-seeking does not lead to optimum arrangements, and may not lead to equilibrium. In models that are more nearly descriptive, such as Lowry's or Hill's, the welfare implications of these tendencies towards equilibrium are difficult to define, but in other cases the states achieved might be related to the performance of the plan in producing desired satisfactions.

This line of development is, I believe, particularly important because the present generation of models produces outputs which are very difficult to relate to the decision-making process. These outputs may, in fact, in many cases be incomplete, in that they do not define many of the consequences that are of interest to decision-makers. In other cases, even given a complete set of outputs, these may be so many and so diverse and our knowledge of the transformation function into an index of performance so fragmentary that the models have not produced much digestible useful guidance. What is here suggested is, therefore, that the process of constructing useful models for prediction may be made to depend on built-in evaluations by locating groups within the models, in such a way that a measure of performance is automatically generated by aggregating these evaluations.

In pursuing this line of investigation, two related cautionary notes must be struck. First, it is perfectly clear that the optimization function which defines the utilitarian satisfaction of individual groups in the locational marketplace and which is necessary to motivate the locating activities in a model may correctly and of necessity disregard externalities and other social costs or benefits which will influence the planning decision-makers' choices. These considerations properly belong in a complete evaluative model. But similar concepts might well be applicable within the process of optimizing from the behavioral standpoint. Their absence suggests a market mechanism which is imperfect from the social point of view. Such a discovery at the interface between predictive modeling and evaluation then reflects back into the policy design process. It suggests the possibility of basic changes (such as user charges) in the plan to be tested, which may in turn induce changes in the models themselves.

407

The second caution deals with the somewhat limited scope of locational models that deal with spatial allocation to the neglect of complete and specific consideration of important social problems. It is true that even a pure locational model can touch upon important aspects of the concentration and segregation of ethnic and lower-income strata of the population, their deprivation of adequate housing and community facilities, and their failure to secure adequate access to suitable employment opportunities. These aspects of the spatial distribution of social problems are far from unimportant in metropolitan decision-making. It is, however, likely that important aspects of education and mobility are going to move increasingly into the center of decision-making, and that these aspects are almost totally absent from locational models. Since these problems press for consideration in budgets and in policy-making, they cannot indefinitely be deferred from systematic and scientific examination in the total metropolitan context. I believe, however, that our current capability for analyzing these problems theoretically and for quantifying relationships through the use of models is very meager. I would anticipate that in the immediate future the developments in these fields will have to be parallel to but not integrated with locational modeling, but that in as little as five years' time, these two strains of analysis and decision-making can be merged.

A GLOBAL PERSPECTIVE

Up to this point, I have conducted the discussion largely on the basis of an inside view of model-building in relation to decision-making. I now wish to step outside of this framework and draw out two major implications from my experience. These implications respectively support the importance of models, and suggest the desirability of cautious limitations in the claims that can be made for them.

The positive claim that can assuredly be made for the models of the foreseeable future is that they will make possible much more accurate and informative projections of the effects of alternative policies. This greater accuracy will rest in part on the analytic studies necessary to implement parts of the model-building process. But more important, the increases in accuracy and insight will result from an increased capacity to deal in detail, and especially in area detail, with large and complex metropolitan systems. This capability will be achieved through the intelligent exploitation of the immense bookkeeping and computational capabilities of the computer.

Insofar as designers and decision-makers can find means by which to relate to the process of computer simulation and projection, there will be immense gains in the fruitfulness and cogency of their own work and thinking. Indeed, it is not too extreme to suggest that the gains that can be achieved by these relations are to some considerable extent independent of the accuracy of the models and of their operational capabilities. The mere exercise of trying to make design and decision considerations sufficiently clear and explicit that they may influence model-building has a remarkably disciplining and clarifying effect. This observation, indeed, suggests that the major focus referred to above on *operational* models is partly in error. Such a concentration may tend to separate the designer and the decision-maker from simulation because it is not couched in their terms and thus becomes an inscrutable mystery. At the same time, the simplistic premises of operational modeling tend to fly in the face of the deepest and most strongly felt experiences of many of those outside the modeling process. This gives rise to a dispute which is in many ways homologous with the dispute between science and humanism.

If, indeed, projection experiments with the metropolitan system can be useful in the senses I have discussed, this success will be a substantial breakthrough in systems modeling. In spite of the extensive present discussion of the success of systems analysis with respect to space engineering, transportation planning, and the like, it still remains true that no successful complete model of a complex biological or social entity has yet been made operational. Thus, for example, there is no successful model of the complete function of a cell, let alone of an organism; nor of a school, let alone of a metropolitan area. The difficulty in modeling such complex systems may be discussed in the same context as certain very deep epistemological problems which arise in relation to planning design and decision-making.

The device which is being used to simulate metropolitan function and which in addition it is hoped can be useful in relieving the planner of some design and decision-making problems, is the digital computer. This computer is sequential and one-dimensional in its operation, very much like the sequential nature of causation in the physical sciences, and the historical development in science and technology as a whole. We may usefully question the extent to which this sequential concept of cognition, causation, and operation can be made to coincide with the complex systems organization at the biological and social level, of which man's mental processes are a part.

This is not to suggest that the cognitive processes involved in design and decision (or the operation of systems to which they apply) are devoid of logic. It implies, rather, that the applicable logic may be more complex than has previously animated our science and technology and our social science predictions. If this suggestion is to any degree correct, it follows that, for some time to come, the most efficient performance of the most complex aspects of the planning process will best be performed by "human computers"—or planners—rather than by electronic digital computers. In my own mind, there is fairly clear separation between the parts of the planning process appropriate for assignment to these different treatments. The boundary between these parts of the process will move in various ways as we gain experience, and depending on circumstances. Considering, moreover, that planning is a social process, there is a strong implication that the human computers who engage in design and decision-making in what we are pleased to call an intuitive fashion, should make their methods ever more widely available and widely understood. Thus, at the same time that we set limits on our immediate ambitions for scientizing the planning process, we must also mark out the path by which personal, intuitive, and subjective processes become the object of some degree of scientific understanding and replication.

It thus appears that an appropriate consideration of this problem may lead in the direction both of more genuine democracy, by narrowing the differences between the elites and the general public, and towards a greater unification of human endeavor by creating a broader common ground between the so-called sciences and humanities.

SELECTED READINGS

Alonso, William. *Location and Land Use—Toward a General Theory of Land Rent.* Cambridge: Harvard University Press, 1964.

Berry, Brian J. L. Department of Geography Research Paper No. 85. *Commercial Structure and Commercial Blight.* Chicago: University of Chicago, 1963.

Chapin, F. Stuart, Thomas G. Donnelly, and Shirley F. Weiss. *A Probabilistic Model for Residential Growth.* Chapel Hill: University of North Carolina, Institute for Research in Social Science, in co-operation with U.S. Department of Commerce, Bureau of Public Roads, May 1964.

Chapin, F. Stuart, and Shirley F. Weiss. *Factors Influencing Land Development.* Chapel Hill: University of North Carolina, Institute for Research in Social Science, in co-operation with U.S. Department of Commerce, Bureau of Public Roads, August 1962.

————. *Some Input Refinements for a Residential Model.* Chapel Hill: University of North Carolina, Institute for Research in Social Science, in co-operation with U.S. Department of Commerce, Bureau of Public Roads, July 1965.

Harris, Britton. "The Uses of Theory in the Simulation of Urban Phenomena," *Journal of the American Institute of Planners,* Vol. 32, September 1966.

————. *Highway Research Record No. 26: Land Use Forecasting Concepts.* Washington: National Academy of Sciences—National Research Council, Highway Research Board, 1966.

————. "Some Problems in the Theory of Intra-Urban Location," *Operations Research,* Vol. 9, September–October 1961.

————. "A Model of Locational Equilibrium for Retail Trade." Paper presented at a Seminar on Models of Land Use Development, Institute for Urban Studies, University of Pennsylvania, October 1964. Mimeo.

————. "Inventing the Future Metropolis." Paper prepared for the Catherine Bauer Wurster Memorial Public Lecture Series, sponsored by the Harvard Graduate School of Design and Massachusetts Institute of Technology. May 1966. Mimeo.

————. "The City of the Future: The Problem of Optimal Design." Paper presented at 13th Annual Meeting, Regional Science Association, St. Louis, Mo., November 1966. Mimeo.

Herbert, John, and Benjamin H. Stevens. "A Model for the Distribution of Residential Activities in Urban Areas," *Journal of Regional Science,* Vol. II, No. 2, 1960.

Journal of the American Institute of Planners. Special issues: *Urban Development Models: New Tools for Planning,* Vol. 31, May 1965; *Land Use and Traffic Models,* Vol. 25, May 1959.

411

Lowry, Ira S. *A Model of Metropolis.* Memorandum RM-4035-RC. Santa Monica: The RAND Corporation, August 1964.

————. *Seven Models of Urban Development: A Structural Comparison.* P3673. Santa Monica: The RAND Corp., September 1967.

Muth, Richard F. "The Spatial Structure of the Housing Market," *Papers and Proceedings of the Regional Science Association,* Vol. 7, 1961.

Orcutt, Guy, John Korbel, Alice M. Rivlin, and Martin Greenberger. *A Microanalysis of Socio-Economic Systems: A Simulation Study.* New York: Harper, 1961.

Seidman, David R. *A Linear Interaction Model for Manufacturing Location,* Penn-Jersey Transportation Study. Philadelphia: Delaware Valley Regional Planning Commission, 1964.

Wingo, Lowdon, Jr. *Transportation and Urban Land.* Washington: Resources for the Future, Inc., 1961.

DISCUSSION OF PART II

COMMENTS BY DONALD J. BOGUE *

To a sociologist, the preceding four papers have three important general implications. The first deals with economic realism. If you review the writings on "urban economics" over the last five years, published in the context of urban planning and primarily written by architects and urban design folk, you find one common message: cities are for people, not for machines. This approach poses a false dichotomy. It implies that we must make the city a place in which people can live in maximum comfort, and the machines must take a back seat whenever they get in the way. The four papers presented here reaffirm the old and very important idea that the metropolis is a mechanism for getting a livelihood, that as an economic mechanism it operates by established principles, and that men and machines must coexist in an environment that meets the needs of both.

We must admit that we can't turn our cities into doughnuts or pretzels at will without taking into account some of the principles that Hoover has advanced. If we attempt to violate principles of location theory, there are certain definite costs that must be paid. Perhaps we can be far more flexible than in the past; but if this is true, it is because the principles have been changed by technological progress, not because we have been freed from these principles. In other words, I believe that city planning must be much more responsible economically than some of its more vocal crusaders have been advocating.

A second general conclusion one can draw from these papers is that we now know much more about metropolitan economics than we did only a few years ago. When I first began working in this area, metropolitan research could be described as being primarily descriptive. The older research plotted transportation curves and density curves, and made maps where the whole object was to "describe the parameters." Today we are testing whole theories, integrating sets of hypotheses into models, and studying the interaction of many forces simultaneously. Urban economics has passed the "takeoff point" as a research discipline.

The third general implication of these papers is that urban planning or metropolitan planning of the millennium type is now clearly recog-

* Director, Community and Study Center, University of Chicago.

413

nized as economically impossible. The notion that we can leap from the sordid slumming present into a perfect future as a result of a grandiose planning program is shown to be economically impractical. We must get from where we are now to where we wish to go, step by step, taking a planned sequence of action, knowing that there is no way that we can discard or shuck off the problems of the present except to solve them—and pay the price.

I have ten specific comments to make.

1. I think that there should be a strong drive in the field of urban economics to substitute direct observation for inferences from indirect data. For example, we need to know directly what are the locational needs of households rather than infer them indirectly from housing market data. We need to study samples of intrametropolitan changes. We need to know "true" desire lines in our transportation surveys; instead of finding out where people live and to what place they must travel, and calling the straight line between origin and destination a "desire line," we should recognize that where people now live is not fixed or given. Many people may dislike their residential location, and many transportation studies are extrapolating these dislikes.

Another example: we need to estimate elasticity of housing and the urban housing market by use of more direct data. Muth's paper shows amazing ingenuity and sophistication in arriving at broad inferences, yet I think his is not a theory of the urban housing market as much as an argument that theory of the urban housing market is possible.

It appears that urban housing events respond much more sensitively to environmental effects than we have thought in the past; even with the crude indirect evidence that can be dredged up from census housing statistics, it is plausible that a much more sophisticated and detailed theory of the housing market could be developed. Refinement in this area is going to come from much stronger doses of direct data based on direct observation. For example, if we had a representative sample of 500,000 instances of housing purchases in which we knew in detail the characteristics of the former occupant, those of the new occupant, and the economic reasons for the move out of one and the move in of the other, we might be in a better position to talk about elasticity.

2. There are certain sociological phenomena regarded as "natural" in economic analysis, which need to be given explicit economic evaluation; some of them are very powerful. For example, Hoover refers repeatedly to a natural desire of entities which are alike to assemble together in a particular area. This applies not only to businesses, but residences as well. Apparently, there is a strong desire for people of

particular characteristics to live near people having the same characteristics and apart from those with characteristics they dislike or that are different. This we can frankly call "segregation," and it can take many forms: occupational segregation, income segregation, educational segregation, ethnic segregation, religious segregation, and racial segregation.

Sometimes we underappreciate the diversity and power of this sociological phenomenon. We think only in terms of racial segregation these days, tending to forget the other forms. Class segregation is an economic good for which people are willing to pay. It has a market value. It needs to be measured as a component of urban life rather than left to run uncontrolled through the analysis as something assumed or something natural. Segregation should be explicitly taken into the analysis and given full attention in the systematic theory of urban structure.

For example, there is a very real question concerning how class segregation arises. One group of people believes it is foisted upon us by urban real estate developers who clear a square mile and build housing to rent or sell all at the same level. Other groups believe this to be a desire on the part of purchasers, which developers only supply. We do not know whether class segregation is increasing or decreasing in its various forms. Do Catholics mind living in Protestant neighborhoods, and conversely? If so, is this dislike increasing or decreasing? These are sociological components that have a very real economic dimension.

Economic discrimination provides another example of an area requiring more attention. Preferential treatment in hiring, in paying salaries or giving promotions, whether on the basis of sex, race, or by other criteria, has a dramatic impact upon intrametropolitan structure. It might well be that if we eliminate economic discrimination and leave economic segregation alone, we will have one form of a metropolis; if we abolish both by some act of magic, we will have another form; if we abolish neither, we will have still another form. I think discrimination, like segregation, has a very real monetary and economic dimension.

3. My third point has to do with longitudinal analysis. For decades now we have been inferring urban structure and urban dynamics from static data. At first we had only data for only one instant of time—and we were lucky to have even that. We have performed correlation analysis and other types of detailed analysis on these cross-sectional data, and from this research have inferred structure and change. Now, we

have census tract population and housing data for thirty cities that run for three decades and data for seventy cities that run for two decades. When the 1970 census is out, data for two decades will be available for at least 180 metropolitan areas, and for one decade, perhaps 250. We can now do longitudinal analysis of metropolitan structures. In addition, the Census Bureau has produced data on retail and service activities by city parts. In the new census cycle this will be repeated, so the time has arrived for intensive longitudinal analysis for the study and explanation of change.

Cross-sectional analysis has dominated sociological and social economic research of this type in the past. I think, for example, that most of Muth's functions are derived from statistical analysis. The time has come for us to think and do research and in a longitudinal vein.

4. Much more attention ought to be paid to new subcenters. For years now we have been speaking of the multinucleus theory of the metropolis. We talk about the central business district, and admit the existence of outlying nuclei, but as yet systematic investigation and theorizing about these subcenters are missing. We have case studies but no rigorous generalized study of the rise of these centers and of their impact on the sector of the city in which they are located and upon the metropolis as a whole. Findings from such a study ought to be incorporated into the models we hope to build in the near future.

Industrial parks, new housing developments, urban renewal: what forces bring these into existence and what effect do they have upon the total metropolis? Answers to questions of this nature are still needed to augment and to be built into our theories, especially through application of the new expanding longitudinal dynamic theory.

5. My fifth point is concerned with the importance of microanalysis. It is quite possible for the game of model building to lead us astray and divert our attention from some important research endeavors. In his paper, Harris points out, as one of a series of dichotomies, that some types of models must undertake to be holistic and others to be only partial. If we try to put a man on the moon too quickly—in other words, if we complete holistic models before we have quantified many of the parameters—the effect can be to slow down progress rather than accelerate it. To be specific, there are types of events occurring in metropolises all over the country, perhaps all over the world, which, if studied on a comparative, minute basis, could yield much information that could then go into models. For example, if we were to take a microstudy of specific public housing developments, now perhaps ten to twenty years of age, in various metropolises, and find out what has

happened to them in their immediate environments and what effect they have had on the metropolis, the results could add a great deal to our knowledge. Or we could take samples of specific large-scale subdivisions that have now reached middle age in perhaps ten or fifteen metropolises, and find out what is happening to them. From such a study we could develop a theory of the life cycle of sub-divisions. As another example: we now have at least a dozen samples of integrated housing in the United States and there are plans to promote racially integrated housing; microeconomic analysis could evaluate the experience of the established integrated housing to dis-cover what principles may be flowing therefrom. While we are en-gaging in macro-model building, I think there is still ample room for microstudies of metropolitan structure.

6. Special economic attention should be paid to urban pathology. Segregation and discrimination may have as much to do with urban structure as accessibility, but the impact of crime and delinquency in lowering land values and hastening the exodus of people from neigh-borhoods also needs to be appreciated and given a place in economic analysis. It has been pointed out that we are dealing only with the characteristics of poverty, rather than the causes. It seems to me that one of the greatest "causes" of poverty is broken homes: the ADC family (Aid to Families of Dependent Children) where the woman is rearing children with no visible breadwinner. That concentration in one large mass of large numbers of pathological families has an im-portant impact on urban structure and future prospects for improving neighborhoods. The location of unemployables is also a major aspect of urban structure. It may be that old recipes of rehousing pathological cases or raising their income may help, but do not resolve the prob-lem. Perhaps planned dispersal is indicated.

7. My seventh point is that there needs to be penetrating analysis of the urban slum housing industry by the economists. How much profit does a block of slum property generate as an investment? What is a typical balance sheet for such business operations? Why is there such poor maintenance of buildings? One of the papers said that buildings could be maintained indefinitely, that slums were a product of poor maintenance. Why, then, do we have poor maintenance in an area of high density? Is this due to a deliberate policy of the investor? Is it due to some characteristic of the tenants which makes maintenance im-possible? Is it due to the fact that the urban slum industry is a marginal industry with insufficient capital and is unable to finance maintenance? We hear rumors of "slumlords," block busting, collusion

between politicians and land owners of slums to evade code enforcement. A very substantial segment of public opinion regards the urban housing slum segment of the urban housing market as a parasitic semi-criminal industry. Is it or isn't it? I think this is a major avenue of work in urban economics.

8. It is quite possible that the urban housing market has yet to go through the phase of economic regulation similar to that which occurred in other phases of the economy. We have the Securities Exchange Commission, the Federal Communications Commission, the Equal Employment Opportunity Commission, the Food and Drug Administration, all as regulatory agencies over some segment of the economy. It might be that there is need for a new one, the Housing Practices Commission, whose duty would be to cover fields of construction, maintenance, sale, and rental of housing with minimum standards and standards of practice. It might be that there is an "invisible hand" guiding the housing market, and it may not be the one that Adam Smith had in mind. This, I think, is worth the attention of economists.

9. The ninth point I make as a demographer. Throughout all four of these papers, there is an assumption of unlimited or uninterrupted population growth. Just as, as Hoover said, we have faith in inevitable and continuing rising income, so there seems to be explicit the idea that the metropolis is going to grow forever. I believe there is a grave danger in this set of assumptions, for they are naive assumptions. Many urban planners may feel that they must desperately try to keep ahead of the baby boom; that all one can possibly do will not be enough. Those days are over.

The birth rate of this country is now low and steadily declining. Metropolitan growth in the '60–'70 decade, the one we are in now, may well turn out to be only half that of the '50–'60 decade. It is quite possible that in the '70–'80 decade, the total population of the nation will grow by only 5 per cent. If particular metropolises fail to attract migration, the whole metropolis could lose population. Many metropolitan areas face this prospect, which is very definitely there in the future. If we are planning for 1980, it is naive to assume that population will double every twenty-five years, or that the suburbs are going to grow like weeds, just because both phenomena have happened in the past.

The truth is that the people of this nation have the knowledge and attitudes needed to control fertility. If we were so minded, for economic or other reasons, we could bring population growth to an absolute zero within five years. This could and may happen. The implications are tremendous; every economist should keep them in mind in making his projections.

10. Harris states that models can be used to demonstrate what the future will be like if certain alternative lines develop. If in carrying out these exercises we take what we now know about city populations in future years, our economic results will be very different from what we anticipated.

For example, the next fifteen years will bring a complete end to illiteracy. The portion of the population that is functionally illiterate with seven years of schooling will be very small. We shall see a complete end to the unassimilated ethnic minority from Europe; a complete end to net rural-to-urban migration. (Already this is diminishing; with 65 per cent of the population living in cities, the rural population is rapidly reaching that stage where the people who are left have a viable economic connection.) I think we will see an escalation of the poverty definition. Instead of a band centered around $3,000, as Ornati has described it, fifteen years from now the band may be centered around $8,000. Our income tax system may well be much more steeply regressive in the next fifteen years. To a sociologist who has watched the functioning of social security in European nations, this is a strong possibility.

In my opinion, there are great opportunities today for collaboration among economists, sociologists, and members of the other social sciences in metropolitan research. By jointly working along the lines of the ten points I have indicated, we can accumulate deeper insight into the structure of metropolitan areas—how they are organized now, and how they will change in the future.

COMMENTS BY ANTHONY DOWNS *

As commentator on these four papers dealing with intrametropolitan development, I was asked to search out and discuss their common themes and implications. However, their diversity, which consists not only in the specific subjects they cover but also in their methods of approach, makes this task quite difficult. Hoover's paper is a general review of our state of knowledge about metropolitan affairs. This precludes him from making any original contributions on this subject, as he readily admits, but his review is wide-ranging. Harris also concentrates on reviewing quantitative models of urban development. However, instead of ranging across the many types of models applied to

* Real Estate Research Corporation.

urban affairs, he narrows his consideration to "optimal, long-range, metropolitan planning, with some considerable emphasis on its spatial aspects." In contrast, both Ornati and Muth make new contributions to urban thinking concerning relatively specialized areas of knowledge. It is true that Ornati tackles his subject in the form of a review of knowledge about poverty in cities. However, he points out that we know so little there is not much to review; therefore, much of what he says seems quite original—at least to me. Muth writes an almost wholly original essay describing his own work in analyzing housing markets, with relatively little review of other existing knowledge concerning the subject.

In spite of this dual diversity of both subject matter and approach, the four papers do have a few common themes and implications. Therefore, I will concentrate on those. I will appear to be focusing more on things I disagree with than upon those I consider to have been correctly set forth by the authors. This one-sided approach (particularly in reference to Muth's paper) tends to overemphasize my apparent disagreement with the authors, although in point of fact I have found very little to quarrel with about their positive assertions. Rather, I question the perspective with which they have approached the problems concerned. But my assertion that an author should have approached his problem from a somewhat different direction is by no means the same as saying his contribution is useless or inaccurate. It merely reflects the difference between his prejudices and mine in grappling with these most complicated subjects.

The Metropolitan Area as a Dynamic Process

The first common theme concerns the authors' over-all perspective concerning life in metropolitan areas. All seem to imply that metropolitan areas and cities should be conceived of primarily as dynamic social processes rather than places or sets of physical structures. It is true that none say this in so many words; nevertheless, I think it is clearly implied by all their papers. Hoover argues that most of our urban problems result from the dynamic shifts caused by the aging of the housing stock, changes in population size, rises in income, and other such factors. Also, he shows how these dynamic factors affect the changing form, structure, and composition of metropolitan areas.

Harris indicates that useful models need to take a very dynamic approach, with careful timing of variables. Ornati is even more explicit, since he conceives of central cities as "anti-poverty machines." That is, he focuses upon the cultural processes that upgrade low-income and other deprived groups in central cities over time. Since these processes require the concentration of poor and deprived persons in such cities, their presence is not necessarily an indicator of failure on the part of those cities. Nor does their presence mean they are "locked in" to a permanent status of poverty. This conclusion is bolstered by his, to me, surprising statement that the *proportion* of poor persons is much smaller in the largest central cities than it is in smaller ones. Perhaps large central cities are more efficient as "anti-poverty machines" than smaller ones, in spite of their *absolutely* larger concentrations of poor persons.

Muth draws another significant conclusion based upon looking at cities in a dynamic way. He correctly argues that there has not been much decentralization of population or activity in our metropolitan areas; rather, what has been called decentralization by many critics is mainly just growth.

How Broadly Should the Dynamic Processes in Metropolitan Areas Be Conceived?

I completely agree that metropolitan areas can best be viewed as dynamic processes, but I do not fully concur with the particular breadths of viewpoint towards those processes chosen by all four authors. Clearly, the breadth of viewpoint appropriate to a given analysis depends upon the specific subject and purposes of that analysis. Therefore, it would be foolish to contend that every paper about metropolitan areas should have the same breadth of perspective. Nevertheless, three of the four authors chose perspectives for their own subjects which I thought were too restrictive.

For example, Hoover describes the function of an urban concentration as "to facilitate contacts." I realize that this is but a single phrase in a very long and complex paper. Yet I believe it accurately reflects his view of the truly most significant function of metropolitan areas. This view meshes with another related, or perhaps identical, theme in much literature about metropolitan areas, which states that the key function of cities is encouraging contacts among diverse persons and interests so as to stimulate maximum creativity and activity. Lewis Mumford is one of the more celebrated proponents of this theme. I certainly agree that this is one of the key functions of metropolitan areas. However, I believe such areas have other equally significant functions not related either to frequency of contacts or diversity.

Any attempt to describe all the functions of metropolitan areas is bound to seem arbitrary and incomplete, since they contain all the rich diversity of modern life itself. Nevertheless, I have found it useful

421

to aggregate these many functions into three admittedly oversimplified ones, as follows:

1. *The upgrading function.* This consists in improving the economic status and providing acculturation to low-income and other deprived groups, particularly recent in-migrants from outside the metropolitan area. It is a key function of central cities, as mentioned above, and provides the focus for much of Ornati's paper on poverty and cities.

2. *The environment-stabilizing or value-reinforcing function.* This function consists in providing an appropriate environment in which middle-income and upper-income persons and families can enjoy their lives. Perhaps the titles I have given to this function are misleading. It really consists in allowing those who "have it made" to enjoy the perquisites of life as opposed to the first function, above, which is to help others not so fortunate enter into this status. The terms "environment-stabilizing" and "value-reinforcing" may impart an excessively static impression of this function; it also involves an improvement in standards, particularly in our technologically dynamic economy. Nevertheless, the emphasis in this function is not so much upon upward social mobility as upon gradual improvement of the status quo.

3. *The economic-base function.* Under this heading, I join together all the diverse aspects of metropolitan life concerned with its economic efficiency as a location for production, distribution, and other value-creating activities. Certainly this function, like the others, could easily be broken down into a number of subfunctions.

Although this classification is admittedly arbitrary and oversimplified, it does lead to certain conclusions relevant to Hoover's description of metropolitan areas. First, the environment-stabilizing or value-reinforcing function is more dependent upon each group's achieving homogeneity of contacts than diversity of contacts. As sociological observers of metropolitan areas well know, members of different ethnic and socioeconomic groups often seek to live with other people similar to themselves. A certain voluntary social segregation and class stratification connected with specific places results from this tendency. Hoover himself makes many observations that reinforce this conclusion. Thus, his analysis verifies that a search for homogeneity of contact is almost as powerful an influence upon metropolitan areas as the need for diversity of contacts.

A second implication is that it may be more fruitful to look at metropolitan areas as consisting of multiple groups with competing interests and different goals than to use very broad goals that apply to everyone.

But even this simple division leads to a conclusion verified by our more complex analysis: certain city functions tend to produce primary benefits for specific parts of the total population who are *not* the primary beneficiaries of other city functions. For example, the upgrading function benefits low-income in-migrants the most. In contrast, the environment-stabilizing function benefits middle-income and upper-income citizens the most. I believe any sophisticated analysis of goals and objectives in metropolitan areas must take account of this "diversity of publics" being served. Undoubtedly, this complicates the analysis, particularly because weighing the benefits accruing to different groups requires essentially ethical or political judgments rather than scientific ones. Nevertheless, a willingness to face this complexity leads to much more useful results than using goals so broad that every group benefits from all of them.

The above discussion implies that one useful form of model building in metropolitan areas would be simulation similar to that described in Ornati's work. By attributing differing objectives to different parts of the metropolitan-area population, the analyst can seek to construct a decision-making model with which he can simulate their possible reactions to various policy alternatives. I believe this approach will eventually prove to be much more useful than models that assume universally accepted objectives.

In my opinion, Muth's paper, also, exhibits a breadth of perspective towards housing markets which is too narrow to take account of all of the significant dynamic elements affecting them. To some extent, this criticism is more a matter of taste than of scientific accuracy. Muth has attempted to illustrate in his paper just how much of the activity in housing markets and cities can be explained on the basis of a sophisticated and fully developed model built almost exclusively upon economic factors. Therefore, he pays little attention to social factors, immobilities, market ignorance, and certain insights that might be obtained by using a broader perspective. It is certainly a valid intellectual and scientific procedure to see how much of a given set of empirical phenomena can be explained from a relatively narrowly conceived set of premises. I have followed this procedure myself at great length in *An Economic Theory of Democracy*.[1] Moreover, I think Muth is unusually capable at carrying out such an analysis. He has a remarkable grasp of the analytical tools he employs, and can "push them" farther and with more ingenuity than any other economist I know in this field.

Yet this narrowness of approach necessarily prevents Muth from dealing with some highly significant factors in housing markets. For one

[1] New York: Harper, 1957.

423

thing, by confining himself to economic analysis based largely on deductive reasoning plus a few empirical observations, he ignores some interesting empirical literature developed in the studies on race and housing sponsored by the Ford Foundation through the University of California. These include Luigi Laurenti's book *Property Values and Race,* the works of Eunice and George Greer, Davis McEntire, Chester Rapkin and William G. Grigsby, and Nathan Glazer.[2] The empirical data developed in these studies might have provided further grist for Muth's well-designed mill. Furthermore, his analysis of equilibrium or near-equilibrium conditions in housing markets tends to ignore the single most important force regarding segregated housing markets in major cities. This force is the rapid expansion of the non-white population resulting from both high rates of natural increase and significant in-migration from outside metropolitan areas. Equilibrium conditions based upon a balance in housing markets between two population groups (such as white and non-white) are simply not going to occur when one of the groups is expanding quite rapidly in the area under consideration (usually a central city neighborhood), and the other group is shrinking. In fact, static analysis of the type used by Muth can be quite misleading when applied to this situation.

Another factor he does not consider is the influence of threats of violence and irrational considerations upon market behavior. I was struck by the ingenious and plausible "boundary effect" argument he advanced to explain why Negroes tend to buy housing primarily on the edge of existing ghettos rather than in all-white neighborhoods some distance away. However, I think an equally compelling force producing this result is the threat of violence and other unpleasantness which Negroes fear, based upon experience of others who have moved into all-white neighborhoods. Such non-economic factors certainly have traceable economic effects. Muth would undoubtedly be able to analyze them quite capably once he admitted them into his model.

A final significant result of Muth's relatively narrow approach to slum housing markets is typical of the conclusions reached by many economic analysts of urban renewal and housing markets in recent years. These analysts correctly point out that (1) as Muth says, "the principal reason for slum housing is the low incomes of its inhabitants," and (2) urban renewal programs which demolish low-quality housing tend *in themselves* to raise the cost of housing to low-income households by reducing the supply of housing available to them. From these correct

[2] All are part of Special Research Report to the Commission on Race and Housing (prepared under the direction of Davis McEntire), University of California Press, 1960.

observations are derived two conclusions which I believe are false. The first is one stated by Muth: "Measures taken to raise the incomes of low-income groups offer the best prospects for solving the problem of poor-quality housing." The second is that urban renewal is undesirable because of its adverse impact upon low-income families. These two conclusions are so widespread that they are worth examining briefly.

It is quite true that increasing the incomes of low-income persons would undoubtedly make them better off. But it does not follow that their housing would improve if the actual amount of housing supply made available *to them* did not rise as fast as their incomes. For example, in the past year, high interest rates have "choked off" the increase in the total supply of housing which had been occurring in the previous few years. At the same time, general economic prosperity stimulated the incomes of consumers, including those in the lowest-income groups. But the resulting gains in income by the latter groups did *not* improve the quality of their housing, since the general increase in "tightness" in the housing market caused vacancies to decline, rents to rise, and maintenance levels to fall off. Furthermore, because of tremendous immobilities in the housing market—such as those caused by racial segregation and imperfections in the "trickle-down" process—great increases in income among low-income persons may not be accompanied by commensurate gains in *their access* to good-quality housing. As a result, higher incomes may simply lead to higher rents with no improvement in housing quality. The only cure for this situation is insuring that the amount of standard housing made available to low-income households goes up as fast as their incomes. It is not likely that the free market will produce this result in the short run, though it might in the long run. But housing quality is experienced in the short run and has key effects therein too, as recent slum riots tend to show.

The second common conclusion—that urban renewal is undesirable because it reduces low-income housing supply—is, in my opinion, likely to be unjustified when viewed in light of the general housing market. In periods when the general housing supply is "tight," as it has been in the last year, then I would concur that actions that diminish the supply of housing directly available to low-income groups—such as the demolition involved in urban renewal—are undoubtedly harmful to such groups. But when the general housing market is experiencing a rapid increase in supply—as it was in the late 1950's and early 1960's—then the harmful impact of urban renewal may be more than offset by these larger changes in the housing supply. In such periods, removal of the worst housing units through demolition may be well worth the resulting marginal decline in the supply of low-income housing, since that decline

425

is being counterbalanced by a general expansion in the supply of all housing. Hence, urban renewal may be quite desirable even to the lowest-income groups in such periods.

The above reasoning leads me to conclude that narrowly defined analyses of the housing market—though they can be extremely useful in extending our insights into the working of that market—should not be used as the basis for broad conclusions about it. Such conclusions can be accurate only if they are based on a more comprehensive outlook which takes into account some of the social factors, irrationalities, and immobilities that Muth has deliberately left out of his study. Moreover, these supposedly "non-economic" factors are particularly crucial in any analysis of slums and poverty. As more and more studies in many fields are indicating, slum residents are essentially the victims of irrationalities and immobilities in society. They are people who "fall into the cracks" between the neat logical categories dealt with in the disciplines of economics and other social sciences. Precisely the "frictional" factors which tend to be ignored by formal model builders are crucial elements in the lives of these deprived people.

The third author whose viewpoint seems excessively narrow to me is Harris. However, my criticism of his approach will be dealt with in the next section. In contrast, Ornati seems to have struck a proper balance between the nature of the subject and breadth of variables and factors he took into account when dealing with it.

Designing Models of Practical Significance to Decision-Makers

In searching for things these four papers have in common, I found myself struck by the absence in all of them of a factor that I regard as particularly important. This is the adaptation of urban analysis to practical needs of political and other decision-makers. These decision-makers have been entrusted with the actual responsibility for shaping public policies towards metropolitan areas. Yet, analysts of urban affairs all too often tend to approach their subjects in terms of "pure" intellectual content and challenge rather than usefulness in decision-making. Undoubtedly, this comment reveals my bias as a consultant to decision-makers rather than an academic student of urban affairs. I certainly recognize that studies of urban life motivated by the intellectual curiosity of the analyst play a highly significant role in the development of our knowledge. Therefore, my feeling that these papers are not well adapted to the needs of decision-makers may be more a comment on my own perspective than a valid criticism of their authors. Nevertheless, I would like to set forth this criticism and some of its implications, particularly because I think it applies to the preponderance of analytic work done on urban affairs in universities.

For example, Harris makes an initial assumption about the nature of his subject which practically guarantees that his conclusions will not be of any practical use to decision-makers grappling with today's problems. In spite of its title, his paper does not really deal with "Quantitative Models of Urban Development," but rather with a special class of such models. The particular class on which he concentrates consists of "optimal, long-range, metropolitan planning" models. Since no responsible decision-makers on this earth have viewpoints dominated by any one of these three traits, the main area on which he focuses attention is almost guaranteed to be irrelevant to practical decisions in metropolitan areas.

Harris may legitimately retort (in fact, he did!) that merely because this subject is not of immediate practical significance to decision-makers does not mean that it has no value. I agree. But I find myself rather repelled by his insistence that decision-makers adapt themselves to intellectual model-builders, rather than vice versa. Thus, he states that, "Insofar as designers and decision-makers can find means by which to relate to the process of computer simulation or projection, there will be immense gains in the fruitfulness and cogency of their own work and thinking" (pp. 408–9). In my opinion, it is more reasonable to expect analysts to develop theories useful to decision-makers than it is to expect practical men of action to change their ways to fit intellectuals' models.

One of the ways in which I believe model builders should adapt their thinking more closely to real-life decision-making is by shifting their attention from grandiose macroscale models to more modest microscale models. Paradoxically, this conclusion seems to contradict my comments in the previous section about proper breadth of perspective. Nevertheless, my intuitive feeling, bolstered by considerable experience in working with practical decision-makers at municipal, state, and federal levels, is that the highest marginal payoff from model building now lies in tackling very particular, narrowly defined problems. After all, suboptimizing can still produce viable models. For example, I think we could learn a great deal by applying the techniques of economic analysis to such limited problems as vandalism and its relation to rehabilitation, how to reduce juvenile delinquency through small innovations which cut down on opportunities for crime (such as getting people to keep their car doors locked), the relationship between property maintenance and the behavior of tenants, particular incentives which might cause slum owners to improve their buildings, and the specific cost-benefit balance of various narrowly defined policies. Small-scale microanalysis models designed to deal with these questions could markedly improve our present purely trial-and-error or purely traditional approaches to them.

In this respect, Ornati's paper struck me as an excellent example of shaping analysis to suit a problem, rather than pursuing it as an intellectual challenge. His analysis of the relationship between migration and the number and proportion of poor in central cities demonstrates a firm grasp of poverty and its eradication as *processes* rather than *states*. This analysis certainly has some cogent policy implications. It is clear that one way to reduce the absolute incidence of poverty is to block the entry of more persons into poverty. This can be done through birth control on the one hand, and by attempting to control immigration on the other. It has long seemed to me ironic that America's success in lifting most of its people out of poverty has been based in part upon its "choking off" any large-scale inflow of poor persons from abroad. Few liberals or economists ever discuss this essential underpinning of our widespread prosperity, since it goes so much against the grain of our image of an "open society." Yet Ornati's analysis reminds us again that the success of any American "war on poverty" depends upon continued prevention of a flooding of our society with foreign poor. However, we cannot block in-migration to central cities from our own rural areas. So anti-poverty campaigns must take into account that the greater their success, the more rural poor will be lured to our major cities. Incidentally, the fact that the widespread nature of our internal prosperity rests upon the exclusion of others is for me a persuasive moral argument for continued aid of some kind to underdeveloped countries abroad, and even within the United States.

Another significant extension of Ornati's arguments can be made regarding the currently popular view that education is a form of investment in human capital. In recent years, many economists have espoused this belief, which Ornati employs in his analysis. However, I think these economists have not extended their arguments far enough. They should also take account of another form of investment in human capital of crucial significance to urban poverty. I refer to the enormous investment of time, effort, talent, money, and love made in children by their mothers. In slum neighborhoods, mothers often fail to make these kinds of investments in their children because the mothers must work, or are too apathetic to do so, or lack the proper knowledge and cultural capabilities. This failure may create a need for compensatory investment by schools and other public agencies in the same children. I believe that it might be fruitful for economists to pursue this line of analysis and its implications in the same way they have regarding formal education in schools.

Ornati's analysis of poverty also confirms several points I made earlier. For one thing, his emphasis that the poor do not form a homogeneous group meshes with my suggestion that policy objectives should be defined in terms of several differing "publics." Also, the fact that entirely different policy approaches to poverty are necessary for different groups confirms the efficacy of developing economic models of a microscale, suboptimizing nature. Finally, he emphasizes that the plight of the poor often results primarily from factors which traditional economic theorists regard simply as "friction" or "minor irregularities" in their analytic models. Thus, if we wish to help the poor, we must concentrate our analytic powers on aspects of social and economic performance which most previous analysts have considered trivial or uninteresting.

The Use of Models to Test Policies

Hoover's paper emphasizes another reason why I believe economists should concentrate more heavily on microscale models designed specifically to test practical policy alternatives. He concludes that the future growth of metropolitan areas will take the form of continued multi-nucleated sprawl. I concur with this conclusion. But I was struck by the uncontrolled nature of the growth he forecasts, and the importance of forces and factors which are essentially exogenous to public policy. This underlines the need for more powerful tools of analysis which public decision-makers can use to formulate and explore specific devices that might influence future urban growth patterns. Certainly, the free market has been and will continue to be a tremendously powerful force generating income and other values for all elements of society. Moreover, I believe that whenever we can entrust particular areas of decision-making to free-market processes with reasonable effectiveness, we should do so to avoid the less-self-correcting deficiencies of bureaucratic or political decision-making. Nevertheless, experience shows that an increasing proportion of activity in urban areas tends to fall within the regulatory sphere of one or more public bodies. Therefore, we have an ever more pressing need for better methods of testing out the policies which might be adopted by these bodies. Economists are beginning to make significant contributions to the tools necessary for such testing, but there is enormously more to be done.

REBUTTAL BY BRITTON HARRIS

It is unusual to find two discussants who are able to comment so coherently on four papers as diverse as those dealing with intrametropolitan development, and to do so with urbanity and cogency. Although I have no very serious disagreement with either commentator, there is the *appearance* of a sharp disagreement with Downs on one particular point. I shall therefore follow his example of restricting the focus of my remarks. I shall use them to try to show that this disagreement does not, in fact, exist.

I think that Downs has taken two different positions in his commentary. In discussing the work of Ornati and Muth and in presenting some of his own original and well-thought-out ideas, he appears to be taking a long view of metropolitan decision-making. He is talking about issues that will not be settled in the next five or even twenty years. Indeed, some of the issues he raises might be treated only by measures that have very little immediate impact and "sex appeal." On the other hand, he takes me to task for taking a long-term point of view and for not advocating the construction of models dealing with problems of, let us say, vandalism, which are the problems of immediate interest to decision-makers. Let me try to see how this dichotomy might be resolved.

In the first place, I think that Downs and I would agree that there are some problems that have to be solved on a metropolitan basis, even though this creates severe difficulties for decision-makers who are locked in to less-than-metropolitan jurisdictions. These problems arise with regard to transportation, air pollution, water pollution, public open space, industrial development, regional development, and many related areas. In the long run, if decision-makers do not exist who can identify their interests with the solution of these problems, they will have to be invented.

In the second place, there are many problems of a long-term nature which, while they have many petty day-to-day manifestations, cannot be managed by salving these irritations, small or large. Two areas in which Downs is particularly interested, education and housing, cannot be solved overnight. We have not begun to explore the workable policy combinations that can ultimately resolve these issues, but we can be sure that in general, when they are found, they will not in themselves prevent next summer's riots. If we do not now have decision-makers who develop the art of combining long-term and short-term solutions with a major emphasis on the long term, we shall once again have to invent them and the political environment in which they can function.

In the third place, I have no basic disagreement with the importance of understanding and modeling problems at the small scale. Indeed, I believe, much to the dismay of some of my colleagues in the model-building fraternity, that unless we fully understand behavior at the microlevel, we are in danger of making egregious mistakes in modeling at the macrolevel. In this work, I believe that there is room for a certain amount of division of labor. I am also inclined to feel that a great deal of very fruitful microanalysis will proceed in response to day-to-day decision-making problems. Such a division of labor should not be a cause for acrimony, and I am sure that there are some who can function admirably at more than one level.

Finally, I think that Downs mistakes my point about the involvement of decision-makers in the modeling process. Let me restate this to say that decision-makers and model-builders have to be mutually involved in the same process and can respectively gain a great deal from this involvement. Neither should be required, however, to accept the other's definition of what is either appropriate or possible. As a result of his involvement in this process, the decision-maker is quite clearly able to make suggestions about new procedures; and at the same time, the model-maker is able to make suggestions about new areas of investigation. Since, in my view, both model-building and decision-making are relatively undeveloped fields, neither group of participants should be alarmed if he turns out to be talking to someone in the other group who does not yet exist. We clearly cannot permit ourselves to be bound either by the present horizons of decision-making or by the present horizons of technique.

PART III

THE URBAN PUBLIC ECONOMY

Dick Netzer*

FEDERAL, STATE, AND LOCAL FINANCE
IN A METROPOLITAN CONTEXT

As a framework for analysis of budget policy—both the revenue and the expenditure sides of the accounts—Musgrave's normative conception is as useful in a metropolitan context as it is in the national context.[1] In the provision and financing of public services in metropolitan areas, how should, and do, the allocation, distribution, and stabilization branches function? Equally important, how do they interact?

Taking them in reverse order, it is apparent that stabilization goals neither should nor can play a *major* role in decisions or urban public services and their financing. They should not, because stabilization objectives should be centrally established and executed within a single national economy. They cannot, because the principal actors, local and state governments, do not possess the money-creating powers ultimately necessary to support functional finance. The subnational governments have such limited flexibility even short of the capacity to borrow without limit, that they can be viewed as more or less passive reactors to, rather than aggressive fighters of, economic fluctuations.[2]

Indeed, the evidence from the Great Depression, as initially interpreted, suggested that subnational governments are actually "fiscally perverse," in that their reactions tend to reinforce fluctuations.[3] That is, they cut back expenditures and increase tax rates in downturns and behave in an opposite fashion in booms, as a consequence of the limitations and pressures they confront. A considerable literature has evolved which questions the validity of the thesis during the Great Depression itself and, more importantly, demonstrates that the thesis has not held in the years since World War II.[4] The general finding is that

---

* Professor of Economics, New York University.

[1] Richard A. Musgrave, *The Theory of Public Finance* (McGraw-Hill, 1959), Chap. 1.

[2] See the list of limitations in Robert W. Rafuse, Jr., "Cyclical Behavior of State-Local Finances," in Richard A. Musgrave (ed.), *Essays in Fiscal Federalism* (Brookings, 1965), pp. 65–66.

[3] The principal interpreters were Alvin H. Hansen and Harvey S. Perloff, *State and Local Finance in the National Economy* (Norton, 1944); and George W. Mitchell, Oscar Litterer, and Evsey D. Domar, "State and Local Finance," in Board of Governors of the Federal Reserve System, *Public Finance and Full Employment* (1945).

[4] See especially Rafuse, *op. cit.*, and Ansel M. Sharp, "The Behavior of Selected State and Local Government Fiscal Variables During the Phases of the Cycles, 1949–1961," *Proceedings of the National Tax Association, 1965.*

the strong secular rise in the scale of state-local finances has overwhelmed cyclical influences. In fact, because of the peculiar sensitivity of the markets for tax-exempt securities to changing credit conditions, there has been some modest counter-cyclical effect.[5] The lack of "fiscal perversity" in the past twenty years has been made possible, to some extent at least, by the institution of some of the changes—notably improvements in intergovernmental fiscal relations—suggested by Hansen and Perloff in their original indictment. But the absence of "fiscal perversity" does not demonstrate that pursuit of stabilization objectives is or can be a significant aspect of subnational public sector budget policy.

As for distribution, the logical solution is Musgrave's: in a federal system, conscious redistributive fiscal adjustments should be made at the central government level. As Musgrave says, "Unless this is done, distributional adjustments at the state level may come to be nullified by interstate movement, and serious barriers to an optimal location of economic activity may be imposed." [6]

Logical or not, the subnational public sector does produce substantial redistribution. This is not necessarily conscious policy, but a consequence of expenditure programs designed for much narrower ends—the relief of destitution, the provision of merit goods (education, health services, etc.) to the poor—and of political compromises in state-local tax policy. This redistribution is the net result of a fairly pronounced "pro-poor" pattern of expenditure incidence, combined with a moderately regressive pattern of state-local tax incidence. Most state-local tax incidence studies have resulted in incidence curves of a modified reverse "J" shape: sharp regressivity at the very low incomes, proportionality over a fairly broad middle-income range, and a small degree of progressivity at the upper ends of the scale. This finding, of course, largely reflects the incidence of the property and sales taxes, dominant at the local and state levels, respectively.[7]

[5] Frank E. Morris, "Impact of Monetary Policy on State and Local Government: An Empirical Study," *Journal of Finance,* Vol. 15 (May 1960).

[6] Musgrave, *The Theory of Public Finance,* p. 181. Musgrave points out that this solution would be more or less similar to one in which Buchanan's "fiscal residuum" (from operations of all levels of government) is equalized and subnational governments depend upon benefit taxes. See James M. Buchanan, "Federalism and Fiscal Equity," *American Economic Review,* Vol. 40 (September 1950).

[7] See, for example, O. H. Brownlee, *Estimated Distribution of Minnesota Taxes and Public Expenditure Benefits* (University of Minnesota, 1960); Richard A. Musgrave and Darwin W. Daicoff, "Who Pays the Michigan Taxes?" *Michigan Tax Study Staff Papers* (Michigan Legislative Tax Study Committee, 1958); University of Wisconsin Tax Study Committee, *Wisconsin's State and Local Tax Burden* (1959); Levern F. Graves, "State and Local Tax Burdens in

Those studies which have examined expenditure benefits generally find that average dollar benefits per family rise very slowly indeed as income rises (no matter what the basis of allocation).[8] The combined result is significant redistribution. For example, the Minnesota study found that expenditure benefits per family were at least twice as great as the tax incidence for families with incomes of less than $5,000.[9]

TABLE 1.
ESTIMATED INCOME REDISTRIBUTION EFFECTS OF THE PROPERTY TAX
AND THE LOCAL SERVICES IT FINANCES, 1957[a]

(millions of dollars)

Money income class	Amount for class	Cumulative
Net additions to income, for class:		
Less than $2,000	315	315
$2,000–3,000	180	495
3,000–4,000	190	685
4,000–5,000	485	1,170
5,000–7,000	280	1,450
Net subtractions from income, for class:		
Over $15,000	740	740
$10,000–15,000	435	1,175
7,000–10,000	275	1,450

[a] Based on data in and underlying Netzer, *Economics of the Property Tax* (Brookings, 1966), Chap. 3, especially Table 3–14. The tax incidence case used is Case II, after federal tax offsets. The benefits incidence case is Case IA. The value of federal tax offsets has been allocated on the basis of the distribution of federal individual income tax payments by adjusted gross income class.

Gillespie's nationwide study found that, as of 1960, the *net* benefits for income classes below $3,000 exceeded 25 per cent of family money income before taxes.[10] An analysis confined to the property tax and the local expenditures it finances estimates that in 1957, when $12.3 billion in local property tax revenues financed about half of local

California," California Assembly Interim Committee on Revenue and Taxation, *1964 Report;* University of Maryland, College of Business and Public Administration, *Maryland Tax Study* (1965); Gerhard N. Rostvold, "Distribution of Property, Retail Sales, and Personal Income Tax Burdens in California: An Empirical Analysis of Inequity in Taxation," *National Tax Journal,* Vol. 19 (March 1966); Dick Netzer, *Economics of the Property Tax* (Brookings, 1966), Chap. 3; Alan D. Donheiser, "The Incidence of the New York City Tax System," New York University, Graduate School of Public Administration, *Financing Government in New York City* (1966).

[8] See, for example, Brownlee, *op. cit.;* Musgrave and Daicoff, *op. cit.;* Netzer, *Economics of the Property Tax.*

[9] Brownlee, *op. cit.,* p. 2.

[10] W. Irwin Gillespie, "Effect of Public Expenditures on the Distribution of Income," in *Essays in Fiscal Federalism,* pp. 122–86.

437

general expenditure, the fiscal process produced a net shift of $1,450 million from income groups above $7,000 to those below $7,000 (see Table 1). The very rough characterization of local government finances in metropolitan areas as of 1962, shown in Table 2, similarly suggests important redistribution, and no doubt substantially understates its extent.

TABLE 2.
CRUDE REDISTRIBUTIVE CHARACTERISTICS OF LOCAL GOVERNMENT FINANCE
IN METROPOLITAN AREAS, 1962[a]

(billions of dollars)

Probable over-all incidence	General expenditure (net of charges)	Financing, excluding charges
Progressive, on balance[b]	14.0 (56%)[c]	2.2 (9%)[d]
Roughly proportional	11.1 (44%)	9.6 (38%)[e]
Regressive, on balance	—	13.3 (53%)[f]
Total	25.1 (100%)	25.1 (100%)

[a] Basic data from U.S. Bureau of the Census, *Census of Governments, 1962*, Vol. V, *Local Government in Metropolitan Areas* (1964), Table 9.

[b] "Progressive expenditures" are defined here, for ease of exposition, as those which have the same redistributive effect as progressive taxes.

[c] Includes education, welfare, health, and hospital expenditure net of charges.

[d] Includes estimated share of intergovernmental aid financed from state and federal income taxes.

[e] Includes local revenues (excluding the property tax) and state aid financed from non-income tax funds.

[f] Includes the property tax.

Distribution policies or consequences ultimately concern individual consumer units. One dimension, the usual measure in incidence studies, is the proximate dimension of incidence by income *class*. Another dimension, important in a metropolitan context, is that of *geographic* redistribution within large urban areas. The fragmentation of tax bases among a large number of political jurisdictions of extremely disparate character, the highly uneven geographic distribution of expenditure needs (notably, residences of the poor) and the possibility of exporting some tax burdens across jurisdictional lines, together suggest that the metropolitan fisc might have redistributive consequences among communities. The usual variant of this is the "suburban exploitation of the central city" hypothesis, aspects of which are discussed below.[11]

Whether or not the hypothesis is valid, it does seem likely that analysis of net fiscal incidence on a highly disaggregated geographic basis—by communities within a single urban area—would produce

[11] See also Wilbur R. Thompson, *A Preface to Urban Economics* (The Johns Hopkins Press, for Resources for the Future, 1965), Chaps. 3 and 7.

rather different results than the more usual aggregative studies. Aggregation tends to reduce the regressivity of the principal local revenue, the property tax, by combining high-housing-consuming suburbanites with low-housing-consuming city dwellers, the former with high incomes and the latter with lower incomes. Effective property tax rates are usually higher in the larger central cities,[12] but these differences are not reflected in the aggregate studies, which apportion property taxes in some relation to housing consumption. In any case, the evidence suggests that the property tax is far more regressive within individual cities than it is on a statewide or nationwide basis.[13] It seems likely that, in reality, the fiscal systems of the large metropolitan areas produce almost no redistribution between the central city poor and the suburban rich, aside from that not insignificant element resulting from the operation of state and federal grant programs.

It is evident that the allocation branch dominates the provision and financing of urban public services; that is, the primary purpose of subnational public finance is the support of goods and services which, for one reason or another, will not be provided in "adequate" quantity and quality in the absence of governmental action. In almost any classified tabulation of local government expenditure—that in Table 2, for example, or the Brownlee classification[14]—allocation branch items predominate.

The allocation branch comprehends the provision of what Musgrave has called social wants and merit wants, and also the provision of a substantial volume of what are essentially private goods but which, because of historical accident or otherwise, fall in the public sector (e.g., water supply in most parts of the country). The problem in the case of social wants is to discover and satisfy consumer preferences as if market solution were in fact obtainable; in the case of merit wants, the problem is to arrive at some type of political settlement. But in all cases some of the usual private sector standards or requisites for optimization apply here as well: the need for adequate knowledge of alternatives and an institutional setting in which this knowledge can be effectively utilized by the participants in the processes; some degree of mobility of factors among uses and over space; the existence of a continuum of alternatives rather than stark either-or choices; and so on.

[12] See Netzer, *Economics of the Property Tax,* Chap. 5.
[13] See Donheiser, *op. cit.*
[14] In O. H. Brownlee, "User Prices vs. Taxes," in Universities–National Bureau of Economic Research, *Public Finances: Needs, Sources and Utilization* (Princeton University Press, 1961), p. 424; see also C. Harry Kahn's comments on Brownlee at pp. 436–37.

The majority view is that these requisites do not exist in the real world of public finance in metropolitan areas. In part, this is because of legal restrictions on the powers of local governments to act. But a far more important source of the difficulty is held to be the fragmented nature of local government in metropolitan areas, which limits mobility, impedes free exercise of consumer preference, and magnifies externalities to the point where they often exceed in magnitude internalized costs and benefits.[15] The argument essentially is that existing institutional arrangements do inhibit optimal solutions—that the financing devices themselves, in the context of a fragmented structure of government, add more or less avoidable imperfections to those inherent in the nature of the public sector. We turn now to an examination of this set of issues.

EFFECTS OF FINANCING ARRANGEMENTS ON THE OUTPUT OF SERVICES

Local Tax Sources

As Table 3 indicates, local taxes finance slightly less than half of the cost of public services in metropolitan areas.[16] And when we speak of "local taxes," we mean the property tax and little else, except for the small number of large central cities (like New York, Philadelphia, St. Louis, and a number of Ohio cities) which obtain significant revenues from non-property tax sources. Moreover, at least some of the intra-metropolitan consequences of the property tax are common to other locally imposed tax devices.

The usual conclusion is that the fragmented governmental structure with its attendant spillovers of costs and benefits leads to: ". . . an allocation of resources to collective consumption that is below the optimum level that would be indicated if all benefits of such consumption were appropriable in the spending community. . . . The inefficiencies, in terms of under-allocation of resources to the public sector, and the accompanying inequities, go a long way toward providing some

---

[15] For the best statement of this, see Harvey E. Brazer, "Some Fiscal Implications of Metropolitanism," in Benjamin Chinitz (ed.), *City and Suburb: The Economics of Metropolitan Growth* (Prentice-Hall, 1964). For a dissenting view, see David Davies, "Financing Urban Functions and Services," *Law and Contemporary Problems,* Vol. 30 (Winter 1965).

[16] Table 3 includes, as revenue, direct state government outlays for highways and public assistance and estimated state contributions for employee retirement; this was done to adjust for differences in the distribution of functional responsibilities among the states.

TABLE 3.
SOURCES OF FUNDS FOR PUBLIC SERVICES IN METROPOLITAN AREAS,
PER CENT DISTRIBUTION, 1962[a]

Source		Per cent of total
Federal and state governments		32.3
Federal aid	1.7	
State aid	19.4	
Other state government funds[b]	11.2	
Local taxes		45.7
Property	39.3	
Other	6.5	
General sales	2.6	
Income	0.8	
User-charge-type revenues		17.4
Charges and special assessments	9.1	
Utility revenue	8.3	
Other local sources[c]		4.5
Total[b]		100.0

[a] Based on data in U.S. Bureau of the Census, *Census of Governments, 1962*, especially Vol. V.

[b] Includes direct state government expenditure for highways and public assistance, and estimated state government contributions to retirement systems for metropolitan area local government employees.

[c] Includes employee contributions for retirement, liquor store revenue, sale of property, interest earnings, and other and unallocable.

Note: Because of rounding, detail may not add to totals and subtotals.

understanding, if not explanation, of the major problems confronting metropolitan America." [17]

In concept, the coexistence of a large number of small governmental units within a single urban area need not lead to undernourishment of public services or other suboptimal results. Tiebout has provided a model, at a fairly high level of abstraction, in which individuals reveal their preferences for public goods much as they do in the course of voluntary exchange in the private sector.[18] Under a set of restrictive assumptions, he views suburban communities as competing for residents by offering differing packages of public services combined with the tax rates required to finance the services; consumers choose among the communities on the basis of their relative preferences for collectively provided vis-à-vis privately provided goods and services. Obviously, to

[17] Brazer, "Some Fiscal Implications of Metropolitanism," *op. cit.,* pp. 144, 145. See also Lyle C. Fitch, "Metropolitan Fiscal Problems," in Chinitz (ed.), *City and Suburb,* for a good exposition of the undernourishment hypothesis.
[18] Charles M. Tiebout, "A Pure Theory of Local Expenditure," *Journal of Political Economy,* Vol. 64 (October 1956).

the extent that this abstraction is applicable to the world we live in, it offers an attractive means of arriving at an optimal solution to local finance problems, a solution which reflects consumer choice.

Unfortunately, Tiebout's restrictive assumptions usually do not apply: mobility and knowledge is restricted; externalities exist; and actual fiscal flows are complex and often unrelated to decisions of individual consumer-voters. Therefore, it is not surprising that the pattern of tax rates and expenditure levels the Tiebout thesis would lead one to expect—a high and positive correlation—is seldom observed in metropolitan areas.[19] In fact, the most common pattern is the opposite one: tax rates and expenditure levels are *negatively* associated. At least, this has been the finding in most reported studies.[20]

The explanation for this appears to lie in the enormous disparities in taxable capacity among the political jurisdictions in the larger metropolitan areas. There is a strong positive correlation between tax base and expenditure levels. The richer communities—those with extensive concentrations of business property (or non-property tax bases) and those dominated by high-value residential property—do spend a good deal more than the poorer communities, by and large. But they do not spend as much more as their superior tax bases would permit. Therefore, tax rates and tax base tend to be negatively correlated; the richer communities provide superior services at lower tax rates.

This is a general description of the pattern of variation among jurisdictions outside the central cities. The central city–suburb comparison presents a somewhat different, but analogous, pattern. Generally, central cities spend significantly more, on a per capita basis, than suburban communities which are, on balance, richer. This is mainly (but not entirely) a consequence of the concentration of poverty-linked public service needs and outlays in the central cities. However, the per capita property tax base in most large central cities is well below that of their surrounding areas.

This has not always been the case. At one time, the central cities had a near-monopoly on non-residential property which offset their parallel near-monopoly on low-value housing. But they have lost the

[19] Indeed, the surprising thing is that this pattern is *ever* observed. But it is, for example, in regard to non-school expenditures and taxes in upper-income Chicago suburbs (the presumed laboratory for Tiebout's observations). See Netzer, *Economics of the Property Tax*, pp. 125–31.

[20] See, for example, *ibid.*, pp. 125–31; Julius Margolis, "Municipal Fiscal Structure in a Metropolitan Region," *Journal of Political Economy,* Vol. 65 (June 1957); and "The Variation of Property Tax Rates within a Metropolitan Region," *National Tax Journal,* Vol. 9 (December 1956); Donald J. Curran, S.J., "The Metropolitan Problem: Solution from Within?" *National Tax Journal,* Vol. 16 (September 1963).

former near-monopoly, with the dispersal of industry away from central locations, while retaining the latter. The upshot is that effective property tax rates in most large central cities exceed those outside the central cities. In most other places the effective rates are roughly equivalent. This is usually explained by existence of important non-property taxes utilized mainly by central cities. On the whole, therefore, tax levels in central cities are significantly higher than in suburbs (as a group). Moreover, these higher tax levels buy services which are inferior in a number of important respects, notably in regard to schools.[21]

Some observers have argued that there is a pronounced observable trend toward reduction in intrametropolitan fiscal disparities—a trend toward uniformity accompanying increased economic specialization within metropolitan areas.[22] To a considerable extent, such observations have been a result of rising expenditures, values, and tax rates on the newly urbanized, formerly rural fringes of metropolitan areas: they have become more like the already developed sections. It is by no means certain that disparities are disappearing within the already urbanized sections of metropolitan areas, and it may be that central city–suburban disparities are *increasing*.

However this may be, the existing disparities afford a rational explanation of the notorious resistance of suburban communities to metropolitan-area-wide solutions to governmental problems, and also an explanation of the observed tendency to control land use for maximum fiscal advantage: the fortunate low-tax, high-expenditure communities seek to preserve their favored positions, a natural response.[23] One result is to insulate part of the metropolitan area's economy from local taxation. The extreme cases are the industrial enclaves with few residents and fewer school children; in effect, industrial property in such enclaves is exempt from school taxation.

These are obvious and special cases of the undernourishment hypothesis. The more general cases fall into two classes. First, given the

[21] For discussion of city-suburbs disparities, see Netzer, *Economics of the Property Tax*, pp. 117–24; Curran, *op. cit.*; Margolis, *op. cit.*; Brazer, *Some Fiscal Implications*; Advisory Commission on Intergovernmental Relations, *Metropolitan Social and Economic Disparities* (1965); Mordecai S. Feinberg, "The Implications of Core-City Decline for the Fiscal Structure of the Core-City," *National Tax Journal*, Vol. 17 (September 1964).

[22] See Jesse Burkhead, "Uniformity in Governmental Expenditures and Resources in a Metropolitan Area," *National Tax Journal*, Vol. 14 (December 1961); Netzer, *Economics of the Property Tax*, pp. 132–35.

[23] On the land use effects, see Dick Netzer, "The Property Tax and Alternatives in Urban Development," *Regional Science Association Papers and Proceedings*, Vol. 9 (1962); and Lynn A. Stiles, "Financing Government in the Suburbs— The Role of the Property Tax," *National Tax Association Proceedings, 1960*.

fragmentation and the disparities, local tax support of redistributive services is likely to be restrained. If the poor are concentrated in already high-tax communities, redistributive services can be more amply supported only by taxing the poor more heavily, a self-defeating proposition; the resources of the rich are not available, since these resources belong to other jurisdictions, those with minor needs for redistributive services. Second, non-redistributive services with heavy benefit spillovers are likely to be undernourished simply because, as noted earlier, the benefits cannot be appropriated by the communities which individually tax themselves for the service. And although all would benefit from a broader base for financing such services, the well-off communities resist nonetheless, since they cannot be sure that a breach in the existing pattern, for financing services affected with major externalities, will not become a much wider assault on their advantageous positions.

Intrametropolitan fiscal disparities thus have both equity and efficiency consequences. Moreover, the efficiency consequences include effects on the location of activity as well as the effects on the level of output of public services. What has been called "fiscal zoning" presumably has some effect on locational patterns; the direction of the effect must be assumed to be suboptimal, away from the pattern which would prevail in the absence of land use controls. There is also likely to be a more direct cause-and-effect relationship: differentials in tax rates within urban areas no doubt have some bearing on location decisions of firms and individuals, and presumably the results are often suboptimal.

The extent of the actual influence of taxes on location is open to question (see below). However, there is no doubt that *fear* of potentially adverse tax influences is a critical factor in state and local tax policy decision-making. It is almost certain that these competitive fears have restrained the increase in local taxes and thus have had feedback effects on the output of public services; this, of course, is not susceptible to quantification.

Anxiety about the competitive effects of tax differentials has given rise to a fairly extensive literature on the subject.[24] Most studies take

[24] Examples are Wilbur R. Thompson, "Importance of State and Local Taxes as Business Costs," *National Tax Association Proceedings, 1957;* Reuben A. Zubrow, "Some Difficulties with the Measurement of Comparative Tax Burdens," *National Tax Association Proceedings, 1961;* and the studies cited in John F. Due, "Studies of State-Local Tax Influences on Location of Industry," *National Tax Journal,* Vol. 14 (June 1961); and Netzer, *Economics of the Property Tax,* pp. 109–10. Perhaps the best analytical pieces are Harvey E. Brazer, "The Value of Industrial Property as a Subject of Taxation," *Canadian Public Administra-*

a whole state as the unit of observation. They generally conclude that "relatively high business tax levels do not have the disastrous effects often claimed for them," [25] mostly because state-local taxes are so small an element in business costs, even in business cost differentials at alternative locations. This conclusion must be accepted with some reservations. For one thing, the usual studies are too aggregative to uncover the marginal cases in which tax differentials are in fact the only significant cost differentials. Such marginal cases surely exist, and as local tax levels rise relative to total income and output, these cases will become more frequent.

Moreover, tax differentials may reinforce, rather than offset, other cost differentials. This is the prevailing situation with regard to manufacturing activities and the central cities. The dispersive tendencies are powerful, even without tax differentials which work in the same direction. Finally, there is the distinction between *inter*regional and *intra*-regional locational effects. Tax rate differentials may not be important enough to offset the major interregional factor cost differentials but can easily be far more significant within a single metropolitan area where other cost differentials are relatively minor.

And tax levels within metropolitan areas do vary considerably among alternative locations. The Campbell study of the New York area, for example, showed a three-to-one range for a sample of twenty-five manufacturing firms among sixty-four locations in the region, a range which surely must affect locational decisions.[26] A more recent study of New York City's finances provides fairly clear evidence that the major business tax differentials which have existed in the area actually have stimulated decentralization of economic activity away from New York City.[27] Indeed, the evidence is so clear that it has had a major effect on recent tax policy decisions in both New York City and its periphery.

Local business tax differentials will affect locational decisions only to the extent that the tax differentials are in excess of the location rents for a given activity at a particular site and of the value of public services provided to firms in return for the tax payment.[28] Ordinarily, the user-charge component of local tax payments is small indeed for business

tion, Vol. 55 (June 1961); and Wolfgang F. Stolper, "Economic Development, Taxation, and Industrial Location in Michigan," in *Michigan Tax Study Staff Papers* (1958).

[25] Due, *op. cit.*, p. 171.

[26] Alan K. Campbell, "Taxes and Industrial Location in the New York Metropolitan Region," *National Tax Journal,* Vol. 11 (September 1958).

[27] See the papers by Leslie E. Carbert, James A. Papke, William Hamovitch, and Henry M. Levin, in *Financing Government in New York City.*

[28] See the exposition in Brazer, *The Value of Industrial Property.*

firms. It is by no means small for individuals, especially in dormitory suburbs, which perhaps partly explains the apparent insensitivity of residential location decisions to local tax rate differentials.[29] There have been few studies of this, but one survey of high-income individuals suggests almost complete insensitivity.[30]

However, because the tax-service nexus is far from clear to individuals within central cities, it is reasonable to suppose that high property taxes on housing in the cities are a serious deterrent to central city housing consumption. The consumer perceives only the annual or monthly cost of housing, 25 per cent or more of which reflects property tax payments in most large central cities; he sees little connection between this cost and the quality of public services offered. He therefore is presumably less willing to pay a high price for the housing-cum-taxes package than in a suburban location, where the connection with public services is far more obvious. To the extent that this is true and that its truth is appreciated, however incoherently, by public officials it may explain, indeed justify, the common big-city policy of taxing housing much more favorably than other types of real property.[31] But this, too, is a circular process, with feedbacks on the output of public services: keeping tax rates low on a large fraction of the tax base restrains the ability of central cities to increase the output of public services.

In summary, then, the prevailing metropolitan area local tax structure—heavy reliance on the property tax by a large number of taxing jurisdictions—appears to restrict the output of public services to a level below that which might obtain under other institutional arrangements. The existing structure also has suboptimal effects on location decisions and land use patterns, and these effects in turn probably further restrict the output of public services. What other institutional arrangements (confining the discussion here to locally imposed taxes) might there be?

For the central cities, at least, a partial solution is to be found in non-property taxes, on personal income and/or consumption (non-

[29] Another explanation may be found in the federal individual income tax offsets to local taxes. See Benjamin Bridges, "Deductibility of State and Local Nonbusiness Taxes under the Federal Individual Income Tax," *National Tax Journal*, Vol. 19 (March 1966); "Allowances for State and Local Nonbusiness Taxes," in Musgrave (ed.), *Essays in Fiscal Federalism*.

[30] James N. Morgan, Robin Barlow, and Harvey E. Brazer, "A Survey of Investment Management and Working Behavior Among High-Income Individuals," *American Economic Review*, Vol. 55 (May 1965), p. 259; this is more fully developed by the same authors in *Economic Behavior of the Affluent* (Brookings, 1966), pp. 169–70.

[31] For an extended discussion of this, see my *Economics of the Property Tax*, pp. 74–85, and *Financing Government in New York City*, pp. 58–61, 710–15.

property business taxes levied by local governments have no obvious advantages, on any score, over business property taxes). Personal taxes of a general nature avoid the serious deterrence to increased housing consumption (which is a goal most large older cities actively pursue with a variety of policy devices) inherent in the property tax. They also afford a means of moderately extending the geographic scope of central city taxing powers, by a form of reverse-suburban-exploitation, that is, taxing those suburbanites who happen to work or shop in the central city to defray part of the "excess burden" of redistributive central city services. But presumably the scope for central city non-property taxation is limited by the locational impact; very large differentials will not work.[32] Perhaps the greatest potential is in central city personal income taxation, partly because so few state governments rely heavily on income taxation.[33] In any event, those large cities which impose some type of income tax do appear able to reduce their reliance on the property tax by more than do the sales tax cities in places like Illinois and California.

De-emphasis of the property tax would tend to reduce the land use and location effects of local tax structures. The process could also be helped by radical reform of the property tax, into a tax based largely on land values (or land value increments). The potential of land value taxation has recently gained new and well-deserved attention.[34]

But the essential need appears to be some mechanism for levying local taxes on a broader geographic base, that is, converting some portion of local taxation into area-wide taxes. The objective here would be to provide for more satisfactory financing of both redistributive services and non-redistributive services affected with major externalities. A corollary advantage of area-wide taxation is that the metropolitan area affords a more satisfactory basis for application of the superior forms of taxation—on income and consumption rather than property—than does a large collection of separate small taxing units. But one cannot be sanguine about the possibilities here. Indeed, one can argue that resort to increased grants from the state and federal governments

[32] It is estimated that, when New York City's sales tax rate was 4 per cent and there was no sales tax in surrounding areas, the tax differential reduced retail sales in New York City—of the types sensitive to and covered by the tax —by close to 25 per cent. See the papers by Hamovitch and Levin in *Financing Government in New York City.*

[33] See Advisory Commission on Intergovernmental Relations, *Federal-State Coordination of Personal Income Taxes* (1965), p. 11.

[34] See Netzer, *Economics of the Property Tax,* Chap. 8; Clyde E. Browning, "Land Value Taxation: Promises and Problems," *Journal of the American Institute of Planners,* Vol. 29 (November 1963); James Heilbrun, *Real Estate Taxes and Urban Housing* (Columbia, 1966).

has been, and will continue to be, the most likely and popular means of spreading the tax burden geographically.

Federal and State Financing

As Tables 3 and 4 indicate, federal and state funds finance some-

TABLE 4.

FINANCING OF PUBLIC SERVICES IN METROPOLITAN AREAS, BY MAJOR FUNCTION, 1962[a]

Function	Expenditures ($ billion)[b]	Sources of funds (per cent distribution)		
		Federal and state governments[c]	User-charge-type revenues[d]	Other local sources[e]
Education	12.4	33	6	61
Highways	4.9	68	5	27
Welfare	2.8	75	—	25
Health and hospitals	1.6	10	25	65
Housing and renewal	1.1	26	30	44
Local utilities	3.2	—	89	11
Other and unallocable[f]	10.1	10	14	76
Total[g]	36.1	31	16	53

ᵃ Based on data in U.S. Bureau of the Census, *Census of Governments, 1962*, especially Vol. V.

ᵇ Includes direct state government expenditures for highways and public assistance, estimated state government expenditure for retirement systems for metropolitan area local government employees, and estimated local government contributions to their own retirement systems. Interest allocated crudely by function and, where possible, retirement system amounts also allocated.

ᶜ Includes, in addition to aids, the state government expenditure described in the preceding note. Functional distribution estimated.

ᵈ Functional distribution partly estimated.

ᵉ Computed as residual; includes taxes, miscellaneous revenues, employee contributions to retirement systems, liquor store revenues, borrowing and net use of cash balances. Net borrowing amounted to $2.8 billion in 1962, about one-seventh of the total in this column.

ᶠ Includes employee retirement system amounts not allocated by function and liquor store finances, as well as other and unallocable general expenditure and its financing.

ᵍ The percentages differ slightly from those in Table 3; that table compares revenue amounts to total *revenues*, while in this table the revenue amounts are compared to total *expenditure*.

what more than 30 per cent of the cost of the public services provided in metropolitan areas. This is on the basis of a broad definition of federal and state financing, to comprehend identifiable direct state government provision of public services in metropolitan areas, as well as the intergovernmental payments through which the external governments help support locally provided services. The most important of such identifiable direct state services are highways and public assistance.

The states differ considerably in their distributions of responsibilities among the state government and the local units.[35] On the average, state governments directly account for about one-third of combined state-local expenditure, but state participation is substantially lower in states like New York, New Jersey, and California and substantially higher in places like Pennsylvania and Connecticut, among the more urbanized states. Greater state aid may or may not offset lower direct state participation, but both factors must be considered in appraising the state role. In some states, like New York, the major intergovernmental problem is in fact the distribution of functional responsibilities, and not state aid formulas and the like.[36]

Federal and state funds, using this broader definition, finance one-third of local education costs (and, of course, nearly all the *public* costs of higher education), over two-thirds of highway and welfare costs, and much smaller, almost nominal, proportions of the costs of other public services in metropolitan areas. It is clear that local revenue sources bear a substantial residual burden in connection with redistributive services (about $2 billion for health and welfare purposes, as of 1962) and that external financing is not of major consequence in connection with other services with major spillovers.

These are 1962 proportions, and the percentages have risen somewhat since then. However, the role of external financing has changed relatively little during the past fifteen years; the really revolutionary expansion of the roles of the state and federal government occurred in the 1930's. This is evident from the following tabulation of the percentages of combined state-local expenditures met from state and federal sources:[37]

	Per cent
1964–65	54
1960	53
1955	51
1950	54
1940	49
1927	26
1902	18

[35] See the paper by Morris Beck in *Financing Government in New York City*. Mushkin points out that differences in the assignment of the welfare function are the most important consideration. See Selma J. Mushkin, "Intergovernmental Aspects of Local Expenditure Decisions," in Howard G. Schaller (ed.), *Public Expenditure Decisions in the Urban Community* (Resources for the Future, 1963).

[36] *Financing Government in New York City*, pp. 29–31, 36–40.

[37] Calculated from U.S. Bureau of the Census, *Census of Governments, 1962*, and *Governmental Finances in 1964–65* (1966).

Financing from taxes levied by higher levels of government tends to overcome spillover problems, disparities in local tax bases and disparities in the concentration of the poor within metropolitan areas; it can also result in greater reliance on taxes with more appropriate distributive effects than usually result from metropolitan area local tax structures. It *can* do these things, although these are not necessarily the explicit reasons for intervention by higher levels of government. More commonly, the motivation for federal action is to encourage the provision of *additional* public services; equalization features are designed to effect this expansion with minimum burdens on taxpayers in the poorer states. In contrast, state government action is usually often justified as a *substitute* for local tax support of a given level of services (notably in connection with state school aid), although some programs give priority to stimulation of local action.

The goals are perhaps of less significance than the effects. Most studies indicate that external grants have strongly stimulative effects. For example, Sacks and Harris found that both federal and state aids in 1960 had strong positive effects on the level of state-local expenditure by state; they also found state aid to be a major stimulative force among local governments within New York State.[38] In fact, in New York State, an additional dollar of state aid for schools appears to result in a net increase of 90 cents in school expenditures.[39]

Bishop, in a study of the New England states as of 1961–62, came up with rather different findings. His conclusions were that state school aids are stimulative, but the stimulative effects were found mainly in the smaller towns. In the larger places, and therefore in the states as a whole on a weighted basis, the primary effect of additional school aid is to reduce local property taxes.[40] This is consistent with other aggregative studies of school aids, but conflicts with the results of smaller-scale comparisons where similar socioeconomic areas are involved. Take, for example, Bergen County, New Jersey, and Westchester County, New York; both are New York suburbs, with similar high income levels and roughly the same population and public school enrollments, and both have large numbers of separate school systems (seventy-four and fifty, respectively). As of 1962, per pupil expenditures in Westchester

[38] Seymour Sacks and Robert Harris, "The Determinants of State and Local Expenditures and Intergovernmental Flows of Funds," *National Tax Journal,* Vol. 17 (March 1964); Sacks, Harris, and John J. Carroll, *The State and Local Government: The Role of State Aid* (New York State Department of Audit and Control, 1963), pp. 120–41.

[39] *Ibid.,* pp. 173–75.

[40] George A. Bishop, "Stimulative versus Substitutive Effects of State School Aid in New England," *National Tax Journal,* Vol. 17 (June 1964).

were about 40 per cent higher than in Bergen, but the bulk of the difference was accounted for by differences in state aid per pupil.[41] This was also true of non-school local expenditure in the two counties. The case that state aid is primarily substitutive would require that local support of local services be lower in Westchester than in Bergen, since state aid is higher and most other variables are similar, but this is not the case.

The structure, as well as the purposes, of state aid programs does permit them to be substitutive. This is not usually the case with regard to federal aid, because of the nature of matching requirements. This, however, does not apply to federal direct expenditure—notably social insurance—which can replace state-local expenditure. It also does not apply to many newer federal grant programs with minor or non-existent matching requirements. For example, the Medicaid provisions of the 1965 federal legislation are expected to *replace* $110 million annually of locally financed expenditure for hospitals in New York City.[42]

The effects of grants-in-aid on the output of public services are thus by no means clear; if the primary purpose of grants is to increase public expenditure, they may, in some circumstances be relatively inefficient means of doing so. However, one approach holds that grants are substantially more efficient in increasing public expenditure than is direct state performance of functions. Campbell and Sacks, in a series of papers, have pointed out that the actual structure of intergovernmental relations, which differs widely among the states, is a major determinant of the output of services in metropolitan areas. They include among the structural variables state versus local direct responsibility, the extent of state aid for local functions, and the nature of the subsystems of local government (with complicated overlapping and differentiation in some northern and western metropolitan areas and great simplicity in most southern areas).[43] Their findings suggest that the output of public services is relatively high where major local responsibility is combined with substantial state aid and relatively low where the substitute is a larger direct state government role.

The evidence on a statewide basis for the fifteen states with the largest metropolitan area populations (in Table 5) tends to support this

[41] Based on *Census of Governments, 1962,* data.
[42] See the paper by Katherine W. Strauss in *Financing Government in New York City,* especially pp. 368–70.
[43] See Alan K. Campbell and Seymour Sacks, "Administering the Spread City," *Public Administration Review,* Vol. 24 (September 1964); Sacks and Campbell, "The Fiscal Zoning Game," *Municipal Finance,* Vol. 36 (May 1964); Sacks, "Metropolitan Area Finances," *Proceedings of the National Tax Association, 1963.*

thesis, although not unreservedly so. Three of the four high expenditure states in the top section of Table 5 have below-average state direct roles

TABLE 5.
PER CAPITA EXPENDITURE AND STATE FINANCING,
SELECTED STATES, 1964–65[a]

State	Per capita state-local general expenditure	Per cent of state-local general expenditure		
		State gov't. direct expenditure	State aid to local gov'ts.	Total, state-financed expenditure
California	$203	27%	25%	52%
Michigan	178	32	21	53
Indiana	176	36	20	56
New York	165	22	24	46
Texas	146	34	15	49
Maryland	146	33	25	58
Connecticut	140	43	9	52
Illinois	138	36	13	49
New Jersey	136	24	10	34
Florida	128	36	16	52
Pennsylvania	126	39	16	55
Ohio	126	28	17	45
Virginia	126	42	16	58
Massachusetts	122	32	19	51
Missouri	121	41	12	53

[a] Includes fifteen states with largest SMSA population, 1960 (77% of U.S. total). Based on U.S. Bureau of the Census, *Governmental Finances in 1964–65*.

and all have well above-average state grants. Four of the six low expenditure states have relatively high state direct roles; all have relatively low state aids. But there are exceptions in all the groups. Moreover, the correlation between expenditure levels and the combined extent of state government financing is decidedly poor.

However, it is easy to see why the thesis might be applicable conceptually, and perhaps also to explain some of the observed deviations. Consider only expenditures with a primarily allocation branch character. Such outlays are likely to be a good deal higher under a local-performance-with-high-state-aid regime than with high direct state performance. This surely would be the case if the marginal propensity to consume allocation branch services is higher in richer communities. In such a case, high-income communities would devote larger portions of their residents' incomes to public services. Equalizing state aids would tend to increase the outlays of the poorer communities, with the strength of this tendency dependent on the form of the state aid.[44] In contrast, state performance would result in an expenditure level suggested by the marginal propensity for public services at the state-wide average personal income level; the result should be somewhat lower public expenditure.

The case is strengthened by the fact that local taxes are deductible for federal income tax purposes. Suppose, for example, that the rate of substitution of public for private goods (that is, the willingness to surrender income for public uses) is invariant with respect to income. The residents of higher-income communities, because of the federal tax offset, would be able to spend more relative to income for local public services without any greater sacrifice of net (after-tax) income. Consider two communities, one in which the residents' average marginal income tax rate is 30 per cent and another in which the rate is 15 per cent. The after-tax cost of a dollar of local public expenditure to the average resident is more than 20 per cent greater in the low-income community. Or, if the willingness to surrender private income is similar in the two places, local expenditures relative to income will be more than 20 per cent higher in the richer community.

But there is no reason to expect this arrangement to work for redistributive expenditures. Indeed, their very concentration in the poorer communities will frustrate any willingness of residents of richer communities to tax themselves to support such services. And, as we have seen, the most important factor making for differences in the direct state role is connected with the locus of the responsibility for that major redistributive service, public assistance. This could explain some of the deviations from the "expected," such as low expenditures in Massachusetts.

At any rate, in concept it does appear that the output of public services might be maximized under a regime in which there is:

1) a high degree of local responsibility for allocation branch services;

[44] The issue here is the relative importance of income as against substitution effects. A general-purpose equalizing grant's effects would be virtually all income effects and would produce a proportionate rise in expenditures, on the assumption that the marginal propensity to consume public services rises with community income. A functional grant would have some substitution effects, depending upon matching requirements and the institutional obstacles to substitution. For example, school grants to independent school districts probably produce less substitution of school for other public expenditures than do school grants to general-purpose local governments.

2) significant equalizing state aid to the poorer communities for such services; and

3) major state (and/or federal) responsibility for redistributive services.

User Charges

As Tables 3 and 4 show, user-charge-type devices finance about one-sixth of public services in metropolitan areas; if state and federal highway-user taxes are classified as user charges, the proportion rises to one-fourth. Relatively heavy reliance on price-like devices to finance urban services seems appropriate. True, user charges are highly inappropriate for redistributive services but, as we have seen, the allocation branch appears dominant in metropolitan finance.

Moreover, within the metropolitan area allocation branch, a significant portion of the output of public services consists of services of an essentially private character, for which the exclusion principle applies: the consumer can be, or actually is, excluded from enjoyment of the service unless he is willing to pay its price.[45] Some of these are affected with no greater externalities than are most privately produced goods and services (water supply, most transportation services, many recreational activities). In such cases, individuals can vary their consumption (within limits) on the basis of price without efficiency losses, indeed with significant efficiency gains. For other services, where major external *diseconomies* are involved (e.g., air and water pollution, traffic congestion), there is an argument for user charges as "social economy" reimbursements or to induce consumers to eliminate the diseconomies their actions produce.

Intuitively, it seems obvious that financing from user charges, rather than from general taxes, should affect the level of output of public services. If the general thesis, that existing institutional arrangements produce undernourishment of urban public services, applies to services that are amenable to user charges but are not presently financed by them, the effect should be a substantial increase in the output of such services. One reason for this is that user charges can overcome the political fragmentation problem. The charge, presumably, is based on actual use of services or facilities, not the domicile of the taxpayer; the demand of "foreign" as well as "domestic" users can be satisfied, on a compensatory basis, by the managers of the enterprise.

There has been surprisingly little systematic empirical investigation of the effect of user charge financing on the output of services. Casual empiricism suggests that there are in fact higher standards of service

[45] See Musgrave, *The Theory of Public Finance*, p. 9.

where user charge financing is employed. For example, the essence of the frequent criticisms of the operations of public authorities is that they produce their own "private opulence amidst public squalor." That is, they utilize their command over user charges to produce unusually high-grade services within their spheres of operation.[46]

Rigorous analysis has been applied to one aspect of this question —the effects of earmarking taxes for specific purposes. Buchanan has developed a model, based on individual fiscal choice, which suggests that earmarking will lead to an efficient solution in which expenditures are higher than would otherwise be the case.[47] An empirical effort to test the Buchanan hypothesis produced negative results—the extent of or change in earmarking seemed to have little effect on expenditure levels.[48] In an earlier paper, Margolis found that earmarking, in the form of school districts independent of general government, tended to reduce school expenditure.[49] He explained this on the basis of a log-rolling theory of voting behavior—the multipurpose expenditure package combines the consumer's surplus for specific projects so that voters accept the entire package rather than lose the specific project. His discussants, however, suggested that "backward log-rolling" is possible as well and that the empirical evidence is far from conclusive.[50] The case, then, must be regarded as not proved, although the Buchanan model is most attractive.

The potential for user charges in metropolitan finance can perhaps be illuminated by a brief review of the extent of user charge financing in metropolitan areas currently, that is, as of the 1962 Census of Governments. As we would expect, charges are of minor significance for services with a major redistributive aspect. *Education* charges amount to about 7 per cent of current operating expenditure, and these are largely school lunch fees, which are far below the full costs of the resources devoted to the program; the subsidy here, of course, is a federal one. *Hospital* charges equal about 35 per cent of current expenditure. The bulk of the revenue is collected outside the largest cities and largest metropolitan areas, where the hospitals serve the general

---

[46] For a more sophisticated view of authorities, see Robert C. Wood, *1400 Governments* (Harvard University Press, 1961), Chap. 4.

[47] James M. Buchanan, "The Economics of Earmarked Taxes," *Journal of Political Economy,* Vol. 71 (October 1963).

[48] Elizabeth Deran, "Earmarking and Expenditures: A Survey and A New Test," *National Tax Journal,* Vol. 18 (December 1965).

[49] Julius Margolis, "Metropolitan Finance Problems: Territories, Functions and Growth," in Universities—National Bureau of Economic Research, *Public Finances: Needs, Sources and Utilization* (Princeton University Press, 1961).

[50] Lyle C. Fitch, pp. 272–73, and William F. Hellmuth, pp. 276–80, in *Public Finances . . . Utilization.*

population and not just the indigent as in the bigger cities. Small-city public hospitals in effect are substitutes for the big-city voluntary hospital. *Public housing* charges (rents) amount to about 90 per cent of current expenditure and in-lieu-of-tax payments; the redistribution occurs here because the federal (and any other public) subsidy is designed to cover all, or nearly all, of the capital costs of public housing.

Turning to allocation branch expenditures, *sewerage* charges are about equal to current expenditure, in the aggregate. But annual economic costs for this heavily capital intensive service are far above current expenditure. Special assessments probably cover about one-fifth of capital outlays. In regard to other *sanitation* services (mainly refuse removal), charges are only about 15 per cent of expenditure. Charges are more commonly utilized in smaller cities and suburbs than in the big cities. Local *parks and recreation,* probably the most rapidly growing urban expenditure, generate charges equal to about 20 per cent of current expenditure. *Fire protection* can be viewed as very much a private good,[51] one which could readily be provided by a privately owned public utility company, but charges are negligible and the service is financed from general taxes.

Transportation services, other than streets and highways, are largely financed from charges. Charges for airports and water terminals substantially exceed current expenditure and probably largely cover debt service costs as well. Public transit systems come close to breaking even in regard to current expenditure; the very large deficits on capital account are concentrated in a very few places, notably New York. Local government parking operations generate large surpluses, in the form of net parking meter revenues, only a small part of which is used to subsidize off-street parking.

Highways are a rather different matter. In 1962, highway expenditure in metropolitan areas totalled $4.9 billion, of which $3.3 billion was financed from federal and state funds. The bulk of these funds were derived from earmarked highway-user taxes, which can be considered as user charges in a very aggregative sense. Users provide the funds, and no doubt at a more ample level than might be the case without earmarking, but there is little connection between user tax payments and specific uses of the roads. Of the locally financed $1.6 billion, about 20 per cent came from user sources, equally divided among local highway-user taxes (mostly licenses and often not earmarked), special assessments for street improvements, and more specific types of charges (mostly tolls). These figures relate to a fairly narrow definition of high-

[51] Ignoring the tiny fraction of fire losses due to fires originating on adjacent properties.

way expenditure. Associated street functions and police traffic control activities probably involve at least $400 million more in expenditure, and generate only minor user charges.

This review suggests significant potential for greater and more sophisticated application of user-charge-type financing. One of the most serious obstacles to effective utilization of pricing devices in financing public services can be traced to the traditional justification for user charges (and analogous taxes) on the basis of benefits received. The benefit principle, however, is concerned with equity, not allocation: how can we equitably spread the costs of public goods among individuals? But this principle is inappropriate for allocation branch decisions on the financing and provision of services with a substantial private character. Efficiency in allocation requires that prices (or other types of charges) and the level of services provided be determined on the basis of the marginal *costs* of the services. More often than not, there is little correspondence between benefit-determined charges and cost-determined charges.

Vickrey had done extensive work on this. In a major paper, he contrasts benefit and cost solutions for a number of urban services, and advances imaginative (and reasonably workable) cost-based charging schemes.[52] A number of these schemes involve charges based on site characteristics, such as land area and frontage; in effect, these are offered as substitutes for the existing benefit-justified taxation of the value of land and improvements, that is, the property tax. The pricing of urban transportation services, on a cost basis, has received more attention than anything else, by Vickrey and by others, especially in Britain.[53] Fairly elaborate and detailed pricing schemes have been advanced, schemes which radically depart from the conventional benefit approach to highway financing.[54] Such proposals have met with a rather negative response in this country, but seem to be on the verge of acceptance in conservative Britain.

A MODEL MULTILEVEL SYSTEM

There is no shortage of proposed solutions to the problems posed by

[52] William Vickrey, "General and Specific Financing of Urban Services," in Schaller (ed.), *Public Expenditure Decisions in the Urban Community.*

[53] See, for example, William S. Vickrey, *The Revision of the Rapid Transit Fare Structure of the City of New York,* Finance Project, Mayor's Committee on Management Survey of the City of New York (1952); Lyle C. Fitch and associates, *Urban Transportation and Public Policy* (Chandler, 1964), Chap. 4; U.K. Ministry of Transport, *Road Pricing: The Economic and Technical Possibilities* (1964).

[54] For a good exposition of this approach, see A. D. Le Baron, "The 'Theory' of Highway Finance: Roots, Aims, and Accomplishments," *National Tax Journal,* Vol. 16 (1963).

the existence of multiple levels of government functioning within urban areas. Solutions include models at high levels of abstraction,[55] comprehensive sets of policy recommendations,[56] and more or less pragmatic "practical" solutions.[57] Most frequently, the theoretical models are efficiency solutions based on individual choice (such as the Musgrave and Tiebout models); they stress spillovers as the basis for allocation branch intergovernmental transfers and relegate redistributive activities to higher level governments. An alternative formulation explicitly allows for differences in consumer preferences as to the "mix of governments" in the provision of services and for changes in this mix as part of the process of adjustment to achieve desired levels of public services.[58] This formulation minimizes the role of spillovers and rejects distinct roles for the various levels of government. It provides the rationale for a "marble cake," rather than a "layer cake," approach to intergovernmental relations, in which federal, state and local governments all perform some services and do some financing of all the major functions, in differing degrees at differing times and places.

No doubt this is an increasingly accurate description of the observed system. However, it affords no normative standards for appraising the system. Any aspect of intergovernmental action can be considered to be efficient, according to this model, in the sense of reflecting changing consumer preferences for the "mix of governments." Moreover, as a positive theory, it provides little basis for estimating the extent or even the direction of expected change.

There are, I believe, real differences in the capabilities of the levels of governments—in their capacity to realize efficient solutions on the basis of more conventional definitions of efficiency—which are closely related to the vast differences in the geographic coverage of the levels. The federal government, after all, does operate throughout a single integrated economy and, moreover, an economy with only minor external flows. Most of the states are in effect regional governments and

---

[55] For example, Charles M. Tiebout, "An Economic Theory of Fiscal Decentralization," in *Public Finances . . . Utilization;* Charles M. Tiebout and David B. Houston, "Metropolitan Finance Reconsidered: Budget Functions and Multi-Level Governments," *Review of Economics and Statistics,* Vol. 44 (November 1962); and Richard A. Musgrave, "Approaches to a Fiscal Theory of Political Federalism," in *Public Finances . . . Utilization.*

[56] For example, Simeon E. Leland, "An Ideal Theoretical Plan of Finance for a Metropolitan Area," in *Financing Metropolitan Government* (Tax Institute Symposium, 1955).

[57] For example, L. L. Ecker-Racz and I. M. Labovitz, "Practical Solutions to Financial Problems Created by the Multilevel Political Structure," in *Public Finances . . . Utilization.*

[58] This is put best in Selma J. Mushkin and Robert F. Adams, "Emerging Patterns of Federalism," *National Tax Journal,* Vol. 19 (September 1966).

comprehend the totality of one or several metropolitan areas.[59] The states therefore can act with only occasional effects on *intra*regional competition. In contrast, a very large part of the total metropolitan area population spills over the boundaries of even the largest of local government units (usually, the county).

Therefore, it seems appropriate to utilize a formulation based upon some kind of systematic differentiation in the roles of the levels of government. The by now conventional models do just this, by confining the lower levels to allocation branch activities, with intergovernmental adjustments for spillovers. The model suggested here follows this pre-scription.

In this model, stabilization and distribution activities and goals are basically federal government responsibilities. In reality, the system does function this way to a considerable extent: direct federal action for stabilization objectives; federal social insurance for stabilization and distribution objectives; and federal grants, the bulk of which (excluding the highway aids) are basically redistributive in purpose and effect. The extent to which this is the case is perhaps best illustrated by contrasting current experience with the federal role thirty-five years ago, when stabilization goals were only partly accepted and ineptly acted upon and when redistribution was hardly an important goal of federal action.[60]

Nonetheless, there is, as we have seen, a substantial redistributive element in the finances of state and local governments, notably in connection with education and with non-federal financing of welfare, health, and other poverty-linked services. Nationwide, the obviously poverty-linked services, exclusive of aids and charges, absorb about 10 per cent of local government taxes; in the large central cities, the figure is closer to 20 per cent. In the model system, this is highly inappropriate: individual local governments would have no financial responsibility for clearly redistributive services.

At present, the state government role in the redistributive services is a large one, via grants and direct performance. Health and welfare

[59] Only 32 of the 219 metropolitan areas are interstate areas. Twenty-three of the 32 have 70 per cent or more of the area's population within the primary state; these 23 include 18 of the 21 areas with 250,000 or more inhabitants. The interstate problem concerns mainly a few large areas. The 6 largest interstate areas—New York SCA, Chicago SCA, Washington, D.C., Philadelphia, St. Louis, and Kansas City—in 1960 had about 7.4 million of their 31.1 million populations in the secondary states. All 213 other areas had only 1.8 million people in the secondary states, about 2 per cent of the total population of these areas. U.S. Bureau of the Budget, *Standard Metropolitan Statistical Areas* (1964).

[60] George W. Mitchell, "The Federal Impact on Metropolitan Finance," in *Financing Metropolitan Government* (Tax Institute Symposium, 1955).

services financed from state taxes amount to about one-sixth of state tax collections. In the model system, federal grants, social insurance and perhaps a negative income tax would supplant state-financed redistribution. But this departure from the ideal is considerably less obnoxious than is redistribution by separate local units from their own resources. In fact, a shift from local to state support, from intraregional to regional finance, of redistributive services would be a major step in the right direction.

This applies, as well, to metropolitan-area-wide financing devices for distributive purposes. In the single-county metropolitan areas the county government can and often does perform this role. In the larger areas there is no such machinery, and the state government can be viewed as a rough substitute for metropolitan-area-wide government. However, in a number of places there is considerable interest in area-wide taxing arrangements. For obvious reasons, the services directly linked to poverty are unlikely candidates for such support. A much more likely candidate is education; but this has an important redistributive character, too.

The model system would provide for area-wide performance and/or financing in another type of situation: where there are major, obvious spillovers among the political jurisdictions within a metropolitan area. The definition here is essentially a technological one, but with a hazy dividing line between spillover services and services whose costs and benefits are largely internal to individual communities. The externalities with regard to education are large ones, but the external effects are as often extraregional as they are captured within a single metropolitan region. This argues for state and national financing, not only for area-wide arrangements. However, for transportation and air and water pollution control, for example, the very large external effects are primarily confined to a single urban area.

Aside from such types of services, there is little argument for area-wide machinery or performance. Indeed, there is a case for having a multiplicity of small jurisdictions to provide and finance allocation branch activities without important externalities. If the jurisdictions had some correspondence to "natural" service areas for the provision of most local services and if the financing devices were specific cost-based charges along the lines suggested by Vickrey, most of the advantages of the Tiebout solution[61] could be realized. That is, the provision of services would be related to revealed consumer preferences.

Carried to its logical extreme, this arrangement would suggest sepa-

[61] In "A Pure Theory of Local Expenditure," *op. cit.*

460

rate special-purpose units of government for a long list of services, with different boundary lines for each set of units. This would entail a huge amount of consumer voting and other decision-making. Decision-making is not costless, which points to the desirability of a more limited number of jurisdictions, but not so limited as to rule out effective consumer choice. The losses in consumer choice through fewer units can be offset by greater reliance upon true pricing arrangements, under which consumers have a genuine choice as to the amount of the service they consume.[62]

This, in outline, is the model system. The real-world departures from it are clear enough: major redistributive elements in purely local finance; absence of area-wide machinery for services with major externalities; a pattern of fragmented local units which is generally poorly designed even to deal with appropriately local responsibilities on the basis of consumer choice. How then can we move toward a better system?

Institutional Strategies

One approach might be through the development of true metropolitan government. By "metropolitan government" in this context, we mean some sort of governmental entity which performs a variety of services (or finances them) over all or a large portion of a metropolitan area—a general purpose agency with full governmental character, analogous to the state or the large central city. As has been noted, metropolitan government in this sense simply does not exist in the United States, except in those single-county metropolitan areas in which the county government plays a large role.

Nearly 100 of the standard metropolitan statistical areas comprise no more than a single county. Of these, twenty-four are located in states in which countywide local government units (county and county school districts) account for 60–80 per cent of total local government expenditure; effectively, such areas now do have metropolitan government. But about half of the single-county areas are areas in which the countywide units account for only about one-fifth of local expenditure, and another fourteen are areas in which the county share is less than 15 per cent. The high-county-share areas are mostly in the South. Expansion of the county role, to a level approximating that found in a number of areas in California (about 30 per cent of local expenditure), affords an obvious way of achieving the reality (but not the name) of metropolitan government in single-county areas (or in multiple-county

---

[62] For a more extended discussion of this, based upon ideas suggested to me by Lynn A. Stiles, see Netzer, *Economics of the Property Tax*, pp. 216–17.

areas with only minor overspills of population from the primary counties).

Aside from this, the chances for true metropolitan government appear to be dim. The idea seems to have little popular appeal. Indeed, labelling an expansion of the county government's role as "metropolitan government" apparently greatly increases the unpopularity of this strategy, as the experience of Dade County, Florida, indicates. It is not difficult to understand the unpopularity of the proposal. First, as noted earlier, the residents of the presently advantaged communities are likely to resist any reorganization which threatens to diminish their existing fiscal advantages. Second, metropolitan government proposals frequently have been urged on the basis of claims for economies of scale over a wide range of functions, claims which are unpersuasive intellectually and which conflict with the superficial evidence of higher unit costs in the large cities.[63] Third, any radical change in that most conservative of institutions, local government, is likely to be acceptable only if the institution is generally perceived to be working very badly indeed. It is probable, as Vernon and Wood have separately argued, that few people other than the experts share this perception.[64]

Ad hoc regional government devices clearly have far more popularity. The number of special-purpose districts and authorities has been increasing rapidly. According to the 1962 Census of Governments, there were (in that year), 5,411 metropolitan area special districts with sufficient autonomy to be classified as independent governmental units, an increase of 45 per cent in just five years. All but 179 of these units were single-function units, distributed by function as follows:

Fire protection	1,174
Natural resources (drainage, etc.)	946
Water supply	764
Sewerage	570
Housing and urban renewal	391
Other	1,387

Some of the relative financial magnitudes are shown in Table 6. The special districts accounted for about 7 per cent of local government expenditure in metropolitan areas, but because they specialize in capital-intensive services, they accounted for 15 per cent of capital outlay. The

---

[63] See Werner Z. Hirsch, "Implications of Metropolitan Growth and Consolidation," *Review of Economics and Statistics,* Vol. 16 (August 1959).

[64] Raymond Vernon, *Metropolis 1985* (Harvard University Press, 1960), pp. 224–28; Wood, *1400 Governments,* pp. 196–99.

TABLE 6.
SPECIAL DISTRICTS IN METROPOLITAN AREA FINANCES,
1962, BY FUNCTION[a]

Function	Special district expenditure		Charges and utility revenue as per cent of special district expenditure
	Per cent of SMSA local government expenditure	Per cent distribution of special district expenditure	
Housing and urban renewal	41	18	46
Water supply	19	12	56
Transit	30	10	103
Sewerage	23	10	24
Airports and water terminals	38	8	64
Electric power	20	6	88
Hospitals	10	6	64
Highways	6	5	N.A.
Parks and recreation	11	4	12
Natural resources	36	4	33
All other	3	18	26
Total	7	100	50
Exhibit: Total capital outlay	15	44	—

N.A.—Not available.
[a] Based on U.S. Bureau of the Census, *Census of Governments, 1962*, Vol. V, *Local Government in Metropolitan Areas.*

most important special district functions are housing, water supply, transit, and sewerage. Their more important functions account for 20 per cent or more of local expenditure. And they rely heavily on user charges, which in 1962 financed 50 per cent of total expenditure, compared to less than 20 per cent for all metropolitan area local governments.

These data overstate the significance of special districts as truly regional mechanisms. Fewer than 300 of the 5,400 special districts spend more than $1 million annually; of these about 80 are housing authorities; 60, water and/or sewerage agencies; 30, hospital districts; and about 30 deal primarily with one or more transportation functions. These large transportation agencies mostly operate on a multicounty basis and a fair number of the large water and sewer districts operate on a countywide basis. But few of the other large districts (as defined here) operate on a geographic basis as broad as a single county. Many, including most of the housing authorities, are confined to a very small segment of their own metropolitan areas.

This indicates that the popularity of the ad hoc district or authority has not been sufficiently exploited to realize the potential for area-wide solutions, where technology or other factors dictate such solutions. The popularity has obvious bases, including the appeal of price-like financing and "business-type" management for quasi-commercial services, and the ease with which debt, tax, and similar limits can be surmounted by the use of the ad hoc governmental entity. The authority or special district by itself, however, is hardly the ultimate in institutional strategies. For one thing, organization on a special-purpose basis does not guarantee that particular local government functions will be performed in an innovating manner. The ad hoc units develop their own institutional biases and blinders (in particular, they are notably resistant to the use of sophisticated pricing mechanisms),[65] and often are hesitant to venture into the new fields their technical competence and equity capital cushions (in the form of amortized revenue-producing facilities) equip them to enter. The continuous generation of new units, which is therefore usually necessary, both complicates the public sector decision-making process and contributes to a fair amount of dead weight losses in the form of political in-fighting.

An even more obvious defect of the ad hoc government strategy is its apparent unsuitability for tax-supported redistributive functions, even where the source of financing is not the major problem. Consider here the experience with housing authorities, very few of which operate outside the confines of a single city; evidently few places are willing to tolerate a situation in which an authority has the power to relocate the central city poor in other parts of the metropolitan area.

The most promising as well as the most crucial strategy is connected with changes in intergovernmental fiscal relations. This strategy can be so characterized for a number of reasons. First, as has been noted repeatedly, the residual responsibility for redistributive services at the local level is a large one and this should be assumed by higher levels of government. Second, the fundamental fiscal imbalance in our federal system has become both more apparent and more openly recognized, by both the experts and the political leaders. In brief, our system places the major responsibility for the provision of the most costly, most rapidly expanding types of public services on the states and their local subdivisions and, at the same time, effectively awards the most productive and flexible revenue sources to the federal government. The data make this clear. In 1964–65, the federal government directly spent $25

---

[65] The Port of New York Authority, in an effort to promote bridge and tunnel traffic in its earlier days, adopted a pricing schedule which results in tolls which on the average are lower in congested peak hours than in the uncongested off-peak hours; although aware that this is in effect "fiscally perverse," the Authority has been unable to bring itself to end this pricing policy.

billion for civilian functions analogous to those provided by state and local governments (excluding social insurance), while state-local governments directly spent more than three times as much, $82 billion.[66] Taking into account grants-in-aid, the federal government financed $36 billion of ordinary civilian expenditure, or roughly one-third of the $107 billion total; state and local agencies financed, from their own resources, the remaining two-thirds.

Between 1952 and 1964–65, a period in which the important changes in the rates of major federal taxes were *reductions,* federal revenues (excluding social insurance) rose by $40 billion. This financed an increase in federal civilian expenditure (as here defined) of $15 billion and an increase in federal grants of $8½ billion. Meanwhile, state and local revenues from their own sources increased by $44 billion, partly reflecting economic growth but also the consequence of repeated tax rate increases and new tax adoptions.[67] With the increase in federal grants, this financed an increase in state-local expenditure of nearly $53 billion, an increase more than three times as great as that in ordinary federal civilian expenditure.

This, of course, is not a new situation. However, this inherent fiscal paradox, always implicit in the system, has become more apparent recently. It is now clear to all who care to see that a normal peacetime full employment situation provides the opportunity at the federal level for what Walter Heller has called "fiscal dividends"—buoyant federal revenues permit, indeed require, some combination of tax cuts and spending increases. Meanwhile, at the state and local level, governments struggle to find acceptable revenue devices, which means new and higher taxes, to match rapidly expanding demand for their services.

Third, recognition of this has resulted quite recently in a number of major new federal (and in some places, state government) programs involving substantial grants-in-aid and also direct federal assumption of responsibility, notably in the education, health, and (broadly defined to include anti-poverty programs) welfare fields. This can be viewed as a belated recognition of the national interest in the resolution of urban problems, with the increase in the federal role likely to level off at

[66] Data adapted from U.S. Bureau of the Census, *Governmental Finances in 1964–65.* Ordinary federal civilian expenditures, as defined here, exclude expenditures for these functions: national defense and international relations, space research and technology, farm price support, interest, and veterans services and benefits. All data in the comparison in this passage exclude social insurance operations.

[67] I estimate that effective tax rates rose, on the average, about 40 per cent, on the assumption that state-local revenues at constant effective tax rates rise about as fast as does gross national product.

a new higher plateau, much as it did between the late 1930's and the late 1950's. Or it can be viewed as no more than the beginning of a continuously expanding federal role. The historical precedents suggest the former interpretation, but there clearly has been change in intergovernmental relations in the past few years.

Intergovernmental Mechanisms

The available mechanisms for altering intergovernmental fiscal roles to enhance the output of urban services (accepting here the conventional undernourishment hypothesis) include fund transfers via conditional or unconditional grants or tax sharing, tax credit arrangements, and shifts in functional responsibilities to the higher levels of government. The potential and appropriateness of the latter, both at the federal and state levels, should not be overlooked.

In reality, both expansion of conditional grants and transfer of functional responsibilities to the federal government have occurred in the past thirty years, often provided for within a single Act of Congress. For example, the Social Security Act itself provided grants to the states for public assistance and, in addition, established a federally administered system of social insurance which was and is a partial substitute for public assistance. Most major pieces of health legislation in recent years have both enriched grants to the states and expanded the direct federal role, especially in medical research. Most of the education legislation similarly provides both grants to the states and federal loans and scholarships for individual students. The anti-poverty legislation and the Medicare legislation contain similar mixtures of grants and direct federal action.

Typically, expansion of the direct federal role involves federal performance of activities not previously performed by *any* level of government, rather than substitution of federal action for actual state-local action. But this is not necessarily the only possible arrangement. In fact, the model used here suggests that the federal government ultimately should handle all income-support programs through expanded social insurance arrangements (including federalization of unemployment insurance, in part to reduce interstate competition to lower payroll tax rates) and probably through the proposed negative income tax as well.

This would substitute for existing federally aided state and local income-support activities. As an intermediate goal, the model suggests immediate state government assumption of the entire public assistance function in the small number of very large urban states (like New York and California) where the function remains largely a local government one and consumes large chunks of locally raised revenues. In addition, there is real scope for direct state government performance, in the absence of metropolitan-area-wide governmental machinery, of allocation branch services with important local spillovers. This is especially appropriate in states that are almost entirely urban.

Distributional considerations and obvious spillovers clearly justify many federal conditional grants, both actual and proposed. But once such cases are accommodated, it is hard to argue for much more in the form of federal conditional grants in this model. Local fiscal strains provide insufficient justification for federal action, which would override local consumer preference in favor of *inaction* and thereby move away from optimality. This lack of justification applies to a fair number of federal grant programs, it would seem, including urban renewal, open-space grants for local parks,[68] and perhaps even mass transportation.

Similar considerations should govern state government grant policy. At this level, much of the discussion traditionally has concerned the question of "anti-urban bias" in state grant provisions and formulas. No doubt there has been some of this, related to malapportionment of legislatures. But some of the apparent rural bias is inherent in the nature of the aided functions. For example, if states provide large highway grants, a substantial share is likely to go to the rural areas where the road mileage is; there is no discrimination if the distribution of combined direct state expenditure and state grants conforms reasonably closely with the distribution of highway use, as it does in many states.[69]

The major problem in state aids may be in connection with large-city school systems. In most large central cities, the combination of relatively few public school children (that is, relative to suburbs) and relatively high business property values produces low state school aid, under apparently equitable state aid programs. But the equity is only apparent. The underlying assumption is that the cost of providing a given quality of education is uniform statewide. If it is not—if the provision of equivalent-quality education in the slum schools is as costly as is frequently alleged—then the conventional state aid formula is discriminatory.

Any number of variants are conceivable, providing for more or less

[68] See Henry M. Levin, "Estimating the Municipal Demand for Public Recreational Land" (Brookings, 1966, mimeo.).

[69] In New York, for example; see Mark A. Haskell, "Highway Finance Policy in New York State and New York City," in *Financing Government in New York City.*

unconditional (or at least very broad-purpose) federal grants to the states. The starting point for contemporary discussion of this type of device is the Heller-Pechman proposal.[70] The principal feature of this plan proposes per capita grants to the states. The plan would distribute a total which is equal to a specified fraction of the federal individual income tax base, a base which increases rapidly as the economy expands. This proposal would impose few limitations on the uses to which the states could put the new funds. Some proposed variants would restrict the use to health, education, and welfare purposes; this is not terribly restrictive, since expenditures for these functions financed from state and local taxes now account for at least 60 per cent of total tax-financed state-local expenditure.

Essentially, the case for unconditional grants rests on the fiscal imbalance argument, pure and simple: the need to transfer rapidly growing federal revenues to subnational governments. Externalities and distributive considerations provide support only for specially tailored federal action in particular functional fields. But general-purpose grants do afford one advantage, even within this model. If there is a federal interest, on the basis of externalities and distributive considerations, in a wide range of local activities, and if the differential degrees of federal interests are very hard to calculate or determine with any precision, then general-purpose grants are appropriate, to economize on decision-making in an atmosphere of indeterminacy.[71]

However, the major arguments for a Heller-Pechman type of plan relate to magnitude and simplicity. If the fiscal imbalance is of major proportions, as seems likely, it is important to develop a mechanism which will transfer large and growing volumes of federal funds and will do so with some assurance. The Heller-Pechman plan has this capability, since the funds provided will rise rapidly and automatically with economic growth. If the total distribution were set at a fixed percentage of the individual income tax base, it would come close to doubling in the next decade, without further action by Congress.

Another part of the argument is that such a scheme is a necessary supplement to expansion of federal conditional grants, since these are not likely to be sufficient to overcome the fiscal imbalance. If condi-

---

[70] See Walter W. Heller, *New Dimensions of Political Economy* (Harvard University Press, 1966); and Joseph A. Pechman, "Financing State and Local Government," in American Bankers Association, *Proceedings of a Symposium on Federal Taxation* (1965), pp. 71–84. See also Walter W. Heller, Richard Ruggles *et al., Revenue Sharing and the City* (The Johns Hopkins Press for Resources for the Future, 1968).

[71] This point was suggested by a comment by Harold Groves in *Public Finances: . . . Utilization*, p. 225.

tional grants are to be the solution, it is not enough to plead state and municipal poverty; one must have a plausible list of new and expanded grant programs, substantial in amount and related to activities in which it is conceivable that Congress may perceive a national interest.

Very large new and radically different federal programs usually have a lengthy gestation period, from initial public discussion to congressional adoption on more than a token scale. Therefore, the list of conditional grant alternatives to the Heller-Pechman route must include measures now in the public eye, if they are to have any effect in the next decade. The proponents of the unconditional grant approach argue that, aside from the poverty-linked services, there are no likely candidates for large new conditional grants. The one exception, perhaps, is in education. But even here, there is some evidence that problems connected with controls, segregation and the public-private school distinction may prevent the federal government from assuming a very much larger role.

The simplicity argument is partly based on the automatic features of the Heller-Pechman proposal. It also relates to the enormous complexity of subnational government in the United States. First, there are real differences in service needs, differences which should not be overridden by highly specified conditional grants which induce governments to take what are to them low-priority actions. Second, the distribution of responsibilities between the states and their local units so varies among the states that simple block grants to the states are far and away the easiest way to effect transfers of resources from the federal government to the state-local sector.

The opposing arguments have three main strands. First, there is the argument that per capita distributions are insufficiently equalizing among the states. To be sure, per capita grants are mildly equalizing (compared to, say, a revenue-sharing scheme in which the origin of the federal tax collections determines the distribution of the grants) and also are redistributive among individuals, if they substitute funds raised from progressive federal taxes for funds raised from more or less regressive state and local taxes. However, the equalizing effect is far less than might be achieved in other ways.

Second, opponents do not accept the essentially political judgment that the scope for large increases in conditional grants is limited. Therefore, they view the Heller-Pechman proposal as essentially competitive with conditional grants, not as a potential supplement.

Third, and perhaps most important, opponents view the simplicity of the unconditional grant and the flexibility it affords the recipient state governments, as major defects, not as virtues. There is no real way of assuring that the additional federal funds provided in this manner will in fact be used to buy additional public services, rather than as a substitute for funds otherwise raised from state and local taxation. There is no assurance that the new funds, even if stimulative in effect, will stimulate the right services, those in which the nation as a whole has the greatest interest, like education. Finally, there is no assurance that the states will share the funds with local governments which so often bear the actual responsibility for the provision of the important services. In sum, the flexibility provides much opportunity for the continued undernourishment of the high-priority urban public services.

But is this apprehension realistic? Are not most state governments, in this urban nation, subject to similar types of pressures, pressures which impel them to maintain (and increase) tax efforts, spend for high-priority purposes, and aid local governments? This is suggested by the uses that state governments have made of their own additional resources in recent years.

Between 1952 and 1965 (to continue the earlier comparison), state government general expenditures financed from their own revenues increased by $19 billion. The states disbursed 40 per cent of this increase ($7.6 billion) in the form of aid to local governments, effecting an increase in the intergovernmental expenditure share of total state budgets. As for the functional distribution, 46 per cent of the $19 billion increase went for education, 14 per cent for health and welfare purposes, 16 per cent for highways, and 24 per cent for all other purposes.[72] In other words, the political pressures within the states led them to utilize their additional revenues in ways which most observers would agree are generally consistent with national priorities, mainly for redistributive-type services. It hardly seems likely that these pressures will change greatly in the years ahead and permit the states to "shortchange" local governments or spend any revenues from unconditional grants on circuses rather than schools.

A final type of intergovernmental mechanism consists of tax credits, that is, credits against specified federal tax liabilities for all or part of specified state (and/or local) tax liabilities.[73] Federal tax credits have existed for forty years in the case of the estate tax and for thirty years in the case of the unemployment insurance payroll tax. The new thing in recent proposals, notably that of the Advisory Commission on Intergovernmental Relations,[74] is that they apply to a form of state taxation

[72] Data adapted from the *Compendium of State Government Finances* for 1952 and 1965.

[73] The standard work is James A. Maxwell, *Tax Credits and Intergovernmental Fiscal Relations* (Brookings, 1962).

[74] In *Federal-State Coordination of Personal Income Taxes.*

470

which, unlike the existing tax credits, is felt by large numbers of individuals—the state income tax. The Advisory Commission proposal is explicitly designed to encourage the states to utilize the individual income tax much more heavily. In two-thirds of the states the income tax is not effectively exploited at present. It is the only major type of tax not used heavily by the state-local sector at present (in the majority of states), and it has various advantages over other types of state-local taxes, notably its lack of regressivity and its high revenue growth potential.

The tax credit proposal makes a good deal of sense if the main impediment to wider state use of the income tax is the fear of interstate competition for economic development: by lowering the net cost to taxpayers, the tax credit will reduce the absolute size of the disincentive feature (although states with high income tax rates will remain in the same *relative* position, short of a 100 per cent tax credit). But if the real reason for reluctance to use the income tax is simply a difference in values among different electorates—a preference for less income redistribution in some states—then the tax credit is an imperfect device for enforcing national uniformity in income redistribution by means of taxation.

In any event, this, like most other tax credit proposals, is concerned more for the "quality" of tax systems than it is for increasing the total output of public services. Its contribution to the latter goal inevitably will be a modest one, in comparison with the approaches discussed previously.

In summary, the analysis here suggests the following as the appropriate courses of federal action, to move toward the model multilevel system of public finance in metropolitan areas (presented more or less in order of the author's priorities):

1. Federal assumption of direct responsibility for all income-support programs.
2. Greatly increased federal financing, presumably via conditional grants-in-aid, of other public programs linked to poverty, programs which redistribute income in kind, such as health and hospital services, social services to children and families and special educational services for disadvantaged children.
3. Expansion of other federal conditional aids *only* to the relatively minor extent that real and substantial interstate and interregional spillovers are involved.
4. A major federal program of general-purpose grants to the states.
5. Some type of federal credit for state (and local) income tax payments.

METROPOLITAN CHANGE AND FISCAL INSTITUTIONS

The model multilevel system utilized for this paper can accommodate a fair amount of urban growth and change. That is, its prescriptions are likely to be as valid (or invalid) a decade hence as they are today. An ideal system may be constant over time, but actual fiscal institutions are not. What is the likely effect of urban growth and change on fiscal institutions? Or putting it another way, in the light of expected environmental changes, are the policy prescriptions discussed above likely to be more or less readily acceptable than they are now?

The most important environmental changes can be summarized in two old bromides. First, the country is becoming more metropolitan in the senses that (a) more of the total population lives in metropolitan areas and (b) more of the metropolitan area population lives beyond the central cities and therefore is likely to be accommodated by a fragmented governmental structure. Second, individual metropolitan areas are becoming more alike, in economic mix, income levels, population composition, and cultural amenity.

These changes together suggest that institutional changes effected in one area are likely to be imitated or replicated in other areas more quickly than heretofore. If the states have the real capacity to be experimenters and innovators, as has been so often asserted by writers and so little demonstrated in practice, this should make for an exciting prospect in regard to forms of governmental organization and arrangements for the provision of public services, including possibly better utilization of user charge devices.

But these processes are also likely to bring about greater uniformity in state-local tax systems. Greater uniformity, in turn, is likely to increase local reluctance to make tax changes which will make the tax system of an individual area or jurisdiction appear to depart greatly from that found in competitive locations. If the state-local sector continues to expand relative to the national economy, with consequent revenue pressures at the local level, solutions in the form of shifting administrative and/or financial responsibilities to higher levels of government will become increasingly attractive. The sheer weight of an increasing metropolitan population would work in this direction, as well. As has been argued earlier, an increasing role for the federal government in regard to redistributive services is highly desirable, but an expansion of the federal role may be on balance inefficient with regard to a wide array of allocation branch services.

It is also a reasonable presumption that intrametropolitan spillovers will increase over the years. This is *not* a consequence of increasing intrametropolitan economic interdependence. Indeed, with the decentralization of economic activity within urban areas, economic interdependence is probably declining; the high point in interdependence was probably reached some years ago when most suburbs were largely dormitories for the central cities. The increase in spillovers is, instead, a result of technological change and linkages and rising aspirations with regard to public services—greater demand for air and water pollution control, for regional park and recreation facilities and for other services which can be provided only on an area-wide basis. This suggests an increasing reliance on area-wide governmental machinery, but more in the form of ad hoc regional machinery than of general-purpose metropolitan government.

Will intrametropolitan fiscal disparities increase? The controversy about whether in fact there is already an observable trend toward uniformity was noted earlier in this paper; the results of the controversy to date are inconclusive. But if in fact there is a shift in the responsibility for redistributive services to higher levels of government, it seems inevitable that disparities in resources relative to needs will decline, not increase. And a reduction in these disparities makes a Tiebout-type solution for the remaining (purely local) allocation branch activities both more feasible and more attractive.

As an aside, it should be noted that one of the more objectionable consequences of existing disparities may be a passing phenomenon in most areas, even in the absence of changes in intergovernmental fiscal relations. This phenomenon is "fiscal zoning," controlling land use to maximize tax base and minimize service costs. Fiscal zoning has its greatest attractions when jurisdictions are very small in geographic extent—when the location of a single large plant or shopping center or residential subdivision can make a real difference in the fiscal position of a small school district or other unit. However, as metropolitan areas grow outward, urbanization increasingly reaches into territory where there are few large jurisdictions rather than many small ones. For example, in the New York region, most of the 1946–60 development occurred in a 1,000-square-mile ring served by 520 units of government; in the current decade, the development is occurring in a 3,600-square-mile ring with 700 units; and in subsequent years development is likely to shift to a 2,000-square-mile outer ring with only 300 units. Fiscal zoning is likely to be considerably less attractive when the average unit covers 10 square miles than it is when the average unit covers less than a single square mile.

Finally, we must note the possible effects of some changes which are national, not merely metropolitan. Increasing population leads to various kinds of resource constraints. These are not absolute constraints, but constraints in terms of relative costs and alternative uses —notably constraints connected with land, water supply, and clean air. It is reasonable to anticipate that such constraints may increase the readiness to use sophisticated pricing mechanisms to ration the existing supply, to curb external diseconomies, and to guide new investment. Technological change has converted such mechanisms from far-out science-fiction notions to immediately practicable schemes, schemes consistent with the increasing perception of our world as "spaceship earth" rather than as one with an abundant exploitable frontier.

SELECTED READINGS

Advisory Commission on Intergovernmental Relations. *Federal-State Coordination of Personal Income Taxes.* Washington, 1965.

Brazer, Harvey E. "Some Fiscal Implications of Metropolitanism," in Benjamin Chinitz (ed.), *City and Suburb: The Economics of Metropolitan Growth.* Englewood Cliffs, N.J.: Prentice-Hall, 1964.

―――. "The Value of Industrial Property as a Subject of Taxation," *Canadian Public Administration,* Vol. 55, June 1961.

Break, George F. *Intergovernmental Fiscal Relations in the United States.* Washington: The Brookings Institution, 1967.

Buchanan, James M. "Federalism and Fiscal Equity," *American Economic Review,* Vol. 40, September 1950.

―――. "The Economics of Earmarked Taxes," *Journal of Political Economy,* Vol. 71, October 1963.

Burkhead, Jesse. "Uniformity in Governmental Expenditures and Resources in a Metropolitan Area," *National Tax Journal,* Vol. 14, December 1961.

Campbell, Alan K. "Taxes and Industrial Location in the New York Metropolitan Region," *National Tax Journal,* Vol. 11, September 1958.

Davies, David. "Financing Urban Functions and Services," *Law and Contemporary Problems,* Vol. 30, Winter 1965.

Due, John F. "Studies of State-Local Tax Influences on Location of Industry," *National Tax Journal,* Vol. 14, June 1961.

Fitch, Lyle C. "Metropolitan Fiscal Problems," in Benjamin Chinitz (ed.), *City and Suburb: The Economics of Metropolitan Growth.* Englewood Cliffs, N.J.: Prentice-Hall, 1964.

Gillespie, W. Irwin. "Effect of Public Expenditures on the Distribution of Income," in Richard A. Musgrave (ed.), *Essays in Fiscal Federalism.* Washington: The Brookings Institution, 1965.

Margolis, Julius. "Metropolitan Finance Problems: Territories, Functions and Growth," in Universities—National Bureau of Economic Research, *Public Finances: Needs, Sources and Utilization.* Princeton: Princeton University Press, 1961.

Musgrave, Richard A. "Approaches to a Fiscal Theory of Political Federalism," in Universities—National Bureau of Economic Research, *Public Finances: Needs, Sources and Utilization.* Princeton: Princeton University Press, 1961.

Mushkin, Selma J. "Intergovernmental Aspects of Local Expenditure Decisions," in Howard G. Schaller (ed.), *Public Expenditure Decisions in the Urban Community.* Washington: Resources for the Future, 1963.

――― and Robert F. Adams. "Emerging Patterns of Federalism," *National Tax Journal,* Vol. 19 (September 1966).

475

Netzer, Dick. *Economics of the Property Tax*. Washington: The Brookings Institution, 1966.

New York University, Graduate School of Public Administration. *Financing Government in New York City*. Final Research Report to the Temporary Commission on City Finances, City of New York. New York, 1966.

Rafuse, Robert W., Jr. "Cyclical Behavior of State-Local Finances," in Richard A. Musgrave (ed.), *Essays in Fiscal Federalism*. Washington: The Brookings Institution, 1965.

Tiebout, Charles M. "An Economic Theory of Fiscal Decentralization," in Universities—National Bureau of Economic Research, *Public Finances: Needs, Sources and Utilization*. Princeton: Princeton University Press, 1961.

———. "A Pure Theory of Local Expenditure," *Journal of Political Economy*, Vol. 64, October 1956.

Vickrey, William. "General and Specific Financing of Urban Services," in Howard G. Schaller (ed.), *Public Expenditure Decisions in the Urban Community*. Washington: Resources for the Future, 1963.

*Werner Z. Hirsch**

THE SUPPLY OF URBAN PUBLIC SERVICES

How urban public services are rendered, and by whom, is a matter of tradition, sometimes almost of mythology, and not necessarily of rational planning.

Government provides urbanites with tangible and intangible services. The former, being more visible, have traditionally occupied our main interest. Direct government participation in rendering tangible services involves building and operating public facilities, requiring decisions of major consequence. Among the investment decisions are what plant to build; how, where, and when to build it; and how to finance it. Among the operating decisions are what quantity and quality of services to render; how, where, when, and for whom they should be rendered; and what, if any, charges to make for rendering them.

While this paper will be concerned primarily with tangible public services, the existence and importance of such intangible services as planning, zoning, and judication should not be underestimated.

My inquiry into the supply side of urban public services will look upon services as resource-using sets of activities (often rendered by a government department) whose objective is to satisfy urbanites' wants and thus enhance their welfare. In an affluent urban America, both pecuniary and non-pecuniary benefits of government services must be considered. The latter relate to cultural and artistic activities, as well as to aesthetic values of natural and man-made (e.g., architectural) beauty. Although, as economists, we are more comfortable dealing with the measurable pecuniary benefits, the prevalence of non-pecuniary benefits must be recognized.

In this paper we will begin with a detailed exploration of urban public service production, emphasizing measurement problems. This will lead directly into a discussion of urban public service production functions, together with some empirical examples. Next, urban public service costs and cost functions will be presented, followed by an investigation of scale economies and the broader issue of urban government consolidation. Thereafter, the supply of urban public services

* Professor of Economics and Director of the Institute of Government and Public Affairs, University of California, Los Angeles.

The author would like to acknowledge helpful criticism given by Eugene J. Devine, Morton Marcus, and David Shapiro. Needless to say that all are accorded full discharge of responsibility.

477

will be investigated, both in relation to the nature of the supply function, the question of who should supply urbanites with services, and how services are distributed by income, race, and community. Finally, a concluding section will point to some topics that appear to be germane, but which, due to the limitations of space, cannot be considered here in detail.

URBAN PUBLIC SERVICE PRODUCTION AND ITS MEASUREMENT: QUANTITY AND QUALITY

Economists have long been concerned with output and its measurement, although only a few have turned to the public sector and even fewer to urban public services. Ridley and Simon, who undertook a major investigation of municipal activities measurements in the late thirties, provide a striking exception.[1] They suggested four possible measures: expenditures, effort, results, and performance. Performance is defined as "the effect of the application of effort."[2]

Lytton, in a pioneer study in the late fifties, attempted to measure the output of certain federal government departments, including the Post Office, the Veterans Administration, and the Internal Revenue Service.[3] His output measurements were mainly in terms of the number of items handled, e.g., papers and letters. As Lytton recognizes, these measures neglect quality dimensions. A study by the Bureau of the Budget went somewhat further in measuring the output of the Division of Disbursement of the Treasury Department, the Department of Insurance of the Veterans Administration, the Post Office Department, the Systems Maintenance Service of the Federal Aviation Agency, and the Bureau of Land Management of the Department of the Interior.[4]

All these studies chose relatively easy government services; part of their output had clearly defined physical characteristics that could be counted. Under the recent impetus of programming-planning-budgeting efforts on all three levels of government, new output measurements are being undertaken on a wide front and major new contributions can be expected.

[1] Clarence E. Ridley and Herbert A. Simon, *Measuring Municipal Activities* (Chicago: International City Managers Association, 1938).

[2] *Ibid.*, p. 2.

[3] Henry D. Lytton, "Recent Productivity Trends in the Federal Government: An Exploratory Study," *The Review of Economics and Statistics*, Vol. 41 (November 1959).

[4] Bureau of the Budget, *Measuring Productivity of Federal Government Organizations* (U.S. Government Printing Office, 1964).

478

Output

Urban public service outputs are those amounts, basically expressed in physical units, that result from, or exit from, the production process, which can be described as follows: Various input factors enter a pipeline in which production converts them into outputs. Since the process takes time, it is usually advisable to assign a time dimension to the production process. Output is measured in terms of the number of basic output units of specified quality characteristics per unit of time. There is another aspect in which time plays a role: Output can be produced at either a steady or a varying rate, which can affect the cost of production as well as the value of the output.

To measure the annual physical output of an urban public service of specified quality, we must first define the basic service unit and estimate the number of units produced per year.

We seem to be more comfortable defining basic output units of goods than of services. Goods are more easily defined because their output tends to have clearly identifiable physical characteristics and can be counted. It makes no difference whether the goods are sold privately or by a government.

A few services have a basic output unit with reasonably well-defined physical characteristics. The best example is water, where the basic output unit is a cubic foot, or acre-foot, of water delivered to the place of use. Perhaps next in ease comes refuse collection. A ton, cubic foot, or container of refuse, collected and disposed of, appears to be a useful basic physical service unit. Should this information not be available, we might fall back on the number of city blocks, households, or persons served. These are less satisfactory basic service units, but their use is often necessary in an analysis of urban public services.

Keeping in mind the nature of the production process, the basic service unit of street cleaning can be a mile or square yard of street cleaned; street lighting: a mile of street lit; police protection: a city block protected from crimes; fire protection: a city block protected from fire; urban transportation: the number of cars moved per minute in rush hour; hospital services: patient days in the hospital; and schools: the number of pupils completing a specified grade, and so on.

In ease of defining the basic service unit, water is likely to be at one end of the spectrum, and hospital services and education on the other. This is particularly so since the number of quality dimensions associated with the unit, and the complexity of these dimensions, tend to be smaller in water than in the other two.

But before considering quality characteristics, it should be noted that defining the basic service unit entails serious conceptual problems, and estimating the number of units produced in a given period is complicated by severe empirical difficulties. These difficulties, however, are not unique to urban public services, and therefore will not be discussed here.

Quality

A basic service unit tends to have numerous quality dimensions. For example, if we consider the person served by a library as the basic library service unit, quality dimensions would be determined by the library's selection and physical conditions of books, availability of books, reading room facilities, help for children in selecting books, reference service, location, and so on.

Quality identification and determination can involve at least three situations. In the simplest case, the service unit has a single quality characteristic. In such a case, the service would produce a single direct result, which, however, can assume different values. Perhaps closest to such a situation comes mosquito abatement, in which the sole purpose is to kill mosquitoes. Assuming that there are no indirect effects, different abatement procedures could produce different percentages of mosquito eradication.

A more common and more complex case involves not a single but numerous quality characteristics—with the possibility of direct and indirect results—each of which can assume different values.

It is important to remember that many government departments are vertically integrated: they produce as well as deliver a service. Under such circumstances, the quality dimensions of both product and delivery service must be considered. For example, a cubic foot of water has important inherent quality characteristics in terms of its physical, chemical, and biological attributes, including hardness, turbidity, temperature, color, taste, odor, mineral content, bacterial count, and so on. Quality characteristics of the delivery process include water pressure, reliable supply, rapid repair, and courteous and correct metering.

The situation is simpler in relation to refuse collection, where all quality issues center on the delivery process.

While quality specification is important in defining physical output, quality evaluation is needed to add up different qualities and types of output; quality evaluations must be made on decisions regarding how much of a certain public service of a given quality to produce (as well as what quality to produce).

The existence of different types and qualities of goods and services is commonplace. For example, the California orange industry grows millions of cases of oranges annually, including many varieties, mainly Valencia and Washington Navel oranges, in many different qualities. Likewise, the quality of fire protection differs among communities. And in our public schools a certain number of pupils finish grades 1 through 12 in a given year, but with differing educational achievement and performance.

For many purposes it is not meaningful to simply add Valencia and Washington Navel oranges, or to list total number of children in our schools. We would often want to separate first graders from high school graduates in measuring the output of schools. When we add up outputs of different types or qualities, we face an index number problem. Each group must be given some weights that hopefully reflect the worth of quality differences. While market prices evaluate relative quality differences, mainly of close substitutes, and admittedly not always perfectly, quality evaluation of public services must seek other methods. It is an extremely difficult undertaking.

Proxies

For most purposes the evaluation of output quality characteristics should be carried out in terms of satisfaction accruing to beneficiaries at the margin. However, we are very seldom in a position to obtain such estimates, or, for that matter, to obtain estimates of any output quality value or output quality. Consequently, we must rely on various makeshift arrangements, mainly in the form of proxies that more or less approximate what we would actually want to estimate.

A variety of proxies for output quality, output quality value, and total output value are presented below. Table 1 shows the proxies, by and large in descending order of their appropriateness.

For example, as shown under category I in the Table, a reasonably good output quality proxy would exist if one, or a few, output quality characteristics could be estimated. Other proxies are absolute, or relative, input quantities, as well as input performance indicators.[5] The process is similar for categories II and III, as shown in the Table.

A search of the literature has shown the following proxy applications: *Absolute input quantities* to approximate education output quality are: average enrollment per secondary school, number of former Woodrow Wilson fellows on faculty, number of American Council of Learned Society award winners, number of Guggenheim fellows on faculty, number of full-time faculty with doctorate, number of volumes in the library, and full-time enrollment in undergraduate education.

[5] I owe this distinction to Morton Marcus of the University of California at Los Angeles.

Input relationships that have been used as proxies for education quality are: annual library acquisitions per full-time graduate student based on a three-year period, members of instructional staff per 1,000 students, and per cent of full-time faculty with doctorate.[6]

An *input performance indicator* applied to education is the number or types of publications produced by university professors.[7]

TABLE 1.
PROXIES FOR OUTPUT QUALITY, OUTPUT QUALITY VALUE, TOTAL OUTPUT VALUE

I. Output quality
    a. Samples of one, or few, output quality characteristics.
    b. Absolute input quantities.
    c. Relative input quantities.
    d. Input performance indicators.

II. Output quality value
    a. Value of one, or few, output quality characteristics, valued in terms of benefits.
    b. Value of one, or few, output quality characteristics, valued in terms of cost.
    c. Output quality or any of its proxies (see I).
    d. Input costs.

III. Total output value
    a. Output value in terms of the benefits of one, or few, quality characteristics.
    b. Output value in terms of the cost of one, or few, quality characteristics.
    c. Output quality value or any of its proxies (see II).
    d. Output quality or any of its proxies (see I).
    e. Input costs.
    f. Physical output performance indicators.

Output quality proxies for fire protection are square miles covered per pumper company, square miles covered per ladder truck company, population covered per pumper company, population covered per ladder company, and average number of building fires per first due pumper company.[8]

Examples of proxies for *output value* can be seen in a few education studies, where one or more quality characteristics—such as incremental earnings due to education—have been used in benefit terms.[9] A some-

[6] For examples see F. Welch, *Measurement of the Quality of Schooling,* Investment in Human Capital Series, Paper No. 65:12, University of Chicago; Albert H. Bowker, "Quality and Quantity in Higher Education," *Journal of the American Statistical Association,* Vol. 60 (March 1965); and Allan M. Cartter, "Qualitative Aspects of Southern University Education," *The Southern Economic Journal,* Vol. 32, Part 2 (July 1965).

[7] Cartter, *op. cit.*

[8] Warren Y. Kimball, "Population Density and Fire Company Distribution," *Fire Journal* (March 1965).

[9] Werner Z. Hirsch and Elbert W. Segelhorst, "Incremental Income Benefits of Public Education," *The Review of Economics and Statistics,* Vol. 47 (November 1965).

what detailed example, using a few output quality proxies in terms of costs, is presented below.

Subcategories IIIa and b might also include the use of property value increases as well as the savings and costs of municipal services associated with urban renewal.[10]

Physical output indicators used in relation to education are performance or achievement test scores, school continuation rates, number of doctorates awarded, doctorates awarded per decade and/or full-time graduate enrollment per year, per cent of baccalaureates who later earn doctorates, ratio of college entrance to high school graduates, number of Woodrow Wilson fellows choosing school in question, and ability of states to retain their own high school graduates in their institutions of higher learning.[11]

Physical output proxies used in urban renewal evaluation are reduction in the following: crime, disease, fires, and juvenile delinquency.[12]

Number of subfunctions performed have been used as an *output measure* by Schmandt and Stephens, who found sixty-five subfunctions of police protection in Milwaukee, Wisconsin.[13]

In relation to hospital services, beds available per 1,000 population and beds used per 1,000 population have both constituted *output proxies*.[14]

Finally, *partial or total input costs* have frequently been used as proxy, for example, wages and salaries, and total current expenditures.[15]

An Example

In the following example output of a relatively simple urban public service is valued in terms of the costs of a small number of quality characteristics. The service selected—residential refuse collection—is simple because it is devoid of vertical integration, the basic service unit is reasonably easy to define and quantify, and the important quality dimensions appear to be relatively few in number.

The output value of refuse collection can be estimated with the aid of the following equation:

[10] James C. T. Mao, "Efficiency in Public Urban Renewal Expenditures Through Benefit-Cost Analysis," *Journal of American Institute of Planners*, Vol. 32 (March 1966).

[11] Welch, *op. cit.*, Bowker, *op. cit.*, Cartter, *op. cit.*

[12] Mao, *op. cit.*

[13] Henry J. Schmandt and G. Ross Stephens, "Measuring Municipal Output," *National Tax Journal*, Vol. 13 (December 1960).

[14] Martin S. Feldstein, "Hospital Bed Scarcity: An Analysis of the Effects of Interregional Differences," *Economica*, Vol. 32 (November 1965).

[15] Welch, *op. cit.*

$$O = \sum_{i=1}^{n} A_i Q_i, \tag{1}$$

where

A_i = number of basic service units of the ith quality per period of time, e.g., number of full refuse containers collected per year,

Q_i = dollar value of the ith quality per basic service unit,

O = value of total output.

We can consider the basic service unit to be a container of refuse collected, and there is relatively little difficulty in estimating the number of containers collected per year. Important quality dimensions are collection frequency, pickup location, and nature of pickup (i.e., whether separation of refuse into garbage and trash is required).

For simplicity's sake we will concern ourselves merely with two collection quality dimensions—pickup frequency and location. Specifically, we will assume that the choice is between one or two weekly pickups and curb versus rear-of-house pickup. This gives us four different refuse collection qualities:

1) Once-a-week curb collection,
2) Once-a-week rear-of-house collection,
3) Twice-a-week curb collection,
4) Twice-a-week rear-of-house-collection.

The cost of rendering these different qualities has been estimated with the aid of multiple regression equations for twenty-four St. Louis City–County municipalities in 1960, with the following results:

$$Q_1 = \$6.13,$$
$$Q_2 = \$12.33,$$
$$Q_3 = \$9.98,$$
$$Q_4 = \$16.28.$$

Thus, Q_3 is about one and one-half times as much as Q_1, while Q_2 is about twice as much as Q_1, and Q_4 is about two and one-half times as much as Q_1.

If, in a metropolitan area

$$A_1 = 5 \text{ million},$$
$$A_2 = 10 \text{ million},$$
$$A_3 = \text{zero},$$
$$A_4 = 2 \text{ million},$$

then the value of total output—*O*—turns out to be about $187 million per year.

URBAN PUBLIC SERVICE PRODUCTION FUNCTIONS

The question of what determines the output of urban public services has largely been neglected in the economic literature. Yet, an understanding of urban public service production functions is essential if we are to deal with efficiency problems, including the substitution of one input factor for another, and the presence of scale economies.

The Urban Public Service Function Concept

The long-run production function for an urban public service describes a multitude of choices open to the government unit responsible for rendering it. It represents the relationship between inputs of productive factors and outputs per unit of time, subject to some constraints. More specifically, it shows what each set of inputs at different scales of operation, with a given state of technology and service conditions, will produce by way of outputs. In more formal terms:

$$O = f(I,S,T), \tag{2}$$

where the following new notations are introduced:

I = input factors,

S = service conditions affecting input requirements,

T = state of technology.

However, frequently the dependent variable is a rather poor estimate of the value of total output. Instead, it is more a physical measure of output units of differing qualities. In such a case, we might want to place a quality variable on the right-hand side of the equation, so as to partial out effects of quality variation upon the dependent variables.

Thus, equation 2 can be rewritten

$$A = f(Q,I,S,T). \tag{3}$$

We will consider in detail some of the variables in equations (2) and (3) concentrating on the three new variables.

Basically, input factors are divided into labor (L), capital (K), and resources or materiel (R). Managerial talent could be included under (L), or be interpreted as human capital (K). Otherwise, a separate input category could be reserved for management.

There are some rather unusual aspects of labor and capital usages of governments. For example, the markets in which policemen, firemen, and teachers are purchased are generally not competitive. Furthermore, government tends to be the predominant, if not virtually the sole, purchaser of these skills.

Managerial talent in government is subject to some notable constraints, as well as incentives, bearing on the type of person and skill drawn from the general pool of labor. Among the constraints are those stipulated by law, the rough-and-tough of politics, and usually relatively low salaries. These constraints are counteracted by non-pecuniary incentives, e.g., political power, and the ability to move up the political ladder, possibly to national prominence.

Finally, the substitution possibilities, particularly between capital and labor, may be more restricted in government than in the private sector. These restrictions may stem not only from the nature of urban public services, but also from the severe difficulties of urban governments to obtain voter approval for capital equipment, especially on the local level.

In considering service conditions affecting input requirements, we can point to a variety of physical, human, financial, legal, and political factors that can make it easier, or more difficult, for governments to provide services of a specified quantity and/or quality. It is easier for a fire department to provide homes with a specified fire protection quality if they are close to a fire house or a fire hydrant (with all-year-round high water pressure), if they are built with bricks rather than wooden material, if they are not surrounded by dry brush, and so on.

Likewise, the ease of collecting refuse depends on density factors: The closer the various pickup locations are to each other, the less time it takes collection crews and trucks to move from location to location. The average distance to disposal sites also affects input requirements.

In relation to education, a child's native ability as well as his motivation and desire to learn can be looked upon as conditions affecting the ease or difficulty with which a given achievement can be accomplished. Population density is a factor, since it bears on the need to bus children to school. School crowding and teacher-pupil ratios, the availability of able, well-trained teachers, and so on, can also impede or advance the educational process. However, some of these variables tend to reflect quality differences and have been used for just such a purpose.

Finally, whenever technology changes, we end up with a new production function. However, we seldom seem to get technological changes that lead to sudden rapid changes in the production function of urban public services. Yet, police departments in cities are beginning to use helicopters, and fire departments of some urban counties have begun to acquire aerial tankers designed to help fight brush and forest fires. Refuse is increasingly disposed of by incinerators in place of landfills. And computers are beginning to play an increasingly important role in various police and fire departments, as well as in administrative offices.

In rendering urban public services, as in private production, three output concepts have analytic value: total, average, and marginal output or product.[16]

Theoretical Considerations

There are two major ways to provide estimates of urban public service production functions. One method relies on technical information supplied by engineers, based on their day-to-day operation or on specially designed experiments. The other method uses *ex post* statistical information—either cross-section or time-series data.

Production functions estimated from technical information benefits from the fact that the range of applicability is known, and results of technical progress can be incorporated with relative ease.[17] A further advantage is that production functions can be estimated from engineering data over a wider range than *ex post* statistical data would permit.

Engineering production functions, however, cannot incorporate managerial capacity as an input variable. As a result, they are mainly applicable to narrowly defined processes, e.g., the cleaning of a particular street, the activities of a refuse collection crew, the operation of a fire fighting unit, and so on. In short, engineering data are best used to estimate process functions—and if managerial (and entrepreneurial) capacity is relatively unimportant, to estimate plant production functions (e.g., a fire station, a school, or a refuse incinerator).

Engineering data must make some assumptions about managerial (and entrepreneurial) capability, since they may represent the most efficiently managed process of an urban service, or, perhaps, some normal or average condition. As a result, engineering production functions are useful for deriving process and plant cost functions used to estimate manpower, capital, and material requirements; but they are inappropriate for the study of scale economies of government units.[18] While they may increase returns in the process of a plant function, the increase may be more than offset by diseconomies of scale in administration.

[16] For a detailed definition and review of applications, see George J. Stigler, *The Theory of Price* (Macmillan Co., 1946), pp. 41–51.

[17] A. A. Walters, "Production and Cost Functions: An Econometric Survey," *Econometrica*, Vol. 31 (January–April 1963), p. 11.

[18] *Ibid.*, pp. 11–13.

The production function of a single city is distinct from that of all cities. For example, short-run managerial ability is virtually fixed in a given government unit, while it need not be for the industry (i.e., all government units). On the other hand, the supply of high school science teachers is not fixed for a given school district; it is, in the short run, more fixed for the industry (all the nation's high schools taken together). Furthermore, even if a specific government enjoys increasing returns to scale, the "industry of governments" might not do so because of limited input supplies, which can result in diseconomies.[19]

Important applications have been found for process engineering data in co-operation with linear programming models. In the linear programming model, technological opportunities of the government unit are expressed in terms of a finite number of activities, and fixed capacities of certain inputs are specified as technical limitations. Computing methods have been developed that permit determination of the most efficient combination of activities in light of specified prices.[20] It must be remembered that linear programming methods are applicable to short-run conditions only, and are not a description of existing conditions but a prescription of what governments ought to do with a specified objective in mind.[21]

Only in a very few instances have engineering data been used to derive urban public service production functions. However, there are a few exceptions. Isard and Coughlin made use of engineering data to estimate requirements for sewers, schools, roads, land, and so on, and their carrying capacity.[22] A sanitary engineering research project of the University of California in the early fifties relied on engineering data that were mainly obtained through time and motion studies. The study addressed itself not only to the question of refuse collection, but also to haul disposal.[23]

[19] *Ibid.*, p. 8.

[20] Harry Markowitz, "Industry-Wide, Multi-Industry, and Economy-Wide Process Analysis," in T. Barna (ed.), *The Structural Interdependence of the Economy* (John Wiley & Sons, 1956).

[21] Benjamin Stevens and Walter Isard, "An Interregional Linear Programming Model," *Journal of Regional Science*, Vol. 1 (Summer 1958); Benjamin Stevens and Robert Coughlin, "A Note on Inter-Areal Linear Programming for a Metropolitan Region," *Journal of Regional Science*, Vol. 1 (Spring 1959); Britton Harris, "Linear Programming and Projection of Land Use," P-J Paper No. 20, *Penn-Jersey Transportation Study: 1963;* and William Garrison and D. F. Marble, "Analysis of Highway Networks: A Linear Programming Formulation," *Highway Research Board-Proceedings*, No. 37 (1958), pp. 1–17.

[22] Walter Isard and Robert E. Coughlin, *Municipal Costs and Revenues Resulting from Community Growth* (Chandler-Davis Publishing Co., 1957).

[23] Sanitary Engineering Research Project, *Analysis of Refuse Collection and Sanitary Land Fill Disposal*, Technical Bulletin No. 8, Series 37 (Sanitary Engineering Research Project, University of California, Berkeley, 1952).

In addition to engineering information and models, *ex post* data can be subjected to statistical methods to estimate production functions. Whether we use cross-section or time-series data, four statistical methods can apply: (1) single equation least squares analysis, (2) covariance matrix method, (3) factor shares method, and (4) instrumental variables. The most commonly used method relies on single equation least squares. In the opinion of Walters, its attractive properties are "the simplicity of computations, the small standard errors of the coefficients, and the high level efficiency in predicting output for given inputs, and . . . if the purpose of the model is to predict output for given quantities of input, the single equation approach will be best." [24]

Indeed, most empirical production functions including those pertaining to urban public services, have been derived by using single equation least squares methods. Because of data difficulties, most urban public service functions have used cross-section data, either from the Census of Government or from special surveys. Unlike time-series data, cross-section data do not need to be deflated; deflation poses almost insurmountable problems. Still, data must often be adjusted and normalized. For example, even if cross-section data are used for labor force functions, labor inputs need to be standardized to allow for adjustment for differences in age, sex, race, and education composition.

Measuring capital is another serious problem. Again, it is less difficult if cross-section data are used. Most likely, utilization of capital varies less between different government units at any one moment of time than it does over a longer period of time. Nevertheless, estimates of cross-section capital stock need to be adjusted for the percentage of capacity employment. For example, Klein made such an adjustment by using the number of train hours as a measure of the input of capital services on the railways. [25]

The use of time-series data would result in further difficult methodological data problems. Standardizing labor input over time into "equivalent man-hours" is no mean task; likewise, the measurement of urban public services output over time, in terms of homogeneous physical units, is virtually impossible. Ways must be found to measure capital over time. The ideal measure of capital for a production function is the volume of capital services, but there is no way to measure capital services. [26] Net capital does not measure it well. To some extent, gross

---

[24] Walters, *op. cit.,* pp. 17–19.

[25] Lawrence R. Klein, *A Textbook of Econometrics* (Row, Peterson, 1953).

[26] Robert M. Solow, "Investment and Technical Progress," in Kenneth Arrow, *et al.* (eds.), *Proceedings, Stanford Symposium on Mathematical Methods in the Social Sciences, 1959* (Stanford University Press, 1960).

capital might be more appropriate, particularly if it could be adjusted to reflect such things as the decline in efficiency of a piece of equipment as it ages. But the capital stock of most governments is a conglomeration of equipment and buildings at different stages in their life cycle, and there seems to be no way to disentangle this bundle. Fortunately, capital plays a relatively small role in many urban public services, and errors from inappropriate handling of capital are therefore smaller than they would be in private industry.

Some Empirical Production Functions

Not all the variables mentioned earlier are needed in certain empirical production functions. For example, there are many short-run situations where technology and service conditions affecting input requirements remain unchanged; therefore the T and S variables can be dropped. Also, if cross-section data of government units in a reasonably homogeneous metropolitan area are analyzed, it is often possible to drop the input variable from the equation.

Let us now look at a few examples of statistical studies that attempt to estimate urban public service production functions. Kiesling has derived an education production function (primary and secondary) for school districts in New York State.[27] Data from the "Quality Measurement Project" of New York State's Department of Education pertain to ninety-seven participating school districts over a three-year period in the late fifties, and were applied to derive a single least squares multiple regression equation.

Kiesling's output proxy was average pupil achievement test score. Inputs were represented by per-pupil expenditures during the first year of the three-year study; quantity was represented by school district size, i.e., number of pupils in average daily attendance; and service conditions affecting input requirements were represented by an intelligence score, i.e., results of Lorge-Thorndike Intelligence Examination. This analysis was carried out for all pupils as well as for six separate socioeconomic groups in terms of the occupation of the family breadwinner; it was designed to reflect the child's motivation and desire to learn.[28]

The regression equation for grades four, five, and six, covering all pupils, was found to be

[27] Herbert J. Kiesling, "Measuring a Local Government Service: A Study of School Districts in New York State," The Review of Economics and Statistics (forthcoming).
[28] The socioeconomic groups were children of professional persons and proprietors; managers and officials; clerks and workers; skilled and semi-skilled workers; and unskilled workers and servants.

$$X_1 = -12.78 - \underline{1.269}X_2 + \underline{4.362}X_3 + \underline{0.174}X_4,[29] \qquad (4)$$

where

X_1 = average achievement test score,

X_2 = size, i.e., number of pupils in average daily attendance (natural logarithm),

X_3 = expenditure per pupil (natural logarithm),

X_4 = intelligence score.

All three net regression coefficients are statistically significant at a probability level of 0.05. The adjusted coefficient of multiple determination is 0.343, and is also statistically significant at a 0.05 probability level.[30]

Production functions for elementary education in Boston were estimated by Katzman.[31] He estimated two separate production functions: the first uses percentage of annual continuation rate as an output proxy, and the second uses reading score.

The two production functions are as follows:

$$O_6 = 43.8 + \underline{2.047}S_{16} - 0.047E_1 + 0.138E_2 + 0.049E_3 + \underline{0.190}E_4$$
$$- 0.006E_5 + 0.035E_6 + \underline{0.097}E_8; \qquad (5)$$

$$O_3 = 174.5 + 8.657S_{16} - \underline{0.889}E_1 + 2.291E_2 - 0.033E_3 - \underline{1.230}E_4$$
$$- 1.048E_5 - 0.654E_6 + \underline{0.393}E_8, \qquad (6)$$

where

O_6 = percentage annual continuation (in school) rate,

O_3 = median change in reading scores between second and sixth grades,

S_{16} = index of cultural advantage,

E_1 = percentage of school crowding,

E_2 = student–staff ratio,

E_3 = percentage of teachers with masters degree,

E_4 = percentage of teachers with one to ten years of experience,

E_5 = percentage of annual teacher turnover,

[29] Kiesling, *op. cit.*

[30] *Ibid.* By far the best statistical fit was obtained in relation to all students of grades 10 and 11, where the adjusted coefficient of multiple determination was 0.810.

[31] Martin T. Katzman, "Distribution and Production in a Big City Elementary School System," *Yale Economic Essays* (Spring 1968).

E_6 = percentage of teachers with permanent status,

E_8 = number of students in district.

In both cases statistically significant regression coefficients—at a probability level of 0.05—are underlined. The coefficients of multiple determination adjusted for the degree of freedom are 0.936 and 0.711, respectively, and are highly significant at a probability level of $0.05.$[32]

In summary, output of education in these studies has been approximated by achievement test scores, reading scores, and annual school continuation rates. In place of input factors, Kiesling used expenditure figures, while Katzman omitted information on this item. From a long list of variables reflecting service conditions that have an effect on input requirements, Kiesling was able to quantify two truly important ones: intelligence score, and occupation of breadwinner likely to affect a child's motivation and desire to learn. Katzman introduced six variables: E_1 through E_6—all of which reflect service conditions and, to some extent, quality characteristics of the school.

The state of technology was not explicitly introduced by either study. Both used the number of students as an additional variable, which is not the most appropriate way of measuring the scale of operation in relation to a production function.

A further statistical production study was carried out in relation to electricity generation, admittedly not an urban public service in the fullest sense. Dhrymes and Kurz used 1937–59 time-series data to estimate long-run electricity generation functions.[33]

URBAN PUBLIC SERVICE COSTS AND COST FUNCTIONS

Governments incur costs in building and operating facilities to supply urbanites with services. We will consider some relevant cost concepts before embarking on an examination of both theoretical and empirical cost functions. This will be followed by a probing into urban public expenditure function studies, which have been quite common in the postwar period.

Cost Concepts

The costs of urban public services are not conceptually different from the costs of activities in the private sector of the economy or in other divisions of government. They may be divided into four components based on the distinction between the nature of the resources

[32] *Ibid.,* pp. 52–53.
[33] Phoebus J. Dhrymes and Mordecai Kurz, "Technology and Scale in Electricity Generation," *Econometrica,* Vol. 32 (July 1964).

employed (operating and capital) and the nature of the payments made (direct and indirect) for a public service. A further useful distinction is between social and agency costs. Social costs entail all the resources required for the activity, in terms of the value in their best alternative use. But they may not equal the costs borne by the urban government that provides the service. The actual payments made by governments to secure the services of resources, and the value of services rendered by resources owned by governments for the production of current agency services, will be called agency costs. Agency payments to labor, and the vendors of materials and services, usually appear in the budget of the agency. To the extent that such resources are used in the production of current services, they are assignable to the current year's costs; if such resources are capital goods (for use in future years), they must be prorated. In current production, a government agency employs goods secured by payments both in the present period and in preceding periods. Where no payment is made for the use of current services, as in capital utilization of a building constructed in a previous year, they are referred to as indirect agency costs; they represent the value of resources (the building's services) in their next best alternative use in the year for which an attempt is being made to establish current agency costs.

As noted in the preceding discussion, agency costs and social costs may not be equal. Other parties, public and private, may incur costs that are not explicitly charged to the agency in question, nor considered in that agency's efficiency and financial deliberations. The same four-part division of costs is applicable. For example, the fire department requires services from the police department in controlling traffic and crowds around a major disaster scene. The police department costs are direct operating costs, but are not part of the fire department's costs. In its inspection and prevention program, the fire department may require certain types of fire extinguishers installed in factories and offices. The owners of these facilities incur direct capital costs when they install the extinguishers. The sprinkler systems of major buildings are part of the capital costs that private parties incur to meet fire department standards, and the services of such systems may be imputed annually as part of the total social cost of fire protection in the community. Fire drills detain workers from engaging in other productive exercises and may be considered as indirect operating costs generated, but not incurred, by the fire department.

In examining the social costs of an urban public service, we can also distinguish between technological and pecuniary externalities. The first entail actions by one unit, in this case an urban government agency, that affect the physical outputs other units are able to derive from their physical inputs. An example is public education, where the efforts of schools result in a more productive labor force for all firms in the private sector. The labor input is changed and with the same quantities of other productive factors, the firms are able to produce greater quantities or qualities of outputs. A pecuniary externality does not affect technical productive relationships, but rather raises or lowers the prices other units pay for certain goods and services. The residents and firms in a city with high-quality fire protection pay lower fire insurance premiums. It would be more costly for each party to provide this high quality service himself than it is when the economies of scale are realized through community service; hence, the costs of fire protection and insurance are lower for each unit.

This issue can also be illustrated in relation to the costs of urban crime. Crime can reduce society's income and wealth in four ways involving technical externalities:

1. Destruction of property.
2. Loss of victim's earnings through death and injury, i.e., decline in net human capital.
3. Earnings which criminals could have earned in a legitimate pursuit instead of pursuing a criminal career or being incarcerated.
4. Costs of crime prevention and mitigation.

While these are true societal losses due to crime, they can bother some citizens and government officials less than the pecuniary externalities, i.e., the involuntary transfers from victim to criminal. These transfers often are quite large, and can hurt financially, physically, and mentally. If those who are hurt are powerful—e.g., in Los Angeles, if they are rich residents of Beverly Hills, Bel Air, Pasadena, or other such communities, as against poor residents of Watts—public remedies might result that incur marginal costs far exceeding the social benefits derived. Thus, the results may be inefficient, yet change the distributional pattern.

We should also note that other standard cost concepts are applicable to urban government services. The distinction between fixed and variable costs, while applicable, is likely to be of less consequence in empirical efforts, since many government services are highly labor intensive; hence, variable costs tend to play a larger part than fixed costs in the total cost picture.

Cost Function Concepts

In developing urban public service cost functions, the focus here will be with an agency's costs, not with social costs of their activities. In line with urban public service production function 3, corresponding agency average unit cost functions can be defined. Long-run average unit cost of a given service is affected by the service quality, quantity, prices of factor inputs, service affecting input requirements, and state of technology. In formal terms:

$$AUC = f(Q,A,I,F,S,T),\qquad(7)$$

where

$$AUC = \text{average unit cost, and}$$

$$f = \text{input factor prices.}$$

Since input factors were discussed earlier, and some manpower problems will be discussed in the supply section, discussion here can be brief. Because urban services are labor intensive, salaries and wages tend to overshadow all other factor prices. Wages usually tend to vary over time, as well as between regions within the United States. However, major differences within any one given metropolitan area would not be expected. Important differences, if any, would tend to be reflected to a major extent in manpower quality.

Some Empirical Cost Functions

Estimation of urban public service cost functions is made difficult by conceptual as well as data problems. We will only cite a few of the conceptual problems: for example, in regard to average unit cost, we must know costs of both inputs (which must be totaled up) and output (as denominator). For those services for which either input cost or outputs are hard to define, great difficulties are encountered in defining the dependent variable.

On the other hand, independent variables present a difficulty in separation: Should they be part of a cost function or a demand function? For example, in the cases of both police and fire protection, the value of the property to be protected has a direct bearing on the cost of the service. At the same time, property values also reflect an ability to pay for the service or, at least, to demand it.

Furthermore, as will be discussed below, public officials have many reasons for not operating along the lowest unit cost function. Matching grants, preservation of positions, and inertia—among other considerations—can encourage government officials to operate above minimum cost.

The empirical difficulties are no less numerous and grave, whether reliance is on Census of Government data or survey techniques. Separation between operating and capital costs is often impossible. One government finances the acquisition of certain equipment out of taxes, while another does so by floating bonds. Further, the issue of renting versus buying equipment and facilities introduces empirical difficulties. Even the same government might not be consistent over time.

As Phelps has pointed out, "Capital cost varies over time depending upon the effects of tightening credit conditions." [34] Information on the effects of these credit conditions is hard to come by.

Because of great conceptual and empirical difficulties, relatively few empirical urban cost studies have been carried out. A few examples will be presented.

Using 1960 cross-section data for twenty-four St. Louis City–County cities and municipalities, an attempt was made to derive a cost function of residential refuse collection.[35] A multiple regression equation with the following values was estimated:

$$X_1 = 6.16 + 0.000\,089X_2 - 0.000\,000\,000\,436X^2{}_2 + \underline{3.61X_3}$$
$$+ \underline{3.97X_4} - 0.000\,611X_5 - 1.87X_6 + \underline{3.43X_7}, \qquad (8)$$

where

X_1 = 1960 average annual residential refuse collection and disposal cost per pickup in dollars,

X_2 = number of pickup units, which appears to be a good proxy of the annual amount of refuse collected,

X_3 = weekly collection frequency,

X_4 = pickup location,

X_5 = pickup density,

X_6 = nature of contractual arrangements, and

X_7 = type of financing.

X_2 is a quantity proxy, X_3 and X_4 are quality variables, and the other three variables reflect service conditions affecting input requirements. Since we are dealing with a short-run cost function of a reasonably homogeneous metropolitan area in one year, there is no need to introduce either the state of technology or input factor prices as independent variables. The multiple correlation coefficient adjusted for degrees of freedom is 0.874. It is statistically significant at a probability level of 0.05, as are the underlined net regression coefficients.

[34] Charlotte DeMonte Phelps, "The Impact of Tightening Credit on Municipal Capital Expenditures in the United States," *Yale Economic Essays*, Vol. I (Fall, 1961).

[35] Werner Z. Hirsch, "Cost Functions of an Urban Government Service: Refuse Collection," *The Review of Economics and Statistics*, Vol. 47 (February 1965).

A second example pertains to sixty-four St. Louis City–County police departments for 1955–56, for which the following multiple regression equation was estimated:

$$X_1 = 3.14 - 0.000\,0103X_2 + 0.000\,000\,000\,00351X^2{}_2 + 0.000\,550X_3$$
$$+ 0.000\,00946X_4 + \underline{0.00315X_5} + \underline{0.00949X_6} - 0.000\,00212X_7$$
$$+ 0.000\,946X_8 + \underline{0.107X_9} + \underline{0.000\,219X_{10}}, \tag{9}$$

where

X_1 = per capita total expenditures for police protection,

X_2 = nighttime population,

X_3 = total miles of streets,

X_4 = nighttime population density per square mile,

X_5 = per cent of non-white population,

X_6 = per cent of nighttime population under twenty-five years of age,

X_7 = combined receipts of wholesale, retail, and service establishments,

X_8 = number of wholesale, retail, and service establishments,

X_9 = index of scope and quality of police protection,

X_{10} = average per capita assessed valuation of real property.

In this equation service quantity proxies are X_2 and X_3; X_9 is a quality proxy, and the other variables reflect the service conditions affecting input requirements. The coefficient of multiple determination adjusted for degrees of freedom is 0.90, which is statistically significant at a probability level of 0.05, as are the underlined net regression coefficients.

The following average unit cost function was estimated for fire protection of the St. Louis City–County area in 1955–56:

$$X_1 = 0.63 - 0.000\,0235X_2 + \underline{0.000\,000\,000\,109X^2{}_2} - \underline{0.0866X_3}$$
$$+ 0.000\,00170X_4 - 0.00206X_5 - \underline{0.000\,0108X_7}$$
$$+ \underline{1.889X_9} + \underline{0.00231X_{10}}, \tag{10}$$

where the following are notations not found in equation 9:

X_1 = per capita total current expenditures plus that service for fire protection,

X_3 = area in square miles,

X_4 = density of dwelling units per square mile,

X_5 = 1950–55 nighttime population increases,

X_9 = index of scope and quality of fire protection.

In this equation, X_2 is a proxy variable for quantity and X_9 for quality. X_3, and X_4, and X_5 are indicative of service conditions affecting input requirements; in a sense this holds true for X_7 and X_{10}, which also reflect quantity, however. The coefficient of multiple determination adjusted for degrees of freedom was 0.82 and is statistically significant at a probability level of 0.05, as were the underlined net regression coefficients.

There are other public service cost functions, but many of them either do not concern urban public services or they pertain to expenditure functions, which are discussed below. Among the bona fide cost studies, some others will be referred to when scale economies are examined.

Empirical Expenditure Determinant Studies

During the last thirty years, a substantial number of studies have been undertaken that were designed to determine factors affecting expenditures of state and local governments in general, and municipal governments in particular. Some have concerned themselves with general spending, while others analyzed specific services.

Colm's study, one of the earliest, used scatter diagrams to find the impact on different categories of state-local spending of income, urbanization, industrialization, and population density.[36] Using cross-section data for 1942, Fabricant found current expenditures of local governments strongly related to population density, urbanization, and income. Significant correlations were also found when these three variables were related to school, highway, public welfare, health and hospital, police, fire protection, and general control expenditures.[37] Fisher repeated the Fabricant analysis with 1957 data, and found that the same variables no longer accounted for as much of the variation in spending.[38]

Sacks and Harris modified the Fabricant approach by adding federal and state aid, respectively, as additional independent variables. They found that level of income and aid payments explained a large part of

[36] Gerhard Colm, *et al.*, "Public Expenditures and Economic Structure," *Social Research,* Vol. 3 (February 1936).

[37] Solomon Fabricant, *The Trend of Government Activity in the United States Since 1900* (National Bureau of Economic Research, 1952).

[38] Glenn W. Fisher, "Determinants of State and Local Government Expenditures: A Preliminary Analysis," *National Tax Journal,* Vol. 14 (December 1961).

the variation in spending, leaving the other variables insignificant; this was particularly true for the more recent data.[39]

In 1964, Fisher categorized the determinants under three major headings: (1) economic variables—per cent of families with less than $2,000 income, and yield of representative tax system as per cent of U.S. average; (2) demographic variables—population density, urbanization, per cent population increase; (3) and sociopolitical variables— index of two-party competition, per cent of population over twenty-five years of age with less than five years schooling.[40]

Finally, Kurnow, using the same data, showed that a joint rather than an additive regression model is more appropriate for the study of expenditure determinants.[41]

In addition, there are a number of more specialized studies, mainly concerned with education.[42]

The most comprehensive nationwide study on city expenditures was undertaken by Brazer who employed five different samples of 1951 data; the large sample contained 462 cities, 3 smaller statewide groups, and a smaller number of very large cities, including the overlying government unit. The analysis was made not only for total general operating expenses, but also for police protection, fire protection, highways, recreation, sanitation, general control, and others. Among the independent variables tested were population density, median family income, intergovernmental revenues; population size, population growth rate, and manufacturing, including trades and services employment. It was primarily the first three that were found to be statistically significant.[43]

Scott and Feder made a multiple regression analysis of per capita municipal expenditures of 196 California cities with over 25,000

[39] Seymour Sacks and Robert Harris, "Determinants of State-Local Government Expenditures and Intergovernmental Flows of Funds," *National Tax Journal,* Vol. 17 (March 1964).

[40] Glenn W. Fisher, "Interstate Variation in State and Local Government Expenditure," *National Tax Journal,* Vol. 17 (March 1964).

[41] Ernest Kurnow, "Determinants of State and Local Expenditures Re-examined," *National Tax Journal,* Vol. 16 (September 1963).

[42] For example, see Edward F. Renshaw, "A Note on the Expenditure Effect of State Aid to Education," *The Journal of Political Economy,* Vol. 68 (April 1960); Werner Z. Hirsch, "Determinants of Public Education Expenditures," *National Tax Journal,* Vol. 13 (March 1960); Sherman Shapiro, "Some Socioeconomic Determinants of Expenditures for Education: Southern and Other States Compared," *Comparative Education Review,* Vol. 6 (October 1962); and Jerry Miner, *Social and Economic Factors in Spending for Public Education* (Syracuse University Press, 1963).

[43] Harvey E. Brazer, *City Expenditures in the United States,* Occasional Paper 66 (National Bureau of Economic Research, 1959).

population. As independent variables, they used per capita property valuation, per capita retail sales, per cent population increase, and median number of occupants in dwelling units. The first two variables, basically reflecting fiscal capacity, accounted for almost all the explained variations in expenditures.[44]

More recently, Pidot undertook a study of 80 Standard Metropolitan Statistical Areas. He found that government expenditures in core areas were significantly related to the level of personal income, size and commercial nature of property base, amount of state aid, population size and density, presence of renter-occupied housing, and, for capital projects, population growth.[45] The study is enriched by a principal component analysis which rests on the assumption that observed data are the work of a small group of independent underlying factors. It identified the following components: degree of metropolitization, wealth level, size, commercial-industrial nature of the economy, presence of old people, receipt of redistributive state aid, and receipt of federal monies.[46]

Finally, brief mention should be made of cross-section studies of governments within a particular metropolitan area. Wood has studied the New York region; Sacks and Hellmuth have studied the Cleveland region; and I have studied the St. Louis region.[47]

All these expenditure determinants studies have serious shortcomings, the single most important one being the absence of a rigorous, logical underlying theory. Expenditure functions are usually related to factors affecting cost as well as demand. In some cases, cost considerations are more strongly emphasized, and in others, demand considerations are more important. Examples of the latter are the Fabricant and Scott-Feder studies.

Local fiscal capacity, as well as federal and state subsidies, are perhaps the most important determinants of local expenditures. These two are the main sources of funds (and again, neither fits well into demand or cost theory). State and federal aid poses some interesting

[44] Stanley Scott and Edward Feder, *Factors Associated with Variations in Municipal Expenditure Levels* (Bureau of Public Administration, University of California, 1957).

[45] George B. Pidot, Jr., "The Public Finances of Metropolitan Government in the Metropolitan United States" (unpublished Ph.D. dissertation, Harvard University, 1966).

[46] *Ibid.*, p. 230.

[47] Robert C. Wood, *Fourteen Hundred Governments* (Harvard University Press, 1961); Seymour Sacks and William Hellmuth, *et al.*, *Financing Government in a Metropolitan Area, The Cleveland Experience* (Free Press, 1961); Werner Z. Hirsch, *Measuring Factors Affecting Expenditure Levels for Local Government Services* (Metropolitan St. Louis Survey, 1957 [mimeo]).

questions which these studies have not yet illuminated, i.e., whether federal and state subsidies are substitutes for or supplements to local sources.

Nevertheless, expenditure determinants studies, while not yielding bona fide cost functions, can advance our understanding of why expenditure levels differ among communities and among services. In some cases, predictions based on these studies can turn out to be reasonably correct.

SCALE ECONOMIES AND GOVERNMENT CONSOLIDATION

What happens to unit costs as governments grow or consolidate? Although this is only one consideration in the debate about the desirability of metropolitan consolidation and/or growth, it is of great interest to both decision-makers and the electorate.

We will first consider some of the theoretical issues concerning the existence or absence of scale economies in rendering urban government services. This will be followed by a few empirical examples together with a critical appraisal. Finally, the larger issue of metropolitan consolidation will be explored.

Some Theoretical Considerations

Our analysis and evaluation of the cost implications of growth or consolidation of urban governments will assume that services are rendered by local governments. We will rely on a quasi-dynamic model in which growth and consolidation can take the form of horizontal, circular, and vertical integration.

A horizontally integrated government controls a number of units all furnishing a single service (such as police protection), and a unified policy is pursued with regard to these units.

If a government unit (or plant) renders a number of services that complement one another, circularity (or complementarity) exists; City Hall is a good example. A circular, horizontally integrated government controls a number of units that furnish complementary services, and a unified policy is pursued with regard to these services and units.

A vertically integrated government controls a number of different operations in the production of ingredients which enter into rendering a service, and a unified policy is pursued. An example is electricity generation and distribution.[48]

In a small community, virtually all services tend to be centralized in a single plant, i.e., City Hall, which, for maximum efficiency, should be centrally located. As the community grows, a number of location-

---

[48] Clearly there can be different combinations of these three basic types.

oriented services will require additional plants. Among the first will be fire protection, which is strongly affected by the time-distance between fire station and property to be protected. Growth usually takes the form of more horizontally integrated service plants.

Consolidation can follow and permit control over more already existing units, that is, further horizontal integration.[49] However, with the exception of centralizing administrative offices, relatively few changes can be made in the short run with regard to school buildings, police stations, fire houses, libraries, sewage and water treatment plants, and so on. The consolidated government will tend to use much of the existing plant, some of which may already have over-capacity use. Only when replacements are built can plant size reflect the needs of the consolidated government; it will seldom operate under genuine long-run conditions. Instead, quasi-long-run conditions are usually encountered.

With these considerations in mind, let us speculate about the shape of quasi-long-run cost functions of some horizontally integrated services. For example, police protection in a small community will tend to face a short-run cost function until it reaches a size where an additional station is needed. Deductive reasoning suggests that this short-run cost function should have a flat-bottomed U shape. Its left-hand portion declines on the assumption that a community needs, on the average, one police officer per 1,000 residents to provide good police protection; around-the-clock service can thus be rendered by a department of no less than four full-time officers. Once these four men are effectively deployed, and serve up to 4,000 residents, the addition of officers will tend to change per capita costs relatively little until territory and distances increase substantially. The end of the flat-bottom will occur when there are some tens of thousands of inhabitants. Yet the police department may seldom operate in the rising expenditure phase, since location considerations produce diseconomies of scale and can lead to the opening of branch stations. Libraries, schools, and parks also have indivisible but highly adaptable fixed plants. The law of diminishing returns applies and leads to a U-shaped short-run cost function. Since all four service units are basically flexible, their average cost functions tend to have substantial flatness.[50]

[49] The following consolidation plants have received most attention: annexation by the core city, city-county consolidation, federation or borough plans, urban or metropolitan county plans, single or multipurpose metropolitan district plans.

[50] The characteristics of a fire house are slightly different in that some portion of the fixed plant, i.e., the fire fighting equipment, is divisible and adaptability is limited. A fire house extends its scale of operation by adding a fire engine and the number of firemen who operate it.

Assuming that services of equal quality are rendered regardless of the scale of operation; that plants are of about equal size, have about equal service functions, tend to be operated at about optimum capacity, and can be readily added or closed; and that factor prices are fixed; the long-run average unit cost function tends to be horizontal.[51] There is some evidence that these assumptions by and large tend to be met.

The conditions that help private industry to benefit from scale economies—lower factor costs, larger and more efficient plants, and induced circular and vertical integration—often do not appear to exist when local urban governments grow or consolidate. Cities and counties, except for labor, purchase a highly diversified array of factors; few of them are in large enough quantities to secure major price concessions. Unionization of public servants, however, can produce diseconomies. Also, the nature of local government services, particularly location consideration, tends to keep plants relatively small. Legal restrictions on salary levels of top officials and on permissible debt interfere with good administration and retard technological economies. At the same time, serious diseconomies can accompany a large local government that loses efficiency because of political patronage and administrative top-heaviness.

On a priori grounds, growing or consolidating urban governments can approximate conditions under which long-run cost functions for horizontally integrated services (which account for 80 to 85 per cent of total metropolitan area government expenditures) will be horizontal. Since, however, some plants (and the caliber of its officials) are of fixed size, the quasi-long-run cost functions will resemble a U with a flat bottom over a very wide range. Furthermore, since most horizontally integrated services incur relatively little overhead, the short-run and long-run functions will tend to approximate one another. They coincide in their flat-bottom portion. Net economies are responsible for a negative slope to the left of this area and net diseconomies for a positive slope to the right of it. The more units are horizontally integrated, the flatter the short-run function.

In a similar way, we could speculate about the shape of the cost functions of circularly integrated services, which seem to account for three to six per cent of total metropolitan area government expenditures. This has been done elsewhere,[52] and it was concluded that on a priori grounds, short-run average unit cost functions for such multi-purpose,

---

[51] Don Patinkin, "Multiple-Plant Firms, Cartels and Imperfect Competition," *Quarterly Journal of Economics,* Vol. 61 (February 1947).

[52] Werner Z. Hirsch, "Expenditure Implications of Metropolitan Growth and Consolidation," *The Review of Economics and Statistics,* Vol. 41 (August 1959).

single plant services could be expected to be U-shaped, with the trough in medium-sized communities.

A similar analysis of vertically integrated services concluded on a priori grounds that the quasi-long-run average unit cost function for water services and sewage services tends to decline until a very large scale of operation is reached.

Some Empirical Scale Economy Studies

To test hypotheses deduced in the previous section, we will examine an empirical study of the average unit cost of different-sized governments performing similar services. Specifically we will consider how average unit costs vary in relation to the size of senior high schools.

Riew analyzed 109 Wisconsin senior high schools using 1960–61 data (92 four-year and 17 three-year high schools).[53] Operating costs per pupil in average daily attendance were correlated with the number of pupils in average daily attendance as a scale measure. Three quality proxies were used—(1) average teacher salary, (2) number of credit units offered, and (3) number of courses taught by average teacher— and two growth variables—(1) growth in the number of pupils and (2) percentage growth in classrooms. A significant parabolic relationship between the pupil cost and enrollment was found to exist. The trough of the cost function was found to be at an enrollment level of 1,675 students. Riew attributed the economies of scale mainly to the fact that senior high schools require a much higher degree of specialization with regard to teaching staff and facilities than do primary schools.

Now let us turn from single plant operations to growth or consolidation which involves services controlled by a single government yet possibly carried out in a number of plants.[54] While it is difficult to develop empirically bona fide quasi-long-run average unit cost functions, those developed in case studies for police protection and refuse collection, discussed earlier, might be considered reasonable approximations.[55] Both of these cost studies used proxies in an attempt to introduce quality as independent variables. For both these horizontally integrated

[53] John Riew, "Economics of Scale in High School Operation," *The Review of Economics and Statistics,* Vol. 48 (August 1966).

[54] For such an analysis, ideally we would like to have time series data of government growth without consolidation, or of government consolidation without external growth. Unfortunately, such data are not available and researchers attempting to estimate quasi-long-run average unit cost functions have been forced to use cross-section data.

[55] Werner Z. Hirsch, *Measuring Factors . . . Services, op. cit.,* and "Cost Functions of an Urban Government Service: Refuse Collection," *The Review of Economics and Statistics,* Vol. 47 (February 1965).

services no significant scale economies were found for communities of 200 to 865,000 residents (and 200 to 225,000 pickup units) in the St. Louis city-county area in 1955–56 and 1960, respectively. Similar results were found for education, while fire protection showed some small economies of scale up to a nighttime population of about 110,000.

A study by Schmandt and Stephens can also be used to test hypotheses about the quasi-long-run average unit cost function of city police departments, whether they have one or more police stations. Schmandt and Stephens analyzed nineteen cities and villages of Milwaukee County, Wisconsin, and correlated per capita police protection expenditures in 1959 with service level and population; no significant scale economies were revealed.[56]

Kiesling checked for economies of scale in primary and secondary New York State schools. He found no economies of scale in school district performance and indeed had to fall back on geographical differences between school districts to avoid finding diseconomies.[57]

A distinctly different approach to the study of scale economies has been developed by Will,[58] whose approach relies on a set of "engineering specifications," which in some manner are related to service level, and service requirement.[59] Specifically, he starts by identifying relevant standard units of efforts for particular services. A unit of effort used for the measurement of any given service is some physical unit, or combination of inputs comprising a work unit, such as a street sweeper and its crew. Ideally, a measurable output of service can be associated with the effort unit, and the output can be stated in terms that permit it to be related to a need index. Once standard units of effort have been identified and described, their costs are estimated.

Professional expertise is also used to estimate service requirements in terms of standard units of effort. Will relies on the work of professional associations and students of public administration to identify the need determinants of urban services. The need indicators are then translated directly into standard service requirements through professional application of the rules established by experts. Finally, cost estimates are made for the total service requirements; these estimates can also be translated into per capita terms.

---

[56] Henry J. Schmandt and G. Ross Stephens, "Measuring Municipal Output," *National Tax Journal*, Vol. 8 (December 1960), p. 374. The partial correlation coefficient relating per capita expenditure and population size was 0.22 which is statistically insignificant for a sample size of 19.

[57] Kiesling, *op. cit.*

[58] Robert E. Will, "Scalar Economies and Urban Service Requirements," *Yale Economic Essays*, Vol. 5 (Spring 1965).

[59] *Ibid.*, p. 33.

Specifically, Will estimated annual per capita standard service requirements for fire protection, in dollars, for thirty-eight cities varying in size from 50,000 to one million. He found per capita standard service requirements for fire protection to vary from $23 to $72.[60] These dollar figures were regressed against city population with the conclusion that, "there are significant economies of scale associated with the provision of municipal fire protection services, at standard levels of service, for central cities ranging from 50,000 to nearly one million in population." [61] The statistically significant geometrical relationship was that of a hyperbola eventually becoming asymptotic to the horizontal axis. Major economies were realized up to a population of 300,000. From there on the economies of scale were barely in existence.

Will mentions some basic shortcomings of his method. "The major weakness discovered was that the most significant standards, those set by the National Board of Fire Underwriters for aggregate recommended service levels, had economies of scale already built into them." [62] Furthermore, the engineering standards used did not reflect the possibility of large cities suffering from top-heavy management, political patronage, and so on.

So far, we have been concerned with horizontally integrated services. Empirical tests of the quasi-long-run average unit cost functions of circularly integrated services hardly exist. However, the administration of school districts with 500 to 48,000 pupils in average daily attendance has been examined in one case study and a U-shaped cost function was discovered with its trough at an average daily attendance of about 44,000 pupils.[63]

Finally, we can point to a few empirical studies testing the hypothesis about the shape of the quasi-long-run average unit cost function of vertically integrated services. For example, Isard and Coughlin have produced operating cost data for 1953 for secondary treatment sewage plants in Massachusetts.[64] A correlation analysis of these data reveals a statistically significant negatively sloping unit cost function.

Nerlove has examined returns to scale in electricity supply, using public utility rather than governmental data. He correlated production costs with physical output and labor, capital, and fuel prices on a firm

[60] *Ibid.,* p. 43.
[61] *Ibid.,* p. 60.
[62] *Ibid.,* p. 59.
[63] Hirsch, *op. cit.,* pp. 239–40.
[64] Isard and Coughlin, *op. cit.,* p. 76.

basis. The coefficient of multiple determination for 145 privately owned utilities in 1955 was 0.93, and statistically significant increasing returns to scale were indicated.[65]

A number of gas and electricity cost studies were also made in the United Kingdom. Lomax found long-run average cost functions declining in relation to gas supply.[66] Likewise, Johnston found long-run average cost of electricity supply declining.[67]

These empirical studies come reasonably close to approximating bona fide average unit cost functions. In addition, there are a larger number of expenditure determinant studies that claim conclusions with regard to the existence or absence of economies of scale. Most of them claim that they were unable to detect significant scale economies,[68] although two studies claim to have detected some economies of scale. Nels W. Hanson uses 1958–59 data for 577 school districts in 9 states with enrollments ranging from 1,500 to 847,000. He applies a simple regression analysis of size of school district with residuals of current expenditures per pupil, adjusted for relationships between characteristics of the adult population and the community and school expenditures. This simple correlation analysis does not adjust for many crucial factors (especially service quality) that can affect unit cost.[69]

Shapiro, using 1957 government data as well as 1960 census data (more or less by inspection), concludes that "local governments in the smallest and the largest county areas within different states tend to have highest per capita revenue and expenditures."[70]

Although expenditure studies are inadequate to shed light on the complicated question of economies of scale in rendering urban public services, the cost studies summarized in Table 2 offer some insight, which can be applied to the broader question about metropolitan consolidation, which is taken up next.

---

[65] Marc Nerlove, *Returns to Scale in Electricity Supply* (Institute for Mathematical Studies in the Social Sciences, Stanford University, 1961), p. 11.

[66] K. S. Lomax, "Cost Curves for Gas Supply," *Bulletin of the Oxford Institute of Statistics,* Vol. 13 (1951).

[67] J. Johnston, *Statistical Cost Analysis* (McGraw-Hill Book Co., 1960).

[68] Among those who claim to have been unable to detect significant scale economies is Harvey E. Brazer who stated: ". . . There is little, if any, demonstrable positive relationship between the population size of cities and their levels of expenditures per capita when other independent variables are taken into account and the sample studied is a large one." Brazer, *op. cit.,* p. 66.

[69] Nels W. Hanson, "Economy of Scale as a Cost Factor in Financing Public Schools," *National Tax Journal,* Vol. 17 (March 1966).

[70] Harvey Shapiro, "Economies of Scale and Local Government Finance," *Land Economics,* Vol. 34 (May 1963).

TABLE 2.
COST CURVE STUDIES OF SCALE ECONOMIES

Name and Year	Service	Type	Result
Horizontally integrated services			
Riew (1966)	Secondary education	S	AUC is U-shaped with trough at about 1,700 pupils
Kiesling (1966)	Primary and secondary education	S	AUC is about horizontal
Hirsch (1959)	Primary and secondary education	S	AUC is about horizontal
Schmandt-Stephens (1960)	Police protection	S & Q	AUC is about horizontal
Hirsch (1960)	Police protection	S & Q	AUC is about horizontal
Will (1965)	Fire protection	E	AUC is declining with major economies reached at 300,000 population
Hirsch (1959)	Fire protection	S	AUC is U-shaped with trough at about 110,000 population
Hirsch (1965)	Refuse collection	S	AUC is about horizontal
Circularly integrated services			
Hirsch (1959)	School administration	S	AUC is U-shaped with trough at about 44,000 pupils
Vertically integrated services			
Nerlove (1961)	Electricity	S	AUC is declining
Isard-Coughlin (1957)	Sewage plants	S	AUC is declining
Lomax (1951)	Gas	S	AUC is declining
Johnston (1960)	Electricity	S	AUC is declining

Note: The following abbreviations are used: S = statistical data; AUC = average unit cost; Q = questionnaire data; E = engineering data.

Urban Government Consolidation

Although all three levels of government play a role in providing urbanites with public services, the actual provision rests mainly with local governments. As shown in Table 3, local government units in 1962 numbered more than 91,000, compared with more than 155,000 in 1942 and 116,000 in 1952. During the last twenty years the number of school districts, townships, and towns has declined, while there has been an increase in the number of special districts and municipalities.

Especially since the end of World War II, profound interest has prevailed to reduce the number of local governments. This has been done primarily through consolidation.

Three major virtues have been claimed for urban government consolidation—savings due to economies of scale, improved conditions for

TABLE 3.
LOCAL GOVERNMENT UNITS, 1942–62

Year	Counties	Townships and towns	Munici- palities	School districts	Special districts	Total
1942	3,050	18,919	16,220	108,579	8,299	155,067
1952	3,049	17,202	16,778	67,346	12,319	116,694
1957	3,047	17,198	17,183	50,446	14,405	102,279
1962[a]	3,043	17,144	17,997	34,678	18,323	91,185
Net change 1942–62	−7	−1,775	+1,777	−73,901	+10,024	−63,882
1962 divided by 1942	1.00	0.91	1.11	0.32	2.21	0.59

[a] 1962 data include Alaska and Hawaii.
Source: U.S. Bureau of the Census, for *Census of Governments* 1942, 1952, 1957, and 1962.

co-ordinated and orderly planning for growth, and equity in financing government services.

The scale economy issue has already been examined. It can be concluded that most government services require relatively close geographic proximity of service units to service recipients; this prevents the establishment of huge primary schools, fire houses, police stations, or libraries. Urban government services are also labor intensive, with wages and salaries often accounting for more than two-thirds of the current costs. The resulting concentration of manpower can increase the bargaining power of labor and this, in turn, increases costs. While there are some economies resulting from bulk purchases of supplies and equipment, such savings can be outweighed by inefficiencies resulting from top-heavy administration and the ills of political patronage in very large governments. Therefore, in terms of economies of scale, governments serving from 50,000 to 100,000 urbanites might be most efficient.

The second claim for consolidation relates to co-ordinated and orderly planning for growth. This can result in a sacrifice of freedom to act individually and independently. Perhaps the most serious questions in this context have been raised by Schlesinger who is convinced that, "Large organizations suffer from a geometric increase in the difficulty of (a) successfully communicating intentions and procedures, (b) establishing a harmonious system of incentives, and (c) achieving adequate cohesion among numerous individuals and sub-units with sharply conflicting wills." [71] He goes on to point out that "large or-

[71] James R. Schlesinger, *Organizational Structures and Planning* (The RAND Corporation, February 25, 1966), P-3316, p. 1.

ganizations find it hard to anticipate, to recognize, or to adjust to change . . . Changes in the environment can only be appreciated by small groups initially. To influence a large organization—to get the prevailing doctrine changed—is a time consuming process, and by the time it is accomplished the new views will themselves be on the verge of obsolescence. This may account for the organizational propensity to zig and zag." [72]

If large organizations are centralized there can be a declining incentive to consider alternatives and an increasing pressure to simply get decisions made. As a result, as McKean points out, large centralized governments may be tempted to neglect the variety of choices open to them. More importantly, they may be inclined to underestimate uncertainties.[73]

A third virtue of consolidation is equity—a somewhat ambiguous concept. Since reliance is placed on both income- and wealth-related taxes for financing urban government services, at best, equity can be attained with regard to one or the other, but not to both. There is also the philosophical issue of whether we benefit from giving all urbanites the same service, since not everybody has the same preference functions.

But even if we agree that increased equity is important as an objective, various fiscal arrangements can be relied upon to attain this objective without a change in government structure. Federal and state subsidies to local urban governments have worked in this direction and have produced similarity in results as shown in studies by Burkhead and Curran. Their case studies of Cuyahoga County, Ohio, and Milwaukee County, Wisconsin, indicate that in the postwar period, per capita expenditures of urban governments have grown increasingly similar.[74]

Consolidation of urban governments is likely to have some distinct shortcomings. It tends to eliminate consumer choice with regard to urban government services. And small local government has sentimentally, but perhaps correctly, been extolled as the last bastion of "town meeting" government. It is the only level at which people in government can effectively meet and engage in democratic dialogue.

Considering the various pros and cons, the conclusion of the Royal

[72] *Ibid.*, p. 19.
[73] Roland N. McKean and Melvin Anshen, "Limitations, Risks, and Problems," David Novick, ed., *Program Budgeting* (Harvard University Press, 1965).
[74] Jesse Burkhead, "Uniformity in Governmental Expenditures and Resources in a Metropolitan Area: Cuyahoga County," *National Tax Journal*, Vol. 16 (December 1961); and Donald J. Curran, S.J., "The Metropolitan Problem: Solution from Within?", *National Tax Journal*, Vol. 16 (September 1963).

Commission on Local Government in Greater London makes much sense:

. . . As many local functions as possible should be given to local authorities of the smallest practicable size. Our reason for this is that we believe that local authorities should be small enough to maintain and promote a sense of community in local affairs, and, if possible, to stimulate the practical interest of electors. On the other hand, we believe that they must be large enough and strong enough financially to carry the necessary staffs for the performance of their functions. The ideal size logistically varies between function and function, and some round average must be produced. We thought that the optimum size would be a minimum of about 100,000 inhabitants, and a maximum of about 250,000, and we thought that these boroughs should be achieved partly by keeping existing boroughs unaltered and partly by amalgamations of the smaller boroughs, urban district councils and rural district councils.[75]

In the postwar period, in spite of early strong advocacy of consolidation, hardly any large-scale mergers and few small mergers have taken place.[76] What are some of the reasons?

The first point one might want to make is that consolidation did not offer as many advantages as the first protagonists claimed. Furthermore, metropolitan areas are heterogeneous in their interests and outlook. While newspapers, real estate interests, banks, retail trade, railroads, and utilities are often vociferous and favor consolidation, large manufacturers selling in the national market and fearing higher taxes, residents afraid of further traffic congestion, air pollution, juvenile delinquency, and others stimulated by industrial growth, appear to oppose it.

The race issue might also have played some part in that white suburbanites were fearful that consolidation would open the gates to Negroes, spreading low-income groups throughout residential areas and resulting in the deterioration of public services and increases in cost.

Another reason has been advanced by Curran, who maintains that "spontaneous integration of the localities swings on the fulcrum of individual self interest." [77] His Milwaukee study does not find any trend toward uniformity in resources of different urban governments. Since local governments would be more unlikely to spontaneously forego advantages in resources, and therefore tax base, grave impediments to

[75] Sir Edwin Herbert, "The Reorganization of London's Government," *The Metropolitan Future: California and the Challenge of Growth,* Conference No. 5 (University of California, Berkeley, 1964), pp. 9–10.
[76] Dade County, Florida, and Toronto, Canada, are the two most prominent consolidations on the American continent in the postwar period, with the first having had numerous difficulties.
[77] Curran, *op. cit.,* p. 221.

consolidation exist. He concludes that the resources position of the central city, in this case Milwaukee proper, whose position has steadily worsened both in property base and in state payments, further darkens the outlook for consolidation.

Finally, consolidation is a revolutionary step—a great departure from the experience of most American urbanites. As such it engenders all-pervasive uncertainties, and many voters appear reluctant to opt for a future that might profoundly affect the qualities of their living.

Even though large scale consolidation of urban governments is not in the cards, some compromises have appeared. Among them are county-wide purchasing efforts, regional planning councils, and the "Lakewood Plan," whereby cities purchase certain services from an urban county.[78]

The federal government has taken a number of steps that can encourage area-wide co-operation. For example, in the National Capital Transportation Act of 1960 Congress declared that the continuing policy and responsibility of the federal government is to encourage and aid in planning and developing a unified and co-ordinated transit system for the Capital region.[79] The Act of 1965 authorizes a system of rail rapid transit to be built within the District of Columbia, but fully capable of extension beyond the District boundaries and not to exceed $431 billion. To this end $150 million were appropriated and a $50 million bond issue authorized.[80]

In the same manner, Congress has encouraged interstate and regional co-operation in the planning, acquisition, and development of outdoor recreation resources,[81] and the Housing and Urban Development Act of 1965 explicitly requires "significant effective efforts" by all available public and private resources in projects designed to beautify and improve open space and other public lands in the nation's urban areas.[82]

SUPPLY OF URBAN PUBLIC SERVICES

A perusal of the literature reveals a great paucity of inquiries into the supply of urban public services. What complicates matters further is the fact that not too much can be learned from theoretical inquiries into private sector supply functions, as will be shown below.

[78] Vincent Ostrom, et al., "The Organization of Government in Metropolitan Areas," The American Political Science Review, Vol. 55 (December 1961); and Robert Warren, "A Municipal Services Market Model of Metropolitan Organization," Journal of the American Institute of Planners, Vol. 30 (August 1964).
[79] Public Law 86–669.
[80] Public Law 89–173.
[81] Public Law 88–29.
[82] Public Law 89–117.

With this in mind, what follows is a brief analysis of the nature of urban public service supply functions and an examination of who supplies urbanites with public services and what considerations should play a role in determining who should be the supplier. Thereafter, an effort is made to shed some light on how, in the absence of a market price, urbanites of different income, race, and location are supplied with services. Finally, a rather unique feature of urban public service supply determination is examined.

Nature of Urban Public Service Supply Function

The supply of an urban government service is related to about the same factors that affect its costs. In addition, the supply also depends upon the government unit's goals. The latter issue greatly complicates the derivation of a public service supply function. There is no good theory that explains the precise goals of governments in general and of urban governments in particular. It appears that most governments have a large number of goals, many of which are rather intangible and often conflicting.[83] Then, too, the chain of causality between individual and collective goals and service procurement is long and complex. There are very few cases, if any, where governments would have the strong profit incentive that is common in private firms.

Marginal cost is an optimality concept that can be used when it can be assumed that some rational maximization (e.g., of profits) on the part of decision makers is pursued. This cannot be done in relation to the suppliers of urban public services, as we have no assurance that the least cost combination of resource inputs, that is, the lowest cost function of an infinite number of such functions, will be selected by the government unit.

There is a second reason why we cannot readily derive a government service supply function from its marginal cost function. It relates to the fact that most urban services are offered in a market with strong monopolistic characteristics. Marginal cost is not a supply curve for a monopolist, because it does not portray quantities offered at respective alternative prices.[84]

---

[83] For example, Martin Katzman finds that one of the major goals of the Boston public schools is to provide Irishmen with employment in the schools. Although this is a goal that one normally would not expect, it is only one of a large number of important goals the schools are likely to have. Katzman, *op. cit.*, p. 102.

[84] The view expressed here does not consider urban public service supply functions as either superfluous or non-existent. This extreme view is implied (erroneously, I think) in a recent statement by Otto A. Davis when he says, "Economists attempting to understand this (allocation) process would do well to discard at least a part of their notions of demand and supply and, hence,

Under these conditions, what can we say about the slope of the urban public supply function? Clearly, we would expect it to reflect the production characteristics of the service—specifically, the presence or absence of technological scale economies. In addition, the unit's effect on factor prices would play an important role. Government units purchasing relatively large amounts of labor inputs will often have some monopsony power and tend to face a positively sloping supply function. In this connection it is less important that the government buys an absolutely large amount of personnel than that it buys a relatively large one in terms of resources available in the area.

For example, should the city of Los Angeles attempt to double its police force in a few months' time, it would have to bid scarce resources away from other places, or from other pursuits, and as a result police salaries would tend to rise substantially. This tendency for salaries to increase is less the result of the very large number of policemen hired than the fact that in the short-run, at prevailing salaries, there are only a given number of candidates available. In relation to this available pool of policemen, demand increases substantially. A similar wage increase might result if Iowa City, Iowa, a much smaller and more isolated town, were to double its police force. On the other hand, if a city the same size as Iowa City, but located within the Los Angeles metropolitan area, were to double its police force, it could tap a rather large supply of policemen to fill the relatively small number of positions opened by it, and barely affect wages and salaries.

The labor supply function has been emphasized because salaries and wages of urban public services often constitute more than two-thirds of current expenditures. Thus, they play an important role in deriving a service supply function whose shape is likely to be strongly affected by that of the labor supply function. Prices of other inputs are unlikely to be affected in a major way by the scale at which they are bought by the government unit.

It is quite likely that both the labor supply and public service supply functions are more or less irreversible. They are irreversible in the narrow sense, since most urban areas have been growing in recent years and most urban public services have increased in importance. Furthermore,

---

the implicit implication that a pricing mechanism is the allocative device in the public sector." Otto A. Davis, "Empirical Evidence of Political Influences Upon the Expenditure Policies of Public Schools," in Julius Margolis, ed., *The Public Economy of Urban Communities* (Resources for the Future, Inc., 1965), p. 111. There is a difference between saying that there is no direct relationship between the marginal cost and the supply function on the one hand and that economists should discard parts of their supply notions.

some services are essential as well as habit-forming, and are virtually impossible to cut back. In this sense then, we have been moving along the supply function from left to right.

But there is a second sense in which labor supply and urban public service supply functions can be irreversible. Even if cutbacks were attempted, an absence of major technological and pecuniary economies of scale, together with some fixed investments, would make us move to the left along a supply function likely to be somewhat higher than the one used to move to the right.

Let us now turn to some aspects of the labor supply functions. While it is useful to look upon the labor supply function of governments furnishing public services in a given urban area as an aggregate, often greater insight can be obtained by breaking it down. For example, there are at least five groups from which teachers may be drawn at the beginning of a school year: (1) a pool of credentialed teachers who return after teaching the previous year, (2) newly trained credentialed teachers, (3) credentialed teachers returning to teaching after an absence, (4) teachers who return to a state with permanent teaching credentials, and (5) teachers with provisional credentials. The supply function of these five groups can differ. For example, the supply of returning credentialed teachers is likely to be related to the number of teachers teaching in a given state during the previous year, number of retirements and deaths in this group, teachers' salaries in the state generally and the school district in particular, teachers' salaries in other areas, and alternative pursuits to teaching. On the other hand, the supply of teachers with provisional credentials is related to the number of persons considered to meet minimum teaching qualifications, ease with which they can obtain provisional credentials, teachers' salaries in the state in general and the school district in particular, teachers' salaries in other areas, and salaries in alternative pursuits.

It is not uncommon to hear reports of shortages in certain classes of urban public employees, such as teachers or nurses.[85] What is often meant by such statements is that there are fewer employees of a certain type than the author of the statement would like to have, even though there may be no shortage in the economic sense. However, not all reported shortages are of this nature. A shortage may be said to exist in the economic sense when quantity demanded exceeds quantity supplied at the prevailing price. In labor markets, this situation is often manifested by job vacancies. We do observe local governments attempting to hire, for example, additional nurses possessing the same qualifications

[85] The rest of this section has benefited from discussions with Eugene J. Devine of the University of California, Los Angeles.

515

as those already employed, at the wage being paid to those currently employed, and finding no more available at that wage.

Several shortage concepts have been advanced in the literature to explain job vacancies. The most widely used concept of shortage relies on price or wage controls; quantity demanded will exceed quantity supplied when a price ceiling is imposed at a level below the market-clearing price. A variant of this, widely utilized by local governments, is the single salary schedule. Employees working under such a schedule may perform different tasks (such as policemen and firemen), or have different alternative opportunities (such as high school physics teachers and physical education teachers), but are paid according to the same salary schedule. Kershaw and McKean found that the single salary schedule was a significant factor in the current shortages of high school teachers in several subject-matter fields.[86] It can also result in job vacancies when a school district is prevented from paying differential salaries for teaching on different grade levels or at different locations within a city.

The concept of a dynamic shortage was applied to the market for engineers and scientists in the fifties.[87] This concept is based on a lag in the response of salaries to a shift in demand.

A firm's demand first shifts when it recognizes that it wants to hire more personnel at prevailing wages, but cannot do so. Vacancies will exist until salaries are raised above the current levels, and will persist if the demand keeps increasing.

Job vacancies may also exist if the economic unit is a monopsonist (which we define here as an employer facing an upward-sloping factor supply curve) and is unable, for some reason, to engage in wage discrimination.[88] Local governments are typically constrained from discriminating in the payment of wages. The existence of monopsony power is also implicit in the two shortages concepts discussed above. If a school district with a single salary schedule faced a perfectly elastic supply curve for, say, physics teachers having certain qualifications, and the wage was set below the equilibrium wage, it would obtain no qualified physics teachers. However, we observe that school districts do obtain

---

[86] Joseph A. Kershaw and Roland N. McKean, *Teacher Shortages and Salary Schedules* (McGraw-Hill Book Co., 1962).

[87] A. A. Alchian, K. J. Arrow, and W. M. Capron, *An Economic Analysis of the Market for Scientists and Engineers* (The RAND Corporation, June 6, 1958), RM-2190-RC.

[88] See G. C. Archibald, "The Factor Gap and the Level of Wages," *The Economic Record,* Vol. 30 (November 1954); and E. J. Devine and Morton J. Marcus, "Monopsony, Recruitment Costs and Job Vacancies," *Western Economic Journal,* Vol. V (September 1967).

Werner Z. Hirsch

some qualified physics teachers at the prevailing wage, but not as many as they would like, implying that these districts face an upward-sloping supply curve. The dynamic shortage concept is similarly applicable only to an economic unit facing an upward-sloping supply curve. If the unit faced a perfectly elastic supply curve, and its demand curve shifted to the right, it would be able to secure all the additional personnel it wanted at the prevailing wage.

Which Government Should Supply Urbanites with Services?

Under fiscal federalism, it is conceivable that federal, state, and local governments could all be actively engaged in supplying urbanites with services. But in line with our American tradition, the federal government has basically taken a back seat, leaving the field to local governments (mainly, counties, cities, and districts) and, to a minor extent, to state governments. In most cases cities cover a smaller territory than do districts and counties. Most districts are parts of one county, although there are a few instances where they embrace more than a single county. Thus, a discussion about which of these three governments might best supply urbanites with services can be related to the efficacy with which local or area-wide governments best perform certain services. In this connection, the determination of whether a given urban government's service is most effectively supplied by a small municipality or a large county or district can be related to three criteria: scale economy, people-government proximity, and multifunctional jurisdictions.

Based in part on a number of economic studies, it appears that the following urban government services are likely to enjoy major economies of scale: air pollution control, sewage disposal, public transportation, power, water, public health services, hospitals, and planning.[89]

Most of the other urban government services for government units of more than about 50,000 inhabitants are likely to enjoy only minor, if any, economies of scale. This does not deny that certain specialized higher education and library facilities can incur scale economies; but these appear to be the exception when compared to the major education and library expenditures.

People-government proximity is favored because in a democracy active participation of citizens in their government is desirable. Services for which close citizen participation appear particularly important include education, libraries, public housing, welfare services, police pro-

[89] Isard and Coughlin, *op. cit.*; Hirsch, *op. cit.*, pp. 232–41; Brazer, *op. cit.*, pp. 437–43; Shapiro, *op. cit.*, pp. 175–86; Marc Nerlove, *Returns to Scale in Electricity Supply* (Institute for Mathematical Studies in the Social Sciences, Stanford University, 1961).

tection, and fire protection. In relation to transportation, planning, parks and recreation, and urban renewal, proximity appears to have mixed benefits, since citizen participation enriches democratic procedure but, at the same time, tends to prevent decisive socially desirable action.

The importance of multifunctional jurisdictions is pointed out by the Advisory Commission on Intergovernmental Relations: "Every unit of government should be responsible for a sufficient number of functions so that its governing processes involve a resolution of conflicting interests, with significant responsibility for balancing governmental needs and resources." [90]

Using these criteria, and granting that income redistribution objectives can be met by federal and state subsidies or other fiscal mechanisms, the following conclusions suggest themselves: Local urban governments, particularly if they serve 50,000–100,000 citizens, can effectively provide education, library service, public housing, public welfare services, fire and police protection, refuse collection, parks and recreation, urban renewal, and street maintenance programs. Services which appear to be best provided on a district or countywide basis are air pollution control, sewage disposal, transportation, electric power, public health services, water, planning, and hospitals.[91]

Service Distribution by Income, Race, and Community

Governments supplying urbanites with services free of charge must decide how much of each service, and what quality, each household or firm is to receive. Since most urban public services are indeed not public goods, some degree of exclusion can be practiced and questions of equity and efficiency must be faced.

Recently Shoup examined criteria for distributing crime prevention in cities. He pointed to at least two major goals governments might have in supplying police protection. The first is one of equality which would be met if every person faced the same probability of having a crime committed against him. The second is a minimization of crime which, "with a fixed amount of police resources available, is achieved when an increment of police input will reduce the number of crimes by the same amount, no matter where it is placed within the city, or at what time of day." [92] He goes on to point out that the marginal cost of preventing one more crime under those conditions would be the same everywhere in the

[90] Advisory Commission on Intergovernmental Relations, *Performance of Urban Functions: Local and Areawide* (Washington, D.C., September 1963), p. 6.

[91] Werner Z. Hirsch, "Local Versus Areawide Urban Government Services," *National Tax Journal,* Vol. 17 (December 1964).

[92] Carl S. Shoup, "Standards for Distributing a Free Governmental Service: Crime Prevention," *Public Finance,* Vol. 19 (1964).

city. Yet achieving this goal will usually leave some of the city's districts more crime-ridden than others. He concludes: "Crime will have been minimized at the cost of distributing police protection unequally . . . Even if the two districts are equal in population, minimization of crime will commonly result in unequal crime rates per capita among districts, because disruptive social forces, aggravated by poverty, are stronger in one than in another." [93]

Relatively little is known about the actual distribution of urban public services by location, race, religion, income class, or other categories—mainly because records are not kept in those terms. Furthermore, there are occasions when some discrimination is practiced that is not necessarily public knowledge.

Education is one of the few services for which attempts to provide some measurements of service distribution have been made. For example, in relation to social class, a study was carried out in the aftermath of the Watts riots in Los Angeles. Martyn took four districts of the Los Angeles school system that mainly serve socially and economically "underprivileged" children—the Watts, East Los Angeles, Boyle Heights, and Avalon school districts—and compared some key characteristics with those of "privileged" school districts.[94] He found substantial inequality in the supply of education when comparing "privileged" to "underprivileged" districts, often favoring the "underprivileged" district. For example, the pupil-teacher ratio in the four "underprivileged" districts varied from 27.8 to 29.7, while that in the "privileged" district averaged 31.9.

While one would expect that a higher proportion of portable classrooms were used in the disadvantaged areas because they have higher growth rates, this proved not to be the case. Average annual expenditures per pupil in average daily attendance for maintenance averaged $30.75 in the "underprivileged" and $28.24 in the "privileged" school districts. Also, expenditures of textbook funds, both per junior and senior high school pupil, were higher in the "underprivileged" than "privileged" districts. The same picture prevailed in relation to expenses of instructional supplies. Finally, while per pupil in average daily attendance annual expenditures for elementary schools was about the same in the "underprivileged" and "privileged" districts, in junior and senior high schools the "underprivileged" school districts spent substantially more than did the "privileged" ones. For example, for junior high schools the "underprivileged" figure was $384 compared to

[93] *Ibid.*, p. 385.
[94] Kenneth A. Martyn, *Report on Education to the Governor's Commission on Los Angeles Riots* (November 1965 [mimeo.]).

$365 for "privileged" districts. And for senior high schools in "underprivileged" districts, the figure was $447 compared to $385 in "privileged" districts.

However, not all figures favored the "underprivileged" districts. If the quality of teachers is measured in terms of permanent versus probationary or conditional teaching certificates, or formal education, or the length of experience, the "privileged" districts were favored.

Some of the distribution characteristics of public education were examined by Katzman in relation to the Boston public schools. He found current costs per pupil in different Boston schools to vary significantly with neither race nor median family income.[95]

Early in the 1960's, Sexton, in a study of the distribution of input measures (such as teacher training, guidance facilities, and so on), in a large city high school system found a systematic bias against lower-income groups.[96]

While Katzman found no significantly statistical relationship between race and income on the one hand and current costs per pupil on the other, he found the two variables strongly related to such output measures as changes in reading score and percentage continuation rate attributed to school inputs, i.e., education quality. He estimated the following two multiple regression equations:

$$O_3 = 74.0 + \underline{0.663S_4} + \underline{0.008S_6} - 0.479S_{12} - 0.127P + 0.982S_{13} \quad (11)$$

$$O_6 = 4.5 + \underline{0.169S_4} + \underline{0.002S_6} - 0.006S_{12} + \underline{0.238P} + \underline{0.532S_{13}}, \quad (12)$$

where

O_3 = median change in reading scores attributable to school inputs,

O_6 = percentage annual continuation (in school) rate,

S_4 = percentage of white population,

S_6 = median family income,

S_{12} = per cent of Irish,

P = per cent of public elementary school participation, and

S_{13} = per cent of voter participation.

The coefficient of multiple determination adjusted for degrees of freedom in the first equation is 0.6320 and in the second 0.8838, and in both cases they are statistically significant at a probability level of 0.05. As before, statistically significant regression coefficients at a 0.05 level of significance are underlined.[97]

[95] Katzman, *op. cit.*, p. 78.
[96] Patricia C. Sexton, *Education and Income* (The Viking Press, 1961).
[97] Katzman, *op. cit.*, pp. 80–81.

On the basis of these partial empirical results, it appears that, under the impetus of federal programs, culturally and economically deprived schools probably tend to have per pupil expenditures equal to, or even larger than, those in advantaged areas. However, the latter tend to enjoy better prepared and more able teachers than the poor schools, possibly the result of the schools' sensitivity to the electorate, as well as teachers' preferences.

A Special Consideration in Supply Determination

Finally, we will briefly consider a rather unique feature of public service supply determination. The amount of services supplied heavily depends upon the amount of money made available and legal directives for its use. Both reflect political constraints and community values. For example, the funds available to government reflect social and political values of the community in terms of its vote on bond issues, tax levies, and officials voted into power.

The legal mandate charges most governments with a responsibility to provide services for everyone: all children must be given an education, all homes must be protected against fire, all citizens must be given access to the courts, and so on. Under such circumstances, the quality is varied more than the quantity of the service. This is best illustrated by working with sets of supply functions, each pertaining to a different service equality.

For example, if, in Figure 1, OM pupils must be educated, we will

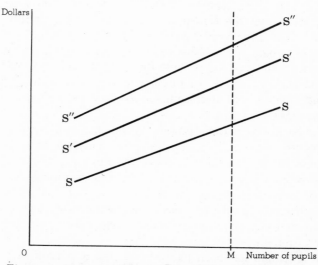

Figure 1. Urban public service supply functions.

seek an intersection with the supply function (having a particular quality) that is consistent with the funds available for the purpose.

FURTHER CONSIDERATIONS IN BRIEF

Time, space, and the state of knowledge requires neglecting a number of important issues. Three of these issues will be briefly presented here, together with a possible framework. They are designed more to help clarify conceptual issues than to lend themselves to empirical inquiries.

First, it is well to note again that urbanites receive pecuniary as well as non-pecuniary benefits, both from the public and private sector. Looking merely at pecuniary income leaves out a decisive portion of important benefits to urbanites in an affluent society. Pecuniary income can be ascertained analogously to national income and is, of course, equal to real product. Non-pecuniary income (or product), does not admit to such an easy definition. Both types of income are produced as a result of labor, capital, and resources being combined by either the private or public sector of the economy.

So far this paper has dealt mainly, if not exclusively, with the production of tangible public services. The concern has been with government building and operating facilities designed to provide urbanites with a variety of services. In addition, government provides a variety of intangible services, some of which can be virtually costless. The very existence of government, and its laws, can create benefits. Government often serves also as a spillover adjuster, mainly by rendering a variety of intangible services. These include planning, zoning, regulation (especially of the transportation-communication utility network), judication, and even persuasion. In this somewhat indirect participation in the urban production process, government mainly provides an environment, and rules to provide for more socially desirable outcomes for all urban transactors. In this capacity, government often attempts to reduce under- and over-compensation of participants in activities in urban areas.

Government has various powers by which it can reduce uncompensated inputs. For example, if a neighbor puts up an unsightly fence or is noisy during the early hours of the morning, adjacent homes are affected in an undesirable manner. Likewise, when one plant pollutes water or air, other plants, recreational facilities, and homes are adversely affected. In all these cases, neighbors bring about uncompensated costs which government zoning, regulation, and judication can prevent or minimize.

Little attention has been paid here to the important fact that urban activities take place on (and between) specific locations, and their resulting spillovers. The cost of overcoming spatial distances and their alternatives deserves careful investigation. It appears useful to differentiate between four basic land uses: residential, commercial-industrial, transportation-communication network, and recreational. Using these four divisions as basic building blocks, a framework can be constructed to elucidate questions in relation to space, intangible services, and non-pecuniary urban output. In such a framework parcels of urban land are assigned to these four land uses, and activities on them ultimately produce urbia's output. Activities on the various urban parcels are parts of an activity vector which makes up a home and business enterprise (private and public), respectively, with the business enterprise constituting an activity of the final urban area output vector—home. Thus, home and business enterprise, respectively, are multidimensional activity vectors. In this setting, government, developer, owner and/or user of home or business enterprise, and neighbor are prime transactors on the urban scene. These transactors engage in activities which convert urban residential (or commercial-industrial) land parcels into house or business activity (that is, the physical shell), and finally into home or business establishment.

In terms of timing and sequence of activities, government usually arrives first on the scene. It plans, zones, and provides certain social overhead, that helps prepare parcels of urban land for development. Thereafter, the developer arrives and builds residential or commercial-industrial property. During this period government and developer take steps to start the conversion of a physical facility into a home and business enterprise. Thereafter, mainly under the initiative of owner and/or user, the conversion into home and commercial enterprise proceeds, with government and neighbors interacting to various degrees.

Thus government virtually continuously participates in the creation of house, business establishment, recreation facility and transportation-communication utility network, and the conversion into business enterprise and home. Government renders both tangible and intangible services, producing pecuniary and non-pecuniary urban output.

Our understanding of how urban public services are rendered is far from perfect. However, there is little disagreement that other sectors of the economy have progressed faster in the last century; they have attracted greater managerial talent and benefited more from gains in science and technology. The paucity of managerial talent in managing the urban public sector has far-reaching implications and is unlikely to be changed—unless urbia offers its high public officials greater rewards and improved training programs.

Local urban governments are unable to depend on their electorate to approve bond issues for modern capital equipment. And their reluctance to finance research is legendary. Both have kept them from progressing very rapidly; fiscal incentives from state and federal governments might have to be relied upon to remedy the situation. Steps in these directions could produce great benefits since providing urban public services depends very heavily on manpower.

These are merely examples of the many aspects of supplying urban public services that remain to be subjected to careful economic analysis so that promising policy recommendations can be derived.

SELECTED READINGS

Brazer, Harvey E. *City Expenditures in the United States.* New York: National Bureau of Economic Research, 1952.

Bureau of the Budget. *Measuring Productivity of Federal Government Organizations.* Washington: U.S. Government Printing Office, 1964.

Fabricant, Solomon. *The Trend of Government Activity in the United States Since 1900.* New York: National Bureau of Economic Research, 1952.

Hirsch, Werner Z. "Cost Functions of an Urban Government Service: Refuse Collection," *The Review of Economics and Statistics,* Vol. 47 (February 1965).

Katzman, Martin T. "Distribution and Production in a Big City Elementary School System," *Yale Economic Essays* (Spring 1968).

Kiesling, Herbert J. "Measuring a Local Government Service: A Study of School Districts in New York State," *The Review of Economics and Statistics* (forthcoming).

Pidot, George B., Jr. "The Public Finances of Metropolitan Government in the Metropolitan United States." Unpublished Ph.D. dissertation, Harvard University, 1966.

Ridley, Clarence E., and Herbert A. Simon. *Measuring Municipal Activities.* Chicago: International City Managers Association, 1938.

Scott, Stanley, and Edward Feder. *Factors Associated with Variations in Municipal Expenditure Levels.* Berkeley: Bureau of Public Administration, University of California, 1957.

Shoup, Carl S. "Standards for Distributing a Free Governmental Service: Crime Prevention," *Public Finance,* Vol. 19 (1964).

Will, Robert E. "Scalar Economies and Urban Service Requirements," *Yale Economic Essays,* Vol. 5 (Spring 1965).

*Julius Margolis**

THE DEMAND FOR URBAN PUBLIC SERVICES

It is strongly felt that urban public services have been the most neglected of all goods supplied in our society. Certainly, a day rarely passes that newspapers do not dwell on a problem that is being "inadequately" or "improperly" handled by local governments. Streets are congested, air is polluted, schools are crowded, police are ill equipped . . . The indictment is long. Is this the usual rhetoric of public debate, or is it indeed true that the urban public services are poorly supplied? And whether one judges the public services as impoverished or munificent, can we state, even approximately, the conditions for "optimal" provision? The answers to these questions are still not available, despite the considerable amount of attention economists have given to urban public services; for the record of sophisticated analysis is not very long. This survey, therefore, is more of a progress report on beginnings and better understood difficulties than a summary of findings.

The first major section of this paper deals briefly with the "facts" of urban public services: What are the magnitudes of expenditures and some of the characteristics of local government considered relevant to the analysis of public services? The second section analyzes public goods. The third examines more closely one means of registering demand—the political process—and some of the political economy models are discussed. The last section discusses the economist-administrative process of determining demand, namely benefit-cost analysis.

SOME DIMENSIONS OF THE URBAN PUBLIC SERVICES

Table 1 shows the per capita expenditures of the nearly 10,000 local governments of the thirty-eight largest Standard Metropolitan Statistical Areas (SMSA's) in 1964–65. Although these figures give a reasonable representation of the activities of local government, they are deceptive in regard to a portrait of urban public services. They ignore the direct services of the state and federal governments in the areas. For instance, the per capita local expenditures of the San Antonio SMSA, the lowest spender of the thirty-eight SMSA's, is two fifths that of New York, the highest spender, but the ratio of state direct expenditures to local for

* Professor of Economics and Engineering-Economic Systems, Stanford University.

Texas is twice that of New York. Clearly, the urban public services in Texas were greatly understated in this table and thereby the national figures are also understated. The major impact of the state services would show up in higher education, highways, welfare, hospitals, and correction.

If we considered the first four categories of Table 1, the combined state and local expenditures per capita for these services in 1964–65 would have been: education—$149.47, highways—$63.15, public welfare—$32.58, and health and hospitals—$27.66.[1]

TABLE 1.
PER CAPITA EXPENDITURES OF ALL LOCAL GOVERNMENTS IN THE
THIRTY-EIGHT LARGEST SMSA's, 1964–65

Education	$123.65
Highways	19.85
Public welfare	25.13
Health and hospitals	18.17
Police protection	17.27
Fire protection	9.87
Sewerage	10.20
Sanitation, other than sewerage	6.34
Parks and recreation	9.04
Water supply	15.34
Other utilities	19.22
Interest on general debt	11.54
General control	7.27
Other direct general expenditures	42.87

Source: U.S. Bureau of the Census, *Local Government Finances in Selected Metropolitan Areas in 1964–65*, Series GF-No. 9 (1966), Table 1.

The federal government is less important than the state as a direct provider, but consideration of its activities would still further change the portrait of urban public services. A purely federal program, the postal services, more intraurban than interurban, spends $27.00 per capita, and there are federal direct outlays on each of the categories usually assigned to state and local: for example, education—$5.42, health and hospitals—$11.91, housing and urban renewal—$4.89. Federal expenditures to serve urban areas need not be incurred within the confines of a local area. Many municipal water supply systems, especially in western states, are at least partially federal; airports and water transportation are heavily federal. Therefore the portrait shown by Table 1 is incomplete, but it is sufficient for this paper which focuses solely on the public services provided by local governments.

[1] U.S. Bureau of the Census, *Governmental Finances in 1964–65*, Series GF-No. 6 (1966), Table 7.

The urban public services are supplied in response to a very complex set of forces. The urban government is expected to show leadership in solving racial problems, youth training, immorality, unemployment, delinquency, poverty, congestion, pollution, and public health, as well as in enhancing the beauty of the area, its cultural endowment and general amenities. We have noted the interventions of state and federal governments, but these are not by single governmental units. Twenty-one federal departments and agencies have 400 regional and subregional offices in the field to deal with state and local governments. There are 170 federal aid programs to state and local projects enmeshed in over 400 separate appropriations.[2] But the multiplicity of federal or state agencies fades in magnitude before the number of local governments. As of 1962, the 212 metropolitan areas contained 18,442 independent local governmental units, less than one-fourth of which were municipalities.[3] But the large number of governments is of no special concern to us except as it relates to an interesting and barely analyzed aspect of our topic—the registering of demand for public services.

As we shall point out later, the fragmentation of government is the basis of the reasonable charge that externalities among governments give rise to inefficient provision of public services, but at the same time we might ask whether the fragmentation encourages or discourages a greater responsivity to the demands of the public. Education is usually provided by an independent school district, the number of fire districts within SMSA's is over one-fourth the number of municipalities. The general consensus is that the special-purpose (usually a single-function) government is neither efficient nor responsive. Usually, however, independent school districts are exempted from this charge. The evidence supporting partial or total government is anecdotal rather than analytical. It is not apparent that a government containing more departments will be a better recorder of the public's wants. There is incomplete evidence that the more complex single government will spend more than the set of independent governments, but this is far from proving that the resultant package of services is better.[4]

[2] Senator Edmund S. Muskie, *Testimony, Creative Federalism,* Part 1. Hearings before the Subcommittee on Intergovernmental Relations, 89th Cong., 2nd Sess., November 16, 1966, p. 2.

[3] U.S. Bureau of the Census, *Census of Governments: 1962,* Vol. V, *Local Government in Metropolitan Areas,* p. 2.

[4] Julius Margolis, "Metropolitan Finance Problems: Territories, Functions and Growth," *Public Finances: Needs, Sources and Utilization,* Universities–National Bureau of Economic Research (Princeton University Press, 1961); James Buchanan, "The Economics of Earmarked Taxes," *Journal of Political Economy,* LXXI, October 1963.

Another dimension of the structure of governments which, though unanalyzed, is relevant to the study of demand, is how the behavior of government is affected by the internal structure of decision making within governments and the external constraints imposed by states. Limitations on taxing or bonding powers, frequency of elections, ward or city-wide representation, city manager versus mayor, are a few among a long list of issues extensively debated in the literature of local public administration. Unless these discussions are meaningless, the different institutional forms should affect either the efficiency of production of public services, or the choice of levels of supply and their distribution within the city. The very extensive writings on local government stress problems and frustrations, where solutions are too often identified with ease or honesty of decision rather than correctness of decision. Unnecessary institutional constraints may be an abomination, but at the other extreme the actions of an arbitrary, dictatorial government may be far from those that could be justified by an acceptable social criterion. So long as there is an economic problem of insufficient resources there will be difficult allocational decisions. The relaxing of constraints on governments does not necessarily mean that the allocational decisions would be superior.

Let us return to some of the quantitative dimensions of the public services. Over the past decade there have been many statistical studies of the variation of urban public expenditures. All of them are incomplete because the data are inadequate to test interesting hypotheses.[5]

The major data shortcoming is the absence of measures of product. A larger expenditure figure is always an ambiguous number. Does a higher police expenditure per capita mean a greater preference for law and order via police services; or does it mean that the crime problem is greater and, therefore, the higher expenditures are needed to reach the same service level; or are the greater expenditures necessary because different urban forms make certain services more costly; or is

---

[5] For a sampling of the different styles of analysis see: Roy W. Bohl and Robert J. Saunders, "Factors Associated with Variations in State and Local Government Spending," *Journal of Finance,* Vol. 21 (September 1966); Alan K. Campbell and Seymour Sacks, *Metropolitan America: Fiscal Patterns and Governmental Systems* (Syracuse University, mimeo, 1966); George F. Break, *Intergovernmental Fiscal Relations in the United States* (Brookings, 1967); Julius Margolis, "Metropolitan Finance Problems: Territories, Functions and Growth," in *Public Finances: Needs, Sources and Utilization,* Universities–National Bureau of Economic Research (Princeton University Press, 1961); Glenn W. Fisher, "Interstate Variation in State and Local Government Expenditures," *National Tax Journal,* Vol. 17 (March 1964); Harvey E. Brazer, *City Expenditures in the United States* (National Bureau of Economic Research, 1959).

there a shift in the composition of public and private provision of services? Statistical studies recognize these problems and they incorporate characteristics of the communities that are addressed to the issues of the nature of the product, but the analysis is unsystematic and inconclusive.

The problem of product definition can be posed in more general terms. Some of these services are the fruits of progress of the economy, others are costs of an urban-industrial society, and too often it is difficult to distinguish. Is a park a therapeutic retreat from the tension of an aggressive society, or is it a place for joy and recreation? Or is this question the same as asking whether the rich man is happier than a poor man?

Urban public expenditures are more variable than one would anticipate, given the relatively high level of national cultural integration. The variation increases when we consider the individual services. Table 2 presents mean per capita expenditures in metropolitan and non-

TABLE 2.
VARIATIONS IN PER CAPITA EXPENDITURES IN METROPOLITAN AND
NON-METROPOLITAN PORTIONS OF FORTY-FIVE STATES, 1957

Public services	Metropolitan		Non-Metropolitan	
	Mean	Standard deviation	Mean	Standard deviation
General expenditures	$148	$37	$134	$47
Education	63	14	69	18
Highway	15	7	20	11
Health and hospital[a]	7	5	6	4
Public welfare	7	8	8	12

[a] Exclusive capital outlays.
Source: Alan K. Campbell and Seymour Sacks, *Metropolitan America: Fiscal Patterns and Governmental Systems* (Syracuse University, 1966), mimeo., Table III–10.

metropolitan areas and a measure of variation. Education is, relatively, the least variable of all of the public services. This uniformity also extends to non-metropolitan areas. It is interesting that the public service with the least variability is the service which has inspired the arguments that, due to externality effects of education, variation should be discouraged and federal aid encouraged.

It is likely that the significant educational grant programs by the states accounts for the reduced variation. The well-known finding that the poorer regions make much greater efforts than the richer in regard to education is primarily accounted for by the much greater effort of the state governments.

Some of the factors giving rise to variation in services are well known, but others are disputed. All studies show the unsurprising fact that income is a major factor. Intergovernmental transfers, when they are included, also are important, but then this structural difference among states should itself be explained. Other variables which are frequently found significant are wealth, employment characteristics, age distribution, size, density. Earlier we commented on the "surprising" variation in public services, but considering the great range taken by the "determinants" of expenditures, it may have been more appropriate to express surprise that the spread was not more. If we had considered the full range of all local governments the differences would have been very great.

Differences among large aggregates like SMSA's are small relative to the differences among the territorial governments which comprise the SMSA's. Every SMSA is reasonably balanced between jobs and labor force, but many cities comprising an SMSA have no jobs except to provide services for residents and some cities have no residents except for a few maintenance personnel. There are cities with no vacant land and others with huge farms awaiting subdivision. There are cities with a minimum lot size of one acre and others densely packed with multifamily units. Cities are differentiated by race, occupation, age.[6] From the fiscal perspective, differences per se cause no problem. We should expect variances in preferences and incomes and therefore variations in services comparable to differences that we would find in the private sector; e.g., the difference in house space per capita between a rich commuter suburb and a poor working-class suburb is probably far greater than the difference in fire department expenditures per capita. But the differences in services that do exist, and even those that might be accounted for by income and taste, do give rise to pressures for uniformity. The statement of disparities of services per capita is almost always associated with an accompanying conclusion that it is deplorable. The goal of uniform public services is possibly as commonly held as the goal of income equality is rejected. The goal of uni-

[6] Advisory Commission on Intergovernmental Relations, *Metropolitan Social and Economic Disparities: Implications for Intergovernmental Relations in Central Cities and Suburbs* (Washington, D.C., 1965); Bernard Frieden, *Metropolitan America; Challenge to Federalism,* Advisory Commission on Intergovernmental Relations, Committee Print of Intergovernmental Relations Subcommittee of the House Committee on Government Operations, 89th Cong., 2nd Sess., October 1966.

formity is a significant factor in the explanation of shift to higher-level financing and provision of services.

EXTERNALITIES IN PUBLIC SERVICES

A metropolitan area is spatially differentiated. Changes in transportation and production technology provide the keys to explain the movements we have observed over time. Important as these factors are, elements of tastes, preferences of households as consumers and workers, also play a major role. In the domain of public services the preferences of households are even more important because consumers are the voters. Households choose a site to optimize their utility, and one of the factors that enters into their utility function is the character of the neighborhood, and for many, the character of the city as well.

A model could be constructed of the distribution of activities among the communities in the metropolitan area which considered only transportation and communication costs, together with individual preferences in regard to housing space, neighbors, and transportation costs (including time). It could solve for rents and for the allocation of space. However, as the computer went through its successive iterations and spun out the model it would find that a special set of constraints would start creating difficulties. The transportation networks linking the units would have to be supplied by a source which made consistent decisions. The model builder might postulate a single decision maker to affect these decisions. In practice, however, the local government units will be filling in the sites on the basis of their own particular interests. The governments are not passive receivers of businesses and households; instead, they seek to encourage specific types of development. Firms want their governments to protect or enhance their competitive positions; households want to protect their neighborhood values; and both groups will be concerned with intra- and extra-municipal consequences of public services. These groups will be pressing for operating rules on the part of their governments fitting in with such interests. The results would differ significantly from those arrived at by the computer.

In the same light, I would not be misrepresenting the fiscal analysts if I said they sought to structure the set of governments so the computer could work out the most efficient allocation, taking into account production externalities and consumption externalities, and not any beggarthy-neighbor policies. In practice, we find local government lines often arbitrarily drawn within a metropolitan region so that each contains a peculiar mix of activities, and we find the local governmental units adopting self-seeking policies to protect their own residents. Two consequences for public services can be noted: neglected externalities and fiscal disparities.

In recent years externality effects, unpriced consequences, have received particular attention. Hirsch, Break and Brazer all stress externalities as a major criterion for the size of local government.[7] None would use it as a sole criterion; they would especially urge consideration of political vitality of a local government, but the presence of externalities is the main basis for their urging that special rules be established by a larger government or that taxes be levied by the larger government. Though they do not necessarily infer a metropolitan-wide government because of such region-wide externalities, they do recommend some fiscal or regulatory transfers to larger governments which would produce essentially the same results.

There is general agreement about which services exhibit area-wide externalities. Air pollution control, sewage disposal, transportation, public health, water supply, planning and urban renewal, arterial streets: all are classified as having area-wide spillovers. With the exception of planning, these tend to be technical services. There is disagreement only about certain of the human resources services. Education qualifies as possessing extensive spillovers, but there is no consensus about public welfare. There is consensus that neighborhood parks, police and local libraries do not have spillovers.

Despite the substantial agreement among the expert observers about spillover effects, a good deal remains unresolved. Much more analysis is required. Education is considered heavily endowed with spillovers since the educated population is mobile and they can and do take their personal investment to other jurisdictions. But the same would be true for any other input enhancing human capacity. Libraries, museums, zoos, and even playgrounds have similar effects. Public welfare, if well organized, should have the same consequence, especially for the children in the welfare families. If police services were effective, individuals raised in an environment of law and order are more likely to accept it at a later point in life. Further, every well-policed area reduces possible successful crimes in the metropolitan area and, therefore, the size of the criminal population throughout the area. Casual analysis could establish spillover effects for almost any service which goes beyond the restricted servicing of specific sites. What we require at

---

[7] Werner Z. Hirsch, "Local Versus Areawide Urban Government Services," *National Tax Journal*, Vol. 17 (December 1964); Harvey E. Brazer, "Some Fiscal Implications of Metropolitanism," in Guthrie Birkhead (ed.), *Metropolitan Issues: Social, Governmental, Fiscal* (Syracuse University, Maxwell Graduate School, 1961); George F. Break, *Intergovernmental Fiscal Relations in the United States* (Brookings, 1967).

this point are empirical studies of the magnitudes of these effects, and the losses involved in ignoring them.

An argument in defense of the presence of educational spillovers is the high residential mobility of the population. But this argument raises in a new light the question of the small government, responsive to the residents. All of the analysts stress the desirable political and consumer sovereignty resulting from the many neighborhood-cities in the metropolitan area. But if the population is highly mobile in terms of residences how does the householder exercise his preference in the community to which he is going to move? Is there any mechanism which can be used to develop a set of governments so that there are reasonably good substitutes? A more important aspect of mobility is the daily mobility in regard to jobs, shopping, entertainment, and so on. The majority of the metropolitan population residing in the suburbs finds itself functioning under several territorial governments, probably paying taxes to each, but able to influence directly only one of them.

I do not mean to urge a regional government solution to the crazy-quilt of governments now existing in metropolitan governments, but I would urge that arguments about externalities or democratic responsiveness should be used with great caution. At the minimum we require a great deal more empirical analysis before we can speak with authority on that score.

A second consequence of the existing patterns of local governments is well recognized, but it goes beyond the scope of this paper so I will only mention it. Since the main source of local funds is property taxes and since commercial and industrial property will be distributed unequally throughout the area, fiscal resources will be distributed unequally. Though city officials are convinced of the necessity of building up a fiscal base through encouraging further industry, the evidence that fiscal strength follows industrialization is inconclusive since the demands for public services also increase with industry. In any case, officials do adopt competitive policies in regard to industrial location. Services are extended to attract industry, and tax increases are resisted for services that are of no value to industry. If such policies are pursued by many cities, and they often are, they are self-defeating, since industry will locate without regard for public action and, as a consequence, the policies adopted could be suboptimal from the perspective of the entire metropolitan area.

DEMAND FOR PUBLIC SERVICES

The demand for an urban public service is not an unambiguous concept. Consider the demand function for private goods. No matter how difficult it is to estimate demand functions for private goods, we usually have observations of amounts purchased during several periods at a reasonably well-identified set of prices. Often these gross observations can be supplemented with information about the attributes of purchasers—for example, their income, race, residence, occupation, etc. But how different it is in the public sector. The consumers of the goods are not the purchasers; the purchasers are a mix of elected and appointed officials who pay with tax revenues; the taxpayers may not be the users of the services and decision-makers may be neither taxpayers nor users. Observations on prices or quantity are rare; costly surveys are often necessary to tell us who uses the services; and the handful of studies of who pays for the services are highly oversimplified. Not only are there several steps between consumer and payer, but often the consumer may not be part of the political constituency which is doing the paying.

Demand analysis for private goods reaches back to individual preferences to motivate market behavior and also to provide a basis to evaluate market performance. Therefore, it is not surprising that the body of analysis developed to understand the demand for public services should also refer back to individual preferences. Certainly it is reasonable to attempt to apply private market analogies to public processes. If successful, we would have a rich body of theory to extend to the huge but neglected public sector; possibly the normative theorems might be transformable into administrative rules. Unfortunately, it is more difficult in the public sector to use predictive tests to judge the usefulness of abstract models and, therefore, discussions about the reasonableness of models will be more common. It is easy to sympathize with the critic who feels that his sensibility is being strained in being asked to accept refined arguments to explain why the resident of New York "demands" more education for the resident of New Orleans, or more wilderness areas in California.

Since there is no body of studies of demand for urban public services, we shall deal with the problems of demand in a more indirect fashion. We shall critically survey some of the recent, more promising developments in economic analysis for the urban public sector and see how they contribute to our understanding of the demand for urban public services. Before turning to the new developments in analysis let us mention, albeit too briefly, the more traditional approaches to the market for public services.

Need rather than demand has been the more traditional basis of planning for public services. Need is sometimes defined in crude terms of "requirements for a satisfactory urban society," but in serious studies it is derived from detailed surveys of service levels that governments are trying to achieve or more sophisticated studies of goals, priorities, and costs.[8] Goals research is an old preoccupation of man. Preachers and political leaders have long felt that they had special insights into the goals of society. Leaders in professional groups, like librarians, planners, or sanitary engineers, felt that they could interpret the public welfare and the implied needs for their services; and now social scientists are joining the search for goals and priorities. The possible establishment of goals and the specification of needs by elites or social processes, though deserving of research, has been beyond the insights of economic analysis. Though the economist's decision-model has become increasingly sophisticated about the form in which to consider objectives, and how to use optimization techniques, it has not progressed in the domain of substantive objectives. The economist's focus is on the utility of individuals; therefore, let us turn to the demand for public service as revealed, though imperfectly, by the preferences of individuals, and to the analytical structures developed with individuals— acting individually or as groups—as major elements.

In the two decades since the end of World War II, there has been a many-pronged attack on the problems of analyzing the provision of public services. The special conditions associated with public, rather than private, supply of goods and services have begun to be subjected to intensive analysis. Brave souls have applied the model of *homo economicus* to explain the political processes by which decisions are made. Welfare economists have extended their models to include public goods and to pay attention to public decision-making.

The analysis of public goods became deeply involved with the studies of the failure of decentralized market structures. It was clear that there was no decentralized market system by which to achieve Pareto optimal levels of public goods,[9] and efforts to derive voting models for political choices have not been successful. Public *goods,* first formulated as the extreme case, is now considered as a special case of externalities, and the difficulties of providing optimal public goods are now attributed to a much broader range of public services. It is far too early to predict where this line of research will go, but it has already been a fruitful source of hypotheses for the study of urban public services. Public goods are provided through political processes, usually considered impervious to economic analysis and, though an optimal political decision-making process has not been devised, the

[8] Leonard A. Lecht, *Goals, Priorities, and Dollars* (Free Press, 1966).
[9] Paul A. Samuelson, "Aspects of Public Expenditure Theories," *Review of Economics and Statistics,* Vol. 24 (November 1958).

study of optimal political systems may suggest hypotheses for the study of political decision making in regard to public services. These two lines of investigation—public goods and economic theory of political decisions—have centered on mechanisms by which a society can be elevated into the welfare economists' utopian world of Pareto optimality.

Another tack—centering on cost-benefit analysis—has borrowed less from these developments in theory and has addressed itself to the more pressing operational questions of how to evaluate the public services and plans to alter them. Applied welfare economics in the form of benefit-cost analysis, which began as an oddity in the evaluation of certain kinds of public works, has merged with the more limited operations-research type of cost-effectiveness studies to form a loosely defined field of programming-planning-budgeting systems analysis of public operations. Though most of these developments have occurred at the level of the federal government, they have percolated down to the local levels. The analytical studies have gained the opportunity to demonstrate their value for the urban public decision makers; they still have to prove themselves as useful techniques by which to evaluate urban public services or to plan them. At the moment, support for their extension is strong but far from universal.

I cannot present a report of the successful fusion of these traditions and their unraveling of problems of the demand for urban public services, but a partial survey of some of the developments in these new research areas does indicate progress, if too little to make us confident as to the obvious correctness of these approaches.

Public Goods

The analysis of public goods is intimately tied to the welfare economists' models of the optimally organized decentralized market economy. A specific allocation of resources would earn the welfare economists' accolade of optimal if the marginal rate of substitution of any two goods for any two consumers would be equal to the marginal rate of transformation in production of these two goods.[10]

The decentralized price-market economy would lead to this desirable outcome under a set of stringent conditions, including the absence of externalities. An externality is an unpriced effect. It may be a benefit received by those who do not pay for it, or a loss incurred by those who are not compensated. In any case the decision makers, who pro-

---

[10] The clearest statement of the condition is in Francis Bator, "The Simple Analytics of Welfare Economics," *American Economic Review*, Vol. 47 (March 1957).

duce the service or those who purchase it, will not make the proper determinations in production or consumption if they lack the pecuniary incentives or guides that "price" supplies. A public good, in its pure form, is an extreme case of an externality. It is defined as a good which, if available to anyone, is equally available to all others. This pure case implies that there are no feasible ways to exclude any consumer from enjoying the good, and the consumption of the good by one consumer does not affect the amount available for all others. Classic illustrations would be a radio signal which blankets an area, a defense system which deters an attack, an act of charity which eases all our consciences.

The difficulty for demand analysis, based on individual preferences, posed by the treatment of public services as public goods, is that there is no voluntaristic procedure by which to signal the decision maker that the benefits of an increment of output are greater than the costs of that increment. The benefit of an increment is the sum of the benefits received by each member of the community. Citizen A is not inclined to offer to pay a sum for a public good if there is a subset of members of the community who benefit and hopefully will pay so that the good will be available to each member of the community, including citizen A. Since it is likely that a reasonably large number of persons will share in this strategic behavior, it is argued that the public goods will be under-supplied—the true demand for the good will not be revealed by the consumers. Unfortunately, the same difficulties of revealing true preferences hold in the case of political decisions of any type of public service which is provided without a price.

The perplexing feature of a public good is that it relies on individual preferences for the evaluation, but without an optimal mechanism to aggregate the preferences. In fact, there may not be any observable individual actions directly attributable to the consumption of the public good. For instance, the community "image" is a public good. Do citizens value the identification of their city as "friendly," "culturally progressive," "an All-American City," a "city of churches," "a city with know-how," "honest"? Certainly many, if not most residents, value these images and public officials' actions are affected thereby in many ways, but short of deciding where you are going to live it is difficult to identify individual behavior which reflects on individual values assigned to the "image." The insistence on individual valuation is perfectly understandable. The individual utility arguments in the evaluation of a public good create a complete, individually-evaluated allocation of resources for private market and public political goods, but it is not clear that this is the best way to proceed to analyze the demand for public services or to evaluate the institutions by which public services are provided. Comparability of public provision with private market choice is a virtue, but it is not a necessity. ·

In the private sector, utility theory provides a preference mechanism for demand analysis; its usefulness lies in its contribution to prediction and to normative judgements about market solutions. For the latter objective, welfare judgements, individual preferences are insufficient since we must rely on a social welfare judgement for distributional rules. It is far from clear that the individualistic basis of public goods analysis contributes to the positive analysis of public services. This does not necessarily nullify its central role for normative analysis, but it does arouse suspicion that it may provide an incomplete basis, possibly a disastrously incomplete one. If these reservations have merit, public goods analysis would provide a weak source for positive or normative demand analysis of the public sector, but the whole field is in much too exploratory a stage for anyone to discourage this line of investigation. But just as it would be in error to prejudge the value of public goods concepts, it would be an error to neglect other approaches to explain or evaluate public services.

Public goods have been defined traditionally by the existence of non-excludability (e.g., the noise I hear from the adjoining freeway cannot be denied my neighbor), but there are at least two other categories which broaden the class and extend the problems of public goods to a major part of urban public services. Non-excludability need not derive from technological conditions of supply but it may be deemed efficient or desirable on some policy grounds.

Wherever the marginal cost of supplying another consumer is zero, it would be efficient to allow the consumer entry without assessing a charge, even if it were technically feasible to charge a price; for example, since no resources are diverted if another car is permitted upon an underutilized freeway, it should not be charged a price even if it were simple to collect the toll. Zero marginal cost is an extreme case of a more general category—marginal costs well below average costs. Many public services are characterized by a large ratio of capital to operating costs or by the establishment of a large network. The bridge or water supply would be an illustration of the first type and a police system illustrates the second. In both cases a very large capacity is required to meet certain peak conditions, but in offpeak periods the costs of another unit of output is very slight. If the system is to be efficiently used and entry is to be controlled by price, then the sum of revenues may be less than the costs though the sum of benefits, or the value of the demand, may be greater than costs. Under these conditions, efficiently designed, exclusion prices will not reveal the benefits of the increment of service.[11]

But the largest urban public service, education, would not qualify as a public good on the technical grounds either of non-excludability or of marginal costs far below average costs. In Musgravian language, public education satisfies merit wants.[12] These services are supplied "freely" to the qualified population and they are financed through the general fisc. They are "private" goods which have become endowed with public interest. Though they are the bulk of urban public services, the literature on public goods is distressingly weak in analyzing them. There is a trend to incorporate them into the general class of public goods, which has both advantages and disadvantages.

One general characteristic of public services which greatly expands the applicability of public goods doctrine, though the goods rarely satisfy the technical conditions, is the great value assigned to uniform treatment in the public sector. Possibly, uniformity of services is a "halo" effect extending from the important doctrine of uniform treatment before the law, but whatever the source of the desire for uniformity, it is very widespread throughout the public services. The goal of uniformity is rarely directly analyzed, but it comes up indirectly in the case of specific public services, where equal treatment becomes one of the attributes of the merit want to be satisfied by the specific service.

Merit Goods

The initial attitude towards merit goods was to see them as imposed on the population by a group of moralists or the intellectual elite or a pressure group with power, but with a recognition that the imposition might be a legitimate activity in a democratic society. Though there existed a modicum of respectability for merit goods, they were viewed with hostility. The absence of a link between the merit goods and the preferences of consumers meant that the individualistic normative model could not handle them and therefore they were outside the realm of normative analysis.

One response to the lacunae in analysis would be to explore more carefully the model of political organization, and to evaluate the role of groups in influencing allocations and the institutions by which the

[11] For a survey of possible pricing rules, see William Vickrey, "General and Specific Financing of Urban Services," in H. Schaller (ed.), *Public Expenditure Decisions in the Urban Community* (Resources for the Future, 1963).

[12] Richard Musgrave, *Theory of Public Finance* (McGraw-Hill, 1959), pp. 13–14.

allocations are made. Hopefully, this search for explanation would give rise to insights about how to formulate a set of normative rules appropriate to group decision making. A second response would be to find ways to transform merit goods to public goods and then apply the body of doctrine developed for public goods. The latter approach has been more common. It is understandable, but not necessarily best, that the economist turned in this direction. The first approach, an examination of the process of political decision, might have cast light on the mechanism by which conflicts are resolved or, in economists' language, resources are allocated, and therefore on the processes through which preferences are revealed. The interpretation of the latter phrase explains inhibitions in turning towards political models. It is likely that the political model, or the analysis of demand as it is revealed through political interchanges, would not reveal the only measure of demand considered meaningful for welfare judgement—a demand based upon individual preferences. But if the public sector is dominated by merit goods and if the analyses of merit goods were not amenable to individualistic models, then normative models based upon individual preferences would be irrelevant for policy and it might be more desirable to explore political models. The moral for research is that more work on the analysis of public institutions is necessary to develop a normative model for policy. But before going into political models, let us look at the transformation of merit goods to public goods—the extension of the traditional normative model to services associated with social values.

In the case of a merit good the individual receives more of the public service than the amount he would have purchased, e.g., he has more low-cost housing, more days in the hospital, or more years in school than he would be willing to pay for himself. Two arguments can be developed to permit this excess to be consistent with Pareto optimality. The first would argue that the receipt of goods by the underprivileged enters into the utility function of the privileged.[13]

The underprivileged, in terms of their preferences, would have been still happier if they had received the transfer in money rather than in kind, but this would not have been as satisfactory to the privileged. The privileged allocate their budget among commodities so as to maximize their utilities, and among the commodities are the incomes of the underprivileged and a set of specific commodities consumed by the

[13] The most complete statement of these arguments deals with intergenerational transfers used in the defense of social discount rate. See Stephen Marglin, "The Social Rate of Discount and the Optimal Rate of Investment," *Quarterly Journal of Economics,* Vol. 67 (February 1963).

underprivileged (merit goods).[14] There is an optimal combination of income transfer and merit goods transfers from the perspective of the privileged. From the perspective of the underprivileged these transfers are constraints, and they optimize within them. Therefore, a Pareto optimality is achievable, but there is one catch. If we assume that the transfers enter the budget functions of the privileged as disinterested charity—i.e., they are only interested in the welfare of the under-privileged and not in the grace of giving—then the utility of the donor increases as much with their neighbor's gifts as their own. Charity is a public good. A day in school for an underprivileged child gives satis-faction to all the privileged. My neighbor's joy does not diminish mine. Clearly, some, possibly most, of us will be tempted to let our neighbor pay for the common satisfactions. A common decision, a public act, is necessary to get the proper amount and mix of transfers. But the decision necessitates a political act, and again we face the difficulty of re-vealing "true" preference for public goods via market or political processes.

Once we convert these merit goods it is difficult to know what should be the limit on the definition of a public good. One of the most in-genious conversions of a merit good to a public good is the assignment of direct benefits to non-users who are potential users. It has been pro-posed that we evaluate parks, museums, and similar facilities not only in terms of benefits to users, thereby treating it as a private good, but that we should assign a demand for the facility to non-users who might want to use it.[15] Note that the commodity non-use is equally available to all and the amount of non-use by one party does not affect the amount of non-use by any other party. At first blush this would seem to be sleight of hand, but it is clear that persons would often pay for an option to purchase something they may never use and which they may hope never to use. An obvious example would be a local hospital. If there were insufficient local private demand the community might unanimously support a tax to represent the wishes of the healthy but fearful. To repeat, the transformation of the merit good to a private-plus-public-good is an illuminating bit of analysis but it still leaves us without a basis for "revealed" preferences except for the actions of the political bodies.

An alternative transformation of merit goods is less extreme. Rather than searching out a public good dimension, a careful, exhaustive enu-

---

[14] The underprivileged need not be the conventionally defined poor; they may be the young or the aged.

[15] Burton A. Weisbrod, "Collective Consumption Services of Individual-Con-sumption Goods," *Quarterly Journal of Economics,* Vol. 68 (August 1964).

meration of all of the externalities is analyzed. From one perspective this is what is done in the preceding case, since a public good can be defined as the polar case of externalities, but the difference in form does make a great difference in the possibility of demand evaluation. Utility interdependence is peculiarly difficult to measure. Private charity provides only a lower limit and, of course, there is no private market counterpart. The externalities sought in this second approach are independent of the utility gains of the recipient of the merit good; one can often find market-type analogies for these types of goods; and, as in the case of public goods, the valuation of the externalities is based upon individual preferences.

Consider the following partial list of benefits of education, other than the increased income of the student:

—improved home environment of children of students,
—social and political stability of an informed electorate,
—less costly collections of taxes,
—mothers can work or enjoy their leisure,
—neighbors find the more socialized child more attractive,
—crime costs decline in community of child's residence and the community to which he migrates.[16]

Most of these gains accrue to specific parties, and they are gains which either reduce costs or increase incomes. They contain some benefits that are difficult to measure, such as improved citizenship, but most of the gains are susceptible of measurement. One of the most astute students of economics of education says that "in principle, the recipients of external benefits from some activity (for example, education) should be willing to subsidize the activity and, indeed, should seek to subsidize it. The voting mechanism and taxation provide the means for subsidization. Analysis of voting behavior may shed some light on the question of whether external benefits are recognized and have an effect on decisions. But regardless of whether or not subsidies are actually paid by 'outsiders,' we need to identify and measure the magnitudes of external benefits to determine the returns on resources devoted to education." [17]

[16] Burton A. Weisbrod, *External Benefits of Public Education* (Princeton University Press, 1964), pp. 24–37; and Werner Z. Hirsch, "Regional Accounts for Public Schools," in Werner Z. Hirsch (ed.), *Regional Accounts for Policy Decisions* (The Johns Hopkins Press, for Resources for the Future, 1966), p. 51.
[17] *Ibid.*, pp. 27–28.

Note the hypotheses of the quotation:

1. The beneficiaries of externalities should be willing to pay.
2. Voting and taxation behavior may reveal whether externalities are perceived and whether they affect decisions.
3. Analysis of benefits is important whether or not beneficiaries pay.

But note also the limitations:

1. Beneficiaries always prefer that someone else pay, and if they can shift burdens they will.
2. If voting were the major institutional channel for public decision making this hypothesis might be reasonable, but voting is not the major institution.
3. As a scientific problem, the determination of the rate of return is of great interest, but its role as an index of demand is conditioned by the peculiar nature of merit goods, unpriced distribution, and the values associated with the political organization.

I shall deal with the problems of measurement of benefits and the rate of return on investment in a later discussion of benefit-cost analysis. At this point, I want to explore briefly the implications that this decomposition of merit goods into groups of externalities has for hypotheses about the state of the public services. What are some of the "idealized facts" that are part of this approach to merit goods? First, merit goods are supplied at zero prices to direct consumers, since it is desired that they consume an amount whose cost is greater than the value it holds for them. The fact of zero prices also holds for public goods, though there is no desire to subsidize the consumers of public goods. Secondly, an optimal supply of merit goods would require an optimally designed voting and taxing scheme or, if possible, a pricing scheme which would have the same results. Both of these sets of "facts" are reasonable approximations. What do they imply for the provision of urban merit goods?

If a good is supplied at a zero price, we can expect an excess demand at that price or, as more commonly described in the "view-with-alarm" literature, an insufficiency of supply. The response to excess demand is that some form of rationing, other than price, is adopted. Typical forms are: congestion (where some persons decide to avoid the service because of quality deterioration); administrative rules limiting access to the public service; an active market in other assets which gives one access to the public service. Let us consider each of the above response patterns.

Changes in land values are often associated with a public improvement. Consider, then, the construction of a park or a playground or a community center. Those who welcome the facility and are prepared to incur costs for them will pay more for a residential site located closer to them. Land values and rents will rise and the sites will be occupied by those who value the facility more.[18] Those who find less of an attraction in the facility and therefore do not value the convenience of living nearby will not be willing to pay the higher rent and will move elsewhere. We are all familiar with upgrading through urban renewal and the consequence to the poor, who were presumed to benefit, being forced to relocate to areas not blessed with the improved facilities. Therefore, we may find the perverse effect: the consumers, who would have generated the greatest externality benefits for others, may not consume, and those citizens who "subsidized" the merit good may find their well-intentioned subsidy captured in capital gains to land, with the consumers of the good paying an indirect price.

The "perversity" phenomenon is only applicable to merit goods, not "public goods" like transportation or fire-fighting systems. The same changes in land values will occur and the same rationing of use by changes in the price of housing will develop, but since the externality benefits are not anticipated, there will be no disappointment.

Though an indirect market price reaction will occur in both cases of zero-priced merit and public goods, in neither case will this price information be sufficient as a guide for public service planning. We shall discuss the index of land values as a guide to public services planning in the section on benefit-cost analysis, but it is clear that the "demand" for facilities by the users will not have been satiated. Rents may ration access but not limit pressures to expand the quantity of services; the "deserving poor" may have been forced away from the park or the better school but they want this free facility in their new location.[19]

A second and more obvious form of rationing is administrative criteria. Education may be limited to age groups, subjects, number of

[18] A precise statement of the pattern of occupation and rent changes would involve an analysis of consumers' surpluses, income elasticities of demand, value of time, density preferences, and so on, which would take us beyond the scope of this paper.

[19] Land value effects are only one type of indirect market. Political corruption could be viewed as another. Legal costs to overcome crowding in courts and regulatory bodies would be still another. There is an abundance of scattered case material dealing with the consumers' adaptation to zero-priced public services, but there has been no systematic study of this process except in water resources and urban transportation.

hours; hospital beds may be restricted to types of diseases; libraries may limit the number of books borrowed; police will be distributed by area or population or crime rate. If the services are free to the direct users, excess demand will exist, administrators will decide who is most "deserving" of the service, and pressures will exist to expand them.[20] Since there need not be any private costs inhibiting pressures on extending the service, the amount of "excess demand" or "undersupply" will appear dramatic.

The "scientific" analysis of this source of excess demand would be the standards developed by professional associations. Librarians, recreationists, educators, almost every branch of the public services seek to expand their services to the rationed populations. The individualistic theory of merit goods finds its justification in the utility functions of the subsidizers, but the professional associations find their arguments in the capacity of their clients to consume their services. Since the associations do not try to estimate benefit, but only "need" under conditions of zero pricing, their representation of demand for their services is limited only by the capacity of their clients to consume. It is not surprising that urban public services do not measure up to the standards and are therefore always painted as inadequate. Though the subsidizers are prepared to extend the supply of merit goods beyond the consumers' willingness to pay, they are often rightfully suspicious of the possible motives of the administrative agencies. If an individualistic basis for merit goods could be established, then rationing rules might be devised to reduce the apparent excess demand. A pricing scheme, if feasible, might still be more efficient but, unfortunately, it is not always feasible. A large part of the new work in public systems analysis is directed towards the rationalization of administrative rules.[21]

If administrative rationing were not adopted, then we are likely to find the most public form of seemingly inadequate supply—quality deterioration. Congestion imposes social costs which then become the rationing device. The government does not charge a price, but quality

---

[20] "The operating agencies can offer some evidence about the demand for their services, for example, the number of unprocessed applicants or the extent of unserviced areas. Unfortunately, the unmet demand for government service always falls short of the resources available to the public sector." Gerald J. Boyle, "The New York City Budget Process," in *Financing Government in New York City,* Final Research Report of the Graduate School of Public Administration, New York University, to the Temporary Commission on City Finances, City of New York (N.Y. University, 1966), p. 216.

[21] For a useful analysis of rules and pricing in regards to a public good, see Allen V. Kneese, "Rationalizing Decision in the Quality Management of Water Supply in Urban-Industrial Areas," in J. Margolis (ed.), *The Public Economy of Urban Communities* (Resources for the Future, 1965).

may deteriorate so that substitute products are chosen—e.g., private schools instead of public schools, private recreation, and so on. But the excess demand, the desire on the part of the actual or rationed user for more of the service at the price he is charged, is great.

In the case of a public good, such as transportation, the social costs provide information, though no incentive, for the government to expand the services. In the case of a merit good, the social costs—quality deterioration—do not provide this information, since we do not know about the reduction in the utility of the externality beneficiaries.

POLITICAL PROCESSES

Rather casual assumptions are often made that political processes will reflect the preferences of consumers or that public decisions should reflect their preferences. However, systematic explorations of the likelihood that the urban political system does succeed in reflecting preferences, or of the conditions where the system could be successful, are extremely few. It would be hazardous to project the trend of these few studies, but I believe that the number of political studies by economists will increase greatly in the next decade. Hopefully, we will enlist the aid of political scientists.

A degenerate case of the political decision-making process is the Tieboutian model of individual choice of local governments.[22] I classify it as "degenerate" because there is no specification of a political process by which the government policies are formed; despite this failing, however, it has a virtue which other political models lack—individuals can move among government jurisdictions. Movement has the quality of resignation from the social contract. Mobility of population is an important factor in local political decisions. A substantial part of local decision making is directed towards attracting activities from other areas or discouraging "their" activities from moving elsewhere.

The Tieboutian scheme was an attempt to solve the public goods problem, but its main impact was to increase the awareness of economists of the value of a competitive model of governments. The model is one of an infinite variety of communities, each with a different package of public services and taxes. Assuming that all private goods are available, at the same price, the individual chooses a site so as to balance off his marginal site costs (housing costs including taxes) with his marginal evaluation of the set of public services. The model, as an argument that public goods will be optimally supplied, is not persuasive since it has no political mechanism to generate the optimal set of

[22] Charles M. Tiebout, "A Pure Theory of Local Expenditures," *Journal of Political Economy,* Vol. 64 (October 1956).

packages to be available to the itinerant households. However, the model did have a salutary effect of reminding the rationalizers of metropolitan government that differences among communities had social advantages, even if there were external diseconomies.

Migration among communities is interesting at several levels. It greatly expands the possibilities of individual choice of a preferred set of public services and style of living, as stressed by Tiebout. It also offers an interesting dimension to the analysis of demand for public services as seen through planning or political processes.

If individuals can be made aware that over their life-cycle they will choose to live in different types of communities, or at least in different neighborhoods within the city, they may be more likely to consider the merits of metropolitan proposals which may benefit areas other than where they live at the moment. If it is less costly to increase their utility by an improved set of options than by improving their neighborhood, then they may accept the more far-reaching solutions. This attempt to focus on the full set of options is part of the strategy of master planning. The record of success of the strategy is poor. Despite the stress on the distant future and the attempt to divert attention away from the immediate and particular, payoffs to specific areas dominate and master plans have not become operating documents.[23]

A third level of interest in intercity migration is the fact that movement is itself a form of "voting." It is this interaction between a market decision, the choice of a site, and the political decision on public services that is particularly interesting.

One of the most common goals of community leaders, especially in suburban communities, is that of fiscal profitability. The criterion they use in evaluating a public act is the change in tax revenue and public costs associated with the act. Though these studies have been primarily concerned with land use policies like zoning and annexation, fiscal profitability considerations are implicit in many other decisions. For example, an improved water supply is more costly, but is this offset by more industry with its larger tax base? The popular base for this criterion is not "profits" to the city treasury, but the assumption that a fiscally profitable decision will result in lower taxes to the remaining residents. Of course, if fiscal profitability is an operational criterion of city leaders, and if individuals make locational decisions on the basis of a value of services-tax cost differential then it might seem reasonable to hypothesize that we might find a confirmation of public decisions in the operations of the market. Land values should rise in the more

[23] For some case material on the problems of master planning, see Edward C. Banfield and James Q. Wilson, *City Politics* (Vintage, 1963), Chap. 14.

"fiscally profitable" cities. The "profits" should be capitalized into gains for the current residents. Immigrants might still face a low tax rate, but higher property values would mean greater interest and tax payments so that in equilibrium the advantage will be lost.

If we tested the above hypothesis of market confirmation of fiscal profitability criteria, it is unlikely to be validated, but the mechanism of market verification of the political leaders' fiscal decisions is suggestive of further hypotheses. Fiscal profitability is generally too crude a criterion. There are interdependencies among land uses that are ignored, and it is silent on the problem of evaluation of the public services. It implicitly assumes a requirements approach. Individual decisions on location will be determined by the costs of the site, including taxes, and the benefits to the purchasers. The benefits would include the value to the individuals of the public services as well as the quality of private facilities available, as shopping districts, job possibilities, social groups and so on. A fiscally profitable decision need not be one where the sum of individual benefits minus costs calculations is positive. Let us consider the consequences of mobility based on fiscal benefits, gains and losses to the residents, rather than just fiscal profits.

Assume that the sum of individual benefits minus costs of the public expenditures were positive and individuals perceived this. In this case, if the residents were randomly drawn from the community at large, the outsiders would perceive the fiscal advantages in the community and land values would rise. Note that the residents first received a fiscal gain, and this was then converted to a capital gain to the asset they held. But the full story would not end at this point.

Not all residents would have received the same fiscal gain, but all of them would receive the same capital gain. The new land values would be the competitive market value, determined by the demand of many residents and outsiders and the supply of the many sites in the city and outside. Each site would receive the same increase in value. The fiscal gain to the residents would be unique to each resident—it would be based upon the utility to him of the public services. After market values adjusted, each resident would find that his housing costs, including imputed rent based upon new site values, would have increased but this increase in costs would be above or below their previously estimated fiscal gain. For those who never had a fiscal gain, continued residence in the community would not be advantageous. For these two groups, costs, including opportunity costs, would be greater than the benefits of the public decision. The composition of the residents would shift to include only those for whom the net fiscal gain was greater than the average. A desirable pattern of public services would result in gains to a majority of the residents and a reshuffling of the population to exclude those who least welcomed the pattern. The population would become more homogeneous relative to tastes for public services and the political leadership would be confirmed in their decisions.

"Voting with one's feet," as developed above, is an interesting model which stresses the importance of mobility and the market for assets which gives access to the fiscal package of government, but it is far from an adequate model of public choice. First of all, it should be pointed out that it is not an optimizing model. Further, it does not contain any discussion of voting by ballot or any other form of political influence.

Any set of public acts would generate a change in the ratio of residential costs to benefits of public services. Migration, according to the pattern outlined above, may take place, but this does not mean upgrading of community welfare but only a greater homogeneity among residents. A poorly designed package of public services would have led to capital losses, migration, a homogeneous community, and a state of welfare well within the utility possibility frontier of the metropolitan area.

In the real world, heterogeneity and political conflict will persist. Some of the heterogeneity can be explained by the costs of moving and differences in economic base. Others may be accounted for by informal political actions which prevent the market from operating. For instance, older, childless couples would be forced out of a growing community because of the higher property taxes. But usually these couples live in older houses which are highly underassessed. The opportunity costs of living in the community have increased but not the cash costs. The "inequitable" property tax administration reduces the political opposition and the speed at which the community becomes homogeneous.

It would be intriguing to explore the question whether voting both by ballot and by feet would solve the public goods problem and give rise to an optimal set of public services (ignoring merit goods, distributional criteria, and externalities among communities). Unfortunately, this is not the place for such a digression. I raise it here because political influence on the provision of public services in a community is exercised both to affect the density of economic activity to achieve growth and capital gains, and also to achieve net fiscal benefits to the residents who are hostile to in-migrants and ignorant of, or indifferent to, capital gains effects. This sharp distinction between utility of services and asset enhancement is drawn too strongly. The protagonist of "better" schools will vote for schools in any event, but his campaign literature stresses that better schools mean better neighborhoods and therefore, the preservation of property values. In turn, the chamber of commerce member who seeks to keep taxes down to encourage industry, jobs, and growth concedes that good schools are useful to attract executives and technicians. Therefore, it would not be too amiss to assume an objective function for political leaders which evaluates public services in terms of benefit and asset position of the residents. But we shall not pursue this model at this point. Before turning to the more explicit political models I would like to amplify a bit the asset-enhancement goal.

A major goal of community leaders is growth of the city. Public services, taxes, and land policies are frequently evaluated in terms of their effects on growth. The declining rate of growth of the central city is a signal of danger, a call to organize counter-measures. But growth in city A can only be earned at the expense of city B. Does it matter greatly to the resident in city A if his new job is located a mile south in the central business district of A or a mile north across the border in city B? For most purposes the resident would not care, and few residents feel strongly about services to attract the firm. But those with large property holdings who stand to gain with increased density feel quite differently. Growth is not only a synonym for progress but it is the source of capital gains. The large investors in land are not mobile, at least in terms of their planning horizons. They are very interested in mobility, but it is the mobility of the in-migrant. It is their heavy investment which makes their payoffs from public activities very different from those of the residents, and which will create difficulties in interpreting the political process as an instrument to evaluate the consumers' demand for urban public services. Goals for land enhancement are not the same as utility optimization.

Let us now turn to the more explicitly political models.

There are several political approaches to the positive or normative analysis of urban public services adopted by economists. The first is identified with the work of Downs and Buchanan-Tullock and is an extension of the classical literature of welfare economics.[24] Most of the research has been theoretical but there have been statistical studies which have sought to verify hypotheses suggested by this literature.[25]

[24] Anthony Downs, *An Economic Theory of Democracy* (Harper, 1957); James Buchanan and Gordon Tullock, *The Calculus of Consent* (University of Michigan Press, 1962); Jerome Rothenberg, "A Model of Economic and Political Decision-Making," in Margolis (ed.), *The Public Economy of Urban Communities.*

[25] James L. Barr and Otto A. Davis, "An Elementary Political and Economic Theory of the Expenditures of Local Governments," *Southern Economic Journal,* Vol. 32 (October 1966); Edward Banfield and James Wilson, "Voting Behavior

The studies substitute political institutions for market processes in linking individual preferences to public expenditures.

A second approach has been to concentrate on the behavior of the legislature, as a political body, and its relationship to the administrative bodies which represent the public services. The legislature is representative of the interests of the electorate, but the connection between the individual and his representative is developed in only a rudimentary way.[26] The substitute for the market would be bargaining among legislators and administrators.

A third approach is much more informal than the other two. There are many case studies of specific public services or cities which introduce political factors to explain decisions or which discuss revisions in government structure. Though politics are important inputs, the authors make no efforts to explore systematically the structure or behavioral characteristics of the political process.

In recent years political scientists have begun to study local political decision-making at a more analytical level.[27] At the moment, economics and political science literature exist side by side and there has been little cross-fertilization, but both sets of studies have short histories and few things travel slower than communications across departmental borders. Hopefully, this insulation will disappear.

The classic form of the political model is to assume that politicians present tax and expenditures options to voters so as to maximize the vote they receive. In this search for political support they will discover the preferences of consumers, innovations in services, and tax alternatives, and they will be motivated to maximize the sum of the fiscal surpluses (benefits minus costs) going to the citizenry. There has been disagreement as to whether a fiscal program which emerges from such a model would result in too large or too small a government or whether it will be inequitable. Certainly, if we can substitute the politician-voter for the entrepreneur-consumer relationship and the election for the marketplace we would have established a very useful means to analyze the demand for public services.

---

on Municipal Public Expenditures: A Study in Rationality and Self-Interest," in Margolis (ed.), *The Public Economy of Urban Communities.*

[26] Charles E. Lindblom, "Decision-Making in Taxation and Expenditures," in *Public Finances: Needs, Sources and Utilization,* Universities—National Bureau for Economic Research (Princeton University Press, 1961); Aaron Wildavsky, *Politics of the Budgetary Process* (Little, Brown, 1964).

[27] Nelson Polsby, *Community Power and Political Theory* (Yale University Press, 1963); Edward Banfield and James Wilson, *City Politics* (Vintage, 1966); Robert A. Dahl, *Who Governs?* (Yale University Press, 1961); Robert C. Wood, *1400 Governments* (Harvard University Press, 1961).

There are many shortcomings to the political model of public finance, or economic model of political decision-making, which have yet to be overcome. A glaring limitation exists in the central role assigned to the voter. It will be difficult for economists to abandon this central role of the voter since it is the most direct means to associate fiscal outcomes with individual preferences. But if one feels there is any merit to Galbraithian strictures in regard to consumer sovereignty, then one should gag at accepting a model dependent upon voters' sovereignty.

A politician certainly wants to be elected and this does require a majority of the vote, but this is usually far less than the majority of eligible voters. The median percentage of adults voting in 461 city elections in 1961–62 was 33 per cent.[28] This is probably an overstatement of community interest. When city elections were held at the same time as state or national the median percentage was 50, and when it was held independently the median fell to 29. When the citizenry are asked to focus on the important local issues free of partisan debate they demonstrate great disinterest. The support of only a relatively small minority of voters is sufficient for the great majority of municipal candidates. This low turnout to vote is matched by ignorance about local affairs and inactivity in regard to campaigns.

The lack of voter interest may be distressing but it is not unreasonable. A single vote is to be cast for a man who is to take a position on a great many issues. An "enlightened" vote would require a tremendous investment of study time. We should not expect any voter to make this investment, given the extremely low probability that his ballot will affect the outcome of the vote or that his candidate will be bound by his campaign promises. If voting were to provide a reasonable register of preferences it would be extremely costly. The ersatz polling which does take place bears little relationship to an "optimal" choice. None of this is meant to disparage the critical role that elections may play in the creation of political stability and also for community improvement, but only that it is not a device by which to discover the demand for public service.

The slender popular base of support for the elected officials encourages the analyst to look for roles to be played by men other than voters and politicians. If there are such other roles, then the politician's function would have to be redefined. To be effective it would be insufficient for him to have gained a majority of votes cast; the support of others would be necessary. Clearly, the politician's objective function would be to maximize his utility, and the inputs to his utility function

[28] Eugene C. Lee, "City Elections: A Statistical Profile," in *Municipal Yearbook: 1963,* International City Managers' Association (Chicago: 1963), p. 83.

would be supplied by a variety of groups in the community. He may have to satisfy that small minority which ensures him a post, but beyond that he is free to respond to many informal pressures. The studies of the political scientists give very little space to the electorate and even the elected officials are usually merged together with a host of other wielders of influence: civic leaders, voluntary commission members, social elites, and so on. Their studies deal with who makes decisions, how they are made, how influence is exercised. Their system, in contrast to the economists' model, is an extremely elaborate scheme. It does not defy formalization,[29] and it should be possible to link it to the economists' concern with the payoffs to individuals of specific public acts and services.

The political scientist's finding of a pluralistic power group—specialized influentials who concentrate their attention on restricted areas, and a relatively small group of influence wielders—is consistent with the facts of urban government, which provides many different services for different groups. The concentration of political power is consistent with a concentration of economic power in the community. In New Haven the ten largest owners of real estate paid almost one-fifth of the total taxes levied by the city, and their taxes financed one-eighth of the city's total expenditures.[30] It is not surprising that with this type of disparity we have a disparity of influence in metropolitan public decision-making. Units with large capital investments in the city are likely to incur much greater political costs to safeguard and enhance their investments. Much of the payoff in public service finally rests in property values and this will mean a market in influence to supplement the electoral aggregation process.

A political model of public finance or an economic model of public decision-making should include the factor that larger property holding will lead to increased political participation and this, in turn, will make planning for space relatively more important than planning for persons. Peculiar competitive practices may develop among cities which may reduce the welfare of the aggregate of persons but increase property values of a subset. I suspect that a model can be constructed which would enable us to construct a demand for public services through political institutions, but it will reflect the distribution of wealth within the city. Of course, the normative properties of this "political" demand curve are dubious.

The normative properties of the second approach of economists to political decision making is equally uncertain. The bargaining adjust-

[29] See Rothenberg, *op. cit.*
[30] Dahl, *op. cit.,* p. 81.

ment models were developed for legislative and administrative haggling which made them most appropriate for the federal and national governments. At the local level the process of adjustment among groups is far less formal and uniform. Trade-offs in support on municipal issues are less manageable or explicit than legislative logrolling. On the whole, the political science studies have tended to be consistent with what could be roughly called bargaining models. These models focus on the decision, the forces affecting it, and the terms. Though insight into the decision process is of great value, it does not enable one to make an independent estimate of demand.

Our political models are not yet sufficiently advanced to tell us how to estimate demand, nor can we be sure that they ever will be successful in that role.

BENEFIT-COST ANALYSIS

In recent years developments in economic theory have tended to confound the economic adviser to the government, while developments in applied economic analysis have excited the public officials to seek out the economist for guidance on public programming and planning. The theorist has deepened the problem of public goods,[31] asserted the impossibility of a democratic social welfare function,[32] denied the existence of a general theory of the second best,[33] and strengthened the arguments against judging a situation that is allocationally superior independent of distributional effects.[34] Despite these admonitions by theorists, the applied analyst has persisted in developing analytical schemes by which to evaluate the design and scale of public services. His philosophical foundations are weak, bureaucratic and political resistances are strong, but his techniques are being rapidly extended to many areas of the urban public services. Water supply[35] and urban transportation[36] were initial areas of application but benefit-cost techniques are being extended to the full range of urban public services.[37]

---

[31] See Musgrave, *op. cit.*; and Samuelson, *op. cit.*

[32] Kenneth J. Arrow, *Social Choice and Individual Values* (Wiley, 1951).

[33] Kevin Lancaster and Richard Lipsey, "The General Theory of Second Best," *Review of Economic Studies,* Vol. 24, No. 63 (1958).

[34] Edward Mishan, *Welfare Economics* (Random House, 1964), Chap. 1.

[35] Jack Hirshleifer, J. DeHaven and J. Milliman, *Water Supply* (University of Chicago Press, 1960); Joe S. Bain, R. Caves and J. Margolis, *The Northern California Water Industry* (The Johns Hopkins Press, for Resources for the Future, 1966).

[36] C. D. Foster and M. E. Beesley, "Estimating the Social Benefit of Constructing an Underground Railway in London," *Journal of the Royal Statistical Society,* Vol. 126 (March 1, 1963).

[37] For a survey of these studies and techniques, see Robert Dorfman (ed.), *Measuring Benefits of Government Investments* (Brookings, 1965); A. R. Prest

Benefit-cost analysis is an attempt to apply in a straightforward way the economic model of choice to a public service. Since the economists' model was developed for a firm with a single owner-manager producing a single product under conditions of certainty, the extension of the model for practical use by government agencies has been a heroic effort.[38] The objective function has been difficult to identify; the absence of markets makes prices very elusive, and public services are instances of increasing returns, indivisibilities, or extensive externalities —areas where economic analysis is still underdeveloped. Given these limitations, and the very few economists who have been involved, the progress has been remarkable.

The structure and theory of benefit-cost analysis have been developed in many papers and I shall not try to review them here. I shall deal with only a few points. The first thing to note is the variety of similar types of analysis: cost-effectiveness, program budgeting, systems analysis, planning-programming-budgeting-system, and so on. All of these studies share a similar frame of reference, e.g., heroic quantification, specification of objectives, analysis of costs and returns, and testing of alternatives. But there are also important differences, and these differences stem from tradition rather than internal logic.[39] All of these studies are directed towards more rational decision-making in government. The distinctive feature of benefit-cost studies is that they are less managerially oriented than the others. Any sharp distinction would overstate the differences, but I believe that the differences are real and significant.

The benefit-cost studies took as their point of departure the welfare of the nation and they paid little heed to the peculiar problems of the

---

and R. Turvey, "Cost-Benefit Analysis: A Survey," *Economic Journal,* December, 1965. For more specific urban references see N. Lichfield and J. Margolis, "Benefit-Cost Analysis as a Tool in Urban Government Decision-Making," in H. Schaller (ed.), *Public Expenditure Decisions in the Urban Community* (Resources for the Future, 1963); Jerome Rothenberg, *Economic Evaluation of Urban Renewal: Conceptual Foundation of Benefit-Cost Analysis* (Brookings, 1967); Harry P. Hatry and J. F. Cotton, *Program Planning for State, County, and City,* State-Local Finances Project of the George Washington University (Washington, D.C.: 1966).

[38] Almost all of the difficulties facing the public analyst also face the analyst for the giant firm. Both find it difficult to specify objective functions, decide on the appropriate discount rate, cope with uncertainty, determine optimal prices, and so on. The literature of optimization analysis for both private and public operations is joined at a highly abstract level, but there seems to be little cross-fertilization at the applied levels.

[39] For a recent review of many of these techniques, see David Novick (ed.), *Program Budgeting, Program Analysis, and the Federal Budget* (Harvard University Press, 1965). An early book on benefit-cost analysis which is in the flavor of the later developments is Roland N. McKean, *Efficiency in Government Through Systems Analysis* (Wiley, 1958).

government. The other studies have been more operationally linked to administrative control of the government agencies. The objective function is defined by the agencies' assignment; the constraints are the political and administrative rules under which the agencies operate. In a continuum of analytical studies ranging from administrative rationality to policy evaluation, the benefit-cost studies would fall at the policy extreme. As a consequence, these studies are less operational—i.e., less useful to agencies who feel they cannot abandon their directives— and the studies focus more on the nature of an objective function derived from an analysis of the public interest.

The classic form of benefit-cost analysis is the search for the single number, the aggregate of benefits less the aggregate of costs. Recognition of the importance of distributional questions, of who receives the benefits and who bears the costs, was slow in coming. For national programs one might argue that distributional questions should be ignored since for the full set of programs redistribution is likely to be nil.[40]

For local programs distributional issues are often critical at two levels. Many local public services are directed towards social problems, such as education, law and order, and poverty alleviation. It is difficult to avoid explicit evaluation of distributional benefits. This distributional question, the income level of the recipients, is one that has been discussed at length in the literature. A second distributional question is peculiar to urban services. Who is the population to be served?

Benefits are crudely defined as prices individuals would be willing to pay for the service if there was some feasible way to assess these prices. Implicit in benefit-cost analysis is the assumption that the desired outcome would be one which would have resulted from perfectly operating private markets, if there had been no technical difficulties leading to public provision. A national government might not be reprimanded if it ignored the benefits of its actions for foreigners, but can we treat so lightly an indifference to benefits of those who live beyond the city borders? The problem of relevant population arises at several levels. Public services may cause an export of population which may create difficulties elsewhere. Public services may cause an import of population with possible losses or gains to exporting or importing cities. And what about the gains or losses of the mobile population? Men may leave the city, independent of the state of public services, and take with them whatever advantages from the public services they had been able to internalize. Residents outside the city use the city's services and, of

[40] There is no evidence supporting this hypothesis. Further, an appropriate goal might be redistribution.

course, residents commute outside. Which of the possible populations should we consider? What are the choices?

If we consider a stationary distribution of residences and activities, but with spillovers, shall the city's analyst consider the benefits wherever they appear in the metropolitan area—for example, a smog control program which benefits the entire area, a road improvement of benefit to through traffic as well as local traffic, a public health program which reduces epidemic possibilities? [41] Since the outsiders are not taxpayers or voters, one would assume that the economic analyst would be directed by his employer, the local government, to ignore these benefits. It is not clear that this will always be done. Central cities may be competitive with their suburbs in regard to a fixed set of economic activities, but they gain as the entire metropolitan area grows. The incidence of benefit to the central city resident of reduced air pollution elsewhere is indirect, and though there are cases of cities considering benefits to non-residents, they are likely to be infrequent.[42] Therefore, the central city may assign a small value to benefits received by the suburbs. The relationship is not likely to be reciprocal. Almost any growth in the metropolitan area benefits the central city; the suburb is primarily in a competitive position with the other cities and therefore less concerned, or possibly feels injured, by the benefits generated to others.

The technological spillins and spillouts create planning difficulties, but it is generally assumed that the people to be considered for benefits analysis are those within the boundaries of the financing authority. This myopic view is even less satisfactory for the case of mobile residents and activities. If an expansion of police activity means a reduction in crime in the city but a relocation of crime to the adjoining city, should we consider as benefits the reduction only and not the offsetting increase? If urban renewal attracts middle-class childless apartment dwellers back to the city to the fiscal benefit of the central city, what about the fiscal loss to the suburbs with its large families requiring schooling? Should the analyst again restrict his analysis to the gains to the city employing him?

What about educational gains to the residents? Mobility increases with education. The more the residents invest in training, the more likely they are to expand the opportunities to them and to encourage them to move elsewhere with their enhanced capacity. "The city" may

[41] For an analysis of these spillouts and spillins, see Alan Williams, "The Optimal Provision of Public Goods in a System of Local Government," *Journal of Political Economy,* Vol. 74 (February 1966).

[42] Los Angeles and San Francisco have adopted water supply programs which have accelerated growth outside the city limits and, in the case of Los Angeles, at a net fiscal cost to the city's residents.

lose this resource, but who is the city? Are the gains to the resident, wherever he later earns his income, to be counted as benefits against the cost of education or only the incomes earned while he remains a resident? Is the road which the resident takes for a week-end in the country as valuable as the one the commuter takes to work in the city?

I believe that the above set of questions is usually answered in terms of the set of occupants of a specific area—for example, a training program that removes a man from welfare is to be considered no more effective than one that encourages him to leave town. Both reduce the city's welfare rolls by the same number. Rothenberg in his study of urban renewal chose the population of the metropolitan area as his reference base, though he recognized that this exposed his analysis to the charge of political irrelevance. The choice of population will become an increasingly serious issue as the number of benefit-cost studies increase. Urban governments are highly place-oriented. Benefits to an area are often merely redistributions within a larger area. People who are mobile may be indifferent among the possible subareas where the "benefits" are generated, but city fathers are not mobile, their jurisdictions are fixed and, therefore, their evaluative frame of reference may be quite different from that of the mobile residents. This conflict poses a problem of professional ethics for the economist-adviser. Does he serve the city official or is his analysis to design a program for the relevant population?

The issue of population of beneficiaries comes up in other forms as well. Consider the educational public service. Certainly the parent is interested in his child's income-earning ability, in his integration into society, in his ability to get along with neighbors. It is equally clear that we are not prepared to trust the parent with the full control over efforts to educate his child. We do not accept parental budgetary allocations as being a proper measure of what the "child" would have been willing to pay. We have strained ourselves in the search for externality effects, many of which can be interpreted as parental "inadequate" demand for education of his child. If we reject parental judgements about willingness to pay in regard to education, should this rejection extend to other urban public services as well?

Benefit-cost studies are based upon individualistic arguments. The benefits are the sum of the prices individuals are willing to pay, but our observations on individuals are restricted to the set of individuals who purchase. Non-purchasers, children in particular, are assumed to be represented by parents. So many of the major urban public service decisions affect children directly that we should feel confident that the parental choice has properly weighted the utility of the child. Urban form, housing design, transportation systems have serious consequences for children. The collapse of mass transportation has had a crippling effect on the mobility of children. At the moment I believe we are exercising implicit political judgements in defining the situations where we accept the purchaser as "appropriate" agent for the family and when to reject him or her. It is not clear that the state should intervene only when parental faults create externalities outside the family. In any case, the "individualistic" assumptions underlying benefits evaluation have to be reappraised more carefully when applied to urban services.

Benefits are the prices which individuals would be willing to pay for the service as estimated by the analyst. In principle, the analyst seeks to avoid interposing his judgement or the judgement of public officials about what individuals *should* be willing to pay, if only they knew their best interest as he does. In practice, tricky concepts like merit goods tempt the analyst to dilute his principles. The conscientious attempt at explicit measurement does not always fully restrain the analyst, but it is still the best discipline. Though there are virtues in accepting the discipline of measurement, it is clear the households are highly inefficient purchasers and they are likely to be inequitable distributors of utilities within the family. Some analysts, in recognition of the facts, reject any reliance on consumers' sovereignty and instead are seeking to discover the needs of the community and establish them as objectives. But let us at least retain individual values, as reflected in people's behavior, as the measure of worth of the services.

The benefit-cost analyst usually seeks out some market behavior which he can relate to the service. He may ask what costs, now incurred, would be avoided if the service was supplied. The logic of the question is that the individual would be prepared to pay at least the saved cost. Illustrations are reduced operating transport costs with a more direct road or reduced medical bills if immunized. But this would be a minimum estimate. Gains should be more than these costs savings.

A second mechanism is to convert the service to an intermediate good, and estimate the enhanced productivity of the individual because of the good. Education is the classic illustration of this method. Increased income associated with increased education is adopted as a measure of what the individual would be willing to pay.

A third approach is to try to find comparable goods which they purchase and since private goods are not often comparable, very subtle reasoning may be involved. Illustrations are commonly found in the park and recreation area. There are private parks which may provide useful information but the more common technique is more indirect. Individuals located at distant points from a park incur travel costs as a

561

function of distance. Attendance at the park is inversely related to distance. The cost of transportation can be interpreted as a price that individuals pay—the higher the price the fewer the "purchasers." [43] With this knowledge of the "imputed" demand curve one could estimate the area under the demand curve and, therefore, the gains to having the park.

Another indirect mechanism would be the values of sites which have differential endowments of public services. Studies of land value differentials related to degree of smog have been initiated. Impact of highways on land values has long been studied. The land value differentials would be the price the individuals would be prepared to pay for the difference between his evaluation of the service and the tax cost he is asked to bear.

The preceding approaches to benefit estimation relate to behavior of individuals. These conform to the classic approaches of benefit-cost analysis, but one of them involves a distortion—the increased income of individuals. There is evidence that income differentials do lead to shifts in education, but there is no strong evidence that the enhanced income measures their willingness to pay. In fact, the whole area of the value of a human life tends to be treated on separate principles. In classic terms, we should ask what the potential victim is prepared to pay to avoid the inevitable or at least to postpone it. Some clues are available—premiums for jobs with greater risk, for example—but instead we have sought social judgements about the value. His income, if he lives, may be enjoyed by him and his family, but it bears little relationship to his price for survival. If we assume that the wife will remarry it also bears little relationship to the loss. There are social processes, such as court decisions or legislative appropriations, which assign values to benefits of lives, and these too have been used in benefit-cost studies, though they do not conform to the individualistic basis of these studies. Essentially, the money income of individuals is a poor index of their welfare. We have all been aware of this, but we have suppressed our objections, because we have been unable to deal with the problem.

One issue in the benefit-cost studies as applied to urban phenomena deserves special attention. It has been suggested that a relatively simple way to judge the value of a public service is to measure the increase in land values or land plus improvements. The latter form, total investment, is a peculiar measure since it includes costs as a measure of benefits. Improvements are the costs of resources necessary to provide the private facilities to exploit the public services. Valuing the public serv-

[43] Marion Clawson and Jack L. Knetsch, *Economics of Outdoor Recreation* (The Johns Hopkins Press, for Resources for the Future, 1966), Part II.

ices as the sum of private facilities would be equivalent to valuing a park by aggregating the costs necessary to reach and use the park. But the private costs are simply the value of the further increment in resources necessary to make the park enjoyable. Though there is little merit in aggregating all improvements, the test of change in land values is a more persuasive measure.

Land values are a measure of the site advantage of an area, and if the city provides special advantages it seems reasonable to hypothesize that these advantages will increase demand for the more attractive space and that the competitive market will bid up the values of land, just equal to the capitalized values of the benefits of the public services. If this hypothesis is valid, then it may not be necessary to pursue all of the byways of benefits evaluation, just the consequences for the market for real property. The public would confirm the public decision by increasing their demand for entry into the city.

The mechanism of land enhancement is usually associated with public works, but the same logic could be extended to any public service. An improved public library makes the city more attractive for some residents and, if no less attractive for others, demand for land in the city will increase and thereby land values. It seems reasonable to assume the same would be true for an improved police force. It is not strange that analysts are tempted to look to land value changes to estimate the difference between the sum of the present value of the public services less the present value of the taxes. Though the adequacy of this measure as a general criterion has not been discussed, a few reservations seem called for.

A major shortcoming in this measure stems from the same problem which plagued the earlier issue of selection of appropriate reference groups. There are many ways to increase land values in one community to the detriment of other communities and, in a significant sense, to the set of communities. Land values increase not simply because of increased advantages to one site but because the advantages do not accrue to other sites and therefore other sites become poorer substitutes. Therefore the best strategy of a city, if it were to seek to maximize its land values, would be to adopt measures which maximized the difference between the sum of its benefits less costs and their neighbors' benefits less costs. For instance, a city's project whose cost equaled benefits among all residents of the metropolitan area but was financed by the city would lower the land values of the city even though the gains to the residents of the city were greater than the costs to the residents. Therefore a facility of this kind, such as a municipal educational TV station, would not be adopted by the city. (A museum attracting tourist traffic and requiring higher private costs by non-residents would rank higher, though the benefits less costs, even for the city's residents, might be lower.)

The problem of reference group can be formulated as a distributional problem within a city. Police can be allocated within a city so as to protect property rather than persons, thereby giving more protection to persons with property. This would encourage a higher-income residential group and greater property values, but at the expense of population change. Land values in the city may increase, but they may not increase in the metropolitan area, and the initial population of the city may have suffered. This set of reactions is suggestive of the urban renewal program.

Benefit-cost analysis is one of the most promising tools by which to evaluate the desirability of public programs, but great care will have to be exercised that as it is applied in the urban areas it does not become situs-oriented rather than people-oriented.

SELECTED READINGS

Advisory Commission on Intergovernmental Relations. *Metropolitan Social and Economic Disparities: Implications for Intergovernmental Relations in Central Cities and Suburbs.* Washington, 1965.

Banfield, Edward C., and James Q. Wilson. *City Politics.* Cambridge: Harvard University and M.I.T. Press, 1963.

Brazer, Harvey, "Some Fiscal Implications of Metropolitanism," in Guthrie S. Birkhead (ed.), *Metropolitan Issues: Social, Governmental, Fiscal.* Syracuse: Maxwell Graduate School of Syracuse University, 1962.

Break, George F. *Intergovernmental Fiscal Relations in the United States.* Washington: Brookings Institution, 1967.

Dorfman, Robert (ed.). *Measuring Benefits of Government Investments.* Washington: Brookings Institution, 1965.

Dye, Thomas. *Politics, Economics and the Public.* Chicago: Rand McNally, 1966.

Hirsch, Werner Z. (ed.). *Regional Accounts for Policy Decisions.* Baltimore: The Johns Hopkins Press, for Resources for the Future, 1966.

Johansen, Leif. *Public Economics.* Chicago: Rand McNally, 1965.

Mace, Ruth L. *Municipal Cost-Revenue Research in the United States.* Chapel Hill: The Institute of Government, University of North Carolina, 1961.

Margolis, Julius (ed.). *The Public Economy of Urban Communities.* Washington: Resources for the Future, 1965.

Musgrave, Richard. *Theory of Public Finance.* New York: McGraw-Hill, 1959.

National Bureau of Economic Research. *Public Finances: Needs, Sources and Utilization.* Princeton: Princeton University Press, 1961.

Netzer, Dick. *Financing Government in New York City.* Final Research Report, Graduate School of Public Administration, New York University, 1966.

Novick, David (ed.). *Program Budgeting, Program Analysis, and the Federal Budget.* Cambridge: Harvard University Press, 1965.

Schaller, Howard G. (ed.). *Public Expenditure Decisions in the Urban Community.* Washington: Resources for the Future, 1963.

Simon, Herbert. *Fiscal Aspects of Metropolitan Consolidation.* Berkeley: University of California Bureau of Public Administration, 1943.

U.S. Congress, Joint Economic Committee. *State and Local Public Facility Planning,* 2 vols. 89th Cong. 2nd Sess., December 1966.

Wildavsky, Aaron. *Politics of the Budgetary Process.* Boston: Little, Brown & Co., 1964.

DISCUSSION OF PART III

COMMENTS BY RICHARD A. MUSGRAVE *

I have the pleasure to comment on three very fine papers, which look at the problem of urban finance from a broad range of views. I will try to stay with the issues that were raised in the papers and have direct bearing on the urban fiscal structure, without wandering off too far into a general discussion of social want theory, which is always a tempting thing to do.

Methodology

I will begin with the methodological side of the matter. It is always said, and rightly so, that it is a bad thing for young economists to be overly concerned with methodology; and since, happily, there are many young people in this field, they should be protected against such enervating concern.

But, on the other hand, this is also a young field of inquiry; and for a young field some methodology may be helpful. Let me note briefly two distinctions that run through the papers, particularly those by Margolis and Netzer. One is the distinction between a normative and a positive theory; the other is that between positive theory and empirical analysis.

As for the distinction between normative and positive theory, the former permits us to evaluate the efficiency of existing institutions, and the latter permits us to predict how the economy will behave. The two need not coincide. Thus we can say on normative grounds that efficient results will follow, under certain assumptions, if firms behave competitively; but accept, at the same time, an empirical finding that markets are imperfect and that business firms act as restrained monopolists, or use markup pricing. Similarly, a normative theory of social wants which derives public goods allocation from individual preferences would not be invalidated by an empirical finding that the determination of municipal expenditure involves many other factors as well.

As for the distinction between positive theory and empirical work, it is the purpose of the latter to test the validity of the former. Empirical work is simply an exercise in testing the usefulness of a positive theory, and a positive theory is useful only to the extent that it leads to empiri-

* Professor of Economics, Harvard University.

cal formulations which can be verified. Thus there is a close linkage between positive theory and empirical results. The final question is how the empirical findings, derived with the help of positive theory, compare with the efficient state of affairs as defined by normative theory.

If these distinctions are kept in mind, we can avoid a certain amount of argument which occurs in the papers. Thus the normative content of Hirsch's expenditure functions may be limited if the functions, in fact, do not reflect individual preferences, but their empirical value may nevertheless be considerable. That much for methodology.

Theory of Local Public Goods

Next I turn to the question of what is special about public-good theory in the local context. In my terms, what special problems arise regarding allocation and distribution branch theory as applied to the local level? The stabilization and growth aspects, which are essentially a matter of central finance, may be passed over in this discussion.

Beginning with allocation, there are two specific features that arise in the local context. One is the fact that residents may choose communities which share their tastes (the Tiebout approach), and the other is the spillover problem. This is the aspect of primary interest here. Benefits or costs may spill over from one region in which expenditure and tax policies are determined, to another which will benefit or suffer but does not share in the cost or enter into the policy determination. We then have the problem of what distortions result and what can be done to render the decision process more efficient.

Unless spillovers of costs and/or benefits result, the basic problems of local and national finance are essentially the same. I am happy to see, therefore, that this is the aspect with which Dick Netzer concerns himself. According to the conventional wisdom handed down from Pigou, and reargued by Burton Weisbrod, the existence of benefit spill-out leads to an undersupply of public services, because the producing unit considers internal (private) benefits only. Netzer takes the same view. But James Buchanan's writings and a recent article by Alan Williams[1] raise some doubts about this.

The most important contribution of Buchanan, I believe, was to draw a distinction between effects on the resource input on the one side and effects on the product output on the other. Suppose that locality A, in supplying service X, generates a benefit spillover to B, while B in supplying itself with the same service does not give rise to a benefit outflow to A. In the absence of negotiations, both A and B may pro-

[1] Alan Williams, "The Optimal Provision of Public Goods in a System of Local Government," *Journal of Political Economy*, Vol. 74 (February 1966).

duce X. By getting together, B may find it profitable to pay A to produce X, and the production site will shift from B to A. In the new situation, total factor input in the production of X may be reduced (since production has shifted to the more productive location) but the level of consumption of X will be increased. Alan Williams' conclusion to the contrary, seems to me to result from an alternative formulation of the problem, which compares an initial situation without negotiation with one in which compensation is made mandatory, rather than with one in which negotiation and compensation are permitted.

Going back to the proposition that the spillover problem is the crux of local fiscal theory, it appears that the problem of fiscal federalism has been solved least where spillovers are most important, i.e., in the very small units and in the metropolitan area. As Netzer points out, if we take the broad structure of federal-state-local finance, the actual arrangement is by no means altogether out of line with his model system. But if we take the town, or especially the metropolitan area, we find that many spillovers occur that are not taken into account, or that policy decisions are made by the residents of a region that is larger than the benefit region. This, I think, is the crux of the matter.

In Margolis' paper, the main emphasis is on a different aspect, i.e., the question of merit wants. These are those awkward types of public wants or public goods which do not fit readily into a social-want theory of the individual preference type. He feels that these are especially important at the local and maybe at the metropolitan level, and hence are the factor which characterizes local finance. I see no theoretical reason why this should be the case, but as a matter of observation it may happen to be so.

I was interested in Margolis' discussion of how to deal with the merit want problem, and how to bring it into the general theory. The possibility of integrating merit wants with interdependent utility formulations is very promising. In this way I can explain the fact that the public gives Mr. Jones milk for his baby rather than money, because it derives utility from the baby having milk, but not from the father drinking beer. I have come to think of this as a useful formulation and have gone some way in reinterpreting my earlier merit-want concept in that direction.

The distinction between social wants and merit wants is one thing, and that between the polar case of social goods (where all benefits are social) and the mixed case (where both social and private benefits ensue) is another. Margolis emphasizes the mixed case in his discussion of externalities. Certain consumption activities which are primarily private have by-products in the form of externalities. This creates a social-good problem basically similar to the polar case where the entire benefit is external, except that it does not call for full budgetary provision of these goods but for partial provision or a subsidy. In other words, we need to move away from a 100 per cent tax finance theory into a theory of subsidies. If there are externalities attached to private consumption, then there should be subsidies. If the externalities are negative, then there should be penalty rates. But the determination of these subsidies and penalty rates can be handled in the context of the individual preference approach. This approach with all its strength and weakness applies equally to the polar public goods case where all the benefits are external as it does to the mixed or subsidy cases.

Returning to the merit goods case, the difficulty is in explaining why society decides what Mr. Jones is to consume rather than to give him cash and let him decide. As noted before, interdependence of utility is one solution. The other is the leadership position, where there is an elite that knows better and has better tastes, which can be imposed in some cases. Perhaps this is true, but it is an uncomfortable position to take.

In addition to the spillover problem, which is the main distinguishing characteristic in local finance, and the importance of merit wants which Margolis emphasizes, one other characteristic of locally supplied public goods may be mentioned. This is the fact, which Harvey Brazer has emphasized, that such goods are typically ones that are not "available to all" but to particular groups only. The policeman on the beat in block 13 gives protection to that city block but not to another. Fire protection in one part of town protects that part but not another. Yet these are services typically financed by the town as a whole. This takes us back to the spillover problem of regional finance. I have argued before that it is at the intralocal level where this whole question is most acute. Not even in Netzer's model case can we have a situation where the supply of all services is determined in particular service regions without any spillover effects. Also, as Margolis has pointed out elsewhere, difficulties of decision-making arise if all service areas are split up and each service is decided upon separately.

To some extent, the problem can be bypassed by finance through service charges. But these are not always feasible, nor are they always desirable where feasible. Where heavy capital expenditures are involved, as is frequently the case with local finance, a real dilemma arises. On one side, if there is no "crowding" and if marginal cost is zero, there should be no charge, because restricting utilization would be wasteful. On the other side, some charges on current services may be necessary to determine whether additional facilities are needed. The problem then is whether to be efficient in the short run or in the long run, and how to develop a multiple price system which does best on both counts. Again, this is a problem that is especially acute in local finance.

Finally, there is the problem of distribution, which is discussed at some length in Netzer's paper. He points to the unfortunate but hardly surprising fact that the wealthy suburbs do not want to support the poor centers, and that this kind of fragmented situation leads to under-supply of services. Indeed, the very mechanism of fiscal location choice tends to create this situation. If I can live with others whose income is high, then public goods will be available to me at a lower price. There-fore, high-income people will move together and try to exclude people with a low tax base, as their presence would increase the cost of services to them. This may be the case simply because increasing numbers require increased services (such as school services) or be-cause presence of a low-income group creates welfare needs. Thus, the higher income residents will set up zoning arrangements to keep these people out (witness the history of the poor laws) and this results in the situation which Netzer describes.

He suggests certain remedies, such as getting away from the property tax base; but he feels, and I think rightly so, that the only fundamental solution is to centralize the redistributive function and let it be dis-charged at the federal level. After this is done, and a tolerable state of distribution has been created, there will be no further objection to letting the wealthy (or people of equal public service tastes) move to-gether if they so wish, to obtain the desired public services. Indeed, this will then be the efficient arrangement. I wonder whether, as an alternative to central redistribution among individuals, it would make sense to adopt a central policy of regional redistribution, so as to equalize (or reduce inequality in) average incomes in all regions, and then leave it to the regions or towns whether they want to be egalitarian or not in their interindividual distributions?

Empirical Aspects

Leaving the theoretical side, let us look at the empirical problems of measurement, which are the primary concern of Hirsch's interesting paper. In a sense this is the most difficult area and where most work needs to be done.

While (or, perhaps, because) I am not an econometrician myself, I am rather dissatisfied with the state of progress in this area. I realize that the subject matter is very difficult, but—and I don't mean this to be taken as an undue criticism—I find that frequently the empirical formulations do not define properly just what it is that they wish to measure.

On the supply side, we have:

1. *The production function* which expresses the technical relationship between factor inputs and product outputs. It is an engineering relationship, but highly important for the public service problem because it deals with economies of scale, both with regard to service levels (for a given service region) and service regions (for a given service level).[2]

2. *The cost function,* which for given factor prices and production functions, permits us to determine the least cost (involving the optimal combination of factors) at which a given output can be produced. Note that this function relates to the supply side problem only. It has nothing to do with consumer evaluation or demand.

On the demand side, we have:

3. *The preference patterns* of individual consumers, telling us how they would wish to allocate their income between different products (public and private), given various relative prices.

In the context of the private market, we can readily go beyond this, and determine (4) *the supply* and (5) *demand schedule* for the market. The supply schedule in a competitive market is derived from the cost functions of the firms, operating under profit maximization. The demand schedule is obtained by aggregating the demands of output which individuals would choose to buy at various prices. It depends on individual preferences and their validation by the level and the distribution of income. Or, alternatively, both schedules are derived empirically (with some difficulty, to be sure) by observing market transactions over time.

In the case of public goods, functions (1), (2) and (3) pose no particular conceptual problem. The much emphasized complaint that it is difficult to define the unit of public service seems to me to apply about equally as much to the case of private goods. But the public good case differs with regard to (4) and (5). As to (4), it seems dubious what is meant by "supply schedule" of public services as distinct from their "cost schedule." In the normative model, the two would collapse

[2] Furthermore, the problem of density enters because the cost per consumer declines if a given service level is shared among more people. This is an aspect of economy of scale which is peculiar to the public-good problem, but which is offset to some degree by the disutility of crowding.

into one, as public services are supplied at cost. More realistically, one might perhaps think of the supply schedule as expressing the politician's response pattern as well as the cost factors, but this may be too subtle a matter to get hold of. Regarding (5), the observed demand for public goods again relates to individual preferences, as in the case with private goods, but the transmission process is now more complex since it also involves the mechanism of political decision-making. In all, there remains a supply side and a demand side to the problem. While they cannot be summarized as readily into market supply and demand functions as for the private good, the two blades of the scissors continue to exist.

Unfortunately, this dichotomy is frequently lost in the statistical measurement of "expenditure functions." While it is of interest as a first approximation to explore by what factors expenditure differentials among communities are explained, our basic interest is not in differences in *expenditures,* but in differences in *service* levels. Given expenditure figures need be adjusted for cost differentials, involving "simple" adjustments for factor price differentials, as well as more subtle adjustments for production function differentials due to such factors as climate, density, or economies of scale.

But even if this is done, the "service level" function does not quite give us what we are after. It combines a mixture of supply and demand factors which need be disentangled if the really interesting insights into the fiscal behavior of communities are to be obtained. To some extent, this might be accomplished by separating demand variables, such as income and demographic factors, from supply variables, such as climatic conditions or wage rates. To illustrate, the cost of a range of service levels for snow removal (i.e., absence of snow on streets) will depend on factors such as snowfall, density, topography, wages and so forth. This is the cost function part of the problem. Service levels provided will then be a function of these costs *and* of demand factors, such as incomes, tastes, and other prices. The general expenditure function is unsatisfactory, both because the dependent variable is poorly defined (i.e., in terms of expenditure rather than service levels) and because the independent variables combine cost and demand factors without due separation. While certain variables may bear on both sides of the picture (density reduces the cost of firefighting per house, but raises demand by increasing the cost of conflagration) a better separation is hardly an insoluble problem.

Thus, it would seem that the first step is to derive cost functions and, as Hirsch has pointed out, this is now being done with regard to various services such as education. The next step is to explain differences in service levels in terms of cost and demand factors. By separating out the latter, insights can then be obtained into consumer behavior with regard to public services; and possibly a third set of variables may be introduced, which characterize the nature of local government and explain the responsiveness of the political mechanism to cost and demand factors. All this is easier said than done, but even if progress is slow, this is surely one of the most interesting directions for empirical research in public finance.

PART IV

POLICY ISSUES

Alan K. Campbell *
Jesse Burkhead †

PUBLIC POLICY FOR URBAN AMERICA

> "What Dante said of his own city may be said of the cities of
> America: they are like the sick man who cannot find rest
> upon his bed, but seeks to ease his pain by turning from side
> to side." James Bryce, *The American Commonwealth*
> (1891).

> ". . . and the Devil, if he did not take the hindmost, at least
> reserved for himself the privilege of building the cities."
> Lewis Mumford, *The City in History* (1961).

An Adam Smith could stand well beyond the threshold of the industrial
revolution in 1776, observe the pin factories around him, and with
great insight prescribe the public and private policies necessary for
strengthening and promoting the growth of the market. A few decades
later a James Madison could also stand well within the changes in governmental organization that were occurring around him, but, with great
insight prescribe those policies that were necessary to strengthen a complex system of intergovernmental relations.

The present authors are neither Adam Smiths nor James Madisons
and are most uncertain of their ability to perceive the existence of the
economic and political forces that are now changing urban society, or
to prescribe for the future. Smith and Madison also had an important
advantage over any contemporary pretenders in the area of public policy prescriptions: there was less to read in their subject matter areas
than is true for urbanists today.

Now that the disclaimer affidavit has been filed, the authors will
wrestle with this diffuse and inchoate subject in three rounds. The first
section of this paper will attempt to examine the large forces that shape
the nature of urban policy, assess their stability, and ask the general
question, "What is new?" The second section will examine recent policy
responses to these forces in being, by looking at two hardware programs
—urban renewal and transportation—and two software programs—education and anti-poverty. The final section will be directed in a hortatory
and prescriptive vein to matters of immediate future policy.

Throughout the paper no effort will be made to separate the positive

* Director, Metropolitan Studies Program, Maxwell Graduate School of
Citizenship and Public Affairs, Syracuse University.
† Professor of Economics, Syracuse University.

from the normative. Value judgments will contaminate both the description of what is and the prescriptions for future policy. The authors do not believe in Lionel Robbins.

THE NATURE OF URBAN POLICY

There are three congeries of forces that come to bear on urban policy. These are, first, the private market; second, the metropolitan governmental structure, including its fiscal dimensions; third, the political structure, to include both the activities of organized political parties and the interest group influences that come to bear on administrators as well as on elected officials.

The Market

It is most difficult to establish a meaningful taxonomy of market forces in the urban area, even when there is a reasonably clear notion of the purposes the taxonomy is to serve. One of the classical distinctions is between those market activities that are "basic" as opposed to "non-basic," or domestic-oriented as opposed to export-oriented. Meaningful distinctions have been established in terms of primary, secondary, and tertiary activity. Those interested in studying the growth of a single metropolitan region, for example in the New York and Pittsburgh regions, have gained considerable perspective by analyzing regional growth patterns in relation to national growth patterns in terms of the mix of activities.

For a taxonomy that is helpful in examining the totality of urban policy problems, a somewhat different structuring may be suggested. First are the market forces that cluster their concern on the central business district. Second are the market forces that center on the development of urban land generally. Third is the market structure for the production of goods and services—the ordinary kind of manufacturing, commercial, and service activity that goes into the cells of the input-output matrix. Each of these groups of market forces could, of course, be further disaggregated, and there are obvious interrelations among them.

If one stands aside to contemplate the play of market forces on the conditions of urban existence he must conclude that a good many of the "problems" that are often described purely in sociological terms are, in fact, the result of the operation of the market. Southern Negroes and Appalachian whites are in the northern central cities because of technological changes in agriculture, particularly southern agriculture. The emigration occurred because income and housing opportunities were better in the North than in the South. The exodus of northern whites to the suburbs is not alone a search for schools and play room for the children. It is also the product of market forces that pushed excess labor from the South into the North, maintained residential property values in old central city areas, and thus facilitated the out-movement of whites.

Market forces, of course, are no more perfectly competitive in their urban dimensions than they are in their national dimensions. A high degree of monopoly power rests in the hands of the middlemen of development—the realtors, the mortgage institutions, the law firms, the contractors and even the architects.[1] The market rather obviously fails to yield anything resembling the highest and best use of land. Central city congestion and urban sprawl are the evident consequences.[2]

Now, of course, it can be argued that the market for urban land is an expression of rational behavior. Profit maximization certainly serves as the guide for private decisions, and land use patterns are responsive to changing costs and demands. But since at least the days of Pigou, economists have been preoccupied with divergences between private cost and social cost where the difference is attributable to external costs that exceed external benefits. No one has ever attempted a balance sheet for a metropolitan area, but casual observation would suggest that the volume of uncompensated externalities generated by urban land use patterns is very high indeed. We do not expect southern plantation owners to assume the full social costs of their technological innovations. We do not expect northern landlords in slum areas to bear the full social cost of their activities. Those checks on market power which operate occasionally and fitfully when market power is national in character, as with utilities and communications, are almost nonexistent at the urban level. No metropolitan area has a Social Diseconomies Board to reparcel the gains and losses that accrue from changing patterns of urban land use.

However well the private market may work in allocating resources for maximizing production, the result may not accord with wise social policy. It may be, as Galbraith argues, that the economists' concerns in the last twenty-five years with the market and with production ". . . have induced a myopia which has kept us from seeing some very great problems which these concerns have left untouched and which in some respects they made more acute."[3] Economic growth, according

[1] For case studies underlying this assertion, see Roscoe C. Martin, *et al., Decisions in Syracuse* (Anchor Books, 1965).

[2] For a discussion of market imperfections and urban sprawl, see Robert O. Harvey and W. A. V. Clark, "The Nature and Economics of Urban Sprawl," *Land Economics,* Vol. 41, No. 1, February 1965.

[3] John K. Galbraith, "The Claims of the Community Against Those of Economics," speech from the conference "Our People and Their Cities," sponsored by Urban America, Inc., Washington, D.C., September 12–13, 1966, p. 2.

to Galbraith, makes little contribution to the solution of those problems normally encompassed in the phrase "the crisis of our cities":

> Economic growth does not provide the public services which mark our progress toward a more civilized existence and which also are made necessary by a higher level of private consumption.
>
> Economic growth does not help those who, because of careless choice of birthplace or parents, poor early environment, absence of educational opportunity, poor health, mental retardation, racial discrimination, or old age are unable to participate fully in the economy and in its gains. On the contrary, it makes this disadvantage more visible and obscene.
>
> And economic growth, we have learned, does not solve the problems of our environment and especially of our urban environment. On the contrary, it makes these problems infinitely more urgent.

If the private market and increased productivity do not automatically contribute to the solution of urban ills, it follows that public intervention is necessary and wise. But intervention requires institutions capable of policy formation, short- and long-range planning, administration, and fiscal support. Do those institutions, which are the building blocks of what has been called the American system of "creative federalism," possess these capabilities?

Governmental Structure

The central characteristic of the local part of the governmental system is fragmentation, both functionally and areally. The unfortunate consequences of governmental fragmentation in the metropolitan region have been commented on so many times that it would be pointless to add to the indictment.[4] The trends and outlook, however, are not without interest.

In 1957 there were 17,984 governmental units in the 212 Standard Metropolitan Statistical Areas. In 1962 there were 18,442 units, an increase of 3 per cent.[5] And these definitions omit a great many governments that are organized as dependent but special districts in suburban areas.

There are almost no counterforces to the continued proliferation of the numbers of governments in the metropolitan area. The centralization of general government authority at the local level proceeds very slowly. In the last decade the loneliness of Dade County has been only slightly relieved by the companionship of Davidson County in Tennessee. Func-

---

[4] Most recently by the Committee for Economic Development, *Modernizing Local Government* (1966).

[5] Advisory Commission on Intergovernmental Relations, *Metropolitan Social and Economic Disparities* (1965), p. 43.

tional centralization continues here and there, of course, as new authorities are established for metropolitan water, transportation, or sewage disposal.

Some years ago Wood pointed out that the multiplicity of governmental units in the metropolitan area was a triumph of the combined forces of administrative specialists and program specialists.[6] The neglected values, he felt, were the political values lost, perhaps forever, to the metropolitan area. Fragmented governments reduce political participation of the citizenry and reduce the responsiveness of the elected officials of general government. Wood's observations continue to be accurate.

The fragmentation of governments in the metropolitan area both mirrors and reinforces the competitive anarchy of the market for urban land. Real estate developers are able to bargain to advantage with numbers of local governments, playing one off against the other to secure concessions in terms of zoning regulations, assessments, and the provision of public services.[7] There are instances where developers will press for a co-ordinated central authority over planning for trunk line sewers or for a uniform metropolitan-wide scheme for house and lot numbers, but, in general, fragmented local government authority has far more advantages than disadvantages for the real estate industry in all of its dimensions.

The fragmentation of local government authority in the metropolitan area is also a major contributor to the generally static character of local finances, and revenue sources in particular. Considering the startling increases in government expenditures in SMSA's in the postwar years, the rigidity in the revenue structure is equally startling. In 1940 the ratio of state grants-in-aid to local revenue was 33 per cent. By 1964 it had increased to only 42.5 per cent. Federal aid programs increased, but because of the changing pattern of welfare, federal grants as a proportion of local expenditures actually declined from 4 per cent in 1940 to 2 per cent in 1962. And the property tax continues in its traditional role, to provide about 85 per cent of locally-raised revenues. Only in the largest cities are there important non-property tax supplements.

There are no significant prospects for change in this pattern of fragmented governmental structures and rigid sources of finance. METRO government is not on the horizon. It is not that the possibility of social invention for governmental structures in the metropolitan area is non-existent. Students of these matters are surely as ingenious as the students of water resources, where social invention has been more promi-

---

[6] Robert C. Wood, "A Division of Power in Metropolitan Areas," in Arthur Maass (ed.), *Area and Power* (The Free Press, 1959).

[7] Martin, *et al., op. cit.,* pp. 245–314.

nent in recent years. The brutal fact is there are too many parties at interest who profit by present arrangements. There is no such thing as regional rationality, and indeed, why should there be? To cite Wood again, few inhabitants have ever looked to local governments to optimize or maximize anything.[8]

Presiding over this system of fragmented local government are the fifty state governments. The basic power of states to make any changes in the system they see fit is unquestioned. Their political ability to adjust local boundaries, however, is much more circumscribed and, in some cases, the restrictions are built into state constitutions.

Although the accepted doctrine of the state's proper relationship to local governments is home rule, practice has not been much influenced by the doctrine.

The diversity of constitutional home-rule provisions; the customary reservations of constitutional and legislative restraint upon the exercise of municipal power, particularly in the all-important area of revenue; and the futility, politically and judicially conceded, of attempting to draw a sharp division between municipal or local affairs or concerns and matters of state concern—all these factors . . . combine to effect a dilution of the political concept of constitutional home rule to an extent which renders it a symbol almost wholly devoid of substantive content and meaning.[9]

The inability of home rule doctrine to influence state-local relations is more a product of the interdependence of the roles of state and local governments than it is a measure of the state's refusal to abide by the rules of the game. Neither federal-state nor state-local relations can be usefully analyzed as relations among relatively independent levels of government. Rather, the system is an interdependent one—a system of interconnected parts. One of the first scholars to make this point was Wallace Sayre in discussing state-local relations in New York State when he argued that "The formal, outmoded doctrines of limitations, separation, and competition stand in the way of both explanation and understanding of the actual, developing relationships between the State government and the local governments." [10]

Despite the states' continual involvement with their local governments, the contribution they have made to maintaining a rational local

[8] Robert C. Wood, *1400 Governments* (Harvard University Press, 1961), p. 198.
[9] *Modernizing a City Government,* Report of The Chicago Home Rule Commission (University of Chicago Press, 1954), p. 309.
[10] Wallace S. Sayre, "Constructive Steps for the Betterment of State-City Governmental Relations," in *A Report to the Governor of the State of New York and the Mayor of the City of New York* (New York State–New York City Fiscal Relations Committee, November 1956), p. 57.

jurisdictional system has been small. In fact, state policy in general has responded very slowly to the fact of metropolitanism.

There are several ways, in addition to modifying the jurisdictional system, by which states can respond, and in some instances have responded, to their growing metropolitanization. These include fiscal assistance either as grants-in-aid to urban governments or by the assumption of direct responsibility for urban-related functions. Another kind of response is to allow local governments to adapt themselves organizationally and procedurally to serve their new and changing metropolitan population. Finally, the states can, of course, make a contribution by requiring local governmental reorganization.

In all of these areas, except the last, the states have done some things —some states more than others.

In the field of intergovernmental aid there has been a continual increase in the amount of state aid, although the proportion of local expenditures so financed has not increased over the past decade. Despite the increasing amount of aid, the pattern of its distribution has hindered its contribution to the solution of urban problems. The earlier bias of state legislatures for rural areas has now translated itself into a bias in favor of suburban areas. There was a time when this rural bias was justified by the distribution of resources. The wealth of the country was concentrated in the urban areas and if minimum levels of government services were to be maintained in the rural areas, intergovernmental aid was necessary. The redistribution of taxable resources, however, within metropolitan areas between central cities and their suburbs raises questions as to the current appropriateness of that pattern.

The average expenditure in central cities in 1957 was $185.49 per capita compared with $159.83 in the outside central city areas, a difference of $27.56. Despite this difference, aid was higher in the area outside the central city, a total of $23.05 compared with $17.81 per capita. The result, of course, was higher taxes in central cities than in outside central city areas, $109.07 compared with $85.78. Although more current data for *all* metropolitan areas are not available, scattered data for specific areas indicate that the pattern of differences has not changed substantially since 1957.

State governments, obviously, are not making any special contribution through their aid system to the solution of the problems of the central cities. Whether the pattern will change is open to question since reapportionment will increase representation for suburban areas more than for cities.

The new federal aid programs are to some degree offsetting the inadequate aid systems of the states. Federal aid to urban areas or for urban problems has gradually increased, beginning with housing and urban re-newal legislation, and moving to the anti-poverty program and aid to education. Perhaps a pattern is developing in which the state govern-ments aid suburban and rural areas, while the federal government takes on the responsibility for central cities.

The states have made considerable statutory changes recently to per-mit local governments to act co-operatively. Normally, these new stat-utes or constitutional provisions authorize local governments to do jointly anything they are entitled to do alone. In addition, many states permit the establishment of metropolitan study and planning commis-sions.

Another kind of permissive legislation is that which allows the trans-fer of functions from one local jurisdiction to another (generally from minor jurisdictions—villages, towns, and cities—to higher levels, pri-marily counties) and from local jurisdictions to the state, especially in welfare, transportation, sanitation, and pollution control. On the whole, however, state assumption of responsibility for new functions has not occurred in those activities which are traditionally urban in character, and fiscal pressures at the state level are likely to hinder any major moves in this direction.

Other examples of permissive legislation could be cited, but the general thrust is clear. There is no evidence that such permissive legisla-tion will make any great contribution to the solution of the fundamental problems that face urban areas. No jurisdiction will engage in co-opera-tion unless it clearly serves its own interest. That interest is likely to be seen as maximizing services and minimizing costs and the maintenance of an environment which fits that jurisdiction's image of itself. The pos-sibility of gain for any particular jurisdiction relates, in part, to the gov-ernmental system operating in the area. For example, co-operation in sharing welfare costs is unlikely when the welfare function is assigned to municipalities rather than to larger jurisdictions.

A few states have moved in the direction of helping their urban areas by establishing departments of local government or of housing and ur-ban development. The establishment of such a department, however, does not guarantee any fundamental change in the role of the state. In fact, in some instances these offices have led to a protection of the status quo, rather than prompting any fundamental changes in local govern-ment organization.

On the whole, the states have not seen it as their function to en-courage basic government reorganization at the local level. Despite the current interest in states, there does not appear to be any under-lying political reason why states should move into more drastic action

584

relative to the local government jurisdictional system. The states did bring about the reorganization of school districts through the use of the carrot of state aid. Obviously they could move in the same direction relative to general local governments. The likelihood of their doing so, however, is reduced by the greater stakes which political parties have in local governments than they had in school districts. Jobs, contracts and elective offices at the local level are important to the continued viability of the parties, and to the extent reorganization threatens this relationship, it will be opposed.

Although the role of the federal government has been primarily in program areas, it may be that its attention will soon be turned to the local government organization question. In fact, the 1966 Housing Act does lend some support to such a trend by supporting the establishment of metropolitan planning agencies. It is possible that the federal government may move to fill the reorganization gap left by the states, just as it has moved to fill the aid gap. This possibility will be more fully examined after a description of some of the present federal aid programs is provided.

Political Structure

The great periods of economic reform in American life were, of course, from 1870 to 1914 and the New Deal years. The politics of reform in these two periods were strikingly similar. The political base consisted of a strong coalition of farmers, small businessmen, and organized labor. The coalition was a national one, with influence primarily on national public policy but also on state and local public policy.

Now the coalition is shattered. There are fewer and fewer farmers; small businessmen work for large businessmen; organized labor is complacent. But if the promise of the Great Society is to be fulfilled, with its emphasis on improving the conditions of urban existence, there must be a political basis for reform and it must have national dimensions. It would appear doubtful that the existing politics of consensus is adequate to the task.

It is no doubt rather old-fashioned to emphasize this, but major new governmental programs do not ordinarily take root and flourish without strong interest-group support. The argument that the new managers of society, armed with the techniques of computerized decision-making, have displaced interest groups is not persuasive.[11] There are civil rights groups, sometimes strong in specific urban areas, but with weak national

[11] For a contrary view see Daniel Bell, "The Great Society, Some Notes on the Adequacy of Our Concepts," Syracuse University, Maxwell School, 1966 (unpublished).

organizations and currently splintered by dissension over strategy, tactics, foreign policy, and ultimate philosophy. There are college students and clergymen, who will, from time to time, lend important support for one or another urban cause, usually associated with civil rights, but spilling over into housing, health, recreation and education. And then there are the poor, who are becoming increasingly visible and vocal, but again, without national organization. It is somehow difficult to imagine that a working political coalition of civil rights groups, college students, clergymen, and the poor can replace the familiar triad of organized farmers, organized labor, and small businessmen.

As for organized political parties whose activities will affect urban policy, the future is somewhat more clear, at least in northern cities. Here it seems very probable that the Democratic party will continue to gain strength both in the central cities and in the suburbs. In the central cities political power will come increasingly to be black power. As this pattern emerges it is likely that the non-black minorities will become increasingly restive with their traditional Democratic party tie. Although not likely to join the Republican party they have already become less reliable Democratic voters. Given the opportunity to vote directly on bond referenda for racial purposes or on such matters as civilian police review boards, they are likely to express some of their resentments.[12]

Meanwhile, the central city Negro Democratic majorities will move increasingly to strengthen their political relations with the federal government in the interests of program support for human resources development.[13] But the outside central city areas, white and less Democratic, will develop further cleavages of interest with the central city. The prospects for a strengthened metropolitan sense of community are by no means bright. As ethnic and political conflicts sharpen on an area basis it will be more and more difficult to organize, finance, and administer metropolitan-wide programs for either physical or human resources development.

In the meantime the traditional interest groups that influence decisions on urban policy will remain influential. That fascinating pluralism that characterizes urban society and which has thus far defied analysis in terms of simplistic power structures will continue to exhibit, as the

---

[12] James Q. Wilson and Edward C. Banfield, "Public Regardingness as a Value Premise in Voting Behavior," *American Political Science Review,* Vol. 58, No. 4 (December 1961).

[13] The ethnic view of urban politics that is suggested here has support in both older writings and recent voting patterns. It has its critics, however. See Raymond E. Wolfinger and John Osgood Field, "Political Ethos and the Structure of City Government," *American Political Science Review,* Vol. 60, No. 2 (June 1966).

occasion demands, a central business district (CBD) "crowd," a transportation "crowd," an industrial promotion "crowd," and other familiar configurations. The resolution of particular urban policy issues will rest in the future, as in the past, on the activities of these and other "crowds" and their relationship to organized political parties. There is a power structure, but few in its ranks will step forward to be identified.

The Pattern of Interactions

The interplay among the three constellations of forces that shape policy in urban America gives rise to certain consequences. Most of these are unpleasant consequences, measured in terms of the unstated value premises of this paper, or in terms of the vision of a Great Urban Society. Public preferences for urban programs cannot be adequately expressed through available mechanisms.[14] The total volume of existing resources may not be efficiently used. Additional fiscal resources cannot be tapped. Program spillovers are substantial, and hence the volume of fortuitous gains and uncompensated losses is large.

Perhaps the most serious policy consequence of all is that the interaction of the market, government organization, and political organization permits the continual pursuit of the policy of containment. The central city ethnic minorities are largely confined to the central city. The aged, the poor, the unemployed, and the sick are kept within its boundaries. And the practice of containment destroys any sense of community responsibility for central city problems, either administrative or fiscal.

The absence of regional responsibility for regional problems gives rise to all manner of seeming policy contradictions. Transportation policy designed to stimulate the holding power of the CBD will also carry persons and goods to the periphery and contribute to urban sprawl. Urban renewal displaces families, in the familiar case, who then contribute to apartmentalization and congestion of existing lower-middle-class housing. Compensatory education for slum children may be bought at the expense of upper-income areas where schools then deteriorate and the parents move to the suburbs. A transportation system that is efficient for automobile manufacturers spills off gross inefficiencies on central city inhabitants. Everything is related to everything else and there appears to be no way to control the interrelatedness.

The strength of market forces is so great in matters affecting regional growth that very often it appears better to join than to combat. This was

[14] For a contrast with this value judgment see A. James Heins, "Some Welfare Aspects of the Metropolitan Problem," Committee for Economic Development, 1965 (unpublished).

certainly the underlying philosophy of the New York Metropolitan Region studies and was made explicit in Hoover's writings about Pittsburgh. In discussing broad national shifts in population, markets, industry, and trends toward suburbanization, Hoover has stated:

Policy in the region, then, should not be directed toward either abetting or combating these trends, but toward the adjustment to them—meeting the problems they raise and exploiting the opportunities they create.[15]

This may well be the only sensible approach for a metropolitan region, but it certainly reduces public policy to a most subsidiary role as compared with private policy. When the public sector rides with the private sector it must also suffer from its externalities.

It is hardly surprising, in the absence of a regional rationality, that land use planning, so central to all that goes on in the metropolitan region, is in such a chaotic state. City planning has traditionally been designed to "maintain existing rental values and improve the circulation of people and the flow of goods." [16] These are laudable goals, but rather narrow ones. Regional planning, where it does exist, is not concerned with land use, but with resource development. As Chinitz has noted, the urban planner now gropes for a strategy, not knowing what to maximize and attempts to move on all fronts at once.[17]

However, in at least some of the aspects of urban program planning, the evident imperfections and contradictions in existing processes appear to have given rise to at least a partial antithesis. The federal government is now making modest efforts to strengthen metropolitan area co-operation where programmatic interests are threatened by the absence of co-ordinated policies in the metropolitan area.

We are obviously past the threshold of federal intervention in the metropolitan area. Federal-city relationships are increasingly strengthened, partially in response to the political party forces noted above.[18] State leadership and state programs for metropolitan areas within their borders are in an uncertain, transitional phase. It would be most difficult to predict whether federal programs will be increasingly subject to some manner of state control or whether the states will be increasingly by-passed. The latter seems the more likely.

[15] Edgar M. Hoover, "Pittsburgh Takes Stock of Itself," in Benjamin Chinitz (ed.), *City and Suburb* (Prentice-Hall, 1964), p. 62. A similar point is made by Wood, *1400 Governments*, p. 174.

[16] John Friedmann, "The Concept of a Planning Region," in John Friedmann and William Alonso (eds.), *Regional Development and Planning* (M.I.T. Press, 1964), p. 503.

[17] Chinitz, *City and Suburb*, pp. 44–46.

[18] Roscoe C. Martin, *The Cities and the Federal System* (Atherton Press, 1965).

There are some new programmatic concerns that, if and when adequately funded, would appear to have sufficient internal dynamic to force some new patterns of metropolitan area administrative rationality. This may be the case with the programs for human resources. If the poverty programs some day expand, particularly in the areas of education and recreation, some greater degree of central planning and funding will emerge from administrative necessity. The day may not be too distant when it will be possible to develop, at least at an informational level, human resources budgets that will comprehend education, health, recreation, and welfare for the whole of a metropolitan area. When that point is reached the technical basis will have been laid for the planning and projection that are now lacking.

In urban economics it is not particularly helpful to assert simply that more resources are needed or that we are suffering from a Galbraith-type imbalance between public and private wants, although both of these assertions are undoubtedly accurate. There may well be an imbalance and our national value pattern may well be distorted. But how are these conditions to be changed?

A formal economic analysis of costs and benefits will not carry us very far in making the large choices. Economists can sensitize their readers to the uncompensated spillovers that arise from existing and frequently conflicting policies. But economic analysis will not, in its present state, provide guides to choices between public and private activities or guides to the allocation of resources among major urban programs. No definition of "need" for a specific public good or for public goods as a whole is yet possible. Preferences can be revealed, and imperfectly, only through the political process.

The same limitations apply to statements concerning the relative mix of federal and state-local resources. No economic optimum can be specified here. As programmatic concerns intensify in particular areas, there will be political recourse to that level of government which proves to be most responsive to the expressed concern. There is no set of abstract preferences or conceptual framework that reveals the appropriate division of intergovernmental resources. Again, preferences will be revealed incrementally through the political process.

URBAN RENEWAL

The nation's seventeen-year experience with urban renewal illustrates the complexity of the interrelationships among market forces, governmental structure, and political structure described in the first part of this paper. The objectives of the urban renewal sections of the Housing Acts of 1949 and 1954 were, it is generally agreed, multiple and often conflicting.[19] This original fuzziness in conception has invited influential interests and groups within the metropolitan area to shape the program to their purposes.

The clearance objectives of the original act have increasingly emphasized the rebuilding of the central business district, reflecting the strength of the commercial and service activities that are concerned with land values and economic activity in the CBD. Urban renewal has become important in building new political forces on the urban scene, as Richard H. Lee of New Haven exemplifies.[20] In terms of governmental organization, urban renewal is a weapon of competition for the central city in its struggle against the suburbs.

The literature and practice of urban renewal abound with polemic and prescription. There is probably no urban program that has evoked so much interest, measured in terms of professional writing, conferences, speechmaking and journalese. The dispassionate student of these matters is thus faced with a most formidable body of data and opinion and also with striking differences in experience among specific renewal programs in specific cities. Every city experience has its own characteristics; generalizations about these characteristics are certain to be uncomfortable.

One of the startling things about urban renewal is the degree to which a major disillusionment has set in in almost all professional writing on the subject.[21] It is not that urban renewal has been attacked violently; rather that it has turned out to be a slow and painful program, and the objectives that it has sought to attain in many cities have not been those of liberal-minded reformers. Somehow there has come to be an in-

---

[19] No attempt will be made here to examine all of the programs, such as the Demonstration Grant Program and the Community Renewal Programs, that are embraced under the rubric of urban renewal. Attention will be directed toward the programs comprehended by the General Neighborhood Renewal Plan.

It may be noted that federal programs for urban housing and community development are characterized by multiplicity, complexity, and parsimony. To cite one small example, under 1961 legislation the Urban Renewal Administration was empowered to rehabilitate dwelling units for demonstration purposes. By the end of 1964 seven such rehabilitations had been completed. (Housing and Home Finance Agency, *18th Annual Report, 1964*, p. 321.)

[20] See Robert A. Dahl, *Who Governs?* (Yale University Press, 1961), pp. 115–40.

[21] For example, Martin Anderson, *The Federal Bulldozer: A Critical Analysis of Urban Renewal* (M.I.T. Press, 1964); Jane Jacobs, *The Death and Life of Great American Cities* (Random House, 1961). For a reasoned rebuttal to Anderson's attack see Robert P. Groberg, "Urban Renewal Realistically Reappraised," *Law and Contemporary Problems*, Vol. 30, No. 1 (Winter 1965); An anthology of relevant literature is contained in James Q. Wilson (ed.), *Urban Renewal: The Record and the Controversy* (M.I.T. Press, 1966).

creased awareness that urban renewal incurs costs, individual and social, many of which were largely unanticipated.

There is an interesting parallel between urban renewal and public housing in the matter of attitudinal change. In the late 1930's many felt that public housing would reform the conditions of existence for the poor in large cities. Fifteen years later almost none cherished this illusion. It has apparently taken fifteen years to understand that urban renewal will not in itself reform the human condition in the nation's large cities.

Urban renewal programs are intended to remedy the conditions of physical deterioration and decay—to restore blighted areas and clear slums. But the terms "blight," "slum," and "decay" are not easy to define nor are the causal factors that contribute to these conditions always self-evident.[22] The general state of affairs is that under certain conditions the market fails to halt deterioration. Private owners have no incentive to redevelop simply because existing investment is more profitable elsewhere or because of the interdependence trap.[23] The "normal" process of replacing deteriorated structures is distorted as the replacement occurs at other sites in the metropolitan area. The task of urban renewal is then to substitute for the existing pattern of private incentives a new mix of public-private activities. As with so many urban programs, the public sector must assume the cost of private spillovers.

The Crucial Elements in Renewal

There are three essential elements in urban renewal programs. The first is the use of the state's power of eminent domain to assist in the site assembly of property in areas designated as slums (or "blighted"). The second is the use of federal funds to write down land values to the point where private development is economically feasible. The third is the requirement to develop a workable plan.

All else that happens in the complex process of renewal is subsidiary to the exercise of these powers; for example, the process of eviction and relocation of families and business firms is a necessary concomitant of site assembly. The search for redevelopers must be undertaken in relationship to the economic feasibility of the new construction. This, in turn, is a function of the values established on the written-down

[22] See Lowdon Wingo, Jr., "Urban Renewal: Objectives, Analyses, and Information Systems," in Werner Z. Hirsch (ed.), *Regional Accounts for Policy Decisions* (The Johns Hopkins Press, for Resources for the Future, 1966).
[23] Otto A. Davis and Andrew B. Whinston, "The Economics of Urban Renewal," *Law and Contemporary Problems,* Vol. 26, No. 1 (Winter 1961).

sites, which depend on the prospective use within the scope of the plan. The large tracts of cleared and desolated land that now characterize so many urban renewal projects, or, in Winnick's phrase, "the awesomely long interval between plan and execution," is often attributable to the fact that land write-downs may not be adequate to assure immediately profitable private reuse of the site.[24]

The Record of Accomplishment

An appraisal of the record of urban renewal is difficult because so few projects have been completed. To the end of 1964, 1,545 projects had been approved for 800 localities; however, only 174 of these were completed in the sense that the last federal payment was made. (Construction by redevelopers was not necessarily completed.) In fiscal terms the record is also modest. From 1949 through 1964 only $4.3 billion in federal funds had been obligated for grants.[25] About $7.6 billion has been authorized from 1949 to the end of fiscal 1966. This scale of operation is far below the reasonable expectations of only a few years ago.[26]

The gains from urban renewal can best be described in such general terms as encouragement to esthetics, the rationalization of traffic problems, the new spur to civic interest in downtown improvements, an improved fiscal base, the construction of cultural buildings, improved sites for industry, the needed expansion of some educational institutions, and an undoubted stimulus to better urban planning.[27] In addition, urban renewal has undoubtedly provided Congressional support for additional funds for federal public housing. Some cities have an improved fiscal outlook as a result of successful renewal projects. It is not yet possible to estimate the private investment multipliers for public renewal funds; experience is too incomplete. However, they may be substantial.

[24] Louis Winnick, "Facts and Fictions in Urban Renewal," in *Ends and Means of Urban Renewal* (Philadelphia Housing Association, 1961), p. 23.

[25] Housing and Home Finance Agency, *op. cit.,* p. 339.

[26] For example, the Colm-Helzner projections, published in 1961, estimated in the "judgment model" that 1970 government expenditures for housing, community redevelopment, and renewal would be $7.9 billion. (Gerhard Colm and Manuel Helzner, "Financial Needs and Resources over the Next Decade: at All Levels of Government," in *Public Finances: Needs, Sources, and Utilization,* National Bureau of Economic Research [Princeton University Press, 1961], p. 15.) New obligational authority proposed for both administrative budget and trust funds under this heading was $2.2 billion for fiscal 1967.

[27] See the excellent discussion in Charles Abrams, *The City Is the Frontier* (Harper and Row, 1965), pp. 155–83.

The Costs of Renewal

While there have been some impressive accomplishments, particularly for a program that has faced so many difficulties in city after city, the costs have been so serious in particular circumstances that any policy appraisal must look at them carefully. The paradox is that the over-all magnitude of renewal is modest, but if more had been done under existing policies the disruption might have been intolerable.

Beyond doubt the most serious cost has been the dislocation and uprooting of thousands of families and small businessmen. To the end of 1964, 185,000 families, 74,000 individuals and 42,000 business firms were displaced.[28] This must amount to more than one million persons. There is simply no way of calculating the time and effort, the disruption in family life, and the social costs of breaking neighborhood ties, friendships, and religious affiliations that have accompanied this involuntary process. In some cases no information is available on the effects of dislocation. A reasonably careful search of the literature, for example, reveals no research to date on the effects of urban renewal on manufacturing activities. What has happened to the hundreds of small manufacturing firms that left their old locations? Have they disappeared? Have they been merged? Do the employees have new jobs? Have the employers retired? The answers are not available.

The same is true of small retailers. No one seems to know where they have gone—whether they are in business elsewhere or whether they have retired. Although the acquisition of condemned property has generally been carried out at reasonably high rates of compensation, there is no compensation for the loss of employment.[29] The ultimate consequences of urban renewal in terms of housing effects are also unknown because so many projects are uncompleted. Thus far the major effect has been to materially reduce the supply of low-cost housing in American cities.[30]

In order for there to be favorable over-all effects on housing, a double disequilibrium in the urban housing market must exist. First, there must be a vacancy rate in low-income housing sufficient to absorb the families that are initially displaced. Urban renewal practice requires that such conditions be certified before demolition can occur.[31]

[28] Housing and Home Finance Agency, *op. cit.*, p. 327.
[29] The Housing Act of 1964 provided for additional financial compensation for relocation for business firms, but does nothing about providing for continued employment.
[30] Scott Greer, *Urban Renewal and American Cities* (Bobbs-Merrill, 1965), p. 3.
[31] For evidence that less than satisfactory procedures are employed for this purpose see Abrams, *op. cit.*, pp. 137–41.

The second disequilibrium is in high-income rental housing, so typically a major component of redevelopment.[32] Here, however, there must be a shortage, not a surplus, if the new high-rise apartments are to be rented at a favorable occupancy ratio.

Needless to say, these two kinds of disequilibria do not always occur in the same city at the same time. In fact, in recent years, with existing trends in the income distribution of the central city, there is more likely to be a shortage of low-income housing than a surplus, and more likely to be a surplus of high-income rental housing than a shortage. In consequence, urban renewal, in the opinion of many observers, eradicates one slum in order to recreate it elsewhere within the city at the same time that high-rise apartment buildings inevitably stand vacant.

There seems to be little doubt that relocation from urban renewal has raised the cost of housing for low-income groups. In a detailed survey made in Syracuse in 1964 it was found that average monthly rents for Negro relocatees increased by 18 per cent, and for white relocatees by 21 per cent.[33] There is no way of determining whether housing quality improved proportionately, although it is known that about 90 per cent of relocatees in the nation as a whole have found standard, not dilapidated housing.

As in any real estate development, urban renewal generates a large volume of unplanned speculative gains and losses. The generous write-down terms plus credit availability that are typically offered to redevelopers have contributed to magnificent windfall gains for a fortunate few.[34] Losses are frequently less conspicuous, although the retailer who suddenly finds that he is just on the edge of the renewal area and all of his customers have been relocated elsewhere would probably argue that he is a conspicuous case.

No balance sheet rendition is possible for urban renewal. To quote Abrams, "Financial benefits cannot be offset against social costs nor an increase in revenues juxtaposed against the myriad peoples evicted from their homes." [35]

The Immediate Outlook

There is a good deal of current disquietude about urban renewal. It may be that urban renewal programs in specific cities have never

[32] Forty per cent of the housing units on project land at the end of fiscal 1964 were for high-income rental. (Housing and Home Finance Agency, op. cit., p. 323.)

[33] Alan K. Campbell, et al., The Negro in Syracuse (University College of Syracuse University, 1964), p. 33.

[34] Abrams, op. cit., pp. 116–27.

[35] Ibid., p. 177.

had very much popular support, but have been sustained in what political vitality they have had by a rather strong confluence of interest groups aided and abetted by intellectual planner-types.[36] Then, given a rather infirm political base, as faulty operations come to characterize a number of projects, public criticism mounts. On the other hand, it is just possible that as more and more projects come to completion and their physical splendors are more evident, the criticisms will abate.

Nonetheless, there are grounds for this disquietude, both in terms of "fundamental questions" and in terms of operating reality.[37] The most fundamental question of all turns on the future of the central business district itself and here, of course, there is no unanimity of opinion whatever. There are those who insist that the CBD and its revitalization are absolutely necessary to the continued health of the metropolitan area. There are those who insist that it is a dying enterprise and that continued dispersal within the metropolitan region is the future pattern. Those who subscribe to this latter view, either because they favor dispersal or because they feel that it is inevitable, necessarily conclude that large downtown projects are doomed to ultimate economic failure. The safe conclusion is that central business districts will thrive in accordance with their ability to attract and hold financial and other service activity. Some will thrive because of urban renewal and others in spite of it. The future form and function of the central city and the CBD in particular is not so clear at this point in time that it is possible to get beyond rather meaningless generalizations.

Another source of disquietude stems from the reasonably well-founded feeling that urban renewal is not an appropriate area for federal intervention.[38] It is by no means clear that the revitalization of central cities is a matter for national action; the costs of non-renewal would appear to be largely local costs with few spillovers; the national benefits from urban renewal are by no means self-evident.[39] The case for a national program is surely not as strong as in the areas of heavy spillovers such as education and health.[40]

[36] See David A. Wallace, "Beggars on Horseback," in *Ends and Means of Urban Renewal* (Philadelphia Housing Association, 1961).

[37] Administrative bottlenecks seem to be endemic. See Greer, *op. cit.,* pp. 106–10.

[38] See Hugh O. Nourse, "Economics of Urban Renewal," *Land Economics,* Vol. 42, No. 1 (February 1966).

[39] The federal commitment is two-thirds of planning and site preparation costs for localities over 50,000 in population, and three-fourths for localities under 50,000 population. The smaller localities account for about 72 per cent of the projects but only 22 per cent of federal funds obligated through 1964. (Housing and Home Finance Agency, *op. cit.,* p. 342.)

[40] As Sidney Webb remarked some decades ago, "It is, to begin with, impossible to make out, with any clearness of principle or consensus of opinion, what are the services of national and of local benefit respectively." (*Grants in*

A third source of disquietude stems from the feeling that the objectives of urban renewal could be achieved by less cumbersome means than the present program. If improved housing is the major goal, for example, this could be attained either by direct income transfers to the poor, or by a combination of an expanded rent subsidy program and public housing.[41] The problems of site assembly in slum areas could be overcome by the use of eminent domain powers unencumbered by existing requirements for redevelopment of large areas within a comprehensive plan. Subsidies for redevelopment could be accomplished much more simply and flexibly by credit subsidies than by relying solely on site write-downs. Indeed, as Winnick has pointed out, we might have had a good deal more private renewal in the last fifteen years from a broader utilization of eminent domain for site assembly combined with subsidized credit facilities at locations that were scattered and not concentrated in a designated renewal area.[42]

But in spite of these objections, programs for urban renewal are very likely to continue and may even be expanded. It is probably too late to reverse the course. Federal funds for programs in central cities do, in some measure, redress the fiscal imbalance between central cities and areas outside the central city. Urban renewal will continue to muster erratic support from central city political parties and from the strong confluence of interest groups represented in the central business district. The immediate future is much more likely to be characterized by efforts to improve the operations of urban renewal than by efforts to terminate it.

Up to now the success or failure of specific urban renewal projects has very often turned on the question, as James Q. Wilson puts it, "Who's in charge?" [43] Renewal responsibilities may be conceived narrowly or broadly. There may be appropriate attention to the relocation of families and business firms or these may be neglected. Aesthetic considerations may or may not play an important part. Fiscal mercantilism, in terms of a preoccupation with the expansion of the property tax base, may or may not dominate the thinking of local government officials. It can only be hoped that as experience accumulates, a broader and more comprehensive view of these complex operations will come to dominate more narrow and parochial interests.

There is some evidence that this is already in process. More and

---

Aid: A Criticism and a Proposal [London: Longmans, Green & Co., 1920], p. 90.)

[41] Davis and Whinston, *op. cit.*

[42] Winnick, *op. cit.*, pp. 31–35.

[43] James Q. Wilson, "The War on Cities," *The Public Interest*, Vol. 1, No. 3 (Spring 1966), p. 30.

more cities are attempting, in a rough sort of way, to follow the New Haven example of viewing physical renewal in conjunction with the renewal of human resources. The community action programs organized under the auspices of the Office of Economic Opportunity will help to further this approach, and, indeed, in some neighborhoods violence and destruction will obviously occur if it is not furthered. We have, by this time, accumulated a good deal of experience on the importance of neighborhood organization to accompany renewal programs.[44] Legislation in 1964 and 1965 has laid the basis for rehabilitation efforts to accompany renewal.[45] The demonstration cities projects may contribute in this area.

In that most crucial matter of all, the provision of adequate housing for displaced families, existing urban policy is obviously most deficient. It may be that this thorny matter cannot be handled successfully without a major national program for a "war on housing" that would considerably exceed the dimensions of the present "war on poverty."

In the meantime, reasonably good progress has been made in the kinds of things economists preoccupy themselves with. Although administrative delays and uncertainties limit the practical applications of the technique, the framework for a systematic benefit-cost analysis of urban renewal projects is by this time well established.[46] Benefit-cost analysis applied to urban renewal projects can contribute importantly to improved decisions with respect to project priority and project scale. When cast in the kind of balance sheet form that Lichfield has devised, benefit-cost analysis can also be extremely useful in analyzing the relative economic impacts on both affected groups and affected neighborhoods. Forces of latent political opposition can thus be uncovered; the externalities may be anticipated and perhaps compensated in advance.

In addition to benefit-cost techniques, economists have contributed

[44] See Peter H. Rossi and Robert A. Dentler, *The Politics of Urban Renewal* (The Free Press, 1961).

[45] William L. Slayton, "Rehabilitation Potential Probed for Urban Renewal, Public Housing," *Journal of Housing,* Vol. 22, No. 11 (December, 1965).

[46] See Jerome Rothenberg, "Urban Renewal Programs," in Robert Dorfman (ed.), *Measuring Benefits of Government Investment* (Brookings, 1965); Nathaniel Lichfield and Julius Margolis, "Benefit-Cost Analysis as a Tool in Urban Government Decision Making," in Howard G. Schaller (ed.), *Public Expenditure in the Urban Community* (Resources for the Future, 1963); Nathaniel Lichfield, "Spatial Externalities in Urban Public Expenditures, A Case Study," in Julius Margolis (ed.), *The Public Economy of Urban Communities* (Resources for the Future, 1965); James C. T. Mao, "Efficiency in Public Urban Renewal Expenditures through Benefit Cost Analysis," *Journal of the American Institute of Planners,* Vol. 32, No. 2 (March 1966); Charles J. Stokes, Philip Mintz, and Hans von Gelder, "Economic Criteria for Urban Redevelopment," *American Journal of Economics and Sociology,* Vol. 24, No. 3 (July 1965).

to the development of simulation models applicable to urban renewal problems, and Wingo has developed an outline for an information system to assist in regional housing policy decisions.[47] This latter, incidentally, is predicated on the realistic assumption that there is no single objective function that can be maximized, but rather a whole series of conflicting and diverse policy goals that must be served by urban renewal programs.

Neither the future of the metropolitan area, nor the future of the central city depends on urban renewal as presently constituted. As Greer says, "In the long run urban renewal will make very little difference in the nature and vitality of the central cities." [48] If the city is to be made a more pleasant place in which to live and work, there are a great many matters other than the physical appearance of the central business district that are important. Employment, income, housing, schools, transportation, cultural amenities, recreation, health—all of these are as significant as physical renewal. The problems arise because physical renewal touches and influences each of these other policy areas.

Planning, public housing, community facilities, code enforcement, neighborhood rehabilitation, and fiscal planning are all tied to renewal. But the local urban renewal agencies lack authority to secure co-operation from other local departments and agencies. No central city in the nation has as yet established an administrative organization that is competent to deal with this complex.[49] And, a metropolitan area organization for this purpose is even farther from view.

URBAN TRANSPORTATION [50]

Urban renewal illustrates an area of urban policy where private economic interests (specifically, in the central business district) have collaborated effectively with local government organization and with local political forces to fill a policy vacuum in a federal government program. Transportation as an area of urban policy cannot be so handily described.

The market forces affecting urban transportation are, of course, very strong indeed, particularly as they center on the automobile.[51]

[47] Wingo, op. cit.

[48] Greer, op. cit., p. 179.

[49] This is not for lack of advice and counsel from professionals. See, for example, the plea for an appropriate administrative organization in Martin Meyerson, Barbara Terrett, and William L. C. Wheaton, Housing, People, and Cities (McGraw-Hill, 1962), p. 308.

[50] The authors are indebted to William Vickrey, Lowdon Wingo, Jr., and Britton Harris for critical comments on an earlier draft of this section.

[51] The classic description of the strength of these forces is to be found in Wood, 1400 Governments, pp. 123–44.

The automobile industry, the petroleum industry, the rubber industry, the construction industry, the suppliers of materials for construction, such as cement and steel—these are the industrial giants of our economy, and to describe their concerns in the pallid phrase "market forces" is a considerable understatement. Consumer interests are weak in comparison with producer interests. The stakes are high; urban transportation costs are now approaching housing costs.

Government organization required to deal with urban transportation problems is fragmented among levels of government, federal, state, and local, and fragmented areally within the metropolitan region. But, although fragmented, some components of the administrative organization have more power than others; state highway departments possess this attribute. Political party organizations, neither in the central city nor in the metropolitan area, have typically depended on transportation as a supportive program, although, of course, there are exceptions. The forces that shape urban transportation policy would appear to play directly on the bureaucracy and its administrative decision structures rather than through the medium of organized political parties.

The Sources of Ultimate Confusion

There are two essential ingredients in the urban transportation complex. The first is the peculiar conditions of supply—a mixture of public and private goods. The second is the large volume of externalities generated by an urban transportation system. The operating realities of these ingredients come to rest on the problem of congestion. This latter has been well described in the literature.[52]

The sources of policy confusion in this area start with the evident condition that the future form and function of the metropolitan region cannot be projected with confidence. There seems to be a general consensus among students of the subject that residential, commercial, and industrial densities in the metropolitan region will decrease over time. But whether the trends will be stronger or weaker than in the past—on this point there is no consensus. Moreover, there is no simple relationship between densities and transportation congestion. Reduced densities may increase congestion on automobile freeways, as the case of Los Angeles suggests. Increased residential densities in the central city and utilization of mass transit will, of course, reduce con-

[52] Wilfred Owen, *The Metropolitan Transportation Problem* (Brookings, 1966); Lyle C. Fitch and Associates, *Urban Transportation and Public Policy* (Chandler Publishing Co., 1964); J. R. Meyer, J. F. Kain, and M. Wohl, *The Urban Transportation Problem* (Harvard University Press, 1965); Edgar M. Hoover, "Motor Metropolis: Some Observations on Urban Transportation in America," (Center for Regional Economic Studies, University of Pittsburgh, 1965).

gestion. But dispersal of employment and residence to a number of centers throughout the metropolitan area might reduce both densities and congestion.

No urban economist or planner can predict with accuracy the location of residential activity, the future of the central business district, the location and composition of industry, or the location and composition of employment in the metropolitan region for ten or fifteen years ahead. But major transportation facilities are planned and constructed now and these facilities, which in some idealized sense, ought to be co-ordinated with the form and function of the non-transport activities of the metropolitan region, in fact, usurp that form and function.

The second source of ultimate confusion lies in the appraisal of the future role of the automobile. The set of urban transportation interests appears to be divided into two subsets: those who like automobiles and those who do not. Curiously enough, these attitudes do not seem to apply to trucks with the same emotional intensity; trucks are rather uncheerfully accepted as inevitable for the present and future efficient functioning of the metropolis.

The confusion surrounding the present and prospective use of the private automobile as the major mode of urban transportation has been well put by Owen:

We have the assurance, therefore, that the problem of congestion in urban areas has been precipitated by the automobile; that the automobile, on the contrary, has been our escape from congestion; that the automobile and mass transportation are both guilty of promoting congestion; and finally that neither is the primary culprit but rather a host of other factors that have resulted, thanks to modern technology, in the successful attempt to crowd too many people and too much economic activity into too little space.[53]

A third source of ultimate confusion lies in the inability to specify an objective function for urban transportation. Is low cost transportation the goal, or is it minimization of commuter time? To what extent are commuters' wishes to be respected, or are preferences to be imposed or altered by administrative authority? Is traffic safety an objective function or a constraint?[54] And, as is customary in any policy matter, even if there could be agreement on the objective function, there remains a whole set of disagreements about the constraints that will be accepted. (This point will be re-examined briefly below.)

[53] Owen, *op. cit.,* pp. 24–25.
[54] See Stefan Valavanis, "Traffic Safety from an Economist's Point of View," *Quarterly Journal of Economics,* Vol. 72, No. 4 (November, 1958).

It is small solace that any possible resolution of urban transportation problems, with existing land use patterns, will always be suboptimal at best. More than 50 per cent of the use of an urban transportation system consists of the journey to and from work.[55] It is possible that if the alternative were available, a great many commuters would prefer to live much closer to their employment. That is, existing patterns embody a large element of social waste when viewed against other possible urban configurations. For at least fifty years the advocates of new towns have pointed out that it is possible to organize a pattern in which employees live within easy walking distance of their employment, and vast resources are no longer required for commuter transportation. Until we have more widespread experimentation with such patterns, we will have no way of judging the efficiency of alternatives.

Operational Dimensions

The general characteristics of urban transportation problems are so well known that little attention need be directed to specific description. The following points may be worth listing:

1) The projection of present trends in automobile usage produces a frightening prospect for increased congestion, traffic accidents, and air pollution.

2) The demands for transportation from reduced densities in urban living, the out-movement of economic activity from the central city, and increased cross-commuting would appear capable of being met only by increased reliance on the private automobile.

3) The private automobile is undoubtedly the greatest generator of externalities that civilization has ever known. Its only possible rival would appear to be warfare among nations. The external benefits in terms of employment and income multipliers are very high indeed; the external costs must be measured in such terms as air pollution, noise, accidents, crime, delinquency, and illegitimate babies.

4) No metropolitan area has been successful in arresting the relative decline in mass transit. Experimentation with off-peak reduced fares, free parking close to subway terminals, and express lanes for buses have occasionally been useful palliatives, but have hardly restored the industry to a state of economic health. The cities that have consciously subsidized mass transit to hold down fares may have engaged in a sound policy with respect to the distribution of income, but the payoff in terms of reduced urban congestion has not been pronounced. Fares

[55] Lowdon Wingo, Jr., *Transportation and Urban Land* (Resources for the Future, 1961), pp. 27–36.

on mass transit may have to be negative if riders are to be attracted back.[56]

5) The dismal outlook for mass transit is not brightened by any hope that we are on the verge of major technological breakthroughs.[57] The technology of mass transit has been laggard, particularly in the United States, but there is no reason to believe this condition will change in the immediate future. There is no one endowed with responsibility for thinking about research and development for the whole of urban transportation. There may be some cost reductions and service improvements, as with the innovations planned for the San Francisco rapid transit system, but these are not likely to lead to major shifts in demand patterns.[58] A new mode of transportation, such as the electric automobile, will undoubtedly reduce air pollution, but probably increase congestion.

6) Since 1956 the most forceful and aggressive entrant on the transportation scene has been the state highway department. Fortified by 90–10 federal funds, with technically competent staffs and encouraged by a strong confluence of interest groups, state highway departments, as the phrase goes, "remake the shape of urban America" by their decisions with respect to urban arterials. City planning departments appear to be rather helpless in the face of state highway departments; suburban planning officials can win an occasional skirmish, but never the war. Local concerns for land use and aesthetics typically lose out to concerns for interarea traffic movement.

7) Fiscal imbalance abounds in urban transportation. State highway funds, except for the arterials, usually stop at city lines, leaving the financial burden of all access roads and streets to the city itself. In 1961, the forty-three largest cities in the nation spent more than twice

---

[56] There appears to be an asymmetry over time in the demand for mass transit; an increase in fares drives passengers away and a reduction in fares does not attract them back. The cross-elasticities of demand among alternative modes of transportation also appear to be relatively low.

Using Chicago data, Moses and Williamson found that at zero prices only one-fifth of area commuters would be diverted to public transportation and that negative prices would be necessary on all modes of public transportation to divert at least 50 per cent of those making the trip to work by automobile. (Leon M. Moses and Harold F. Williamson, Jr., "Value of Time, Choice of Mode, and the Subsidy Issue in Urban Transportation," *Journal of Political Economy*, Vol. LXXI, No. 3 [June 1963], p. 264.)

[57] Meyer, Kain, and Wohl, *op. cit.*, pp. 309–33; Fitch, *op. cit.*, pp. 170–208.

[58] The innovation gap in urban transportation was discussed at the Summer Study on Science and Urban Development, sponsored by the Department of Housing and Urban Development and the Office of Science and Technology. Most of the proposals for improvement centered on bus transportation, and some will undoubtedly be encouraged by HUD.

as much on facilities and services for motor vehicles as these cities received from user tax receipts, plus federal and state grants.[59]

8) Patterns of housing segregation also accentuate the crisis in urban area transportation.[60] The Negro ghettos surrounding the central business district have contributed to the out-movement of white middle-class families or, viewed in another way, the increases in property values in these areas have made it possible for white families to sell at a profit and move to the suburbs. However, central business district employment opportunities for Negroes have so declined that the absence of adequate transportation facilities from the ghetto to available employment erects a further barrier, thus limiting opportunities. The presence of the Negro ghettos also discourages the private redevelopment of middle- and upper-class housing near the central city and thus increases the demands of suburbanites for commuter facilities.[61]

Obstacles to Rationalization

It is not at all clear whether urban transportation is the economist's meat or the economist's poison. There have been a great many well-funded research programs on urban transportation systems and economists have frequently participated in these research efforts, although the techniques and methods of analysis have usually been dominated by engineers. Many of these studies have been sharply criticized.[62] In one critique of the Chicago transportation study it was found that the report did not explore the available alternatives in pricing policy, that it assumed a constant level of use for mass transit, and that it neglected the effects of highway development on the location of residences.[63]

The origin and destination studies which so often are the starting point for urban transportation studies are, of course, a reflection of existing preferences and not of preferences that will obtain at the time the next major increment in the system is constructed five to ten years hence. Commuter preferences for alternative modes of transportation apparently are systematically biased in favor of the automobile by

[59] Fitch, *op. cit.,* p. 138.
[60] John F. Kain, "The Big Cities' Big Problem," *Challenge,* September–October 1966, pp. 5–8.
[61] For further elaboration of these points see Meyer, Kain, and Wohl, *op. cit.,* pp. 144–67.
[62] See Richard M. Zettel and Richard R. Carll, *Summary Review of Major Metropolitan Area Transportation Studies in the United States,* Institute of Transportation and Traffic Engineering, Berkeley, 1962.
[63] John B. Lansing, *Transportation and Economic Policy* (The Free Press, 1966), pp. 279–91.

virtue of the fact that most commuters are not required to pay anything approaching the marginal cost of facilities or the marginal congestion costs inflicted on each other. Commuters may also be ignorant of the marginal costs they do bear and of existing and feasible but unavailable alternatives to automobiles. However, while it is difficult to determine whose superior wisdom should be substituted for the preferences of the "ignorant" commuters, it is clear that techniques for increasing cost consciousness would improve decisions.

Benefit-cost techniques that have been employed for transportation studies have likewise come under criticism.[64] There has apparently been a tendency to count land value increments but not decrements. The estimates of the value of travel-time savings are uncomfortably astronomical. Non-monetary values tend to get converted somehow into monetary values.[65] The benefits from the avoidance of accidents are difficult to estimate and the equation that will relate fatal and non-fatal accidents has not been discovered.

But even if these difficulties could be removed there would be serious conceptual limitations on the use of benefit-cost analysis in a study of urban transportation economics. If benefit-cost analysis were to be used, as it so often is in water resource development, simply to estimate whether the ratio is more or less than 1.0, or for purposes of ranking projects, the conceptual difficulties would probably not be severe. But for the analysis of urban transportation investment, benefit-cost analysis must assume the additional burden of benefit assignment.[66]

Suppose that some rough-and-ready rule of efficient resource allocation is adopted such that individuals or groups who are benefited assume the costs of an increment of a locally financed arterial, and, as usual, there is a choice between user charges and general property taxes. If the arterial highway feeds into the central business district we must now resolve the age-old question of the extent to which improved access yields measurable benefits that have been transferred to CBD property owners, and the extent to which the reduced congestion is properly a benefit to be assigned to the commuter. Even if the

[64] As usual, the analytical framework is better than the practice. For an excellent study of the former, see Herbert Mohring and Mitchell Harwitz, *Highway Benefits* (Northwestern University Press, 1962).

[65] Tillo E. Kuhn, "The Economics of Transportation Planning in Urban Areas," in *Transportation Economics* (National Bureau of Economic Research, 1965).

[66] In water resource projects the benefit assignments are not in every case linked with requirements that project costs must be assumed by the beneficiaries. The assumption of cost is handled by "traditional practice." The beneficiaries of navigation and flood control, for example, are not required to assume costs, but the beneficiaries of power investment, industrial and municipal water, and irrigation are expected to assume an assigned share of project costs.

aggregate benefits could be estimated for the CBD, there would be further problems in the division of this benefit among landowners, employers and vendors.

There is further difficulty in ascertaining whether reduced congestion, and hence reduced commuting time, is a benefit that should be priced out and assigned to the motorist. If we treat the "congestion time" of the Wall Street executive who commutes daily to Westchester County by automobile at its opportunity cost, some very large values, hence high benefits and high user charges, will result. But this commuter time may have been previously capitalized in higher executive compensation rates or lower suburban land values.

Even if the capitalization issue could be resolved, there would remain the suspicion that the automobile industry, which enjoys such very large external benefits from arterial highway construction, should somehow be asked to assume a part of the cost of urban transportation investment.

It does not appear to be possible to specify the objective function for an urban transportation system. Suppose that it was determined that the proper goal is to minimize the total annual cost of transportation in a given urban region. Then one might establish as constraints the minimization of accidents, the maximization of access to the central business district or to other employing or vending centers, the minimization of pollution, and the minimization of congestion on highways. The value of these constraints might be established by some sort of rough community consensus.

But it may be that cost minimization is not the appropriate goal. It may be that it is travel time that should be minimized, subject to a cost constraint that would reflect community judgment. This approach would require imputations for commuter time, but only the marginal time should be counted. That is, it must be assumed that the commuter's original choice of residence reflects a tradeoff between housing values and commuter time. He should be required to pay only for transportation improvements that reduce commuting time below what it was when his residence was purchased.[67]

The third possibility for an objective function would be to attempt to determine what users want, presumably by some kind of questionnaire or interview technique, aided by pricing experiments, and assume that user preferences would reflect the appropriate time-cost tradeoffs.

[67] The valuation of travel time is one of the thorniest of all urban transportation problems. See Moses and Williamson, *op. cit.*, pp. 247–64; Mohring and Harwitz, *op. cit.*, pp. 162–80; James R. Nelson, *The Value of the Time of Human Beings* (Brookings, 1967, forthcoming).

Unhappily, the concept of "user" is not unambiguous and it would be difficult to weight the preferences of such diverse users as commuters, local truckers, shoppers and common carriers, or to handle the multi-purpose trip.

It is possible, of course, to forget about the refinements of benefit-cost or a systems analysis and proceed simply with Vickrey-type solutions.[68] Vickrey does not specify objective functions. He finds that the price of automobile use is far below its marginal cost, although he is quite ready to point out that marginal cost figures are very hard to come by. In these circumstances an economist must instinctively move to raise price and, as is well known, Vickrey's proposals take the form of various metering devices to permit additional charges for the use of arterials into and out of the city and for the use of city streets.

The proposals are ingenious and appealing. They are designed almost wholly to reduce congestion by discouraging the use of the automobile. They are firmly grounded in traditional market price practices for resource allocation, and, if adopted, would undoubtedly improve access to presently congested areas. However, they would be certainly opposed by a solid phalanx of motorists, employers, and commercial establishments in the central business district who fear a reduction in the volume of traffic. If adopted, Vickrey-type solutions might have interesting results. Motorists may be willing to pay much higher user charges. If so, more facilities will have to be constructed.

Vickrey-type solutions may be subject to some worries about the theory of the second best. There is increased awareness that the introduction of a greater degree of marginal cost pricing in one segment of a monopolistic market may not, in fact, move the whole market toward an optimum. However, present practice is so far from marginal cost pricing that perhaps these fears may be laid to one side.

Program Improvements

Transportation has been subsidized in this country since colonial times; every mode of transportation has been supported at least occasionally from the general revenue. As a nation we seem to be addicted to providing more transportation than users are willing to pay for directly. It may be, of course, that the external benefits of this policy have been so substantial as to provide adequate justification; certainly there is no evidence that the practice will be discontinued in the immediate future. The tradition is strong even if the externalities cannot be measured with precision.

[68] See William Vickrey, "Pricing as a Tool in Coordination of Local Transportation," in *Transportation Economics, op. cit.*

This tradition has its programmatic advantages. Transportation planning and urban transportation investment need not be bounded by the constraints of user tax revenues. Unfortunately, as has been noted, we are never quite sure what the proportions should be between user taxes and general revenue or the extent to which market mechanisms should be employed for rationing purposes.

The commonly proposed administrative solution to the problems of urban transportation is the establishment of a strong regional transportation agency. There are, of course, transportation agencies that possess a limited range of functions and responsibilities in a number of metropolitan areas in the United States. There are no areally comprehensive regional transportation agencies with authority to control investment and establish rates and services for all modes of transportation within any metropolitan area, although an increasing number of limited function agencies are being established to qualify for the modest federal, aid under the Urban Mass Transportation Acts of 1964 and 1966.

The creation of a regional transportation agency does not eradicate the confusion that abounds in community aims and objectives with respect to urban transportation, nor will it resolve the conceptual difficulties that now block the path of "rational" investment decisions. Although a regional transportation agency may be able to use cost-benefit analysis more imaginatively than has occurred to date, such an agency will not in itself untangle cost-benefit infirmities.

The proponents of strong regional transportation agencies are almost never precise in the powers and duties that should be accorded such an agency. Confronted by program conflicts and administrative confusion, the terms "co-ordination" and "co-operation" always have a certain amount of magic incantation to which no one is immune. Unfortunately, the incantation will not resolve the problem of who is to be co-ordinated and at what price.

The further difficulty is that urban transportation may not be a very good functional basis for organization. The experience of water resources management is instructive on this point. A strongly endowed regional water resources agency will necessarily dominate at least a part of the program concerns of other functional areas, such as recreation, conservation, and regional programs for industrial location and promotion. In other words, a strong regional water resources agency will push other agencies around. This would be the case and with a vengeance for a strong urban regional transportation agency. Land use patterns—including residential, commercial, and industrial location, and hence urban form and structure, including segregation and desegregation policies—would be subsidiary to decisions concerning transportation. There are very few metropolitan regions in this country where the transportation crisis is so severe that all else must yield before it.

It must be concluded that the hopes for program improvement should not rest too heavily on the establishment of regional transportation agencies. At the very best, such an agency can serve as a broker to conciliate the parties at interest. It will not be in a position to resolve conflicts between central city and outside central city interests; it may mediate them. A regional transportation agency will not make mass transit suddenly viable; it may make modest contributions to maintaining its existence. A regional transportation agency might be able to accomplish a modest degree of articulation between planning for access roads to the central business district and planning for parking facilities for the central business district, and to view this problem, at least, as amenable to systems analysis.

There are other modest accomplishments that may be expected from regional transportation agencies. The multiplication of such agencies could move us slowly towards a pattern of federal grants for urban transportation as such rather than federal grants almost solely for urban highways.[69] It may also be possible for a regional transportation agency to begin to pursue the possibilities for joint optimizing of land use and transportation.[70]

It has not been demonstrated that there is an ideal urban form or an ideal urban transportation system. The outcomes within particular metropolitan areas will, of course, represent compromises that vary among areas in accordance with existing physical facilities, economic feasibility, and consumer choice.[71]

The automobile continues to be the villain of the piece. There must be many urban planners who dream at night that the private automobile has just disappeared from the scene. These dreams must give rise to further visions of enhanced administrative authority—authority that would endow some agency with the power to limit automobile use. Such demands are very likely to be heard increasingly in the next decade.

Fortunately or unfortunately, as the case may be, for local governments to impose solutions on the local citizenry is a most difficult matter. Indeed, urban conflicts are often resolved not on the rule of majority but on something between that and the rule of unanimity.

[69] Kuhn, *op. cit.*, p. 316.
[70] Britton Harris, "Urban Transportation Planning: Philosophy of Approach," (University of Pennsylvania, Institute for Environmental Studies, 1966).
[71] Owen, *op. cit.*, p. 121.

Strong minorities probably block policy change even more often in municipalities than in the U.S. Senate.

It is necessary to reach the unhappy conclusion that only partially ameliorative solutions are in sight; nothing dramatic is in prospect. Automobile congestion may be moderately relieved by efforts to shift preferences toward mass transit. Motorists may be mildly discouraged by higher tolls and fees. Congestion and air pollution will increase. Regional transportation agencies will multiply, with their powers slowly enhanced.

URBAN EDUCATION

Public education, as an area of urban policy, has a number of unusual characteristics as compared with other program areas. Market forces, as described above, appear to have limited influence on the volume of resources devoted to education, or on the operation of the educational enterprise. The construction industry does not appear to be as effective a lobby for school-building programs as is the road-building industry for highways. Even the textbook and instructional equipment industries do not have evident impact in proportion to their established interests.

Likewise, public education has historically stood apart from the direct influence of political parties and from the structure of urban government. In practice, the administration of public education has very often been treated as a unique form of public service, as it was once described by Beard.[72]

However, the traditional isolation of public education from the rest of government is now being reduced. Educational issues are increasingly political issues—federal, state, and local. The business community perceives that an improved educational system in urban areas has a relationship to economic growth. Other urban programs impinge on education. The highway system opens the suburbs to middle-income whites, thus destroying the traditional basis for support for urban education. But urban renewal programs seek to counteract this by incorporating educational facilities in redevelopment plans.

The contemporary problems of urban education are very much the product of standard patterns of suburbanization. The redistribution of population between suburb and central city has created disparities in population characteristics. The conventional and generally accurate description is that the poor, less educated, non-white Americans are stay-

[72] Charles A. Beard, *The Unique Function of Education in American Democracy* (National Education Association, Education Policies Commission, 1937).

609

ing in the central city while higher-income white families and a great deal of the industrial sector moves to the suburb, taking their tax base with them. Although this description must be qualified somewhat in terms of the size of the metropolitan area and region of the country, the larger the metropolitan area, the more accurate it is.

The educational problems created by this redistribution of population and tax base are the objectives for which recent federal aid to education was designed. Although some of the aid will go to rural areas, the bulk of it will go to the cities where more and more of the disadvantaged are concentrated. This use of federal aid for the purpose of overcoming the educational disadvantages of the underprivileged is a new development. As the *Report of the National Advisory Council on the Education of Disadvantaged Children* points out,

Only five years have gone by since educators first began to recognize and define the special problems of educational disadvantage—and at first, very few educators at that. Less than three years have gone by since these first definitions of educational disadvantage began to win a reasonably wide recognition leading to a political climate favoring a federal commitment to large scale compensatory education. Less than one year has gone by since that federal commitment through Title I has become a reality.[73]

The demands for aid to education, of course, go back farther than does the recognition of the special educational needs of the socially and economically disadvantaged. Prior to this recognition, and particularly in the post-World War II period, the greatest demands for aid to education came from the suburban areas that were feeling the pinch of increasing enrollments and a resulting need for physical facilities.

While the political appropriateness of federal aid was being debated, studies showed that investment in education for urban white males brought returns higher than physical investment in manufacturing industry. Economic growth in the United States was discovered to be attributable in good measure to investment in human resources.[74] Under the GI Bill of Rights 7,800,000 World War II and Korean War servicemen were provided with additional educational opportunities. The Veterans Administration stated that "as a result, they raised their income level to the point where they were expected to repay, through taxes, two and a half times through their lifetimes the fourteen and a half billion dollars the program cost."

Equally dramatic are the statistics that demonstrate the social costs

---

[73] November 25, 1966, p. 11.
[74] Gary S. Becker, "Under-investment in College Education?", *American Economic Review*, Vol. 50, No. 2 (May 1960); Theodore W. Schultz, *The Economic Value of Education* (Columbia University Press, 1963).

of inadequate education—social costs in terms. of delinquency, crime, insufficient earnings for a decent life, family instability, etc.

Overcoming Obstacles to Federal Aid

The combination of the need for new facilities in the suburbs and the obvious economic advantage of investment in education were given new political significance with the launching of Sputnik. The educational system of the country came under general attack from those who believed that students were not required to learn enough. Progressive education was often depicted as the cause of the so-called educational failures. There is no doubt that this concern for educational quality increased local expenditures for education and, in the process, undoubtedly increased state aid for education. Most of the increase, however, appears to have come in the suburbs rather than in the city.

This concern for the quality of education also produced the National Defense Education Act. Designed to improve educational offerings in fields related to national defense, it authorized aid for specific purposes and provided it to those school districts with sufficient initiative to apply for it. Again the result was primarily aid for suburban districts since it was these districts which had the necessary initiative and professional competence to make the required effort.[75]

Despite these modest improvements in the support provided education, the concern was not sufficient to overcome the political resistance to a more general kind of federal aid. That resistance reflected the sharp division in the country over the issue of public support of parochial education.[76] Although public opinion polls showed a clear majority of voters favoring aid to education, that majority disappeared whenever preference had to be stated for or against aid to parochial schools. The political roadblock was finally overcome with the landslide victory of the Democrats in 1964, a compromise on the parochial school issue, and the obvious decline in the quality of central city education.[77] The aid provided, therefore, was not general aid but aid for all the educationally disadvantaged. Within this context the program had special meaning for the central cities of the country.

The deteriorating relative position of central city schools began to

[75] Paul E. Marsh and Ross A. Gortner, *Federal Aid to Science Education: Two Programs* (Syracuse University Press, 1963); Frank J. Munger and Richard F. Fenno, Jr., *National Politics and Federal Aid to Education* (Syracuse University Press, 1962).

[76] Munger, *op. cit.*

[77] For an analysis of the constellation of political forces which produced the Elementary and Secondary Education Act of 1965, see Philip Meranto, *The Politics of Federal Aid to Education in 1965* (Syracuse University Press, 1967).

become clear in 1957. That year marks the point at which expenditures per pupil in the suburbs caught up with and began to pass expenditures per pupil in the city. In 1957, for the thirty-five largest metropolitan areas, current expenditures per student were $303 in the suburbs and $310 in the city. By 1962, however, the suburbs had forged considerably ahead. Current expenditures per pupil for the suburban areas were $439 compared with $376, a difference of $63 per pupil. Although later data are not available for all the thirty-five largest metropolitan areas, a check on some of these areas indicates that the gap is still there. Whether it is growing or remaining about the same is not yet clear.

Educating the Disadvantaged

During this period of suburban educational improvement, research concerning the disadvantaged made it clear that the educational problems for this group of students was much greater than for those who went to school in suburban communities. Careful studies have demonstrated again and again that the single best predictor of educational achievement is the family background of the pupil. On the average, the higher the income of parents, the better the performance of the students. Income is undoubtedly a proxy measure for many other family characteristics.[78]

Further, it became clear that educational programs were essentially designed by middle-income people for middle-income students. Educational materials were loaded with examples and illustrations drawn from the life of the suburban child. Teachers are drawn from this same income stratum and were trained in schools of education or liberal arts colleges by faculty who came from the same background and who live as a part of that community.

These findings demonstrate that a different kind of education was needed for the disadvantaged child, and that present personnel and practices cannot do the job. Curriculum has to be revised, teacher training changed, and teaching methods adjusted to fit the students. To do all these things will require time and resources—most of all new and massive resources. A recent study of education in Chicago and Atlanta high schools finds that small incremental differences in the input resources for education will not do the job.[79]

[78] For a review of these studies see Jesse Burkhead, Thomas G. Fox and John W. Holland, *Inputs and Outputs in Large City Education* (Syracuse University Press, 1967); Thomas G. Fox, "A Study of Educational Resource Transformation within a Large City Public High School System" (Syracuse University Graduate School, unpublished doctoral dissertation, 1966).

[79] Burkhead, Fox and Holland, *op. cit.*

TABLE 1.
CURRENT EDUCATIONAL EXPENDITURES PER STUDENT, TOTAL EDUCATIONAL
EXPENDITURES PER CAPITA, AND TOTAL NON-AIDED EDUCATIONAL
EXPENDITURES PER CAPITA (TAX PROXY) FOR CENTRAL CITY
AND OUTSIDE CENTRAL CITY AREAS: 1962

City	Current education expenditures per student		Total education expenditures per capita		Total non-aided education expenditures per capita	
	CC	OCC	CC	OCC	CC	OCC
New York	$536.88	$684.34	$ 77.29	$194.05	$47.10	$127.88
Chicago	408.51	473.69	66.09	112.60	50.78	92.15
Los Angeles	437.14	555.54	101.01	174.83	64.82	115.50
Philadelphia	397.75	492.96	54.69	105.59	37.24	81.42
Detroit	461.67	434.10	93.78	128.08	70.16	88.59
Baltimore	366.07	421.61	80.50	112.82	60.67	81.21
Houston	290.09	450.35	63.75	143.85	32.42	91.87
Cleveland	370.59	459.50	65.01	113.74	58.25	100.98
St. Louis	386.58	423.73	55.31	100.70	37.11	75.87
Milwaukee	377.90	469.38	65.20	124.75	51.77	112.84
San Francisco	466.77	546.29	69.19	172.17	45.47	113.48
Boston	385.46	465.36	50.32	100.87	43.78	93.09
Dallas	301.96	325.40	74.42	100.37	47.29	61.63
New Orleans	271.87	233.05	41.74	66.63	12.68	27.62
Pittsburgh	368.00	450.98	51.19	96.05	39.76	61.52
San Diego	414.63	538.95	105.13	156.29	67.70	92.42
Seattle	409.89	415.72	89.39	138.86	46.93	58.83
Buffalo	447.03	561.20	59.27	137.32	33.82	77.52
Cincinnati	373.11	577.74	62.80	118.29	55.07	95.24
Memphis	227.58	245.71	48.74	96.59	26.54	64.25
Denver	418.30	380.74	81.19	151.07	67.13	116.37
Atlanta	272.52	287.80	57.42	90.49	36.17	51.47
Minneapolis	414.31	441.45	61.42	157.05	41.91	109.56
Indianapolis	352.87	467.92	69.83	144.17	51.30	116.28
Kansas City	409.19	350.67	75.09	156.54	54.40	126.33
Columbus	327.40	332.06	61.25	98.08	51.97	69.77
Newark	496.21	522.23	93.80	112.08	78.32	100.04
Louisville	301.44	477.73	42.81	134.33	25.28	106.31
Portland (Oregon)	421.59	480.14	79.37	149.10	58.32	95.58
Long Beach	426.33	555.54	85.99	174.83	51.08	115.50
Birmingham	194.43	223.89	49.93	61.49	18.23	23.64
Oklahoma City	269.23	291.67	67.16	83.76	43.97	70.37
Rochester	580.05	573.07	79.35	158.58	54.79	91.53
Toledo	377.71	511.85	80.08	160.51	71.54	113.00
St. Paul	415.51	441.45	58.10	157.05	40.37	109.56
Norfolk	265.43	288.65	47.42	87.51	29.53	59.23
Omaha	282.58	394.90	49.48	136.83	43.88	126.37
Mean	376.33	438.38	68.69	126.17	47.23	83.80
Standard deviation	83.61	106.77	16.04	31.45	14.94	25.54
Coefficient of variation	22.1%	14.4%	23.4%	24.9%	31.6%	30.5%

Source: U.S. Bureau of the Census, *Census of Governments, 1962.*

This study concluded that:

The negative findings of this research are not unimportant in themselves. When it is discovered, for example, that class size is not a significant determinant of scores on achievement tests in high schools in Chicago and Atlanta, this does not mean that class size has no possible effect on educational outcomes. It simply means that *within the range of class size variation* in these cities, there is no effect on outcome. An incremental reduction in class size from 32 to 30 does not produce measurably significant gains in output; an increase in materials and supplies per pupil from $7 to $9, for example, will produce no measurably significant gains in output. But these findings tell us nothing about outcomes over a larger range of variation. A reduction in class size from 30 to 10 may produce extremely significant gains. We will never know until we try.[80]

Early efforts to meet these newly discovered needs have not been notably successful. Even with the new federal funds successes have been few. After spending a summer observing federally sponsored programs, the National Advisory Council on the Education of Disadvantaged Children reported that:

For the most part, however, projects are piecemeal, fragmented efforts at remedial or vaguely directed enrichment. It is extremely rare to find strategically planned, comprehensive programs for change based on four essential needs: adapting academic content to the special problems of disadvantaged children, improved in-service training for teachers, attention to nutrition and other health needs, and involvement of parents and community agencies in planning and assistance to school programs.[81]

The Council, in defining what was needed, says:

Time and again at professional meetings and in print, eminent education authorities have enunciated a detailed methodology for "starting where the child is," for liberating children to learn by individualizing instruction, substituting discovery for lecture, emphasizing concrete experience in advance of abstraction, recognizing that disadvantaged children tend to be "physical learners." These authorities have gone further by stressing a need to look beyond conventional school practices for widening the child's total learning environment—involvement of parents as motivators, exposing children to community resources, bringing the world of school into realistic harmony with the world of work, and providing simple guarantees that a child is reasonably well fed and clothed and medically sound of body as a prerequisite to learning. To a child whose whole world is darkened by the mood of hope-bereft adults (parents and teachers alike), by ignorance

[80] *Ibid.*, pp. 93–94.
[81] *Op. cit.*, pp. 2–3.

of patterns of life outside an urban or rural slum, and the physical stresses of hunger, poor teeth, and faulty vision, it is hardly a welcome favor to pile an extra hour of remedial drill upon an unsuccessful school day. To this child, new opportunity must be offered in large, variegated, carefully tied packages, designed to change a life outlook, not merely a report card.[82]

After stating these needs, the Council reports, "Yet, by and large, we are still at the stage of offering remedial fragments—often uninteresting ones, at that." [83]

Political leaders, responding to the difficulties of providing compensatory education, are calling for increased funds. Sargent Shriver has suggested that the practices begun in Headstart be extended into the first, second, third, and grades even beyond, in the regular school year. Harold Howe, Commissioner of Education, has suggested that we must halve class size in central cities, with classes of no more than fifteen students.

If these moves are to be made, the cost will be very high. The present level of federal support is clearly insufficient. At present, aid under Title I, which is where the bulk of the money for education of the disadvantaged is, averages about $25.00 per pupil for total public school enrollment. For some specific cities the figures are: $24.39 per pupil in Los Angeles; $37.19 in San Francisco; in Chicago, $57.50; and in New York City, $60.53. Seldom does the amount of federal aid received by any city close the gap in per student expenditures between the city and its suburbs.

Even if the money is all concentrated in the schools with disadvantaged pupils the present aid will be insufficient. In this regard it is important to note that the proportion of disadvantaged students needing special education is greater than is indicated by the general white–non-white population distribution. One of the measures of this difference is the contrast between the proportion of non-white people in the total city population and the proportion of non-white in the public schools. This difference in population and enrollment proportions is a result of age distribution, family composition, and the greater tendency of white parents to send their children to private and parochial schools. Table 2 shows, for 1960, the proportion of the total population of the largest cities which was non-white and the proportion of public school enrollment which was non-white. For all cities the disparity has increased since 1960.

[82] *Ibid.*, pp. 8–9.
[83] *Ibid.*, p. 9.

TABLE 2.
NON-WHITE POPULATION CONTRASTED WITH NON-WHITE SCHOOL
ENROLLMENT FOR FIFTEEN LARGEST CITIES: 1960

City	Per cent non-white of total population	Per cent non-white of school population	Difference in proportions of non-white school enrollment and non-white population
New York	14.0	22.0	8.0
Chicago	22.9	39.8	16.9
Los Angeles	12.2	20.5	8.3
Philadelphia	26.4	46.7	20.3
Detroit	28.9	42.9	14.0
Baltimore	34.7	50.1	15.4
Houston	22.9	30.2	8.7
Cleveland	28.6	46.1	17.5
Washington	53.9	77.5	23.6
St. Louis	28.6	48.8	20.2
Milwaukee	8.4	16.2	7.8
San Francisco	14.3	30.5	16.2
Boston	9.1	16.4	7.3
Dallas	19.0	26.0	7.0
New Orleans	37.2	55.4	18.2

Source: U.S. Bureau of the Census, *U.S. Census of Population: 1960, Selected Area Reports, Standard Metropolitan Statistical Areas,* and *General Social and Economic Characteristics, 1960.*

The Politics of Increasing Educational Resources

Assuming the need for increased resources to be allocated to public education, the issue becomes the political potential for such an allocation. The outlook is not bright. The present fiscal responses to socio-economic characteristics and the system of local school government tend to reinforce each other. The decision-making unit at the local level, the school board, responds not to the general problems of its metropolitan area or of its state but rather to the district which it serves. Since these districts tend to homogeneity in socioeconomic characteristics, particularly in the suburbs, the inevitable result is a pattern of resource allocation which reflects the nature of the districts involved. Again the relevance of the present fragmented system of local government to substantive policy is demonstrated.

A redrawing of school district lines, causing the districts to reflect more accurately the total population distribution of the metropolitan area, would change this environment and might cause a more equal distribution of educational resources between city and suburb. The growing demand by national educational leaders for metropolitan-wide school districts is based on the belief that such a distribution would be the result.

The political possibility is not great that this partial solution will be adopted. There are no substantial political forces at the appropriate level of government demanding it. But even if there were, its potential for accomplishing the right kind of change in resource allocation is questionable. It is true that a redrawing of boundaries which would include city and suburb in the same district might raise expenditure levels in the city. It might, simultaneously, lower expenditures in the suburbs. The present competitive situation, which is particularly important among suburban school districts, but which probably does have some impact on central city school expenditures, causes per capita and per student expenditures to be higher than would be the case if common, metropolitan-wide school districts were established.[84] In other words, metropolitan-wide districts might tend to greater equality in suburban and city expenditures but might simultaneously lower average total expenditures. City expenditures would be higher, suburban expenditures lower.

To correct the present distribution of resources, however, requires more than simply equalizing expenditures between city and suburb. The need is for an unequal distribution of resources in order to accomplish genuine equality of educational opportunity. Such a goal raises a serious ideological problem for the educational community. The California report explains this dilemma when it says,

With respect to the adequate provisioning of slum schools, one factor is the view of local school authorities that each school, regardless of the nature of the pupil clientele served, must be equally treated. It is said that the public demands that staffing ratiis, expenditures for instructional materials and supplies, etc., be approximately the same for all schools of a given grade level. Further, this view is reinforced by the code. Section 1054 of the Education Code, Statutes of 1963, states: "The governing board of any school district shall maintain all of the elementary day schools established by it with equal rights and privileges as far as possible." [85]

The kind of increased local tax effort which would be required to meet the needs described here seems highly unlikely. The fiscal bind in which most cities find themselves is well known. Further, the behavior

[84] David Ranney, "School Government and the Determinants of the Fiscal Support for Large City Education Systems" (Syracuse University Graduate School, unpublished doctoral dissertation, 1966).
[85] Senate Fact-Finding Committee on Revenue and Taxation, *State and Local Fiscal Relationships in Public Education in California* (Senate of the State of California, March 1965), p. 60.

of the city school boards indicates that they are more tax- than expenditure-conscious. There seems to be a tendency to calculate how much tax increase the community will tolerate rather than to concentrate on the expenditure levels necessary to do the educational job.

A school principal in New York City describes the situation well when he says:

I have regard for the Board of Education, but it has never fully recognized that it ought to be functioning as the representative of the children—all children, but most particularly poor children, who have the fewest representatives in power. The Board should continually be making strong statements about the urgent need for money and services. So far, the Board has represented education in a taxpayer's style. It ought to keep haranguing the city to the point at which a real exploration takes place of how to get the essential funds. Sure, there'd be some complaints from parts of the citizenry, but it would be useful to get those complaints out into the open. And the middle class as a whole would not really oppose this kind of push. The middle class is always passive—alienated from its own beliefs. It doesn't even know it *has* beliefs until things are stirred up. We ought to make education *the* basic industry in this city.[86]

Whether school boards fight as hard as they should for increased expenditures is perhaps a moot point. The difficulties, however, of raising substantial additional funds locally are sufficiently great that it seems unlikely the funds will be raised at this level. Thus, the resources will have to come from outside—from either state or federal aid. Further, that aid, if it is to serve the problem of education for the disadvantaged, will have to be pointed specifically to this problem.

Redirecting Aid

The present aid pattern discriminates against cities. If aid is to serve the purpose outlined here, this characteristic will have to change. The other relevant finding about aid is its impact on local school expenditures. It does raise these expenditures but not as much in cities as the full amount of the aid. If the aid is intended to be fully additive to local effort, therefore, policies will have to be adopted to accomplish this end.[87]

The more important issue, however, is whether aid can be made to reflect the kinds of problems it must solve. Thus far aid at the state

[86] Nat Hentoff, "The Principal," *The New Yorker,* May 7, 1966, pp. 82–85.
[87] Alan K. Campbell and Seymour Sacks, *Metropolitan America: Fiscal Patterns and Governmental Systems* (The Free Press, 1967).

level has not moved in that direction. There is, however, some evidence that state legislatures are beginning to think in terms of compensatory education. New York, California, and Connecticut have all begun to move in this direction. The amounts of money involved thus far are small and compensatory education does not appear to have much political strength.

Reapportionment may aid in correcting the present distribution of aid as between suburbs and cities. Since the Supreme Court decision, insisting on the one-man one-vote principle, there has been much speculation as to what the increase in metropolitan representation in state legislatures will do to state policies and through such policies to state-local fiscal relationships. The uniformly higher aid pattern outside of metropolitan areas, when measured on a state-by-state basis, is consistent with the pre-reapportionment representation pattern.

More complex is the situation as it relates to suburban areas. Although these areas are underrepresented in state legislatures, even more so than central cities, they have done relatively well in terms of the amount of state aid they have received. This result is undoubtedly related to the historical situation when these areas were rural and to the set of functions which state legislatures have decided over the years to aid. These aided functions make up a larger part of the package of services in suburban areas than in central cities. The suburban areas thus receive more aid relative to their fiscal burden than do central cities.[88]

Since reapportionment will increase suburban representation, it follows that the present aid advantage which these areas possess might be retained or even enhanced. On the other hand, it is possible that a reapportioned state legislature will be sufficiently metropolitan-oriented to show concern—not only for suburban problems but for those of the city as well. The result could be an increase in education aid as well as other types of aid to central cities. The evidence on this point is not yet in.

In part, the ability of cities to improve their aid position will depend on the amount and kind of political influence they can bring to bear on state legislatures. To date such influence has not been great. Once the resource issue ceases to be a question of local tax rates, school boards seem to play a relatively small role. School administrators, apparently, are somewhat more involved and perhaps most involved of all are organizations of teachers. The role of teachers, however, is not usually concerned with the issue of increasing aid to disadvantaged schools.

[88] *Ibid.,* Chap. 3.

They are more concerned with such matters as salary scales, pension systems and working conditions.[89]

There is some evidence that some city leaders, particularly those involved in the health of their city, have become increasingly concerned about the quality of education provided in their cities. The relationship of education to economic development is believed by many of them to be important. There are, therefore, a number of cities, of which Atlanta is one, where efforts are being made by community leaders to get greater school aid from state legislatures. If this movement should spread it is possible that a coalition of local business leaders, school board members, school administrators, and teacher organizations could bring substantial pressure to bear on behalf of increased education aid to cities. No such coalition now exists.

Federal aid, as noted above, has been redirected to the cities. The present federal aid program is designed specifically to deal with the problem of the education of the disadvantaged. Politically, this aid has grown out of national rather than state and local political forces. It is a product of the demand for increased aid from national professional associations, plus other national interest groups. The major breakthrough occurred in 1965 when the church-state issue was sufficiently compromised to permit both the National Education Association and Catholic groups to support the program.[90]

The question, therefore, about federal aid is not one of principle but adequacy of funds. The demand for funds from other government activities, particularly the Vietnam war, has undoubtedly held down the increase in resources allocated by the national government to education. Again, there is no evidence of much activity on the part of local school boards to increase federal aid.

Overcoming Educational Disadvantage

Even if the political obstacles to increased resources are overcome and if educational bureaucracies are sufficiently shaken to undertake really new and comprehensive programs, the issue of what is necessary to overcome educational disadvantage is still unresolved. The recent Coleman study seems to indicate that nothing short of income integration in the schools will help the disadvantaged students.[91] Good teach-

---

[89] Alan Rosenthal, "Pedagogues and Power: A Descriptive Survey," *Urban Affairs Quarterly,* Vol. 11, No. 1 (September 1966); "The Strength of Teacher Organizations," *Sociology of Education,* Fall 1966.

[90] Meranto, *op. cit.*

[91] James S. Coleman, *Equality of Educational Opportunity,* U.S. Department of Health, Education and Welfare, Office of Education (U.S. Government Printing Office, 1966).

ing does apparently make some difference, but classmate associations are more important. Students from a background of poverty respond academically well to the atmosphere of a school with a large representation of students from a middle-income background.

Although the Coleman study draws no policy conclusions from its findings, others have been less hesitant. In general, the study has been used to support the need for school integration. A typical statement of this is made by Christopher Jencks when he argues:

> . . . the Report finds that Negro students do better in predominantly middle-class schools and worse in predominantly lower-class schools, but that racial integration has little or no independent effect. Integrating poor Negroes with poor whites, in other words, probably does no good. Integrating poor Negroes with middle-class Negroes might do as much good as integrating them with middle-class whites, but as a practical matter there aren't enough middle-class Negroes to go round. (One reason for this is that 40 per cent of all white-collar Negroes send their children to private schools—an incredible finding which deserves study.) For the foreseeable future class integration will be impossible without racial integration as well.[92]

Not all, however, accept this view. The more militant part of the civil rights movement has been moving more and more in the direction of demanding a rebuilding physically, socially, and educationally of the ghettoes rather than insisting on integration.

Since the Coleman study findings raise some doubts about the effectiveness, at least for education, of this alternative it has produced a rather vigorous dissent from some of the civil rights leaders. Floyd McKissick, president of the Congress of Racial Equality, maintains that the really significant finding is that "A Negro child's achievement is very highly correlated with his feeling that he can control his own destiny." Adding this finding to two others—Negroes do not show as much conviction that their personal behavior can affect what happens to them and that good teachers are much more important to Negroes than whites—McKissick argues, "My point is that even if better teachers, a changed student culture, middle-class schools and ability to control one's own destiny are the critical variables, they do not compel the conclusion that integration is the *sine qua non* of learning for Negroes.

"In fact, total reliance on integration—which amounts to reliance on acceptance by the white man—is at direct odds with that sense of 'control over one's destiny'."[93] What is needed, claims McKissick, is to

[92] Christopher Jencks, "Education: The Racial Gap," *The New Republic*, October 1, 1966, p. 24.

[93] "Is Integration Necessary?", *The New Republic,* December 3, 1966, p. 35.

give parents some real involvement in the schools their children attend. They need a sense of power, real power. If they have this the children will respond and integration will not be necessary.

Whether necessary or not, integration is not likely, in the foreseeable future, to involve more than a small part of the Negro community. Both the physical and political obstacles appear to be insurmountable. First, the disadvantaged are concentrated in wide geographic areas within many cities. To redistribute these pupils throughout the metropolitan area, which would be necessary to achieve integration in the future, would require a transportation network so extensive and costly that it is both physically and politically impractical.

Obviously, there are neighborhood school districts where the redrawing of attendance areas within cities and perhaps the redrawing of district lines between cities and suburbs would substantially alter the present student balance in the schools. Where this is the case, however, political resistance is likely to be stiff. The recently discovered attachment of many people to the neighborhood school has produced powerful political support for present district lines and attendance areas. To assume that such changes could be accomplished on a metropolitan-wide basis is unrealistic.

There is, in fact, an inverse relationship between the intensity of political opposition to accomplishing some redistribution of pupils and the size of the area and proportion of the population involved. In cities where the proportion of disadvantaged students, particularly the proportion of Negro students, is relatively low (thereby making the redrawing of attendance area lines a meaningful alternative), the political resistance seems capable of preventing any substantial changes. Boston is a good example of this situation. On the other hand, where the political strength of the disadvantaged is great enough to initiate some change, the high proportion of students and large areas involved present a practical limitation on how much can be accomplished in this manner.

An alternative to the decentralization of disadvantaged students is the much-discussed creation of education parks or campuses which would contain many more pupils than the present single-building schools. By drawing on a larger enrollment area, school campuses would be able to concentrate services and would contain a more heterogeneous population, thereby, presumably, providing a higher quality of education for all students.

The concentration of disadvantaged students also would be lessened by the return of middle-income families from the suburbs. It had been anticipated by some students of urban affairs that urban renewal would contribute to such a return. This reversal of the outward flow of people would be beneficial in two ways: the mix of students in the schools would be improved and the tax base for supporting education would be strengthened. However, the contribution of urban renewal to revitalizing the central city has not been great. Much of the current disappointment over urban renewal has resulted from a failure to recognize the importance of low-quality education as one of the primary factors motivating the move out of the city. It seems apparent that physical redevelopment, unless it is accompanied and closely interrelated with a variety of social improvements, particularly improvements in public education, will not attract the suburbanite back to the city.

What has emerged from this controversy about integration and all of the studies which preceded it is that the total environment is what causes educational disadvantage and it is therefore necessary to change that total environment.[94] Fiscal, political, and governmental obstacles all stand in the way of such a change.

The first effort at a general attack was the Anti-Poverty Program, an effort, as will be shown, that is now in serious political difficulties. Recently, the Congress approved yet another approach with its passage of the Demonstration Cities bill. Political support for this program also appears to be weak.

None of these approaches possesses the political support that education does. The issue is whether that support will allow for differential aid to cities. There is already a good deal of political backlash being felt in Washington from the states and their school districts. The demand is that aid to education be made general, that the states and the school districts be allowed to decide for what students it is to be used. If federal aid takes this route it will result simply in more education for everybody, with the suburbs maintaining their distinct advantage over central cities.

CITIES AND THE WAR ON POVERTY

This is an awkward time to survey urban policy in the alleviation of poverty. There is an abundance of writing about the characteristics of poverty in America. There is an abundance of divergent sociological theory. There are reasonably well-developed economic techniques for choices among alternative investments in human resources. But there is a shortage of informed experience in the administrative aspects and

[94] Patricia Sexton, *Education and Income: Inequalities in Our Public Schools,* (Viking Press, 1962); H. Thomas James, J. Alan Thomas, and Harold J. Dyck, *Wealth, Expenditures and Decision-Making for Education* (Stanford University Press, 1963); Fels Institute of Local and State Government, University of Pennsylvania, *Special Education and Fiscal Requirements of Urban School Districts in Pennsylvania, 1964;* Burkhead, Fox and Holland, *op. cit.*

the human outcomes of both old and new programs. Therefore, attention will be directed primarily toward a description and a limited appraisal of the activities embraced under the jurisdiction of the Office of Economic Opportunity.

The Anti-Poverty Program, made up of a variety of specific programs, plus provisions for locally designed community action program packages, represents, according to its champions, "A new comprehensive, co-ordinated and focused approach." The program is represented as a war on poverty, and President Johnson claims it represents "a total commitment by the President, and this Congress and this Nation to pursue victory over the most ancient of mankind's enemies." [95] The President insists that the victory must be *total*.

Although the Anti-Poverty Program is not designed exclusively for the poor in cities, it does have central significance for urban areas. The redistribution of population within metropolitan areas has brought a "disproportionate" number of those who are in poverty categories to live in central cities. Of the 47 million families in the United States, 9.3 million have incomes under $3,000 (the usual figure used for drawing the poverty line), and of these, 5 million live in cities. Although poverty is relatively more important in proportion to population in rural areas than in the cities, this fact does not reduce the significance of the Anti-Poverty Program to cities.

Of the total amount thus far appropriated by Congress and expended by the Office of Economic Opportunity, 29.1 per cent of it has been spent in rural areas, the rest in urban areas. Even the programs designed to alleviate rural poverty make a direct contribution to cities. Many of the rural poor, if they are to make a decent living, will have to move to cities. If the Anti-Poverty Program prepares them for urban living and employment, the cities will be the beneficiaries.

The recent concern with poverty in the United States has produced a vast array of statistics describing who and where the poor are. Of the 9.3 million poverty families in the United States, 4.3 million live in the South, 6 million have less than nine years of schooling, 2 million are Negro, 2.3 million have a woman as head of the household, 3.2 million are elderly. In addition, 60 per cent of the families in this category have never earned over $3,000 per year, while 40 per cent have never earned over $2,000.

It is for these people that the War on Poverty is being waged and that war is supposedly concerned with fighting causes rather than symptoms. In contrast, the New Deal social programs were designed to help people get through brief periods of economic distress and, in addi-

[95] President's Message on Poverty to the Congress, March 16, 1964.

tion, to guarantee the elderly some measure of economic security—but only for the elderly who were employed during their working years. The New Deal programs were not concerned with long-term poverty nor with the social and economic conditions that give rise to what has become known as the cycle and culture of poverty.

In contrast, the War on Poverty is designed to break the cycle and to undermine the culture. Underlying the War on Poverty is the hope that it will create an environment of opportunity. President Johnson, in his message on poverty, called for the realization of "an America in which every citizen shares all the opportunities of his society, in which every man has a chance to advance his welfare to the limits of his capacities." This emphasis on opportunity gave the bill its title: The Economic Opportunity Act of 1964.

What kind of opportunities was the bill designed to provide? The Advisory Commission on Intergovernmental Relations lists five:

One, the opportunity *for youths* to acquire skills and to complete their education. . . .; two, the opportunity *for communities* to develop and carry out community action programs—to strike poverty at its source in the cities and in the country-side; three, the opportunity for *"dedicated Americans"* 18 years of age and older to serve as volunteers in a domestic "Peace Corps"—VISTA (Volunteers in Service to America)—to help States and communities to fight the war against poverty; four, the opportunity for *certain hard-hit groups* to break out of the pattern of poverty. . . .; five, the opportunity for *a concerted national attack* on poverty by establishing the Office of Economic Opportunity, in the Executive Office of the President.[96]

The War on Poverty is not an income maintenance program. It is not designed to provide people with either the income or services necessary for a minimum standard of well-being. Financed in its first full year at a cost of approximately one billion dollars, it is clear that the amount of direct help it supplied would be insignificant. One student of the problem estimates that:

The 34.6 million persons identified as poor needed an aggregate money income of $28.8 billion in 1963 to cover their basic requirements. Their current income actually totaled about $17.3 billion, or only 60 per cent of their estimated needs. Some of the deficit could have been—and no doubt was—offset by use of savings. By and large, however, it has been well documented that the low income persons who could benefit most from such additions to their meager resources are least likely to have the advantage of them. And it is not usually the poor who have the rich relatives.[97]

[96] ACIR, *Intergovernmental Relations in the Poverty Program* (U.S. Government Printing Office, April 1966), pp. 1–2.
[97] Molly Orshansky, "Consumption, Work and Poverty," in Ben B. Seligman (ed.), *Poverty as a Public Issue* (The Free Press, 1965), p. 69.

The economic philosophy underlying the Anti-Poverty Program, as commonly stated, is that many of the poor lack the skills and education to find employment in an automated society. The OEO programs are then designed to attack this "structural" problem. At the same time, there must be concern with levels of aggregate demand. The tax reduction of 1964 was intended to provide the attack on this aspect of employment opportunities. The loan programs are intended to meet the needs of relatively small groups of the deserving poor.

Whether income redistribution would be a better strategy for a war on poverty, it is not the strategy which has been adopted. Instead, the Congressional Committee majority, in its report endorsing the program, said, "The philosophy behind the Economic Opportunity Act of 1964 is not that existing wealth should be redistributed but that the poor people can and must be provided with opportunities to earn a decent living and maintain their families on a comfortable living standard." [98]

The War Plans

How, then, is this opportunity environment to be created? The Act provides a number of specific national programs intended to assure such an environment and, in addition, provides a means, through Community Action, for communities to develop such an environment at the local level.

The specific programs include:

1) *The Job Corps:* This program provides vocational training opportunities for men and women ages 16 to 21 in institutional facilities. In addition to improving the skills, education, health, and outlook of these youth, the program provides conservation and other community service activities to the states and communities in which facilities are located. (Title I-A.)

2) *The Work Training Program* (known as the Neighborhood Youth Corps): Payment is provided by the federal government for up to 90 per cent of the cost incurred by local project sponsors under contract to help youth in the 16 to 21 age group to (1) remain in school; (2) return to school if they have already left the classroom; and (3) obtain work experience and develop work habits if they are out of school and out of work. These objectives are met by providing employment opportunities which combine education, as well as training and work experience. (Title I-B.)

3) *The Community Action Program:* The purpose of this part of the Act is to provide stimulation and incentive for urban and rural communities to mobilize their resources to combat poverty. (Title II-A.)

4) *The Adult Basic Education Program:* This activity provides 90 per cent federal grants to state educational agencies to carry out remedial edu-

[98] Committee on Education and Labor, *Report on the Economic Opportunity Act of 1964,* June 30, 1964, p. 2.

cational programs for persons 18 years of age and over. These programs are operated locally by school districts and other educational agencies. (Title II-B.)

5) *The Rural Areas Loan Program:* Designed for attacking the problems of rural poverty by raising and maintaining the income and living standards of low-income farm and non-farm families, loans under this program are made to farm and non-farm families living in the country or in small towns to help them finance small businesses, trades or services such as well-drilling, carpentry, trucking and other income-producing activities. Loans are made to farmers to buy livestock and farm equipment, to buy an interest in co-operatively used equipment, to develop water supplies, farm land and buildings, to buy operating materials to pay farm operating expenses. (Title III-A.)

6) *Migrant Agricultural Employees Program:* Funds are for loans, loan guarantees, and grants to help states, local governments and private non-profit groups to expand current efforts and to set up new programs for special needs of migrant workers and their families. The program provides education for adults as well as children, with day-care centers and adequate housing and sanitary facilities along the road and in the camps. (Title III-B.)

7) *The Economic Opportunity Loan Program:* Designed to assist in establishing, preserving, and strengthening small business concerns and improving managerial skills employed in such enterprises and to mobilize for these objectives, private as well as public, managerial skills and resources, the OEO director may make, participate in, or guarantee loans repayable in not more than fifteen years to any small business concern or to any qualified person seeking to establish such a concern. (Title IV.)

8) *The Work Experience Program:* This program provides up to 100 per cent of federal funds to public welfare agencies or local sponsors for state and local projects designed to improve the employability and increase the capability for personal independence of needy persons, particularly unemployed men and women who are family heads. (Title V.)

9) *Volunteers in Service to America (VISTA):* Called the domestic peace corps, this activity is volunteer-served in very much the same way as Peace Corps volunteers, but in the United States rather than abroad. Its purpose is to recruit, select, train and (1) upon request of state or local agencies or private non-profit organizations, refer volunteers to perform duties in furtherance of programs combating poverty at state or local level; and (2) in co-operation with other federal, state, or local agencies involved, assign volunteers to work (a) in meeting the health, education, welfare, or related needs of Indians living on reservations, of migratory workers and their families, of residents of the District of Columbia, the Commonwealth of Puerto Rico, Guam, American Samoa, the Virgin Islands, or the trust territory of the Pacific Islands; (b) in the care and rehabilitation of the mentally ill or mentally retarded under treatment in non-profit mental health, or mental retardation facilities assisted in their construction or operation by federal funds; and (c) in connection with programs or activities authorized, supported, or of a character eligible for assistance under the Economic Opportunity Act. (Title VI.)[99]

[99] These descriptions of the various titles of the Economic Opportunity Act are adopted from *ibid.,* pp. 204–61.

The only one of these programs which was in some sense new was Community Action. The other proposals had already been suggested or, in fact, enacted by one House of the national legislature.

The Job Corps and Work Training proposals had already been passed by the Senate in the Youth Opportunities Bill. A work study program for college students was considered but dropped in 1963 as part of the National Defense Education Act, and the Peace Corps provided a model for the VISTA program. Actually, a somewhat similar activity was underway in a number of cities under the sponsorship of former President Kennedy's juvenile delinquency program which was directed by the then Attorney General, Robert Kennedy.

There was the precedent, too, of the Ford Foundation-sponsored Gray Areas Program. The Foundation, beginning in 1960, had concerned itself with experiments for the education of the disadvantaged. Out of these experiments the Foundation decided to support a number of rather large-scale co-ordinated attacks on all aspects of deprivation including jobs, education, housing, planning, and recreation in a number of selected cities.

According to the Foundation, the purpose of these grants to the cities of Boston, New Haven, Oakland, Philadelphia, the state of North Carolina, and to Washington, D.C. was "to help local government and private organizations confront the human problems of slums and gray areas—changing neighborhoods characterized by family breakdown, low income residents, and newly arrived groups from rural areas." [100]

Is the War Being Won or Lost?

Is the War on Poverty a success? The question is in many ways a meaningless one. The program had been in full-scale operation for some two years at the time this paper was prepared, and a great deal of that time had been spent in simply getting the organization operating and in experimenting with a variety of approaches, particularly in the Community Action sector of the war.

In some instances direct services are being provided to individuals and it is possible to examine some numbers. In October of 1963 there were 730,000 young men and women between the ages of sixteen and twenty-one who were out of work and out of school. It is for this group that the Job and Neighborhood Youth Corps are designed. What are the characteristics of the trainees? Sargent Shriver describes them in these words:

The average Job Corps enrollee today is reading at about fourth grade—

[100] *American Community Development* (The Ford Foundation, 1964), p. 1.

628

4.5, 4.7; although he has been in school for seven years he is still down in the fourth grade. Eighty per cent of them have never seen a doctor or a dentist. Forty-seven per cent of those eligible to take them have flunked entrance tests to get into the Army, Navy or Air Force. On the average they are about ten pounds underweight. Forty-five per cent of them come from broken homes, sixty-five per cent from a family where the head of the household, male or female, is unemployed. Fifty per cent come from homes where they are on relief. Ninety per cent of them are unemployed, when they come to us, and of the ten per cent who do come to us having been employed, they have been working on an average for $.80 an hour.[101]

Of 63,000 Job Corpsmen who had been or were in the program as of October, 1966, 10,000 had graduated and 29,000 were still in the program. The difference is composed of dropouts and dischargees. Although there has been some difficulty in following the Youth Corpsmen once they leave camp, a recent study indicates that 50 per cent of the 10,000 who have graduated are now placed. Of these, some 70 per cent are in the Armed Forces, with the others back in school. It is estimated that as of January 1, 1967 there are 25,000 graduates who have places in either jobs, the Armed Services, or school. For those who have jobs, an intensive study of 465 graduates indicates that their average earnings are $1.71 per hour, in contrast to the $.80 an hour earned by those who had jobs before they entered the Job Corps.

These numbers are small, but the program is new. It appears that, on the whole, the success of the Job Corps camps has been substantial, although the cost is high. In fact, some congressmen expressed astonishment when learning that it costs more for a year's training in a Job Corps camp than it does for a year's education at Harvard. The present average cost is $7,800 for a full year. Most enrollees stay for only nine months and the cost is therefore $5,850 per enrollee.

The Neighborhood Youth Corps is able to accommodate many more young people than the Job Corps. Since the participant in the Neighborhood Youth Corps stays in his own community and lives at home, there is no need to provide the physical facilities necessary for the Job Corpsmen. Some 500,000 young people have been, or are, enrolled in the Neighborhood Youth Corps Program. For those who are in school the cost is $650 per year; while the cost for those out of school, which includes training, is $1,700 per year. There apparently are no figures as to the ability of the program to train participants for permanent employment, but scattered evidence indicates that the program has had considerable success. The generally favorable view of it held by congressmen is evidence that it does not have the political difficulties ex-

[101] U.S. Senate, Committee on Appropriations, *Hearings* on H.R. 18381, 89th Cong., 2nd Sess. (October 17, 1966), p. 419. (Hereinafter cited as *Hearings.*)

perienced by both the Job Corps and the Community Action programs.

Although very little information is available on the success of Community Action activities, something is known of the kind of activities in which these agencies are engaged. These include (1) remedial and non-curricular education; (2) employment, job-training, and counseling; (3) health and vocational rehabilitation; (4) housing and home management; (5) welfare; (6) consumer information, education, and mutual aid; (7) legal aid and the provision of information on the rights of the poor; and (8) the establishment of neighborhood centers.

Although the Community Action portion of the Anti-Poverty Program was designed to allow local communities to develop their own programs, the tendency has been for the federal government to mandate certain activities within this program and make funds available to only those local agencies who will sponsor such activities. Headstart, for example, is a part of the Community Action Program but is designed by Washington although administered at the local level. Actually over half the money appropriated for Community Action for the fiscal year 1967 is earmarked for designated programs, and of these Headstart has the lion's share. Headstart is popular with Congress and does not raise the political issues other programs do. There were 560,000 young people participating in summer Headstart programs in 1965 and it is anticipated that equally large numbers will continue to participate.

Over-all, the Anti-Poverty Program has begun some interesting and useful training programs. It has, in some instances, provided legal help to the poor; in some cases it has aided the poor in obtaining the established community services to which they are entitled. On the whole it has not drastically improved the lot of the poor. Perhaps in time it will, but the political environment does not seem, at the moment, propitious for providing the necessary resources.

Many now argue that the approach of the War on Poverty is wrong. Both conservative and liberal economists are today demanding that either a negative income tax or a guaranteed annual income be provided for all. Once an income floor is established it will be possible for the poor, to the degree they wish, to move themselves out of poverty. Another version of income maintenance advocated by some is family allowances. Long used in Canada and Europe, there are those who maintain that this is the proper approach for dealing with the problem of poverty.

The Politics of the War on Poverty

Many suggested, at the time the poverty program became law, that it was in for political trouble. Those predictions were right. The program had great difficulty with Congress during the 1966 session and ended with considerably less money than recommended by the President. The final appropriation was some $137 million less than the President's proposal of $1,750 million. Further, the cuts were often made in those programs which were the most original contribution of the anti-poverty concept. Freedom of choice for Community Action agencies was reduced, political participation of the poor discouraged, and the Job Corps severely criticized.

Even if the total $1,750 million had been appropriated by Congress, many cities would have had to take cuts in their on-going programs. OEO Director Shriver gave these examples:

New York, to carry on for this fiscal year what it is already doing, nothing new, no increase in any program, needs $48 million. Under this Bill, with $1,750 million we would have $40 million for New York. Turn to Boston: To do what Boston is already doing, Senator Saltonstall, we would need $6.7 million. We will have $5.1 million for Boston. . . . To do what Providence is doing now would require $1.9 million. Providence, under the best circumstances, as we foresee them now, will get $1.6 million. Washington, D.C., to do what it is doing now would require $11.8 million from us. In this fiscal year, it will get $9.1 million.[102]

Why these difficulties? First, of course, there is the pressure of the Vietnam war on the nation's fiscal resources. But if there must be domestic cuts, why the Anti-Poverty Program?

One of the most important reasons is that the Anti-Poverty Program did not, even at the beginning, have a strong political base. The program had neither major interest group support nor did the political parties see it as a source of popular support. The business community was either indifferent or hostile and the poor themselves, almost by definition, were unorganized. As Patrick Moynihan explains, "The origins of this effort simply cannot be explained in deterministic terms. It was more a rational than a political event. Men at the center of government perceived the fact, to use the term by which *The Economist* described the origin of President Johnson's message on conservation, that ugliness, like poverty, is all around them and that the powers of government might eliminate it."

In the words of Miller and Rein:

The War on Poverty was not propelled by the organization of the poor in rural areas and in large cities demanding their "economic rights." Nor do the prospective political demands of the poor seem to be great enough to "require" that a "war on poverty" be launched in 1964. If there had not

[102] *Hearings*, p. 430.

been such a movement in 1964, it is doubtful whether there would have
been mass pressures for such an activity in that year or in the succeeding
one. . . . The War on Poverty is in advance of the political pressures of
the day. This is the achievement of the war; this is its weakness.[103]

Without a strong political base it was inevitable that the program
would run into political trouble. There was an undertone of resentment
from groups which had, themselves, at one time lived in poverty and
who had managed, and in their judgment on their own, to rise from it.
Individual congressmen, testifying or commenting on the bill, delighted
in citing stories of how their parents had managed to bring their families
out of poverty or how they, by their own successes, had proved the
validity of the Horatio Alger interpretation of the American reality.[104]

No new public policy passed since the end of the war touches a
rawer nerve in the American body politic than does this one. It intrudes
at a point where American society is most ambivalent. On one side
there is a strong strain in the American national ethos of charity and
equality—especially equality of opportunity—and on the other of individualism, an individualism which demands that every man is responsible for raising himself by his own bootstraps.

These competing values have always produced serious political consequences for public welfare. Welfare has never enjoyed as much political popularity as most other functions of government, be they the
functions of education, highways, or even of police and fire protection.

The provision in the Community Action part of the program which
requires the participation of the poor in the formulation and administration of the program simply added fuel to this potential blaze of opposition. Normally organized outside the regular channels of government, Community Action agencies are required by the Act to include
the poor on their governing boards. This inclusion of non-members of
the normal governing groups in a community led to resentment and it
became a politically significant resentment when demands were made
on City Hall and established governmental agencies for more and
better services. Big city mayors quickly saw the program's potential for
the development of an organized political opposition. They saw the
possibility of the new Community Action agencies, with their neighborhood boards, growing into a rival political organization, possessing
even a ready-made system of ward organizations.

[103] S. M. Miller and Martin Rein, "The War on Poverty, Perspectives and
Prospects," in Ben B. Seligman (ed.), op. cit., pp. 276–77.

[104] Representative Griffin expressed the experience of many when he said, "My
father worked most of his life in a plant; and I worked my way through school
and I believe I do know a little bit about poverty." Quoted in Elinor Graham, "The
Politics of Poverty," Ben B. Seligman (ed.), op. cit., p. 237.

Protestations against this independence were made by many mayors to the President. The Office of Economic Opportunity found it necessary to modify their demands for participation by the poor. All in all, it brought into the open much of the smoldering resentment of large parts of the community against special assistance for the poor. The opposition was greatest in the larger cities and tended to concentrate on programs established to aid Negroes. When racial protests and riots were on the front pages of newspapers, the public was not impressed with the official explanations of causation. Rather, the unrest was interpreted as simply a lack of appreciation of what we (the middle and lower-middle income whites) were doing for them (the non-white poor).

Whatever the political consequences of the participation requirement, it was put into the Anti-Poverty Program for specific reasons.

[It] . . . . is based on extensive studies by psychologists, sociologists and community organization workers. Its purpose is to give the poor an effective voice in determining community policies that affect them as impoverished persons and citizens. It also aims to involve them in carrying out the specific anti-poverty programs. By encouraging the poor to become involved in decision-making and administrative processes, the participation requirement seeks to help overcome the psychology of dependency which pervades the "other America" and is manifested in the hopelessness, apathy and hostility of the poor.[105]

Experience undoubtedly is too brief to determine whether the participation by the poor has had the beneficial results intended. It is clear that in many communities it has roused the ire of officialdom and the establishment, particularly the community service establishment. OEO has considerably softened its administrative enforcement of the participation requirement and Congress has further reduced its significance by cutting back on the amount of federal money available to finance community-originated proposals.

The Job Corps, too, has met considerable political resistance. This resistance comes primarily from the communities in which Job Corps camps are located. Incidents of unfriendly contact between Job Corpsmen and local citizens have received national publicity and close attention by Congress. Some camps have been closed and Congress has reduced the amount of money the President requested for the Job Corps, and even that request was tailored to fit the known political environment. It is clear that this program will not be a growing one. In fact, there is a strong possibility that it will be phased out.[106]

[105] ACIR, *op. cit.,* p. 52.
[106] Senator Spessard L. Holland (D-Florida) expressed the sentiment of much

More popular is Headstart and, to a somewhat lesser degree, the Neighborhood Youth Corps. These programs do not involve any local political activity. They are framed primarily by Washington bureaucrats and only administered at the local level. As long as their costs remain relatively modest they will probably not have much political difficulty.

Government Structure and the Anti-Poverty Program

Although the Anti-Poverty Program was designed to co-ordinate federal efforts in fighting poverty, it actually fragmented responsibility at the federal level and added impetus to further governmental fragmentation at the state-local level. To the extent that governmental fragmentation is a deterrent to effective policy formulation and execution, the War on Poverty has added to the difficulties.

At the federal level the Office of Economic Opportunity was, in the words of Sargent Shriver, to focus the general attack of the government on poverty. Shriver said, "This is an authority which the President wants because he wants to be at the focal point with respect to this aspect of our domestic effort." Such focusing caused programs to be assigned to OEO which normally would have gone to the regular departments of the Executive branch. Although OEO was required by law to co-operate with other agencies, the fact is a new administrative agency was created, thereby dispersing responsibility.

Not all programs, however, were assigned to OEO, which was given direct responsibility for only the Job Corps, Community Action, and VISTA. Neighborhood Youth Corps was assigned primarily to the Department of Labor, the Adult Basic Education Program to the Office of Education, Economic Opportunity Loans to the Small Business Administration, the Work Administration Program to the Department of Health, Education and Welfare, and the Rural Loan Program to the Department of Agriculture. In all instances OEO played a secondary role; primary administrative responsibility was placed elsewhere. A federal council was created at the departmental level to co-ordinate all these programs, but this was not much different from other notoriously ineffective interdepartmental committees.

It seems likely that Congress, uneasy about the political criticisms from home concerning the poverty program, will gradually dismember OEO. Many of the education programs will be transferred to the Office

---

of Congress when he said, "I can easily see why the conferees in the House appropriation bill both thought not very highly of the Job Corps because that has been the opinion in my State, it is a general opinion, and the feeling has been that it cost much too much and it has had much too small a result, and there are too many of the so-called graduates of the enrollee group who have not shown the results which were anticipated." *Hearings, op. cit.,* p. 440.

of Education. Certain kinds of training will be moved to the Department of Labor, and it is just possible that those aspects of Community Action which manage political survival will be assigned to the Department of Housing and Urban Development. All in all, the effort at pulling together the various strands of the federal government's social program into a co-ordinating central agency directly responsible to the President has not worked. The failure is both administrative and political.

The loss is reasonably serious, not only in terms of administrative co-ordination, but also in terms of program evaluation. The central staff of OEO has made quite good progress in analyzing and evaluating alternative programs for human resource development. The continued dispersal of the anti-poverty programs among other agencies will reduce the operational usefulness of such systematic evaluation.[107] The possibilities for extending this kind of analysis, usually undertaken in benefit-cost terms, will be greatly increased as more experience with anti-poverty programs becomes available.

The general ill repute of state government in the Executive branch was made clear by the OEO administrative arrangements. ". . . the role of the States in the draft bill was minimal." [108] Some members of Congress protested this treatment but the Administration witnesses for the program were firm in their opposition to any significant role for the states. Shriver, when asked about the role of the states, argued against those senators (Javits and Tower, to name but two) who championed the states. A Republican substitute for the anti-poverty bill sponsored by Representative Peter Frelinghuysen would have simply provided money to the states (in Heller-Pechman fashion) which would design their own programs.

Forty-nine of the fifty states have established anti-poverty state offices and do provide technical assistance to local agencies. Governors do have the power of veto over local programs although, under a 1965 amendment, the Director of OEO may override such a veto. This power had not been used as of mid-1966. In two program areas there is a requirement for state plans: Adult Basic Education and Work Experience.

[107] Economists other than those associated with OEO have also made important contributions to the analysis of human resource programs. See, for example, David A. Page, "Retraining under the Manpower Development Act: A Cost-Benefit Analysis," in John D. Montgomery and Arthur Smithies (eds.), *Public Policy*, Vol. 13 (Harvard University Press, 1964); Gerald G. Somers and Ernst W. Stromsdorfer, "A Benefit-Cost Analysis of Manpower Retraining," paper for Industrial Relations Research Association, 1964.

[108] ACIR, *op. cit.*, p. 78.

Although the states have gradually assumed a co-ordinating role, their financial contribution has been small. Many local agents contend that the state agencies are mostly a nuisance. It is clear that without federal impetus there would have been few, if any, state anti-poverty programs.

At the local level, the inevitable tendency of the champions of a new or even partially new function of government is to insist that their programs be administered apart from the established governmental institutions. The perpetrators of the War on Poverty were not exceptions. Although the turn-of-the-century argument against administration by traditional government agencies revolved around the supposed untrustworthiness of politicians, the justification in the early sixties was new. No longer was it "dirty politicians" who could not be trusted, but rather it was "the Establishment"—the network of existing leadership and agencies that had long been responsible for administering important programs for the impoverished. It was felt that local government was the "establishment" in many communities or shared the role with private groups. The issue was of particular concern with respect to assuring proper sensitivity to racial minorities who constitute a large portion of the poor.[109]

Another reason given for a separate agency was that in many jurisdictions there was no single comprehensive governmental unit which covered the appropriate area for a local Anti-Poverty Program. School districts, towns, and cities were all considered in most instances inappropriate relative to their jurisdictional area. Although the county in many instances covered a sufficiently large area, there were objections to its use "because of its shortcomings as an effective organization and focus of effective political leadership in many places in the county." [110]

As of the 30th of September, 1965, there were 513 Community Action agencies in operation, and 73.9 per cent were private non-profit agencies while the remainder were tied to regular governments. Of those tied to normal governments, 7 per cent were city agencies, 7.6 county agencies, and the remainder scattered between Indian tribal councils and public institutions of higher education.

It is obvious that the organizational structure selected by those responsible for making the war plans on poverty did not make any contribution to lessening the fragmentation of government. Since public housing is run by independent authorities, since school districts are usually independent of their general government jurisdiction, and since

[109] ACIR, *op. cit.*, p. 25.
[110] *Ibid.*, p. 26.

urban renewal agencies tend to have considerable autonomy, it was unlikely that close co-ordination of federal programs, which has not been accomplished at the federal level, would be accomplished at the local level.

Without co-ordination at the federal level and with the states neither possessing nor really desiring this power, and with local anti-poverty agencies fighting for their political lives, the hoped-for, focused, co-ordinated attack on poverty has simply not come off.

It was, perhaps, this disappointing experience which finally encouraged Congress to enact the Demonstration Cities Bill. Whether this program will add to or subtract from fragmentation remains to be seen. One of the strongest arguments for it was that it would reduce the fragmentation of the federal impact at the local level.

Beset by political difficulties, its administration fragmented, its Presidential support weakened, and many of its congressional champions defeated in the 1966 congressional election, the anti-poverty agency and its director, Sargent Shriver, were, at the end of 1966, in considerable political trouble.

Whatever the governmental and political difficulties, experience with the program makes clear that victory, total or otherwise, over poverty will not be easy. It is clear that the modest efforts thus far to provide an "environment of opportunity" are not sufficient. New approaches, probably some version of a guaranteed income, are necessary substantive additions to present efforts. Such a revision of tactics in the War on Poverty will not emerge from consensus politics.

NEW DIRECTIONS—INCREMENTALLY

In the polemics surrounding American urbanism and metropolitanism there is a persistent demand for a unified *federal urban policy*. It is argued that no such policy exists today, and that the present attacks on urban problems are piecemeal, fragmented, inconsistent, and unco-ordinated. An overriding urban policy would make possible, it is believed, the meshing of specific programs into a meaningful framework.

Such a condition will never exist. The American decision process simply does not work that way. Policy changes are incremental, not sweeping. New directions are tried, but with caution. Perhaps it is true, as Lindblom argues, that this concentration on small incremental changes is reasonable ". . . given the limits on knowledge within which policy-makers are confined." [111]

Whether reasonable or not, American urban policy is made in this

[111] Charles E. Lindblom, "The Science of 'Muddling Through,' " *Public Administration Review*, Vol. 19, No. 2 (Spring 1959), p. 87.

way. The bits and pieces of that policy are in those programs described here, together with a great many others. The others include scattered site public houses (more talked about than practiced), rent subsidies (little money), air and water pollution control (beginning to move), and the more grandiose, just-enacted metropolitan planning requirements and Demonstration Cities program. A more complete list would include, as well, the long-established programs for mortgage guarantees and for public housing.

Obviously over-all national economic and employment policies have significance, too, for urban policy. The federal commitment to high levels of employment makes a contribution to the well-being of metropolitan areas. But the need for specific urban social policies is one measure of the degree of failure of national macropolicy. Fiscal and monetary policies that are successful in the aggregate do not guarantee sufficient employment or sufficient income to maintain all people in society at a minimal economic level. Further, the private market, particularly in land, has not produced a distribution of human activities within metropolitan areas which is satisfying to very many. That market, often influenced by government policy, has unleashed forces contributing to the deterioration of the central city and the dispersal of population across the adjoining countryside. Transportation, pollution, social segregation, and fiscal problems are among the results.

It is not surprising that these consequences have created a demand for a national urban policy. The difficulty with the demand is that it assumes agreement about what the problems are, their causes, and the kind of urban society desired. There is, in fact, no general agreement on any of these prerequisites to an urban policy and it is, in part, this lack of agreement which has produced the variety of ad hoc approaches to urbanism and metropolitanism that today, together, constitute urban policy.

Although a single national policy produced by rational analysis and proclaimed as binding is not possible, it is useful to examine what the content of such a policy might be and the process by which it could be formulated. The first step in such an analysis must be identification of the forces responsible for the problems.

There are two broad classes of forces and although the classes overlap they are sufficiently distinct for separate analysis. One class might be described as the physical or hardware problems. These relate to the present distribution of activities within metropolitan areas—where people work, live, and recreate, and the movement from one activity to another.

The second class relates to the social or "soft" problems produced by the low living standards imposed on a significant portion of the population living in metropolitan areas. Tying these two classes of problems together is housing. This has both physical dimensions, the maintenance of minimum structural standards, and social dimensions, the behavior patterns of neighborhood groups.

Since these two classes of problems have different impacts in cities and suburbs it is sometimes useful to distinguish between the two. On the whole, however, there is too much overlap in this classification. The "soft-hard" dichotomy serves better.

The Distribution of Activities

The redistribution of activities throughout large urban areas has produced what has become called the Spread City.[112] Market forces in land use are spreading urban activities over a wider and wider area. The new spread pattern, although traditional wisdom deplores it, has its champions. One student, for example, finds "in the dissolution of the urban settlement a liberation of human energies and a proliferation of opportunities for human interaction." [113] Those opposed to the present pattern claim its costs are too high relative to the needed public investment in social overhead and, further, that it tends to eliminate the cultural and social advantages of a more compact city. It is argued that it is technologically possible, today, to build highly compact, densely populated cities. Only in cities, it is contended, is it possible to have fine symphony orchestras, great libraries, dynamic museums, quality educational institutions and first-rate theatres. Without a healthy, compact center these activities will die or disperse, and dispersion will inevitably lower quality and availability. Further, the social heterogeneity represented by the city is seen as preferable to the presumed dull, unimaginative conformity of the communities in a spread city pattern.

Both market forces and governmental fragmentation promote the spread city. But even if these are allowed to operate unhindered, it does not follow that there is no need for physical development policy. The champions of a decentralized urbanism do not defend the present unorganized pattern which has been produced by the new spread pattern. Some kind of multicentered urban area is more often advocated with resulting communities resembling the long-championed New Towns.

[112] Regional Plan Association of New York, *Spread City,* Bulletin 100, 1962.
[113] Melvin M. Webber, "Order in Diversity: Community Without Propinquity," in Lowdon Wingo, Jr. (ed.), *Cities and Space, The Future Use of Urban Land,* (The Johns Hopkins Press, for Resources for the Future, 1963), p. 18.

What the New Town is supposed to provide is what the standard suburb leaves out: good transportation, good timing of community facilities, good public utilities, good open space, and good over-all design. Above all it is concerned with the better use of land.[114]

If there is to be a preferred physical pattern, New Towns or otherwise, it can be accomplished only if present functional policies in such areas as transportation, utilities, urban renewal, and land use controls are designed to accomplish that pattern. The difficulty, of course, is that the present arrangement of governmental institutions does not permit a hard decision to be made about whether it is compact cities or spread cities, or something in between, that government policy should promote. It may be that the issue is not what urban policy ought to be, but rather the provision of a mechanism for making that decision.

Requirements for comprehensive planning, which are integral parts of more and more federal programs (highways, airports, open spaces, urban renewal, mass transit) represent a recognition of this need. In the Housing Act of 1966, this comprehensive planning requirement has been generalized. After June 30, 1967 any local government jurisdiction seeking federal aid for physical improvement will have to advance its aid request through a metropolitan planning agency. In the words of the Act,

All applications made after June 30, 1967 for federal loans or grants to assist in carrying out open space land projects, or for the planning or construction of hospitals, airports, libraries, water supply distribution facilities, sewerage facilities and waste treatment works, highways, transportation facilities, and water development and land conservation projects within any metropolitan area shall be submitted for review to any area-wide agency which is designated to perform metropolitan or regional planning for the area within which the assistance is to be used. (Title II, Sec. 204.)

The passage of this provision culminates a long-time effort by Senator Muskie to encourage metropolitan-wide regional planning with real power. The Act does not require the regional unit to approve the plan of the local jurisdiction, but if it comments unfavorably it goes back to the local jurisdiction who may either change it to meet the criticisms or it may be passed on with the unfavorable comments to the appropriate granting agency in Washington. That agency, according to the Act, shall

[114] Ada Louise Huxtable, "First Light of New Town Era Is on Horizon," *New York Times*, February 17, 1964, p. 28. There is a vast literature on New Towns. A good over-all view is contained in Frederic J. Osborn and Arnold Whittick, *The New Towns: The Answer to Megalopolis* (London: Hill and Leonard, 1963).

review the comments and recommendations "for the sole purpose of assisting it in determining whether the application is in accordance with the provisions of federal law which govern the making of the loans or grants." In other words, if there is no requirement for comprehensive planning in the specific federal grant programs under which the local government is applying, the Washington agency has no legal power to consider the recommendations of the metropolitan planning agency. Even with this limitation, however, a seemingly significant power grant is made by the Act. Many specific federal programs do have comprehensive planning requirements. Further, the Act will establish on a permanent basis many metropolitan planning agencies. These agencies will compete for power with other units and will, on occasion, win.

The development policies that may be adopted by these regional planning agencies are, of course, not known. They must have representation on their governing boards from the elected officials within the area. These officials are not likely to approve any drastic revision in present patterns. Nevertheless, these new requirements do represent one of the first efforts by the federal government to influence governmental structure at the local level.

Instead of a hard decision for spread or compact cities, direct attacks within specific functional areas will continue to be made. Highways will be built, and perhaps a few mass transit systems. Pollution will be partially controlled and some downtown rebuilding will continue. In the suburbs there is a possibility that new communities will come to take on more recognizable shape than has been true of the leapfrogging spread of the past. It is possible that private industry will find the creation of New Towns a profitable enterprise. Already Reston, in Virginia, and Columbia, in Maryland, are pointing the direction. The federal government policy, which has already attempted to make easier the creation of New Towns through providing grants to local jurisdictions for borrowing ahead for public utilities, is helping. That help will probably increase.

New Towns in-town, essentially to help cope with the social problems of the central city, have also been suggested.[115] In this case, the proposal is for the creation of well-serviced, reconstructed "new" communities within cities. Not only would such towns provide new and improved housing but, in addition, new and improved community facilities —schools, playgrounds, neighborhood centers, shopping areas, and the like.

[115] Harvey S. Perloff, "New Towns Intown," *Journal of the American Institute of Planners,* Vol. 32, No. 3 (May 1966), reprinted as Reprint No. 57, Resources for the Future.

The New Towns in-town concept might well become attached to the currently discussed public-private corporation for the rebuilding of certain sections of cities. The administrative model most often cited is Comsat. The hope is to combine, as in the case of Comsat, private and public capital for the rebuilding of depressed sections of cities. The advantage such an approach would have over present urban renewal is greater administrative flexibility and, perhaps, more use of the supposed innovative spirit of the private sector. Although it is not clear why this could not be done through a full-fledged public corporation, such as TVA, the American bias in favor of the private sector may be controlling. The only thing really new about the proposal is the administrative device it would create. The need for massive public subsidy would remain.

None of this discussion of new approaches to physical development is meant to imply that a new national urban policy is about to be established. Rather, there will continue to be a variety of approaches, incremental in their impact. It is possible, however, that the increments will evolve into a new package of programs which will move policy in a new direction. As is evident from programs already tried, whatever is done will be costly. There is no way to remake or even to maintain urban America at its present standards without substantial public resources. Most of these resources will have to be provided by the national government.

Socially Sick Cities

Living throughout America but concentrated in its great central cities are families and individuals whose income is inadequate to maintain a minimum standard of well-being. The urban poor are characterized by poor education, bad health, inadequate housing and an apathy encouraged by the environment. The poor have been trapped. The Anti-Poverty Program and federal aid to education are two approaches for dealing with the problems created by these conditions; other approaches are obviously necessary.

Government policies to increase aggregate demand reduce the numbers of persons in poverty. But the success of programs specifically designed to provide training for the kinds of skills needed in an urban society is less clear. Many of those who are unemployed, and particularly Negro teenagers, may be victims of a vague and ill-defined alienation that is a product of slum living, discrimination, low motivation, and the apparent anti-Calvinist attitudes of the culture of poverty itself. If this is the case—and it is impossible to document—the improvement of skill levels, which is the aim of all the training programs, will bring

642

very modest results and indeed may only increase the level of frustration.

The Demonstration Cities Program, proposed by the Administration and enacted by Congress in 1966, is an effort to bring together the various social approaches of the federal government into a concentrated attack on the central city conditions which, it is believed, produces this environment. The purpose of the Demonstration Cities approach is, in the words of Congress,

to improve their [cities'] physical environment, increase their supply of adequate housing for low and moderate income people and provide educational and social services vital to health and welfare.

In more specific terms, Congress says that

the purposes of this title are to provide additional financial and technical assistance to enable cities of all sizes . . . to plan, develop and carry out locally-prepared and scheduled comprehensive city demonstration programs containing new and imaginative proposals to rebuild or revitalize large slum and blighted areas, to expand housing, job and income opportunities, to reduce dependence on welfare payments, to improve educational facilities and programs, to combat disease and ill health, to reduce the incidence of crime and delinquency, to enhance recreational and cultural opportunities, to establish better access between homes and jobs, and generally to improve living conditions for the people who live in such areas, and to accomplish these objectives through the most effective and economical concentration of coordination of federal, state and local public and private efforts to improve the quality of urban life.

Again, the federal government, as in the metropolitan planning provisions of the same Act, is attempting to force local communities to think through and plan their own programs. Unable to organize a comprehensive attack from the federal level, the national government is attempting to provide the incentive necessary to accomplish such coordination at the local level.

In order to encourage such comprehensive planning the federal government is making aid available for such planning. Thus far no money has been appropriated for the actual conduct of programs, only for their planning. It remains to be seen whether Congress will respond once the local communities have formulated their own plans.

Even assuming money will be made available to local communities, the issue of whether enough is known about causation to make such plans effective is an open question. Theories are abundant; practical successes are few. The difficulty of providing educational services in a meaningful way to the disadvantaged has already been examined. The issue of motivation remains unsolved. Perhaps it is true that the present generation of disadvantaged is different from past generations. "Was there any evidence other than impressions that the immigrants of fifty years ago had aspiration and hope in addition to their economic poverty, while the present poor lack aspiration and tend to pass on their impoverished economic and spiritual state from one generation to another?" [116] The evidence is not conclusive.

The problems are so serious that small-scale experimentation is insufficient. Massive undertakings are necessary. The politicians must be prepared for failures and they, in turn, must prepare the public. Thus far no new generation of metropolitan leaders has appeared willing to take the kinds of political risks implied.

The New Technology and Cities

Modern technology has been blamed as the cause of the problems of urban America and, in turn, is often offered as the solution. If only the resources and energies that have gone into the development of the new technology necessary for modern defense systems and for space exploration had been applied to cities, it is argued, their problems by now would be solved. In addition, there are those who maintain that there is a substantial technological spin-off from the advances in defense and space which, if applied to city problems, would make a major contribution to their solution.[117]

There have been, perhaps, a few by-products of space research which have some relevance to city problems. They are not many and they are not spectacular. As John H. Rubel, vice-president of Lytton Industries, suggests, "It would be wholly accidental if technologies valuable to space projects should turn out to be economically valuable in cities." [118]

It has been suggested, however, that even though there has been no substantial technological spin-off from space research and development, it is possible that the space program does indicate a method by which new city technology might be developed. Again, quoting Rubel, "Missiles and space projects use systems analysis. They require multi-disciplinary teams. The problems of space are very complex. Likewise cities and city problems are complex, in many ways much more so. Surely they, too, call for multi-disciplinary teams. Ergo, runs this argu-

[116] Ben B. Seligman, "Introduction," in Ben B. Seligman (ed.), op. cit., p. 15.

[117] National Aeronautics and Space Administration, Conference on Space Science and Urban Life, NASA SP-37 (U.S. Government Printing Office, 1963).

[118] "Defining the Role of the Private Sector in Overcoming Barriers to Urban Betterment," Harvard Program on Technology and Society, October 20–21, 1966, p. 7 (unpublished).

Campbell and Burkhead

ment, why not use the systems approach?" [119] Arguing that this is too simple a translation of the space experience into city development, Rubel urges that a market place for urban technology be created.

Out of this market will grow a new technology for specific kinds of urban development. Rubel suggests that:

In short, if you could set up a project for the creation of a new city from scratch and offer the job to private industry and set up project goals in terms of the performance of a dynamic system, you would see new industry spring up within the framework of existing firms to meet the new needs. Soon the multi-disciplinary teams would be assembled. The relevant analytical techniques would be applied; the new methods, the new technologies, the new insights would begin to emerge. The new insights and the new technologies would include wholly new species of engineering and technology.[120]

Rubel argues that such a development could take place only in new cities. It could not be done with old cities. There are simply too many obstacles in the way. Further, he maintains that his experiment will work only in a situation in which "the project owns or effectively controls the ownership of virtually all the land in the city and surrounding it for a considerable distance. This is an absolute requirement."

Rubel's insistence upon new cities and public ownership of lands points to the major political difficulties which face the rebuilding of urban America. The space technicians would not have had the success they have had if they faced some of the political obstacles that stand in the way of urban redevelopment.

If there were citizens on the moon who owned real estate and who voted and possessed other political resources, the space program would not have proceeded as smoothly as it has.

All of this does not mean that technology cannot make a major contribution to the solution of urban problems. One wonders if the money now being expended by the Department of Housing and Urban Development (HUD) for the perpetuation of the old technologies in cities might not be better spent in research and development. There is no provision in the American system, in either the private or the public sector, to supply basic or applied research to the problems of cities. The resources entering this field are minimal and even those HUD has tried to secure from Congress have been denied. The housing industry, the automobile industry, and other established interests in the market sector fear the possible consequences of major research in these areas and often erect effective barriers.

[119] *Ibid.*, p. 7.
[120] *Ibid.*, p. 13.

645

Government and Politics of Urban Redevelopment

The metropolitan planning provisions in last year's housing bill may point the direction in which the federal government will move in attempting to influence the structure of local government. These provisions are a beginning in the establishment of one kind of significant region-wide governing institution. If the federal government decides to move further in this direction, the Heller-Pechman proposal of general grants provides a possible means.[121] Governmental reorganization, as has already been suggested in a bill filed by Representative Henry S. Reuss, could be tied to such a general grant system. Much of the criticism of the general grant proposal lies in the insistence that state and local governments are not strong enough, good enough, or innovative enough to deserve these grants. The Reuss bill suggests that no grants be provided to any state until it submits a plan for the modernization of its state-local governmental system.

Beyond the politics of reforming local government structure is the politics surrounding the various functional areas relevant to city building. Highways are politically strong. They will continue to be built and, in many instances, will be the principal influence determining urban form. Education has its political strength and will undoubtedly continue to receive more funds, but whether education aid will be pointed in the direction of solving central city ills is by no means clear. Welfare and anti-poverty are weak politically. Urban renewal has changed its political support from the liberal to the chamber of commerce community. Whether this weakens or strengthens the program is not clear, but it does mean that it will be directed to saving downtown rather than providing housing to low-income families.

Emerging political configurations do not bode well for many urban programs, but these configurations do possess greater potential at the federal level than at state and local levels. The federal constituency does provide a base which makes it possible, particularly for the President, to move in new directions without sacrificing his potential for reelection. As has already been demonstrated, federal politics do not limit innovation to the extent that state and local politics do.

There are a variety of explanations for the difference between state and local and federal politics, but perhaps most significant is the fiscal bind in which state and local governments find themselves. The result

[121] See Walter W. Heller, *New Dimensions of Political Economy* (Harvard University Press, 1966); Joseph A. Pechman, "Financing State and Local Government," in American Bankers Association, *Proceeding of a Symposium on Federal Taxation* (1965). See also Walter W. Heller, Richard Ruggles, *et al., Revenue Sharing and the City* (The Johns Hopkins Press, for Resources for the Future, 1968).

is that state and local politics tend to be tax politics, while federal politics are more nearly program politics. Further, a local office-holder and, to a somewhat lesser extent, a state office-holder must constantly fear the creation of "a pocket of opposition." A president, because of the size of his constituency, can balance off opposing groups with favoring groups. This is not easy at the state and local level. The local official may create a vigorous opposition group by the placement of a physical facility—a highway or a garbage disposal unit, or by sponsoring a social program such as a police review board. The opposition group may vote in the next election on the basis of this one issue. The creation of the opposition group does not, however, automatically create a countervailing group. The rest of the community is likely to vote on a variety of issues and thereby the political future of the local office-holder is threatened by the "pocket of opposition."

These political facts of life make it inevitable that within the present structure of metropolitan governing institutions urban policy leadership will have to come from the federal level. Such leadership will not create a unified single urban policy for America. It may move, however, in the direction of co-ordinating present programs, modifying conflicting ones, and perhaps even grasping a new idea like New Towns—both in-and-out-of-town—and perhaps even new cities.

There is not, however, a single large pro-city pressure group with much political muscle. In order to create policy in this field the politician must bring together disparate political forces, often with no interests in common, and try to build a substantive package which has sufficient appeal across pressure group lines to be politically acceptable. In many cases these programs will be designed by the bureaucracy, as was the case with the poverty program. But in every case there must be strong political support, existing or emergent, to overcome the conflicting and anarchic influences that now make every urban policy exclusively incremental.

SELECTED READINGS

Abrams, Charles. *The City Is the Frontier*. New York: Harper and Row, 1965.

Burkhead, Jesse, Thomas G. Fox, and John W. Holland. *Inputs and Outputs in Large-City Education*. Syracuse: Syracuse University Press, 1967.

Campbell, Alan K., and Seymour Sacks. *Metropolitan America: Fiscal Patterns and Governmental Systems*. New York: The Free Press, 1967.

Chinitz, Benjamin C. (ed.). *City and Suburb*. Englewood Cliffs: Prentice-Hall, 1964.

Committee for Economic Development. *Modernizing Local Government*. New York: CED, 1966.

Fitch, Lyle C., and Associates. *Urban Transportation and Public Policy*. San Francisco: Chandler Publishing Co., 1964.

Friedmann, John, and William Alonso (eds.). *Regional Development and Planning*. Cambridge: M.I.T. Press, 1964.

Greer, Scott. *Urban Renewal and American Cities*. Indianapolis: Bobbs-Merrill, 1965.

Jacobs, Jane. *The Death and Life of Great American Cities*. New York: Random House, 1961.

Maass, Arthur. *Area and Power*. Glencoe: The Free Press, 1959.

Margolis, Julius (ed.). *The Public Economy of Urban Communities*. Washington: Resources for the Future, Inc., 1965.

Martin, Roscoe C. *The Cities and the Federal System*. New York: Atherton Press, 1965.

————, et al. *Decisions in Syracuse*. New York: Anchor Books, 1965.

Meranto, Philip. *The Politics of Federal Aid to Education in 1965*. Syracuse: Syracuse University Press, 1967.

Meyer, J. R., J. F. Kain, and M. Wohl. *The Urban Transportation Problem*. Cambridge: Harvard University Press, 1965.

Mohring, Herbert, and Mitchell Harwitz. *Highway Benefits*. Evanston: Northwestern University Press, 1962.

Mumford, Lewis. *The City in History*. New York: Harcourt, Brace and World, 1961.

National Bureau of Economic Research. *Transportation Economics*. New York: National Bureau of Economic Research, 1965.

Osborn, Frederic J., and Arnold Whittick. *The New Towns: The Answer to Megalopolis*. London: Hill and Leonard, 1963.

Owen, Wilfred. *The Metropolitan Transportation Problem*. Washington: The Brookings Institution, 1966.

Rossi, Peter H., and Robert A. Dentler. *The Politics of Urban Renewal*. New York: The Free Press of Glencoe, 1961.

Schaller, Howard G. (ed.). *Public Expenditure Decisions in the Urban Community.* Washington: Resources for the Future, Inc., 1963.

Seligman, Ben B. (ed.). *Poverty as a Public Issue.* New York: The Free Press, 1965.

"Urban Problems and Prospects," *Law and Contemporary Problems,* Vol. 30, Winter 1965.

"Urban Renewal," *Law and Contemporary Problems,* Part I, Vol. 25, Autumn 1960; Part II, Vol. 26, Winter 1961.

Wilson, James Q. (ed.). *Urban Renewal: The Record and the Controversy.* Cambridge: M.I.T. Press, 1966.

Wingo, Lowdon, Jr. (ed.). *Cities and Space: The Future Use of Urban Land.* Baltimore: The Johns Hopkins Press, for Resources for the Future, Inc., 1963.

————. *Transportation and Urban Land.* Washington: Resources for the Future, Inc., 1961.

Wood, Robert C. *1400 Governments.* Cambridge: Harvard University Press, 1961.

SUBJECT INDEX *

Access linkages in urban activities, 241–45, 271*n;* influence on land use, 291–300; relation of population density to, 318–30
Adult Basic Education Program, 626–27, 634, 635
Advisory Commission on Intergovernmental Relations, 2, 470–71, 518, 580*n,* 625
Affluence, 20, 22, 67, 71, 270–72
Age of dwelling units, 320–30 *passim.*
Age 65 and over: prevalence of, in the "poverty band," 23; "age-mix" variables in money income, 70, 72; "Senior Citizens" communities, 270*n;* proportion of population in central cities, 346–47
Aging of a city: impact on urban structure, 20; a factor in spatial patterns of development, 269–70
Agriculture: differentiation in cultivation of land areas, 83–86; technological changes causing migrations from farms, 578
Air pollution, 60, 460, 473, 601, 602
Anti-urban bias in state legislatures, 467
Appalachia, 166, 354
Area Redevelopment Administration, 1, 166
Automation, 105
Automobile: a factor in outward movement from cities, 22, 271, 273, 315; problem of traffic congestion, 599, 602; effects on urban transportation, 600, 601; externality costs of, 601; visions of future limited use, 608

Baltimore, 131, 135, 388
Bergen County, N.J., 450–51
Birth control, 428
Boston, 262, 390, 400, 401, 491, 520, 622

---

* References to tables and figures are in italics.

Budget, Bureau of the, 148*n,* 166
Buffalo, 130, 131, 132, 134, 389
Building and occupancy codes, 307, 418
Bureaus. (*See other part of title.*)
Burgess zonal land use models, 17, 249*n,* 252, 255–56
Business. *See* Central business district

California, 133*n,* 135*n,* 341, 449, 461, 480, 617, 619
CAPSBURG: defined, 356*n;* use of in community-action evaluation, 356–58
CBD. *See* Central business district
Census, Bureau of the, 190*n,* 191*n,* 192, 193, 200, 208*n*
Census data: lack of for a given place for points in time, 63; of Manufacturing (1940–60), 78*n;* of Population, 78*n,* 192*n,* 203, 253, 320*n;* of Transportation, 162, 176; of Business, 260; of Governments, 462
Central business district (CBD): as a focus of accessibility, 240, 255, 259; activities grouped in, 255; intensive land use in, 291–92; relation of population density and housing to distance from, 293–98, *296,* 300–302, 320–30 *passim;* question of revitalization vs. dispersal of, 595, 623
Central-place hierarchy, 91, 92, 261, 266
Central-place theory, 5, 25, 83, 86, 87, 135–37, 261, 262, 386, 387
Chevan demographic transportation model, 396
Chicago, 24, 60, 62, 126–33 *passim,* 150, 250*n,* 297*n,* 300, 309–10, 311, 312, 344, 346, 348, 387, 615
Chicago area transportation study, 2, 392, 396, 603
Children: investments in social services to, 428–29, 471; functioning of school boards regarding, 618. *See*

651

NAME INDEX*

Abrams, Charles, 39, 592n, 594, 648r
Adams, F. Gerard, 317n, 331r
Adams, Robert F., 458n, 475r
Alberts, William W., 331r
Alchian, A. A., 516n
Alevizos, John P., 261n
Alonso, William, 79r, 85, 90n, 249n, 253n, 331r, 369, 393, 394, 411r, 648r
Al-Samarrie, Ahmad, 141n
Ames, Edward, 100n
Anderson, Charles Arnold, 227r
Anderson, Martin, 312, 331r, 590n
Andrews, Richard B., 43n, 267n
Anshen, Melvin, 510n
Archibald, G. C., 516n
Arnold, Robert K., 182r
Arrow, Kenneth J., 516n, 556n
Artle, Roland, 185r
Ashby, Lowell D., 181r, 182r

Bailey, Martin J., 304–5, 307, 308, 312, 331r
Bain, Joe S., 556n
Banfield, Edward C., 549n, 552n, 553n, 565r, 586n
Barlow, Robin, 446n
Barr, James L., 552n
Barringer, Robert L., 398n
Bartholomew, Harland, 285n
Bator, Francis, 538n
Bauer, Raymond A., 185r
Beale, Calvin L., 184r
Beard, Charles A., 609
Beck, Morris, 449n
Becker, Gary S., 227r, 303–4, 331r, 354n, 355n, 362r, 610n
Beckmann, Martin J., 91–92, 139r
Beckwith, A. E., 261n
Beesley, M. E., 294, 331r, 556n
Bell, Daniel, 585n
Berman, Barbara R., 183r
Berry, Brian J. L., 5, 82n, 91, 92n, 137n, 139r, 182r, 184r, 249n, 250, 261n, 269, 386–89 passim, 411r

Birkhead, Guthrie S., 565r
Bishop, George A., 450n
Blank, David M., 332r
Blumenfeld, Hans, 392
Bogue, Donald J., 184r
Bohl, Roy W., 530n
Borchert, John R., 139r
Borts, George H., 165, 183r, 184r
Boulding, Kenneth, 106
Bowker, Albert H., 482n
Bowman, Mary Jean, 227r
Boyle, Gerald J., 547n
Brazer, Harvey E., 37n, 440n–446n passim, 475r, 499, 525r, 530n, 534, 565r, 570
Break, George F., 475r, 530n, 534, 565r
Bridges, Benjamin, 446n
Browning, Clyde E., 447n
Brownlee, O. H., 436n, 439n
Bryce, James, 577
Buchanan, James M., 436n, 455n, 475r, 529n, 552, 568
Burkhead, Jesse, 443n, 475r, 510, 612n, 648r
Burns, Arthur F., 129
Bush, Vannevar, 161n

Cadwallader, Mervyn L., 99n
Campbell, Alan K., 232n, 445n, 451n, 475r, 530n, 594n, 618n, 648r
Caplovitz, D., 349n, 362r
Capron, W. M., 516n
Carbert, Leslie E., 445n
Carll, Richard R., 603n
Carroll, J. Douglas, Jr., 257, 388
Carroll, John J., 450n
Cartter, Allan M., 482n
Casey, M. Claire, 206
Caves, R., 556n
Chamberlin, Edward H., 86n
Chapin, F. Stuart, 398, 411r
Chevan, Albert, 396
Chinitz, Benjamin C., 79r, 181r, 278n, 282n, 440n, 475r, 588, 648r

---

* r refers to authors listed in Selected Readings.

665

Designed by Gerard A. Valerio
Composed in Linotype Times Roman by The Colonial Press Inc.
Printed offset by The Colonial Press Inc., on P & S, SF
Bound by The Colonial Press Inc., in Columbia Bayside Chambray